# A MATTER
# OF TRUST

T0044065

## Praise for the book

'Meenakshi Ahamed has brought us a brilliant, important, sparkling and definitive study of a part of American history that is growing more crucial by the day. *A Matter of Trust* is essential reading at a moment when the United States and India are all the more central to each other, and when valiant democracies around the world are in danger.'
—Michael Beschloss, *New York Times* bestselling author and NBC News Presidential Historian

'Meenakshi Ahamed has brilliantly combined her talent as an accomplished journalist with her assiduous historical research to tell the tale of two great democracies. She brings to life the leaders in both countries, with their views and prejudices. A masterpiece.'
—Strobe Talbott, Former Deputy Secretary of State and President of The Brookings Institution

'Meenakshi Ahamed has given us an authentic, thoughtful and accessible account of a relationship characterized by paradox and progress. She tells the tale of the highs and lows of that relationship in all its drama, with strong and idiosyncratic personalities on both sides. Today's transformed India–US relations could determine the future not only of one-fifth of humanity but of the Asian Century. This is a book with a serious message—one to read and savour.'
—Shivshankar Menon, Former National Security Advisor, Ambassador to China and Foreign Secretary

# A MATTER OF TRUST

## INDIA–US RELATIONS FROM TRUMAN TO TRUMP

### MEENAKSHI AHAMED

HarperCollins *Publishers* India

First published by HarperCollins *Publishers* 2021
4th Floor, Tower A, Building No. 10, Phase II, DLF Cyber City,
Gurugram, Haryana – 122002
www.harpercollins.co.in

2 4 6 8 10 9 7 5 3 1

This edition published in paperback in India by HarperCollins *Publishers* 2022

P-ISBN: 978-93-5489-455-8
E-ISBN: 978-93-9032-721-8

Typeset in 11/14.7 Minion Pro at
Manipal Technologies Limited, Manipal

Printed and bound at
Thomson Press (India) Ltd.

 HarperCollinsIn

This book is produced from independently certified FSC® paper
to ensure responsible forest management.

*For*
*India & Hayes*

# Contents

| US PRESIDENTS | INDIAN PRIME MINISTERS |
|---|---|
| Harry S. Truman<br>1945–1953 | Jawaharlal Nehru<br>1947–1964 |
| Dwight D. Eisenhower<br>1953–1961 | Lal Bahadur Shastri<br>1964–1966 |
| John F. Kennedy<br>1961–1963 | Indira Gandhi<br>1966–1977 |
| Lyndon B. Johnson<br>1963–1969 | Morarji Desai<br>1977–1979 |
| Richard M. Nixon<br>1969–1974 | Charan Singh<br>1979–1980 |
| Gerald R. Ford<br>1974–1977 | Indira Gandhi<br>1980–1984 |
| James E. Carter<br>1977–1981 | Rajiv Gandhi<br>1984–1989 |
| Ronald W. Reagan<br>1981–1989 | V.P. Singh<br>1989–1990 |
| George H.W. Bush<br>1989–1993 | Chandra Shekhar<br>1990–1991 |
| William J. Clinton<br>1993–2001 | P.V. Narasimha Rao<br>1991–1996 |
| George W. Bush<br>2001–2009 | Atal Bihari Vajpayee<br>1996–1996 |
| Barack H. Obama<br>2009–2017 | H.D. Deve Gowda<br>1996–1997 |
| Donald J. Trump<br>2017–2021 | I.K. Gujral<br>1997–1998 |
| Joseph R. Biden<br>2021– | Atal Bihari Vajpayee<br>1998–2004 |
| | Manmohan Singh<br>2004–2014 |
| | Narendra Modi<br>2014– |

# Part One:
# 1945–1947

# Chapter 1

# Introduction

O N THE TWENTY-SECOND OF SEPTEMBER 2019, FIFTY THOUSAND Indian Americans gathered at the NRG stadium in Houston, Texas to welcome the prime minister of India, Narendra Modi. Billed as the 'Howdy Modi' event, it was the largest gathering of supporters ever assembled in the United States for a foreign head of state. The event organizers, the Texas India Forum, a new non-profit entity, announced that not only had all tickets been sold out, there was an additional waitlist of ten thousand. The programme was broadcast to millions of people around the world in Hindi, English and Spanish.

Security was tight. Attendees began patiently lining up as early as 6 a.m. to make their way through the extensive security checks. Although massive rains had caused destructive floods in the days leading up to the event, that morning the sun came out and the weather in Houston was as sultry as ever. People wore everything from casual T-shirts to formal dress befitting an Indian wedding. There was palpable excitement in the air as the crowd eagerly awaited the sharing of the podium by the leaders of the two countries that mattered so much to them. Several US politicians were in the audience, including Republicans Ted Cruz and Pete Olson of Texas, and Democrats Raja Krishnamoorthi of Illinois and House Majority Leader Steny Hoyer.

When Modi arrived, the crowd's enthusiasm surged. They chanted his name, drowning out the entertainment. President Trump, the guest of honour, arrived late after stopping for a briefing on the recent floods. Modi greeted Trump outside and, holding his hand, brought him into the stadium. This was Modi's show, and he exuded confidence as he welcomed Trump to the stage. As they stood side by side, looking out at the stadium full of Indian Americans waving both the Indian and American flags and chanting their names, one could not help noticing that the shouts for Modi far exceeded those for Trump. Both leaders gave speeches dutifully affirming their friendship. Modi's was long, but Trump, to his credit, remained standing and nodded respectfully through it all.

Modi's popularity with the Indian diaspora was on dramatic display at the 'Howdy Modi' event. He used the occasion to rally support for Trump with a slogan '*Ab ki baar, Trump sarkar*' (This time, it's Trump time). He asked the crowd—his 'family' he called them—to join him in giving Trump a hand for combating terrorism and for being a friend to India. The crowd responded with cheers. He was trying to convey to Trump that he had the power to deliver Indian American votes. It was a bold message by an Indian prime minister on American soil.

The scene in 2019 Houston was a far cry from the reception India's first prime minister, Jawaharlal Nehru, received on his maiden visit to the US in 1949. The Indian American community was small and politically insignificant at that time. India was a poor country attempting to stand on its feet after years of colonial neglect. Badly in need of aid, India hoped the world's most powerful democracy would help, but it was viewed with indifference by the Truman administration.

Nehru, refined, erudite and respected by many world leaders for having helped win Indian independence, felt it was beneath him to beg for aid. He expected the US, with its wealth and its history of fighting colonialism, to step forward to help India. President Truman, convinced Nehru was a communist because he had chosen to remain non-aligned, mistrusted him. Meanwhile Dean Acheson, the legendary US secretary of state, a staunch cold warrior, treated him with condescension.

Nehru's daughter, Indira Gandhi, accompanied him on the trip and had her own unpleasant encounter with John Snyder, Harry Truman's treasury secretary and personal friend. Snyder arrived somewhat inebriated at a dinner in Washington, DC given by Dean Acheson in Nehru's honour and proceeded to harangue guests about foreigners trying to extract money from the US. It was an inauspicious start to their relationship.

When India became the world's newest and largest democracy in 1947, relations between it and the US, the world's most powerful democracy, should, by all accounts, have been friendly. Neither country had expansionist geopolitical ambitions of its own and both believed in self-determination as the bedrock principle of government.

As Nehru himself so eloquently said when he addressed Congress during his visit to the US capital on 13 October 1949:

> The voices of India and the United States may appear to differ, but there is much in common between them. Like you, we have achieved our freedom through a revolution, though our methods were different from yours. Like you we shall be a Republic based on the Federal principle, which is an outstanding contribution of the founders of this great Republic. We have placed in the forefront of our constitution those fundamental human rights to which all men who love liberty, equality and progress aspire—the freedom of the individual, the equality of men and the rule of law. We enter, therefore, the community of free nations with the roots of democracy deeply embedded in our institutions as well as in the thoughts of our people.[1]

Although both countries subscribed on paper to the same set of values—including a commitment to secularism, a belief in free and open elections, civil liberties and free speech—during those early years, these two nations, which theoretically seemed destined to be partners, found themselves all too often at loggerheads, pursuing conflicting objectives and hobbled by cultural misunderstandings.

The two countries entered the post-war world with remarkably different worldviews and saw things through very different cultural lenses. Though India was poor, it saw itself as an ancient civilization that brought a distinctive approach to politics. It had achieved independence in a uniquely Indian way through Gandhian non-violence and believed that elements of that philosophy might be applied to the conduct of international relations. The contrast between its position in the world and how it saw itself made it unusually prickly.

The leadership of newly independent India was united in wanting to remain neutral and keep its options open with regard to alliances in this new bipolar world. A new term was coined to express this policy: non-alignment. Having rid itself of colonial domination, India was loath to sign away its newfound independence by aligning so quickly with any country. It needed to stand on its own, both to see if it could and to prove to its people that it was strong enough to protect them on its own. India did not want another country to dominate it ever again.

The US, on the other hand, saw itself as pitted in a Manichean struggle against the Soviet Union, a conflict that was ultimately about the choice between good and evil, in which countries had to choose sides. Its closest ally was the United Kingdom and the British used their alliance with the US to make sure the US left India under their jurisdiction.

To analyse how India and the US have dealt with each other, it is not enough to understand how the foreign policy bureaucracies in the two countries went about making calculations in their own national interests. The tone and temperature of relations between the US and India during the first half-century after Independence was largely determined by the personal interactions between the leaders of both countries.

The story of post-independence India is intimately intertwined with the story of the Nehru dynasty* and the overarching influence of this one family on Indian politics for almost half a century. The Nehrus were educated overseas, secular, outwardly westernized and liberal, yet their relations with US leaders were often strained. Nehru, the towering Indian political figure of his era, was India's first prime minister from 1947 until his death in 1964. After a brief interregnum following his death, he was succeeded by his daughter Indira Gandhi in 1966, who held the position of prime minister for the following eighteen years except for a short period from 1977 to 1980. She was assassinated in 1984 and succeeded by her

---

* The Nehru dynasty includes Indira Gandhi and Rajiv Gandhi as well as Vijaya Lakshmi Pandit, Jawaharlal Nehru's sister. Indira Gandhi was Indira Nehru prior to her marriage but is often confused as belonging to Mahatma Gandhi's family. As Nehru and Gandhi were both founders of India and closely associated, it is an easy mistake. By the time she entered public life, Mrs Gandhi was already married and had taken her husband's name.

son Rajiv Gandhi, until his own death: by a suicide bomber wearing an explosive belt in 1991.

Nehru thought deeply about issues, was a prolific writer and enjoyed intellectual exchanges. He developed close relationships with several US ambassadors including Henry Grady, Chester Bowles, John Kenneth Galbraith and Ellsworth Bunker. Each in their own way influenced Nehru, who valued their expertise and respected their views. Nehru chose to remain non-aligned during the Cold War, which put him in the crosshairs of President Truman and Secretary Dulles. Although he was open to Eisenhower's overtures, and came to appreciate President Kennedy when the US came to India's rescue in 1962 after China attacked India, Nehru never got over his reservations about America.

When Prime Minister Nehru took office in 1947, he retained the external affairs portfolio until his death in 1964. It was his worldview, convictions and bias that came to define Indian foreign policy. Nehru saw himself as a world statesman and spokesperson for Asia. He advocated for communist China's recognition at the UN and inserted himself in the Korean War hoping that as a 'non-aligned' country he could be helpful. He merely ended up irritating the Americans.

Nehru's stature and independence of action were undermined during those early years by India's constant need for food aid. Erratic monsoons and a cycle of famines and floods became an obstacle to his plans to modernize India and put him in the position of being a supplicant to US largesse, which affected relations. Americans, especially Congress, expected gratitude if not political support from recipients of its aid. India came to be seen as 'an object for American charity not strategy'.[2]

India's refusal to censure the Soviet Union over its interventions in Eastern Europe and Czechoslovakia added to the deep suspicions of US officials towards Nehru. In retaliation they decided to restrict the amount of food aid sent to India, a move that Nehru viewed as essentially immoral, and he refused to concede to American demands.

The US often appeared arrogant. Its use of its wealth and power to bully smaller countries created a great deal of resentment in India and turned Indians anti-American. Truman, Eisenhower and Kennedy all tried unsuccessfully to resolve the Kashmir dispute and attempted to use aid to pressure Nehru to make concessions. The US would finally agree to leave the issue for India and Pakistan to resolve between themselves.

When the US decided to enter into a military alliance with Pakistan, a mantle of mutual suspicion settled over the relationship. Eisenhower tried to diffuse the tension by inviting Nehru to his home in Gettysburg, a historic civil war site, located two hours from Washington, DC by car.[†] The two men discovered they liked each other and relations between the countries eased.

When Kennedy became the president in 1961, he tried to court India early on. Relations did not go well initially until he sent his wife Jackie Kennedy to India on a goodwill tour in 1961, during which she charmed Nehru, took India by storm and accomplished more for diplomacy than the most experienced diplomat.

The following year, communist China invaded India at almost the same time as the Cuban Missile Crisis, during which the Soviet Union and the US faced off in the most alarming confrontation of the Cold War. Caught totally unprepared and humiliated by China's military successes, Nehru appealed to the US for assistance. Kennedy's quick response helped enormously to improve relations.

The US ambassador to India, John Kenneth Galbraith, played a central role in cementing the relationship between the two leaders but, unfortunately, neither Kennedy nor Nehru lived long enough to build on these developments and retreat from the negative course the relationship had taken under the previous administrations. Kennedy was assassinated in 1963 and Nehru, by then in his seventies, was ill and died in 1964.

Relations with the US were shredded when Mrs Gandhi became the prime minister in 1966. Jawaharlal Nehru and his daughter Indira were very different people. Nehru himself was fully committed to democracy and did everything in his power to make sure India remained a secular, multicultural state. In contrast, Mrs Gandhi's political decisions were not

---

† In 1863, President Lincoln delivered a famous speech called the Gettysburg Address on the site of the civil war battlefield after the war to bring the US together ended. This battlefield is in Gettysburg, Pennsylvania and has great significance for US military history.

grounded in any deep commitment to democratic principles. She relied upon a handful of left-leaning advisors in her cabinet and valued loyalty above all else. No US ambassador ever broke through her icy façade. Unlike her father, she had little interest in the larger global stage and was far more concerned about consolidating her power within India.

Indira Gandhi was insecure, autocratic and possessed little of Nehru's intellectual interests or charm. Hostage to a coalition government which included the communist parties, she spoke out against US policy in Vietnam, infuriating President Johnson. As a result, Johnson pursued a vindictive policy towards India, using food aid as a weapon at a time when India was facing famine. Mrs Gandhi, who seldom forgot a slight, felt India was being humiliated and never forgave him.

Relations further plummeted when Nixon became president. While Nixon and Kissinger went all out to court Pakistan as a conduit to China, Mrs Gandhi defied them by supporting Bengali aspirations for independence from Pakistan. In a lightning military strike, India defeated Pakistan, winning Mrs Gandhi the adoration of all Indians and the wrath of Nixon and Kissinger. She abandoned non-alignment and moved decisively into the Soviet camp by signing a friendship treaty with Russia in 1971. The Nixon years were the lowest point in India–US relations. Nixon was famously caught on tape describing Mrs Gandhi as 'that bitch'.[3]

It was only after Mrs Gandhi's assassination at the hands of her own bodyguards in 1984, and her son Rajiv's assassination in 1991, that the Nehru dynasty's power began to erode. Under new leadership, India was able to reform its domestic policies, putting it on a path to growth and making it an attractive strategic partner for the US.

Three events occurred since 1990 that advanced US–India relations dramatically and elevated them into a strategic partnership.

The first was Indian economic reforms, which took place in the 1990s. After Rajiv Gandhi's assassination, the Congress party freed itself of the socialist policies that had strangled growth and pushed India uncomfortably close to the Soviets. It was able to develop new priorities and mechanisms for growth based on sound economic judgement under the guidance of Dr Manmohan Singh, an academic economist, who would later become prime minister. The government embarked on a series of much-needed economic reforms and India's gross domestic product accelerated, averaging from 4 to 5 per cent in the 1970s to 5 to 6 per cent in the 1990s and, more recently, to over 7 per cent in the 2000s.[4]

After the Cold War was over, India tried to shed its 'third world' image and align with Western interests, projecting a commitment to the basic ideas of European Enlightenment. 'The creation of a new partnership with the West became the central preoccupation of the Indian foreign policy establishment in the 1990s.'[5] The US also shifted its focus from global politics to global economy. India's reforms coincided with Bill Clinton taking office, ushering in a decisive change in the US attitude towards India. Clinton recognized the economic potential of India and the role it could play in balancing China's rising economic threat.

China was not only an economic threat to the US but was catching up with the US militarily, and India's emergence as a global economic force made it a viable counterbalance to China in Asia.

The second force for change was President George W. Bush. He was the unlikely hero of the US–India story who transformed the relationship between the two countries. Although the Bush presidency is associated with three big disasters—9/11, the Iraq war and the global financial crisis of 2008—he built a partnership with India, an initiative that for India was as significant as Nixon's opening to China.

In 2008, Bush concluded a landmark agreement with India, just weeks before Barack Obama was elected president. The nuclear deal was a historic achievement in the history of the two countries and one of the most difficult negotiations the two sides had ever engaged in. It was accomplished by an extraordinary personal effort by Bush and his secretary of state, Condoleezza Rice. Prime Minister Manmohan Singh, the quiet, soft-spoken father of India's economic reforms, was the perfect partner. Despite pushback from his opponents, he staked his government and almost resigned in order to get the deal accepted in India. Bush wiped away years of mistrust and grievances that had accumulated and become entrenched on both sides. He said he did it because he believed the two countries shared common core values—freedom and democracy—and because he was convinced it was the right thing to do.

The third factor was the growing influence of the Indian diaspora in the country. Indian Americans are one of the fastest-growing ethnic groups in the US and account for almost 1.5 per cent of the population.[6] According to a Pew Research Survey, there are almost 4 million Indian Americans in the US and they have the highest per capita income of any group in the country, averaging $100,000. Vivek Wadhwa, who teaches at Stanford University, found that by 2012, Indian American entrepreneurs helped found 16 per cent of the start-ups in Silicon Valley even thought they represented just 6 per cent of the population.[7] Many major Fortune 500 companies are headed by Indian Americans—the heads of Google, Microsoft, Adobe, Mastercard, Sun Microsystems, The Gap and, until 2018, Pepsi are all immigrants from India. They donate to political causes, are courted by politicians and are interested in good relations between India and the US.

By 2000, Indian Americans were becoming organized. The diaspora played a critical role in the passage of the nuclear deal through Congress. The Indian embassy recruited Indian Americans to help persuade recalcitrant members of Congress to pass the legislation involving the nuclear deal. The Indian lobby had become aware of its political clout.

When President Obama was elected in 2008, it looked as though the world's most powerful democracy and the world's largest democracy had both attained maturity and transcended the ghosts of their past. The US had elected its first African American president in a landslide election, and India had a Sikh prime minister, a Muslim president and an Italian-born Catholic woman was head of the ruling Congress party. Both countries seemed to embrace their secular, multicultural identity.

In 2010, their values and world outlook were aligned. President Obama, increasingly concerned about China's growing military power, built on the relations Bush had established, and elevated India's status to that of a strategic partner. We seemed to be at a juncture in history where shared values and mutual interests would determine India–US relations rather than the predilections of personalities.

But neither Obama nor Singh could have predicted how many of their policies and established conventions their successors would undo. In the years that followed, India and the US underwent a profound change in their political culture, electing populist presidents. Trump and Modi both rode in on a wave of anti-Muslim sentiment and, despite being outsiders in their own parties, reshaped their respective parties in their own image. Convinced of the power of their own charisma, they attempted to change existing norms and relationships.

Trump's doctrine of 'America First' and his natural instinct towards isolationism were a stark contrast to the global perspectives of George W. Bush or Barack Obama.

In India, the demise of the Nehru dynasty resulted in the disintegration of the Congress party, which had for so long tried to maintain the tradition of liberal democracy. It was replaced by the Bharatiya Janata Party (BJP), which believed in a Hindu nation and which began to undo the legacy of Gandhi and Nehru and convert India from a country based on secular principles to one based on Hindu nationalism.[8]

Trump viewed international relations in transactional terms, placing little value on continuity. New Delhi watched with concern as he reversed many of the policies of his predecessors, including withdrawing from the Trans-Pacific Partnership, the Iran nuclear deal and the Paris Climate Agreement that both Modi and Obama had invested so much effort in.

Modi, recognizing early on that to maintain good relations with the US required catering to Trump's ego, went out of his way to court him. He filled a cricket stadium with 1,00,000 people to greet Trump on his thirty-six-hour visit to India. Trump responded well to the flattery and was willing to put aside trade disagreements till after his India visit.

Seventy years of India–US relations has shown that despite the two countries being democracies, not only are they far apart culturally but the intersection of their critical interests is relatively modest. Therefore, the only time when the relationship has developed any real momentum is when one of the leaders has been willing to make a leap of faith.

# Chapter 2

# Independence

THE MUGHAL DYNASTY WAS AT ITS ZENITH WHEN THE EUROPEANS first arrived in the sixteenth century looking for trade concessions in India. 'Hindustan' was renowned in the West for its textiles, spices and jewels. Angus Maddison, the renowned economic historian, calculated that the per capita output of Mughal India was comparable to that of France and England. Other studies confirm that by 1650, India's GDP was on a par with Europe and approximated 80 per cent of the prevailing British GDP per capita.[1] Whereas in 1700 India accounted for a quarter of the world economy, by the time the British left in 1947, its share of the world economy had fallen to below 5 per cent.

The Industrial Revolution that propelled Europe towards growth and prosperity also set off competition among the Europeans for global economic domination. By the middle of the eighteenth century, as America began to assert its independence, the Europeans pushed east and south into Asia and Africa in search of new conquests.

Through the ebb and flow of history, the Indian subcontinent had been invaded from the north by many hordes, including those of Tamerlane, Genghis Khan and their descendants. Like Europe, independent kingdoms of various sizes proliferated. Dynasties came and went through the centuries. Some invaders managed to conquer vast portions of the subcontinent, but they were seldom able to hold on to it for more than a century. At no time did India, as a political entity, resemble the cartographic boundaries it holds today.

The Mughal court was luxurious and sophisticated. It attracted artisans, traders and scholars from all over. Much of this was documented in the accounts of visitors who travelled through India. Its rulers engaged in a flourishing foreign trade spanning the Middle East to China. The Mughals were exceptional architects and they built some of the world's most magnificent monuments, including the Taj Mahal. Their lives were full of grand romances and equally grand rivalries. But by the eighteenth century they were in a deep decline. Their greatest weakness was the failure to establish an organized system of succession. It created an incentive for fratricide and even patricide and corroded the dynasty from within. Parts of the Mughal Empire fell into the hands of the Hindu rulers, but the real contenders for the spoils were outsiders, who were waiting for an opportunity to gain a foothold in India. They now stepped into the breach.

By the time the British government took over the East India Company's interests in India in 1858, the ailing Mughal emperor barely controlled Delhi. Powerful princely states, headed by Hindu maharajas, that were once under Mughal sovereignty had long since restored control over their kingdoms. Many were warring with each other and the landscape on the subcontinent resembled Europe with its many fractious countries.

The East India Company, along with the Portuguese and the French, had begun trading primarily in the coastal areas on the fringes of India in the mid-1700s. Under the ingenious and rapacious Robert Clive, the Company moved inland and evolved from a mere trading outpost to a mini state. By 1800 it had accumulated a standing army of a quarter of a million locally recruited men, headed by a handful of British officers.

The growth of the colonial powers was opportunistic. As local kingdoms collapsed or devolved into civil war, the Company stepped in and took control. Initially it was done to provide stability, so its mercantile interests could flourish. Much of the infrastructure it developed was to protect the company's commercial investments, but the meddling in the internal politics of India's princely states became extensive—and increasingly controversial.* There was little oversight over the Company's conduct

---

\* The EIC recruited armies and began to levy taxes. For a full account refer to *Anarchy: The Relentless Rise of the East India Company* by William Dalrymple.

in the colonies as long as its coffers remained full. Its relations with the local population deteriorated and its indifference to the grievances of the Indians it controlled fomented a growing resistance to its presence.

In 1857, some troops of the Company's sepoy[†] army mutinied and shot several British subjects. During the Sepoy Mutiny, sometimes known as the First War of Independence, the rebels tried unsuccessfully to rally around the ageing and bankrupt Mughal emperor in Delhi to launch a movement to expel the British from India. The British Crown stepped in and, in 1858, took over from the East India Company, bringing the Indian colony directly under its control. The dying Mughal dynasty came to an inglorious end as the British did away with the façade that India had an effective 'Indian' ruler by imprisoning the Mughal 'emperor'.

The British government dissolved the East India Company in 1874, and in 1877, Queen Victoria was crowned 'Empress of India' in a spectacular pageant held in Delhi and attended by the Prince of Wales that was meant to awe the natives. The British now controlled a patchwork of approximately 52 per cent of the Indian subcontinent, with the rest nominally remaining in the hands of various maharajas.[‡] In 1911, the capital was moved from Calcutta to Delhi. To commemorate the occasion, King-Emperor George V and Queen Mary held an imperial durbar to which 'Motilal Nehru was among the elite Indians commanded "to be in attendance at Delhi"—that, he commented to his son,[2] the future prime minister of India, "'is a funny way of inviting a gentleman.'"[3]

---

†     Sepoys were locally recruited Indians who joined the British Indian Army.

‡     The British exerted considerable influence over the princely states. The extent of British influence depended on the state and the ruler. The maharajas collected taxes, and British law did not apply in their domain. If a crime was committed in British India and the criminal escaped to 'independent India', he could not be prosecuted unless the maharaja chose to hand him over. The existence of the independent states was a constant threat to British dominance. The Crown posted representatives to the courts and interfered relentlessly in their internal affairs in an attempt to ensure the maharajas were puppets who were compliant with British demands.

A new city, New Delhi, was built by architect Edwin Lutyens to rival the glorious Red Fort of the Mughal emperors.[§]

Once the Crown took over from the East India Company in 1858, it began to move British families, missionaries and cultural institutions into this ancient land. They layered racial inequality on to a society already burdened with a caste system. The British government never lost sight of the fact that India existed to furnish the needs of Britain. Its primary purpose in India was to furnish raw material for British factories and provide manpower at times of war. The British became increasingly harsh in their dealing with their colonies, investing the minimum needed to keep them functioning. Railways were built to ease the transportation of goods being sent to England. Schools were built to provide sufficiently educated locals to staff its vast administration that was necessary to collect taxes, maintain order and run India.

The Indian economy stagnated, while India's commodities fuelled the Industrial Revolution in England. 'British colonial policy in India deliberately stifled trade with the rest of the world, arrogating to Britain all the useful Indian exports. Indeed, the relative weight of India in the world economy plummeted during the two centuries of British colonial domination and the effective economic growth rate of the country was, on average, zero.'[4]

Over time, sustained discrimination bred resentment and fuelled nationalism. In the aftermath of the First World War, leaders like Mahatma Gandhi who had studied in England recognized the inequities they were being forced to tolerate at home. Gandhi had spent time in South Africa before returning to India, where he had taken a stand against colonialism. On his return, he launched a unique form of protest against British rule through the principle of non-violence. It would attract international admiration, including from Martin Luther King, Jr, the leader of the civil rights movement in the US who adopted some of Gandhi's teachings and methods.[¶]

---

[§] New Delhi was built seven miles from Old Delhi, the walled city of Shahjahanabad which was built in the 1600s and remained the capital of the Mughals until the British siege of Delhi in 1857.

[¶] Nelson Mandela was also inspired by Gandhi and adopted his teachings.

The 'half-naked fakir', as the British prime minister Winston Churchil had once described Gandhi, inspired the entire country to join the 'Mahatma' to evict the British from India. Among his followers was Jawaharlal Nehru, a young, aristocratic lawyer who had recently returned from England, having studied at Harrow and Cambridge, before studying law in London. He was passionate about Indian independence and quickly endeared himself to Gandhi.

## Nehru and Gandhi

When Nehru was a fourteen-year-old boy, he would run to get the newspaper every morning to follow the latest Japanese exploits during the Russo–Japanese war. In his autobiography, he confessed that he was excited when he heard of Japanese victories during the war, and 'mused of Indian freedom and Asiatic freedom from the thralldom of Europe'.[5] Nehru found colonialism an affront to human dignity and took pride in Asian nationalism. His political awakening began when he was an adolescent, but when he was a young man of twenty-seven, he met Gandhi and his life changed forever.

Nehru was mesmerized by Gandhi when they first met in Lucknow in 1916. He persuaded his father Motilal to get to know the man who would become his friend and mentor. Gandhi had already attracted a following by the time Nehru entered his orbit and Motilal could see why his son was drawn to him. They both recognized that Gandhi was no ordinary man and that he had both the charisma and wisdom to guide the forces that were rising to drive the British out of India.

Motilal was a lawyer and approached the issue of Indian independence from Britain as a constitutional matter to be managed through legal reform. He had been a member of the Congress party for several years, but he was a moderate. Gandhi, who was twenty years older than Nehru, was an activist. He developed his thinking when he was a young lawyer fighting colonialism in South Africa. He refined his approach and became more radical on his return to India and organized a grassroots movement that inspired the entire country, putting them on a path to peaceful resistance to foreign domination. Motilal's home, Anand Bhavan

(Abode of Happiness), became a frequent meeting place for the leaders of the Congress party.

Although father and son both supported Gandhi, Motilal was anxious about his only son risking arrest and courting danger. Jawaharlal Nehru had been born in 1889 to much fanfare and celebration. Infant and maternal mortality was still high—Motilal's first wife and child had both died and he had lost his first child by his second wife. For the first eleven years of his life, before his sister 'Nan' was born, Nehru was the only child, spoiled by the women in the family and fussed over by a retinue of servants.

The Nehru family led a privileged life. European governesses and English tutors educated the children and the Nehrus were close to being aristocracy without being official members of a royal family. They were Kashmiri Brahmins who had migrated to Delhi in 1716, shortly after the death of Emperor Aurangzeb, the last of the great Mughals.** They fled Delhi after the 1857 mutiny[6] and moved to Agra, where Motilal Nehru was born in 1861.

Motilal hired private tutors for his children. One of them, Ferdinand T. Brooks, was a twenty-six-year-old theosophist who exposed Nehru to the teachings of Annie Besant, a theosophist and early supporter of Indian independence, but, more importantly, he introduced Nehru to the wonders of science. They set up a small laboratory in the house where they conducted experiments and the young Nehru was captivated.

Later, he was convinced that science was the path to progress. In a 1938 message to the Silver Jubilee Session of the Indian Science Congress, Nehru told the gathering: 'Science is the spirit of the age and the dominating factor of the modern world. Even more than the present, the future belongs to science and to those who make friends with science ... it was science alone that could solve these problems of hunger and poverty,

---

** The Mughal Empire reached its territorial zenith under Aurangzeb, encompassing most of the Indian subcontinent from Afghanistan in the west to Burma in the east and Kashmir in the north to large parts of the peninsula in the south. After Aurangzeb, the Mughal Empire disintegrated, creating opportunities for the British to take over. In 1857, the last Mughal emperor barely controlled Delhi and its environs.

of insanitation and illiteracy, of superstition, of vast resources running to waste, of a rich country inhabited by starving people.'[7]

When Nehru was sixteen, he was sent to England to study at Harrow, followed by Trinity College at Cambridge University, where he was exposed to a stimulating world of ideas. He continued to study science but read widely and developed a taste for poetry—one of his favourite verses was the opening lines of Algernon Charles Swinburne's 'The Roundel,' which he loved to quote.

After graduating from Cambridge, Nehru moved to London and studied law to please his father. He spent two years in the city living the life of a young society gentleman, acquiring a taste for champagne and fine wine, and became involved in London's rich cultural life. He attended lectures by John Maynard Keynes and Bertrand Russell, and was introduced to Fabian socialism. He absorbed the prevailing attitudes about America being an overly materialistic society, commonly held among many of his British acquaintances.

By the time he returned to India in 1912, at the age of twenty-one, he was fully anglicized in speech and manners. But despite his seven years in England, Nehru felt deeply rooted in India and never saw himself as anything but Indian. He had always stayed in close contact with his family throughout. His wealthy and indulgent parents had sent for him twice during the seven years so he could spend his holidays at home. His Western education and years overseas did not leave him untouched. He was deeply influenced by his exposure to the West and said of himself: 'I have become a queer mixture of East and West, out of place everywhere and at home nowhere.'[8]

Nehru returned to India full of admiration for the British. It was after the infamous Jallianwala Bagh massacre in 1919, when peacefully assembled citizens were gunned down by British soldiers in a walled garden, that Nehru became radicalized. He came to realize that the British had two dimensions, one enlightened, the other deeply racist. He now devoted himself full time to the cause of independence, participating in protests and marches, and quickly became one of the key leaders of the freedom struggle.

Nehru met Gandhi the same year as his wedding to Kamala, and of the two events, his patriotic fervour for the freedom struggle evoked more passion in him than his marriage. The marriage had been arranged by Motilal soon after Nehru returned from London in the traditional Indian manner. Kamala was a Kashmiri Brahmin, with soft hazel eyes and light skin. Tall and slender, she had a gentle personality and had been brought up in a loving household. Her move to her in-laws' home was difficult. She lacked the educational background of her sisters-in-law and husband and found them intimidating. She withdrew into a shell and never became Nehru's friend, soul mate or confidante. Twenty-one months after their marriage their daughter Indira was born.

Nehru's absences did not allow their relationship to develop and they began to lead increasingly separate lives as he got caught up in politics. Kamala began to suffer from bouts of ill health, and shortly after her marriage she started a long struggle with tuberculosis.[9]

Nehru was not particularly empathetic about ill health. One of his pet peeves was Indians who whined about their illnesses. He would urge his daughter Indira to run and exercise daily. 'I was unused to illness or lying in bed with fever or physical weakness. I was a little proud of my health, I objected to the general valetudinarian attitude that was fairly common in India.'[10] Nehru once told Indira tongue-in-cheek that speaking of illness and disease, except in the case of necessity, should be forbidden by law. He urged her to read Samuel Butler's novel *Erewhon*, in which illness was considered a crime and the sentence was commensurate with the severity of the illness. When Indira was very ill and in a sanatorium in Switzerland, being treated for what was likely tuberculosis, he wrote to her: '[Y]ou are wise enough to realize that health is not merely a physical condition. It is very much a mental affair.'[11]

Nehru's indifference towards his wife for much of their marriage upset their only child, Indira. She held her father responsible for her mother's suffering and her resentments against her father manifested themselves during her adolescence in ways that hurt his feelings. Towards the end of Kamala's short life, Nehru came to appreciate his wife and regretted not valuing her qualities more. After Kamala died at the age of thirty-seven, he kept some of her ashes and asked that they be mingled with his when he died. It was a sentimental gesture, an attempt to make up after she was gone for what he seemed unable to do when she was alive.

Nehru spent almost thirteen years in and out of prison during India's struggle for freedom. Indian jails were overflowing with members of the Congress party and the Indian elite who had joined the independence movement. It became a badge of honour to serve time for the cause. Nehru endeared himself to the people when they saw him being beaten by the British police during protest marches. He was admired for standing up to the British and refusing special treatment for himself.

While in prison, Nehru wrote several books, including a delightful history book for his daughter called *Glimpses of World History*. He was a prolific and elegant writer and his prose a pleasure to read. He also wrote hundreds of letters to friends, colleagues and relatives. His letters to his daughter have been compiled into a book. One of his most enduring legacies is a series of 400 letters, covering five volumes, which he wrote to his chief ministers as prime minister.

Nehru's fiery speeches, tireless campaigning and personal sacrifice propelled him towards the leadership of the Congress party and made him the anointed favourite of Gandhi. Gandhi was his mentor and they shared a similar vision for independence, but religion was one of the areas where Nehru occasionally disagreed with the older man. Gandhi was a deeply spiritual man and accepted the spiritual beliefs of other people as long as they were not prejudiced.

Nehru would get impatient with Gandhi for injecting religion into politics. When Gandhi decided to fast until death to show his disapproval of the British attempt to divide the people by creating separate electorates in September 1932, Nehru was distraught. He wrote: 'I felt angry with him at his religious and sentimental approach to a political question, and his frequent references to God in connection with it. He even seemed to suggest that God had indicated the very date of the fast. What a terrible example to set!'[12] He despaired at what would happen to the movement if Gandhi died for what he felt was an insignificant cause compared to the greater cause of freedom.

Nehru acknowledged that religion was important to people—after all, he lived in a family where the women were devout practising Hindus— and in his fifties, he himself was attracted to Buddhism and its concept of the 'middle path'. Addressing a gathering of Buddhists, he said, 'The message of the Buddha may well solve the problems of our troubled and tormented world.'[13] His study was full of busts and figurines of Buddha, but he was repelled by much of what passed for religious instruction that preyed on people's ignorance or prejudices.

Nehru despised any form of superstition or religious dogmatism, believing they encouraged intolerance and inhibited the honest exchange of ideas. He believed in the concept of free will and put his faith in ethics. Nehru was determined that India should be a beacon of tolerance. Most of all, he insisted that India have a firmly secular identity. He knew that a diverse country like India—where the natural inclination, cemented by years of the caste system, was to exclude 'the other'—would always be vulnerable to fracture.

For Nehru, Gandhi was irreplaceable. According to his biographer, Michael Brecher, Nehru was formal in his dealings with most men and Gandhi was the only man he was close to, both professionally and personally—a mentor, spiritual guide and friend whom he could confide in. Even though they came from different worlds—Gandhi had been raised in a modest, middle-class, orthodox Hindu household, while Nehru was the ultimate Indian aristocrat—they were both united in their common goal to achieve independence for India.

### India, FDR and Empire

In the lead-up to the Second World War, India had tried to negotiate with the British to win independence in return for providing manpower during the war. Hoping to enlist American help, Nehru had written to President Franklin D. Roosevelt about India's aspirations to be freed from colonial rule and requested his support, assuring him that the Indians would do their best not to submit to the Japanese, who were then threatening India's eastern border during the war.

Roosevelt tried to persuade Churchill to accept the forces of history and grant India its freedom, but his advice fell on deaf ears. Churchill was an unapologetic imperialist. When Gandhi launched his campaign of non-violent resistance to British rule, Churchill was apoplectic and 'raged that Gandhi ought to be lain bound hand and foot at the gates of Delhi, and then trampled on by an enormous elephant with the new viceroy seated on his back.[14]

Churchill had long been an obstinate opponent of Indian independence. He famously said: 'I have not become the king's first minister to preside over the liquidation of the British Empire.'[15] With few strategic interests in India, Roosevelt was unwilling to push Churchill further and invoke his displeasure.

The United States was the most powerful country and FDR the most powerful politician in the world. FDR was elected an unprecedented four times as president. He had grown up in the sophisticated environs of elite east coast institutions and was related to former president Theodore Roosevelt. His record is all the more remarkable as he was struck by infantile paralysis (polio) at the age of thirty-nine and suffered considerable degeneration in his legs. His towering personality and agile intellect more than compensated for his physical disability. Having guided the country through the difficult years of the Great Depression that followed the crash of 1929, and then steered it through the Second World War, he was admired abroad as well as at home.

President Wilson's fourteen points, which formed the basis of the US position at the Paris Peace Conference in 1918 and supported self-determination for all people, inspired Indian leaders. The documents had laid the foundations for the League of Nations and subsequently the United Nations, which came into existence in 1942. Nehru's expectations of US support for Indian independence was further reinforced by the declaration of the Atlantic Charter in 1941.[††] But the British viewed the freedoms afforded by the document as applicable primarily to Europe. The US saw it differently. According to the historian H.W. Brands, 'the failure of Americans to contradict Churchill's narrow construction of the Atlantic Charter provoked considerable dismay'[16] among Indian leaders.

---

†† The Atlantic Charter was a joint declaration between Britain and the US respecting the right of all peoples to choose the form of government under which they would live.

There were several US officials, such as Wallace Murray at the State Department, who felt the British policy in India was misguided. Although it had no sympathy for colonialism, the US found itself in an awkward position as it was a British ally. Under Secretary Wells worried that with a war raging, Europe was its priority, and although India's struggle for independence was worthy, Roosevelt's decision had to 'turn on the "question of expediency".[17] It is a misconception to conclude that the US did little to help India's nationalist aspirations. 'Robert E. Sherwood's *Roosevelt and Hopkins* (1950) makes it clear that at this time Roosevelt urged Churchill to settle the India question.'[18] According to Arthur Herman, 'Like any alliance, the "special relationship" between Britain and the United States, and the bond between Roosevelt and Churchill, had its shaky moments, almost all of them came over India.'[19]

Close to 2,50,000 US soldiers were stationed in India along the China–Burma–India border. They had come at the behest of the British government to assist in the war effort. In March 1942, Roosevelt had decided to send his personal friend and confidant, Colonel Louis Johnson, to India as an 'observer'. Indian nationalists conveyed to him that they would support the allies during the war but, in turn, they wanted independence from colonial rule.

Louis Johnson's presence in India made the British uncomfortable. He got along well with Nehru and made friends with many of the leaders of the independence movement, who naturally hoped that the US would support their aspirations, having fought its own independence from the British. Tensions over Johnson's presence reached a head when the British dispatched Sir Stafford Cripps to India in March 1942 to try to work out an arrangement with the nationalists to assist the war effort in return for a gradual timetable for independence.

According to Henry William Brands, 'Roosevelt directed Louis Johnson … to mediate between Cripps and Viceroy Linlithgow on the one hand and Nehru and the Congress party on the other. The appearance of Johnson as a deus ex machina threw a momentary scare into the British.'[20] Cripps was a liberal and sympathetic to India, but the proposal that Johnson came up with exceeded his instructions from Churchill.[21] The mediation failed as soon as Churchill gained assurances from Washington that they would not seek to use the Cripps Mission as leverage in the Lend-Lease agreement.‡‡

The British had become paranoid about any friendship between India and the US. They were looking for people to blame for inciting the nationalists who wanted the British to leave India. In the end, the British left because it was inevitable. 'The choice, then, was coercion on a large scale or independence—and British resources were inadequate to retain power by force.'[22]

The warm rapport between Johnson and Nehru was aborted when a severe intestinal infection compelled Johnson to leave India suddenly. It was a condition that would afflict several US ambassadors subsequently stationed in India, including Galbraith and Moynihan. The British were relieved as they viewed any relationship between India and the US, particularly with Indian leaders involved in the freedom struggle, as a threat to their status quo.

The failure of the US to influence Churchill left the Indians somewhat bitter. Many leaders of the independence movement felt disappointed by the country that claimed to uphold the very aspirations of freedom, liberty and equality that India was trying to attain. Louis Johnson's warmth and friendship had raised false hopes among the freedom fighters who had convinced themselves that America would support their cause once Johnston spoke to his president. When Louis Johnson left, there was no one to counter the subtle anti-US messaging that was being fed to Nehru and other leaders in the Congress party by the departing British. The British, in their anxiety to preserve their status in India, were prepared to sabotage any potential relationship from developing between the US and India. Jagat Mehta, who was in the foreign service and got to know Nehru, believes that this was when Nehru first became disillusioned with the US.[23]

---

‡‡ The Lend-Lease policy of 1941 was an arrangement that President Roosevelt devised to help his European allies defeat Hitler without giving up American 'neutrality' during World War II. It claimed it was lending and leasing military and other aid and equipment to Britain. Eventually, it was used to supply $50 billion in aid to over thirty countries worldwide. This continued until the war ended in 1945. (Source: Office of the historian, US Department of State.)

Ultimately, in the early days of the Cold War, India was viewed as a British domain and was far removed from American interests. The US remained deferential to Britain when it came to its former colonies. FDR, who was intensely engaged with the British on a far larger political landscape across the globe, did not see any political mileage in antagonizing Churchill on India's account. He had said his piece; Churchill was uninterested in his advice and so he did not pursue it.

Relations between Churchill and the Indians continued to deteriorate. In 1943, the Bengal famine devastated the region where the US soldiers were based. Cyclones and tidal waves washed away crops, homes and people. The war prevented the flow of food and the British, distracted by the war in Europe, failed to alleviate the shortages. Appeals for aid were made to the US, but when the US Congress finally agreed to consider aid to India, 'Britain, not desiring to see this agency, and with it the Americans, operating in India, refrained from formulating an official request for assistance.'[24] Upwards of three million people starved to death and Churchill refused to send food relief to the region.

## Independence

When independence came in 1947, Nehru was not only Gandhi's choice to become India's first prime minister but also the unanimous choice of the people of India who adored him. If Gandhi was the father of the nation who guided India to independence, Nehru became the undisputed leader of independent India. He was the country's first prime minister and served from 1947 until his death in 1964.

The independence movement in India united Indians of all religions and ethnicities in a common cause.[§§] The British, in a policy of 'divide and rule', used religious differences to try to weaken the coalitions against them. They supported the Muslim League against the Indian National Congress, hoping to maintain their own primacy. But they had

---

[§§] Although the most prominent leaders of the freedom movement were Gandhi, Nehru and other Hindus who belonged to the Congress party, there were several Muslims leaders in the party as well.

miscalculated. The desire for independence was too deep and, by 1945, the freedom movement's momentum had become unstoppable. The peace marches and massive non-violent protests eventually brought the British government to the negotiating table. In 1946 it agreed to grant India its independence, but it was to be partitioned along religious lines into two states, India and Pakistan.⁵⁵ Partitioning the country was a highly complex task in a subcontinent where co-religionists had lived together since the 1500s.*** They accounted for a quarter of the population and were fully integrated into the country.

Sir Cyril Radcliffe, a British barrister who had never lived in India, was tasked with the unenviable job of drawing the lines to partition India in five weeks. Gandhi and Nehru were opposed to Partition, but it was the cost they had to pay for independence.

Pakistan had declared itself an Islamic state, but India chose to remain secular. With 45 million Muslims representing 20 per cent of the population in 1947, India had more Muslims than Pakistan after Partition. Gandhi and Nehru fought the founders that leaned towards making India a 'Hindu' state. They were determined to keep India secular and multicultural, and a state based on the rule of law and a constitution, not religion or ethnicity. This was of paramount importance to Nehru and Gandhi.

Lord Mountbatten was sent to India as the last viceroy to oversee the transition to independence. It proved to be a wise choice. Unlike some of his predecessors, he treated Nehru as his equal and developed an immediate rapport with him. They had both been born to privilege, attended the same schools, and found they had much in common. Mountbatten's wife, Edwina, fell in love with India and developed an intimate relationship with Nehru. Her ties to Nehru and India would result in a long and lasting friendship between the two families that

---

⁵⁵ Some Muslim leaders led by Jinnah demanded a separate state for Muslims. They did not want to live as a minority population in a Hindu-dominated country. Ironically, during the Mughal period, which lasted roughly from 1550–1700, most of northern India was a Hindu country ruled by Muslims, who were a minority.

*** At the time of Partition, Hindus comprised approximately 66 per cent of the population and Muslims 24 per cent.

would outlive the transition to independence. It was a friendship that helped smooth over the many challenges thrown up by the indelicacy inherent in the relationship between a recently rejected ruler and its subjects. As the British left India, their most significant influence on Nehru was Mountbatten. The British used him as their instrument of influence. Nehru took Mountbatten's advice seriously, sometimes to India's detriment, as in the Kashmir question when he acceded to the viceroy's advice to refer it to the UN.

Mountbatten remained in India as governor general through the transition period, along with the British commander-in-chief of the army and his staff. Quickly realizing that the army may not be in a position to manage the transfer if violence erupted, the British government decided to advance the date of Independence by a year to August 1947.[†††]

The transfer of power in India, for all its pomp and show, was one of the most poorly planned and hopelessly mismanaged operations in British history. Conducted in haste, approximately 14 million people were displaced, crossing the border with inadequate security. Estimates vary, but 5,00,000 to 2 million people died, almost entirely at the hands of mobs, slaughtered by religious fanatics. Gandhi and Nehru's worst fears were realized as violence raged across the subcontinent for months.

The division of assets between the two countries, including military stores, financial reserves and water rights, was not completed before Independence. This led to extensive friction after the countries parted ways. The situation was set up for conflict between the two new countries.

Despite maintaining a low profile during Partition so as not to be held responsible for its failures, the British wished to continue to exert their influence in South Asia and retain their military bases. They wanted to ensure they could maintain their connections in the two countries and protect their commercial dominance. They pressed to have a British national remain as head of the army. Nehru felt this was incompatible with a country's sovereign status as he did not believe that the army chief could be loyal to two masters. As a compromise, in order to ensure a smooth transfer, an interim agreement was reached that would last for

---

††† The original date for Independence was August 1948.

a year. Field Marshal Auchinleck was to assume overall command of the armies of both India and Pakistan as the supreme commander, and Commander-in-Chief Lockhart would head India's defence forces while General Gracey would do the same in Pakistan.

In addition, a special defence committee was formed, and Mountbatten was appointed as its chairman. Several members of the Indian government were unhappy about this arrangement as it made the new Indian cabinet subordinate to the defence committee, putting national security in the hands of foreigners. They felt that, at the very least, Nehru himself should have been appointed the chairman, not Mountbatten, and worried that Nehru was unduly influenced by the British. However, as Nehru was India's most experienced and trusted leader when it came to foreign affairs, the country accepted his decisions. As events in Kashmir would soon show, the fears of the sceptics would prove to be justified.

Although the British granted India and Pakistan independence in 1947, they only had legal jurisdiction over some 52 per cent of the country. The remaining 48 per cent of India was officially independent of the British and ruled by individual princely states. Each maharaja had to be persuaded to join either India or Pakistan. They could opt to remain independent, although the British advised them that such a move would not be in their interest. Prior to Independence, the interim Indian government embarked on a remarkable mission to convince 565 maharajas and minor rajas to join India so it could maintain its geographic integrity. Most did in return for retaining special privileges. Kashmir was one of the three holdouts and it would have serious domestic and foreign policy consequences for many years.‡‡‡

The country that Nehru inherited when he finally became prime minister in 1947 was impoverished, undeveloped, unhealthy and backward. Like most colonial enterprises, the British had invested just enough in India

---

‡‡‡ The other two were Hyderabad and Junagadh. Both had Muslim rulers and Hindu majority populations. Hyderabad was in the middle of the Indian peninsula and landlocked. It was eventually taken over by force. Junagadh was on the western border and the ruler opted for Pakistan but was prevented from doing so by his political base, which was composed of Hindus who wanted to stay with India.

to keep the wheels of the empire running, but the Bengal famine of 1943 killed 2–3 million people, crippling India's food supplies and exhausting its resources for several years. With literacy rates at a pathetic 12 per cent, the human resources needed for future development of the country were in short supply. Life expectancy hovered between thirty and forty years, and the average Indian survived on less than a rupee a day.[25]

Nehru created the framework for India's economic development. During a trip to the Soviet Union in 1955, he had been impressed by what he saw. The abject poverty that existed in India was not visible in the Soviet Union. The Soviets seemed to have attained an acceptable standard of living for their citizens. Nehru hoped to emulate this example and lift the teeming millions in India out of the grinding poverty that enslaved them to moneylenders and middlemen. He was convinced that education was the best route and invested in the future. Although the Soviet political system had little appeal for him, as he was firmly committed to democracy and a free press, he decided to adopt parts of their economic model. He was looking for ways to pull India out of its state of subsistence and put it on a path to growth.

Eighty per cent of India's population was employed in the agricultural sector in 1947, many of them on subsistence farms, and indentured labour was common. It was an unproductive system and merciless to the poorest farmer without means to credit. Most of India still lived in rural areas. Nehru wanted to emulate the Soviets, hoping to eliminate dire poverty and shift the economy towards manufacturing and technology. He decided India needed a planned economy based on a system of five-year plans, with an emphasis on industrial growth and investment in technology. It was a popular approach among the global development community at the time, including the World Bank, which was encouraging countries to set up planning commissions and five-year benchmarks. It did not all work precisely as Nehru envisioned, and there were many compromises along the way, but his legacy lingered for years after he was gone. He decided to invest in education and science to create a foundation that would supply India with the resources and manpower to propel it towards this goal.

Nehru set up the All India Institute of Medical Science (AIIMS) and encouraged the expansion of medical schools. The proliferation of medical professionals helped drive down mortality rates and there was a rise in the life expectancy rate over the next decade. This resulted in an explosion of the population. According to the census of India, the population in 1950 was 361 million, but by 1961 it had increased by almost a third to 438 million.

Nehru started the famous Indian Institute of Technology (IIT). In order to ensure they would be world-class institutions, he invited other countries to collaborate in setting them up, making sure India did not become reliant on any one country. Domestically, India owes Nehru a great debt. Its goal to pull itself out of poverty and into the twenty-first century is closer to being realized thanks to the investments he made and the priorities he set at Independence.

No country benefitted more from its collaboration and investment in IITs than the US. The institutions spawned many of the engineers who later fanned out throughout Silicon Valley and are currently employed at Microsoft, Google and other large tech companies, providing the US with highly skilled engineers to fulfil the growing demand for manpower in the technology sector. Fifty years after its initial investments, the US has reaped the dividends with a vibrant Indian American community creating both capital and growth in the US.

From the very first five-year plan, Nehru's emphasis was on educational institutes, industrialization and developing India's technological base, and these are the very investments that have contributed to making India into an economic power in the twenty-first century.

For Nehru, the path to progress was through science. It was more than a field of study for him. It was a way of life he was fully committed to. He viewed science philosophically, as a path to choose instead of religion. 'What is a scientific approach to life's problems? I suppose it is one of examining everything, of seeking truth by trial and error and by experiment, of never saying that this must be so but trying to understand why it is so ... of having an open mind, of trying to imbibe the truth wherever it is found.'[26]

Many of the aspects that are most admirable about modern India stem from the legacy Nehru left behind. He was ethical, incorruptible and set a standard that no prime minister since measured up to. By the time he became prime minister, Nehru, like Gandhi, had become a national icon, and people revered him. He was treated like a demi-god and Indians called him 'Panditji' (honoured teacher). Nehru, who was by instinct a private person, remained a lonely man for most of his adult life. He became more isolated by being put on this pedestal and retreated further into himself.

India emerged as a newly born, independent country just as the world was being divided into two ideologically opposed blocs of nations. The American diplomat George F. Kennan articulated in his famous 'Long Telegram'§§§ from Moscow, in February 1946, a policy of containment and confrontation towards the communist bloc. On 5 March 1946, Winston Churchill delivered a speech advocating for a 'special relationship' with the US. He warned about the dangers of communism and Russian expansionism declaring, 'an iron curtain had descended upon the continent'. The contours of a new world order had emerged out of the rubble of the Second World War. On one side stood the liberal democracies of the West, led by the United States and including all of Western Europe. On the other side stood the Soviet Union, the satellite countries of Eastern Europe that had fallen under its sway after the end of the war and China.

India chose to remain neutral or 'non-aligned'. Most foreign diplomats who got to know Nehru during this period agree that Nehru's choice of non-alignment was not anti-Western. It was just pro-India. Having just come out from under the yoke of colonialism, he was reluctant to see India submit to any sphere of influence. With the world just entering the Cold War, a policy of non-alignment carried some risks. Remaining neutral during this period ran the risk of isolation, but for Nehru it was not a matter of cost and benefit. He believed it was the most principled and honourable course.

Nehru took it a step further. He wanted to be recognized as the leader of emerging nationalist movements around the world and believed in

---

§§§ George F. Kennan, a highly respected American diplomat who was posted in Moscow, had observed Stalin and become alarmed at the aggressive projection of Soviet power, both in Eastern Europe and the countries abutting the Soviet Union. He feared the expansion of communism and warned about it in what came to be known as the 'Long Telegram'.

Asian unity. His first speech at the UN General Assembly in Paris, on 3 November 1948, called for Europe to recognize Asians as equals. 'Nehru made clear that India would develop an active concern in world affairs, pursuing an independent policy compatible with her own national interests.'[27] His biographer, Sarvepalli Gopal, notes that Nehru's objectives were not clearly defined and 'appeared to consist primarily of vague and rather grandiose hopes of closer ties between the Asian countries and even the formation of two or three Asian federations' in the beginning.[28]

Nehru's vocal support of the nationalist aspirations of newly emerging nations at a time when the Western powers were primarily concerned with curbing the advance of communism put him at odds with Western interests. With the world entrenched into a polarized state, he was convinced that neutral countries would become essential corridors for communication between countries that did not have relations with each other. His non-alignment policy is perhaps one of his most enduring legacies.

# Chapter 3

# Kashmir*

WHILE INDEPENDENCE WAS BEING CELEBRATED ON THE subcontinent with euphoria, a sense of foreboding consumed the maharaja of Kashmir. He had watched with trepidation as, one by one, the princely states had been absorbed by the newly created nations of India and Pakistan. Kashmir, famous for its lush green valleys and cool mountain streams, where Mughal emperors spent their summers to escape the scorching heat and dust of the Indian plains, was strategically important and coveted by both countries.

Embedded like a crown above the subcontinent, the Himalayan mountains crest its northern frontier, Pakistan lies to its west and India cups its southern perimeter. Inspired by the rich fauna and fragrant flowers, the Mughals used it as their summer capital, laying out magnificent gardens filled with flowers and fruit trees. The Shalimar Garden built during Emperor Jehangir's reign still survives in Srinagar, the state capital. The mountains, landscape, food and people bear little resemblance to the heartland of India.

Maharaja Hari Singh had resisted pressure to give up his kingdom. His ancestors had ruled the state for the past one hundred years. Hari Singh was

---

* The official title in 1947 was the State of Jammu and Kashmir. It included the valley of Kashmir, Jammu, Gilgit, Baltistan and Ladakh. After 1948, Jammu, Ladakh and the valley of Kashmir remained with India, while the rest became Pakistan-administered Kashmir, commonly known as 'Azad Kashmir'. For the purposes of this book, Kashmir refers to the Jammu and Kashmir state.

a Hindu and head of the Dogra clan. Before the partition of India in 1947, the state's population was roughly 77 per cent Muslim and 20 per cent Hindu.[1] Kashmir encompasses a complex community. Hindus are dominant in Jammu, while Buddhists form the majority in Ladakh. The Muslims belong to the Shia, Sunni and Ismaili sects, including some ethnic Hazaras and Tajiks. It was also home to several mystical Sufi sects. Jahanara, the daughter of Emperor Shah Jahan, who built the Taj Mahal, had written a book on the Sufi saints of Kashmir in the seventeenth century.[2]

The maharaja had come under intense pressure to give up his dream of independence and choose between joining India or Pakistan. Mountbatten had visited the state and tried to meet with him to discuss Kashmir's options, but not wanting to be put under pressure to make a decision, the maharaja had pleaded illness. Muhammad Ali Jinnah had tried to visit him on three occasions but had similarly been turned down.

Kashmir's prime minister[†] had urged the maharaja to join Pakistan given its majority Muslim population, but the maharaja hesitated, hoping to somehow retain his independence. In order to buy himself some time, he signed a 'standstill' agreement with Pakistan in August 1947. Under the agreement, Pakistan took over the telegraph and some communication responsibilities in the princely state with the anticipation that the maharaja would eventually bring it into the Pakistan union.

Nehru neglected to make sure that India secured a similar arrangement. He was preoccupied with the influx of refugees coming into India from Pakistan and attempting to control the communal riots that had broken out around the country. He was also dealing with the more immediate problem posed by the accession of the princely state of Junagadh to Pakistan.[‡]

The upheaval of Partition in neighbouring India and Pakistan had increased tensions between religious communities in Kashmir. Refugees

---

† Ram Chandra Kak was the prime minister of the princely state, prior to Justice Mehr Chand Mahajan, who became the first prime minister of Jammu and Kashmir after it acceded to India.

‡ Junagadh, on India's western border with Pakistan, was one of the three holdouts. Its ruler was a Muslim and opted to join Pakistan. His subjects were primarily Hindu. India was busy trying to intervene to force a plebiscite.

fleeing the violence had come to the state, bringing with them tales of horror. The maharaja wanted, at all costs, to avoid importing the problems of Punjab to his state.[3] Aside from limited incidents, there was no widespread communal fighting in Kashmir until 1947.[§]

The maharaja began having second thoughts about his arrangement with Pakistan when it began to exert pressure on him by blocking trade and supply routes to his state. He fired his pro-Pakistan prime minister and decided to replace him with M.C. Mahajan, a legal scholar and Supreme Court justice in Lahore. Mahajan was close to the Indian National Congress leaders, and the deputy prime minister Vallabhbhai 'Sardar' Patel in particular.

Mahajan was hesitant to take on such a difficult job at a complex time, but the maharaja's wife personally came to Lahore to convince him to accept the position. They met at Faletti's Hotel in May 1947, where the maharani and her sixteen-year-old son, Karan Singh, tried to persuade him over tea to accept the offer. According to Mahajan, it was the young prince whose entreaties touched his heart. 'I said I would think it over.' And he agreed to visit His Highness if he were officially invited to Kashmir. On the first of September, he received a formal invitation and agreed to meet the maharaja. The monsoon was in full swing, the roads were impassable, and he arrived at his destination via a combination of horseback and military wagon. Part of the journey was endured on foot until he was rescued by a passing lorry.[4]

At the urging of Nehru, Patel and Mountbatten, Mahajan took up his new position later that month, and began to explore the terms under which Kashmir would accede to India. The maharaja realized that remaining independent was unrealistic in a landlocked country but was hesitant to proceed with the administrative reforms that Nehru insisted on. Nehru's

---

§   In 1947, during the months of October and November, there was a series of attacks on the Muslim population in Jammu led by the Rashtriya Swayamsevak Sangh, a Hindu right-wing paramilitary organization. It was a communal carnage in which, according to some estimates, close to 1,00,000 Muslims lost their lives. (Source: Christopher Snedden, *Understanding Kashmir and Kashmiris*)

ancestors were from Kashmir and, much as he wanted Kashmir to be a part of India, he wanted the Kashmiri people to legitimize the union.

The nationalist Congress party led by Gandhi and Nehru had built strong affiliates in many of the princely states. It had links with the secular National Conference party headed by Sheikh Abdullah, who was pro-Congress and a close friend of Nehru. Like Maharaja Hari Singh, he would have preferred independence for the state, but faced with a choice between India and Pakistan, he preferred Kashmir remain with India. Nehru was confident that a government under Sheikh Abdullah would remain loyal to India.

Nehru insisted that the maharaja install a government headed by the sheikh. Abdullah was charismatic, educated, a brilliant orator and easily the most popular leader in the Kashmir valley. Nehru did not believe the accession would be viewed as legitimate without the endorsement of the Muslim population, and for this Abdullah was key. There was only one problem—the Sheikh was despised by the royal family whose authority he had challenged.

The maharaja rejected Nehru's demands to let Sheikh Abdullah form a representative government as he felt Nehru was asking him to sign away his kingdom. The maharaja knew that with Sheikh Abdullah, he would have no role in the state's future, because 'the Sheikh had built his popular movement not just around a demand for democracy, but more specifically around the expulsion of the Dogra dynasty'.[5]

The maharaja's indecision regarding his kingdom's future created room for interested parties to change the dynamics on the ground by generating tension within the community. Passions were inflamed and the conflict over Kashmir was set into motion, and it became a festering wound that never healed. Since Partition it has been and remains today one of the most contested pieces of real estate, despite the efforts at mediation by the United Nations and several US presidents.

## Accession: The Start of the Dispute

The communal fires of Partition had barely died down in India when the new government was faced with its first external crisis as Pakistan-backed insurgents infiltrated the Kashmir region in October 1947 to instigate an insurrection and depose the maharaja. Several theories exist about the origins of the invasion. Pakistanis assert that Hari Singh was a cruel despot who discriminated against his Muslim subjects and the raiders entered Kashmir to support their religious brethren. In their counter complaint to the UN, they would use the term 'genocide' to describe the treatment of Muslims in Kashmir. The Indians, in contrast, argued that once Pakistan got wind of the maharaja's overtures to India in September, it sent in raiders to overthrow the Dogra dynasty and take the state by force, relying on Islamic sentiment to turn the tide in their favour.

Regardless of their motivations, the facts were that non-Kashmiris entered the state from Pakistan and gathered Kashmiri Muslims along the way in a rebellion to oust the maharaja. The maharaja, not realizing the scale of the invasion, was hoping his small army would repulse the attack. He went with his new prime minister to survey some of the villages that had come under attack and quickly saw they were outnumbered.

Initially, the maharaja turned to the British prime minister, Clement Attlee, for assistance and asked him to request Pakistan to withdraw the raiders. Pakistan denied any involvement and London maintained its distance from the finger-pointing.

With key towns rapidly falling to the invaders and the security of his government threatened, Hari Singh realized he had backed himself into a corner and was negotiating for help from a position of weakness. The royal household went into a state of panic, worried that help may not arrive in time.

The main palace, situated on top of a hill overlooking the city of Srinagar with a stunning view of the lake, had all its fountains and chandeliers designed by the French craftsman René Lalique. The queen's romantic palace nestled in a cove of lotus flowers on the lake where she spent afternoons entertaining guests. There were several other palaces and hunting lodges that dotted Kashmir, full of magnificent carpets and antiques acquired in Europe on foreign travels.

The queen's palace was now swarming with priests offering prayers and fortune tellers predicting what the next few days would bring. Rumours of the advancing rebels ricocheted through the palaces, embellished at each retelling and creating further waves of anxiety.

As Srinagar inched towards a state of siege, Earl Mountbatten, who was known to be pro-India, saw an opportunity to bring Hari Singh to heel and suggested that Nehru condition India's assistance on an accession agreement, which the maharaja had, until then, refused to sign. Mountbatten argued that, if the maharaja agreed to join India before it sent help, it would legitimize Indian involvement and prevent Pakistan from considering India's intervention an act of war. Once order was restored, a plebiscite could be held to determine the future of Kashmir.

Although Nehru and Patel were ready to assist the maharaja, they hesitated to force the accession issue on him at gunpoint. They felt that the maharaja, as an independent ruler, had the right to seek assistance from India. But forcing accession at the same time would complicate a delicate negotiation best handled separately.

With the raiders practically knocking on the palace gates, 'faced with a desperate situation, the Maharaja was at last prepared to shed his earlier reluctance to appointing Abdullah to office. An assurance to this effect was given to the Government of India and the Governor General speedily accepted the instrument of accession, concomitantly noting India's intention to consult the people once law and order had been restored'.[6]

Had the maharaja believed that Pakistan would have offered him better terms and greater autonomy, he could have negotiated to join Pakistan as they had already entered a standstill agreement. Pakistan did not like Sheikh Abdullah any more than the maharaja did, as the Sheikh was aligned with Nehru; therefore, Pakistan would not have insisted that Abdullah head a government in Kashmir and would have been happy to see him exiled to India. One can only conclude that the maharaja had decided that, as independence was unrealistic, India was the best option for Kashmir.

Pakistan argued that it was geographically exposed without Kashmir, but it also believed that the Hindu ruler had no moral right to join India given the population's Muslim majority. Nehru rejected the demographic argument as India had more Muslims than Pakistan and was a secular nation. For him, having Jammu and Kashmir be part of India became increasingly important as a symbol of India's secular credentials.

The legitimacy of the accession agreement and the state's status were challenged by Pakistan and became the cause for three wars between India and Pakistan. Jammu and Kashmir became the repository of grievances between the two countries, involving several generations of politicians and encompassing issues ranging from identity politics to terrorism. It has outlived the Cold War and, like the Israeli–Palestinian conflict, threatens to turn into the twentieth century's hundred-year war. Several US presidents tried and failed to move the countries to a resolution on the Kashmir issue and it remains one of world's potential nuclear flashpoints.

## Rift with the British

Maharaja Hari Singh deposited the crown jewels at the state treasury and left Srinagar on the evening of 26 October 1947. As darkness fell, they drove through the hills for Jammu, taking whatever rubies, pearls and other valuables in the convoy of cars that carried him to safety. V.P. Menon, who had undertaken the difficult task of integrating the princely states into an independent India, flew to Jammu to meet him. On his arrival at the palace, he 'found it in a state of utter turmoil with valuable articles strewn all over the place'.[7] The accession document was signed later that night.

The maharaja could not conceive then that he would never be allowed to return to his kingdom. In his absence, his administration collapsed. Sheikh Abdullah and the Indian Army's divisional commander, Major General Thimayya, restored some order. In April, Nehru replaced Mahajan with Sheikh Abdullah. He gave the maharaja a ceremonial title without any real powers and excluded him from all negotiations involving the future of the state.[¶]

¶ In April 1949, Nehru deposed the maharaja in favour of his eighteen-year-old son Karan Singh, who was an admirer of Nehru and inspired by the vision of independent India. He was amenable to Nehru's reforms and Abdullah. The maharaja felt betrayed by both Nehru and his son and in a fit of anger turned the crown jewels over to the state. Abdullah, who was

With the maharaja out of the way and the path clear for a democratic government in Kashmir, Nehru tried to mobilize troops and move them into the state to prevent it from falling to Pakistan. He met with stiff resistance from Mountbatten and the British generals, who did everything they could to slow him down, as the politicians in London were reluctant to support India, and did not want India to take unilateral action against Pakistan that would disadvantage Pakistani claims in Kashmir. Realizing that their interests were not aligned, Nehru began to confer privately with Indian Army officers and, in the end, sent a Sikh battalion to Kashmir rather than the famous Gurkhas officered largely by the British.

Under the transition agreement, the Pakistani and Indian armies were still headed by British generals, who were wary of being caught in a war between the two ex-dominions while still commanding armies on behalf of the new governments. The British generals stayed in constant touch, keeping each other fully informed about rebel movements. However, they did not share this information with the Indian prime minister or cabinet on the premise that, as Jammu and Kashmir was not part of India, they were not obliged to divulge this information to the Indian government.

The relationship between the British commanders and the Indian leaders soured during the transition period. Deputy Prime Minister Patel thought that Field Marshal Auchinleck had been partial to Pakistan in dividing the military supplies between the two countries at Partition and pressed for his removal. Auchinleck resented having his integrity questioned and Mountbatten had to intervene with Nehru to smooth things over.

Pakistan's first governor general, Muhammad Ali Jinnah was also frustrated with the British. He wanted to respond to Indian troop movements into Kashmir with an all-out attack on India. But in the early years of independence, not only were all the high-ranking officers in his army British, even the lower level personnel of the technical branches of the Pakistani services were British.[8] His commanding officers took their

---

now head of the government in Jammu and Kashmir, kept them under lock and key. The royal family never saw them again. Karan Singh later served as the state's governor. A long legal battle to recover the family jewels remains unresolved to this day.

orders from Auchinleck, who remained the supreme commander of both armies. He was not about to have British officers go to war against each other on behalf of client states. Though initially this stymied Jinnah's plans to wrest Kashmir by force, it helped Pakistan in the long run, as British empathy lay with Pakistan. At this stage, the British were playing a positive role by averting a war that neither side could afford so early in their nationhood.

The British Army chiefs** and Mountbatten alarmed London when they warned that the two former dominions were preparing for war, but much to India's disappointment, London's focus was on the prevention of war rather than on reining in Pakistani aggression.

Pakistan, due to the raiders, now held part of Kashmir. As Indian troops began to retake Kashmir and drive the invaders out, Nehru requested the army chiefs to provide Indian troops with adequate supplies and equipment, but General Lockhart, supposedly at the head of the Indian Army, refused. Nehru had also by this time learnt that Lockhart, whom he found difficult to deal with, had been aware of the rebel preparations for their raids into Kashmir but had chosen not to share this information with the Indian government.[9] When the invaders from Pakistan had entered Kashmir on 22 October, General Gracey of the Pakistan Army alerted General Lockhart of the Indian Army 'that a force of 5,000 tribesmen had entered Kashmir and seized Muzaffarabad and Dornel'.[10] He also warned that they were about to attack other strategic areas right up to Poonch and that the trucks and arms they were using could only have been obtained through the assistance of the Pakistani authorities.[11] This information was not conveyed to Nehru or Patel.

Though few British officers remained in the Indian Army, a schism developed between them and the Indian senior officers. The former tended to confide in the British ambassador while the Indian officers conferred with Nehru and Patel. Within the British government, sentiment shifted away from India. The British officers had demonstrated that their loyalty was to the Crown rather than to the new government of India.

---

** Pakistan's army chief was Gracey Smith. India had diversified its high command after Lockhart's departure.

The Indians concluded that the transition arrangement, which was to have lasted until 15 August 1948, had too many conflicts of interest and should be terminated in November 1947. This action did, however, cost India some goodwill with the British and had some inherent disadvantages for India. Auchinleck's departure also removed a critical plug that had prevented the two armies from going to war against each other. The ending of the transition arrangement also meant that the communication link between the two opposing armies ceased to function. India no longer knew the Pakistan Army's intentions.

Pakistan, knowing that it needed the British, retained all its British officers, both during the transition and after it ended. British officers developed close relations with their Pakistani colleagues. As a consequence, British policy was often more favourably disposed towards Pakistan. This carried over to Whitehall, and the British government became more pro-Pakistani.

The Pakistani leadership had once observed the closeness of the Nehru–Mountbatten relationship with concern. After the breach between the Indian government and the British generals, they went out of their way to court the British. Once Mountbatten left India, the special glue holding Indo-British relations together seemed to dissolve. The timing was favourable to Pakistan as Western interests, focused on oil and Iranian nationalism, were increasingly becoming preoccupied with the Middle East. Pakistan was viewed as a useful Muslim ally, and the British saw a role for them beyond South Asia.

In December 1947, prior to the reference to the Security Council, Pakistan had stepped up its raids across the Poonch border in Kashmir. Reports were coming in of abductions and massacres. Nehru was under intense pressure to respond with military action. Pakistan's prime minister, Liaquat Ali Khan kept reiterating that its actions were a response to atrocities inflicted on Muslims by the maharaja and others. This is when Nehru began to lose hope that a bilateral solution could be negotiated.

Mountbatten tried to mediate between India and Pakistan and began a round of unsuccessful negotiations to resolve the differences over Kashmir. He was able to somewhat persuade Nehru to make concessions due to their special relationship, but he found the Pakistanis insufferable.

Frustrated by the lack of progress, Mountbatten asked Prime Minister Attlee to try his hand at resolving the disagreement, but Attlee was not interested.

Within the British government, there seemed to be varying views on Kashmir. Mountbatten tried to get the maharaja to join India, while his colleagues in London tilted towards giving it to Pakistan. Mountbatten was pro-India and close to Nehru and felt disheartened that London had turned its back on India. London made it clear to him that it was not fully behind his idea of Kashmir's accession to India.

Lacking the support of his government, Mountbatten slowed things down by conferring with the British army chiefs to hinder supplies and troops for the clearance of the raiders out of Kashmir. He persuaded Nehru that a new international organization in New York, the United Nations, was an impartial forum whose purpose was to address disputes similar to the one they were dealing with.

Getting nowhere with the Pakistanis and finally realizing the time of his handover period was running out, he proposed the withdrawal of troops to be followed by a plebiscite conducted by the UN.

While most Indian cabinet members did not like the idea of an outside entity conducting the plebiscite, Nehru was swayed by Mountbatten and reluctantly agreed. Pakistan initially rejected the proposal. After rounds of fruitless negotiations, the Indians came to believe that Pakistan was not negotiating in good faith. They also became increasingly suspicious of the British. The Indians concluded that the British had not been even-handed; they had asked India for restraint without penalizing Pakistan in any meaningful way for starting the crisis and had not insisted that Pakistan withdraw its troops. They also believed that the British prevented them from pushing the Pakistani-backed invaders out of Kashmir by force, which at the time they had the capacity to do and which could have ended the crisis.

Much against the view of Patel and Gandhi,[12] based on Mountbatten's advice, India filed a complaint at the Security Council on New Year's Day in 1948, under Article 35, Chapter 6 of the UN Charter. What Nehru had most wanted was for the UN to acknowledge that Pakistan had unlawfully assisted irregular troops in infiltrating Kashmir with the intention of taking over. He wanted the UN to censure Pakistan for the initial unlawful act but then have its people determine the fate of the state.

The intention of filing a complaint with the Security Council was to contain Pakistan's ambitions and provide cover for India should it decide to go to war with Pakistan to get rid of the 'raiders'. It was a 'specific reference', not a general one. However, once the fateful Pandora's box had been left with the UN, many hands tampered with it and, once opened, India lost control of the narrative. This probably counted as Nehru's greatest foreign policy blunder and possibly one of the factors that prevented a timely resolution of the dispute.

Pakistan responded to India's complaint with its own accusations that ran several pages longer than India's and expanded the dispute beyond Kashmir. It denied India's accusations, refuted the accession as illegal and immoral and claimed that the invasion took place due to atrocities inflicted on the population by the despotic maharaja. India had gone from being an injured party whose territory had been 'invaded' to a mere party in a disputed territory.

From the Indian perspective, the villain in the Kashmir episode at the UN was Phillip Noel-Baker, the secretary of state for Commonwealth relations, who, along with the British foreign secretary Ernest Bevin, took a pro-Pakistan line at the UN. Although there were many people more familiar with the subcontinent in the British cabinet and military, who may have been better informed and more even-handed in their judgement, the Foreign Office and the Commonwealth Relations Office took the lead on the Kashmir dispute.

Bevin and Noel-Baker's primary focus was Britain's interests in the Middle East. As explained by Noel-Baker:

> The Foreign Secretary has expressed anxiety lest we should appear to be siding with India in the dispute between India and Pakistan over Kashmir which is now before the United Nations Security Council. With the Situation as critical as it is in Palestine, Mr Bevin feels that we must be very careful to guard against the danger of aligning the whole of Islam against us.[13]

With oil interests at stake and the Middle East inflamed over Palestine, the Foreign Office was far more concerned about preserving British relationships there. Pakistan now became important as part of a pan-Islamic front to preserve their interests in the Middle East.

Once the Kashmir issue was brought to the UN, the original complaint was marginalized. India was incorrect in its naïve assumption that it was the aggrieved party and Pakistan would be automatically censured. Noel-Baker, who had reliable confirmation from British generals that the initial raid into Kashmir had been undertaken with Pakistan's support, not unsympathetically predicted: 'I understand the anger and frustration which they must feel at the continued support, which, we do not doubt, their opponents in Kashmir are receiving from Pakistan. Nevertheless, it was a dangerous miscalculation on India's part to hope that the Security Council would condemn Pakistan as the aggressor and authorize India to send her troops into Pakistan.'[14] However, once at the UN, Noel-Baker did an about-face and told the Indian delegation that 'from his own sources he was satisfied that Pakistan had provided no assistance to the raiders'.[15]

The British line at the UN, which they pressed on the US as well, was that Pakistan's intrusion into the state was a justifiable response to the repression of Muslims by the maharaja, that Pakistani military troops should police the state and that Abdullah should be kept from taking power. The Foreign Office felt they could manipulate the Indians and advised Noel-Baker that 'by playing on [India's] respect for legal processes we might get them to accept whatever the Security Council can be brought to recommend'.[16]

When Noel-Baker arrived at the UN, he embarked on what can only be called a lobbying campaign on behalf of Pakistan. His instructions from Attlee were fairly general. London's primary concern was to avoid war between its ex-dominions. Noel-Baker was to encourage India and Pakistan to find a solution, avoid going to war and reassure Pakistan that they were not siding with India. He was to lean on India's sensitivity to global opinion to find a resolution and to play on India's respect for legal process in order to get it to accept the findings of the UN Security Council.

The British trusted their officials to work in the Crown's best interests in what used to be a far-flung empire. They were used to giving senior officials a wide berth to conduct government business. Only on rare occasions would an emissary be reprimanded.

Instead, Noel-Baker started canvassing his European allies on the Security Council to pass resolutions to bring all Kashmir disputes under UN control. Noel-Baker's proposals included a plebiscite as soon as possible, to be carried out under UN's auspices, and he argued for the presence of both Pakistani and Indian troops in Kashmir. This would establish equal rights for Pakistan, ignoring the legality of the accession agreement. The introduction of Pakistani troops into what was technically now Indian territory was unacceptable to the Indians.

Noel-Baker then turned up the dial to a dangerous level. He introduced the idea that the democratically elected government headed by Sheikh Abdullah, which had replaced the monarchy, be disbanded and replaced by a neutral entity like the UN. This would remove a major obstacle for Pakistan.

Although Sheikh Abdullah was famously difficult to handle, and occasionally toyed with independence, he was secular and had shown no interest in joining Pakistan. Nehru was confident that Kashmir would remain with India so long as Abdullah remained at its helm. The Sheikh was a skilled politician and trusted by the state's Muslim subjects. He had spent most of 1949 negotiating special provisions with New Delhi to grant Jammu and Kashmir substantial autonomy to govern its internal affairs under Article 370 of the Indian Constitution.[††]

The debate in the Security Council slid from consideration of an illegal invasion to a plebiscite and a new government in Jammu and Kashmir. Pakistan was not asked to remove the offending invaders to re-establish neutrality. Instead, the state was being asked to disband a democratically elected government voted in by its people.

Noel-Baker's strategy to isolate India at the UN put India at a severe disadvantage. The US, Belgium and other allies 'simply supported the policy which we consistently recommended and ... to abandon the non-committal line which they were adopting when the council's work began'.[17]

---

[††] The Indian Constitution was adopted in 1950. Article 370, which was decreed in 1954 by a presidential order, limited India to Jammu and Kashmir's defence, external affairs and communications, among others.

Nehru and the Indian cabinet were shocked by the British betrayal at the UN and requested an adjournment on 12 February 1948. They were trying to work out a way to remove the whole Kashmir saga from the UN.

Mountbatten had put India in a terrible predicament by pushing Nehru to take the Kashmir complaint to the UN, where the British had been able to not only expand the UN's oversight on Kashmir but also stack its Western allies against India. India had fought side by side with these same countries during both world wars and felt their ingratitude deeply. Nehru was slow to understand the shift in British policy and could not believe that India, which had been so critical to the British Empire, could be jettisoned so easily and treated as unimportant.

Nehru sent a telegram to Attlee expressing his anger at what had transpired at the UN. Mountbatten, Cripps and other India hands were alarmed by Noel-Baker's pro-Pakistan tilt at the UN and communicated their misgivings to the British prime minister as well. No doubt Mountbatten had also conveyed to Attlee that London was risking its relationship with India, but the only action Attlee took was to request Noel-Baker to tone down the British resolution without recognizing India's sovereignty over Kashmir. Attlee, to Nehru's astonishment, pressed India to accept the barely modified resolution.[18]

On 27 February 1948, the Commonwealth Affairs Committee of the British cabinet met for the first time. Noel-Baker was given a clearer and more even-handed set of instructions that were contrary to the ones he had tried to promote. Attlee gave Noel-Baker a dressing down about his excessively pro-Pakistan agenda that was not authorized by London.

The Chinese had now rotated into the presidency of the Security Council. They came up with a set of proposals that were fair and acceptable to India.‡‡ The US, whose policy had thus far been to follow the British line, seemed to think it could be a breakthrough, but Noel-Baker was not done

---

‡‡ The proposal had three parts: restoration of peace by calling upon Pakistan to withdraw the raiders, request that India appoint a plebiscite administration with UN-nominated directors and a request that India broaden the interim government with representatives from all major political groups. (Source: Dasgupta, *War and Diplomacy in Kashmir*, 127)

meddling. Despite his promises to Attlee, he tried to alter the Chinese proposals to accommodate Pakistan and, by April 1948, the Chinese proposal that had looked so promising when it was first introduced in March bore little resemblance to its original form. Although Attlee was not pleased and Nehru was furious, they agreed for a UN commission to be sent to Kashmir to make an independent assessment of the dispute.

## The UN and the US

By 1948 the sun had begun to fade across the British Empire. Although the British still viewed themselves as masters of the universe, they no longer held the exalted position they enjoyed before the Second World War. Faced with severe economic pressure, they nevertheless still tried to exert their political influence internationally and viewed Americans in a supporting role.

The United States was preoccupied with its effort to rebuild Europe after the war and its newest threat of communism. It had little interest in mopping up after the British in Asia absent compelling economic interests. When the Kashmir issue was brought to the UN in January 1948, the US was happy to follow the British lead on its ex-dominions. Far more pressing on the international agenda was the Palestinian mandate and the Arab anger over a Jewish state, which was going to play to Pakistan's advantage once the Kashmir issue was put under an international lens.

Noel-Baker proposed sectioning Jammu and Kashmir into military zones and having both Pakistani and Indian troops stationed in the state under a neutral UN-appointed military commander. The US was hesitant to dismiss India's legitimacy to Kashmir via the accession and unwilling to go along with Noel-Baker's plan. Under Secretary of State Robert Lovett 'was cool to the British proposal, which he surely knew would have been unacceptable to the Indians had it been introduced at the United Nations'.[19] In an internal note on Kashmir, written on 11 January 1950, the US seemed sceptical of Pakistan's assertions of Indian aggression and more inclined to agree with the Indian position.[20]

Noel-Baker then began to push the US State Department to support his proposals and strategy. He suggested that the US take the lead in promoting his proposals to the UN as he did not want them to appear as British manoeuvres. Noel-Baker's attempts to advance his ideas as an American plan initially persuaded Nehru that it was so. Long distances and slow communication created some confusion until Nehru was briefed by N. Gopalaswami Ayyangar, his representative at the UN, about the true source of the plan.

US Secretary of State George Marshall had reservations about Noel-Baker's proposal and saw grave danger in proceeding with a scheme that would be so injurious to India. He understood that for a plan like this to work, all parties needed to be brought on board and compromises needed to be made. Unfortunately for India, the US was not willing to contradict the British at this stage and certainly not over Kashmir. Without investing in a friendship with the US, Nehru had no one in the Western alliance looking out for India's interests.

Nehru's natural orientation was pro-British due to his intense friendship with the Mountbattens. Years of fighting the British and dealing with their arrogance had not diminished his goodwill towards them. He generally gave them the benefit of the doubt until he was disappointed, as he had been by their army commanders.

Noel-Baker's persuasive lobbying moved the US attention away from the initial complaint that India had made regarding Pakistan's invasion and made it focus on the goals of the United Nations Commission for India and Pakistan (UNCIP). Noel-Baker pushed for holding a plebiscite as the solution to the problem. US Ambassador Austin, who had been appointed by President Truman as his representative to the United Nations and was the one dealing with the Kashmir problem, found both sides vexing. The US representative had firm instructions that no further dismemberment of the subcontinent was to be supported. Jammu and Kashmir as an independent country was also not presented as an alternative.

At its creation, Pakistan needed a separate identity. Islam was the unifying factor that politicians could use to delink Pakistan from 'Mother India'. The bulk of Pakistan's population came from the two divided states of Punjab and Bengal, which had large Muslim populations. The Muslims in both states shared the same language, culture, music and food as their Indian neighbours; the critical difference was their religion. Religion was the wedge that the leaders of Pakistan used to separate the people and form their own identity, so that each time Nehru, Gandhi and other secular Indians insisted they were but one community, it felt like a denial of Pakistan's legitimacy rather than an embrace of brotherhood. From Pakistan's perspective, Kashmir, therefore, belonged to Pakistan due to its Muslim-majority population.

UNCIP,[§§] headed by Josef Korbel, arrived in Pakistan on 5 July 1948, at the peak of the monsoon season. The delegation quickly discovered the accusations and deceptions that were at the heart of the Kashmir dispute. By now the two sides were entrenched in their positions and increasingly sceptical of a fair solution. UNCIP received a tepid welcome by Pakistan on its arrival. 'It soon became quite evident that the Pakistan Government felt most uncertain about the Commission's policy and intent and preferred to wait and watch. The press, less diplomatic than members of the government, did not disguise its mistrust.'[21]

Sir Zafarullah Khan, Pakistan's elegant and articulate representative at the UN who was also the minister for foreign affairs, dropped a bombshell. Contrary to Pakistan's public denials, he informed the Commission that three Pakistani brigades had been operational inside Kashmir since May 1948. Upon questioning, he also admitted that the UN had not been informed of their presence. Earlier, he had made it clear to Noel-Baker that if 'the United Kingdom pursued a policy favourable to India, the present pro-British government in Pakistan might be swept away and its successor go over to Russia'.[22] It became clear to Korbel and his team that Pakistan was, as India had complained to the UN, behind the original invasion. It was also clear that Pakistan had no intention of withdrawing from the territory it held or retreating from its claim to the state.

Indians were still incensed about the perceived injustice of the UN attitude. They felt they owned the moral high ground, more so now, as there was little ambivalence about the war being waged by regular Pakistani soldiers. The Commission was receiving letters about the war's impact on

---

§§ UNCIP was headed by Joseph Korbel, father of Madeleine Albright, secretary of state under President Clinton.

the population and the worsening of relations. Sheikh Abdullah conveyed, through a private channel, a message to the Commission that the dispute would likely be fought out.

Having departed Pakistan without any encouragement from the government and a hostile press, Korbel and his team arrived in Delhi three days later, hoping for a better reception. Korbel reported that Nehru was in a pensive mood, but a somewhat calmer press gave the delegation conditional approval to proceed.

During a long discussion with Nehru, Korbel wrote that he confirmed his distaste for war and preference for peaceful solutions. He pointed out that India had achieved its independence in that manner, but Pakistan had opted for force to get its way. Nehru confirmed to the commissioner that he wanted Kashmiris to decide their future and supported a plebiscite as long as the Pakistanis withdrew their troops.

The meeting ended badly when Korbel asked if Nehru would make a gesture of concession to Pakistan and Nehru lost his equilibrium and shouted: 'You seem not to understand our position and our rights. We are a secular state which is not based on religion. We give to everyone freedom of conscience. Pakistan is a medieval state with an impossible theocratic concept. It should never have been created, and it would never have happened had the British not stood behind this foolish idea of Jinnah.'[23]

The Pakistanis were no less dramatic. Ghulam Mohammad Khan, the new governor general of Pakistan, said: 'Nehru hates the mere existence of Pakistan and wants to destroy us. Well, he can do so. He has an army and weapons; we have none. He can march to Karachi, come to this house and thrust a dagger into my heart. I may die, but I will never surrender.'[24]

The Security Council had suggested that the Commission try to establish a coalition government but, after many meetings with various members of the two governments, it became apparent that the hatred and mistrust that had developed between the two countries would make this a non-starter. Nehru remained obsessed with his demand that the UN condemn Pakistan as the aggressor, which it was not prepared to do.

Some members of Nehru's cabinet were convinced he had made a mistake by taking the Kashmir problem to the UN and giving in to British demands. India probably had the military strength to push the invaders out and take back most of the occupied state. Pakistan would then be in an untenable security situation. India would effectively be able to control the water supply to 19 million of the 35 million acres of irrigated land in Pakistan. Any diversion of the water supply would be the end of Pakistan's independence as a country.

Nehru realized that the Kashmir dispute was not playing well internationally and that the rest of the world did not share his moral indignation. India's unique reputation of having attained freedom through non-violence had put Gandhi and India on a pedestal, and the fighting over Kashmir was eroding India's claim to the moral high ground.[¶¶] But Nehru was not Gandhi. Gandhi had studied the British carefully. He appreciated what was good about them and used it to India's benefit. Nehru was smitten by the Mountbattens and unable to accept that British priorities were no longer with India.

Partitioning Kashmir was emerging as the only viable solution that could be acceptable to both parties until a better solution was found. A ceasefire resolution in three parts was put forward. First, both governments agreed to issue the ceasefire within four days of acceptance of the resolution. Then, as a nod to India, Pakistan was asked to withdraw its troops, which represented a material change in the situation since it was presented to the UN. This placated Nehru, though it lay some distance from the original boundary that was claimed. The last part affirmed that a plebiscite would be held once law and order were restored.

When UNCIP arrived, hostilities between India and Pakistan had grown so ominous that the Commission decided that a ceasefire was the more urgent priority and set about trying to establish a boundary. Alarmed at what seemed an escalation in the crisis, the Commission decided the ceasefire would stop hostilities and create conditions that might enable a plebiscite which would finally end the dispute.

---

¶¶  This would be the first of several occasions during his time as prime minister when Nehru would abandon the principle of non-violence that Gandhi had so carefully nurtured. It had not only set India apart from other nations, but won it admiration internationally.

Both parties to the dispute had disagreements with the formulation the UNCIP came up with, but its eventual acceptance in the two countries differed. Ayyangar, who was India's representative to the UN, called the resolution a 'remarkable piece of work'. According to Korbel, there was a fiercer struggle in Pakistan and Zafarullah 'hurled interrogations at me until I was exhausted. He assured the Commission of his complete trust in its integrity, but suspected India.'[25] India accepted the resolution two weeks before Pakistan, and when Pakistan finally sent its approval, it came with so many disclaimers and conditions that the Commission had to consider its answer 'tantamount to a rejection'. It had taken the Pakistanis almost a month to send their response.*** The work continued with the Commission trying to incorporate the new requirements. Finally, a ceasefire was ordered one minute before midnight on 1 January 1949.

Although the plebiscite would never come to pass, the Commission's ceasefire held its original form for, more or less, sixteen years. It was later replaced by the Line of Control, which remains the internationally recognized boundary between the two countries. Tensions over Kashmir continue to dominate relations and have been a cause for concern internationally. The US has intervened on several occasions when conflicts between India and Pakistan have arisen to prevent any escalation between the two nuclear armed states. In a speech to parliament in February 1953, Nehru said: 'Our Union with Jammu and Kashmir can only be based on the wishes of the people of Jammu and Kashmir; we are not going to achieve a union at the point of a bayonet. Our policy, therefore, should be to try and win them over instead of frightening them. We must not disturb the status of Jammu and Kashmir but let it remain a separate entity in the Union of India.' He also pledged to leave Kashmir if the people requested they do so, saying: 'If the people of Kashmir do not wish to remain with us, let them go by all means; we will not keep them against their will, however painful it may be to us ... Our strongest bonds with Kashmir are not those that are retained by our army or even by our Constitution ... but

---

*** The Commission adopted the resolution on 13 August 1948. Pakistan sent its conditional approval on 6 September.

those of love and affection and understanding and they are stronger than the Constitution or laws or armies.'[26]

Unfortunately, Nehru was unable to live up to the high ideals expressed in the speech. He tried early on to accommodate some of the early proposals put forward during Mountbatten's tenure, including the plebiscite. On 2 November 1947, he made a public offer to hold one under UN auspices and announced his intentions over a radio broadcast.[27] It was only after the Kashmir problem was referred to the UN and the British upheld Pakistan's claims that he backed away, as he felt the UN was no longer a neutral mediator.

Since then there has been a steady erosion in relations between Srinagar and New Delhi over successive governments. Kashmiri resentment about having their fate decided by outsiders continues to inflame separatist passions in the Valley, while the seemingly permanent presence of almost 5,00,000 Indian troops in Kashmir has contributed to human rights abuses and resentment among the civilian population.[28]

In September 2019, Prime Minister Modi's government revoked Kashmir's special status under Article 370.

Nehru and Gandhi had always hoped that one day Indians and Pakistanis would become close once the pain of Partition was over. Despite his differences with Jinnah and Liaquat Ali Khan, therefore, Nehru tried to avoid an open breach. He, at the very least, wanted to leave the door open for the possibility of unity, but failed to realize that these cultural ties were themselves a deep threat to Pakistan's identity. As time went on, Kashmir became the lightning rod that severed cultural and economic links between the two countries, making it one of the most dangerous hotspots on the planet.

# Part Two:
# 1947–1964

# Chapter 4

# Truman and Nehru: A Culture Clash

FRANKLIN D. ROOSEVELT DIED OF CEREBRAL HAEMORRHAGE ON 12 April 1945. Although his health had always been a concern, his death still came as a shock to the world. The following month, Germany surrendered, and the war shifted from Europe to Asia. In August 1945, the US dropped atomic bombs on Nagasaki and Hiroshima. By 2 September, the Japanese surrendered, bringing down the curtain on the Second World War.

India was regarded as a bulwark against communism in Asia, even though it was considered a backward country. When Chester Bowles chose to go to India as ambassador in 1951, President Truman was shocked he had actually selected India. Bowles remembers the president saying: 'Well, I thought India was pretty jammed with poor people and cows wandering around the streets, witch doctors and people sitting on hot coals and bathing in the Ganges, and so on, but I did not realize that anybody thought it was important.'[1]

President Roosevelt had been a towering statesman and respected by world leaders. In contrast, Truman was a neophyte in foreign affairs until he became president. The son of a farmer, he was a haberdasher from Independence, Missouri, a small town on the outskirts of Kansas City, and was probably the most well-attired president in US history—he owned ninety-six pairs of shoes, including twenty-one pairs of slippers, several of which were hand embroidered.[2]

He had been the vice president for just eighty-two days when FDR died. Despite his years in public service, Harry S. Truman had relatively little experience in international affairs and brought a parochial mindset to the presidency. As vice president, he had attended just two meetings with FDR and was excluded from briefings on world events and kept in the dark about the Manhattan Project* until he became the president. Ironically, even Stalin knew more about America's nuclear programme from his spies than the vice president. When Truman met Stalin at Potsdam, Germany, and hinted that the US possessed a weapon that was very destructive, the Russian head of state was already aware of what he was referring to.

His friend Justice William O. Douglas's observations about him were scathing: 'Truman was ... very provincial. He knew very, very little about what went on in the world ... of course, when he was President experts brought him all sorts of information ... but he started with very little understanding. Truman did not know the world of ideas. He did not know the world of philosophy. He did not know the world of religion. He would give me long lectures about the Persians, and they were the demonstrations of the greatest ignorance I have ever known from a person in a high, high place ... he was a very, very ignorant man at that level.'[3]

When India became independent, Truman was busy with the pressing need to rebuild Europe. India was viewed as a distant country with no direct bearing on US political interests. In 1947, the State Department had not even formulated a coherent South Asia policy. US strategic interests in the region were limited, confined to critical raw materials of war such as mica, thorium and manganese. India was seen as a potentially important source of manpower in the event of a global war between the US and the Soviets, as well as a stabilizing force in Asia.[†]

Truman would grow during his presidency to meet the challenges of the Cold War. He helped put in place the architecture of alliances that provided the framework of US foreign policy for the next fifty years. The Marshall Plan or the European Recovery Program, the North Atlantic Treaty Organization (NATO) and the treaty with Japan were accomplished under his administration. They ensured security and peace in Europe

---

* The code name given to America's efforts to develop the atomic bomb.

† Many of the Indian soldiers who fought for the British in the two world wars were recruited from Punjab and were primarily from the Muslim and Sikh communities.

and, by any measure, have been among the most successful alliances. His interest did not extend to India and he remained uninformed about the country.

Secretary of State George Marshall, the most powerful voice on foreign policy in the immediate post-war period, was sympathetic to newly independent nations' attempts to free themselves of the influence of their former colonial rulers and had displayed some scepticism about British attitudes towards India. However, the US, wholly preoccupied with Europe, Japan and Russia, and lacking its own strategy towards India in the years immediately after its independence, followed the British lead in the subcontinent and considered India a part of the British sphere of influence.

The first Indian problem faced by the State Department was the crisis in Kashmir. Secretary Marshall was unconvinced by the British position on Kashmir, which seemed to him to tilt too far in Pakistan's favour. But Britain was too important a buffer against the Soviets in Europe, and Cold War considerations prevented Marshall from raising objections to British policy on Kashmir.‡

The British tried to influence other countries of the Western alliance to accommodate Pakistan's position on disputes at India's expense. As Canada's foreign secretary, Lester Pearson, wrote in his journal: 'West Pakistan seem much easier to talk to, more like ourselves, than the Indians. They seem franker and more straightforward, more vigorous. Of course, this apparent difference may be partly the result of "suggestion". The British, with few exceptions, will tell you that the Paks are a better people, more "our type", you know; so when you arrive here you subconsciously look for this difference.'4

According to the Canadian ambassador to India, Escott Reid, Western politicians and visitors felt they could relate better to Muslims, as the culture of Islam was closer to the West. 'With the Arab world the West shares a common heritage of Aristotelianism and of Hellenistic thought; with Russia there is the common bond of Byzantine tradition and, more recently, of the mainstream of nineteenth century European philosophy;

---

‡    For a full explanation, see Chapter 3.

With China we share an essentially practical if not pragmatic outlook ... India, on the other hand, has almost no intellectual or religious roots with the West.'[5]

There was also a general perception that Pakistanis were the superior fighting force and could supply the West with men in the event of another world war. Reid suggested that 'there was in the US government, in the Pentagon and, to some extent, in the State Department, a strong view based on the reading of [Rudyard] Kipling, that the martial races of India were in the north, and much of that was now Pakistan. And therefore, the sensible thing for us to do was to cosy up to these martial races; they would be a great value to us in the fight against communism, and we ought to certainly give the military assistance to and maybe have an alliance with Pakistan.'[6]

Without a robust South Asia policy in the US, it was the ambassadors and leaders of the two countries who played a key role in developing the relationship.

## A Good Beginning: The First US Ambassador to India, Henry Grady

The first US ambassador to arrive to India in 1947 was Henry Grady, an inspired choice. Nehru, who had retained the portfolio of minister for external affairs, was the key person on the India side and, luckily, they hit it off.

As Ambassador Grady and his wife sailed into Bombay in late June 1947, the temperature soared to almost 48 degrees Celsius in the plains. It was one of the hottest summers on record. The date for the transfer of power and the partition of the subcontinent had been moved up to 15 August, but the migration of populations had already begun. Grady had just a few weeks to present his credentials and make an initial round of introductions before the chaos of Partition set in. At a dinner party given for the Americans on the fourth of July, he found the Mountbattens and Nehru charming and Jinnah pompous. Jinnah, a private citizen at the time, insisted the American ambassador call for an appointment to see him rather than dropping by.[7] In Grady's opinion, 'had Jinnah been less difficult, many of the problems which beset India following the achievement of independence could have been and doubtless would have been avoided'.[8]

Just after midnight on 14 August 1947, the eve of Independence, violence erupted all over Delhi and in many of the border states. The outgoing British government had not made adequate preparations for security and, in the ensuing days, thousands of civilians were massacred by communal mobs. Ambassador Grady's mostly Muslim household staff was moved to the Old Fort for safety. Some took refuge in a mosque. Grady experienced the chaos of Partition first-hand:

> Before we had troops for protection, two of our embassy staff moved in with us. One had a pistol and the other a shotgun. At midnight we three would march in military formation around the house to see that there were no prowlers. Our head servant, Shakoor, a Muslim, showed great bravery, not only in connection with getting food but also in connection with getting people to the safety of camps when passions were running high and killings were frequent. During the worst night we experienced, when the mob was moving in the direction of our compound and was not more than two blocks away, he went with our station wagon and picked up our Muslim servants only two hours before the mob came, demanding that the British head of the household turn the servants over to them.[9]

During this period Nehru and Gandhi were both preoccupied with trying to stop the bloodbath. Nehru walked into rioting crowds unprotected to stop the fighting at great personal risk. It took almost three months after Independence to calm the inflamed religious tensions.

As Nehru turned his attention to the task of governing, the country was in terrible economic shape. Nehru wanted to bring India into the twentieth century. Industrial development, science and technology were the essential ingredients in his plans for India's development. In this, Grady could not have been more helpful.

Grady had a doctorate in economics, had been to India before and had studied its industrial capacity for the war effort. In August 1941, he had been sent by Roosevelt to visit various countries in Asia to purchase raw materials for the war and had visited India to source mica and minerals needed in the production of spark plugs used in planes. In April 1942, he spent five blisteringly hot weeks in India preparing a comprehensive survey of the country's industrial resources and its potential capacity to meet demand in case the war necessitated it.§

When Nehru became the prime minister, one of his greatest challenges would be supplying food to a country that had still not recovered from the 1943 famine. Although the rains had come on time in 1947, food stocks were low and heavily dependent on the monsoon. and food security was a constant concern. Nehru was desperate for ideas and expertise—Grady had both.

Nehru grilled Grady for hours on his ideas for India's economic development. To help develop the plans for dams to generate power, Grady used his contacts at Bechtel and Knudsen, though he encountered resistance from India on accepting help from foreign companies. The American approach was to hire the best company to do things in the most efficient way possible. Instead, wishing to learn how to do things and not be dependent on others, India wanted partnerships.

Despite their differences, Grady and Nehru shared a sense of humour, believed in the other's sincerity and got along. The Gradys were an older couple who had not been groomed within the diplomatic service with all its protocol. They exhibited a more relaxed attitude that put Nehru at ease. According to Nehru's sister, Vijaya Lakshmi Pandit, who got to know them well, his 'lovable' wife Lucretia 'had a most disturbing habit of referring to her friends without mentioning their names ... She once introduced Tara⁵ to a guest in her home as "the daughter of our beloved across the seas", much to the bewilderment of the person being addressed, who was left in the dark as to who Tara was!'[10] The Gradys would remain good friends with the Nehru family long after their official relationship ended.

Grady quickly established a friendship with Nehru—they often dined together—but Nehru's frequent consultations with Grady on

---

§ This came to be known as the Grady Plan.

⁵ Tara, short for Nayantara, is Vijaya Lakshmi Pandit's daughter.

economic matters made the British uneasy. The British considered India their territory and were nervous about the Americans replacing them. Attempting to protect their commercial and political influence in India, the British had used Mountbatten and other people close to Nehru to warn him against the United States.

Grady was aware that the British were trying to sabotage the India–US relationship. He would later write: 'The British refused to see the United States as a partner in India.'[11] They warned Nehru against 'dollar imperialism.'[12] Grady, an Irish Catholic, sympathized with people who had been colonized and felt strongly that State Secretary Dean Acheson should not accommodate British colonial interests and work towards developing strong independent ties with India, Iran and other countries.

Grady's warm relations with Nehru helped the prime minister to develop a more positive view of the US. Grady encouraged him to visit the US and Nehru became interested in the idea of visiting this beacon of technological advancement and modernism. He also hoped that the US would open its arms and help support India.

Unfortunately for India–US relations, barely a year after he arrived in India, Grady was transferred to Greece as an overstretched Britain handed over the responsibility for the security of Greece and Turkey to the US. He sailed from India in June 1948.

## The Cold War Edges In

The year 1948 was pivotal in world politics. Stalin made two aggressive moves in Europe that sent shockwaves through the Western alliance and raised the risk of another world war. The first was in February 1948 when the Soviets helped engineer a communist takeover in Czechoslovakia. The second was the Berlin Blockade in June 1948. The Cold War polarized the world, and the Russians under Stalin embarked on an aggressive strategy in Europe. As far as Truman was concerned, you were either with the West or with the communists. Non-alignment as a foreign policy option was unacceptable to him.

In 1948, Nehru and the Congress party were in the Western camp. They were negotiating to join the Commonwealth at the time and were wary of the Soviets, irritated by their support of the Left in India. In February 1950, Nehru wrote: 'If there is a World War, there is no possibility of India lining up with the Soviet Union whatever else she may do. It is obvious that our relations with the United States as with the United Kingdom in political and economic matters are far closer than with other countries.'[13] In those early years after Independence, he viewed the Soviets as expansionist and found their constant interference in the local politics of different countries appalling.

Nehru was not a believer in communism. He believed in the goals of greater equality, but not at the expense of free speech and open elections. For all the good economic intentions of the Soviets, he thought the suppression in their system excessive. But he was less judgemental about alternative forms of government than someone like Truman, for whom everything was black or white.

Nehru saw the movements in Asia through the lens of nationalism— as anti-imperialist rather than anti-Western. He was convinced that eventually ancient Chinese culture would dominate any political structure imposed on its people, and communism as practised in China, if it survived, would be benign. Nehru did not see China or Mao Zedong, chairman of the Communist Party and ruler of China, as a threat to India at this stage and was willing to recognize the legitimacy of the Mao government as the new reality. Nehru was to prove wrong in his assessment of China. India was one of the first countries, along with the USSR, to recognize the People's Republic of China and establish diplomatic ties with Beijing.

Nehru's views carried little weight in US policy circles. He did not have the international stature nor the popularity in the US for his advice to matter. Instead, his views came to be seen as an irritant. In 1948, the US was more worried about the threat from Russia in Europe. The Cold War would only extend to Asia once the Korean War began.

Truman was convinced that Nehru's insistence on pursuing a policy of non-alignment was a cover for pro-communist sympathies and his views on Nehru hardened. When William O. Douglas, an American jurist and politician, was about to depart for India on one of his summer trips, Truman called him in: 'If you're going to go to India there is something I would like to have you do … I'd like to have you spend as much time as you could with Mr Nehru to find out if he's a communist ... He sat right in the chair you're sitting in, and ... if I ever saw a communist, there's a communist. And I'd really like to have you spend some time with him and smoke this fellow out and find out where he really stands ... I can smell these communists a mile away. And this man Nehru sure looked like a communist to me.'[14]

When the justice returned after two weeks and several lunches, dinners and private conversations with Nehru in India, he reported back to Truman that Nehru was no more a communist than they were. The president was unmoved. According to the justice, giving his report on Nehru to the president was like 'shouting into a hurricane. There was no possibility of any kind of bridge or access or understanding at all between Truman and Nehru. Not for any shortcomings on Nehru's part because he's a pretty worldly man. He gets along with all sorts of people. But they don't breed that kind of a person around Independence, Missouri.'[15]

Given President Truman's antipathy towards Nehru, it was difficult to see any relationship emerging that could overcome such deep prejudices. In addition to the sceptics in the White House, there was a group of right-wing hawks on Capitol Hill that was fervently anti-communist and distrustful of non-alignment, which they did not see as 'neutral'. They refused to acknowledge the possibility that new nations might want to remain neutral between the superpowers in deciding what was in their best interests.

The polarities in the world escalated in intensity and danger when the Soviets first detonated a nuclear bomb in September 1949. The following month, Mao established control over China but was not recognized by the Western alliance. Nehru, who viewed himself as a champion for Asia and the new post-colonial nations, expended a fair amount of political capital trying to convince the West to recognize Mao's China as the legitimate government and have it recognized at the UN. This infuriated the US.

With Henry Grady gone, there was no American ambassador to smooth ruffled feathers or promote Nehru to a US administration that had little time for him or for India. Henry Grady's replacement, Loy Henderson, was a cold warrior who never developed the close relations his predecessor Grady had had with Nehru.

## A New Ambassador: Loy Henderson

Henry Grady had managed to circumvent the British on his arrival in India and established a direct connection to Nehru. His close relations had caused great consternation in the British Foreign Office. When Loy Henderson was appointed to replace Grady, the British decided to intervene and control the relationships between Nehru and the US right from the start.

Henderson, at Bevin's request, paid a courtesy call to the Foreign Office in London on his way to India in the summer of 1948. He was startled by the conversation. The British tried to prejudice him against the Indian prime minister, and told him that Nehru had made 'vituperative attacks' on the United States at an imperial conference in London, and that he had threatened to withdraw from the Commonwealth if the United Kingdom's relations with the US were closer than their relations with India. They portrayed Nehru as a petty, irrational, unstable man who needed to be restrained.[16]

The astounding conversation continued after dinner and became even more disturbing. As Henderson later reported, 'He [Bevin] wondered whether I would mind if Sir Archie, after his arrival in India, would refrain from showing any particular friendliness towards me and the American embassy, and if from time to time he would be publicly critical of the United States. I told Mr Bevin that I did not think that the idea was good and that I would mind very much. I said that I thought Nehru would understand sooner or later that we were playing some kind of game.'[17]

On Henderson's arrival in India, the Canadian high commissioner made a similar proposition although not in quite as blatant a manner as the British. Once again, the proud American stood his ground and the Canadians quickly backed off. They were simply following instructions from Her Majesty's government and seemed relieved not to have to participate in the charade.

Henderson was a Soviet specialist and had helped formulate the Truman Doctrine, which agreed to provide military and economic assistance to democratic countries in order to help them resist terrorists and communists. Henderson was a cold warrior and distrusted Stalin.

He was initially willing to give Nehru some latitude on developing his foreign policy. However, as time wore on, he grew increasingly impatient with his policy of non-alignment. Unlike his predecessor, he did not develop close relations with Nehru. Henderson was formal, restrained and entrenched in the bipolar world of the Cold War.

With Henry Grady's departure, the goodwill between the US and India diminished. Dean Acheson had replaced George Marshall as secretary of state and neither he nor Ambassador Henderson warmed to Nehru or India. 'Mr Acheson seldom became involved in South Asia, which he considered a secondary theatre.'[18]

When a resolution in the UN to condemn the action in Czechoslovakia was voted on, India abstained, a decision that was misinterpreted by the US as being pro-communist. India had just gone through a bruising session at the UN where the British had lined up the US and other nations against India and supported Pakistan's claims in Kashmir. Nehru was recovering from what he saw as a Western betrayal led by the British and had requested an adjournment. The Indians were wary of supporting actions that would establish a precedent for UN interference in the internal affairs of a country. India's vote at the UN reflected its concerns over its implications for Kashmir rather than a stand on communism.

With Stalin threatening Europe, the US in 1948 was intent on preserving the Western alliance at all costs and keeping Britain within the fold. The US was willing to disregard its own reservations about British behaviour towards its former colonies and, to India's dismay, followed British direction at the UN.

When Britain left India, it owed its former colony close to 1.134 billion pounds sterling.[19] During the war, the money on the war effort spent in India was paid for in rupees. In return, Indian banks were credited with IOUs issued in sterling. The US had also spent a considerable amount of money in India supplying its troops to counter the Japanese threat in Burma. The British had deposited the US dollars in London and although it was credited to India's account, it was never sent to India. It became part of the IOUs.

Nehru had planned to use the sterling balances to finance capital investment needed to modernize Indian industry. Immediately after the war, Britain was close to insolvency and unable to pay off these debts. Instead, they negotiated an agreement under which the debt represented by the sterling balances would be liquidated over an extended period. In addition, Britain debited against India's credit balance a variety of payments, including such items as civil service pensions to be paid to the members of the Indian Civil Service who had served in India under British rule. Britain also charged India for old army equipment and military supplies left behind at Independence. In 1949, when the sterling was devalued, the value of these balances was cut by a third.

Some of the sterling balances belonged to Pakistan. Sardar Patel, the deputy prime minister, and other Hindu nationalists considered holding the money hostage to force a resolution on Kashmir. It speaks to Gandhi's high moral standards that he went on a fast on 13 January 1948 to convince the Indians. 'The cabinet decided ... to make immediate payment if Gandhi wished it.'[20] He was fully supported by Nehru. On 30 January 1948, two days after he broke his fast, he was assassinated by a Hindu fundamentalist.

The British were worried that the US was encroaching on their economic turf internationally and were concerned about keeping it away from their former colonies. The US had been putting pressure on Britain to dismantle the system of imperial preferences so that it could have access to markets in its prior colonies, but it set its demands aside. Once the Cold War set in, the goal of the US was to have a strong Britain to resist the Soviets. The US decided not to interfere with British foreign policy towards the Commonwealth countries.

India also pursued its self-interests. With Mountbatten gone, Nehru succumbed to domestic political pressure to incorporate the state of Hyderabad into India by force in 1948.[**] This princely state had been one of the three holdouts that had not immediately joined India or Pakistan. Having united India and calmed the riots, Nehru turned his attention to economic development and governing. With a famine looming, and the sterling balances unavailable, despite having large reserves of positive

---

** Hyderabad was the richest princely state. Lying in India's southern peninsula, it was fully encircled by India.

sterling balances on the books, Nehru had to seek foreign aid to feed his people.

Although relations between the US and India were somewhat unstable, Nehru needed to raise funds to help India achieve its economic goals and decided to accept President Truman's invitation to visit the US in October 1949.

## A Disastrous Visit

The State Department and the White House had agreed that it would be helpful to invite Nehru to visit the US and possibly ease tensions between the two countries. Ambassador Grady was pleased that his friend was planning to visit his country. He had encouraged him to visit technological centres and meet with scientists in the US. Nehru was also excited about the trip as it was to be his first trip to the US, and he was anxious for it to go well. 'I have met a large number of Americans and read a good number of books on America. And yet I am not really acquainted, in the intimate way one should be acquainted ... I am receptive if I want to be and I propose to be receptive in the United States ... I want to see their good points and that is the best approach to a country. At the same time, I do not propose to be swept away by them.'[21]

The president sent his plane to London to pick up Nehru as India did not yet have an aircraft with service to the US. The State Department put in an enormous effort to plan the trip with sensitivity: 'We decided that the theme of his visit was going to be the "discovery of America".[††] He had never been here before, we were going to open the doors to him. And so much of what we organized, the statements we prepared ... dealt with this theme ... Nehru was obviously touched, and Nehru's response to that welcome was warm and friendly, so we all thought, "gee whiz, we're off to a good start". It went rapidly downhill.'[22]

After the initial greetings on arrival, the discussions between Truman and Nehru did not go down well. The discussions were stalemated by

---

[††] This was a tribute to Nehru's book, *The Discovery of India*, which he wrote in prison for his daughter Indira.

differences over China, India's early recognition of the Mao government and the impasse over Kashmir. The interactions between Dean Acheson and Nehru, if anything, hardened their differences rather than softening relations. They both found the other arrogant and condescending.

According to Nehru's biographer, 'Loy Henderson had informed [C.D.] Deshmukh, Nehru's financial advisor, that Truman would give Nehru anything he asked for, but Nehru refused to beg or to do more than state India's requirements for food and commodities in general terms. The result was that at a time when there was a glut of wheat in the American market and it would have been easy to make (as was widely expected) a gift of a million tons, India was not offered even special terms.'[23]

Nehru felt that the US—being the wealthier, older democracy—should have 'offered' help and provided money to a new, emerging democracy, that it was demeaning to ask for help, and that gentlemen should not put one another in that position. The US attitude was that if you need our help, you need to ask and show gratitude. It was as much a cultural divide as anything else. India's needs were caught between Nehru's pride and US expectations of charity.

Aside from the two official meetings where things did not go well, some of the more distressing interactions took place over the lunches and dinners that had been arranged in Nehru's honour. Dean Acheson hosted a formal dinner for Nehru at Anderson House. Indira Gandhi attended the dinner with her father and was seated near Ambassador Matthews, who described the unfortunate scene: 'Unfortunately, a little late and obviously having stopped somewhere for more than one or two bourbons and branch water, John Snyder rolls in and sits down about three seats from Indira … Well, he sure as hell didn't know who Indira was, and at that point didn't care, and started talking about these foreigners who come over here and take our money away from us.'[24] Ambassador Matthews said he and others tried to talk over Snyder but he could see that Mrs Gandhi was 'seething' at the discourtesy and Matthews agreed that she had every right to be.

After dinner, Dean Acheson invited Nehru home for a private talk but felt that Nehru never relaxed. 'I was convinced that Nehru and I were not destined to have a pleasant personal relationship. He was so important to India, and India's survival so important to all of us, that if he did not exist—

as Voltaire said of God—he would have to be invented. Nevertheless, he was one of the most difficult men with whom I have ever had to deal.'[25]

At a lunch in New York, organized for Nehru to meet with titans of industry and banking, brash American behaviour was on full display. One of the participants bragged about the collective wealth of the Americans in the room. Rather than being impressed, Nehru found this utterly tasteless. It played to the prejudices about American materialism he had inherited from the British. The White House dinner was just as bad, with the main topic a discussion about the 'relative merits of Maryland and Missouri Bourbon whiskey'.[26] For Nehru, a teetotaller, the evening must have been painful.

According to Nehru's biographer, S. Gopal, the trip was not entirely a failure. Nehru's visit with Einstein was rewarding and he enjoyed good press coverage in general. But it was hard to deny that the most critical part of the visit did not go well. As noted above, Acheson found him 'one of the most difficult men' to deal with. Aside from their disagreements on Kashmir and China, Nehru simply refused to view communism through the satanic lens that the US did, and his tendency to lecture when he felt he was in the right did not endear him to Washington.

Truman came to the conclusion that Nehru 'just doesn't like white men'.[27] This was an ill-informed view based on shallow observations, as Nehru was good friends with a large number of white administrators, including Mountbatten and former political advisors. He also enjoyed a good rapport with former US ambassador Henry Grady.

As the trip concluded, Dean Acheson 'threw cold water on Loy Henderson's idea of a $500 million aid programme. The Indians would have to tough it out with loans and self-reliance. The National Security Council (NSC) at year's end downgraded India's importance to US security, and policymaking remained reactive'.[28] Vijaya Lakshmi Pandit, India's ambassador to the US, tried to follow up on aid requests with little success. As the food situation in India became dire, she had put in a request for 2 million tons of wheat to Dean Acheson's office in July 1950. Tom Connally, the chairman of the Senate Foreign Relations Committee, had responded that it was unlikely to be appropriated by Congress. The following year, in January 1951, he explained, 'Our relations with India are not very good, are they? Nehru is giving us hell all the time, working against us and voting against us.'[29] Senator Henry Cabot Lodge concurred, 'The record of India co-operating with us is very disappointing.'[30]

India had sent Nehru's sister, Vijaya Lakshmi Pandit, as its ambassador to Washington. It was a significant appointment due to her closeness to the prime minister. Washington in 1950 was very much a man's world. M. Stanley Woodward, who was chief of protocol, worried about her placement at official dinners and whether she should be invited to go with the men after dinner to have cigars and discuss politics or retire with the women for coffee and gossip. Madame Pandit made it clear she was going to join the men. In her memoirs, she described Dean Acheson as 'charming and polished' but said he found her difficult to accept as her country's official representative. On one occasion Acheson said, 'Why do pretty women want to be like men?'[31] After an infuriating conversation with Speaker of the House Sam Rayburn, to whom she tried to explain that India was not 'Hindu' India, he condescendingly replied, 'Oh, you have Muslims in India! Honey, why didn't you say so earlier?'[32]

For their part, the State Department and other officials found Madame Pandit arrogant and saw in her shades of her brother. Although she established some good individual friendships in Washington during her tenure, by nature she was proud and not a trained diplomat. She did little to smooth the bumps left behind by Nehru's visit.

## The Korean War

The differences over the Korean War were the final discord that strained relations between the US and India to the point where they were becoming difficult to retrieve. The Korean War was the first international crisis that tested India's neutrality, and Nehru's ability to manage relations with the two warring blocs of nations.

Shortly after Independence in 1947, the Korea problem was brought before the UN. Initially, Moscow had preferred the Korean people decide their own fate, but the US had wanted to take it to the UN. The majority of the members, including India, had passed UN resolution 112(11) recognizing the 'rightful claims of the people of Korea to independence', but instead of allowing the people of Korea to participate in the UN debate, the resolution established a United Nations Temporary Commission on Korea.[33] India became its chairman, and its goal was to unify Korea and oversee elections. The Soviets, who controlled North Korea, did not provide the UN access to the north, and the elections that were held in the southern zone, controlled by the US, voted in Syngman Rhee. He had excluded left-wing parties from participating in the election and Nehru's efforts to convince Rhee to include the North had been rejected. 'As a reaction to the attitude of Mr Syngman Rhee, India did not recognize the South Korean government headed by him.'[34] Rhee never forgave Nehru or India. The attempts at reunification failed and, on 9 September 1948, North Korea declared itself a separate state.

India as a nation was barely three years old when the North Koreans invaded South Korea on 25 June 1950. Two days later, the UN Security Council passed a resolution condemning the action. Although India joined in the resolution, both India and the UK persuaded the US to pass a less robust resolution than the US had originally wanted.

The US followed up with another resolution, expanding its mandate to protect Indochina (Myanmar, Thailand, Malaya, Laos, Cambodia and Vietnam) and Taiwan from communism. This time India abstained, worried that the US was expanding its reach into Asia. Nehru became increasingly suspicious of US intentions when it took the lead with troop deployments to Korea. Although nominally under the UN, by placing the largely US troops under the command of a US general, it became a US-driven war in all but name. The US now wanted its allies to support them with troops, but Nehru was alarmed that General MacArthur, whom he considered a dangerous warmonger, was appointed as commander rather than someone from a neutral country. The UN force in Korea was largely US-supplied.

Although Truman had committed US forces as early as 30 June 1950, just five days after the North Korean invasion, he waited for several weeks before he told the American people. On 19 July, he informed them that US troops had been sent to Korea and by September that year, US troops and arms were flooding into the Korean peninsula.

John M. Vorys, a Republican congressman from Ohio, advised Truman to 'get some Asiatic peoples in the fighting to help us, not just other white people', so that 'it wouldn't look so much like "white man's imperialism"'.[35] Nehru, who had retreated to a more neutral position, only agreed to send medical personnel, disappointing Americans. The US saw itself as pitted in an epic struggle against the Soviet Union. To President Truman, it was a choice between good and evil.

Initial US intervention met with severe losses. MacArthur's landing at Incheon turned the war around for the US and, seeing a path to possible victory, MacArthur pushed the war to the 38th parallel.[‡‡] Nehru had reliable intelligence from his embassy in Beijing that the Chinese would join the war if the UN crossed the 38th parallel. Any Chinese intervention would have escalated the war in an uncontrollable direction.

Desperate to prevent this, Nehru launched an international campaign for a ceasefire. The Chinese had used him before to convey messages to the US and others in the West and the Soviet Union saw India as neutral. The Indian initiative to dial down the fighting in Korea was a multipronged affair. Krishna Menon, India's high commissioner to the UK, made the rounds in London and the UN; Ambassador Vijaya Lakshmi Pandit met people in Washington, and S. Radhakrishnan talked to the Russians in Moscow, where he was serving as ambassador.

The US dismissed the Chinese threat to enter the war as a bluff. India tried to draft a resolution at the UN to have China recognized and to negotiate a ceasefire, and though Nehru had the support of many developing countries, the Western alliance was reluctant to antagonize the US and collectively voted against Nehru's resolutions.

Nehru's information on the Chinese had been correct. His warnings had been ignored by the US to their detriment. On 8 October 1950,

---

‡‡  After the Second World War, Korea was divided at the 38th parallel north, a latitudinal line that demarcates North Korea and South Korea. The north went to the communists and the south to the democrats.

the UN troops crossed the 38th parallel. By 25 October, that year, the Chinese crossed the Yalu River and entered the war. 'By late November two hundred thousand Chinese troops had crossed the border and begun to move south, routing the divided UN forces in North Korea.'[36] After November 1950, the situation in Korea deteriorated into a long stalemate, with heavy losses on both sides and no end in sight.

The US was determined to find some sort of victory, but much to their irritation, India, the UK and Canada worked hard on crafting a peaceful solution in Korea. The US had now dug its heels in, and while British involvement was unwelcome but tolerated, Indian attempts to find a solution made the US apoplectic.

As one historian wrote: 'In New Delhi was the prickly and moralizing Prime Minister, said by a friend to be "flattered" by Britons and Canadians to think himself the "only living statesman" to carry the "banner for those seeking world peace". In Washington sat the ironic bon vivant, four years Nehru's junior, who belittled moralistic poseurs and believed US power more than anything else kept the peace.'[37] Acheson found Nehru irresponsible and, though he liked some Indians, by and large, the country and its inhabitants 'gave him the creeps'.[38]

Nehru wanted to keep the Cold War out of Asia and hoped to constrain the war from spiralling out of control. He believed India could be a moderating influence and inserted himself into the Korea debate, which strained relations between India and the US, but he thought he was justified. It was an Asian war; the Chinese had used him to convey messages to the US and others in the West, which gave Nehru the ability to negotiate with both sides and be heard. He invested enormous energy in trying to negotiate a ceasefire through 1951–52 and an end to hostility, but the main actors viewed him as an interloper.

The Soviets did not appreciate India's involvement any more than the US. The Soviet Union under Stalin was not close with India, and Stalin had treated both Nehru and Mao with condescension. Central to the Indian initiative for a ceasefire was the admission of China to the UN and the granting of China a seat at the Security Council. The Soviets had no interest in elevating China to an equal status. It suited the Soviets to have China drain US resources in Asia.[§§]

Nehru was hopeful that truce talks would eventually lead to an end to the war, but they got derailed over the issue of the forcible repatriation of prisoners of war. The US and the UN urged that prisoners should have the freedom to decide their own future; in contrast, the Chinese communists wanted all prisoners to be forcibly repatriated. Only 73,000 out of 1,70,000 POWs were willing to return home, causing great embarrassment to the Chinese.[¶¶]

On 19 November 1952, Krishna Menon, India's representative to the UN, submitted a draft resolution without consulting the US or its Commonwealth allies. It was a revision of earlier plans essentially supporting the principle of non-forcible repatriation and establishing a commission at the end of the war to take custody of the prisoners. The Russians, who still exerted considerable influence over Chairman Mao, prevented the Chinese from accepting it. Andrey Vyshinsky from the Soviet delegation attacked the Indian resolution on the floor of the UN, calling it 'pathetic', 'ludicrous' and 'camouflage for horrible American policy'.[39] After the Soviet reaction, the Chinese backed away from the negotiations, which had broken down. To Nehru's credit, despite the vitriol he faced from Russia and the retraction from China, he refused to retreat from the resolutions the Indian delegation had proposed.

Acheson was lukewarm to the plan, and Nehru threw his hands up telling his sister, Mme Pandit, that 'the world is determined to commit suicide'.[40] He was worried that Menon had neglected to consult with all the parties, even though he had come up with a plan that aligned with what they approved of. The war dragged on without a conclusion, draining

---

§§ Acheson sent a note to Nehru citing his objections to giving communist China a seat at the UN, the confiscation of US property from the consulate in Beijing, hostile actions against US citizens in China and support to communist insurgents in Asia. Source: Frankel, *Nehru looks East*, 54.

¶¶ I have seen different estimates. According to Francine Frankel, UN's final estimate, on 6 March 1953, was that 83,000 POWs were pro-communist and willing to be repatriated. Of the remaining 50,000, 35,000 were North Koreans and 15,000 Chinese who were unwilling to be repatriated.

men and resources on both sides. On 11 April 1951, General MacArthur was relieved of his command. Truman belatedly recognized he had escalated the war by crossing the 38th parallel and inciting the Chinese. With American prestige at stake, finding a face-saving path to peace was proving difficult.

The Korean War limped through the remainder of the Truman administration without either side willing to make concessions. In June 1951, there was a breakthrough when the Soviets proposed a withdrawal of troops from both sides of the 38th parallel without the earlier demand that the US depart the Korean peninsula. They also, significantly, put aside the earlier demand that Formosa's (Taiwan) seat at the UN be given to Mao's China.

Most Americans supported an end to the war, but by then Truman was facing domestic problems from Senator Joseph McCarthy, who accused the administration of appeasement. With elections around the corner, and an increasingly vocal anti-communist right-wing group on Capitol Hill led by McCarthy, President Truman did not have the political will to resolve the Korean War. Not to mention, the seventy-eight-year-old volatile leader of South Korea, Syngman Rhee, a rabid anti-communist, who stood in the way of peace.*** A ceasefire was not agreed upon until 1953 when the Eisenhower administration took over.

The Korean War had established the US as the major power in the new bipolar world. Although Britain had weaned itself off the Marshall Plan that had rebuilt Europe after the Second World War, it was a shadow of its former self. The Commonwealth had divided interests and could not make up for the loss of its empire. The British were losing their influence internationally and the US was rapidly stepping into the breach.

The Korean War saw the rise of Krishna Menon's influence on Nehru, and his increased authority over foreign policy as he got involved with the Canadians during negotiations over the fate of POWs.

---

*** Secretary John Foster Dulles was accused by some critics of colluding with Rhee into provoking North Korea to attack so that the US could enter the war and roll back the advance of communism in Asia.

In October 1951, the US Congress passed the Battle Act. It prevented any country engaged in the trade of embargoed items with the communist bloc from receiving US aid. India had an abundance of thorium nitrate, an embargoed item, and badly in need of funds, saw this as an unreasonable constraint, particularly once the Korean armistice was signed. A Polish freighter had left India in 1953 with a ton of thorium nitrate bound for China. Nehru told George B. Allen, the US ambassador, that India could not be bound by US law and have another country determine who it should trade with. He emphasized that he could not accept aid with strings attached.

Finally, the situation was resolved when the US agreed to buy the thorium themselves. Another source of conflict was the assumption that poor countries like India were better off focusing on raw materials and leaving manufacturing and skilled enterprises to the West. 'The Indians would never get their processing plant running: they were incompetent, and no self-respecting westerner would help them.'[41] Indians thought this smacked of colonial attitudes and began to view Americans as 'grasping materialists … willing to subordinate human concerns to the pursuit of profits'.[42] It is a clear example of the sparring that took place between the two countries when the US would attempt to bully smaller countries like India.[43]

As the Truman administration turned its attention to domestic politics and elections, its foreign policy concerns shifted back to the Middle East. Loy Henderson was posted to Iran in September 1951 as nationalist sentiments threatened Western interests there, and Chester Bowles jumped at the chance to replace him as ambassador to India, much to everyone's surprise, as India was considered a 'maximum hardship' post. Acheson was confident Bowles would do better than Henderson and he was right. It was a fortunate change for India's relations with the US.

Bowles arrived in November 1951, full of enthusiasm, ideas and empathy for India. Unlike his formal and patrician predecessor, he was casual; he had forgotten to bring a formal suit when he arrived and had to borrow one to present his credentials. In many ways he was the perfect ambassador for his time. India was still in its 'Gandhian phase' and simplicity was appreciated. Chester Bowles and his wife would host parties where they invited common people, served local food, enrolled their children in Indian schools and learnt Hindi. By treating Indians as equals and appreciating their culture, Bowles differentiated himself from his European counterparts and quickly won over the Indian community.[44]

Bowles saw 'India as the political and economic key to a free and stable Asia'.[45] He made it a point to become close to Nehru and understand his priorities. He pushed the US to step up aid in support of India's First Five-Year Plan and promoted the idea of aid without strings in respect for India's neutralism.

When he arrived, Bowles found Nehru somewhat bitter towards the US. John Foster Dulles had negotiated a peace treaty with Japan. Nehru, who viewed himself as a leader in Asia, was one of the only major figures in Asia not consulted by Americans. It had hurt his pride.

In the winter of 1951, when the rains failed, famine loomed in India. It requested a loan to buy 2 million tons of American wheat. The US Congress demanded a more favourable, pro-US foreign policy in exchange, in spite of Bowles explaining to them that aid with strings attached would create resentment in India.

Mutual distrust between the countries poisoned aid negotiations. Just as Truman was requesting Congress for food aid to be sent to India, Nehru spoke out against US policies towards China and Korea, enraging members of Congress, who resisted helping India. When the first shipments of food landed in India, Nehru publicly criticized the Japan Peace Treaty, which smacked to the US of ingratitude. 'If Nehru's person was not exactly at the centre of troubled US–Indian relations, his aversion for Western capitalism and self-importance ... combined to make Washington consider Indian foreign policy particularly irritating and pretentious. Bilateral ties were in the hands of men hugely different in character and personality.'[46]

Negotiating his path through the Cold War was not easy for Nehru. Stalin was far from friendly to India and would occasionally attack India as being a lackey of the West. The US was reluctant to give democratic India, a poor new country, a helping hand and was less generous than it could have been. The Commonwealth provided India with some allies and prevented Pakistan from lining up its members against Indian interests. But it meant having to contend with a great deal of criticism at home.

Nehru's hope was that the newly independent countries in Asia would come together under some shared umbrella that engendered cooperation and provide a counterweight to the cold warriors. That is why he was so persistent about pushing for China to be recognized by the UN. Nehru's enthusiasm for Asian cooperation did not always serve him well. It prevented him from ascertaining Chinese interests and their attitudes towards India.

Nehru believed that his policy of non-alignment was the only way to protect India from the extreme hostilities of the new bipolar world and maintain neutrality in the event of another world war. India's recent experiences at the UN had left him disillusioned about the ability of the intergovernmental body to be an objective party. His Buddhist beliefs influenced him towards seeking the middle ground in politics.

Chester Bowles, while he did not subscribe to Nehru's policy of non-alignment, found much in it to appreciate. Bowles endeared himself to the Indians by advocating on their behalf with Washington, and, as a consequence, was increasingly viewed by his own government as suffering from 'clientitis'.††† He got personally involved in appropriating aid for India and came to Washington in January 1952 to fight for an increase in India's aid programme. He found that Truman and the White House, despite their distrust of Nehru and what they considered his communist leanings, more willing to help India than the US Congress. He underestimated the lobbying effort that was required to convince Congress that India was worth supporting. Without the full backing of the State Department or the president, as a lone ambassador he was unable to persuade Congress to open its purse strings, and annual aid levels remained below $200 million and would continue to drop further in the next administration.

In November 1952, Dwight D. Eisenhower was elected as the new president and the fraught relationship between Nehru and Truman

---

††† This is a term used in the US State Department when ambassadors get seduced by the country they are posted in and lose perspective of who they are supposed to serve.

came to an end. The short, fourteen-month interlude of the Bowles ambassadorship, which helped smooth over the somewhat singed relations with Washington, was too short to put India–US relations on a better trajectory. Without the support of the State Department or the White House, or a compelling geopolitical cause, there was nothing that bound the two countries together.

# Chapter 5

# Eisenhower: Vying for Asia

THE INDIAN CABINET WAS AWARE THAT KRISHNA MENON WAS destroying India's image in the US. G.L. Mehta, the Indian ambassador to the US, found him so destructive, he twice submitted his resignation to Nehru. Menon would sweep into Washington, take over meetings, be rude to sources who had been carefully cultivated by the Indian ambassador, or other embassy delegates, and leave town having ruined relations they had spent months nurturing.[1] 'He took every possible opportunity of rubbing the US government on the wrong side. He was a lone operator who carried out secret negotiations with the United States Government without keeping the Indian Ambassador informed.'[2]

Indian diplomats both feared and despised him. 'Every single Indian Ambassador to the United States starting from Vijaya Lakshmi Pandit, through B.K. Nehru, had repeatedly protested bitterly to the Prime Minister that all the good works for Indo-American relations done by the Embassy for a whole year was demolished by one single appearance by Krishna Menon on American television. The poor Ambassador was also subjected throughout the year to repeated complaints by India's friends about Krishna Menon's anti-American utterances which were naturally assumed to represent the views of the Prime Minister himself.'[3]

Secretary of State John Foster Dulles complained to President Eisenhower that Menon was pushy about getting appointments and 'using the name of Nehru ... he is, as you probably know, a very adroit and unscrupulous maneuverer who likes to have his finger in every pie.'[4] Messages from powerful leaders such as John D. Rockefeller and

Senator Sherman Cooper, who later became ambassador to India, tried to persuade their Indian friends to get Menon to tone down his anti-American vitriol. They conveyed their misgivings to senior members of the Indian government who they hoped would convince Nehru to restrain Menon, but the Indian leadership, including President Dr Radhakrishnan, seemed reluctant to confront Nehru. Vijaya Lakshmi Pandit, who was exceptionally close to her brother and disliked Menon, had been unsuccessful. Others felt it was pointless to try as it seemed to be a blind spot with the prime minister. Emboldened by Nehru's protection and unchecked by any superior authority, Menon became insufferably arrogant as Nehru continued to entrust him with important foreign policy assignments. Although he was Nehru's intellectual confidant and global trouble-shooter, as the historian Sunil Khilnani agreed, Menon was 'one of the most reviled figures of the Cold War era'.[5]

The most flamboyant display of Menon's ego took place on 23 January 1957, when he gave a nine-hour speech at the UN defending India's position on Kashmir. At first, members of the UN were annoyed to be subjected to such a tediously long speech. But when Menon spoke uninterrupted, not even stopping for a bathroom break, they were simply stunned. When he was finally done, he ran to the delegates' lounge and fainted; doctors had to be summoned. The whole dramatic event was caught by the photographers and journalists and splashed across newspapers the next day. It had no favourable impact on India's position on Kashmir but added to his eccentric image.

This was not the first time Menon had fainted. 'Living for years on the drug Luminal, frequently fainting, or speaking incoherently in public, obsessed with an infatuation and closely shut in by an imaginary circle of his enemies, his behaviour had become increasingly unpredictable. Even in 1950 ... he had sent Nehru a telegram on the Japanese peace treaty which was so clearly dictated while under the influence of drugs that Nehru had to order him to withdraw it.'[6] What is remarkable is Nehru's tolerance of Menon's behaviour and willingness to sublimate India's interests to protect his friend.

Initially, Menon was just an advisor to Nehru and lived in London, where he had resided for most of his adult life. He had helped Nehru with the publication of his books and after India became independent, Nehru appointed him as India's high commissioner to the UK, but the appointment was not a success. Nehru received several complaints from the British about Menon's less than diplomatic behaviour. Nehru overlooked Menon's lack of social graces, and—for reasons few could explain—trusted him and elevated him from advisor to special representative at the UN.

Nehru had found Menon invaluable when India was negotiating to become a member of the Commonwealth. It was Menon who worked out the legal mechanism that enabled India to be a member without having the English monarch be India's head of state, even though his unrestrained sarcasm and abrasiveness often diminished his intellectual contribution. Eventually, bending to mounting pressure from his friends in London, Nehru brought Menon to India as an advisor. Menon had not lived in India since childhood and was initially reluctant to return. He had few close friends in India and no political support. His entire focus was Nehru, who indulged him, reciprocating his friendship and loyalty.

Nehru sent Menon to New York to represent India at the UN. He was tasked with ensuring that the Soviet Union supported India's position on Kashmir. Menon's presence in New York would have a long-lasting impact on India and be damaging for its relations with the US and other Western countries. Nehru eventually brought Menon back to India and promoted him to the powerful position of minister of defence. The latter was a position for which Menon was wholly unqualified and his failures during the war with China would eventually end his career, much to the relief of the rest of the cabinet.[*]

Nehru and his sister had always been close. He relied on her feedback in countless ways, especially once he became the prime minister and

---

[*]   There has been a great deal of speculation regarding Nehru's loyalty to Menon. His closest family and friends in their letters and memoirs have found it hard to explain. Some explanations given were that Menon lived in London and was helpful during Kamala's illness in Switzerland. Others say he helped Nehru edit his books and get them published in the UK. Some allude to his handling Nehru's finances overseas but none seem to fully explain the extent of loyalty that Nehru displayed, especially when it ran counter to India's interests.

was unable to leave India for extended periods. According to Michael Brecher,[†] Vijaya Lakshmi Pandit became an invaluable link to the most important diplomatic centres in the world for her brother; having served as ambassador to Moscow and Washington, she was a vital source of information for him until Krishna Menon entered his inner sanctum. The two became rivals who treated each other with disdain. They both competed to influence Nehru, but Menon seems to have come out ahead.

Several diplomats remained perplexed over the inexplicable hold that Menon seemed to exercise over Nehru in foreign affairs. Had Gandhi not been assassinated, it is possible the Menon would not have been able to exercise the level of influence on Nehru that he did. Gandhi dealt with the British and other countries with wisdom and grace and, despite their disagreements, won India's independence and the eventual respect of his adversaries. It was not until the China disaster in 1962 that Nehru was finally forced to dismiss Menon.[‡]

Menon did manage to make a few friends in the international community. During his younger days in London, he had helped to promote the idea of Indian independence among the left-wing intellectuals in London as well as some Labour politicians. Bertrand Russell, Aldous Huxley, Stafford Cripps and Michael Foot were among those he converted.[7] The Canadians found him very helpful during the negotiations over the Korean War. Lester Pearson, the Canadian foreign minister, worked closely with Krishna Menon during the discussions that led to the UN General Assembly approving the Indian resolution regarding the prisoners of war in December 1952. Although the Chinese rejected it at first, it formed the basis for the final agreement that was adopted in 1953, which brought an end to the war and the final resolution of how to manage the prisoners. According to Escott Reid, the Canadian ambassador to India:

Krishna was the brilliant, constructive negotiator and draftsman. He went from delegation to delegation in New York, from capital to capital, and from ambassador to ambassador in New Delhi, working

---

†    Biographer and friend of Nehru.

‡    See following chapter.

out his compromises … which led to the armistice, and the formula which led in January 1954 to the final disposition of the prisoners of war. His achievements were remarkable. He earned, however, few plaudits and much abuse, especially from the Americans.

Perhaps Krishna Menon's increasing irritability in dealing with the United States was in part the result of his learning that the United States Government was, at this time, through the US information service, helping to finance a publication in India which attacked Menon with even greater vigour than that with which he attacked the United States. The British High Commission knew of this; I knew of this; presumably Menon knew of it. The publication was *Freedom First*, the organ of the Indian Committee for Cultural Freedom. The attack on Menon which it published was entitled, 'Is Krishna Menon pro-communist?' For a man like Krishna Menon who was highly strung, anxious and often on the verge of a nervous breakdown, it was like putting a flame to his scars and insecurities deepening his antipathy that had already been seeded by Laski and the Socialists in Britain.[8]

By the time Menon's career ended in 1962, he had inflicted a great deal of damage both within India and in its relationship with the US.

Foreign diplomats avoided him as he tended to lecture them and could be dismissive or downright rude. The few good ideas Menon had on Korean war prisoners or on international events such as the Suez crisis were accompanied by such a caustic personality that he failed to advance India's interests internationally.

## The Eisenhower Administration

By the time the Eisenhower administration took over in 1953, the world's two superpowers—the US and Russia—were firmly locked in the Cold War. They tried to extend their alliances beyond Europe with countries that would support their political views. The neutral or non-aligned countries that India was a leading member of were under considerable pressure to choose sides. Much of the pressure on India came from the US.

The Soviets were less aggressive with countries like India and Egypt and played a long game, offering friendship, trade and aid before approaching them for alliances.

Nehru pushed back against US pressure, insisting on the right of a country to exercise its freedom by considering policies on a case-by-case basis rather than blindly following the policy set by another country's priorities. He adamantly advocated for peaceful co-existence and this put him at odds with the most important man in the US foreign policy department, John Foster Dulles, President Eisenhower's powerful secretary of state.

New Delhi hoped that the incoming Eisenhower administration might present an opportunity to build new relationships, but when Eisenhower appointed Dulles as secretary of state, Indians were shaken. They were not alone; the British were equally distraught about his appointment. When Anthony Eden, the British prime minister, first heard that he was under consideration, 'he went so far as to "express the hope" privately to Eisenhower that Dulles would not receive the appointment as Secretary of State'.[9] British diplomat Sir Alexander Cadogan thought he was the 'woolliest type of useless pontificating American'.[10] It was not clear from his comments whether Sir Cadogan was being generally rude about Americans or confining his remarks to Dulles.

On paper Dulles had all the right credentials to be secretary of state but, in reality, he lacked charm and grace, both essential ingredients for diplomacy. His grandfather John Foster and uncle Robert Lansing had both served as secretary of state under presidents William Harrison and Woodrow Wilson, respectively. Dulles was exposed to international affairs at a young age when he accompanied his uncle to Europe at the time the Treaty of Versailles was being negotiated. In contrast to Eisenhower, who saw first-hand the bravery of the Europeans fighting in the Second World War while serving in the US armed forces, Dulles saw a Europe that was divided and tired after the First World War and considered them weak and incapable of working for the collective good. As the secretary of state, he saw a defunct colonial system and a Britain and France in decline. His superior attitude upset the Europeans, who picked up on his lack of empathy towards them.

In an otherwise flattering portrait of the new secretary, James Reston of the *New York Times* voiced people's fears when he wrote that Dulles 'might be tempted to use the power of office to launch something of a crusade'.[11] Dulles had a reputation of viewing everything through a moral lens: 'Christianity versus Communism, spirituality versus atheism, he defined the Cold War explicitly as a moral rather than as a political or economic conflict.'[12] Dulles had studied Stalin's *Problems of Leninism* and kept a well-worn copy on his nightstand. He had met the Soviets in the fall of 1945 at the Council of Foreign Ministers, an organization of the foreign ministers of the US, Britain, France and the USSR, and decided they could not be allies in a post-war Europe as their interests were now in conflict. He believed Soviet communism was godless and, therefore, immoral.

By 1950, Dulles became obsessed by the communist threat and worried that the Chinese were expanding their influence in the East. He felt containment alone was insufficient to address the threat. He believed in collective security arrangements and wanted 'fainthearted allies and fence-sitting neutrals' to line up behind the US leadership and rally in support of its dynamism.[13] He thought non-alignment was a moral betrayal and failed to understand the forces of nationalism. His one-dimensional, anti-communist lens, filtered through heavy doses of Christian morality, prevented him from understanding nationalist leaders like Prime Minister Mossadegh of Iran, President Nasser of Egypt and Nehru, and only succeeded in alienating him from them. He even irritated Churchill, who sarcastically commented: 'Mr Dulles makes a speech every day, holds a press conference every other day and preaches on Sundays. All this tends to rob his utterances of real significance.'[14]

A thick-set man who occasionally slurred his speech, spoke in a flat voice that lacked passion, and was reported to suffer from bad breath, Dulles was simply charmless. Eisenhower was not enthusiastic when his name was initially proposed for the job, but he saw that Dulles would be valuable domestically in placating the extreme right wing that had become vocal under Senator McCarthy and the anti-communists within the government.

Earlier, President Truman, a Democrat, had made a similar calculation. It helped that Dulles was a successful corporate lawyer with extensive contacts and a formidable legal mind. He recruited Dulles to serve in his administration to negotiate the treaty with Japan after the war and help with its passage on the Hill, relying on him to persuade the more conservative Republicans. Dulles had failed to consult with Nehru on the Japan treaty and India had refused to sign it.§ Nehru attacked the treaty and its snub of Soviet and Chinese interests. He signed a separate treaty with Japan and felt vindicated when Acheson later said, '[N]ever was so good a peace treaty so little loved by so many of its participants.'[15]

Eisenhower liked to remain above partisan disputes. He sometimes gave the impression that he was not fully engaged in the details of his policies and allowed his more aggressive secretaries like Dulles to set policy. But, in reality, he was fully informed about the issues. While the two men could not have been more different when it came to style, Dulles and Eisenhower were often on the same page on issues of substance. Eisenhower was gracious, conciliatory and genuinely interested in views that differed from his own. He even indicated to Nehru when they met that he could appreciate the choice India had made to be non-aligned.

Having commanded the Allied forces and led them to victory in the Second World War, he was universally admired by leaders across the world. At the Geneva Summit in July 1955, Anthony Eden and other European leaders were 'overshadowed by Eisenhower's personality and performance. By a near unanimous judgement he was the leading figure of the conference ... In every encounter he projected an earnest and pacific intent, a serious yearning for reconciliation, a readiness to grant the other side a rectitude no less than his own. All this produced a sense of trust.'[16] By the time his administration ended, the US was unquestionably the leader of the post-war world. Eisenhower's stature and personality had as much to do with the acceptance of the US in this new role as did its economic power.

---

§   Truman had asked Dulles to help negotiate the Japanese peace treaty. He felt using a Republican would help with its approval on the Hill. Dulles had trouble from the Pentagon and the British on the terms. He was reluctant to impose harsh reparations for war damages having studied the results of the Treaty of Versailles.

The US had established itself as the dominant military power in the non-communist world, ushering in a new role for it in world politics. Advances in technology had enhanced American air power, with the new B-52 bombers capable of delivering nuclear weapons and the massive Forrestal supercarriers. The US now boasted the most advanced weapons system in the world.

Eisenhower had been a soldier for most of his life. Having seen the ravages of war first-hand, he was convinced that 'there is no alternative to peace'. His political philosophy as president was driven by this determination. Although Eisenhower respected the Europeans and admired the sacrifices they had endured during the Second World War, he was careful not to be associated with their colonial impulses. Eisenhower believed that the most effective way to contain the communist threat was through collective security arrangements. He had personally experienced the critical role that allies had played during the war and strengthened US ties with its allies abroad when he came to power. Eisenhower did not always share their strategic vision and preferred a less aggressive projection of American power than they would have liked, but minor differences did not undermine the basic principle that underpinned his foreign policy objectives of making NATO, SEATO and other similar alliances the bedrock of US commitments.

Domestically, Eisenhower's goal was to have a balanced budget and not to live off the inheritance of future generations. The most obvious way to accomplish this quickly was to allocate fewer resources to defence now that the war was over. Only Eisenhower, the revered military commander, could do this without criticism from the right-wing hawks. In many ways, he was a pragmatic leader. He was a conscientious housekeeper and held his Midwestern values close to his heart during his presidency. Eisenhower worried about bankruptcy and extravagance in government and that expenditures would spiral out of control in trying to stay ahead of the Soviet Union. His worst fear was for the Soviets to determine US tax rates and defence expenditures by engaging the US in an arms race.

Eisenhower had grown up in Kansas in a middle-class home and worked his way up through the military to become supreme commander of the Allied forces during the war. With communism threatening the American way of life and the Cold War dividing the world, Eisenhower was calm, reassuring and understated; he projected a sense of security with voters.

## Korea's Rocky Conclusion

One of Eisenhower's goals was to end wasteful wars, and he strove to end the Korean War early in his administration. By 1953, Americans had grown increasingly weary of the war and, as casualties began to mount, the polls showed that Americans were not convinced they should be there. 'Soldiers fought and died for meaningless hills with names like Heartbreak Ridge and Bloody Ridge. One small promontory without any strategic significance … changed hand eleven times. During peak fighting, 1,500 Americans died near this barren hill every week. A year into the war, on Memorial Day 1951, Eisenhower had quietly despaired over the waste. He wrote in his diary: "Another Decoration Day finds us still adding to the number of graves that will be decorated in future years. Men are stupid."'[17] When he became president, he promised to end the war.

At an NSC meeting on 11 February 1953, all options were put on the table, including using nuclear weapons strategically if it could end the war quickly. Dulles pushed to use pre-emptive power against the communists, but Eisenhower hesitated. Eisenhower worried that the stakes were too high and the risk of annihilation too real. 'Eisenhower had repeatedly stressed to Dulles and his other advisors that preventative war was not an option. He resolutely believed that any military confrontation with the Soviet Union would inevitably involve nuclear weapons.'[5] Dulles had been conflicted about the bombings of Hiroshima and Nagasaki. He saw the results of nuclear war in moral terms and found it reprehensible, but also felt US power could not be compromised. Although Eisenhower hesitated to have a confrontation with the Soviets, he seemed less concerned about

---

5    Eisenhower was more concerned about a confrontation with the Soviets than with communist China, which did not at that time possess nuclear bombs.

the strategic use of nuclear power in Asia and actively discussed its limited use in Korea if it accomplished a quick conclusion to the war.

Although the debate continued without a decision being taken, the fact that the US would even consider the use of nuclear weapons so soon after the horrific results in Japan revealed a degree of callousness among US foreign policymakers towards Asia.

When Stalin died in March 1953, new opportunities in international relations opened up. Under Stalin, the Soviets had supported the communist faction in the Korean War. Stalin had watched with satisfaction as the US extended their troops and resources in a prolonged conflict that began to lose the sympathy of the American people. But the duumvirate of Khrushchev and Malenkov came under pressure from the Chinese and Koreans to end the war as they had done all the fighting, depleting their resources, and suffered the heaviest losses.

Stalin's death provided the Russians and the Chinese with the perfect face-saving excuse to retreat from the stalemate of the Korean negotiations. Neither side was winning and with Eisenhower and Dulles now driving US foreign policy, the threat to China and North Korea had suddenly escalated as the Republicans were thought to be more aggressive. China's brilliant and suave foreign minister, Zhou Enlai, on his return from Stalin's funeral, suggested that the Chinese would be prepared to come to an agreement that both sides would find acceptable and quickly resumed negotiations to end the war.

In April 1953, Eisenhower delivered his famous 'Chance for Peace' speech, but despite his proposals to curb military expansion, he mulled over the potential benefits of a few tactically placed nuclear bombs. Eisenhower had launched an intensive bombing campaign in Korea to keep up the pressure on the Chinese: 'In May, American warplanes started bombing hydroelectric plants, dams and irrigation canals. Much of North Korea was blacked out and flooded, and with the rice crop ruined, the country faced famine.'[18]

The following month, Dulles was dispatched to India to inform Nehru that the US was contemplating the use of nuclear weapons. The two men did not take to one another. Nehru, a firm secularist, was impatient with Dulles's moralizing religiosity. Dulles, in turn, found Nehru obdurate, and his unwillingness to side with US interests irritated him. Dulles left for Pakistan, having conveyed Eisenhower's message to Nehru with the assumption that Nehru would share the information with the Chinese. The visit seemed to have accomplished its objective, although Nehru later denied he had passed along the message.

On 30 October 1953, Eisenhower would officially approve NSC-162/2, which was a policy that allowed for the use of nuclear weapons to be used as a deterrent to the growing communist threat. This NSC resolution encouraged the US military to both develop and rely on its nuclear arsenal, giving it greater priority than before. The threat of nuclear weapons, on top of the losses already incurred, was too high a price, even for Mao. Despite Nehru's denials, the message reached the Chinese that the US would not rule out the use of nuclear weapons. Zhou Enlai subsequently made concessions based on the earlier Indian resolution passed at the UN in 1951, in which Menon and B.N. Rau, India's representative to the UN Security Council, had proposed a solution to the conflict over the disposition of POWs. The issue of repatriating Chinese prisoners of war had held up an armistice in Korea in previous negotiations. The UN and the US had wanted voluntary repatriation and the Chinese had insisted that all Chinese nationals be returned to China.

An agreement was finally signed in May 1953.** The Chinese nominated India to head the repatriation committee and the Indian Ministry of External Affairs cabled its missions overseas that it was going to be part of the process. On 8 June 1953, the US and China signed a prisoner of war agreement. The Neutral Powers Committee became the effective mediator and based its decisions on the principles laid down by the Geneva Convention.

Canada, like India, wanted to moderate both China and the US's policies, which they viewed as overly hard-line. India's role had become increasingly controversial as President Rhee, a fervent anti-communist and darling of the US right wing, despised Nehru and wanted India to

---

** It was agreed that those who wanted to return would be given safe passage; the prisoners who refused to be repatriated would be given time to reconsider and be interviewed. Any POWs who still insisted on remaining would be handed over to the UN.

have no role in Korea. He almost torpedoed the agreements by an act of sabotage. On the night of 18 June, he released 40,000 North Korean POWs who had refused repatriation and they disappeared. The Americans were shocked at his behaviour. Rhee justified his actions to General Mark Clark, the UN commander in Korea, saying, '[W]hat is uppermost in my mind is the fear that if the Indian armed forces, a thousand or more, come to guard these boys to help the communist brainwashers grill them and indoctrinate them for two or three long months, urging them to go back to the communists, the Korean people will not let them alone.'[19] General Clark, who had initiated the prisoner exchange in Korea, was understandably furious.

Eisenhower shared his displeasure to Rhee through Ambassador Ellis Briggs, but Rhee was adamant that Indian soldiers not be permitted to enter the Republic of Korea in relation to the POWs. Nehru thought the US was making a mistake trying to appease Rhee when such an important agreement was at stake. The Chinese and the Americans were anxious to proceed with the truce and decided not to let this incident prevent the agreement from going forward.

Following the armistice in July 1953, a Korean peace conference was organized to decide Korea's future. In order to placate a volatile Rhee, the US requested that India be excluded. Henry Cabot Lodge explained that Rhee was adamant India not be involved, despite the support of many in the British Commonwealth that they participate in the talks. India was unable to get the two-third vote at the UN needed to override the US vote. The US had lined up most of Latin America and Pakistan and voted against India's inclusion, despite all the work India and Nehru had done to resolve the Korean conflict. China, which had used India as an intermediary during the early phases of the Korean War to pass messages back and forth to the US, turned its back on India too. The US, sensing that the Indians were no longer useful in reaching out to the Chinese, wanted them out of the Korean equation to appease Rhee. Britain, Australia, Canada and New Zealand voted to keep India in, but the US blocked their votes.

The Korean War exposed Nehru's naïveté. The Asian unity that he had tried so hard to promote had proved to be an illusion. Although his commitment to non-alignment allowed him to negotiate between the various parties in an impartial manner, his lack of allies undermined his efforts and isolated India when it came to getting votes to be included in the conference. Nehru was outflanked by the Western alliance at every level.[††]

India continued to be responsible for 21,700 POWs who refused to be repatriated to North Korea or China. Six thousand Indian troops under the command of General K.S. Thimayya were responsible for the POWs on behalf of the Neutral Nations Repatriation Commission. By 24 September, the Indian force took charge of 22,604 POWs from the UN command, and 359 POWs from the Chinese and North Korean command.[‡‡] According to the terms, the Commission was dissolved ninety days after its establishment at its seventy-ninth meeting, on 21 February 1954.[20] By all accounts, General Thimayya, who was chairman of the Commission at the time, did an exemplary job.

India's role in the Korean War had complicated relations between the two countries and irritated the US, but once it ended, Eisenhower reached out to Nehru and invited him to visit Washington. He wrote in his diary that ending the Korean War was his greatest achievement as president.

## Diverging Interests

The Indians were alerted during Dulles's trip to New Delhi, in May 1953, that the US was planning to provide military aid to Pakistan. In

---

[††] Pakistan and the US voted against India during the Korea conference, which also struck a blow to the negotiations. The US had pulled out its firepower to placate the South Korean president Syngman Rhee, who insisted India be excluded from the conference. The US had put its ambassadors to work in various capitals to line up the UN votes against India. Escott Reid, Canadian high commissioner to New Delhi, commented, 'The Americans were at their most bloody-minded vis-à-vis the Indians in this period.' Churchill sent Nehru a private note of appreciation for not making it into an international incident and compromising the armistice.

[‡‡] According to Dennis Kux in *Estranged Democracies*, the Indian custodian force of 6,000 took charge of 22,604 Chinese and North Korean POWs and 359 UN soldiers who wanted to remain with the communists. Each of them had to be interviewed to ascertain their preferences regarding repatriation.

an announcement, which did not endear him to the people while he was in the country, Dulles said that the US 'had no present plans that would bring it into a military relationship with Pakistan which could be reasonably looked upon as unneutral as regards India'.[21] The Indians found this an odd statement to make. It seemed to imply that arms to Pakistan were under consideration and the US was trying to gauge India's potential reaction.

Dulles flew to Pakistan after his India visit, where he was treated like royalty. Ayub Khan, Pakistan's charismatic British-educated general,[§§] was enthusiastic about an alliance with the US and promised Americans bases, manpower and whatever else they needed. Dulles left impressed with Pakistan's potential as a suitable ally in Asia. Ayub Khan followed up by courting the US and visited Washington to promote Pakistan with the Pentagon, the Hill and the White House. He wanted American arms, aid and protection from India.

Ayub Khan was aware that the US–Middle East alliance was imperfect. Egypt's Nasser was a nationalist and unlikely to join the alliance, and Iran was still suspicious of the West after their treatment of Mossadegh, while Iraq was keeping its distance. Sensing an opportunity, he sought to exploit the situation and pushed the US for an alliance and aid in return for co-operation in the Middle East. Nehru's insistence on non-alignment had alienated the US and Ayub Khan was quick to take advantage of Nehru's inflexibility and offer Pakistan to them as its most compatible ally in Asia. Starting in the 1950s, the seeds of US–Pakistan cooperation began to germinate at India's expense and the US 'tilt' to Pakistan would, to a large extent, influence US–India relations.

Nixon followed Dulles to India in October 1953. Eisenhower had asked the vice president to visit Asia to assess where the frontlines of communism lay and to ensure there was no further communist expansion in Asia. Dulles had helped shape Nixon's views and may have prejudiced him against Nehru and non-alignment. The two men met regularly and often had drinks together to discuss world affairs. They both held strong

§§ Ayub Khan took over Pakistan's presidency in a military coup in 1958. He remained the president for ten years.

views about communism and judged countries by their willingness to pledge allegiance to the US.

Nixon was welcomed in India with an enthusiasm that Dulles was denied. Nehru spent several hours in discussions with Nixon on Asian affairs. The US subscribed to the French position in Indochina and backed Bo Dai, the last emperor of Vietnam, who was viewed as a vassal of the French colonial regime. Nehru thought he was corrupt and a charlatan and disagreed with the US position. Nehru would be proven correct. The US was increasingly stepping into France's shoes in the Far East and began to view Vietnam as the linchpin in staunching the spread of communism.

Nehru was under the impression that he had communicated his concerns to a sympathetic Nixon and that they had had an amicable exchange. He had been impressed by Nixon and hoped that his concerns would be conveyed to the US president. Instead, Nixon took an anti-Indian stance. After his meeting with Nehru, he made statements to the press that were unsympathetic to India and Nehru's positions. Nehru felt puzzled and betrayed. Nixon's press conference would not be forgotten by Mrs Gandhi or by the Indian government. There was no ambassador capable of overriding the tensions created by the visit and it left Nehru and India suspicious of US intentions. It was also the beginning of the US–Pakistan military alliance. The US began discussions to give Pakistan $25 million in military aid. Nixon promoted the alliance with Pakistan while objecting to India supplying thorium nitrate to China.⁵⁵

George Allen, the acting US ambassador to India, delivered a letter, on 24 February 1954, to Nehru from Eisenhower that formally informed him of US intentions to supply arms to Pakistan. The letter laid out the strategic reasons underpinning the decision as serving US interests in the Middle East. The letter read: 'Having studied long and carefully the problem of opposing possible aggression in the Middle East, I believe that consultation between Pakistan and Turkey about security problems will serve the interests not only of Pakistan and Turkey but also of the whole

---

⁵⁵ The Battle Act barred US aid to any country trading in strategic goods with communist China. India considered this an imposition on its sovereignty.

free world. What we are proposing to do, and what Pakistan is agreeing to, is not directed in any way against India.'[22]

Nehru read the letter presented to him by the career foreign service officer filling in as ambassador, who had failed to impress Nehru during his tenure in Delhi. Nehru smiled, looked silently at his cigarette for a few minutes and calmly told Allen that he was concerned by the consequences of the new policy. India did not see military aid to Pakistan as a 'neutral' act. Nehru felt that the US was bringing the Cold War to South Asia, where the only conflict since Independence had occurred between India and Pakistan. He pointed out that the arms would most likely be used against India. Allen, having failed to build a relationship with Nehru, did not perceive the depth of Nehru's reaction and did not communicate the impact of the US action to Washington or temper its impact on Nehru.

Perceptions about US motivations reached a new low in India. Indians felt that the US had increased tensions in the region. In a letter to his chief ministers, Nehru wrote cynically of the US as being unable to 'think of anything else but of getting bases all over the world and using their money power to get manpower elsewhere to fight for them.'[23]

One of the advantages of having talented ambassadors in difficult diplomatic posts is their ability to maintain good relations between countries and smooth over misunderstandings. During Eisenhower's first term, there were long gaps when there was no effective US ambassador to India. Allen and Dulles had failed to establish a rapport with Nehru, Menon was wrecking US relations and G.L. Mehta watched helplessly as relations suffered.

## Plebiscite in Kashmir

Eisenhower would be the first in a long line of US presidents who would attempt to resolve the Kashmir problem but, like the Arab–Israeli conflict, it would evade a solution. Kashmir was viewed as a potential flashpoint for a future conflict in Asia. Anxious to find a resolution, the president asked Paul Hoffman,*** head of the Ford Foundation, to go as his emissary to India to try to bring the parties closer together.

Henry Byroade, a rising star at the State Department, had taken over from George McGhee as head of the Bureau of Near Eastern, South Asian and African Affairs. The fact that these regions, encompassing many newly independent countries, were lumped together showed the low level of attention they received at the State Department where European affairs and Russia dominated. Byroade, along with some of his colleagues, believed that the most viable solution was to partition the state of Jammu and Kashmir. He thought Hoffman would be a good person to explore the idea with India and Pakistan and sent him to the subcontinent in April 1953.

Nehru preferred to work out a bilateral solution on the border with his counterpart in Pakistan, based on the ceasefire line drawn by the UN with minor adjustments, but this had not been acceptable to Pakistan. Hoffman and Bunker worked behind the scenes and probably came the closest to bringing the parties together towards a resolution, but, as always, it unravelled at the last minute.

Nehru welcomed Mohammed Ali Bogra, prime minister of Pakistan, with enthusiasm when he visited India in July 1953. He agreed to hold a plebiscite in Jammu and Kashmir in August, and communicated his acquiescence to Bogra, but the talks unravelled when Nehru discovered that the US has secretly entered into a military alliance with Pakistan.

Nehru had publicly declared on more than one occasion that a plebiscite could take place, but he had become increasingly suspicious of US interests in the region and wished to retain control of how it would be conducted. Rumours had been circulating in Delhi that Adlai Stevenson and Dulles had been encouraging Kashmiri independence in the hope that the US would get bases in Kashmir. Nehru opposed Admiral Nimitz's appointment as plebiscite administrator, preferring a neutral country

---

*** Paul Hoffman was also former chief of the Marshall Plan.

from a small state that would not try to influence the outcome. The US was offended as Nimitz was universally admired in the US.†††

In a letter to his chief ministers, Nehru justified his accusations: 'I have no doubt that American agents have been the cause of some mischief both in Kashmir and Nepal. I have little doubt that it is American help that has brought about the last change in Iran. With all this background, I am not prepared for an instant to accept an American nominee whoever he may be.'[24] Although the Pakistanis did not disagree with Nehru while in Delhi, when they went home they requested Admiral Nimitz be appointed. Pakistan took an increasingly tougher line, with the US backing it, and the talks stalled.

Nehru's opposition had hardened in the face of the US–Pakistan military alliance, despite assurances from Bogra that the arms Pakistan received would not be used against India. Dulles was consumed with containing communism and had no patience for Nehru's non-alignment policy. Nehru backed away from any international intervention in Kashmir and asked the UN to remove American personnel from their team in Kashmir. His dislike for the US became intensely personal.

## Looking East

Nehru had helped convene the Bandung Conference in Indonesia. It was held, on 24 April 1955, to bring Asian countries together who had emerged from the yoke of colonialism. The goal was to express their solidarity and neutrality, and freedom from foreign domination. All forms of governments were included, but it was difficult to get any concrete agreements on trade or to vote as a bloc at the UN. Nehru was one of the key spokespersons, but China resented him trying to represent all Asians.

––––––––––––––––––––
††† In reality, Sheikh Abdullah had become dispirited by the attitude of Hindu nationalists and begun to explore the idea of separating from the Indian mainland. It was not generated by the US but the politics within India, but for Nehru, who was firmly committed to a secular state, it was unacceptable that the desire for Kashmiri independence could be a response to internal squabbles. It was easier to believe that outsiders were trying to undermine Indian unity.

India had offered a plane to transport Zhou Enlai and his party to Bandung, but at the last minute he changed plans and decided to get there on his own. The Indian aircraft carrying other members of the Chinese delegation blew up over the South China Sea. There were no survivors. It was said to have been an act of sabotage by the Taiwanese. Despite the setback, Zhou put on a dazzling show as a diplomat, making China's presence a factor to be reckoned with in Asia. After the Korean War, China was no longer willing to allow India or anyone else to act as its intermediary and made that clear at Bandung. Moscow could no longer count on them to be subservient. The power dynamics in Asia were shifting and Khrushchev decided India could be an important ally in containing an increasingly belligerent and independent China.

With the West courting Pakistan at India's expense, an opportunity for the Soviets presented itself when the US began its military aid relationship with Pakistan.

India realized that, with the US backing Pakistan, a severe imbalance had been created in the region. Nehru began to revaluate whether Moscow should be cultivated to redress the situation. Stalin's demise made a friendship with the Soviets more palatable. Having been adamantly opposed to bringing Cold War politics to South Asia, Nehru now found himself caught in its net with the newly formed US–Pakistan alliance and decided to visit Moscow in June 1955 to explore India's options. He received a rousing welcome. He had borrowed many ideas from the Soviets for his economic plans but had been careful to maintain the integrity of his non-aligned status. He would be risking his principles if he created an alliance with Moscow.

Nehru was impressed with the outward signs of progress when he visited Russia. He saw that, in the absence of wealth, there was adequate food and clothing for the masses, and this made a deep impression on him. The emphasis on education for all and scientific progress were goals to which he aspired for India. He truly believed that a 'well-read and well-trained society is not likely to submit for long to many restrictions on individual freedom'.[25]

The Soviets also sought to woo India and offered to propose India as a sixth member of the UN Security Council. Although Nehru demurred, he was flattered. It was far more than either the British or the Americans had offered. Anthony Eden was concerned enough about the warming relations that he invited Nehru to London for a debriefing. The *New York Times* took a more sarcastic tone in an editorial published on 24 June 1955. From Nehru's perspective, he began to soften his views about the Soviets post-Stalin. He thought he could be a catalyst, bringing them together with the West.

Soviet Premier Bulganin and Khrushchev visited India in December 1955 and spent almost a month in the country. It was an unprecedented visit with effusive crowds greeting them everywhere they went. On the diplomatic front, Nehru won important concessions from the Soviets. They agreed to support India's claim to Goa and, in a clever move, offered to change their position on Kashmir at the UN from neutral to supporting India. From then on, the Soviets would prove to be a reliable vote for India on the Kashmir issue and use their veto power at the Security Council to protect Indian interests. Although India was hardly a high priority for the US, it was considered a beacon of democracy and a frontier state against the expansion of communism in Asia. Nehru's push for Asian unity, regardless of shared political structures, and the Soviets aggressive cultivation of India as an ally was a threat to US interests in the region. The Suez crisis provided a bridge over what had until then been a troubled relationship.

## Suez Crisis

British diplomat Anthony Nutting described the Suez as the 'dying convulsion of British imperialism'. It would end Anthony Eden's career, do away with the Egyptian monarchy and bring Eisenhower and Nehru closer together. 'Americans also sensed that the tectonic plates of history had shifted at Suez ... they recognized that British civilization was giving way to its own.'[26]

Nasser, the thirty-seven-year-old military officer who had taken over Egypt in a military coup and made himself the head of state in 1956, had nationalized the Suez Canal, freeing it from British control. He did this in retaliation to the World Bank and the Western countries reneging on a commitment to finance the construction of the Aswan Dam. He claimed that the tariffs from the Suez Canal would finance the building of the dam.

The World Bank had done extensive studies and confirmed the viability of the Aswan Dam project, but British reluctance and US irritation with Nasser's recognition of Red China turned the project into a political issue and it stalled. Without congressional support, the project lapsed. For Nasser, the livelihood of his people was at stake and he was furious that they were being used as political pawns. His decision to nationalize the canal elicited anger from the British, who wanted to teach him a lesson.

Dulles believed the US had no constitutional basis for military action in the Middle East and the British needed to work this out by themselves. Eisenhower and Dulles were cool to the British maintaining their colonial prerogatives and had sympathy for the Arabs, who wanted economic and political independence from them. Churchill dramatically warned the US not to act against British interests and supply arms to Egypt, in case they were used against 'white people'. Further, according to foreign policy expert Derek Leebaert, 'Churchill made other threats. Perhaps he'd withdraw British troops from Korea, he told the administration, if he didn't receive support for British rights in Egypt.'[27]

The US did not supply arms to Egypt because the administration viewed Nasser as an opportunist and did not trust him. But they had no intention of 'shooting their way down the Suez'[28] if they were denied passage. Eden's paranoia was perhaps fuelled by his health conditions and his dependence on Benzedrine. In high doses, the drug can make a person irrational and paranoid.

The British enlisted the French and Israelis to invade Egypt on 29 October 1956. Eisenhower was furious. Not only had Americans been kept in the dark, he was worried that the Soviets, sensing an opportunity, might get involved by offering to help Egypt, thus escalating the crisis. A week later, he decided to go to the UN to pass a resolution condemning the invasion and putting considerable pressure on Britain and France to quickly accept a UN-sponsored ceasefire.

Aware that Nehru was close to Nasser, Eisenhower requested his support at the UN.‡‡‡ He wrote: 'I venture to suggest that it would be most

---

‡‡‡ Nehru had considerable influence among Liberal British MPs and neutral countries. Eisenhower suspected that Churchill could be behind the Suez aggression.

helpful at this juncture if you could personally use your great influence with the British government to urge that they accept that plan without qualifications.' He also asked India to provide troops for the UN forces in Egypt.[29]

Nehru was happy to support the US as it aligned with his own position. He had great respect for Nasser's goals for his people. He did not agree with Western perceptions that Nasser was a threat to peace. The US felt that Nasser had acted impulsively and displayed instability when he sank thirty-nine vessels in the Suez Canal, but Nehru saw it differently: 'Nasser is the best of the group of Egyptian army officers and others for whom he is spokesman. Under present conditions, if Nasser were removed there would come into power someone who would be more inimical to the West and more unreasonable in his actions than is Nasser.'[30] He agreed Nasser was immature when he took power but believed he had come a long way.[31] Nehru also thought that the British and French had acted rashly. The Suez incident strained relations between the transatlantic allies, but it forged new connections between Nehru and Eisenhower. The US was striking out on its own, making decisions independent of and in opposition to its European allies and forming new ties.

Eden also realized that continuing the assault on Egypt was economically unsustainable. London's dollar reserves had fallen by '$57 million in September and $84 million in October. But the November panic drained away $279 million, or 15% of London's total dollar reserves. With close to three quarters of Europe's oil supply coming from the Middle East, half of which needed to go via the Suez Canal, Europe was barely getting 10% of its allocation from the region.'[32] The US used this to put pressure on Britain to withdraw from Egypt.

Nehru and Eisenhower found common ground on the Suez crisis. Nehru's views on Eisenhower softened and he realized that the president had no sympathy for colonial inclinations. Eisenhower used this as an opportunity to reach out to Nehru and they began a correspondence that lasted through his presidency. Nehru had not publicly condemned the Soviet action in Hungary that was taking place in parallel, but he later privately admitted to Eisenhower when they met in Gettysburg that he had been horrified by the naked aggression of the Soviets in Hungary although he did not share the West's fear that they were pursuing world domination.

According to Escott Reid, Nehru was slow to denounce the Soviet suppression of the Hungarian revolution because he thought the Western powers were trying to deflect attention away from 'what he considered to be the dangerous, arrogant, imperialistic aggression of Britain and France against Egypt'.[33] The USSR had propped up a pro-Soviet regime in Hungary in 1949 that was despised by the people. The turnout during the elections in 1947 had been abysmal. There had been little appetite among the civilians to support the communist candidates who ran for office. An uprising, on 23 October 1956, demanding free elections was brutally crushed by the pro-Soviet government headed by Erno Gero and, by 25 October, Soviet tanks entered Kossuth Square and began to gun down demonstrators. As students lay dying, Nehru clearly stated he did not think others should interfere in the internal affairs of another country. He had Kashmir at the back of his mind. It would become his Achilles heel in determining, as in this case, India's response to action in world affairs.

By the end of October 1956, Imre Nagy had become premier of Hungary. He requested that the Soviets withdraw and declared Hungary neutral. The Soviets re-entered Hungary. On 5 November 1956, UNESCO was about to open its conference in New Delhi and with two injustices taking place—one in the Middle East with the British and French as the aggressors, and the other in Europe with the Soviets as aggressors—non-aligned India was once more the arbiter of the world's conscience.

A vote was taken at the UN on 6 November 1956 for the Soviets to withdraw their troops. The US wanted India to censure the Soviets. The phone rang at Nehru's residence at 1 a.m. to ask how India should vote. Krishna Menon in New York was making the request. Nehru was exhausted. He was swamped with work and told Menon to use his judgement. Menon abstained, much to the annoyance of the US and other Western countries. India was intensely criticized for its vote but Nehru, never one to blame others, took full responsibility for it.

## A New Equation

India may have been the reason why Sherman Cooper got married. After a period of months without an ambassador, followed by George Allen, who lacked any real connection to Nehru, Eisenhower appointed Senator Sherman Cooper of Kentucky as ambassador to India. There was just one minor glitch; the senator was single. He was dating Lorraine Shevlin, a vivacious woman who had been married twice before to aristocratic men, spoke Russian fluently and was a talented linguist.

Cooper had attended Yale and Harvard, was tall, handsome and had served with General Patton in the war. He was also forgetful, notoriously unpunctual and needed 'looking after'. Lorraine, who was friends with Jacqueline Bouvier (Kennedy) and the 'Georgetown Set',§§§ was the perfect match for him, and Dulles decided they should get married. He called Cooper into his office, offered him the ambassadorship and persuaded him to marry Lorraine Shevlin before he left on his assignment for India. Dulles exclaimed, 'Nobody should be our ambassador in India without a hostess'![34] The two were married right after his swearing-in ceremony. Nehru immediately took to the couple, and they were a big hit in New Delhi social circles and maintained their relations for years after their assignment ended. Despite having spent just a year in India, Cooper would become an India hand in Washington and India would count him as a valued friend in government. Although Krishna Menon stunted any achievements due to the strained relations during his short assignment in the US, Ambassador Cooper developed good relationships in India and wanted to help. He became an effective advocate for India in Washington—he persuaded colleagues to support increases in aid levels for India and assisted in their passage through Congress.

In December 1956, Nehru visited the US for a second time. It was a contrast to the previous visit, which had been disappointing for both sides. Eisenhower invited Nehru to his farm in Gettysburg for private talks away from the press and official staff. They excluded Dulles and Menon, and

---

§§§ 'The Georgetown Set' was a group of influential elite friends of journalists, spies and government officials from the Washingtonian neighbourhood.

over two days had fourteen hours of conversation. They drove up from Washington, spent some time walking around the farm with a soft rain falling. The setting was informal, and the farm was unpretentious but cosy. The two leaders exchanged views on Asia, communism and non-alignment, and aired their misunderstandings over warm suppers.

Nehru was able to share with Eisenhower his vision for India's economic development and Eisenhower developed a better appreciation for non-alignment and Nehru's neutrality, and even saw some purpose to it.

They did not emerge from the meetings with any concrete agreements, but Eisenhower wanted to send a subtle message to the British that he was establishing his own relationships with world leaders and that the US could not always follow the Europeans. The Suez debacle had shown the US that it needed to follow its own path and disentangle itself from Britain's colonial baggage.

Eisenhower promised to help India with increasing US economic assistance. Congressional resistance had been difficult to overcome but the two developed a mutual respect for each other's values and limitations. Nehru was far more temperate about US aid to Pakistan after this historic meeting, and Eisenhower did everything he could to support India on the Hill. He also sent messages to the British, the French and the World Bank to boost lending to India. Prior to Nehru's visit, Congress had appropriated $75 million for India and the White House had managed to supplement this to $360 million in August 1956, in a package to be implemented over three years. Eisenhower convinced his administration that if they did not help India, the Soviets would step in. Eisenhower, along with a group of progressive economists, were rethinking their approach to development and aid and were less concerned about the size of India's public sector versus the private sector.[35] Ellsworth Bunker had been appointed ambassador to India to replace Senator Cooper and he met Nehru during this US visit. He would become one of the most respected and admired US ambassadors to India.

Nehru had based India's economic development model on the Soviet system of five-year plans. India's First Plan, out of necessity, had focused on agricultural development. After the 1943 famine, the primary concern of the government was to feed its people and ensure the country's food supply. The Second Plan addressed growth and Nehru's vision of modernizing India. The emphasis was on industrial development. This required capital which was scarce. By May 1958, the government had to revise its plan and adjust the budget based on available resources.¶¶¶ India had already depleted its foreign exchange reserves and had a hard time attracting foreign investments. Its balance of payments deficit over that last three years was $1,317 million.[36] It had difficulty attracting US investors as the big projects in steel and oil were state-sponsored—as only the government had the resources—and the US was reluctant to invest in state-owned enterprises.

In 1959 when the Democrats, including Chester Bowles, Sherman Cooper and John F. Kennedy, swept Congress, India found in them advocates to protect its interests. Kennedy, in particular, saw India as a beacon of democracy and Nehru as a font of wisdom in the East. In an article in the October 1957 issue of *Foreign Affairs*, he described India as 'the leading claimant for the role of broker middle state in the larger bipolar struggle'. He also delivered an 8,000-word speech to his senate colleagues on 25 March 1958 to try to convince them to support aid to India.[37]

Although he could not help with US direct investments, Ambassador Ellsworth Bunker oversaw a significant expansion of US aid to India through a combination of quiet diplomacy and powers of persuasion, particularly in the agricultural sector. Having spent years as a lobbyist for the sugar industry, he had many friends in Congress and understood how to work the corridors of power. He was a quiet, elegant man and proud to trace his family back to the 1600s. He was a meticulous dresser who conducted himself with dignity and exuded a sense of calm. He was trusted by everyone and enjoyed the confidence of the State Department. He never tried to aggressively promote India in the way Bowles did, but steadily worked to expand aid to India by building a powerful case about the growing Soviet influence in the region. With his efforts, US assistance grew substantially from $400 million in 1957 to a record $822 million in

---

¶¶¶ Part A: $9,450 million. Part B: $630 million would be undertaken if funds were available.

1960.[38] The Indian agriculture minister, S.K. Patil, signed a $1.276 billion PL480**** food bill with the US in May 1960.

Ambassador Bunker promoted helping India to develop an atomic power plant under the 'Atoms for Peace' programme and used the Russia card to push for its approval, warning Congress that if they did not assist India, Russia would. The Russians were aware that Nehru was looking for large industrial projects to take India forward and were happy to provide India loans on exceptionally favourable terms. India was seeking to develop a steel mill and it became a litmus test of US willingness to support India's vision for its industrial development.

This was a distinct shift from the earlier US attitude towards India on aid. Nehru always found it difficult to ask for assistance and Ambassador Allen, unlike Bunker and Cooper, who wanted to genuinely help India, wrote a hard-headed letter to Dulles in August 1953, displaying a rather cynical attitude towards India. 'It would have been preferable … if we had insisted on clear-cut request by GOI for our assistance. Instead, we skirted around question of request and agreed to Indian position that GOI merely let us know, in answer to our inquiries, how much GOI lacked in funds … continuation of this essentially dishonest fiction would be fraud on American people … and place US–Indian relations on false and therefore unsound basis.'[39]

After Partition, the sharing of water sources was a major unresolved issue that was a source of conflict between India and Pakistan. The US, with the World Bank, sponsored the Indus Waters Treaty that was worked out in 1959. It was a dramatic change from the Truman years during which there had been no interest in India's development as a country.

Towards the end of his term, Eisenhower decided to visit India. Helped by Ambassador Bunker, he concluded that non-alignment was acceptable, and even welcomed, and expressed a desire to see India for himself. In December 1959, he became the first US president to visit an independent India. Eisenhower confided to Lord Plowden, head of the Atomic Energy

---

**** The Public Law 480 was a piece of legislation that was signed by President Eisenhower. It allowed poor countries to purchase food from the US on concessional terms. President Kennedy renamed it the 'Food for Peace' programme. India was able to pay the US in rupees.

Commission, that he arranged his three-week trip to Europe and the Middle East just to get to India.

During his four days in India, Eisenhower spoke to Parliament, addressed the masses at the Red Fort, visited the Taj Mahal and spent time with Nehru. Millions lined the streets to greet him, and he was met with enthusiasm wherever he went. It was a public relations triumph. During the discussions, Nehru brought up the problems India was having with a newly assertive China. Increasingly belligerent actions along disputed border areas had become a headache for India in recent months. Nehru, who had always supported the Chinese, was disappointed by their behaviour and worried at their intransigence. When China killed nine members of an Indian police patrol and contested 37,000 square miles of territory, Secretary of State Christian Herter, who had replaced Dulles, called for a negotiated settlement.[40] He was far more balanced towards India. Eisenhower and Ambassador Bunker agreed that if Indians requested military aid from the US they would provide it.

In May 1960, two weeks after Eisenhower and Bunker had conferred, the US approved the sale of a Fairchild C-119 transport aircraft to India to help supply its Himalayan defences. A few weeks later the US received a request for Sidewinders. Although the president and Ambassador Bunker approved the sale, there were several pro-Pakistan holdouts in the military hierarchy who were still suspicious of Nehru and against the sale. They eventually persuaded the president to change his mind. The intelligence base in Peshawar had led to close cooperation between the Pakistani military and its US counterpart. The deepening military relationship between the two countries would prove challenging for India. To make matters worse, Krishna Menon, the new defence minister, utterly despised by the US, was representing India on the arms purchase, which doomed the sale.

Nehru and Eisenhower met one last time during the United Nations General Assembly in New York at the end of Eisenhower's term in 1960. Eisenhower had persuaded Nehru to attend and support him on disarmament. The session was taken over by Khrushchev's theatrics. The Soviets had just shot down a U-2 spy plane that belonged to the US Central Intelligence Agency (CIA) from Peshawar and Khrushchev had thundered during the UN session in protest, getting the Soviet delegation to pound their shoes on the delegate desks. Both agreed that the Soviet leader was being overly dramatic and unhelpful. He had also unsuccessfully tried to undermine the structure of the UN. Eisenhower and Nehru, who had developed a rapport through their visits and correspondence, met on the side and discussed China, the Congo and the dim prospects for disarmament. Nehru was tired and Eisenhower was at the end of his term, and both knew that they were not solving any major problems in the world, but the two men had developed a friendship that enabled them to accommodate each other's differences.

John Foster Dulles had died of colon cancer in May 1959 after suffering bouts of abdominal pain for two years. With him and Menon out of the political picture, Nehru and Eisenhower had done much to dissipate hostilities between the US and India just by reaching out and spending several hours talking together. Under Eisenhower's leadership, the US enjoyed eight years of peace. He had nurtured collective security arrangements that would ensure peace in Europe and Asia for decades and warned the world to be alert for the dangers of the growing menace of the military industrial complex. The world did not listen to his words of wisdom.

# Chapter 6

# Nehru and the Kennedys

INDIANS CELEBRATED WHEN THE YOUNG, HANDSOME PRO-INDIAN senator from Massachusetts won the presidency in 1960. They had not forgotten Vice President Nixon's visit and his subsequent press conference where he had made anti-Indian statements to journalists. JFK, on the other hand, had supported aid appropriation for India when he was a senator and was friends with Chester Bowles and Sherman Cooper, all supporters of India on the Hill.

There was something magnetic about John F. Kennedy that fascinated people all over the world. He drew a sharp contrast to the ageing men that occupied the world stage—Khrushchev, de Gaulle, Macmillan and Nehru. His glamorous wife, Jackie, added to the glittering aura that surrounded him.

When Kennedy first met Nehru in 1951, he was a thirty-four-year-old, two-term congressman from Massachusetts. While visiting India with his brother Robert, he had arranged to meet Nehru, who was renowned both as India's leader and as a spokesperson on the world stage for the emerging newly independent countries. Non-alignment was gaining traction across Asia and Africa. By this stage, even Winston Churchill, who had resisted India's independence and had never warmed to Nehru, was calling him the 'light of Asia'. Kennedy had read all about the Indian leader and was looking forward to meeting the man who had become a legend in his lifetime.

Kennedy was a fast and voracious reader. According to his biographer Arthur Schlesinger, he read 1,200 words a minute. He read constantly—

during meals, in the bathroom, while getting dressed. He loved the world of ideas and could quote from the Greeks and the Romans as well as American historians. Kennedy knew that Nehru was erudite and had written several books. He hoped Nehru would have some wisdom to share and that he could learn something from him.

Nehru, who knew very little about the congressman, treated Kennedy with indifference when they met. Kennedy had been warned that, when Nehru became bored, he would tap his fingers together and look at the ceiling. When he was president, Kennedy related the story of how Nehru, after ten minutes of their first meeting, started to 'tap his fingers and gaze abstractedly at a spot over his visitor's head'.[1] It is to his credit that he did not allow Nehru's behaviour then to prejudice him in his future dealings with the prime minister.

Jackie Kennedy, in an interview she gave to Schlesinger, recounted how she would be cold to people with whom her husband had difficulties, but was always thrown off when he was gracious and warm to them and would carry on as though they were good friends. According to her, Kennedy did not bear grudges when it came to politics.

Of all the neutral countries, Kennedy regarded India as the linchpin in Asia against the creeping influence of communism. As early as 1959, he saw India and China competing for the economic and political leadership of Asia and the respect of the newly independent countries. He believed the country that won that race would shape Asia's future and was certain that it was in the US interest to back India. Kennedy admired Nehru as an intellectual leader who was committed to individual liberty and his nation's independence. He recognized that Nehru provided the sort of leadership that was essential to the development of Asia. He understood that people were tired of colonialism, and the desire for independence and nationalist movements did not constitute a threat to US interests.

Earlier, in 1958, Kennedy had called on Americans to 'renounce the proposition that "we should enter every military conflict as a moral crusade requiring the unconditional surrender of the enemy". The stereotypes of the fifties, he thought, were not only self-serving but, worse, did not provide a useful way of thinking about international affairs.'[2] Unlike Dulles, he did not find Nehru's stand on non-alignment hazardous to US interests. He had made a decision early in his administration to redress the balance in the US relationship in South Asia by cultivating India.

## Galbraith: The Admired Ambassador

Perhaps the most significant decision that Kennedy made regarding India was the appointment of Harvard professor John Kenneth Galbraith as ambassador. They met when Kennedy was a student at Harvard and Galbraith was his advisor. Later, when Kennedy became a senator, he turned to Galbraith for advice on economic policy and met with him on a regular basis. Galbraith eventually became one of Kennedy's counsellors when he ran for president and remained a trusted member of his inner circle through his presidency.

While Galbraith was ambassador, the secretary of state, Dean Rusk, was largely excluded from decisions regarding India. Although Rusk brought solid foreign policy credentials to the job, Kennedy found him lacking in vision. Rusk, a long-time State Department official who had been close to Dean Acheson, was formal, conservative and bureaucratic. He was not a personal friend of Kennedy and was never part of the inner circle, unlike Galbraith. Rusk was a cold warrior and did not share Kennedy's interest in India. When it came to India, it was understood that Galbraith was in charge. Not only did he have access to the Indian prime minister but he had a direct line to Kennedy, and he let everyone know it.

India was fortunate to have, in Kennedy, a US president who was predisposed to help and, in Galbraith, an ambassador who was decidedly pro-India. This confluence of relationships could not have come together at a more opportune time for India as it was about to be confronted with the first external threat requiring military aid from the US. Nehru had aged, and he was not the energetic leader he once was. Galbraith found himself in the unique role of advising his own government and also becoming an unofficial advisor to Nehru during this critical period. He would become the most trusted and highly regarded US ambassador to India.

By the time he arrived in New Delhi, Galbraith already enjoyed a close relationship with Nehru. He had spent time in India in the 1950s and his expertise in economics and agriculture had provided him with an entrée to

Nehru, who was in the throes of developing the Indian economy. Galbraith treated Nehru as his intellectual equal, which greatly pleased him. His easy access to Nehru and his academic credentials gave him a status that was the envy of the diplomatic corp. He was the only US ambassador whose charms Mrs Gandhi succumbed to. She confided to her friend Dorothy Norman, 'It's awfully good for the muscles just to look at him!'[3]

At six feet nine inches, with slightly greying hair, the brilliant and supremely confident—many would say arrogant—Galbraith brought his own distinctive style to the ambassadorship. Born in Canada, he had graduated from Berkeley with a doctorate in economics before becoming a professor at Harvard. He arrived in India in the hottest months and, like some other ambassadors, would suffer chronic stomach ailments. He also suffered from headaches, sinus problems and had trouble sleeping. His journals are full of references to popping pills and pain medications to cope with his health problems, all of which miraculously cleared up when he left India.

Galbraith's dispatches from India were widely circulated in Washington and admired for their wit and acerbic observations. He described the Saudi ambassador to India as 'a vast man, exceeding in diameter even the late J. Falstaff. He was not built for the desert and all the camels should be grateful that he took up diplomacy.'[4]

The irony of India's attitude towards aid did not escape his humour: 'We had a session on steel with the Minister Swaran Singh. He would like us to finance the fourth steel mill under public ownership with no interference by us with construction or operation, although we would have an opportunity to advise. The Indians can be a bit exacting in the requirements we must meet if we are allowed to help them.'[5]

He was notoriously sarcastic without any regard for rank or seniority, even when the object of his insult was his own government. In a missive to the White House, when he was particularly irritated by a delayed response to an action he considered urgent, he chastised them: 'I might plead for speed here so you could put the bite on Bhutto. May I also remind all hands that just as Washington considers it prudent to remind ambassadors to move with all firmness, vigour and determination, so ambassadors are entailed in characteristic humility to ask Washington to collect itself effectively for supporting action. I notice with mild distaste my feeling that while I should be expected to move GOI with some celerity, the tempo USG must be taken as given and very deliberate at that.'[6] It was unlikely that any other ambassador could have gotten away with such a note to the White House, but Galbraith did not have to clear his dispatches through the State Department. He usually went over their heads directly to the president of the United States.

Galbraith had decided that the best way to overcome the dyspeptic relationship between the two countries would be to bring Nehru and Kennedy together on the premise that if these two leaders, who shared similar worldviews and a sense of humanity, met, their differences would melt away. A state visit to Washington was arranged for November 1961. Galbraith proposed a low-key, no-fuss visit, though the president was sceptical, having had some experience before with heads of state who asked for 'no fuss' but were disappointed when none was made.[7] At Galbraith's suggestion, they arranged to greet Nehru at the Auchincloss residence in Newport.*

## Another Disastrous Visit to the US

Nehru arrived in New York on 5 November 1961. Despite his long journey, he was taken to the television studio of *Meet the Press* and subjected to an aggressive interview by Lawrence Spivak. Kennedy met Nehru at the naval base and brought him by boat on the *Honey Fitz* to the Auchincloss residence but made the mistake of pointing out all the grand mansions of the wealthy on the way, saying, 'I wanted you to see how the average American family lives.'[8] Kennedy's attempt at humour was lost on Nehru, and the conversation went limp. Nehru was immediately put off by '[t]he affluence and glitter with which Kennedy was surrounded'.[9] It grated on him.

---

* The Auchincloss residence was the family home of the first lady, Jackie Kennedy's parents. Located in Newport, Rhode Island, it was also known as the Hammersmith Farm.

Although Nehru, like Kennedy, had been born into wealth and privilege, he had turned his back on material comforts under Gandhi's influence. Years of fighting for his country's independence and seeing the immense poverty that the majority of his countrymen endured made talk of material wealth offensive. Kennedy's unfortunate joke reminded Nehru of his first trip to New York when he had found conversations that focused on materialism and wealth distasteful.

In contrast, Nehru and Eisenhower had got on well. They were of the same generation and he respected what Eisenhower had achieved during the war. More significantly, Eisenhower projected a simplicity when they met at Gettysburg that Nehru had found sincere.

The atmosphere did not improve much once they arrived at the White House. While Nehru was sweet to Mrs Kennedy and their daughter Caroline, who greeted him on his arrival, he was tired and difficult to engage even when the conversation turned to Vietnam. There were long awkward silences and the atmosphere became heavier with each passing minute. Nehru may have been reluctant to discuss Vietnam as he was not a fan of President Diem and was wary of the US involvement there. India had intervened in Laos and worked with Moscow to make sure Laos remained neutral, but Nehru saw no further role for India in Southeast Asia any more.

Mrs Gandhi, who had accompanied her father but had no official designation, was obliged to have lunch with Mrs Kennedy instead of the men, which Jackie quickly saw annoyed her. They did not take to each other. Mrs Kennedy found Mrs Gandhi to be 'a bitter, pushy, horrible woman ... who always looked like she'd been sucking a lemon ... Who when marriage and love and all those things don't turn out right, it all goes back inside you and the poison works inside like an ulcer. She's a truly bitter woman, she's the kind of woman who's always hated Jack.'[10] The young wife of the president had been unduly harsh, but she had seen something—a suffering that others around them had missed.[†]

---

†    In her interview with Schlesinger, Jackie displays great resentment towards both Nehru and Mrs Gandhi for not responding to the effort that she and her husband were making to welcome them and extending their friendship. She thought it was impolite. She became very fond of Nehru when she visited India later.

At the state dinner, Mrs Gandhi irritated her hosts when she 'assailed the President about American policy, and praised Krishna Menon, the professional anti-American of New Delhi'.[11] She seems to have gone out of her way to annoy her hosts, considering she was not an admirer of Menon. When Chester Bowles was ambassador, she went to his home to complain about Menon and his devious ways, so it must have had more to do with the state of her inner turmoil than her actual views. What likely slipped under the radar of the CIA, and the multiple people who were managing the trip on both sides and preparing the briefing documents, was that both father and daughter were somewhat compromised during the state visit. Prime Minister Nehru was likely suffering from a health issue and Mrs Gandhi was almost definitely going through some form of depression.[12]

B.K. Nehru, the popular Indian ambassador to the US, tried to rescue the visit that was quickly becoming a disaster. He invited people to meet Nehru at the embassy to provide them another opportunity to meet him in a more relaxed environment. Under normal circumstances, Nehru would have relished the opportunity for an intellectual exchange of ideas and conducted himself with poise. He was an elegant man and knew how to captivate an audience, but he just was not himself.

B.K. Nehru had seen Nehru perform with charm and skill during foreign trips. He was puzzled by his prime minister's behaviour. At first, he put it down to jet lag and fatigue, but he later began to suspect that Nehru was unwell. 'There were moments during his visit when the old Jawaharlal returned but for long periods, he was spiritless, listless, uninterested in his surroundings and uncommunicative—the very reverse of Jawaharlal as he normally was.'[13]

B.K. Nehru had arranged for the 'best and the brightest' to meet Prime Minister Nehru over breakfast. Nehru, normally a stickler for punctuality, arrived twenty minutes late, and when he emerged from the car there was white foam at the left side of his mouth. The ambassador wiped it away and noticed that Nehru's gait was slow; he forced a smile of greeting and sat limply, but 'his answer was slow, meandering and sometimes irrelevant'.[14]

It is entirely possible that Nehru experienced a minor stroke or that he was suffering from an acute bladder infection that had disoriented him. Despite B.K. Nehru's observations, no attempt was made to get him medical attention. In retrospect, it seems almost criminal that Nehru's health was neglected, and his trip compromised.‡ Nehru died two and a half years after his visit to the US.

We now know that Mrs Gandhi was in a state of deep depression that year. In a letter to Dorothy Norman, a month before her trip to the US, she told her that she was miserable, and when she returned to the US in March 1962, she wrote to Norman again telling her how low she felt. 'Heaven alone knows how I am going to survive this trip! The tiredness seems to reach deep inside and I am so depressed!'[15]

Mrs Gandhi had developed a deep friendship with an American woman, Dorothy Norman, with whom she maintained a correspondence that spanned thirty-four years. The letters, remarkable for their honesty, are intimate and trusting. She pours her heart out in them, revealing her deepest secrets, insecurities and desires. Given her later conflicts with the US, it is ironic that her most trusted confidante was an American.

President Kennedy attempted to engage Nehru during their private talks in Washington. He shared confidences with him and tried to elicit his opinions but, in the end, gave up exasperated. Of the prime minister, he said, 'It was like trying to grab something in your hand, only to have it turn out to be just fog. It was all so sad: this man had done so much for Indian independence, but he had stayed around too long, and now it was all going bit by bit.'[16] It was the worst state visit Kennedy had had.

Kennedy had begun the visit with great hopes for the relationship, but he was terribly disappointed. He thought Nehru was on the decline and, though he wanted to help India, his earlier enthusiasm for the country cooled after the visit. He felt that, with Nehru at India's helm and unwilling to hand over power to more energetic leadership, economic progress would be difficult to achieve even with American assistance. 'The President, as I gathered later, was left with the impression that the Prime Minister was "finished".'[17]

---

‡   Nehru suffered a stroke in January 1964 followed by renal complications. He died in May 1964. He likely had started to suffer from cardiac issues by 1961. He also had a history of bladder infections.

Kennedy's charms were not entirely wasted on Nehru during the infamous visit. Nehru later told his minister, M.J. Desai, that he was 'impressed with the cordial atmosphere during all his talks with the president, and it was the first time in his discussions with an American or Soviet head of state that it was possible for both sides to lay their cards completely on the table. Nehru said several times during and after the trip that President Kennedy is one of the most honest and most moral world politicians of our day.'[18] This was high praise coming from Nehru but his kind words did not find their way to Kennedy.

Americans were left with the impression that Nehru had aged and was tired or indifferent to his relationship with the US. The only person Nehru seemed to warm to was Jackie Kennedy, who charmed him and whom he invited to visit India.

Despite his disappointing encounters with Nehru, Kennedy found something compelling about India's experiment with democracy. He was quick to notice that Nehru responded positively to Jackie and immediately agreed for her to accept Nehru's invitation to visit India.

A month after Nehru returned to India, Jackie's trip to India was postponed because India forcibly took over Goa to almost universal censure from around the world.

## Goa

Goa rises from the sand like a thorn on the side of India. It was a Portuguese colonial port outpost on India's western coast, south of Bombay, and the last vestige of India's colonial past. India had tried unsuccessfully since Independence to convince Portugal to voluntarily give up its tiny territories in India. Ellsworth Bunker, Eisenhower's ambassador to India, had met with Nehru and suggested that 'Goa might be purchased from Portugal in the manner in which the United States had bought Louisiana from France'.[19] Nehru had liked the idea, but Portugal was not interested. For the Portuguese, Goa was a symbol of its once glorious past.

When Indian efforts failed, they stirred up local sentiment against the Portuguese. The resulting unrest provided India with a pretext to intervene and take over Goa by force. In the month after Nehru visited the US, India invaded Goa on 17 December 1961. The military operations lasted two days and were conducted by land, sea and air. They resulted in twenty-two Indian and thirty Portuguese fatalities.

The integration of Goa into India was politically popular in India. Indians considered it taking care of 'unfinished business'—evicting the last of the Europeans from India. Krishna Menon was one of its biggest promoters. He justified the takeover by claiming that Indian fishermen were being fired on by Portuguese military personnel.

The West uniformly condemned the Indian action. Portugal dramatically put on a show of public mourning, with silent marches accompanied by religious symbols moving through its streets in funeral-like processions. Films and theatre performances were cancelled. Portugal sank into a state of depression and called on its NATO allies for support.

By unilaterally invading Goa, India had violated Articles 33 and 37 of the UN Charter that required a peaceful resolution to the dispute, failing which India was required to submit the disagreement to the Security Council. With the searing experience of Kashmir in the background, India did not trust the UN to reach a decision favourable to India.

Leaders like Indonesia's President Sukarno followed the events in Goa carefully to see what the consequences for India would be, as they had similar situations in their own countries. They would all have liked to exercise the freedom to push the colonial powers out without going through the UN. It was precisely the sort of situation that the US wanted to avoid. The US was particularly chagrined that someone of Nehru's stature was undermining the UN's processes.

The US delegate at the UN, Adlai Stevenson, rebuked India and tried to pass a UN resolution against the action, joined by the UK, which felt obliged to support Portugal. But the resolution was defeated by a Soviet veto. The Soviets were becoming a reliable friend to India in substantial ways. While no one in the US was sympathetic to colonial sentiments, India's use of force in Goa was objectionable. Galbraith was the lone voice in his government willing to speak up in India's defence, icily noting that he did not intend to 'carry added burden of defending domination of millions of black men by a few thousand whites from minor European despotism'.[20] However, he informed Nehru that the use of force undercut

India's moral high ground as the nation of non-violence. Nehru seemed hypocritical, preaching peace internationally while using force at home.

Nehru and Desai and other members of the Indian diplomatic community were sensitive about the reaction internationally and in the US. Members of the Indian government saw that Goa had damaged India's prestige overseas and compromised Nehru's moral leadership, but they refused to confront Nehru. They defended him to the outside world saying Portugal had left him no alternative.

Galbraith was well aware that the negative world reaction had disturbed politicians and the press in India, who took pride in India's image as a promoter of non-violence. He decided, '[I]t was up to India to do its own repair work and letting them stew in their isolation for a while and worry about the way they were perceived internationally might do them some good.' In an extremely ill-timed visit, Menon visited the US on 22 December 1961, which Galbraith likened to 'the use of a gasoline hose as a fire extinguisher'.[21] Earlier Galbraith had told Desai that India had been utterly callous of US public opinion. If they had to send someone to smooth relations, they could not have chosen a representative of the Indian government that invited more explosive reactions than Krishna Menon.

On 18 January 1962, Kennedy wrote Nehru a letter expressing his disappointment about the way Goa had been handled. White House officials were angry that they had been given no prior indication about India's intentions when Nehru had come on a state visit to Washington the month before. They felt it undermined the trust they were trying to build with India. The letter was long, candid, but not unfriendly in tone.

On a philosophical level, Kennedy's letter argued that resorting to force is never a good option. He reminded Nehru that all countries 'have a capacity for convincing themselves of the full righteousness of their particular cause. No country ever uses force for reasons it considers unjust.'[22] He said it was harder to work with India for peace in the Congo while India was using force in Goa. It also undermined the UN as an international arbitrator of disputes. Closer to home, and on a more practical level, the president elaborated on the negative impact the use of force had on aid appropriations for India from a Congress that was already reluctant to give money to it and other third world countries.

Nehru replied that at the time of his visit, he had not made the decision to invade Goa forcibly, but circumstances had compelled him to act. Jagat Mehta believes Nehru was not entirely wrong, as his natural inclinations were pacifist. According to Mehta, Nehru had assured Kennedy during his US visit that Goa would be resolved without force. He was unable to keep his word because Menon put pressure on Nehru, telling him 'that he either had to be pro-imperialist and tolerate Goa or side with the nationalists'. While Nehru was in the US, Menon pushed him into a corner on Goa. He was aided by public sentiment that had been stirred up, which quickly overtook events, pre-empting Nehru's ability to consider alternative resolutions.

In the end, internal memoranda within the US government indicate that the US decided not to respond to Nehru's letter and to drop the matter. A tiny port remnant of Portugal's colonial past was not important enough to the US to make it a cause. Even the NATO countries did not want to make an issue of it. But India's prestige, along with Nehru's, had been tarnished and India's tendency to preach to others was compromised.

The misunderstandings over Goa led the US to postpone Jackie's visit. In the end, Nehru was concerned about his image overseas and wrote to President Kennedy to smooth things over. He explained his position and, while he defended his actions, he apologized for any misunderstanding arising from not informing the White House.

The reinstatement of Jackie Kennedy's visit was the olive branch. Just as she had charmed Khrushchev and de Gaulle, Nehru too melted and communications between Nehru and Kennedy became more cordial. Jackie's visit was arranged for March 1962 and would be one of the most extensively covered events by the media.

## Jackie: The Royal Visit

Jackie Kennedy's goodwill tour to India was one of the most glamorous events to grace New Delhi since Independence. She arrived on 12 March 1962, with sixty-four pieces of luggage and, according to *Life* magazine, she changed outfits about twenty-two times during her nine-day visit. Jackie Kennedy's sister, Lee Radziwill, accompanied her. Her entourage had several staff and included her hairdresser. Dozens of journalists covered the trip. All the major networks sent reporters including NBC's Barbara Walters.

Painters and decorators had been spinning around the embassy grounds for days, rearranging furniture, touching up peeling paint and polishing all the brassware. The ambassador, John Kenneth Galbraith, was treating it like a royal visit, personally supervising every detail to ensure perfection. Everything from the floral arrangements to the guest list had been carefully curated. Galbraith even insisted on a rehearsal dinner to make sure that, on the actual day, the event would flow as seamlessly as possible. The embassy staff had been instructed to give the visit the highest priority and all other matters of state had been put on hold for the month.

Jackie Kennedy was well known for her refined taste. She despised Victorian mirrors, adored regency furniture and, above all, loved the classical ideal. One of her first undertakings as first lady had been the restoration of the White House. She was responsible for having it and several momentous neo-classical buildings in Washington designated as historical monuments. Jackie had a perfect figure and impeccable taste in clothes. Designers loved to dress her, and she became a fashion icon. Photo spreads of her and the handsome president filled all the magazines. As Jay Mulvaney, author of *The Clothes of Camelot*, wrote, 'Jackie approached the task of wardrobe creation with a serious discipline.'[23]

During her three days in Delhi, Nehru gave Jackie his undivided attention and insisted she stay at his residence in the guest suite that Edwina Mountbatten often used. At a dinner hosted by him, Nehru led Jackie down the stairs after dinner and they sat on the steps in deep conversation while the guests stood at a distance, straining to catch a sentence here and there. Neither of them, both stoically private individuals, divulged any details of their conversation.

After three days in the capital, Jackie and her party left for Agra, Udaipur, Jaipur and Benares. She was enchanted by the Taj Mahal and returned to enjoy it by moonlight, seeing it twice in the same day. Crowds lined the streets and greeted them wherever they went. Jackie had charmed the prime minister, impressed the maharajas and was gracious to the ordinary people she met. The press loved her. If the objective of the trip was to enhance goodwill between the two countries, it was a diplomat's dream.

At the young age of thirty-two, Jackie Kennedy had proved to be an invaluable asset to her husband. She had earlier smoothed over a tense relationship between Kennedy and Khrushchev by showing an interest in the Soviet space programme and the fate of the dog that had been sent into space. She had made a good impression on de Gaulle when she had discussed Malraux's books and spoken to him in flawless French.

Now, she had softened the edge that had resulted in the sour aftermath of Nehru's visit to the US five months earlier and followed by India's takeover of the Portuguese colony of Goa. Her goodwill trip restored the balance and the dust settled. She emphasized India's cultural heritage and was the first American to add glamour and colour to the images of a poor and famine-stricken India that people were otherwise used to seeing.

The advancement of relations could not have come at a more essential time for India. As the movement of China's army across the Himalayas cast a shadow over India, US support would become vital to its survival.

# Chapter 7

# The War with China

O N 16 OCTOBER 1962, TWO URGENT MEMORANDA WERE WAITING on the desk of the national security officer at the White House. The first, from the State Department, warned that clashes on the Sino-Indian border had escalated to a dangerous level. The second contained top-secret CIA documents obtained through U-2 reconnaissance imagery, which showed that offensive Soviet intermediate range missiles had been delivered to Cuba.[1]

The winds of war were gathering, pitting the communist world against the non-communist world. In the West, the world's most powerful democracy, the United States, was facing down the world's most powerful communist country, the Soviet Union, and its client state, Cuba. The US and the Soviets were nuclear powers and any aggressive move carried the threat of annihilation were it to escalate to war.

Ten thousand miles away in the high Himalayas, in a desolate area where little grows and habitation is a struggle, India, the largest democracy in the world, was entangled in an increasingly open border conflict with China, the most populous communist country in the world.

Nehru had sought to maintain good relations with China since India's independence in 1947. Pan-Asian unity was one of Nehru's principal foreign policy goals and he had tried to be an advocate for China.[2] In a period when China could count on few friends internationally, he had spent a good deal of his political capital attempting to convince Western countries to admit communist China to the UN, even though India's efforts met stiff resistance.

Nehru found it difficult to imagine China as an adversary after the pledges of solidarity agreed to at the 1955 Bandung Conference. China and India, along with several other Asian and African countries, had agreed to five core principles called 'Panchsheel' to ensure peace and non-aggression among the participants.

Beneath the outward show of friendship lay some unresolved issues between the two that predated Independence. Relations began to significantly deteriorate after the 1959 revolt in Tibet when the Chinese marched into Tibet and sealed its borders.* India and China periodically had minor border clashes but when China occupied some 12,000 square miles of territory claimed by India in Assam and Ladakh, the honeymoon between the two countries was over.

According to Indian Foreign Secretary Jagat Mehta, one of the first foreign service officers recruited by Nehru after India's independence, 'The idea that once the European imperialists left Asia, the newly independent countries would live harmoniously was based on hope more than reason.'[3]

## Origins of the Dispute

In January 1959, Zhou Enlai claimed that British imperialists had drawn the border between China and British India without consulting the Chinese. Disputes over borders originally drawn unilaterally by the British over a century ago have been the cause of wars, large and small, across the world. Such conflicts persist in Africa and the Middle East.

India's border with China was first drawn by the British imperialists in the 1890s with the goal of containing Russian expansion in Asia. At first, Britain recognized Chinese suzerainty in this remote region, including over Tibet, believing that Chinese ownership would prevent the steadily increasing Russian encroachment in the region. But by the 1800s, the enfeebled Manchu dynasty lost control over vast tracts of China's territory to the Russians.[4] As China proved too weak to be an effective deterrent to Russia, influential imperialists in London supported a forward policy

---

\*    The Chinese considered Tibet a part of China and viewed this as an internal matter. India saw it differently.

and promoted a more expansionary policy of British India's frontiers. The British began to survey this remote frontier region and maps with varying borders began to circulate, which would cloud political discussions about the border well after the British left India.

Among the most disputed areas between India and China was the Aksai Chin, a barren, frozen plateau, 17,000 feet above sea level. It was of little use to India but was an important access path for China to reach the Sinkiang province.

The Chinese attempted to define their southern border by sending an emissary to survey it in 1880. China first voiced its claim to Aksai Chin in 1896 to George McCartney, the British representative in Kashgar. China supported its claim with a map drawn by W.H. Johnson in 1865, showing the Aksai within China's territory. McCartney seemed to agree at the time that China's claim to all of the Aksai Chin region was legitimate. A British intelligence report from the same year also confirmed his observation.[5]

In 1899, the British tabled a new idea. In an official submission made to Peking, they proposed that the Aksai be divided into two, with one half going to Sinkiang and the other to become part of Tibet. There was no reply from the Chinese. As a consequence, in the absence of an explicit rejection by China, Lord Curzon decided to go ahead and treat the new proposed boundary as accepted.

In 1910 the Chinese tried to reassert their authority in Tibet and around the tribal areas bordering the region but, when the Chinese government collapsed in 1911, there was a power vacuum in Peking, which emboldened proponents of the British forward school to expand their influence throughout this region. Fearing China incapable of being an effective buffer, they revised their maps without official clearance from London. The latest maps showed all of the Aksai within British India.

Following the nationalist revolution in China, even formerly moderate British officials converted to the forward school. In 1912, Britain sought to expand its influence in Tibet and help it attain autonomy from China. Tibet declared its independence in 1913, but never succeeded in ratifying its independence from China through any formal agreement. The Chinese did not believe it served their interests to negotiate from a position of weakness. They preferred instead to wait and play the long game.

In 1914, China, Tibet and British India gathered at the Simla Convention to try to forge an agreement on the frontier. The multiple maps that had been drawn over the previous thirty years, showing different configurations of the border—one with all of Aksai in China, one with half in China and half in Tibet, and the most recent showing it in British India—provided fodder to the different sides.[6] At the conference, Britain helped Tibet secure its autonomy from China, and Tibet and Britain signed a treaty. China remained internally so weak that it was not in a position to challenge the two, but it refused to sign any agreements and the conference ended in failure. In 1919, Britain tried to force China to resume negotiations by threatening to recognize Tibet as an independent country, but China demurred.

The situation on the Chinese border thus remained in limbo until India's independence in 1947. On the map, British India held several hundred square miles of territory that China claimed belonged to it. But these various lines drawn on different maps remained a theoretical exercise. Nothing changed on the ground. None of the powers had any physical outposts in this forbidding part of the world and life carried on as before.

Aside from the Aksai, other parts of the western areas were never delineated with a clearly defined border. Instead, a no man's land was allowed to exist between China and India.

To the east, Sir Henry McMahon drew boundary lines that cut through jungles, torrential rivers and areas inhabited by inhospitable tribes. Britain's aggressive forward policy saw the steady erosion of Chinese authority that had traditionally dominated the region.

During the Second World War, when the Japanese were at India's doorstep, the British realized how vulnerable India's eastern border was and converted the McMahon Line into its permanent boundary. This unilaterally assigned border was thus inherited by India in 1947, and India insisted it belonged to it by right. The Chinese did not view the issue through the same lens. They insisted the border should be a matter for negotiation. 'The withdrawal of British power from the subcontinent in 1947 prepared the way for a reversal of the balance that had existed across the Himalayas.'[7]

In the early 1950s, India noticed that maps in China depicted India's claimed territory as lying within China. Initially, when Nehru brought this to Zhou Enlai's attention, he brushed it off and said the maps had not been updated. During Nehru's highly successful visit to China in 1954, at the height of Indo-Chinese friendship, Zhou brought up the border and implied that the Chinese accepted the McMahon Line in the east as an 'accomplished fact' and, since China's relations with Burma and India were friendly, it was inclined to recognize the line. The Aksai Chin was never broached by either party on this visit.

In 1958, India discovered the Chinese had built a road in the Aksai Chin. Nehru lodged an official protest with Peking and asked for information regarding a missing Indian patrol. The curt reply from the Chinese made it clear that they thought the Indians had been trespassing on Chinese territory and the troops had been detained.

Facing increasingly angry parliamentarians, Nehru reassured Parliament that India viewed its boundaries as sacrosanct, regardless of Chinese maps. The Indian government decided, at this point, to start installing posts along the border and actively patrolling sections of it.

In 1959, a revolt broke out in Tibet. The CIA, with collusion from India, arranged for the Dalai Lama's dramatic escape over the Himalayan mountains to India. Hundreds of Tibetan refugees followed him, and the entire episode became an international embarrassment for China.

When the Chinese announced that they would be marching into Tibet, India reacted with alarm, warning China that it was harming its reputation internationally. China responded that 'if unfriendly governments used the exercise of China's sovereign rights in Tibet as a pretext for further obstruction of her UN membership, that would only be another demonstration of her hostility'.[8] It was a sharp rebuke to India that any attempts to interfere would not be tolerated.†

The façade of Indo-China friendship ruptured. Nehru was pilloried in the Chinese press as a 'stooge of Western interests'. It was a far cry from his

---

† China wanted to make it clear to India that it should not expect to leverage its support of China's membership to the UN for any territorial concessions in Tibet or elsewhere.

visit to China in 1956, when massive crowds everywhere had cheered him. Nehru's dream of Asian solidarity disintegrated.

In the interest of preserving his dream of Asian unity, Nehru glossed over China's aggression in Tibet and turned a blind eye to the brutal repression of Chinese citizens. He viewed the convulsions in China as temporary symptoms of a nation struggling to regain its identity and exorcising decades of domination by Western powers. He did not subscribe to Western fears of a communist sweep across Asia and was convinced that ancient Chinese culture with its deep roots would ultimately triumph over communist ideology.

From 1958 on, Zhou Enlai and Nehru exchanged a series of letters to try to resolve the border issue between the two countries. Visits were exchanged between the two prime ministers and various proposals discussed. China seemed willing to concede the McMahon Line in the east, with minor adjustments, provided it could retain the Aksai Chin in the west, which it needed to access Sinkiang province. As far as the Chinese were concerned, the Aksai Chin was of no practical use to India and would be challenging for India to defend. Much to China's bafflement, an inflexible India rejected the proposal.‡

Nehru found himself backed into a corner. By making stirring public speeches about the integrity of India's claims, he had inadvertently whipped up public sentiment against China. Each time Nehru and Zhou were to meet, the Indian press exploded with editorials applying pressure on him to resist giving into Chinese 'demands'. Parliament and the press were suspicious of Nehru's resolve towards China and, after 1959, Nehru was on the defensive regarding his China policy, with Parliament questioning his attitudes given the extreme vitriol expressed towards both India and Nehru in the Chinese press.[9] Members of Parliament worried that Nehru,

---

‡ 'A man of great sensitivity and familiar with symbolism, Zhou was offended when on a visit to India, in 1953, Mrs Indira Gandhi, acting as hostess for her father at a reception for Zhou, greeted him dressed in Tibetan clothes given to her by the Dalai Lama.' Zhou confided this to the Pakistani ambassador to Beijing, Sultan Muhammad Khan, and seemed convinced Mrs Gandhi was sending him a political message. (Source: Sultan Muhammed Khan, *Memories and Reflections*, 103.)

in order to preserve his dream of Asian solidarity, might soften and sell India short. Democracy in India had a loud voice. Zhou had no such political constraints.

Negotiations only work if approached in good faith. Nehru never came to the table with any concessions. All India had to offer were demands and its friendship which, given the recent hostility, held little value for China. Indian attempts to lobby on behalf of China at the UN had come to naught. As a poor country, India was of little economic value to China.

China came to the discussions with a deal and proposed an east-west swap. They were willing to recognize the India's claims in the east in return for India acknowledging China's claims to the Aksai Chin in the west. Xu Yan, the authoritative Chinese analyst of the 1962 war, outlined Mao's approval of the offer based on China's weak international security position at the time.[10] Indians, on other hand, refused to negotiate on any part of the border. Members of the Chinese delegation reported being shocked at Nehru's inflexibility and his refusal, as they saw it, to understand their point of view.[§] When they suggested freezing the borders until some indefinite calmer future, they were rejected. After the failure of the summit talks in 1959, both sides hardened their positions.

## Drift to War

After 1960, an aggressive forward policy was adopted by India. Both sides began to flex their muscles and violate the existing line of 'actual' control. Skirmishes took place in 1961 and began to escalate through early 1962. A split developed between the army and New Delhi.

The army, well aware of its limitations, had reservations about the forward policy. It was wary of unnecessarily provoking the Chinese over territory that was of marginal importance to India and logistically difficult to supply and defend.

But in the political arena, sentiments had already overtaken practical considerations. Parliament was against any concessions to China and,

---

§   The Chinese reported this to East European diplomats. (Source: Maxwell, *India's China War*, 158).

for the first time, the opposition dared to question Nehru's policies and warned him against appeasement. Nehru vacillated. He tried backing away from the war rhetoric: 'My whole soul reacts against the idea of war anywhere,' he would declare in speeches. But he also told Parliament that, while he preferred diplomacy to war, he would fight for India's sovereignty if it became necessary.

When the Chinese took over an Indian controlled post at Thag La, roughly five kilometres north of the McMahon Line, Nehru told his army chiefs to 'throw the Chinese out' as though it was a simple task. The battle drums were growing louder by the day but there was no review of military resources or preparedness. Army officers, who tried to warn New Delhi that the army was ill-equipped for war, were silenced or pushed aside.

India began to hatch a military operation codenamed 'Leghorn'. The plan was to surprise and evict the Chinese from the Thag La Ridge in the Aksai Chin region. The troops were told to prepare for battle. The Chinese supply posts were just a few miles behind the ridge while the Indian supply routes were unnavigable. Supplies would have to be airdropped. Not only were the logistics challenging, but also it was unclear to the Indian Army if Thag La was part of India or China.

The person in charge of India's armed forces was Krishna Menon, who, through his careful cultivation of Nehru, had become the minister of defence. This eccentric, anti-Western, left-wing intellectual had no knowledge about military affairs and was incapable of providing the military or Nehru with strategic options or guidance during this critical time. His personal insecurities had led him to push aside competent commanders who disagreed with him and to replace them with a bunch of yes-men without the necessary planning skills. The odds seemed stacked against India.

As news of the border clashes trickled into the press and the Chinese incursions into Indian territory became known, the calls for Nehru to act became a clamour. There was no public relations team to manage public sentiment, which was becoming increasingly impulsive and almost irrational in its demands.

Nehru found his choices limited. A constitutional amendment had been passed by the Supreme Court of India that prohibited the concession of any of its territory without being ratified by an amendment to the Constitution.⁵ Nehru, at this stage, was politically strong enough to steward a constitutional amendment** allowing him to concede territory in the western sector in exchange for recognition of the McMahon Line, a solution along the lines proposed by China. China had struck a similar deal on its border with Burma. But the give and take of diplomatic negotiations eluded Nehru. He was ageing, tired and trying to micromanage too many arms of government. He lacked the expertise and technical knowledge of the equipment and manpower needed for conducting and winning a war. The war that came turned out to be a debacle.

## The Sino-Indian War: An Indian Disaster

On 8 September 1962, a Chinese military unit penetrated India's North East Frontier Agency (NEFA) at Dhola, two miles south of the McMahon Line. A flurry of notes was exchanged back and forth between the two countries as each accused the other of violations and demanded that it withdraw its troops. Both sides were intransigent and rejected the charges levelled by the other.

Dhola Post had previously been in Chinese-occupied territory until India unilaterally decided that it belonged to India. A few months earlier, despite the army's misgivings, it was instructed to take Dhola over as part of the forward policy.

By mid-October 1962, communication between India and China broke down.

China, which had been amassing well-equipped troops and placing them in position along the border for some time, occupied the high

---

⁵ In 1958, Nehru had ceded some minor territory to Pakistan to settle boundary disputes. It was challenged in the courts, and in March 1960, the Supreme Court upheld the challenge. The government was informed that any compromises on territory to China would have to go through a constitutional amendment. (Source: Maxwell, *India's China War*, 153.)

** A constitutional amendment was passed that prevented anyone from conceding any territory belonging to India without going through the courts.

ground. Chinese soldiers, many of whom had been stationed on the Tibetan Plateau for years, had become acclimatized and had appropriate clothing. The Chinese army had been building roads and facilities for years, so its logistical capabilities were far superior to that of India. Its supply lines were a few hours long as opposed to a trek of several days for the Indian troops.

By contrast, Indian soldiers were woefully unprepared. They were still in their summer cotton uniforms, wholly unsuitable for altitudes of 14,000 feet. They were underequipped, under-rationed and un-acclimatized. The roads on the Indian side were shoddy or non-existent. To engage the enemy, Indian soldiers were forced to trek up steep mountain jungles on foot with inadequate footwear. They had to cross the Namka Chu River, which, at that time of the year, was a torrent twenty to fifty feet wide, with sheer banks that were twenty feet high. Many soldiers lost their lives just getting to their battle posts.

When the fighting broke out, Indians were on the defensive. The soldiers had left their base in the plains, on 6 October, in cotton uniforms with one blanket, carrying only fifty rounds per man and light weapons. They were compelled to leave the rest of their equipment behind in their march to the Karpo La Pass at 16,000 feet.[11]

The entire mission was a death trap. The supplies for the troops had to be airdropped but they often missed their target and ended up in Chinese hands. The bedraggled troops became demoralized when they finally arrived at Namka Chu and discovered that there were no supplies waiting for them. The drop zone had been closed for days due to bad weather and only a third of the supplies dropped at nearby Tsangdhar had been recovered.

'Once he [General Kaul] saw the military situation, I thought he would abandon all talk of evicting the Chinese,' wrote General J.P. Dalvi. 'Subsequently, our gloom was borne out by events when reports of pulmonary disorders, chilblain and even frost-bite poured in. Many died at Tsangdhar. The battalions arrived exhausted and without the most elementary requirements for battle. They had been hard on rations and without protection against the cold for many days. Kaul himself bemoans these happenings, without realizing that they were the direct result of his own orders.'[12]

General Kaul had never commanded troops in battle but he had been chosen by Menon to head the operation because he was willing to follow the orders of the politicians in Delhi and suspend his own military judgement. He clashed with the other more experienced generals who pointed out the difficulties of the operations or refused to send their men into what was essentially a suicide mission.

Kaul replaced General Umrao Singh when Singh raised objections to the government's forward policy and explained the difficulties of executing Operation Leghorn. He was transferred and his warnings ignored. When Kaul arrived via helicopter at the battlefront, he developed a pulmonary disorder due to the altitude and had to be carried around by porters. His state could hardly have inspired his troops.

On 11 October 1962, Kaul was airlifted to Delhi for a meeting with Nehru, Krishna Menon, the cabinet secretaries and senior members of the army. This would have been the perfect opportunity for him to brief the government in a responsible manner by providing them with an accurate account of the situation on the ground. Instead, he told them what he thought they wanted to hear. He knew that India could never win and would likely suffer heavy losses but decided not to tell the truth. Nehru abdicated his responsibility by leaving the decision to the generals and no one rescinded the order to proceed with Operation Leghorn or to revaluate the forward policy.[††]

Some of the soldiers who participated in the war and later recounted their experiences were appalled at the decision-making process. The higher authorities had obviously assumed that it would be easy to beat the Chinese. Otherwise, one cannot imagine how such an order to engage the enemy could have been issued by the highest in the land to the ill-equipped, ill-clothed, ill-prepared, fatigued, disillusioned and disorganized troops of 4th Infantry Division to engage the enemy. 'One can imagine the mental state of the Brigade Signal Officer when, on arrival after an exhausting

---

†† Putting Operation Leghorn into action would escalate the conflict and risk all-out war.

journey, he discovered that the generating engine to charge the wireless batteries had not fetched up. A porter had dropped the charging engine in a deep khud on the way from where it could not be retrieved … But we were in for a still bigger shock when it was discovered that almost all the secondary batteries had arrived without any electrolyte … How could communications be established … It was a calamity.'[‡‡]

## Thirteen Days in October

As temperatures cooled in the high Himalayas, with the first signs of snow appearing and the inflamed border tension raging, Washington was in its own state of nervous agitation. On 15 October 1962, U-2 flights, authorized by the president, had flown missions over western Cuba and collected evidence confirming earlier reports that the Soviets had been building missile sites there.[13]

The next two days were a carousel of meetings with CIA and Pentagon officials at the White House. Everyone was on high alert, working round the clock, and no one was getting any sleep. There were endless talks with lots of coffee and cigarettes and participants bound together with tension. The joint chiefs were advocating a first strike, but Kennedy hesitated.

On 18 October 1962, he met with the Soviet foreign minister Andrei Gromyko and told him that the US would not tolerate Soviet missiles in Cuba. Gromyko denied their existence.

The following day, Defense Secretary McNamara laid out three options before Kennedy. The president decided that, in order to de-escalate and retain room to manoeuvre, his best option was a naval blockade instead of a bombing campaign or total war. He called it a 'quarantine', one level below a blockade, which was considered an act of war. Moscow was busy trying to manage the fallout, and Gromyko sent Kennedy a message saying the missiles were to aid Cuba's defence capabilities and should not be misinterpreted. The *Baltimore Sun* carried an article describing food

---

‡‡ In his book, Major General K.K. Tewari said the batteries and electrolyte were dumped by the porters because of their weight. Some porters, Tewari suspected, were in the pay of the Chinese. (Source: Tewari, *A Soldier's Voyage of Self Discovery*, 105–106.)

shortages and economic hardship in the Soviet Union, indications that it had internal weaknesses not previously known to the administration.[§§]

On 22 October 1962, President Kennedy shared the photographs showing the missile sites with the US Senate. The US military alert system was moved to DEFCON 3.[¶¶]

Fidel Castro, Cuba's charismatic prime minister, mobilized his armed forces. Castro, a communist revolutionary, had seized power in a coup in 1959. In a dramatic address, President Kennedy told the US that the Russians had turned the island of Cuba into an atomic base from where they could bomb the US. He said that the US faced a grave threat and explained his decision to implement a blockade of Cuba. The president blamed the Soviets for creating the crisis and said the Cubans and Castro were mere pawns in Moscow's hands. He made it clear that he would not stop short of military action to end what he called a 'clandestine, reckless and provocative threat to world peace'.[14] He called on the UN to consider a resolution for the dismantling and withdrawal of all offensive weapons in Cuba. Simultaneously, Ambassador Kohler of the US embassy in Moscow delivered a message from President Kennedy to Khrushchev warning him that should the war escalate, there would be no winners.

On 23 October 1962, tension in Washington mounted as reconnaissance photographs over Cuba revealed Soviet missile sites were ready to launch. As navy warships took up their positions and surrounded Cuba, Khrushchev accused Kennedy of intimidation, but Kennedy refused to back down. He reminded Khrushchev that Soviet activities in Cuba had all been undertaken in secret.

Ambassador Galbraith met with Nehru and senior members of the Indian cabinet to explain the Cuba action and 'count on their restraint and UN support'. He was assured that he would have it.[15]

Nehru by now had realized that India was on the defensive in the war with China and needed American help. On 26 October 1962, Nehru wrote to Kennedy laying out India's position in its border war and requested his

---

§§   This information helped the White House pressure the Soviets.

¶¶   DEFCON refers to defence readiness condition or the state of military preparedness and there are five categories, increasing in severity from 5 to 1.

support. Kennedy responded with empathy and offered his assistance. 'I know I can speak for my whole country when I say that our sympathy in this situation is wholeheartedly with you … I would wish to give you support as well as sympathy.' The president authorized Galbraith to translate the support into action.[16] On receiving the president's warm response, Nehru requested US military assistance.

On 24 October 1962, Soviet ships approached the quarantine line. All eyes in the US were tracking their path. The air in the White House was thick with tension as with each passing minute, they faced the increased prospect of an inevitable confrontation were the Soviets to cross the line. The military went to DEFCON 2 for the first time in its history. The White House tried to anticipate retaliatory actions by the Soviets in case the US was forced to open fire on Soviet ships. It worried that the Soviets could retaliate in Berlin or that the missiles in Cuba would find US targets. These were some of the many scenarios played out at the Pentagon just as the Soviet ships reach the quarantine line. As the two countries faced each other on the sea, the Soviet ships received radio orders to hold their positions. They stood down and reversed course, and a war was averted.

Kennedy's gamble paid off. He did not yield to pressure from his military to engage in a first strike, knowing how quickly events could spiral out of control. He won the admiration of the world and showed he had nerves of steel. The stand-off on the high seas worked for Kennedy. The Soviets had driven their ships right up to the blockade and the two sides had faced each other, but in the end the Soviets blinked. The Soviet ships did not attempt to cross the line. The US, for its part, allowed a Soviet freighter through that was not carrying arms.

On 25 October 1962, Kennedy sent a letter to Khrushchev placing the responsibility of the Cuban Missile Crisis on the Soviet Union. On 26 October, Khrushchev agreed to remove all missiles from Cuba if Kennedy publicly announced he would not invade Cuba.

On 27 October, a U-2 pilot was shot down over Cuba, presenting a new dilemma for Kennedy. The incident threatened to renew the crisis in a way that neither country wanted. He was under pressure to respond militarily and Moscow was anxious about the confrontation spiralling out of control. In an attempt to diffuse tensions, Kennedy sent a letter to Khrushchev promising not to invade Cuba and offered to end the quarantine if the Soviets removed all their missiles from Cuba. Moscow agreed but wanted the US to dismantle its missiles in Turkey. After intensive negotiations, a deal was struck behind closed doors.

On 28 October, the Cuban Missile Crisis was over, though the blockade remained in place until 21 November. Khrushchev announced the dismantling of the Cuban missiles on Radio Moscow and the US reduced its threat levels. Nehru sent a warm letter of congratulations to President Kennedy on the handling of the crisis and began to regard him with greater respect and appreciation.

While Washington was focused on the Cuban Missile Crisis, Moscow was trying to maintain its image as a powerful friend to India while also keeping an eye on the Sino-Indian dispute. As the Soviets were involved in the Cuban Missile Crisis at the same time, they needed China's support in case of any unexpected escalation with the US, and they were not in a position to repudiate China for their new friend India. They would await the end of the crisis to reveal their preferences.

China had grown increasingly suspicious of the Soviets after the Longju incident in 1960 when China had clashed with India. The Chinese later said that the Soviets 'by assuming a façade of neutrality and "making no distinction between right and wrong", in merely expressing regret over the Longju clash had, by implication, shown a preference for India and condemned China'.[17] The Chinese had begun to view the Soviets as corrupt and unfriendly to China. Although their relationship had become strained, it was not obvious to the rest of the world. The two communist countries began to subtly compete against each other by pursuing separate alliances in Asia and elsewhere, but tensions between them remained below the radar of the West.

Nehru took a leaf out of Kennedy's book and, on 20 November 1962, addressed the Indian public on the Chinese attack and the threat to national security. The Chinese had opened a third front near the Burmese border and five more posts fell into their hands. Prime Minister Nehru said, 'We must build up our military strength by all means at our disposal.' Nehru denounced the Peking regime as 'a powerful and unscrupulous opponent, not caring for peace or peaceful methods'.[18]

While the White House had been busy with Cuba, India was trying to fend off a heavy assault by the Chinese in the east. The Chinese captured an Indian airstrip in Walong, Arunachal Pradesh, on 16 October 1962, in retaliation for Indian incursions against Chinese outposts in the area. The Indian army was pushed several miles south. The following day, Indians suffered heavy losses in NEFA and retreated to the Se La Pass. India also lost ground to China in the west in the Ladakh region. The war was turning into a disaster for India.

On 19 October, China broadcast accusations claiming that India had been the aggressor in Ladakh and NEFA, and that China had tried to negotiate a solution to the border dispute in good faith but India had refused to meet it halfway. The Chinese were laying out justifications for launching an all-out attack, which took place at five the next morning.

On 20 October, the Chinese crossed the Thag La Ridge and continued to Tsangdhar. Indians were routed, and the brigade commander, Brigadier Dalvi, was taken prisoner while trying to retreat with his troops to safety in the Chip Chap valley in the west. The Chinese overran many of the posts established by India during its forward policy. With many of its brigades now decimated, by 21 October, India could no longer deny its humiliating defeat.

Until then the public had been fed glowing accounts of the status and preparedness of the Indian Army and its superiority to that of China. They now discovered the truth. Newspapers that had carried false accounts of India's successes at the front, fed to them by the Ministry of Defence, now had to disavow them.

On 22 October, the headline in the *Baltimore Sun* ran, 'India Sees No Limit to Chinese Drive in Northeast, Says Reds Press Offensive all along Himalayas'. India was now confronted with a military disaster as thousands of Chinese troops descended in endless waves across the ridges along its northern frontier.

The Chinese announced that they had captured 947 Indian prisoners of war. India estimated that, between 20 October and 16 November, it lost at least 1,623 soldiers. Nehru declared that the border conflict now constituted total war.[19]

The Indian public felt betrayed and demanded explanations. A contingent of ministers confronted the prime minister and insisted Krishna Menon be fired from his job. Nehru reluctantly removed him as defence minister and took over the portfolio.

With India's northern sector crumbling, the US was getting anxious about the advance of communism in Asia. Although the US was preoccupied with the Soviets, it had kept a close eye on the Sino-Indian conflict through Galbraith in New Delhi.

China, in the meantime, launched a public relations offensive, writing to several communist and non-aligned countries to explain its position on the border war with India. Nehru received offers from Nasser and others to help mediate the dispute but, captive to his domestic constituency, turned them down. India countered by sending its own letters to various governments outlining its position. Most countries declined to take sides. Only the British came out in support of India, hardly surprising since the Indian position rested on boundary lines originally drawn by British cartographers.

As the Cuban crisis died down, there were fewer international problems competing with India's for Kennedy's attention. In India, the situation in the Himalayas continued to get more desperate and, as the Chinese continued to advance, Indian morale collapsed. The Indian public wanted Krishna Menon's head. A group of ministers went to Nehru and demanded Menon be removed from office entirely. On 30 November, Nehru reluctantly removed him from the cabinet.***

India had the good fortune of having someone from Kennedy's inner circle as ambassador. Throughout the Sino-Indian War, the line of communication between the US and India was kept open by the efforts of Galbraith, who had a direct line to Kennedy. Nehru, knowing he was sympathetic to India, trusted him and sought his advice. Galbraith was not shy about his connections at the very top on both sides and made sure everyone knew of them. He was able to keep the power centres in

---

*** Menon had earlier been relieved of his post as defence minister, but Nehru had retained him in the cabinet without a portfolio. He was now dismissed from the government.

Washington within reach and accessible at the time of need, especially Secretary of State Dean Rusk and Phillip Talbot, assistant secretary of state for Near East and South Asian Affairs.

Galbraith's sympathies during the Sino-Indian War lay squarely with India. He had urged Washington to officially recognize the McMahon Line as the legitimate border and argued that it would advance US ties in India, but he did run into resistance from his staff and the State Department personnel who had yet to catch up with the progressive new attitude towards India that Kennedy and his team advanced. Part of the resistance to India was a direct result of Nehru's insistence on non-alignment. Kennedy was less prejudiced about non-alignment than his predecessors or members of Congress.

In an interview he gave, Lindsey Grant, who was the economic officer at the US embassy during this time, said Galbraith 'managed to push through a US government position endorsing the Indian view of the border, whereas our view—and I think the India desk rather shared it—was that it was none of our business, that we should have left that whole question of borders for much longer resolution between them … He simply wanted to take the Indian position.'[20]

When the Sino-Indian War broke out in October 1962, the White House was fully preoccupied by the Cuban Missile Crisis. Kennedy trusted Galbraith and gave him the authority to manage the situation in India as he saw fit. Galbraith met with Nehru on an almost daily basis and it was due to his efforts that arms were airlifted to India on time. His efforts during the war would make him the most beloved US ambassador to India.

The Sino-Indian War forced India to shed its innocence, step into the real world and face some harsh truths about its shortcomings. Nehru, the idealist, was now in his declining years and his leadership was no longer up to the task.

## Non-Alignment and the Aid Dilemma

Nehru's policy of non-alignment became increasingly difficult to maintain given India's need for Western military assistance. Moscow had moved from studious neutrality over the border dispute to pushing the Indians to negotiate with China, which it had needed on its side when it confronted the US over Cuba.

China had carefully chosen to launch its attack at a time when the US and the West would be preoccupied, and the Soviets could not afford to be neutral.

The rift between the two communist countries had been developing for some time, though it was barely perceptible to the Western world. China had viewed with disapproval the Soviet decision to actively court India by providing it with substantial development assistance and making a public display of its friendship. It had thought the Soviet decision to sell India MiG fighter jets was particularly egregious.[†††] China was now able to demonstrate to the Russians that they were misguided in their choices and, in their time of need, the communist countries needed to stand together.

India was disappointed with the change in the Soviet attitude and, in response, made a conscious decision to move closer to the US. But the acidic treatment meted out to Americans by Krishna Menon over the years had left scars. When Galbraith met with M.J. Desai on 29 October, to discuss the press briefing regarding India's request for military aid, Galbraith stressed that Indians should make clear that their request for aid had come from the prime minister.[21] Galbraith knew that securing an appropriation of aid was a difficult task and associating Menon's name with the request would likely kill it in the US Congress.

American arms began arriving in India in the first week of November 1962 during a lull in the fighting. Pakistan objected vociferously and even held a national day of protest. The US tried to calm its fears. India offered to sign a non-aggression pact with Pakistan and promised that the arms would not be used against it. With Indian troops committed to the UN in the Congo and several stationed along the border with Pakistan, there was a pressing need to arrive at some resolution with Pakistan so that the troops could be transferred to the China front where they were desperately needed.

---

[†††] India relished using Soviet-made MiGs on the Chinese.

With a war raging on its borders, and an economy in tatters, it required a superhuman individual to lead India at this critical juncture. As Nehru approached his seventy-third birthday, he had visibly aged. Although there was no indication, he had barely two years left to live. Galbraith could see the pressure Nehru was under. His speech in Parliament, on 9 November 1962, was 'long, at times vague, a little repetitious, and not inspiring … There was also an uproar when he defended General Kaul.' When Galbraith visited Nehru that evening, he found him 'deathly tired and I thought a little beaten.'[22]

Earlier in the year, on 30 March, Nehru had collapsed while on a visit to an antibiotics factory in Maharashtra. It seems he was suffering from an enlarged prostate that had pushed into his bladder, resulting in chronic cystitis. He was evaluated at the All India Institute of Medical Sciences but declined surgery, which would have incapacitated him for two months. Instead he was treated with medicines.[23] The condition must have deteriorated considerably, as he suffered from acute symptoms of cystitis for the next eighteen months.

It is hard to imagine the compromised state within which decisions were being made in Delhi at a time when the country was facing its biggest challenge since Independence. Until the war with China, Nehru's decisions on foreign policy had gone unchallenged. According to Jagat Mehta, who worked closely with Nehru in the Ministry of External Affairs, 'We believed in Nehru, we didn't think for ourselves. For the first ten years we just followed Panditji and he allowed himself to believe he was a world statesman.'[24] The China war exposed the structural weakness within India's administrative process, where Nehru had become more like a king surrounded by sycophantic courtiers and where truth and reality did not align with disastrous consequences.

After the Sino-Indian War, Nehru became politically vulnerable. A younger generation of politicians began to attack him in ways to which he was unaccustomed. Even old friends and loyal supporters began questioning his policies. Many now spoke about jettisoning India's non-alignment policy. J.B. Kripalani, a one-time president of the Congress party and friend of Nehru's, said, 'The government's long-time policy of non-alignment no longer fits national needs.'[25] Although many in the

Indian government let it be known that they were prepared to drop the policy, Nehru's identity was so tied to it that abandoning it, even during wartime, was inconceivable.

Nehru was in talks with Russia and members of the communist bloc for assistance, although the amounts under discussion were trivial compared to what India was receiving from the West. Between 1951–61, 53 per cent ($3.3 billion) of the aid to India came from the US, whereas the Soviet bloc only contributed 15 per cent, with other free-world nations making up the rest.[26] Turkey initially agreed to provide India assistance, but Pakistan protested, and Ankara quietly withdrew its support. But the question of military assistance and non-alignment was suddenly rendered irrelevant on 14 November 1962, when the Chinese broke the lull in fighting with another massive attack.

## Humiliation

By 19 November, the Sino-Indian War had turned into a rout. The oil fields in Assam were threatened and, with the Chinese poised at the mouth of the plains of Assam, the tribal areas of Manipur, Naga and Tripura were vulnerable. These were areas that India had trouble controlling at the best of times, as it had been a challenge since Independence to bring them under its administrative control. It would not take much for China to wrest them away from India. Nehru, for the first time, confronted the possibility of losing the north-eastern part of the country to the Chinese. A sense of doom spread over Delhi.

Nehru became utterly despondent. Realizing that he had no choice but to turn to the US, he dispatched two letters to Kennedy pleading for help, both written on 19 November within hours of each other.[27]

According to India's ambassador in Washington, B.K. Nehru, the original communications Nehru had with Kennedy in early November 'went counter to our policy of non-alignment. [But they] continued to be dignified.' The telegrams that followed were so 'pathetic' that, as B.K. Nehru read them, he could hardly contain 'his sorrow and shame'.[28] The second telegram, he later recalled, 'was so humiliating that I found it difficult to prevent myself from weeping'. B.K. Nehru decided to put it in his desk and not share its contents with anyone at the embassy.

The letter was delivered to President Kennedy through Carl Kaysen who, like many South Asia hands at the State Department, had grown impatient with Nehru's lectures on non-alignment. Kaysen could not resist taunting the Indian ambassador, 'So your spirit couldn't stand even a minor attack for two weeks. Churchill went on fighting single-handed without any help from anybody for two whole years; you have collapsed in fifteen days.'[29]

According to Bruce Riedel, a senior State Department official working on South Asia, successive Indian governments denied the existence of the letters for years afterwards. The State Department acknowledged they had received the letters but kept their contents secret and the John F. Kennedy Library had heavily redacted them at the request of the Indian government until 2010, when they were finally made available to the public.[30]

On 21 November 1962, Galbraith wrote: 'Yesterday was the day of ultimate panic in Delhi, the first time I have ever witnessed the disintegration of public morale—and for the first time, I began to wonder what the powers of resistance might be. The wildest rumours flew about the town. Several told me that General Kaul had been taken prisoner. This was denied rather succinctly in the evening by President Radhakrishnan, who said, "It is unfortunately, untrue."'[31]

With the Chinese advance threatening to change India's boundaries, the frontline against communism seemed to be collapsing. The priority was to airlift arms. The US immediately airlifted military supplies including C-130 aircraft to India. Galbraith suggested sending the Seventh Fleet into the Bay of Bengal as a demonstration of support to India, and to indicate to China that the US was serious. Separately, a team under Averell Harriman, special advisor to the US president, was dispatched to India to discuss India's long-term defence requirements and how best to meet them without inflaming Pakistan. Menon's departure eased the path somewhat for appropriating funds from Congress, which was told the US was helping 'democratic India' resist the attack from 'communist China'.

# Ceasefire

On the morning of 21 November 1962, just as the policy of non-alignment was being discarded and US arms were arriving in India, China announced a unilateral ceasefire, which was to commence at midnight and extend along the entire front. Effective 1 December, China agreed to withdraw its troops to positions behind the line of 'actual' control, which existed before hostilities broke out on 7 November 1959. The Chinese went a step further and said they would observe this withdrawal regardless of the Indian reply, though they hoped for a positive response. If, however, the Indians took advantage of the withdrawal and continued to fight, the Chinese reserved the right to fight back. They suggested that both sides meet to discuss an overall border settlement.

Although the fighting ceased on 22 November, India did not immediately officially acknowledge the Chinese proposal or recognize the ceasefire until 23 November. A prickly exchange ensued between Zhou Enlai and Nehru with Zhou accusing Nehru of not responding to China's magnanimous gesture and Nehru responding with sarcasm.

The Chinese had worked on two fronts: they had tried to resolve the border dispute through negotiations. Although one can question their sincerity, it was a diplomatically skilful manoeuvre for international consumption. Due to India's intransigence, they decided to teach her a lesson militarily. But first, they ensured that they were dug in at all the high positions. They built roads and barracks and took time to cultivate the border states. They chose to begin hostilities only when the US was distracted by the Cuban crisis and when Moscow would need China's friendship the most. Understanding the value of public relations, China reached out to neutral countries to explain its position and pre-empt India, knowing that Nehru enjoyed good relations with many international leaders. The final stroke of genius was the unilateral ceasefire to prevent the US from getting too committed to India. China did not want to furnish India and the US with a reason to gloss over their differences and develop an alliance against it. China emerged from the war as a power to be reckoned with.

Although the war had been a disaster for India, it opened an opportunity for the US–India relationship that had not existed before. India needed the US and the US had a president who wished to cultivate a friendship with India. After the war, Nehru began to gradually appreciate President Kennedy's sincerity with regards to India and relations began to quietly improve.

## The Quid Pro Quo of Aid

Nehru recognized that India had been living in a dream world and he was now fully preoccupied with building up India's defence capability. 'We are quite clear that the Chinese are making a bid for leadership not only of Asia but of the communist world and this too only is a first step in their bid for world leadership. Chinese hostility to the USA and to Western countries generally has been known for a long time ... latest Chinese campaign against the recent Test Ban Treaty is yet another illustration of their grand design. They detest any accommodation or understanding between the USA and the USSR or any easing of international tensions which comes in the way of their Asian and global ambition.'[32]

Nehru believed that China was less interested in territory and more interested in intimidation and political pressure as it viewed India as an obstacle to Asian domination. He felt that China encouraged third-world countries to adopt militant, revolutionary attitudes and was against stable democratic regimes.[33]

The US was highly motivated to help India. It was determined to counter the prestige China had acquired with its victory. But it also wanted to ensure that Pakistan remain in the US sphere of influence and not try to cut an alliance with China. The US well understood the sensitivities generated by any arms build-up between India and Pakistan and needed to walk a fine line between them.

President Kennedy had responded to Nehru's letters asking for help with lightning speed. He called an emergency meeting attended by McNamara, Rusk, McCone, Talbot and Harriman to help assess India's military needs. Within hours, Harriman was leading a team to Delhi. The

Harriman mission arrived in Delhi at 6 p.m. after an eighteen-hour flight on the same day as the ceasefire.

India had gone from a policy of accepting very little military assistance from the US to a very long laundry list of requests. It had both short-term and long-term needs. Initially, Washington had, along with the British, rushed aid to India on the heels of the Chinese advance. Later, in December 1962, during a summit meeting between Kennedy and Macmillan in the Bahamas, they jointly pledged $120 million in military assistance to India.[34]

India was determined to build up its military but was short of capital and resources. It did not have the foreign reserves to do this on its own. In 1962, India's GDP was $36,800 million and its foreign balance was 3 per cent of its GDP.[35] India was shocked out of its complacency by the war with China and wanted to increase its military strength in inverse proportions to its resources. There were figures of $1.2 billion floating around.[36] India's requests were wildly unrealistic.[‡‡‡] It was Harriman's job to ensure that India had the arms necessary to deter China and convince Pakistan that the US was not acting against Pakistan's interests, while basing the numbers in reality.

The US projected India's needs at $300 million over three years. While initially the hope had been that this would be split fifty-fifty with the UK,[37] the US soon realized that the British were reluctant to contribute in equal parts to what it thought was required.[38]

In a memorandum that stated the Kennedy's views on the subject, his concerns about the British are clear: 'While we should make every effort to bring the UK along on further aid, we should not limit ourselves to their preferred pace. It is unrealistic to expect that the British will go fifty-fifty even on a $300 million program.'[39]

Kennedy, like other US presidents, hoped that he could resolve the Kashmir dispute and there was a strong contingent within the administration that wanted to link US aid to a resolution on Kashmir. Galbraith warned against doing this, believing that pressure on India at a

---

‡‡‡ Pakistan had received $800 million in military assistance from the US.

time of weakness would be counterproductive. But the British, who were part of the US aid consortium, insisted Kashmir be part of the equation.

The British knew that knitting Kashmir into any aid agreement would upset the Indians, but the Macmillan government was more sensitive to Pakistani demands than to the Chinese threats to India. General Ayub Khan of Pakistan launched a lobbying campaign warning both the US and Britain that military aid to India would jeopardize their relations. The conservative Macmillan government, which had historically been more sympathetic to Pakistan than India and which was itself vulnerable to possible Chinese retaliation in Hong Kong, was less concerned about the threat of the spread of communism. Domestic political concerns were also influencing support for India in the UK, with Labour supporting India and turning the situation into a partisan issue.

The British aid mission to India was led by Duncan Sandys, who created considerable tension between the British mission and the Americans. Galbraith had an exceedingly low opinion of the British and Duncan Sandys, in particular. He wrote to Kennedy warning him that the British were not helpful: 'May it be known that I view with continuing alarm … that Sandys may return to the subcontinent and I regard this as the irresponsible failure to tell the British when this talk of the glint in Sandys eye comes up how disastrous this would be. I am, in fact, persuaded that at any time we seem to be close to agreement he will be back with the hope of propping up his admirably unpromising career and presumably with his talk of CENTO nuclear deterrents and the rest.'[40]

As a once-grand imperial power in the subcontinent, the British did not want to be embarrassed by their meagre financial contribution and kept pressing America to lower the aid commitment so that their component could remain small. 'British extremely anxious to concert aid policy with US in hope American actions will not embarrass UK in its relationship with India and Pakistan. In brief, UK wants US to go slow.'[41]

Kennedy had to write to Macmillan, who resisted helping India without a quid pro quo on Kashmir. The US got so frustrated it hinted to the British that, although it would like them as partners, it would 'understand if you feel you must at least temporarily stand aside.'[42]

The war altered the relationship between the US and India. 'We continued to talk in terms of non-alignment but we had become, in fact, the allies of the United States in their confrontation at least against China.'[43] Although military aid was limited to $80 million after extensive consultations with the British, the political price was a dialogue on Kashmir. The pressure to link Kashmir to aid relief angered Nehru, who could not 'afford politically to negotiate the Kashmir dispute after having suffered a defeat at the hands of the Chinese'.[44] It was damaging to his psychological state and insensitive to public sentiment.

In May 1963, India sent a team led by T.T. Krishnamachari to London and Washington to follow up on the Harriman mission. TTK, as he was known, was to work out the terms for military assistance to India with the respective countries. He encountered difficulties in the UK, which was not willing to commit to any specific numbers and made it clear that the amount that India was requesting was out of the question. When he arrived at the London airport, he told two Indian correspondents that he had been treated well in the US and hoped he would be in the UK as well. The US had adopted a 'yes, but' approach to India's request. The UK was reluctant to make any commitments. The US confirmed its intent to support India, but the pace and extent of the assistance would be linked to factors like Kashmir.

In response to President Kennedy's enquiry about how the Indians felt about the Kashmir negotiations, TTK honestly said that India thought the West was 'taking advantage of a friend in her hour of need'. Kennedy tried to explain that members of Congress were convinced that Nehru had it within his power to settle the issue if he chose to, but TTK told him no Indian politician could make a quick decision on Kashmir, that India had no intention of attacking Pakistan and a politically palatable settlement was essential.[45]

In a letter to President Kennedy, written on 31 May 1963, Prime Minister Nehru wrote, 'I think that no one can be more eager to bring about normal and satisfactory relations between India and Pakistan than we are. But ... this cannot be achieved by methods of blackmail and undue pressure taking advantage of the Chinese menace.'

Indians were well aware of the quid pro quo on Kashmir. When requests for transport planes, high-performance fighters and advance pilot training were made, it was hinted that progress on a Kashmir resolution would help speed up these procurements. Both the US State and Defense Departments began to see that this 'bazaar' approach was eroding Indian goodwill and Kennedy decided to drop it.[46]

In the end, India did agree to talks with Pakistan on Kashmir, but after six rounds of negotiations with little progress, all sides ran out of steam and abandoned their efforts. Nehru, who had no intention of yielding to US pressure on Kashmir, sent Sardar Swaran Singh as his representative to the talks. Swaran Singh had the ability 'to go on talking forever without saying anything, which resulted in completely wearing out his well-wishers. The talks ultimately fizzled out.'[47] By the time the sixth, and last, round of talks took place in May 1963, with Secretary Rusk leading the Americans, everyone was deeply discouraged. He understood that any settlement short of the other's capitulation would be domestically unacceptable to either side.

Aside from military assistance, India had turned to the US and the West for investments in its overall economic development. Nehru's priority for India was to industrialize, and for this India needed steel and power. Two massive projects that needed funding were launched. One was a power plant at Tarapur, the other a steel plant called Bokaro.

## Bokaro

Bokaro would expose an ideological fault line between the US and India that would be almost as difficult to bridge as non-alignment.

Nehru's central economic goal at the time was to industrialize the economy. Believing that the export potential for Indian manufactured goods was limited, he went the route of investing in industries that would cut the need for imports. Moreover, he believed that, in a country like India, purely relying on the private sector would be insufficient. The private sector in India lacked the capital, the technology and the necessary long horizon to invest in heavy import-substituting industries like steel or machinery.[48] As a consequence, he believed that India should be a mixed economy with heavy involvement by the government in some of these so-called 'mother' industries. This approach brought him in direct conflict with the US, which believed that economic development should be led by the private sector. If capital or technology was necessary, US companies could supply it through foreign investment. It was a fundamental difference in economic ideology that drove a wedge between the two countries.

The steel plant at Bokaro was for many Indians a symbol of the country's bid for industrial independence. It was to be the showpiece of India's fourth economic five-year plan. There were extensive negotiations between the US and India for its funding. Even though Kennedy became involved and personally gave it his backing, the US Congress was reluctant to give money to such a massive state enterprise and refused to go along. The negotiations over Bokaro dragged on for several years. The US wanted to benefit American business interests and funding a state-owned enterprise put constraints on corporate profits.

Galbraith worried that the US would be perceived in India as selfish and insensitive to India's needs. He warned: 'The Left is already delightedly sensing a return to the days when Washington provided most of the ammunition for local anti-Americanism … Aiding the Bokaro plant is necessary for affirmative reasons … Support to a steel plant symbolizes as nothing else but our interest and participation in Indian economic development … The fact that the US Congress was unmoved and refused to approve the funds reflected the cultural chasm between the two countries.'[49]

Chester Bowles, who had taken over from Galbraith, saw the project falter. He realized the US might not, after all this time, come through with the funding and sent a warning. In a cable on 13 August 1963, he wrote, rather darkly, 'If Congressional decision on Bokaro is adverse and Soviets then agree to build it, as many assume they will do, it does not follow that world will come abruptly to an end or that our position in India will be destroyed overnight. But it is no understatement to say that we will have suffered very serious setback at a particularly crucial and uncertain stage in our relations with India.'[50]

In the end, Bokaro became an embarrassment to both sides. Kennedy had been helpful to Nehru during the China war and, in 1963, Nehru graciously offered to withdraw India's request for US funding for Bokaro.

Kennedy sent Nehru a letter expressing his thanks and telling him that the withdrawal also safeguarded India's aid appropriation from being held hostage to the project. They had learnt to cooperate and appreciate each other's political constraints. India ended up building Bokaro with Soviet help.

Tarapur, the nuclear power station near Bombay, was approved before Galbraith left India to return to Harvard in May 1963. The cost of $80 million to build it was approved by the US Congress. India agreed to use US-supplied enriched uranium and, after excruciating negotiations, agreed to the controls the US required. Tarapur would plague relations between the two countries, like other forms of US assistance.

Nehru wanted to industrialize but also to be self-reliant. He wanted India to manufacture items in India, not just import them. The US was more interested in supplying arms and planes, as it benefitted US businesses. It was a fundamental difference in national interests that came between the two countries.

The Soviets, on the other hand, were consistently helpful to India as they had none of America's ideological baggage regarding state-owned businesses and sympathized with a strategy of public ownership of industry. They committed to finance a much smaller steel plant in Bhilai. In addition to supplying India with MiGs, the Soviets agreed to set up a manufacturing plant in India. On 17 August 1963, the government of India announced the formation of a state-owned company that would manufacture Soviet supersonic MiG fighter jets and other aircraft in India. Initially, two factories were to be set up with a capital of 250 million rupees.[§§§] The Soviets were able to get a great deal of propaganda mileage out of their apparent commitment to Indian development.[51]

## Lives Interrupted

Despite congressional impediments, Kennedy intervened several times to help push aid through for India. Kennedy personally intervened when Senator Stuart Symington tried to cut aid appropriation for India. When

---

§§§ The Indian rupee was equal to 18.75 pounds sterling at the time.

India was raising funds for Bokaro, he tried to promote its benefits for US–India relations.

In November 1963, Ambassador Bowles was in Washington to attend a meeting that he had scheduled with President Kennedy. Bowles had recently finished working out a military defence package for India with TTK and Y.B. Chavan, India's new minister of defence, and he wanted the president's approval. It was a watered-down version of the earlier proposals—$375 million over five years, a figure Kennedy thought Congress might approve. The new ambassador to Delhi never got his 26 November meeting with the president. On 22 November, Kennedy was assassinated in Dallas. India mourned Kennedy's death, knowing it had lost a friend.

The Sino-Indian War had seemed to break Nehru's spirit. His vision of Asian brotherhood proved to be a mirage, non-alignment was proving unrealistic in India's current condition, and his leadership was being questioned. By the time the war ended, Nehru's health, once so robust, had dramatically deteriorated.

The demands of governing a country as diverse as India, constantly at risk of famine and flood, while trying to maintain national unity, keeping communalism at bay and sustaining an international profile as a leader of the emerging countries had finally begun to take its toll. On 6 January 1964, Nehru suffered a mild stroke while he was attending a session of the Congress party. He insisted on returning to work after a period of rest. In the early hours of 27 May 1964, he suffered a rupture in his abdominal aorta and took his final breath.

Nehru had devoted his life to India and had been prime minister since India had become independent in 1947. On his bedside table were the following lines from Robert Frost's poem:

The woods are lovely, dark and deep,
But I have promises to keep,
And miles to go before I sleep,
And miles to go before I sleep.

# Part Three:
# 1964–1976

# Chapter 8

# Johnson and Shastri: All Too Brief

VICE PRESIDENT JOHNSON WAS SWORN IN AS PRESIDENT ON board Air Force One, an hour and a half after President Kennedy was declared dead on 22 November 1963. The images of the assassination—the bright morning in Dallas, Texas, the presidential motorcade winding its way through Dealey Plaza, with Kennedy and the first lady in an open car, waving to the crowds, the stinging sound of the fatal shots being fired, the president's bloodied head rolling back—were replayed over and over again on TV screens across the nation as people watched transfixed in horror.

Lyndon B. Johnson insisted that the still-dazed Jackie Kennedy fly back to Washington with him to endorse him in his new role as president, among Kennedy supporters.* The nation was still in shock as it watched Jackie Kennedy emerge from the aircraft in her blood-stained clothes. She had decided not to change because she wanted the country to see what had been done to their president.[1]

## An Accidental President

Johnson had spent most of his professional life on the Hill, but none of his political experience prepared him for the circumstances he found himself in on that fateful day in November. Stepping into Kennedy's shoes proved to be a daunting task. Johnson, like Nixon, found himself diminished by

---

* Johnson was always conscious about power and the best ways to trap it.

the glare of the Kennedy glamour. Competing for the nation's affection against someone as handsome, talented and dynamic as the young president was hard enough, without death making Kennedy a tragic hero. Johnson had to heal the nation and allow it to grieve, while finding a way to make his mark.

The circumstances of Johnson's elevation to the presidency were unusual. His inauguration was overshadowed by Kennedy's funeral, which was attended by the largest assembly of foreign dignitaries since the funeral of Edward VII in 1910. Among the guests were nineteen heads of state and ninety-two royal families from around the world.[2]

After the funeral, President Johnson began to take over a disconsolate Kennedy administration.

Johnson clung to his Texan roots. Unlike Kennedy, who had been the young energetic outsider, cultured, charming and enjoying the company of intellectuals, he seemed to take pride in being boorish. As vice president in 1961, much to the embarrassment of the embassy officials accompanying him on a trip to the Taj Mahal, Johnson let out a Texan yell to test the echo—as tour guides often did to demonstrate the acoustics to visiting tourists.[3]

Johnson had little exposure to foreign affairs. He had spent his entire career focusing on domestic politics and, apart from a couple of trips abroad, he had little experience interacting with foreign leaders. After the funeral, with the world watching, he found himself thrust into a whirl of one-on-one meetings with the most important heads of state. He was slipped five-by-eight information cards about the leaders and managed to handle himself with skill and grace, greeting U Thant, de Gaulle and Mikoyan with appropriate remarks.[4]

Johnson's father came from a small farming community in Texas where making ends meet was a constant struggle. He had married up, and his wife Rebekah had exposed her son to the world of books and public speaking. Johnson was well read and his letters to his mother from college are replete with references to the books he was reading. He was deeply attached to his mother, but he admired his father.

Johnson's father was a large presence in his childhood and dabbled in local politics when Johnson was still a young child, eventually getting to the state level and serving five terms in the Texas House of Representatives. Johnson's father remained rough around the edges despite his years in the Texas state legislature. He prided himself on his roots and ability to connect with his constituents. Johnson, who sometimes travelled with him through rural Texas, soaked it all in.

Johnson was drawn to powerful men and cultivated them in order to advance his career when he came to Washington, and became the ultimate Washington insider. By the time he became president at the age of fifty-five, he had spent almost twenty-five years in Washington, thirteen years as a congressman representing the tenth district of Texas, and twelve years in the Senate, first as Senate majority whip, then as the minority leader and, finally, as the Senate majority leader from 1955–61.

Ever since Roosevelt had coined the slogan that identified his administration as the 'New Deal', each US president had come up with a catchy phrase to define his government. Truman called his a 'Fair Deal' and Kennedy called his the 'New Frontier'. Johnson tried to distinguish himself by naming his the 'Great Society'—he wanted to build an equitable and just society.

Robert C. Weaver, the first African American to be appointed to a cabinet-level post, was brought in by Johnson. He measured Johnson by his achievements rather than his promises. 'I think Kennedy had an intellectual commitment for civil rights and a broad view of social legislation. Johnson had a gut commitment for changing the entire social fabric of this country, and after the 1964 election he had a large majority and was an adroit strategist.'[5]

Robert Hardesty, Johnson's speechwriter, felt that Kennedy could not have achieved what Johnson did because he did not have his skills in getting things done. 'Kennedy started things, an awful lot, good things, too, but he could never get the bills passed. There were some who say he would have done it if he'd had more time, but I don't think so. I don't think he knew or even cared very passionately. Johnson did.'[6]

Johnson was remarkably astute when it came to the ways of Congress. He knew how Washington worked, which committees were important and the players one needed to massage to get things done on the Hill. If anyone had the skills to get his legislative agenda through Congress, it was Johnson. It was one of the reasons that Kennedy had chosen him as a running mate.

Following Kennedy's death, Johnson took advantage of the surge of sympathy to quickly pass the Twenty-Fourth Amendment, abolishing poll taxes. In July 1964, less than eight months after becoming the president, he signed the historic Civil Rights Act into law. In the space of two years, he succeeded in passing some of the most progressive social legislation in US history. A year later, he introduced and then passed the Voting Rights Act as well as Medicare and Medicaid.

Despite his years in Washington, Johnson maintained the persona of a Texan cattle farmer. He often misjudged the impact of his behaviour on individuals and could be crude, especially in male company. While such behaviour was common among the back roads of Texas where he grew up, it raised eyebrows in the drawing rooms of Washington. Bill Moyers, who was close to Johnson, thought that the president saw himself as an actor and spectator at the same time: 'He always was outside the process looking at himself. This was a flaw at times, and I think helped to bring him down.'[7]

Wilbur J. Cohen, Johnson's secretary of health, described a visit to his ranch thus: '[A]fter we finished our business we went out and rode around the ranch. He started to tell us in the most vulgar language about the breeding of cattle, referring to all sorts of sexual characteristics of the animals and of people … An hour later while watching the sunset, he talked eloquently about the land, about the hill country, about the sun, about the seasons, about his hopes and aspirations for people. Pure poetry.'[8] Within one hour, President Johnson had gone from being presidential and dealing with matters of state to acting like a local farm hand and to then turning poetic and philosophical.

Women often found the president intimidating. He was a towering figure at six feet three inches tall, and weighing 210 pounds. Elizabeth Goldschmidt, despite being part of his family's inner circle, said, 'With the physique he had, plus his acting ability, he could be a terrible bully. He would shake his hand under your nose, stride up and down, raise his arms. He knew exactly what he was doing.' Marianne Means, an influential *Washington Post* columnist, made a similar observation: 'He was always on, always manipulating, never happy without some kind of human exchange or confrontation. It was more than a performance, because you felt he was reliving an experience.'[9]

Mrs Gandhi, who was always very prickly about the way she was treated, reacted negatively to Johnson's aggressive behaviour when they disagreed on policy. His resorting to bullying in an attempt to get his way with her created a significant rift in the relationship between the two countries. Johnson believed in exerting power to do good and he expected gratitude in return. This did not go over well in India when it came to food aid.

Johnson particularly seemed to enjoy subjecting senior members of his government to uncomfortable situations. He would famously relieve himself on the toilet while having a conversation about policy or conducting a meeting, as though such conduct was normal. It was extreme behaviour that displayed a need to manipulate people. Aside from his contradictory personal behaviour that veered from charming to domineering, Johnson was a remarkably successful and progressive domestic president even though his foreign policy failures ended his presidential ambitions.

When he became president, Johnson inherited a growing American involvement in Vietnam. In August 1964, Congress passed the Gulf of Tonkin resolution authorizing the president to pursue military action in Vietnam. Focused as he was on the US elections in November 1964, Johnson left the US–India relationship in the hands of Secretary of State Dean Rusk and the new US ambassador to India, Chester Bowles.

Unfortunately, Bowles's second term as ambassador to India would prove to be less successful than his first. He was appointed under less than favourable circumstances. He had been deputy secretary of state under Rusk and the two did not get on. Bowles had strong views and was not shy about expressing them. Rusk, who was formal and reserved, found Bowles intemperate. It did not help that Bowles had been a contender for his job.

As the acting secretary of state in 1961, while Rusk was away, Bowles had come across classified documents on the 'Bay of Pigs' operation. The plan entailed arming and training 1,200 Cuban exiles who opposed Castro to secretly land in Cuba, and convince the local population to join them in overthrowing the prime minister. The mission was to be conducted by the CIA. Troubled by the plan, which he thought risky, Bowles had made his views known to Rusk and others. When his reservations were leaked to the press, he lost the confidence of Kennedy's inner circle despite his protestations of innocence. Robert Kennedy, suspecting Bowles to be behind the leak, never forgave him, calling him a 'gutless wonder'.[10] Bowles's reservations were well founded. The plan failed spectacularly, with 100 exiles killed almost immediately on landing and 1,100 captured. Castro used the incident to solidify his control in Cuba, and his accusations against American imperialists trying to undermine their small country and their peasant revolution resonated with the people of Cuba.

As deputy secretary, Bowles had not been shy about disagreeing with the Asia policies of either the White House or the State Department. He was against putting American troops in Asia, which he thought would provoke China. He believed that the State Department was too eurocentric and obsessed with communism. He thought it should focus more on the development of the aspirations of Asian and African countries.

Bowles came to be viewed as dangerously soft on communism by hardcore cold warriors like former Secretary of State Dean Acheson, prominent journalist Joseph Alsop, and even the former ambassador to India, Loy Henderson. They made no secret of their views, and some of their contemptuous remarks about Bowles were widely circulated and made their way back to the president.[11]

Mistrusted by Secretary Rusk and having greatly annoyed the Kennedys, Bowles was eased out as deputy secretary. He was given the position of 'roving ambassador' and eventually offered the ambassadorship to India. By the time Bowles came to India in the summer of 1963,[†] he had lost his standing at both the State Department and the White House. Although he arrived under a cloud, India graciously welcomed him.

But India had also changed. The war with China had weakened his old friend Nehru politically, and he could see that Nehru's health was failing. The question, 'After Nehru who?' had become the most frequent topic of conversation at diplomatic gatherings.

The legendary Galbraith had just departed and even Bowles, a popular figure in India, would never rise to his stature. He worked hard to complete

---

† Bowles arrived in India in mid-July 1963.

the military aid package that Galbraith and Harriman had set into motion. India had many friends in the Kennedy administration, as Johnson had retained many of the Kennedy appointees. Even after Johnson took over many of them, like NSC staff member Robert Komer,[‡] they were still trying to help India by pushing the new administration to support the military aid package.

The White House sent General Taylor, chairman of the joint chiefs of staff, on a mission to India to assess its military needs. He arrived in India in December 1963 and visited many army units along the Chinese border. By the middle of March 1964, President Johnson's administration seemed willing to give India a package of $100 million annually for five years.[12]

The US insisted that F-104s, the supersonic fighters which it had supplied to Pakistan and which India desperately wanted, were off the table.[13] The Pentagon, always sensitive to Pakistani objections, argued that they would be of limited use against a Chinese attack. The US refusal to supply India with F-104s created enormous bitterness in India. Despite India's preference to diversify away from the Soviets, it found it had little choice but to continue to rely heavily on Soviet arms.

According to Bowles's memoir, *Promises to Keep*, by May 1964, Washington and New Delhi were close to a tentative agreement on an arms deal that met most of India's requirements. President Johnson had agreed to it, and Y.B. Chavan, India's minister of defence, came to Washington to finalize the deal. The final meeting to nail everything down was scheduled at the White House at noon on 28 May 1964.

Once more fate intervened. On 27 May Nehru died. Just as the November 1963 meeting with Kennedy never took place because of his assassination, this meeting was postponed. Instead of gathering to finalize the arms deal, Chavan, Rusk and Bowles found themselves boarding a plane to attend Nehru's funeral.[14]

A historic opportunity was lost. According to Bowles, although the White House continued to support the deal, in the following months Ayub

---

‡    Johnson would refer to Komer as 'the India lover' and ask him why he insisted on being so nice to India and not to his 'good friend Ayub'. General Ayub Khan had impressed Johnson on his vice-presidential trip to Pakistan.

lobbied against the military package. The Pentagon was pro-Pakistan and Rusk backed away from it. Without Kennedy to champion it, and lacking an effective lobby, the nascent military cooperation faded.§

Bowles told Washington that US policy was driving India to the Soviets as their prime supplier. Komer agreed that slowing the military assistance was 'at a real expense to our bilateral relations'.[15] He found it ironic that 'we face today a paradoxical situation in which our de jure ally Pakistan is in fact moving closer to Red China, while we see a major common interest with neutralist India in meeting the ChiCom⁵ threat'.[16]

When Johnson became president, he had asked Defense Secretary Robert McNamara to prepare a paper concerning the importance of economic aid to India and Pakistan. McNamara concluded that it was essential for economic and political stability and the avoidance of chaos. He argued that aid was compatible with US national interests as the major threat to the US in Asia was China: 'The principal danger is the aggressive expansionism of communist China, which seeks to drive out US power and influence and to establish US hegemony over two thirds of the people of the world.'[17] Johnson, however, had been raised in the halls of Congress and was more focused on the return on the aid investment and the domestic impact on American farmers rather than Cold War concerns.

## A Momentous Passing in India

The combination of cajoling, bullying and persuading that Johnson employed to promote his domestic agenda did not deliver similar rewards when dealing with foreign affairs. Johnson developed an obsession over food aid to India and the passion with which he decided to pursue this interest came close to ending the fragile goodwill that the Kennedy administration had taken such pains to promote.

---

§   Kennedy had personally decided to help India. With many in the Congress and Pentagon against India, it was hard to push through without the backing of the president.

⁵   Short for Chinese communists.

In November 1963, when Johnson was suddenly catapulted into office, Nehru was an ill man. Following a stroke in January 1964, Nehru deteriorated rapidly until his death on 27 May that year. During these first few months, events in India barely registered in Johnson's thoughts. In this period, the accidental president was busy consolidating his position among the Kennedy people and preparing for the upcoming election.

Nehru's death was not unexpected, but when it came India felt stripped of its mantle of security. He had kept India neutral and while other newly independent countries were giving way to dictatorships, communism and military juntas, he upheld his commitment to democracy and kept the world's largest democratic experiment alive. India had free elections, a free press, was secular and its people had the freedom to speak out.

Rusk and Galbraith, along with other US officials, flew to India for Nehru's funeral, bringing with them some members of the Indian delegation that happened to be in Washington negotiating the military assistance programme initiated under Kennedy.

One and a half million people attended Nehru's funeral. A twelve-day mourning period was declared. Despite Nehru's dislike of religious rituals, 'Pandits, sadhus, lamas, Muslim divines and Christians had made their uninvited entry into the house ... Each after his own fashion recited prayers for the dead. No one had informed them that their prayers violated the last wish of this image of the enlightened man. His unchanged will had specified: "I wish to declare with an earnestness that I do not want any religious ceremonies performed for me after my death. I do not believe in any such ceremonies and to submit to them, even as a matter of form, would be hypocrisy and an attempt to delude ourselves and others."'[18]

Speculation about Nehru's successor had begun weeks before he died. When the end came, it proved to be a surprisingly smooth transition.[**] The Indian National Congress's president, K. Kamaraj, consulted with the

---

[**]   There were several contenders for Nehru's job. Mrs Gandhi was one power group and there was a group called 'Menonites' who supported Krishna Menon. TTK was also mentioned. Mrs Gandhi did not support Shastri.

key power brokers in the party, known as the 'Syndicate',[††] as well as with critical legislators. They settled on Lal Bahadur Shastri. Morarji Desai, a highly competent administrator and senior member of the party, had originally been the front runner. If seniority had been the only criterion, he would have become the prime minister, but he had been persuaded by the Syndicate to withdraw from the race. He was viewed as too independent and somewhat abrasive.

## Shastri: A Brief Pause

The adjective most commonly used to describe Shastri was 'diminutive'. He was barely five feet tall, unassuming in manner and provincial. Some referred to him as 'Little Sparrow'.[19] He seemed an odd choice to follow in Nehru's footsteps. Nehru was cosmopolitan, confident of his place in the world, recognized as a world leader, a prolific author as well as the undisputed leader of India.

Unlike Nehru, Shastri had no international profile. He had not gone to any of the exclusive universities and schools in the West that Nehru and the Indian elite had attended and lacked the polish associated with the sophisticated circles Nehru moved in. Shastri had followed Gandhi's admonition to study at local institutions and was largely self-taught. He had read Marx, Engels, Laski, Kant, Huxley, Hegel and several other thinkers popular at the time. He especially worshipped Bertrand Russell and had devoured all his work. On his first visit to London as prime minister, he asked to meet Russell. Harold Wilson, who was the British prime minister at the time, volunteered to invite Russell to meet him. But Shastri apparently told him, 'No, I must go to see him. He is my mentor.'[20]

Some of Shastri's critics expressed concern over his lack of experience, particularly in foreign affairs, but he was a skilled conciliator and had a reputation for being above corruption. He had held cabinet-level posts in the railway and home ministries late in his career, but had discharged his

---

[††] The main kingmakers in the Syndicate were Congress Party President Kamaraj, who controlled four states in the south, Atulya Ghosh, who controlled many of the votes in eastern India, and S.K. Patil from Bombay, who influenced a quarter of the INC.

duties with integrity. When a railway accident occurred during his watch that involved several fatalities, he took responsibility and resigned. In the last couple of years prior to Nehru's death, he had been by his side, helping him manage the affairs of the country as minister without portfolio. Nehru trusted him. Although this had reassured members of his party, for many, he still remained an unproven commodity.

Shastri was chosen primarily because he was not controversial. The Syndicate thought they could manage him. Nehru had run the country almost like a monarch. No one had dared question him. With his passing, the senior party members saw an opportunity to finally exert some control on the decision-making process.

Shastri was in poor health when he became the prime minister. He suffered from cardiac problems that made him seem weak. He had suffered a mild heart attack soon after assuming office, but what he lacked in physical vigour, he made up for in determination and an inner self-confidence.

Shastri quietly but quickly asserted his authority after being sworn in. He took the first steps in moving the country to the centre and away from Nehru's socialist policies. Nehru had held the external affairs portfolio through all seventeen years of his tenure as the prime minister. Everyone deferred to him on foreign policy and assumed he was the leading expert in the country. Shastri, who like Johnson, had little experience in foreign affairs and barely any exposure to foreign leaders, set about reducing the power of the prime minister in foreign policy. He set up a committee to evaluate and subject policies to an analysis and review process.

Shastri appointed L.K. Jha as his principal secretary to oversee and coordinate all the government secretaries. He also appointed Swaran Singh as minister of external affairs. Swaran Singh had discharged himself admirably during the Kashmir talks and could be counted on to be loyal.

Shastri made it clear that he believed that India had veered too close to the Soviets and that the country would now pursue a more balanced relationship with the big powers. Visiting US officials immediately picked up the change in atmosphere. Harriman, in a cable to the State Department in Washington, stated: 'I feel today quite a new attitude towards US and the world situation reflected by Indian officials as well as press. I almost felt I was in a different country.'²¹ What gave Harriman pause was the newly appointed foreign minister. Americans feared that Singh continued to retain the old prejudices about the US that had dogged their relations for so long.

In many respects, given her high profile, excellent French and familiarity with the international political situation, it would have made sense to offer Mrs Gandhi the post of foreign minister. She had travelled with her father, already knew most of the heads of state and was familiar with all the policy issues. Shastri saw two major drawbacks in appointing her to such a prominent position. The first was a disadvantage to India. There were many Western politicians, especially in the US, who had been put off by Nehru's policies and had found him arrogant. Shastri worried that appointing Mrs Gandhi would not give him a fresh start, as many would view her as a continuation of her father's policies. The second was a risk to his authority. He was concerned that she might not heed his directions if they contradicted what her father had believed in and, if she chose to challenge his authority by following her own path, she would weaken his office.

Nevertheless, Shastri felt obliged to give Mrs Gandhi a cabinet post. He made sure it was not a critical one and put her in charge of the Ministry of Information and Broadcasting. He must have known that Mrs Gandhi would consider this a political snub.‡‡ Infamous for holding grudges, she had the grand prime minister's house that Nehru lived in made into a memorial for her father. A far more modest house was selected as the new official residence of the prime minister. Shastri did not seem to mind. He was a follower of Gandhian principles, led a simple life with few material possessions and preferred traditional Indian clothes and simple home-cooked meals.

Although reluctant to travel due to his heart condition, Shastri decided he would make the long journey to the US. He was keen to develop a closer relationship with the West and recognized that the US was India's

---

‡‡ Mrs Gandhi resented the changes Shastri made to the government and felt that he was repudiating the Nehru legacy. She seldom lost an opportunity to be critical of his government. For more, see Inder Malhotra, *Indira Gandhi*, pp. 82–87.

largest aid donor and important to its survival. The rains had failed in 1964 and 1965 seemed no better. Food stocks had dropped to precipitously low levels. With the country desperately in need of food aid, a trip was planned for June 1965.

The US had arranged for General Ayub Khan to visit in April 1964, just before Shastri's visit, but Johnson abruptly cancelled it at the last minute. According to Ambassador Dennis Kux, Johnson was stung by the remarks on Vietnam made by the Canadian prime minister, Lester Pearson, after he had met with President Johnson. Johnson was very sensitive about his Vietnam policy, and wanted to avoid a similar occurrence with Ayub Khan. He worried that Pakistan had begun to establish an alliance with China and did not want Ayub to embarrass him. To appear to be even-handed, he thought it best to cancel both Ayub's and Shastri's visits. The decision offended India, which disliked being coupled with Pakistan. It was also a personal blow to Shastri, who had gone out on a limb to be supportive on Vietnam at a time when many Indians were against American involvement in yet another Asian country.

In a telegram to Bowles, the under secretary of state, George Ball tried to soften the decision. 'You can approach Shastri in such a way as to lead him to feel that a postponement of his visit until fall is in the interests of India. In our view, it would not be useful for him to come while the aid bill is pending, in spite of the fact that the Indian attitude on Vietnam has been generally helpful.'[22]

India found its relations with the US frustrating as they were always subordinate to the US–Pakistan axis. India viewed itself as a large country and a reliable democracy and resented being hyphenated with Pakistan. India seemed unable to develop a bilateral relationship with the US without Pakistan sabotaging the effort. In order to maintain the balance, India reluctantly accepted the hand of friendship from Moscow.

In October 1964, Khrushchev, a vocal supporter of India, was pushed out of office. Khrushchev had never recovered his reputation after the Cuban Missile Crisis, when the Soviet Union had to back down after Kennedy called its bluff. His inclination for flashy, headline-grabbing acts, from sending the first dog into space to challenging the US in Cuba, had unsettled the conservative members of the Kremlin. When Khrushchev visited the US in 1959, he hit 'the headlines with his professed desire to visit Disneyland and making sure he was introduced to Marilyn Monroe. During the Soviet premier's visit to Hollywood, the screen goddess implausibly made a short speech in Russian welcoming him.'[23] (Monroe was coached by Natalie Wood, a fluent Russian speaker.)

After Khrushchev left the scene, India lost a reliable friend. This made Shastri's desire for a better relationship with the US even more urgent. The US president, however, did not appear to be interested in forging new friendships in South Asia.

## 'Your Ass Will Be Hanging from a Yardarm'

President Johnson had left his administration's policies towards South Asia in the hands of the State Department. But he assumed a very different posture when it came to food aid. When the renewal for food aid came up in the fall of 1964, just three months after Nehru had died, Johnson abruptly put everything on hold.

Having experienced poverty growing up, Johnson was sensitive to the needs of the poor, but he did not believe in handouts. It was a philosophy he applied to foreign aid. Convinced that no country should take US aid for granted, he began a revaluation of food supplies to India in September 1964. He wanted to ensure that India continued to show that it was doing something to increase its own food production. His new policy would have dire consequences.

Johnson could sense that foreign aid to India was losing support in Congress. Over the years, Nehru's inflexible non-alignment policy had eroded the goodwill of many congressmen, who were showing little inclination to appropriate money for a country that did not support the US in the international arena. Johnson's instinct that India did not have enough of a lobby on the Hill to push back against his new position proved correct.

In September 1964, when PL480 that had been approved by the Kennedy administration ended, Johnson only renewed a one-year programme supplying 4.5 million tons of wheat. In the spring of 1965, the unsuspecting

Indians, unaware that a reappraisal was going on in Washington, requested a new two-year programme of 10 million tons of wheat.

No one on either side expected a denial. Without warning, in June 1965, the president surprised his own bureaucracy, and the Indians, by calling a halt to routine approval of new aid commitments to India (and to Pakistan), demanding a 'hard new look ... before we spend a lot more money'. On 9 June, Johnson announced that new assistance for India and Pakistan would have to be personally approved by him until Congress voted on the fiscal 1966 aid bill.[24] It was an unprecedented level of micromanagement by the president.

In the spring of 1965, India was on the verge of a war instigated by Pakistan. By June, the monsoon looked as if it was about to fail. With a drought on the horizon, Johnson's timing seemed cold-blooded.

Johnson would later claim in his memoirs that he was genuinely concerned about India's dependence on foreign sources of food and that he was trying to prod Indians to increase production. He was worried that India's population was overtaking its ability to feed its people and America could not be counted on to endlessly provide it with surplus wheat.

He became seemingly obsessed with the problem of India's food shortage. One historian wrote, 'What was unusual was not so much Johnson's support for a change in Indian farm policy as his intense, obsessive personal involvement. For the next two years, Lyndon Johnson, in effect, became the US government's "desk officer" for PL480 food aid to India.'[25]

Orville Freeman, the US agriculture secretary, worried about the lack of progress in India's agricultural growth and supported taking a hard line towards it. In response to US pressure, Shastri tried to move resources from industry, a priority sector under Nehru, into agriculture where most Indians were employed. He appointed a new agricultural minister, C. Subramaniam, who developed a blueprint to move India towards self-sufficiency.

Freeman and Subramaniam put together a reform package for India that was signed in Rome on 25 November 1965.[26] Johnson made clear that future aid to India would depend on the plan being implemented, though he warned Freeman that, 'if anybody finds out about this, your ass will be hanging from a yardarm'.[27] He did not wish to be blamed for using food as a negotiating weapon when people were starving.

Only after the new policy was announced did Johnson authorize the next wheat shipment and an additional $50 million fertilizer commodity loan, the first economic aid assistance since the 1965 war, when all assistance except for food had been stopped. Johnson believed, 'No man can compel another—except at knifepoint—to do what he does not want to do.'[28] He did not think coercion was a bad thing if persuasion failed.

Johnson's 'short tether' policy had, on the surface, been a success. According to Komer, Johnson deserved credit for pressuring Indians to restructure their five-year plan in a way that raised agricultural output after 1966. 'There has been a radical turnaround in India's agricultural output, and I think LBJ deserves far more credit for that than he will ever get from the Indians.'[29]

It was true that Johnson had badgered India into reforming its agricultural sector. But it came at a cost. It was seen within India as yet another example of US bullying vulnerable nations. Rather than the US seeming strong, Shastri had been made to look weak. At a time of looming famine and war, Johnson came across as callous and insensitive.

The US began to be viewed negatively by Indians. 'In February 1963, a public opinion poll revealed that 63 per cent of all Indians considered the United States India's 'best friend' while only 7 per cent so referred to the Soviets. In June of this year (1965), the same question resulted in a stand-off between the United States and the USSR of 32 per cent to 32 per cent.'[30]

## Ayub, Pakistani Pressure and the Build Up to War

President Ayub Khan grew increasingly paranoid as the Kennedy administration angled the US away from Pakistan and tried to form a friendship with India. This grew into alarm after the 1962 war when the US swept into action to help India with military assistance against China. Pakistanis increasingly viewed US assistance to India as a direct threat to themselves.

Pakistan had been receiving military assistance from the US since Dulles had fallen under Ayub's spell during the Eisenhower administration. Since then, the respective military officials had set up relationships that they now had an interest in protecting. Ayub had provided the US with a base in Peshawar, which the US used for spying on Russia. This had made Pentagon officials vulnerable to Ayub's veiled threats to rescind the offer if the US were to offend Pakistan by its growing friendship with India.

India had long been critical of the US military assistance to Pakistan. It argued that the Patton tanks and motorized artillery provided by America would be most useful in a war with India, fought on the Punjab plains, not for defending Pakistan's mountainous border with the Soviet Union or China, were either of the latter two countries to attack South Asia or the oil fields of Iran.

Ayub had proved to be a masterful diplomat and made sure that Pakistan was on good terms with China and the Soviet Union. Since Khrushchev's removal, the Soviets had reached out to Pakistan in an attempt to balance their relations in South Asia. In 1961, Moscow had agreed to provide technical and economic assistance to Pakistan's petroleum industry. Over the next couple of years, Ayub also raised loans from Moscow and, more importantly, persuaded the Soviets to take a more neutral stand on Kashmir.[31]

In 1962, China and Pakistan had come to a border agreement on Pakistan-controlled Kashmir. After the 1962 war, China, having lost India as a friend, was actively courting Pakistan for strategic balance against India and the Soviets.

In 1961, President Ayub put pressure on the Kennedy administration to follow through on Eisenhower's commitments to supply Pakistan with a squadron of F-104s. Kennedy admitted that US military assistance in South Asia was unbalanced and far too pro-Pakistani. However, he gave in to the Pentagon's recommendations and Pakistan received the planes. Nehru had been disappointed. It reinforced Eisenhower's warnings, as he left office, about the 'military–industrial complex'.[§§] In the wake of

---

§§ When President Eisenhower left office, he gave a speech warning the country about special interests and, in particular, identified the military–industrial

the India–China War in 1962, as the imbalance started being redressed, Ayub did his best to prevent India from receiving the military assistance it required, especially the desirable Patton tanks and F-104s.

India's defeat at the hands of the Chinese convinced Ayub that India was militarily weak. He calculated that, provided he could prevent India from procuring sophisticated American arms, he had a window of opportunity to act in Kashmir. Once India was able to replenish its arms portfolio, Ayub's freedom of action would be limited.

'The death in 1964 of Nehru, the only prime minister India had since Partition, provided Ayub with an opportunity to test his theory that India might break up within fifteen to twenty years.'[32] Zulfikar Ali Bhutto, who was Pakistan's foreign minister at the time and a hawk when it came to India, put enormous pressure on Ayub to seize India's moment of weakness to wrest Kashmir away from it. Ayub, being more cautious than his hot-headed minister, while understanding that Kashmir was the prize, decided to test the waters in a barren, largely uninhabited area on the west coast just above Bombay.

The first skirmish took place in the Rann of Kutch, Gujarat, an area of 23,000 square miles of marshland, sand dunes and low-lying salt beds that lie underwater for part of the year. The area sticks out like two thumbs into the Arabian Sea. Pakistanis had been infiltrating the northern border for some weeks. In February 1965, India decided to evict Pakistani border troops from a fort they were occupying in an old town called Kanjarkot. Pakistan sent in Major General Tikka Khan, commander of Pakistan's 8th Infantry Division, to counter the Indian action. By April, the two armies had moved into forward positions under their respective brigade commanders.

Fighting began on 8 April 1965 and continued for two weeks. The terrain was hard to fight in, and neither side gained much ground. The air chiefs called each other and agreed not to participate, in order to deescalate the conflict. Indians were anxious about their troops being stranded if the Rann flooded and withdrew on 27 April. The crisis subsided as quickly as it had

complex, a nexus between the nation's military and defence industry that could influence public policy.

begun. The British decided to intervene and dispatched Duncan Sandys to mediate a truce, and the two sides retreated to their original positions.**

Harold Wilson sent a ceasefire request to Ayub Khan and Shastri on 28 April 1965. UN Secretary General U Thant also asked for a cessation of hostilities. The conflict, called the Battle of the Bets,*** was referred to an international tribunal. On 30 June 1965, a ceasefire came into effect and, on 19 February 1968, the International Court of Justice recognized India's claim to the northern border but gave Pakistan 802 square miles, including Chad Bet and Kanjarkot, the original place where conflict began. The US, the UK and Pakistan were relieved that India agreed to international mediation. Nehru's general inclination was to reject outside help. They noted the new direction in India's foreign affairs.

Both sides declared victory. After the loss of face in the Sino-Indian war, not losing was winning for India. 'For Pakistan, it was a victorious war, out of which it learnt a wrong lesson that it could win a cake-walk victory in Kashmir. This fake sense of victory whetted the Pakistani appetite for Kashmir. This led to the September war ultimately.'[33]

Since Independence, both countries had insisted, with some legitimacy, that Kashmir was rightfully theirs. It became a toxin that would poison their relations and distort their foreign policies for the next seventy years. Every US administration at some point harboured a hope that it could help resolve the dispute. In the end, every administration gave up in frustration. Pakistan kept trying to internationalize the issue, hoping that the US or the international community would put pressure on India. India, meanwhile, resisted all attempts to allow foreigners to intercede, relying on the Soviets during the Khrushchev years to thwart Pakistan's efforts at the UN by exerting their veto power in favour of India.

Pakistan saw the Kennedy administration as pro-India, but Kennedy had, at least, tried to mediate between the two sparring countries.

---

** Pakistan claimed that as the Rann of Kutch was submerged under water for a part of the year, the law of the sea should determine the border. This would put it south of where the Indians occupied it. It would run through the middle of the area. The Indians refuted this claim as spurious.

*** Two settlements on raised mounds, Chad Bet and Biar Bet, were the principal objectives of the fight.

President Johnson did not wish to get entangled, and in January 1964, John McKesson from the State Department sent a memo to the national security advisor, McGeorge Bundy, stating, 'We believe we should "back off" somewhat from our previous active substantive role on the Kashmir issue in the Security Council.'[34] He suggested that they wait to see how things developed.

Two months later, Robert Komer sent a memo to Bundy suggesting the US not return to the 'business as usual' relationship with Pakistan. He recommended that they take a firmer line with Pakistan. 'We can subsidize their development, protect them against Indian aggression, continue to seek a Kashmir compromise, but we cannot back them in leaning on India. Moreover, we've never had a better opportunity for the necessary readjustment of our Pak relations to rectify the overcommitment we slid into in 1954–60. Mao's attack awakened the Indians, while Ayub's flirtation with the ChiComs has belatedly made us all realize that Pakistan's overriding concern is to use us against India.'[35] The changed attitude within the State Department towards Pakistan may have been one of the contributing factors that convinced Bhutto and Ayub to try to take Kashmir by force.

In November 1963, shortly after Kennedy's assassination, the Lok Sabha had a debate on Kashmir and discussed revoking Article 370 of the Indian Constitution, integrating Kashmir into the Indian Union and removing its special status. Although no steps were taken, just the fact of the debate provoked hysteria in Pakistan.

A month later, in December, a holy relic, a piece of the Prophet's hair kept in the shrine of Hazratbal in Kashmir, went missing. Apparently, the theft took place at 2 a.m. when the guards were asleep. The incident created an uproar not only in Kashmir, where fifty thousand mourners waving black flags crowded the street in front of the shrine, but also across Pakistan. A massive hunt was launched, and within a month, the hair was recovered, authenticated and restored to the shrine. Pakistan accused India of being incapable of looking after Islam's heritage.

These two incidents, along with the eviction of thousands of illegal Muslim immigrants in the eastern state of Assam, set things ablaze.[†††] With Nehru near death, India looked weak. Ayub decided that the time had come to launch an attack on Kashmir.

Ayub's plan to liberate Kashmir was called 'Operation Gibraltar'. The idea was that irregular forces under Pakistani army's direction would infiltrate Kashmir and stir up unrest and get the local population to rise against the Indian government, and as the disturbances spread, the regular army would enter the fray in 'Operation Grand Slam'. 'The Indians would then either sue for peace or the US-led international community would force a settlement of the Kashmir dispute in favour of Pakistan.'[36] The Pakistani cell that was established in 1964 to carry out this plan included the secretary of the foreign ministry, the head of the army and the defence director of the intelligence bureau.

The Pakistani irregular forces were divided into units with dramatic names of Muslim military heroes such as Salahuddin and Tamerlane. They were to penetrate the ceasefire line and conduct acts of sabotage behind the Indian forces stationed along the Line of Control (LOC). The operation began on 24 July 1965. Pakistan claims they sent 3,000 men. India says it was closer to 30,000.[37]

Their instructions were to mingle with a crowd attending a Muslim religious festival at a tomb on 8 August, then head to Srinagar the next day to join local politicians marking the anniversary of Sheikh Abdullah's arrest, and from there take over the airfield and radio station, proclaim a revolutionary council and ask Pakistan to intervene. This would be the signal for Pakistan to cross the border.

The plans, ambitious and long on drama, fell short on details and planning. The historian Shuja Nawaz describes the fiasco that ensued. 'Most of the commanders of the infiltrators, if not all, did not speak Kashmiri. Their local contacts had not been established, the assumption being that anyone whom they approached would be anti-India and pro-Pakistan. Even minor details such as the conversion of weights and

---

[†††] The refugees had come from East Pakistan.

measures in Indian-held Kashmir to the metric system had escaped them, so they would stand out when they approached anyone to make purchases with the Indian currency they carried for their operations. Many Kashmiri peasants, fearful of Indian reactions, turned in the infiltrators.'[38] Although the uprising the Pakistanis had hoped for did not materialize, it created some initial confusion for the Indian Army, as it followed so closely on the Rann of Kutch episode.

Once India had determined that the Kashmir unrest was not instigated by local elements but backed by Pakistan, it decided to retaliate. Captured infiltrators provided intelligence about the operation. The Indian Army attacked Pakistani outposts in the high Himalayas along the LOC at Kargil and Sunjoi and were able to capture the Haji Pir Pass. Pakistan had some success in Titwal, Uri and Poonch on the Indian side of Kashmir. By 1 September 1965, the Pakistani army had pushed the battle across the LOC into Chhamb and Jaurian, but this time Indians were prepared and waiting for them.

There was intense fighting, with both sides taking casualties. Pakistan, having the strategic advantage on the ground, threatened to cut India off from its ground access to Srinagar. Had the Pakistani army managed to capture Akhnoor in Jammu, it would have been able to cut of the supply routes into Kashmir from India.

Shastri recognized that he had to make a bold decision to avoid defeat. As he paced up and down in his office, his aide, C.P. Srivastava, recalls him saying, '*Ab to kuchh karna hi hoga!*' (Now we will have to do something!) He decided to invade the heartland of Pakistan, ordering Indian troops into Pakistani Punjab and taking a war that Pakistan had started to its very doorstep in Lahore.

Ayub Khan had grossly underestimated Shastri. The Indian invasion of Punjab took Pakistanis completely by surprise. Nehru would probably never have contemplated such an action. The disagreements with India had always centred on Kashmir; an invasion in Punjab by India, though always a possibility, was never realistically considered.

On 6 September 1965, Indian soldiers marched to Sialkot and Kasur and reached the outskirts of Lahore. Ayub had to pull his troops from Kashmir and race to defend Punjab. Operation Gibraltar and Operation Grand

Slam proved to be a total failure. None of the objectives were realized by Pakistan. Indian Kashmiris did not revolt, and the Pakistani army failed to hold any terrain or take any critical cities in Kashmir.

As the war expanded, both sides deployed their air forces and brought in their tanks. Pakistan took the Khem Karan area in India's Punjab. Indian forces crossed into West Pakistan on 6 September but met stiff resistance at Chawinda and Sialkot. One of the largest tank battles since the Second World War took place at Chawinda. The battle involved over 1,500 tanks and ended when the ceasefire went into effect on 23 September 1965. India lost close to 120 tanks and Pakistan lost about forty. The heavy fighting took its toll on both sides.

Neither side had achieved its military objectives. Pakistan was unable to capture Kashmir or any major city in the Punjab and, while India held on to Kashmir, it did not make it to Lahore. By mid-September both sides were exhausted and looking for a way out of the inconclusive war.

India's army chief, General Chaudhuri, told Shastri that their frontline ammunition was used up. He had misinformed Shastri. India had actually used up only 14 per cent of its frontline ammunition whereas Pakistan had used up close to 80 per cent. India, despite its heavy tank losses at Chawinda, still had twice the number of tanks that Pakistan had. Shastri, unaware of India's ability to sustain a longer confrontation, agreed to the ceasefire.[39]

The war lasted seventeen days. India lost 3,000 men and Pakistan 3,800. India held 758.9 square miles of Pakistani territory and Pakistan had gained 210 square miles of Indian territory.[‡‡‡]

The US had cut off arms to both countries once hostilities began, and both sides were low on supplies. On 22 September 1965, the UN Security Council demanded a ceasefire. India and Pakistan accepted immediately, and the fighting ended.

In an interview he later gave, Komer was explicit about the US role in ending the war. 'Our cutting off military aid to both sides was a major reason why they had to go for compromise. Ayub could see that if the war

---

‡‡‡ India's gains were in Sialkot, Lahore and Kashmir region while Pakistan's gains were in Sind and Chhamb. (Source: GlobalSecurity.org, 'Indo-Pak war of 1965,' 11 July 2011)

continued much longer, he was up the creek. He would run out of military resources. That was why he had to go to Tashkent.'[40]

## Peace and Death in Tashkent

The US had annoyed both India and Pakistan during the war. Pakistan considered it an act of betrayal for the US to cut off military supplies when the war began. India was furious that the US allowed Pakistan to use American-supplied arms against India when it had specifically provided assurances that the arms were for the sole purpose of fighting communists. The Soviets, on the other hand, had emerged as the more neutral party and a more reliable friend to India. Although they could not match the US in terms of the aid amount, they had consistently helped India after Stalin's death and agreed to its demand to build MiGs in India. where the US had failed to fulfil its obligations, the Soviets were more willing to share their latest technology with India and had stepped in to help with critical projects like Bokaro.

The Soviet offer to mediate the peace agreement in Tashkent, Uzbekistan was acceptable to both countries. The US went along with their involvement. As Rusk explained, 'We encouraged the Russians to go ahead with the Tashkent idea, because we felt we had nothing to lose. If they succeeded in bringing about any détente at Tashkent, then there would be more peace in the subcontinent between India and Pakistan, and we would gain from that fact. If the Russians failed at Tashkent, at least the Russians would have the experience of some of the frustration that we had for twenty years in trying to sort out things between India and Pakistan.'[41]

The Soviet effort was a success. Premier Kosygin turned out to be a skilful diplomat and the agreement that was signed was hailed as a huge achievement internationally. Shastri, who spent a considerable amount of time with the Soviet premier, raised the possibility of peace talks with Hanoi (North Vietnam) on behalf of President Johnson.

While Shastri was in Tashkent negotiating the end of the 1965 war with Pakistan, Johnson was focused on food aid rather than the peace plan. The acting secretary, George Ball, sent a telegram to the US embassy in London stating Johnson's position: 'We have had difficulty explaining to Congress why we are pouring our diminishing surplus stocks into an India that is not moving towards self-sufficiency. To continue to do so may be doing them a disservice … We still face a problem of whether it is prudent or wise to provide resources to two nations that are more obsessed with each other than their own development.'[42]

Johnson *was* obsessed. A team headed by Clarence Eskildsen of the US Foreign Agricultural Service had been instructed to go to India on a special mission for the president. They were asked to make an independent assessment to ensure that Indians were complying with the agricultural reforms they had promised to undertake. This was despite all the reassurances after the Rome agreement that India was doing everything it could. 'It is important that we keep as much pressure on Shastri, in particular, and the Indian government, in general, as much as possible. To date they have conformed to our wishes in general terms … a number of actions have been taken and instructions issued in New Delhi. However, that does not mean that the Indian bureaucracy and the Indian states are acting.'[43]

Freeman, agriculture secretary, was instructed by McGeorge Bundy to delay the departure of the food aid until the outcome of the Tashkent negotiations was clear. The goal was to make sure India had conformed to Johnson's requirements prior to a Shastri visit, which they anticipated would take place in February. But Shastri never made it to the US. Just hours after signing the Tashkent agreement, he suffered a fatal heart attack and died.

One of Shastri's last duties as the prime minister was a gracious letter he wrote to President Johnson, on 6 January 1966, informing him of his discussions with Kosygin regarding Hanoi.[§§§] He also thanked the president for his generosity in dealing with India's food crisis, though he was likely aware that it was not just congressional hesitation but Johnson's obsession with 'self-help' and tough love that put India into a food-insecure situation in the middle of a famine and a war.

---

§§§ Harriman had met with Shastri in Delhi and conveyed President Johnson's request to Shastri that he bring the issue up with the Soviet premier.

Johnson's attempts may have been better received at a time when India was in a more stable agricultural environment and could build up its reserves. Johnson had a willing partner in Shastri but dealt with him ruthlessly. Recognizing that what had been accomplished at Tashkent was a real achievement, Johnson said, 'Shastri died the right way in the cause for peace, not at the end of a gun barrel.'[44]

Shastri, who was so reluctant to travel because of his heart condition, had barely been prime minister for eighteen months when he passed away in Tashkent. The Indian delegation returned to India with a peace agreement and a coffin.

# Chapter 9

# Mrs Gandhi

W HEN PRIME MINISTER SHASTRI DIED SUDDENLY IN TASHKENT in January 1966, the Syndicate convened once again to select the next prime minister. Once again, Morarji Desai was the preferred candidate of the right wing, and once again the Syndicate prevailed in rejecting him. Worried they would be unable to bend Morarji to their will, they opted for Mrs Gandhi as the more pliable of the two. It would take just a few months before they realized they had grossly underestimated her, and they would come to regret their decision.

Mrs Gandhi had the benefit of a ringside seat in governing the country. When Nehru became the prime minister in 1947, Mrs Gandhi moved into his official residence with him. She gradually evolved from being her father's hostess to becoming his right hand and confidante. She was already familiar with her father's colleagues, many of whom she had known all her life, and eventually got to know all the players across India's political spectrum—their strengths, weaknesses and alliances. She met with all the heads of state and other dignitaries that visited India, travelled with her father on his foreign trips and campaigned all over India during elections on behalf of the Congress party.

In the 1957 election, she visited more constituencies than any other politician, representing her father and the Congress. Though Mrs Gandhi had a thin voice that did not project,* it became apparent to members of the party that she was a vote-getter. She benefitted from the name recognition and association with both her father and Mahatma Gandhi,

---

* As she got older and more confident, she improved. Prior to becoming PM, she asked economist–politician Ashok Mitra to help coach her.

and thousands would show up wherever she went to hear her or even just to see her. She found the people's response to her personally gratifying.

Mrs Gandhi was gradually given official responsibilities within the party. Initially, she paid her dues in soft areas like child and women's welfare, but in 1959, she was offered the top position as president of the Congress. In January 1959, the *Herald Tribune* called her the 'woman to watch'.[1] When the Syndicate placed Mrs Gandhi in the position of leading the nation, no one foresaw that she would dominate the party and Indian politics for the better part of the next twenty years.

## An Interrupted Childhood

Indira Priyadarshini Nehru was born in India on 19 November 1917, as the First World War raged in Europe and Russia was being convulsed by the October Revolution. A Scottish doctor delivered her amid much celebration—she was the first born of Motilal Nehru's only son, Jawaharlal Nehru. Although her grandmother was disappointed that she was not a boy, the rest of the family was overjoyed.[2]

According to family lore, the family patriarch Motilal Nehru had chosen Indira's mother as the bride for his only son because her horoscope predicted great glory for her future lineage. Indira grew up in a luxurious forty-two-room mansion with over a hundred servants and, indulged by her grandparents, she was a happy, boisterous child. Her idyllic childhood was interrupted, however, when her family joined the freedom movement. They travelled around the country organizing protests and spending months at a time in jail. Going to jail for protesting British rule had become a badge of honour.[†]

This inevitably meant that Indira was often at home without her father. Under Mahatma Gandhi's influence, Jawaharlal Nehru became one of the leaders of the independence movement and was continually on the road campaigning.

---

† Nehru, his father, and sister Vijaya Lakshmi all joined the protests. Nehru spent long periods in jail. Later, Vijaya Lakshmi and Indira would as well. Although Indira's father was the main participant, her mother, aunts and grandfather were also active in the freedom movement and spent time in jail.

As is often unavoidable in large families, tensions existed. Indira's young mother, Kamala, was not as sophisticated as her westernized in-laws. When her husband was away, she was often ignored and made to feel inferior. Her mother's frequent humiliations at the hands of some family members cast a shadow over Indira's otherwise happy childhood. She adored her gentle mother, and tried to stand up for her, but she was a child, and her anger fell on deaf ears. Indira singled out, as her mother's main tormentor, her vivacious, brilliant aunt Vijaya Lakshmi Pandit, who also lived with them, and she never forgave her.

Vijaya Lakshmi adored her brother and was her brother's confidante after he returned from England. When he became the prime minister, she served as Nehru's ambassador to the Soviet Union and the United States. After Nehru married Kamala, they lived in the family home, Anand Bhavan, along with all the other relatives, as was the custom. Nehru's sister used her closeness to him to isolate Kamala, her shy sister-in-law.

In 1924, while her husband was away, Kamala gave birth to a premature baby boy who did not survive. Nehru was in prison at the time and was unable to comfort his grieving wife. Indira sensed her mother's loneliness and felt miserable for her.[3] Kamala's health began to deteriorate soon after and Indira became even more protective of her. Later in life, though Mrs Gandhi was often cold and calculating with people who enjoyed power and privilege, she displayed genuine compassion for the underprivileged, the poor and the dispossessed.[‡]

Indira's relations with her aunt suffered a fatal blow when she overheard Vijaya Lakshmi casually remark that she (Indira) was ugly and stupid.[4] Indira was thirteen at the time and the words seared her. No one contradicted her aunt or came to Indira's defence. After this incident, the confident and chatty Indira, who ran around Anand Bhavan like she owned it, morphed into a quiet, moody child given to silences.[§]

---

[‡]   Mrs Gandhi was genuinely distressed and moved to tears when she visited the refugee camps in 1971 after the war with Pakistan. She was very empathetic towards the rural poor and women when she went around India.

[§]   According to Pupul Jayakar, Mrs Gandhi brought up the incident two weeks before her assassination.

While Nehru was in prison, Indira wrote a bitter letter to him complaining about the treatment of her mother: 'Do you know anything about what happens at home when you are absent? Do you know that when mummie was in a very bad condition the house was full of people, but not one of them even went to see her or sit a while with her, that when she was in agony there was no one to help her?' She went on to admonish him and said it was only when he came home that people asked after her mother, implying their hypocrisy.[5]

In dealing with her father, Indira learnt that he suffered when she did not respond to his letters and gave him the silent treatment. Silence was a weapon that she used throughout her political career to communicate her disapproval or to simply unnerve people.[6] For instance, Mrs Gandhi subjected both the German chancellor and the British high commissioner to her silent treatment in 1967.[¶] She refused to engage with Moynihan when he visited her as ambassador, as she was displeased when the US resumed arms sales to Pakistan.

After 1930, as the political situation intensified, the Nehru household became a magnet for all sorts of politicians and hangers-on. Kamala began to participate in freedom marches. A frequent visitor to the house was a young radical named Feroze Gandhi. With Nehru in prison, he made himself indispensable to Kamala, who was fully engaged in the independence movement when her health allowed. His constant presence in the Nehru household brought him into close contact with Indira, who began to trust him and was grateful for the attention he gave her mother. She found herself drawn to him. Feroze proposed to her when she was barely sixteen, but they decided to keep their relationship a secret.

## Health Troubles and Heartache

Indira's education had been erratic due to her father's absences and her mother's illnesses. When she was eight, her mother was diagnosed with tuberculosis (TB). Indira moved with her parents to Switzerland for

---

¶ The German chancellor had requested that Mrs Gandhi delay recognizing East Germany. (Jayakar, *Indira Gandhi*, 204).

a year and a half in 1926 so that her mother could undergo treatment there. She was enrolled in L'Ecole Internationale and became fluent in French. She learnt to go back and forth to school alone. It was a far cry from the dozens of servants who waited on her at home, but she adjusted admirably.

A few months later, in the summer of 1926, Indira was sent to a boarding school at Chesieres, where she was miserable. The school was run by an unpleasant couple whom students found oppressive.[7] She transferred to L'Ecole Nouvelle in Bex, operated by an enlightened headmistress, where she blossomed. Mrs Gandhi retained her ties to the school long after she left.

On her return to India, her attendance in school was erratic and unmemorable until, at the age of sixteen, she enrolled in Santineketan, a progressive school started by Rabindranath Tagore.** She fell in love with the carefree atmosphere, writing to her father, 'everything is so artistic and beautiful and wild'.[8] Later in life, she said of her time there, 'For the first time in my life, I was removed from the atmosphere of intense political living.' She was able to explore her passion for all things cultural, especially Manipuri dancing, and let go of the bitterness and anger that she had built up. One biographer describes it as the place 'where her mind and soul unfolded'.[9]

Indira's idyllic time at Santineketan was cut short when her mother's illness worsened in April 1935. With her father still in prison, Indira had to accompany her mother back to Switzerland for treatment.†† The journey by sea and train was long and difficult. Her mother's health was precarious, and Indira, responsible for her mother's care, was continually anxious. As Kamala deteriorated, Nehru was released from prison so he could join his wife and daughter.

During those months in Europe, father and daughter grew closer, travelling together when Kamala was well enough to be left alone. Feroze Gandhi, meanwhile, had arrived in Europe to study at the London School

---

**  Tagore was a Nobel laureate and Santineketan was a progressive school for the arts.

††  Kamala Nehru spent two years in Swiss sanatoriums from 1926 to 1927.

of Economics. He arrived in Switzerland as Kamala's health worsened. On 28 February 1936, just thirty-seven years old, Kamala died in the sanatorium surrounded by Nehru, Indira and Feroze. Her mother's illness tightened the bond between Feroze and Indira. They continued to secretly see each other throughout their college days in England.

Nehru was very keen for Indira to attend Oxford. In those days, proficiency in Latin was a requirement for admission, and it became a challenge for Indira, who had never had the opportunity of studying it. Always pragmatic, she saw little value in being proficient in a 'dead language'. She attended Somerville College in Oxford and then returned to India before graduating as she, like her mother, was continually ill and weighed just ninety pounds.

Mrs Gandhi suffered from bouts of ill health since early childhood. Being with her mother in the Swiss sanatoriums may have also exposed her to TB, a cure for which only became widely available in the 1950s.

Indira left Oxford in 1940 without graduating, spending time in a TB sanatorium in Les Fresnes before returning to India. The family kept her illness a secret. While her health did improve markedly in the 1950s, she continued to be afflicted by ailments such as kidney problems and anaemia. It is a testament to her courage that she never gave in to her physical weakness or let it compromise the demanding schedule that her political life entailed.

Socialism developed a following in Europe and many Indian students studying in England came under its influence. They embraced the argument that the colonialism which had stunted development in India was a direct product of capitalism. Among the converts were Feroze Gandhi and P.N. Haksar. Haksar's family, like the Nehrus, were originally from Kashmir and knew each other. He had attended Motilal's funeral where he remembers 'Indira Nehru standing in one corner looking utterly forlorn and dishevelled'.[10] Haksar, who had seen the devastating impact of the Spanish flu in 1918 when it swept through India, had been inspired to become a doctor, but discovered he had no appetite for dissecting animals, a requirement in the training process. He was mild-mannered and philosophical, and a great cook, preparing wonderful dinners for

Indira and Feroze while they were in England—he was one of the few Indians overseas who was let in on the secret of their relationship.

After Indira returned to India in 1941, she told her father that she planned to marry Feroze. Her family tried to talk her out of it, but she was unmoved, and their reluctance made her even more determined. She was fiercely independent, not intimidated by authority and had the ability to stand up for herself—all traits that would be repeated during her political career. Mahatma Gandhi was brought in to mediate. After he gave the marriage his blessing, the family conceded.[11]

Indira and Feroze's marriage was not a happy union. Mrs Gandhi was torn between her loyalty to her father, whom she felt obliged to look after, and being with her husband. She also had to juggle her responsibilities as Congress party president after 1959, and Feroze began to feel neglected. There were rumours of him having affairs.[12] Initially, she tried an unconventional arrangement by splitting her time between the two, but it became increasingly taxing. She, along with her children, gradually moved in permanently to Teen Murti Bhavan, her father's residence, and close to the centre of power.[13]

In an intimate window into her marriage, Mrs Gandhi poured her heart out in a July 1959 letter to Dorothy Norman, with whom she had developed a deep friendship. 'A veritable sea is engulfing me. On the domestic front, Feroze has always resented my very existence, but since I have become President (of the Congress party) he exudes such hostility that it seems to poison the air.'[14] But when Feroze died prematurely of a heart attack in 1960, at the age of forty-eight, she was devastated and wrote to Dorothy about her shock and sorrow at losing him even though they had drifted irrevocably apart. Although she admitted her marital problems in private, publicly she denied her marriage was anything less than perfect.

Mrs Gandhi's personal interests were in all things cultural—she especially enjoyed fine textiles, dance and the arts. She found great solace in nature, though she was terrified of thunderstorms. Her happiest memories were of the time she spent in Santineketan pursuing her artistic interests. Had she been born into a non-political family, or at a different time, she may have taken a different path and been a happier, less conflicted person. She was, however, born at a time of political upheaval and her family was at its epicentre. She was almost predestined to be sucked into the vortex of national affairs.

By 1960, after twelve years of a gruelling schedule at her father's side while he was the prime minister, Mrs Gandhi was worn out.[‡‡] Her full-time duties to her father and her own responsibilities within the Congress party began to weigh on her, and her steadily disintegrating marriage added to her burdens. Emotionally spent, she began to complain about frequent episodes of depression.

Indira Gandhi was a private person and did not dare disclose her feelings to anyone in India. Instead, during a correspondence that spanned thirty-four years, she revealed her doubts, misgivings and feelings about herself and her life to Dorothy Norman.

By 1960, Mrs Gandhi had grown increasingly dissatisfied with her life. She was not contemplating a career in politics and seemed tired of India. On 11 April 1960, just six years before she became the prime minister, she wrote: 'I am not doing anything and not wanting to do anything. It is not a satisfactory feeling. I must find the right vocation.'[15]

On 17 October 1961, she again wrote of depression: 'My own mood had changed, and I am in the depth of depression, for no special reason.' In April 1962, she was once again feeling low: 'I just don't know *where* I am. The body is there—grinning, talking, but it's just a shell. The real me is non-existent. Is it dead or dormant? It's *most* depressing and I miss me, if you know what I mean.'[16]

Her most agonizing letter was written on 13 October 1963. The war with China had ended. Her father was three months away from his stroke and must have exhibited signs of declining health. His popularity had eroded; the once-invincible leader seemed vulnerable. She must have been under considerable strain from managing the deteriorating circumstances. She wrote:

---

‡‡ She had effectively become Nehru's gatekeeper and go-between from 1955 onwards. He was so busy that he often passed minor issues to her for handling. (Vasudev, *Indira Gandhi*, 257).

My need for privacy and anonymity has been growing steadily these last three years until now I feel I cannot ignore it without risking some kind of self-annihilation. Privacy, unfortunately, is not possible for me even in the remotest corner of this subcontinent. I have had people presenting their cards and their problems even at the foot of the Kolahai glacier (16,000 ft high)! ... I can claim to have done my duty to my country and my family all these long years. I don't for an instant regret it, because whatever I am today has been shaped by these years. But now I want another life. It may not work out ... But at least it deserves a trial.[17]

She then wrote that she had seen the perfect house in London and wished she could buy it and work outside India.

One explanation for her frustration is revealed, just before her father's death. In a letter dated 8 May 1964, she said: 'The whole question of my future is bothering me. I feel I must settle outside India at least for a year or so and this involves earning a living and especially foreign currency ... The desire to be out of India and the malice, jealousies and envy, with which one is surrounded, are now overwhelming.'[18]

Nineteen days after she wrote the letter Nehru died. Her desperate need to change her life seemed doomed. In another eighteen months, she would be the prime minister. Nothing in these letters indicates any desire for a life in politics or a vision for herself as the inheritor of her father's job. She had, in fact, displayed considerable antipathy towards politics. It makes the events after 1966 even more extraordinary.

## Mrs Gandhi: The Politician

Although Indira Gandhi spent years by her father's side, she lacked his education and intellectual depth. Nehru had an enquiring mind, was a highly nuanced thinker and although he was passionate and occasionally impulsive, such as being moved by Gandhi and his ideas when he first met him, he generally arrived at his convictions after years of thought and study.

Mrs Gandhi's education had been constantly interrupted. She never completed a degree and her academic interests were limited. She had always been more interested in the arts and her knowledge of economics and history was thin. She was often called a socialist. She rejected being labelled and subscribed to no particular political philosophy. She would say, 'I am not pro and con any "-ism" but I do believe in certain principles and social and economic policies.'[19] But her principles often shifted and were not always clear, even to her main advisors.

Nehru firmly believed in democratic ideals and behaved accordingly. Mrs Gandhi, by contrast, made no attempt to build a consensus. She would listen to people's opinions, but she had a proclivity to authoritarian behaviour and could be imperious. Growing up wealthy and privileged, and watching people treat her father and grandfather with extreme deference, gave her a sense of entitlement.

Whereas Nehru acted on his principles, Mrs Gandhi did what was expedient. Charanjit Yadav, a Congress politician who had come out of the communist party, said that 'she never had the principled approach and humanism of Nehru'.[20] The difference in their attitude could be seen as early as 1959 when her father was dealing with the political problems created by the communists in the Kerala government. A correspondent from *The Hindu*, E.K. Ramaswami, asked Nehru whether he was going to dismiss the communists from government. Nehru replied, 'Throw them out? How? What do you mean? They've also been elected!' From behind him, sharply came Indira's voice, 'Papu, what are you telling them? You're talking as Prime Minister.' She turned to Ramaswami and other correspondents and said: 'As Congress President I intend to fight them and throw them out.'[§§]

Mrs Gandhi was, above all, a pragmatist. When the communists became a problem for her, she did not hesitate to put them down. And later, when she needed them in her fight against the Syndicate, she allied with them. As the party president, she pushed the prime minister to act according to the Congress's wishes. But when she took over the prime ministership, she

§§ The communist party had been elected to office in Kerala on 5 April 1957. Their unscrupulous governance had made them unpopular. (Vasudev, *Indira Gandhi*, 276).

refused to be pushed around by the party. She said: 'The world, at large, is not interested in excuses for failures. The world is interested in who wins. Very few care to find out why one has lost. It is success and victory which matter.'[21]

Mrs Gandhi's election as Congress president had prepared her well for the top job. It taught her how best to leverage power within the party and whom to trust. When she was prime minister, she once said, 'I am not a political person.'[22] Although on the surface it seems like a lack of self-awareness, she may have been referring to her inner conflicts given the extraordinary lengths she would go to consolidate power in her hands.

Mrs Gandhi was better at tackling large political crises than the mundane aspects of running a government. She preferred short memoranda to long policy briefs. Her inability to focus for long periods of time on intricate policy discussions could lead to embarrassing situations. P.N. Dhar, one of her chief advisors, recounted one such incident when Mrs Gandhi met with the shah of Iran in his palace in Tehran. While the shah was discussing the oil industry, Mrs Gandhi lost interest and turned to watch the birds in the window. Dhar said that he and Swaran Singh tried to cover up by taking notes and hanging on the shah's every word.[23]

Mrs Gandhi was confident in her political ability, but was intellectually somewhat insecure, relying on others for non-political decisions, particularly when it came to economic policy. When things went wrong, as they did after her interaction with the Johnson administration, she reacted badly.

## Johnson and Mrs Gandhi

Mrs Gandhi inherited a poisoned chalice when she became the prime minister. India had concluded an uneasy truce with Pakistan. The US aid embargo to both countries had encouraged Pakistan to align with China. Between the two hostile countries, India was caught in a pincer grip that extended from east to west all along her northern front. It would remain a constant threat.

Internally, there seemed to be no relief from the economic crisis. The Indian economy was running on empty. Factories were operating below capacity and unemployment was rising. The distribution of foodgrains was inefficient, and productivity was low. The results of the agricultural reforms were slow to kick in and food stocks were at the mercy of Johnson's 'short tether' policy. India was in a precarious state with its balance of payments due to increased imports of foodgrains, which it had to buy in the international market. The inflation rate was 12 per cent in 1965–66 and rising. Commodity prices were shooting up and everyone in the country seemed to be suffering.

Mrs Gandhi would have to make the trip to the US that Shastri had planned before he died. India desperately needed the food aid. Johnson told the Indian ambassador, B.K. Nehru, in February 1966, that he was open to a meeting with Mrs Gandhi as he was having difficulty appropriating the funds from Congress for India, and it would be useful to explore other options with her. Although he did not commit to providing any emergency food aid to India, he invited Mrs Gandhi to visit.

The US was anxious that Krishna Menon not get resurrected as one of her advisors and Ambassador Bowles brought up the subject when he met Mrs Gandhi to extend Johnson's invitation to visit Washington. He was reassured that she considered him an adversary as he had worked against her nomination as prime minister.[24]

Mrs Gandhi arrived in Washington, DC at the end of March 1966. Calling it a goodwill tour, she confided to journalist Inder Malhotra that her main task was to obtain food and foreign exchange for India without appearing to ask for them.[25] Bowles softened up Johnson by telling him of Mrs Gandhi's admiration for him, her sympathy for his predicament in Vietnam and her gratitude for the aid provided to India by the US.

The state banquet for Mrs Gandhi on 28 March 1966 was a success. She had stopped in Paris to have her hair done, dressed beautifully for the occasion and turned on her charm. The national security advisor, Robert Komer, dryly observed: 'She set out to vamp LBJ and succeeded.'[26] To avoid dancing with the president, which would not have gone down well in India, she arranged to leave the dinner early.

The next day, B.K. Nehru hosted a dinner in Mrs Gandhi's honour at the Indian embassy, which Johnson attended. Breaking protocol, Johnson surprised everyone by staying for dinner,⁵⁵ eclipsing Vice President Hubert Humphrey, who was the intended guest of honour. He and Mrs Gandhi got on well. He was in an expansive mood and effusive in his praise for her, proclaiming that he would make sure that 'no harm came to this girl'.[27] He also promised 3 million tons of food and 9 million dollars in aid.

Mrs Gandhi understood she was living in a world dominated by men who were perpetually condescending towards women. When she took over Shastri's position, older members of the Congress party, who had been against her nomination, mistook her reserve for shyness and called her 'goongi gudiya', or 'dumb doll'. Johnson's treatment of her, like a girl in need of his protection, may have grated but she was on a mission. Earlier, the Indian ambassador had asked her how she wanted to be addressed by the president. After some thought, she had imperiously said, 'You can tell him my cabinet colleagues call me sir.'[28] The ambassador decided it was best not to convey the message.

Internal discussions within the US reveal that the US government officials wanted to make sure that the euphoria of the visit did not lull India into complacency by believing that the US would bail it out. Johnson made clear that their aid needed to be part of a consortium and, although the US would help spearhead the process, India needed to do some work to get food commitments from other countries. India also needed to continue to prove it was working towards self-sufficiency. India was expected to work with the World Bank on economic reforms to satisfy the US Congress that its aid dollars were being spent productively. Mrs Gandhi had to adhere to performance levels in return for the help.

## One Political Problem after Another

On 6 June 1966, under pressure from the US and the World Bank, Mrs Gandhi devalued the Indian rupee by 37 per cent, from 4.76 to 7.50 against the US dollar. The war with China and the increased imports of food

---

⁵⁵ The president usually visits for thirty minutes on a 'return' call for a visiting head of state.

due to two consecutive droughts in 1965 and 1966 had contributed to the depletion of reserves. A second war in 1965 had put additional stress on the economy.

Before leaving for the US, Mrs Gandhi discussed the possible impact of devaluation with a small group of advisors. Ambassador Nehru warned her that the International Monetary Fund had indicated it would make devaluation a precondition for any further loans to India, so it did not come as a surprise to her when George Woods, president of the World Bank, made the same point to Ashok Mehta of the Planning Commission.

Though the select group of economists that Mrs Gandhi consulted recognized that monetary devaluation was unavoidable, there was an outcry in India when it occurred. Mrs Gandhi had not consulted the Syndicate before making the decision. The public reaction was surprisingly emotional and negative—it was as though the country had been auctioned at night. Politically it proved to be a disaster, and economically it was not the success for which its proponents had hoped. Furthermore, the increase in aid that was anticipated as a result of the devaluation did not materialize. After the devaluation episode, Mrs Gandhi no longer trusted the advice of the US or the World Bank economists.[***]

Until mid-1965, aid to India had been managed by the US embassy in Delhi, USAID and a small group of Indians from the government. They had, with some minor complications, managed to work out a generally supportive aid programme for India. Plentiful wheat reserves in the US made supplying India with foodgrains relatively routine. After Johnson became the president, this comfortable working arrangement changed.

Orville Freeman, the secretary of agriculture, demanded that India adhere to the Treaty of Rome, which stipulated that it meet certain agricultural reform benchmarks in return for the food aid. All through 1966, bureaucratic infighting delayed the implementation of a comprehensive schedule for the food aid programme, while people continued to die.

---

[***] Mrs Gandhi felt that the West, including the World Bank, left her at the altar during this episode, as the large investment and increased aid she was expecting as a result of devaluation did not take place.

Mrs Gandhi, who had suffered stinging political blowback from the devaluation episode, was disappointed when the aid that Johnson promised during her visit took its time in arriving. She had been accused by the Left of having sold out to the US with little to show for it.[†††] Her instinct was to push away from being taken for granted by the US. She felt she needed to assert her independence and prove that the US was not dictating terms to her. In July 1966, she visited Moscow and agreed to a joint communiqué critical of US policy in Vietnam. Johnson was predictably furious.

During Mrs Gandhi's visit to the US, Johnson had indicated that he would help India as long as he saw progress in relations. He was grateful that the traditional anti-American rhetoric that emanated from India had disappeared and called India a 'deserving friend'. He famously said: 'Let it never be said bread should be so dear and flesh and blood so cheap that we turned in indifference from her bitter need.'[29]

Mrs Gandhi's negative comments about the US bombing campaign in Vietnam infuriated Johnson, who insisted on gratitude from recipients of US largesse. He soured on India and his recent goodwill vanished. An element of vindictiveness crept in in his dealings with India, especially where he knew it would hurt the most: food aid. He insisted that India's feet be held to the fire in what came to be known as the 'ship to mouth' policy.

Johnson decided to monitor every single shipment of grain going to India. He delayed the movement of grain even when his own staff pleaded with him to order the shipment to prevent starvation.

As head of the USDA, Freeman was acutely aware that food supplies in the US were precipitously low. This was due to a drought in the US in 1966 and the massive amounts of food America had sent to India during the previous two years. Johnson may have been genuinely worried about inflation and the mounting cost of the Vietnam War, but his personal handling of the shipments went beyond the obsession he had developed during Shastri's tenure of making India more self-reliant.

Johnson began keeping track of India's weekly rainfall and rebuffed hawks like Freeman and Rusk who were generally inclined to be tough,

---

††† Krishna Menon was one of her most vocal critics.

but noted the dire situation in India. In November 1966, they were urging Johnson to urgently release a two-million-ton wheat shipment. At one point during the crisis, Mrs Gandhi had to call Johnson and beg for the food. Her press advisor, Sharada Prasad, recalled her clenching her fingers around the telephone during the conversation and, while she was friendly and charming on the phone, she was furious inside; when she hung up, she said, 'I don't ever want us ever to have to beg for food again!'[30]

Johnson relented only when the US press, reporting on the famine, found out about Johnson's 'tough love' policies and made him look heartless. Just before Christmas, Johnson finally released 900,000 tons of PL480 wheat.

Johnson may have done India a favour. India's Green Revolution had begun, but it was accelerated under Johnson's rough treatment. Mrs Gandhi was so incensed that she travelled the country with C. Subramaniam and various scientists to ensure that agricultural reform and food self-sufficiency became the country's top priority, but she never forgave Johnson. Her antipathy towards the US became entrenched and, after Johnson, Nixon made it irredeemable.

After the Chinese exploded a nuclear device in October 1964, India tried to get reassurances from the nuclear states that they would be protected under a 'nuclear umbrella'. India wanted a UN-sponsored guarantee against a Chinese nuclear threat but neither the US nor the Soviets were willing to provide such a commitment. They came up with the Non-Proliferation Treaty (NPT) instead, compelling countries that did not possess nuclear weapons not to develop them in return for certain guarantees. India rejected the NPT as it felt it did not provide the country with the needed protections. India made it clear that it had no intention of developing a nuclear weapon, but it refused to sign what it considered to be an unequal treaty. Its steadfast refusal to budge on this issue created suspicion and friction between the US and India for years.

The new US ambassador to Pakistan, Eugene Locke, was a Texan.[‡‡‡] He was a friend of Johnson's and pushed to re-arm Pakistan. In April

---

[‡‡‡] He was appointed in May 1966.

1967, Washington agreed to let Pakistan buy spare parts on a case-by-case basis. Bowles argued it was against the embargo imposed on India and Pakistan after the 1965 war. But by 1967, Bowles's star had dimmed. He was dismissed in Washington as an advocate for India rather than the US. In US policy circles there was much frustration and fatigue with India and a willingness to cautiously reopen a window to Pakistan.

In May 1967, just before the Six-Day War broke out in the Middle East, India's foreign minister M.C. Chagla delivered an anti-Israeli speech at the UN. It predictably drew sharp reactions from the US. Chester Bowles went to see Mrs Gandhi and gave her what she considered a lecture. She confided to Pupul Jayakar: 'It is better that we die than give in to the constant pressure from the USA.'[31] Pakistan held much the same views as India on the Arab–Israeli conflict, but it avoided publicly criticizing US policy.[§§§]

Mrs Gandhi was not unsympathetic to Israel or the Jews. Nehru and Gandhi had tried to allow German Jews to immigrate to India during the Holocaust. It was the British who had refused to let them in. India's official policy on Israel was partly governed by the need to placate the sentiments of the Muslim population in India. Nevertheless, Mrs Gandhi could well have diffused the situation by giving a press conference and smoothing things over. Instead, her anger at the US, for the humiliation it had put India through during a famine, had made her obdurate. She could not overlook a slight even in the interest of her country. For her, politics was personal.

Johnson also took exception to India's remarks. For the rest of the year he sat on the food shipments despite the fact that Congress had authorized their allocation for India. Bowles was excluded from the decision-making process while Johnson studied the dates of grain shipments from American ports to India.

The Soviet Union had increasingly become India's main ally, even though Moscow's handling of India and Pakistan had become more balanced since Tashkent. Sensing an opportunity to displace the US, the

---

§§§ The US had many Jewish members of Congress who were committed to a pro-Israeli policy.

Soviets had offered to sell arms to Pakistan and Pakistan had, in turn, responded by distancing itself from the US and not renewing the lease on its base in Peshawar. India had little choice but to follow these new developments with some discomfort. Its relations with the US had soured and it faced a belligerent China on its border.

By 1968, the tide had turned against Johnson. The US was shaken by anti-war protests and civil rights marches, and Johnson found himself fully preoccupied by Vietnam. The US now had 485,000 troops in South Vietnam; almost 16,000 soldiers had died and close to 100,000 others had been wounded. Americans thought that US involvement in the war was a mistake, and the president's approval rating regarding his handling of the war was at 28 per cent. Discouraged by his political prospects as the elections geared up, he stunned the nation when he announced in March that he would not run again. His approval ratings rose to 57 per cent overnight.

At 6 p.m. on 4 April, Martin Luther King, Jr was fatally shot. He died an hour later. It was a reminder that the country was still divided and not everyone had signed on to Johnson's progressive social programme. In June, Robert Kennedy, who had become the front runner of the Democratic Party, was assassinated. The year 1968 was turning bloody. Johnson had wanted to use the Democratic Convention to highlight the achievements of his administration with a film that was prepared for the occasion. The Kennedy clan now requested the screening of a video on Robert Kennedy and his service to the nation. Johnson was in no position to refuse. Once more, just as his inauguration had been eclipsed by the tragic demise of a Kennedy, his departure from politics was overshadowed by another Kennedy. With Robert Kennedy gone from the Democratic field, the path to the presidency began to look increasingly promising for Nixon.

When Soviet tanks rolled into Czechoslovakia in August 1968, it ended Johnson's hopes of bringing an end to the Vietnam War through a final summit with Premier Kosygin. It also shelved Senate ratification of the Nuclear Proliferation Treaty—an achievement Johnson hoped would be part of his legacy.

Although privately many Indians deplored the Soviet action in Czechoslovakia, India felt it had no choice but to support the Soviets. With a belligerent China and Pakistan allied against them and relations with the US strained, it abstained when the UN Security Council condemned the Soviet action, further irritating US officials.

Caught up with their respective domestic politics, the two countries receded from each other's consciousness.

## Mrs Gandhi Crushes her Opponents

Indira Gandhi needed to consolidate her position within India. The year 1967 was an election year. Devaluation, inflation and famine had taken its toll. Congress had fared poorly at the polls. It won 283 out of 516 seats. The Syndicate was crushed, and its members lost their seats. Mrs Gandhi had won with a comfortable margin but so had Morarji Desai, who had secured an overwhelming majority of votes. He decided to challenge her leadership in the party. In order to placate the various power brokers, and in the interests of unity, Mrs Gandhi was obliged to take him on as deputy prime minister and gave him the finance portfolio. It was a bitter pill, but she needed time to assess her options.

Mrs Gandhi recognized that there was an expanding group of young radicals within the Congress party, which was becoming increasingly impatient with the old guard. They admired her revolutionary spirit and had thrown their support behind her. She began to build a political base within the party that would be loyal just to her. The Congress party began to split into two camps. The old guard coalesced around Morarji and the young radicals rallied around Mrs Gandhi.

Bank nationalization became a lightning rod. Morarji was in favour of free markets and against nationalization but saw the trend was against him. So, as a compromise, he reluctantly agreed to the social control of banks. This committed banks to give loans to farmers and small enterprises. Towards that end, in May 1967, a ten-point programme was announced.¶¶¶

---

¶¶¶ The ten-point programme contained changes to land reform, nationalization of insurance, creation of land ceilings and abolishment of titles and privileges to royal families including privy purses.

Mrs Gandhi had no particular ideological fixations and was unschooled in economics. She lacked the depth of knowledge her father possessed to evaluate the merits of the arguments presented to her. After the devaluation debacle, she had rejected the liberalization argument and relied on the advice of a small group of left-leaning members, which came to be known as her kitchen cabinet. P.N. Haksar, T.N. Kaul and a couple of others were all left-wingers who pushed her towards an anti-US, socialist position on most things. The young radicals in the party pushed to get rid of the privileges of the maharajas and nationalize the banks. Finance Minister Morarji Desai disagreed. He had agreed to the social control of banks and that was as far as he was willing to go.

On 19 July 1969, in a decision taken in the utmost secrecy, Mrs Gandhi nationalized the banks. The move was organized by her economic advisor I.G. Patel, L.K. Jha, governor of the Reserve Bank of India and C.S. Seshadri from the finance ministry. Her trusted advisor, P.N. Haksar helped prepare the legal justification. They persuaded her to limit the bank nationalization to Indian banks.[32]

Morarji was stripped of his finance portfolio. Mrs Gandhi decided that the agricultural sector had been denied access to credit and the focus had to shift towards a more socialist form of government. She tightened controls on exports and imports, nationalized insurance, coal mines and the oil industry. She reserved labour-intensive products to be manufactured by small-scale enterprises and came close to banishing foreign investments, under the Foreign Exchange Regulation Act, 1973. Nehru would have blanched at her left-wing turn. She was effectively shutting India off from the world when it came to trade and industry.

Morarji was horrified and resigned as deputy prime minister. Kamaraj, the old kingmaker of the Syndicate, had returned to Parliament in a by-election and together with Morarji decided that Mrs Gandhi was irresponsible and needed to be removed from office. In May 1969, an opportunity presented itself to Mrs Gandhi by which she was able to strengthen her hand against her opponents. The president of India, Zakir Husain, a figurehead but with powers nonetheless, died.**** She was able to outmanoeuvre the Syndicate and prevent their candidate Sanjiva Reddy from becoming the president. Vice President V.V. Giri, who had been helpful to Mrs Gandhi during the bank nationalization, ran as an independent and became the fourth president of India.

The old guard of the Congress party had seen enough. They put pressure on the party president, S. Nijalingappa, to expel Mrs Gandhi from the party. On 12 November 1969, the Syndicate held an inquisition where she was tried in absentia and found guilty of indiscipline and defiance of the party leadership. It was hinted that she tried to 'sell' India to the Soviet Union and they chided her for subverting the democratic process by creating a cult of personality where loyalty to her, rather than the party, was paramount. Some of the accusations would turn out to be prophetic. After eighty-four years, the Congress party split in two. Mrs Gandhi led the faction called Congress (R) with 297 seats. The Syndicate became Congress (O).

Mrs Gandhi had lost her majority in Parliament when the party split but managed to cobble together support from the communists and some independents. She survived a no-confidence vote and reshuffled her cabinet, bringing the intelligence bureau directly under her control. Having rid herself of the party bosses, she felt liberated. She called elections a year early, anxious to be validated by the people.

Mrs Gandhi was guarded and formal in the confines of Delhi, but she was warm towards—and found it easy to connect with—the women in villages. During various jobs in the Congress party or on the campaign trail, trudging through the back roads and remote towns of India, she had spent years dealing with women's issues and knew she had the support of the common man. Communicating with the masses was of utmost importance to her and she would spend hours perfecting her speeches. Her secretary, P.N. Dhar, said she would fly into a rage if a prepared speech

---

**** In the event of a weak government, the Indian president has the authority to dismiss or appoint the prime minister. If the party split or Mrs Gandhi was faced with a no-confidence vote, she would need an ally in the president. As the vice president, V.V. Giri had authorized the bank nationalization.

did not meet her expectations. In return, she was genuinely moved by the poverty she saw, and she promised to end it. She began to use her popularity with the masses to overwhelm her opponents.

Over 150 million people voted in 520 constituencies on 17 March 1971. Congress won in a landslide. Mrs Gandhi won a two-thirds majority in the lower house, taking 325 seats. Her opponent Congress (O) was wiped out. It only won seventeen seats. She was elected as the uncontested Congress party leader.

The Syndicate had grossly underestimated her popularity among the ordinary people. She had spent years travelling with her father around the country and had gone to every state and canvassed during the 1957 and 1962 elections. During the Sino-Indian War, she was the only person of distinction who went to the frontlines to express solidarity with the soldiers. She did the same during the 1965 war with Pakistan. She displayed more courage and concern than all the men in the cabinet. The people remembered.

By 1971, Mrs Gandhi had become a master politician. She had bested her opponents by getting her mandate directly from the people. She was impatient with the democratic methods of consensus adhered to by both her father and Shastri and had become something of a demagogue. She made it clear that she expected people in government to be loyal to her personally. Party and country came second. Because she encouraged the cult of personality, portraits depicting her as the mythical goddess Durga emerged. She relied on the masses to support her against those resisting her lapses, and civil discourse dissolved into hooliganism.

Mrs Gandhi was a stark contrast to her father, who would have recoiled at her actions. Nehru considered his office a sacred trust and never abused it. He accepted decisions made by the Congress party even though he did not always agree with them. Mrs Gandhi paid lip service to the Indian Constitution, never displaying any commitment to it. The end justified the means for her, whereas, for Nehru, the means was everything.

# Chapter 10

# Nixon: Tortured Relations

O N 8 NOVEMBER 1970, A TROPICAL CYCLONE BEGAN TO FORM over the South China Sea. For several days, fishermen at sea had noticed the gathering clouds and darkening sky. By 10 November, the storm entered the Bay of Bengal. Picking up intensity, it sped across the Indian Ocean towards the subcontinent. East Pakistan lay directly in its path.

An early warning radar had been recently installed in East Pakistan near the Burmese border, but the only advisory picked up by residents was from an Indian radio station. It signalled that a severe storm was approaching. As the morning skies turned menacingly dark on 11 November, worried fisherman hurried back to shore, struggling through dangerously choppy waters.

East Pakistan was separated from West Pakistan by 1,000 miles of Indian territory. It straddled two of the subcontinent's largest rivers—the Ganges and the Brahmaputra. The two mighty rivers converge in the middle of the country, before flowing into the Indian Ocean.

The land is densely veined with rivers and streams and forms a massive delta as the waters criss-cross their way across the plain. Islands form and disappear depending on the season. There is a continual tug of war between the rich silt-laden rivers rushing into the bay and the ocean backing into the land. The inhabitants of this area and their livelihoods are constantly subject to nature's unpredictability. The mud deposited by the rivers makes for fertile crops, but constant flooding and saltwater from the sea disrupt development. Many people live in makeshift or raised dwellings as the ground beneath their feet is often submerged. Borders and boundaries are in flux, hostage to the monsoon's vagaries in any given year. In 1970, this cartographic challenge created problems, not just for Pakistan's two separated wings, but also for India.*[1]

There were very few roads and barely any infrastructure or electricity beyond the main cities in East Pakistan in 1970. Earlier that year, on 23 October, the government's early warning system had cautioned people of an impending storm and urged evacuation. In the end, the cyclone had not been as severe as forecast. Three weeks later, despite government officials being fully aware of the approaching cyclone, the message sent out was vastly understated. In any case, the early notification system was rudimentary and, as much of the country lacked electricity or radios, it was difficult to disseminate information, especially where it mattered most.

Just before midnight, on 11 November, as people slept, the storm made landfall with lashing rain, winds gusts between 115 and 150 miles per hour and a devastating twenty-five-foot tidal wave. The cyclone tore its way through the country, wiping out villages and entire communities. It ripped the clothes off of people, shredded houses and huts and flung the bodies of cattle and people indiscriminately. The tidal wave submerged entire villages and an estimated 500,000 people perished, making it the worst natural disaster in recent memory.

Sydney Schanberg, of the *New York Times*, describes the condition in horrifying detail: 'Bodies, human and animal, were everywhere—stuck in

---

\*    'India and Bangladesh began the exchange of over 160 enclaves—small areas of sovereignty completely surrounded on all sides by another country in August 2015—and, in doing so, ended a dispute that has lasted almost seventy years. For cartographers and others curious about geopolitical oddities, however, it was the end of an era. The exchange between India and Bangladesh means that the world will not only lose one of its most unique borders, but it will also lose the only third-order enclave in the world—one surrounded by an enclave surrounded by an enclave surrounded by another state. It is confusing, so let me spell it out: Dahala Khagrabari, the third-order enclave in question, was a part of India, surrounded by a Bangladeshi enclave, which was surrounded by an Indian enclave, which was surrounded by Bangladesh.' (Source: Adam Taylor, *Washington Post*)

trees, lying in rice paddies, beginning to surface from the small ponds where they had sunk. Most were of strangers carried miles by the awesome wave, sometimes even from distant islands.

'People wandered naked, wailing the names of kin who did not respond. Over 9,000 marine fishing boats were lost, along with 60 per cent of fishermen. The rice crop, East Pakistanis' staple food, was wiped out and an area of 8,000 square miles destroyed.'[2]

With 500,000 people dead or missing, and food supplies gone, the cyclone had created a massive humanitarian crisis. Helicopters were required to drop food shipments because the country was largely inaccessible after the storm. Water, clothing and shelter were desperately needed, but the response from Islamabad was inadequate. Even though Pakistan's military government had all the necessary equipment and logistical capability at its disposal, there seemed to be no national relief response being organized on the scale or timeline needed to avert a humanitarian disaster.

On 21 November 1970, the *New York Times* reported that the United States had sent six helicopters that had not yet arrived. The Pakistani government had deployed only three aircraft for relief work: a seaplane, a small land plane and just one helicopter. The Indian government had offered to help but had been turned down. The West Pakistanis had no desire to expose any internal weakness to a country that was a sworn enemy nor to provide it with an opportunity to appear as the saviour of the East Pakistan Bengalis.

## Crisis Begins to Mount

Amid all of this, Pakistan had been gearing up for national elections to be held on 7 December 1970. The objective was to transfer power from the army to a democratically elected civilian government. After over a decade of military rule, General Yahya Khan, who took over the government in 1969, had announced his intention to restore democracy. The elections were to be based on the principle of one man, one vote.

Relations between the East and West Pakistanis had been fraying for some time. Partition had arranged a marriage between two distinct and very different cultural communities on the basis of their shared religion.

However, over the years their cultural differences proved greater than the bond of religion. The uneven treatment of the East Pakistan Bengalis by the West Pakistanis pushed them towards separation.

Rawalpindi, the seat of Pakistan's military, had always held the reins of power. Dominated by the Punjabis, who looked down on their co-religionists, the Bengalis had felt discriminated against racially, economically and politically.

In 1970, the population of West Pakistan was approximately 61 million. East Pakistan's population of 76 million outnumbered the West by 25 per cent. On election day, the Bengalis of East Pakistan went to the polls in record numbers. The memory of government indifference to the suffering created by the cyclone was fresh in their minds and the election turned into a referendum on Yahya's government. East Pakistan voted as a block and swept its candidate, Mujibur Rahman, and his party, the Awami League, into power. Mujibur won 160 of 162 seats in East Pakistan. Although Bhutto won in West Pakistan, Mujibur won overall as East Pakistan had more seats due to its substantially larger population. As the winner, Mujibur had the mandate to form the new government.

Mujibur Rahman was born in British India in 1920. He became involved in politics at an early age, joining the protests to end colonial rule. When the British left in 1947, they oversaw the partition of the Indian subcontinent into two countries along religious lines. India declared itself a secular country. Although the majority of its citizens were Hindus, a substantial Muslim population remained within India. Pakistan, in contrast, declared itself an Islamic state. It was allocated land where Muslims were a majority.

The contours of the new country of Pakistan—two swaths of land separated by a thousand miles—prevented any real assimilation and doomed the two sides to perpetual conflict, which contributed to the inevitable decoupling of the country. The religious knot that was the premise for the merging of two distinct and culturally diverse populations into a cohesive unit began to fray almost immediately after independence from the British.

Since Partition in 1947, Mujibur had become disillusioned with the leadership of the newly independent Pakistan and resented the unequal relationship.

In 1948, West Pakistan's Muslim League announced that Urdu should be made the official language of Pakistan. This incensed the Bengalis of East Pakistan. Most Bengalis neither spoke nor understood Urdu. Strikes and protests broke out. Insult turned to injury when Jinnah, on a visit to Dhaka University in March, declared, 'While the language of the province can be Bengali, the state language of Pakistan is going to be Urdu and no other language. Anyone who tries to mislead you is really an enemy of Pakistan.'[3] Protests were led by the Muslim Students' League and Mujibur was one of its leaders. He and several student leaders were arrested. Although they were released later, Bengali resentment against West Pakistanis had set in.

In 1949, Mujibur co-founded the Awami League, whose agenda was autonomy for East Pakistan. In 1952, West Pakistan tried once again to impose Urdu as the state language. Predictably, East Pakistan objected. In 1956, Awami League leaders pushed ahead with their demands for provincial autonomy under the new constitution of Pakistan. During this period, Mujibur was in and out of jail, wearing his arrests as a badge of honour and burnishing his credentials as the leader of the Bengali cause.

In 1966, matters came to a head when the Bengali nationalist parties under Mujibur's leadership put forward a six-point plan that, in essence, was a bid for autonomy. The plan called for a federal system with representation based on population. The central government was to be restricted to foreign affairs and defence. The implementation and collection of taxes would remain with the province, and an agreed-upon sum would be paid to the centre. The programme even suggested separate currencies and foreign exchange earnings accounts, but most egregious, in the eyes of the West Pakistanis, was the demand for a militia under local control.

To government officials based in Islamabad, this was nothing short of sedition. They viewed this as a demand for secession, and to them it spelled the end of Pakistan. In 1968, Ayub Khan, the military chief and leader of Pakistan, had Mujibur and thirty-five others arrested in what is now famously known as the Agartala Case. They were charged with going to Agartala in Tripura, India to enlist Indian support for establishing an independent country for the Bengalis of Pakistan.

As the trials began, testimonials about coercion by the government inflamed the East Pakistani public, which stormed the court and demanded the case be withdrawn. The government eventually dropped the case. Everyone was released, but the call for an independent Bangladesh had begun.

Bengali grievances were not just about the preservation of their language and culture. The deep-rooted economic disparity and inequitable allocation of resources between the two wings had been a festering sore since Partition.

The centre of government resided in West Pakistan. Dominated by West Pakistanis, the focus in the early years was on industrial development. East Pakistan was 95 per cent rural and depended on agricultural goods. That put East Pakistan at a disadvantage, both in terms of investment from the centre and development opportunities. The resulting income disparities were significant.

## Table 1: Per capita income in East and West Pakistan (1959–60 prices, in Pakistani rupees)[4]

| YEAR | PAKISTAN | WEST PAKISTAN | EAST PAKISTAN | EAST–WEST GAP |
|------|----------|---------------|---------------|---------------|
| 1949–50 | 311 | 338 | 287 | 51 |
| 1959–60 | 318 | 366 | 278 | 88 |
| 1969–70 | 424 | 537 | 331 | 206 |

| YEAR | SPENDING ON WEST PAKISTAN (IN MILLIONS OF PAKISTANI RUPEES) | SPENDING ON EAST PAKISTAN (IN MILLIONS OF PAKISTANI RUPEES) | AMOUNT SPENT ON EAST AS PERCENTAGE OF WEST |
|------|-----------|-----------|-----------|
| 1950–55 | 11,290 | 5,240 | 46.4 |
| 1955–60 | 16,550 | 5,240 | 31.7 |
| 1960–65 | 33,550 | 14,040 | 41.8 |
| 1965–70 | 51,950 | 21,410 | 41.2 |
| Total | 113,340 | 45,930 | 40.5 |

Source: Reports of the advisory panels for the Fourth Five-Year Plan 1970–75, Vol. 1, published by the Planning Commission of Pakistan.

East Pakistan suffered a significantly poorer economic outcome, in large part, due to the deliberate pro-West and anti-East wing policy adopted by the central government in Islamabad. For instance, despite having 60 per cent of the population, East Pakistan's share of central government development expenditure was as low as 20 per cent during 1950–51 to 1954–55, only to peak at 36 per cent during the Third Five-Year Plan period, that is, from 1965–66 to 1969–70. To aid the process of industrialization in the western wing, the central government systematically transferred visible as well as invisible resources away from the East to the West. West Pakistan imposed a complicated tax structure that depleted resources in East Pakistan and transferred them to the western wing. Foreign aid was rationed out disproportionately as well, and foreign revenues generated by the East were systematically moved to Islamabad.[5]

The 1970 election results widened the rift that had developed between the two wings. Bhutto received 81 out of 138 seats in West Pakistan and not a single seat in the East. Mujibur swept the polls in East Pakistan, winning 160 out of 162 seats but none in the West. The country fractured. Due to his numerical advantage, Mujibur was declared the duly elected winner. The outcome of the election, placing a Bengali as head of state, was unpalatable to both West Pakistan's Zulfikar Bhutto, head of Pakistan People's Party, and the military.

The law required that the new government draft a constitution and take charge within 120 days. General Yahya Khan set 3 March 1971 as the date for the new government to be installed. Bhutto, still seething at his loss at the polls, threatened to boycott the new government. General Yahya Khan was caught between the democratic imperative of recognizing and accepting Mujibur as the newly elected leader of Pakistan and a coalition of West Pakistanis led by Bhutto who refused to accept the outcome of the election. To Yahya Khan's credit, he urged the two frontrunners to work out a power-sharing arrangement. Despite several meetings, no agreement was worked out that satisfied either party. Mujibur offered Bhutto effective control over the West, with himself heading an autonomous East Pakistan. He was rebuffed. The talks went nowhere. Yahya either lacked the leadership skills to push an agreement through or, as many have suggested, was simply inebriated much of the time and no match for Bhutto, who was determined to run Pakistan. A senior minister had warned Yahya earlier that if Bhutto did not become the prime minister within a year, he would literally go mad.[6] Bhutto's ambition was matched by his arrogance. In 1963, President Kennedy complimented him, saying, 'If you were American you would be in my cabinet.' Bhutto's rather ungracious response was, 'Be careful, Mr President, if I were American *you* would be in *my* cabinet.'[7]

With negotiations between Bhutto and Mujibur at an impasse, and pressure mounting from all sides, Yahya Khan stalled. He postponed the seating of the new government to 25 March 1971. BBC correspondent Owen Bennett-Jones observed that 'the future of East Pakistan depended on a struggle among three men: West Pakistani General Agha Mohammed Yahya Khan, a habitual drunk; Sheikh Mujibur Rahman, a professional agitator; and Zulfikar Ali Bhutto, a political operator par excellence.'[8]

Experts who have studied this period in Pakistan's turbulent history agree that Mujibur neither intended nor wanted the break-up of Pakistan. What he desired was regional autonomy. After all, he had just won the election to lead the entire nation. Why would he prefer to lead only a part of it? What transpired in the next few days convinced Mujibur that Yahya Khan and Bhutto, backed by the military, were united in their resolve to prevent him from forming the government.

Once it became clear that the West, led by Bhutto, was looking for ways to avoid handing over power to Mujibur, strikes broke out all over East Pakistan. Mujibur Rahman took his grievances directly to the people. On 7 March 1971, he gave a speech accusing Yahya Khan of not keeping his word and betraying democracy. Protests in East Pakistan turned violent. The more militant Awami League members went on a rampage, killing several West Pakistanis and other non-Bengali Muslims derogatorily referred to as 'Biharis' at the time.[†]

This was an excuse to intervene that the army was waiting for. The army, dominated by the West Pakistanis, wanted to teach the Bengalis a lesson.

---

† 'Biharis' were Muslims who had migrated after the partition from mainland India. They were recruited into the military and police that was dominated by West Pakistani Punjabis and given preference over the Bengalis.

It was immediately mobilized to suppress the agitation that had become widespread. In a last-ditch effort to negotiate a settlement, Yahya, Bhutto and Mujibur met on 22 March. They failed to reach an understanding, and on 25 March, Yahya Khan flew back to West Pakistan with Bhutto following him.

## Operation Searchlight

At 11.25 p.m. on 25 March 1971, an uneasy stillness settled over Dacca (now Dhaka). As the residents of the city slept, the army prepared to assault the city. As darkness covered their tracks, four American-made M-24 tanks rolled stealthily through the streets of the capital of East Pakistan. Their first mission was the university where most of the students were studying or asleep. No one suspected the army would attack its own citizens. The army selected two dormitories as its first target, Iqbal Hall housing Muslim students, and Jagannath Hall housing Hindus. Shelling began and within five minutes thirty people were dead. The soldiers who accompanied the tanks ran through the buildings killing whomever they could. 'Within a quarter of an hour 109 students were dead. The bodies of the Muslim students were dragged up to the roof of Iqbal Hall, where they were left to the vultures. The bodies of the Hindu students were heaped together like faggots‡ and later in the night, six students, who had been spared, were ordered to dig a grave for them. After they had dug the grave, they were shot.'[9]

Professors and intellectuals were next. Hindus, in particular, were targeted for killing. Simultaneously tanks and soldiers moved through the capital, killing people and destroying property. Police stations were set ablaze with officers in them. Shockingly, members of the army itself, the East Pakistan Rifles, were mowed down because they were Bengalis. Foreign correspondents holed up in the Intercontinental Hotel reported that Dacca was in flames.

---

‡ According to the dictionary, the term refers to a bundle of sticks bound together. It could also mean a ball or roll of chopped liver.

At 1.30 a.m. tanks arrived at Mujibur's home. Truckloads of soldiers surrounded his house and opened fire. Mujibur gave himself up; remaining calm, he told them that violence was unnecessary. He was arrested and flown to West Pakistan. Later, the soldiers returned to get his family, and finding that they had fled, they destroyed his house.

At 2.45 a.m. reporters heard machine guns firing into a crowd. The building housing the newspaper *The People* was set on fire. Soldiers then burnt down a bazaar before moving on. By the end of the blood-soaked night, 7,000 people were dead and 3,000 others were under arrest.

A curfew was imposed on Dacca and foreigners were confined indoors. It was two days before Archer Blood and Scott Butcher from the US consulate were able to venture out in their diplomatic vehicles. They saw a scorched city with dead bodies strewn everywhere. They contacted aid workers, the press and friends in Dacca. People described the cruelty and chaos created by the army action. The consulate cabled Washington describing the bloodbath but was told to tone it down.

The Pakistani army was not done yet. Over the next several months, organized massacres were conducted across the country. Human Rights Watch estimated that three million people were killed.

Anthony Mascarenhas of Karachi's *Morning News* was embedded with the West Pakistani army and provided a first-hand account of the atrocities in an explosive article called 'Genocide'. It exposed the naked brutality of the army's actions to the world and changed the history of the war.

The army had decided to invite a handful of reporters to show them how they successfully dealt with the 'freedom fighters' in what they hoped was a public relations exercise to showcase their effectiveness. But what Mascarenhas saw shook him to his core. His wife Yvonne Mascarenhas remembers him coming back distraught: 'He was absolutely shocked, stressed, upset and terribly emotional.'[10] He realized he could not write the article from Pakistan, as everything was checked by the military censors. Worried he would be shot if he tried, he left for the safety of London, on the pretext of visiting a sick relative. Once there, he headed straight to the *Sunday Times*. Mascarenhas told Harold Evans, the editor, that he had been an 'eyewitness to a huge, systematic killing spree and heard army officers describe the killings as a "final solution".[11] Evans promised to run his account of the war. An excerpt below:

> On the night of 25 March—and this I was allowed to report by the Pakistani censor—the Bengali troops and paramilitary units stationed in East Pakistan mutinied and attacked non-Bengalis with atrocious savagery.
>
> Thousands of families of unfortunate Muslims, many of them refugees from Bihar who chose Pakistan at the time of the Partition riots in 1947, were mercilessly wiped out. Women were raped, or had their breasts torn out with specially fashioned knives.
>
> Children did not escape the horror: the lucky ones were killed with their parents; but many thousands of others must go through what life remains for them with eyes gouged out and limbs roughly amputated. More than 20,000 bodies of non-Bengalis have been found in the main towns, such as Chittagong, Khulna and Jessore. The real toll, I was told everywhere in East Bengal, may have been as high as 100,000; for thousands of non-Bengalis have vanished without a trace.[12]

Mascarenhas then recounted that a 'second and worse horror' unfolded with West Pakistan's army taking over the killing. He said that as the army fanned out, they had lists of people that were to be liquidated. These included Hindus, rebels, members of the Awami League and the intelligentsia. The lists were not accurately followed and he describes many shocking killings that took place with no due process and a disregard for human life if the suspect was a Bengali.

For six days, Mascarenhas travelled with the officers of the 9th Division, headquartered at Comilla and saw at close range the 'kill and burn' missions: 'I saw Hindus, hunted from village to village and door to door, shot off-hand after a cursory "short-arm inspection" showed they were uncircumcised. I have heard screams of men bludgeoned to death … I have seen truckloads of other human targets and those who had the humanity to try to help them hauled off "for disposal" under the cover of darkness and curfew.'[13]

He wrote that he was repeatedly told by senior military officers and civil servants that 'we are determined to cleanse East Pakistan once and for all of the threat of secession, even if it means killing off two million people and ruling the province as a colony for thirty years.'[14]

Rape was used as an instrument of war to humiliate and destroy morale. The government of Bangladesh estimated that 200,000 women were raped during this period. The numbers and the brutality are just staggering. A report prepared by the American journalist Susan Brownmiller documents thousands of women who were abducted and imprisoned in rape camps and violated night after night, for months. She writes that women, and even young girls, were sexually assaulted by up to eighty men a night. A thirteen-year-old survivor who was interviewed said she was gagged to stop her screams during such attacks. One survivor, Yasmin Saikia, now a professor at Arizona State University, testified that when her fellow captives died from torture, she and other victims were forced to dig their graves.

Bina D'Costa, a peace and conflict specialist, tracked down an Australian medical doctor who, under the auspices of Planned Parenthood and the World Health Organization, had been brought in to treat some of the women and perform abortions at the end of the war. He reported that the women told him that rich and pretty captives were kept for officers and the rest of the women were distributed among the ranks. 'The women really had it rough. They didn't get enough to eat. When they got sick, they received no treatment. Lots of them died in those camps.'[15] He also reported that they were all malnourished, exhibited many deficiency diseases and had venereal diseases.

As news of the genocide spread, people began to flee. Half the inhabitants of Dacca and Chittagong left, looking for safety in the countryside. Many escaped to India. The soldiers attempted to close the borders and installed checkpoints everywhere, but the Bengalis' superior familiarity with the terrain helped them evade the troops. By the end of May 1971 almost three million refugees had entered India. The Pakistani civil war had, all of a sudden, spilled beyond its borders and into India.

As India struggled to feed and house the refugees streaming in, internal political pressure mounted on Mrs Gandhi to intervene in Pakistan's civil war and help the Bengalis. India now had a pretext to join the war. The East Pakistanis, betrayed by their government and shocked by the brutality of reprisals, demanded immediate independence.

## The White House

Over 10,000 miles away in Washington, DC, the White House and the State Department followed the events in South Asia with increasing alarm as Pakistan unravelled and slid into civil war. The cables arriving from the US embassy in Dacca were not encouraging. Telegrams from Dacca reported that the Pakistani authorities had unleashed a 'wave of terror' against their own citizens in the East and were killing unarmed civilians. They also described that houses were being torched and families killed as they ran out of their homes to avoid the fire.[16] Even National Security Advisor Henry Kissinger, who was decidedly pro-Pakistani, thought Yahya's actions 'reckless'.[17] The army was behaving ruthlessly. Yahya Khan and his generals conducted what amounted to ethnic cleansing. Samuel Hoskinson, a member of the National Security Council, presciently warned that doing nothing would reflect poorly on the US when history books were written.[18]

Seeing the horror on television, the American public was appalled. They empathized with Bengali aspirations for independence. Shocked by Pakistani atrocities and concerned about India's mounting refugee crisis, the US government's response was mixed. Members of Congress, led by Edward Kennedy, wanted the White House to censure Pakistan. They were joined in large part by the State Department. The White House alone remained a bastion of pro-Pakistani hardliners.

The crisis erupting in South Asia could not have come at a worse time for President Richard Nixon. He was in the midst of establishing his foreign policy legacy by engaging with communist China. Yahya Khan was an integral part of his plans. The last thing he wanted at this moment was the distraction of Pakistan's civil war.

In 1967, the year before his successful campaign for the president's office, he wrote a paper for *Foreign Affairs* making the case for bringing China out of isolation. Nehru, of course, prior to the 1962 war, made the same argument but the West had not been prepared to heed his advice. Although sceptics viewed Nixon's suggestions as ambitious and unrealistic, he persisted. When Harry Robbins and H.R. Haldeman first told Kissinger about Nixon's determination to visit China, Kissinger, unaware of his resolve, responded, 'fat chance'.[19] He mocked the president's idea and told his staff, 'Our leader has taken leave of reality; he thinks this is the moment to establish normal relations with communist China. He has just ordered me to make this flight of fancy come true ... China!'[20] Conservative Republicans expressed concern about Nixon's willingness to make friends with a communist country. They had not forgotten that, just four years earlier, the Red Guards had burnt down the British embassy during the Cultural Revolution and tried to force Donald Hobson, the British charge d' affaires, to apologize in public for his country's conduct.[21]

Nixon most wanted to be remembered and admired for his leadership in world affairs. He once confided to Theodore H. White that the country could run itself domestically without a president but that, for foreign policy, the president was essential.[22]

Nixon had inherited an unenviable set of foreign policy problems. The war in Vietnam had scarred the country and he was determined to end US involvement in Southeast Asia. Student protests had become a perpetual public relations headache for the administration. Nixon insisted peace not be bought at the expense of American honour, and the tortured negotiations to withdraw from Vietnam bled through most of his presidential tenure. With Russia, a country for whom he seemed to display little affection, he pursued negotiations with muscular diplomacy. He pushed to limit the arms race and vigorously pursued the Strategic Arms Limitation Talks (SALT), but his relations with Russia remained inconsistent with a one step forward, one step back pace through his presidency. Nixon's most enduring and transformational policy, however, remained the opening of relations with China. Bringing China into the global economy was to change the entire world's economic and political landscape forever.

After being elected president, Nixon decided he wanted to run foreign policy from the White House. Although he appointed his friend William Rogers as secretary of state, he hired Kissinger to be his own foreign policy man in the White House. Together they conducted all important negotiations. Both thrived on secrecy and power, and they set the foreign policy agenda for the US, circumventing the State Department. This inevitably led to friction between Secretary of State Rogers and Kissinger. The two fought over turf and continually tried to undermine one another.

Although he derided them publicly, Nixon liked to surround himself with Ivy League intellectuals. Moynihan, his domestic policy tsar, and Kissinger, who ran foreign policy, were Harvard professors. He let them compete for his attention and did not seem to care that tension between his advisors caused morale to plummet. The atmosphere was infused with distrust and apprehension as cabinet members spied on one another and taped each other's conversations.

Nixon was a loner, unlike most politicians, and he disliked dealing with people. He told Haldeman, his chief of staff, that he wanted to build a wall around himself.[23] He told Haldeman that 'his job was to keep other people away from his two offices. Haldeman memos were the President's preferred medium of communication.' He relied on Haldeman to negotiate tensions within the White House and doing the firing and insulting. He was not above manipulating people and preying on their insecurities. He displayed a streak of meanness and sometimes tested Kissinger's loyalty by making anti-Semitic remarks, such as calling him a 'Jew boy'.[24] The Nixon tapes reveal that, despite his grasp of politics, Nixon was often crass and unpresidential.

Nixon's accumulated insecurities growing up may have contributed to his flawed personality. He was born in Loma Linda, a small town in California. Although his memoirs gloss over his childhood hardships, his early years, by all accounts, seems emotionally bleak. His father was crude, harsh and unsuccessful for much of his life. He lost two brothers to tuberculosis at an early age. His deceased older brother had been his parents' favourite, with the charm and good looks that Nixon lacked. His mother, whom he adored, was caught up with making ends meet and nursing her sick children. Luckily, Nixon excelled in school and this asset was his ticket out of oblivion. He had hoped to go to Yale but was unable to afford the expense; so his first exposure to the wider world was Duke University Law School. Although he did well there, he was not a social success. His contemporaries at college described him as tense, awkward and a workaholic, more often hunched over books than in a circle of friends. He was nicknamed 'Iron Butt' in law school for the long hours he sat studying.[25]

Journalist Tom Wicker describes Nixon walking in the lobby of the US Senate 'slowly, shoulders slumped, hands jammed in his trouser pocket, head down ... preoccupied, brooding and gloomy'.[26] This was his appearance when he was the vice president at age forty-four, with a bright future ahead of him. The description captures the darkness inside him, to which so many of his colleagues alluded. He was, by all accounts, an introverted and lonely man. Only four people had regular access to him. Kissinger and Moynihan, recently recruited to join his team, were among them. All his staffers slowly understood his need for solitude as he became more formal and aloof, preferring communication via memoranda.[27]

At college he developed a lifelong antipathy towards privilege and, to his credit, as president he pursued domestic policies that were significant and enlightened. He oversaw the desegregation of schools in the south, committed $100 million in federal funds to combat cancer, established the Environmental Protection Agency and put a man on the moon.

Despite his personal shortcomings, Nixon is largely responsible for the new world order that we live in today. His initiative to integrate China into the world politically and economically was as transformational as it was visionary.

## Nixon Opens China

The Nixon administration's early feelers to China expressing an interest from the US to begin a dialogue were initially met by Chinese reserve. Approximately 134 formal meetings had taken place on and off for well over a decade in Europe, without any threads of connectivity established. The endless yet superficial minuet had formalized into a sterile non-relationship. Nixon was determined to change that. Early on he instructed Walter Stoessel, Jr, the US ambassador in Warsaw, to initiate communications with Chinese diplomats at a social event. Kissinger recounts the incident thus: 'The setting for this encounter was a Yugoslav fashion show in the Polish capital.' The Chinese diplomats, apparently caught by surprise, fled the scene. According to Kissinger, one of the Chinese diplomats later recalled leaving in order to avoid a conversation with the Americans who were trying to engage them. Undeterred, the American diplomats chased after them shouting that President Nixon wished to talk with the Chinese. This undignified and far from diplomatic approach did result in an invitation to Stoessel from the Chinese ambassador in Warsaw to resume talks.[28]

Of the many countries that Nixon visited when he was in government, he singled out Romania and Pakistan as potential conduits through which to pursue the relationship. He also decided, with Kissinger, to conduct negotiations in secret, just as they were doing with Vietnam and the Soviets. For a while, communications were sent on a dual track, but ultimately, the Romanian channel was abandoned with Pakistan alone playing the central role in Nixon's grand scheme to engage China.

The Chinese also seemed to prefer the Pakistanis. The US and the Chinese worried that the Russians would obtain information from the Romanian channel and sabotage the fledgling relationship. The White House also kept the State Department in the dark to prevent China sceptics from interfering with their plans. The prospect of a visit by a sitting US President to China would be a bombshell. It would certainly make every global power pay attention, and secrecy appealed to both Nixon and Kissinger.

Yahya Khan met with President Nixon in October 1970. Nixon asked him to communicate to the Chinese that he would be willing to send a high-ranking emissary to Beijing and considered a Sino-American rapprochement 'essential' to his policies.[29] Yahya Khan conveyed the message when he visited China mid-November as the cyclone was destroying the eastern part of his country. In his memoirs, Kissinger recounts (with some impatience) that it took three weeks, until 8 December, to receive a response, which was relayed by Pakistan's Ambassador Hilaly in Washington.[30] One wonders if Kissinger was oblivious to the disaster that had engulfed his Pakistani friend. It is telling that, in his description of events in a later portion of his book, he relates questioning Yahya Khan about the security of his status as the president of Pakistan, given the imminent elections. It was clear that the overriding priority for Nixon and Kissinger was Pakistan's reliability as a conduit to China rather than its integrity as a country.

By early 1971, Kissinger and Nixon began to focus on the rapidly deteriorating situation in Pakistan. Their primary concern was to help the current regime stay in power. The scale of human suffering from the fallout of the cyclone and civil war did not move them to intervene on behalf of East Pakistan, despite the news coverage and entreaties from their embassies in Dacca and Delhi.[§]

While Nixon and Kissinger anxiously awaited the Chinese response, Mrs Gandhi had been swept back into office after winning elections in India. Meanwhile, in Pakistan, political temperatures were at a boiling point. On 13 March, having consulted with senior officials earlier in the week, Kissinger decided on a course described by a State Department official as 'massive inaction'.[31]

There was some confusion among members of the US Congress and the State Department, who were reading reports from multiple sources of the deteriorating conditions in East Pakistan. Unaware of the White House's secret China enterprise, they could not understand the reluctance of the president to censure Yahya Khan.

Although many fingers have been pointed at various elements for the break-up of Pakistan, it is clear that Mujibur would not have pushed to secede had Yahya Khan honoured the election results and allowed him to form a government. He communicated as much to Archer Blood, the brave US consul in Dacca.[32]

The failure of the March talks between the principals, followed by the repression that began on the night of 25 March 1971, torpedoed any possible reconciliation and drew East and West Pakistan and their allies into a confrontation that would have adverse consequences for India's relationship with the US.

## Dissent from Dacca

Archer Blood arrived in Dacca in March 1970 to take over as the head of the US consulate in East Pakistan. Blood was tall, serious and handsome

---

§   The US did provide humanitarian relief for the cyclone but did not put pressure on Yahya to stop the killings that began in March 1971.

in an athletic sort of way. He was familiar with South Asia, having been posted in Dacca for a short stint in 1960. He had enjoyed exploring the country with his wife Meg. He was pleased to be posted back to Dacca after a rather unhappy assignment in Greece, where the interdepartmental rivalries of Washington had inserted themselves. His career so far had been ordinary. Nothing he had done until this point suggested a man who would put his career on the line by standing up to his government in Washington for a set of principles.

Blood had observed that economic development had been minimal since his last visit. East Pakistan was visibly poorer than its counterpart in the west. NGOs and aid agencies descended on the country in droves, each with its own prescription for progress, and it was clear that they were helping East Pakistan more than Islamabad.

Archer Blood began to understand the depth of East Pakistan's grievances after the cyclone hit. He and his wife drove around and saw the devastation first-hand. They observed the lack of assistance from the West Pakistanis in alleviating the suffering but had not yet understood that this was the tipping point that would split the country.

Initially, despite his empathy for Bengali aspirations for independence, Blood believed that Bhutto, Mujibur and Yahya should work out a compromise. The massacres inflicted on the East Pakistanis by the army after the breakdown of talks in March 1971 changed his views. The entire consulate was appalled at the killings and called it a genocide. He felt his conscience demanded that he speak out. His consulate sent cable after cable describing in detail the horror that was unfolding in East Pakistan. Although his colleagues at the State Department were sympathetic, the White House was determined to support Yahya Khan and it ignored him. On 6 April 1971, in a last-ditch effort to call attention to the bloodbath, Archer Blood drafted a cable, signed by almost every member of the consulate in Dacca, which would effectively end his career in government.

The 'Blood Telegram', as it came to be called, was a dissent cable. Rarely used, and only under extraordinary circumstances, the purpose of a dissent cable is to formally lodge an objection to official US policy. The Blood Telegram declared that the US policy towards East Pakistan was morally bankrupt, and that the US government had an obligation to speak out against the genocide. Blood purposely sent it out unclassified, knowing that would give it the widest possible distribution.[33]

Kissinger was livid. He told Nixon that the Dacca consulate was in open rebellion. By the end of April 1971, Blood was recalled and, though he could not fire him, Kissinger made sure he languished in the backwaters of the State Department for the rest of his career.

## Principles at Stake

Ambassador Keating in Delhi supported the views of his colleagues in Dacca and said, 'this is a time when principles make the best policies'.[34] A well-respected former Republican senator from New York, he was troubled by the genocide next door and repeatedly tried to convince the White House to restrain Yahya. Despite having been a loyal Nixon supporter, the president called Keating a 'traitor' privately for challenging his Pakistan policy. Keating considered himself a friend of Nixon and had defended his unpopular Vietnam policies in India. In a private meeting with Kissinger at the White House, he requested an honest explanation for what he considered an inexcusably biased policy. Kissinger admitted the policy was being driven by Nixon's special feelings for Yahya.[35] Although Kissinger expressed sympathy for the ambassador's perspective during the meeting, behind his back both Nixon and Kissinger dismissed his views Nixon complained that he had been influenced by India. Kissinger who seemed to miss the irony pandered to his boss explaining, 'They [Indians] are superb flatters, Mr President. They are masters at flattery. They are masters at subtle flattery. That's how they survived 600 years. They suck up—their great skill is to suck up to people in key positions.'[36]

'Operation Searchlight', as the 25 March crackdown in Dacca came to be known, created an exodus of people fleeing to India. Initially, the refugees were a religious mix of people who had demanded independence and were being persecuted by the West Pakistani army, but by April 1971 it was mainly the Hindu Bengali-Pakistanis who were fleeing what many Indians saw as ethnic cleansing. Sydney Schanberg described the systematic targeting of Hindus by the Pakistani army: 'The Pakistani army painted big yellow "H's" on the Hindu shops still standing ... The army forced Moslems friendly to Hindus to loot and burn Hindu houses; the Moslems were told that if they did not attack Hindus, they themselves would be killed.' He reported that of the more than six million Bengalis who are believed to have fled to India to escape the terror, at least four million were Hindus.[37] Although the Indian government had begun to canvas Western countries to help manage the problem, it kept the Hindu/Muslim demographic from the Indian press as many were concerned it might inflame tensions among the religious groups in India. East Pakistan's Hindu population at the time of Partition was 22 per cent approximately; by the 2011 census, it had dropped to 8.5 per cent.[38]

For months, the Gandhi government had been watching the unfolding mess next door. Stung that its offers of help were rejected when the cyclone hit, it now had to deal with the consequences of Pakistan's political intransigence. The Indian press ratcheted up calls to intercede, while Islamabad accused India of encouraging the dismemberment of Pakistan by aiding East Pakistan's armed movement, the Mukti Bahini, and to Mujibur's independence movement.

There was no doubt that an independent Bangladesh would be beneficial to India. Pakistan and India had gone to war in 1947 and again in 1965, with a cold peace in the intervening years. India had always been obliged to defend itself on two fronts. Converting East Pakistan from a foe to an ally would give India considerable leverage over Pakistan. However, in March 1971, despite the obvious advantages of intervention, Mrs Gandhi held out as she fully expected Mujibur's independence movement to prevail and for East Pakistan to become an independent country.

The two countries—the US, firmly allied with Islamabad, and India, equally supportive of Mujibur—watched each other with growing suspicion and anger. India, unaware of the China initiative, was also baffled by US refusal to rein in Yahya Khan in light of all the press and media attention to the atrocities perpetrated by Islamabad.

On 10 May 1971, despite Yahya's troubles, Kissinger sent a message to China's premier Zhou Enlai via the Pakistani channel. It conveyed that President Nixon was prepared to visit Peking and that he, Kissinger, would come as the emissary to prepare for the visit.

As the summer deepened and temperatures rose to unbearable levels, India embarked on a worldwide campaign to involve other countries in the political crisis in Pakistan. On the strength of having to shelter close to six million refugees, Mrs Gandhi pushed the international community to pressure Pakistan to seat Mujibur Rahman, respect the election results and stop the killings so its citizens could return to their homes. She knew that Pakistan was not prepared to have a government headed by Mujibur, nor take back the refugees, most of whom were Hindu. Was she being disingenuous? Parliament, the news media and human rights activists at home were all calling for her to intervene, but she understood that she would be criticized by the world if she intervened militarily without seeking international support for a political solution.

India embarked on a public relations campaign. Mrs Gandhi sent her diplomats out to various countries to present India's perspective and request their help. The international response was lukewarm. Although some offers of aid were made, the rest of the world preferred to treat the situation as an internal problem for Pakistan to manage. Nobody offered any assistance to resolve the political situation. Mrs Gandhi was particularly stung by the lack of support from the non-aligned nations. Her external affairs minister, Swaran Singh, took India one step closer towards war by making statements indicating that India would be prepared to take matters into its own hands if Pakistan did not reverse course.[39]

## Drawn Daggers: US-India

On 18 May 1971, Mrs Gandhi warned Pakistan in a speech that 'India was fully prepared to fight if the situation is forced upon us'.[40]

Nixon and Kissinger, propelled by their dislike of India, were convinced that Indians were planning to destroy Pakistan. Kissinger said that reliable sources had informed him that India was planning to attack and take over East Pakistan. On 23 May 1971, Nixon ordered all aid to India would be cut off if it launched an attack, despite knowing that India, a poor country, was having trouble feeding the refugees. He told Kissinger, 'By God, we will cut off economic aid.' In June he told Kissinger that '[he] wouldn't … help the Indians, the Indians are no goddamn good.'[41]

India would eventually host 10 million refugees.⁵ The World Bank estimated that the refugees were costing India $700 million for six months. The US provided about 15 per cent of the costs and India bore 70 per cent, which it could ill afford.⁴² Cholera had broken out in the overcrowded camps and thousands had died. The numbers became unmanageable.

The Indian embassy's efforts to persuade the United States to rein in Pakistan having failed, it decided to appeal directly to the US Congress and the American public. Indian embassy officials appeared on television networks and college campuses and gave interviews to newspapers. They hoped that exposing the public to Pakistani atrocities would pressure the White House into action. Kissinger was annoyed; he issued a directive that Ambassador L.K. Jha should not be received by any official above desk officer.

Nixon was unmoved by India's predicament and complained that 'the goddamn Indians' were pushing for war. Kissinger, who was not particularly fond of the Indians, wound him up, chiming in that 'they are the most aggressive goddamn people around'.⁴³ In the recently released transcripts of White House tapes, Professor Gary Bass describes Kissinger as contemptuously condemning the Indians and calling them 'a scavenging people'.⁴⁴

In the meantime, communications with China had progressed and on 31 May 1971, Yahya conveyed an invitation from Peking for Kissinger to visit for talks. This was the news that the White House had been anxiously awaiting. Nixon and Kissinger immediately began planning Kissinger's secret visit to China with Pakistan as the conduit. It became crucial to them that Yahya remain in power and India not rock the boat.

On 28 May 1971, in the hopes of buying time, Nixon had written to Yahya and Mrs Gandhi. He urged Yahya to show restraint and to lean towards a political rather than military solution. This advice seemed a bit late as thousands had already been killed and over three million refugees had fled with others following them. His note to Mrs Gandhi

---

⁵    According to the UNHCR, 10 million is the universally accepted number of refugees that arrived in India during this period, though the numbers varied depending on when the reporting took place.

was a veiled directive not to intervene militarily, but it was couched in the language of diplomacy meant to obfuscate.[45] A handwritten message from the president to be gentle with Pakistan was circulated to the State Department and the CIA.[46]

The president liked the Pakistanis. They were always gracious, never criticized his policies and went out of their way to orchestrate his engagement with China. He had visited South Asia in 1953 as the vice president and was given the royal treatment in Pakistan. He felt Pakistan was a country he could work with and placed it in his friends and allies camp. As the vice president, he became an advocate for Pakistan, promoting a strong alliance and supporting its request for military aid. But it was when he visited as a private citizen that his loyalty was cemented. The Pakistanis treated him with the same deference as they had when he was in office. This left a lasting impression on Nixon, who loved pomp and ceremony and was sensitive to his status. He told Haldeman and Kissinger that he considered Yahya a 'real leader' and 'very intelligent'.[47] Yahya, in return, proved his worth by working tirelessly to help Nixon connect with China.

Yahya Khan grew up in the military. He became a general at forty and by forty-five was the commander-in-chief. He bragged about his mistresses and ability to down a bottle of scotch a night. Nixon had taken to this man with his bushy eyebrows, hearty personality and hard drinking ways but, as Yahya dithered and events in his country spun out of control, he conceded with sadness that his earlier assessment of Yahya's skills as a leader were overly optimistic.

Nixon habitually complained of the US liberal elites' partiality for India and was irritated by the State Department's perspective on events in South Asia, which he considered overly pro-Indian.

Nixon disliked India and despised Mrs Gandhi. At a National Security Council meeting on 16 July 1971, he called the Indians 'a slippery, treacherous people'.[48]

Nixon's antipathy for India and Mrs Gandhi had deep roots. His childhood experiences had instilled in him a suspicion and dislike for people of privilege. Mrs Gandhi, with her elite pedigree, belonging to the ruling class, represented everything Nixon loathed. Her haughty personality and left-leaning politics alienated him. He once expressed an admiration for her astute ability to win elections. Aside from that one attribute, which as a politician he appreciated, he had little interest in her or India. The seemingly irrational reaction to her may have an explanation in the past. Nixon was known to hold deep grudges and seldom forgot a slight.

Nixon's first exposure to India had been in 1953 when Nehru was the prime minister. Nixon had not warmed to him either. He described Nehru as 'brilliant, haughty, aristocratic, a man of quick temper and enormous ego'.[49] It is hard to imagine how he would have known about Nehru's temper or ego first-hand. He and Nehru did not spend much time together on his visit. It was also unlikely that a man as cultivated and refined as Nehru would have lost his temper in front of him. Nehru, unlike Nixon, never used profanity.

While some of what Nixon wrote about Nehru's political charisma was positive, it was mostly based on hearsay. His conclusion about Nehru remained unflattering, 'Of all the world leaders I have met, Nehru would certainly rank among the most intelligent. He could also be arrogant, abrasive, self-righteous and suffocating. He had a distinct superiority complex that he took few pains to conceal.'[50]

Nehru's policy of non-alignment was a red flag for Nixon, who considered socialist leanings unacceptable. Nixon complained that Nehru lectured him about the politics of the region and accused him of being obsessed with the dangers of a militaristic Pakistan. In his book, Nixon wrote: 'Though his [Nehru's] words concerned Pakistan's supposed threat to India, his demeanour foreshadowed the time eighteen years later when India's Soviet-supplied army, under his daughter's leadership, dismembered and threatened to extinguish Pakistan, a goal I may have helped to deny them by "tilting" US policy in the conflict towards Pakistan.'[51]

Nixon's inability to connect with Nehru was not surprising. Nehru was everything he was not: debonair, confident, wealthy and privileged. He was an intellectual who had written many books and was revered in his country. Nixon was socially awkward and insecure. He lacked Eisenhower's gravitas or Kennedy's easy charm. It is entirely possible that Nehru treated the much younger man somewhat dismissively. He often lectured if he thought someone intellectually naïve or uninteresting, which would have burned someone as insecure as Nixon.

Mrs Gandhi piqued Nixon even more than her father did. In 1967, when Nixon was out of office, he visited the region. Having come earlier as the vice president with all the fanfare that accompanies the office, it must have been unsettling to meet the same people but be treated without consideration. He called on Mrs Gandhi who had recently become the prime minister. 'She had seemed conspicuously bored, despite the short duration of their talk. After about twenty minutes of strained chat, she asked one of her aides, in Hindi, how much longer this was going to take. Nixon had not gotten the precise meaning, but he sure caught the tone.'[52] He recalled that when he visited Pakistan, even when he was out of office, they laid out the red carpet for him. The contrast could not have been greater and, for a man as thin-skinned as Nixon, it significantly influenced his attitudes to the two countries. He was never able to overcome his anti-Indian prejudice and it compromised his ability to evaluate the subcontinent's conflict dispassionately.

Nixon's response to Mrs Gandhi was so visceral that it wasn't until the full content of the White House tapes were released that the extent of his prejudices were revealed. These tapes, which were kept from public view until this year, lay bare Nixon's shocking racism towards Indian women: 'Undoubtably the most unattractive women in the world are the Indian women ... The most sexless.' He then compares them unfavourably to black Africans whom he also diminishes by saying they have animal-like charm, 'but God, those Indians, ack, pathetic. Uch ... To me, they turn me off.'[53] And in another conversation, he wondered how they could reproduce.

In his memoirs, Kissinger wrote that his choice of words for Mrs Gandhi was unprintable, with the words 'witch' and 'bitch' being the less profane adjectives he used for her. Kissinger's analysis of the president's dislike was the following: 'Nixon and Mrs Indira Gandhi ... were not intended by fate to be personally congenial. Her assumption of almost hereditary moral superiority and her moody silences brought out all of Nixon's latent insecurities.' Kissinger's own view of Mrs Gandhi was not much better. He said that 'Mrs Gandhi had few peers in the cold-blooded calculation of the elements of power.'[54]

A year into Nixon's presidency and before the Pakistani crisis, when assistant secretary of the State Department, Joseph Sisco, suggested to Kissinger that Nixon write to Mrs Gandhi, he replied: 'He won't do it. He doesn't like her ... He doesn't include Indira in those he loves.'[55]

A decade after the Bangladesh Liberation War was over, Nixon still blamed India for the break-up of Pakistan, refusing to acknowledge Pakistan's role in its civil war. He was unable to come to terms with the contradictory facts on the ground and the evidence that his own government had provided.

## Kissinger's Role

Henry Kissinger tipped the scales further, driven by his desire to please Nixon. He had grown up in a conservative Jewish family, wore thick glasses and had a heavy German accent. He was much more a Harvard academic than a dashing diplomat. Nixon plucked him from a respectable but predictable life to become the first face of foreign policy in his administration. Although Kissinger had been a close advisor to Governor Rockefeller, it was Nixon who placed him in the limelight by making him his closest White House advisor. The short, stocky intellectual became a media star and on every Georgetown hostess's 'most wanted' list of dinner guests.

The masseur at Nixon's San Clemente hideaway once remarked that 'he [Kissinger] did not have a muscle in his body'.[56] But this was Washington and proximity to power the aphrodisiac. Only in Washington would Kissinger be considered the sexiest single man in town. His name was linked with various actresses and he enjoyed dinner at the homes of political power brokers. He often leaked information to columnists at these dinners and would make disparaging remarks about the president behind his back.

With his dazzling intellect and deep grasp of history, one would have expected Kissinger to temper Nixon's prejudices and guide his more extreme responses towards a more nuanced and diplomatic solution.

Surprisingly, the Nixon tapes** and Haldeman's diaries suggest a man obsessed with retaining power within the administration, emotionally unstable to the point that the president wonders if he was 'losing it', and sycophantic to the extreme. Whenever Nixon expressed anger towards the Indians, rather than calming things down, Kissinger often exacerbated the president's anger by adding his own negative commentary. Rather than playing a constructive role as advisor and bringing Nixon around to evaluating the cables on the Pakistan crisis in a rational manner, Kissinger encouraged Nixon's tirades on India and the State Department. Although Kissinger engaged in normal dialogues with Indian officials, Haldeman's diaries and the Nixon tapes display a rather hysterical man who was given to self-aggrandizement, treated people in his office badly and was consumed by petty rivalries.

The highly anticipated trip to Peking, codenamed 'Operation Marco Polo', commenced on 1 July 1971. The plan was for Kissinger to visit Asia, including a quick trip to New Delhi, followed by a stop in Pakistan. In Pakistan, he was to feign stomach trouble for two days. With that as an excuse not to be seen in public, he was to fly secretly to China courtesy of the Pakistanis and consummate the relationship with Peking. Everything went according to plan. He arrived in Pakistan on 7 July and on the 9th he was in Peking. A real stomach ache materialized for him as he left Delhi, later called the 'Indian revenge' by the Indian media. It was not severe enough to interfere with the carefully choreographed visit to China. On 11 July, after intensive talks with Premier Zhou Enlai, an invitation for Nixon to officially visit China was issued. Kissinger returned triumphantly to report on his trip to the president. On 15 July, Nixon announced to a stunned world that he would visit China. China's isolation from the international community was effectively over.

The announcement sent shockwaves through Moscow, Saigon, Hanoi and New Delhi. In one stroke, Nixon had pulled off a stunning diplomatic coup. The Soviets, who had been dragging their feet on the SALT talks,

---

** Audio recordings of conversations between President Richard Nixon and his administration officials, family members, and White House staff, between 1971 and 1973.

became more amenable upon seeing their rival China form a friendship with their Cold War adversary. The façade of communist camaraderie was punctured, and India, bordered by hostile China on one side and a Pakistani civil war on the other, set off to balance the equation by signing a treaty with Russia.

The view from New Delhi was grim. China, which had humiliated India in 1962, had a close relationship with India's arch-enemy, Pakistan. The two allies bordered India on its eastern and western flank in the north.

Although China was supposedly an ally of its communist brethren, the Russians, in reality, fissures had developed in the relationship. Since 1962, India had tried to balance alliances in the region by cultivating relations with Russia. The Soviets, wary of the Chinese, had gone out of their way to befriend India as their relations with China had devolved from big brother and comrade to sibling rivalry.

The balance of power in the subcontinent was fragile. India, the largest democracy in the world, did not enjoy the support of the US, the most powerful democracy in the world. India's democratic development was still attempting to shake free from the culturally entrenched feudalism that had existed for centuries. Nehru, one of the founders of modern India, had borrowed heavily from the socialist template of development. India's non-aligned policy was not anti-Western. It was a response to colonialism and its sentiment was misunderstood by Western leaders, who tended to view the world through the lens of the Cold War.

Time and again, the US voted for Pakistan and against India's interests. However, India had not anticipated that the US would line up with a communist country against India. The US–Pakistan–China nexus was a blow to India, and it provided the pro-communist and pro-Russian factions in Mrs Gandhi's government ammunition to push her towards a Soviet alliance. With a potential war looming with Pakistan, Mrs Gandhi's closest advisors, D.P. Dhar and P.N. Haksar, persuaded her that a formal alliance with the Soviets was essential to India's interests. On 9 August 1971, Russia's foreign minister Andrei Gromyko and Swaran Singh, his counterpart in India, signed a friendship treaty. The Soviets, although disinclined to actively participate in other countries' territorial wars, nevertheless agreed to supply India with arms and the heavy water used in nuclear reactors.

The reaction in Washington was understandably cynical. Kissinger quipped that 'the Soviets will be surprised to learn the depths of Indian ingratitude'.[57] They also rightly pointed out that this relegated India's non-aligned policy to the dustbin of history. Mrs Gandhi at this juncture accepted a long-standing invitation to visit Washington to soften the blow. She was not as enthusiastic as some of her left-leaning advisors about the treaty with the Soviets. She thought her visit to Washington could serve the dual purpose of redressing the balance somewhat and exploring US intentions in East Pakistan. Unfortunately, the visit was a failure.

The Indian embassy had heard rumours that Mrs Gandhi was not going to be treated with dignity, and the Indian ambassador had called Kissinger to complain. There was some issue about whether Mrs Gandhi would be put up at Blair House where most world leaders stayed. Kissinger called Ambassador Mosbacher, who was in charge of the arrangements, to smooth things over and to make sure the prime minister was received cordially.[58] Interactions among the officials swung between forced cordiality to outright antagonism.

Earlier, in August 1971, Kissinger had given Ambassador Jha a dressing down. He threatened to cut off aid to India if it were to attack Pakistan. He launched into the friendship treaty India had signed with Russia and pointed out clauses he found disturbing that would oblige India to support any aggressive actions by the Russians in Europe. He then softened his attack by saying India was a potential world power, and Pakistan would always remain a regional power and that, in his view, independence for East Pakistan was inevitable.[59]

The level of distrust on both sides was so high by this point, and the personal animosity of the leaders towards each other so deep, that diplomacy could not to dissolve the tensions.

After a brief stop in New York, where she charmed a gathering of intellectuals and sympathetic friends, Mrs Gandhi arrived in Washington on 4 November 1971. The disdain the two leaders felt for each other was palpable as they stood together at official ceremonies. Both sides were on guard. Kissinger and Nixon were convinced that Mrs Gandhi wanted to dismember Pakistan and that India's insistence that Pakistan negotiate with Mujibur was tantamount to asking Pakistan to surrender. They viewed the subcontinent's crisis in Cold War terms: India was an ally of the Soviets and consequently in the wrong camp. They did not acknowledge the irony of Pakistan and the US lining up with China.

Despite Nixon's gracious but bland remarks at the state dinner, the Indians were not placated. They were upset that Nixon had made no reference to the refugees or the suffering of the Bengalis. Mrs Gandhi's toast was ridiculed and dismissed by the White House as an anti-Pakistan diatribe.

The next day Nixon was raging about how much aid the US was giving to an ungrateful India. Kissinger fanned the flames: 'I wouldn't be too defensive, Mr President, because these bastards have played an absolutely brutal, ruthless game with us.' Kissinger then urged Nixon to be polite with her in public but tough in private.[60] The meeting between the two leaders in the Oval Office was bitter and uncomfortable. Neither gave ground or tried to understand the other's perspective. Kissinger called it a dialogue of the deaf. Nixon thought Gandhi was a warmonger and she thought he had enabled genocide. Veiled threats were exchanged. Nixon hinted that, if India entered the war, it would spill over to involve the superpowers, and possibly China.

Whatever little goodwill these two democratic countries might have had towards each other evaporated that day. The contentious meeting and harsh accusations, followed by threats ended any pretence of cordiality between the two leaders. Their personal animus for each other doomed relations between the two countries. The now infamous tapes containing Nixon and Kissinger's discussion of the previous day's interaction are a testament to the vulnerability of a relationship between countries to the personal likes and dislikes of their leaders and their inability to transcend their prejudices.

The final insult that buried the relationship took place when Mrs Gandhi returned to the White House for her farewell meeting. She was kept waiting for over forty-five minutes. Samuel Hoskinson, Kissinger's aide, surmised this was a power play by Nixon to establish who was in control. The pettiness of the interaction was complete. The agenda for the meeting was a discussion of non-confrontational issues. The Indians thought it pointless to bring up Pakistan again. Both sides were entrenched in their unshakable beliefs about the others' complicity in the crisis. Their differences unbridgeable, the summit ended with each convinced that the other side had made war inevitable.

The postmortem of the visit between Nixon and Kissinger, caught on the Nixon tapes, has been quoted extensively by historians working in this area. The tapes are notorious for the insulting manner in which Nixon and Kissinger discuss the Indian prime minister and India. Mrs Gandhi, who seldom revealed her strategy even to those in her orbit, would exact her pound of flesh within the next few weeks.

## War

On Monday, 22 November 1971, Haldeman wrote in his diary, 'Henry [Kissinger] burst in at noon to say that the radio and TV reports that India has attacked Pakistan. He has no confirmation. By 9:00 tonight he still didn't have any confirmation. Our vast intelligence network doesn't seem to be able to tell us when a couple of major nations are at war, which is a little alarming, to say the least.'[61]

Kissinger called it a naked case of aggression. Nixon wanted to officially condemn India with Kissinger ratcheting up the invective. 'India is outrageous ... those sons of bitches ... let's not kid ourselves—that means Pakistan will get raped.'[62]

Indian troops had been building up their presence along the East Pakistan border for several months prior to the outbreak of war. With large Pakistani troop presence in East Pakistan sent to subdue the rebels, Indians were on high alert. With the Bengalis fleeing East Pakistan and crossing the border to India, the Indian Army was preparing for an escalation in tensions. Skirmishes between the sides had been frequent.

On 7 November 1971, the New York Times reported that the Indian Army had crossed the border to take out Pakistani guns that were shelling a town in India. Delhi was in an uproar at the shelling and decided to move aggressively. Mrs Gandhi, who had claimed the moral high ground saying her troops would not cross the border even when provoked, was exposed. Publicly she was still calling for a diplomatic solution, insisting that Pakistan hold talks with Mujibur. Secretly, she was preparing for war.

On 21 November 1971, Indian infantry troops launched an attack on Boyra in East Pakistan. The Pakistanis retaliated but the initial round went to the Indians. Sydney Schanberg managed to find his way to the frontlines. It was closed to all non-combatants, but he succeeded in befriending officers in the Indian Army, and witnessed them pushing into Pakistani territory towards Dacca.

The Indian plan was to launch a full-scale attack in East Pakistan on 4 December 1971, but Pakistan surprised Indians and pre-empted them in the West. On 3 December, at 5.30 p.m., Pakistan hit India's major airfields in the north, shelling Indian positions all along the western border. Yahya Khan had taken inspiration from the Israeli Six-Day War of 1967, hoping for a lightning strike.

The war that the Indians had been preparing for had finally arrived. India would claim that she was attacked first and responded in self-defence, although there was plenty of evidence that the war was already under way on the eastern front. Yahya Khan and Mrs Gandhi both took to the airwaves to announce that war between their countries had begun. The three generals leading the war on the Indian side were a Jew, a Parsi and a Sikh. They were well-prepared, with the Jewish general, J.F.R. Jacob, as commander of the eastern front.

The Indian Air Force quickly established control over the skies in East Pakistan, while the infantry pushed its way to Dacca. Supported by the Mukti Bahini and the badly abused local population, Indians were treated as liberators. The surge of local support effectively quashed any hope for a Pakistani victory. The Indians raced to the finish line in the east, anxious to win before the United Nations or any other intervention could compromise the outcome of an independent Bangladesh. By 6 December, the war in the East was all but over and India recognized the new country of Bangladesh. By recognizing East Pakistan as an independent country, India was attempting to avoid accusations of territorial expansion or being labelled an occupier.

The battle on the western front had not gone as smoothly for India. Pakistanis were defending their own land, not the land belonging to Bengalis. The fighting was fierce, with punishing losses on both sides.

Nixon predicted India would win in a war with Pakistan and Yahya would be demolished. But Nixon, ever loyal to his Pakistani friend, insisted on supporting him to the end. He said: 'Yahya is a thoroughly decent and reasonable man. Not always smart politically, but he's a decent man.'[63] Nixon and Kissinger had not displayed any empathy towards the Bengalis. The projections made by Kissinger's staff and the State Department on the possible outcome of a war had prepared them for the inevitability of independence for Bangladesh. If anything, they expected it, having admitted that Yahya's crackdown had been reckless. Their primary concern was West Pakistan and Yahya's survival.

They plotted various ways to bolster Pakistan, such as cutting off military aid to India, as well as $100 million in food aid and loans. The State Department suggested that parallel actions be taken against Pakistan to maintain neutrality. On 3 December 1971, a Washington Special Action Group (WSAG) meeting was convened, the minutes of which were subsequently leaked to the columnist Jack Anderson, who made them public. During the meeting Kissinger instructed everyone to 'tilt' to Pakistan, explaining, 'I've been catching unshirted hell every half hour from the president, who says we are not tough enough. He really does not believe we are carrying out his wishes. He wants to tilt toward Pakistan, and he believes that every briefing or statement is going the other way.'[64]

## Triangulation

Kissinger instructed George Bush, the administration's US representative to the UN, to condemn India. Bush and Kissinger met secretly with the Chinese in New York City to obtain China's support in the Security Council. Kissinger got carried away and imbued the war as a great power conflagration, despite there being no facts on the ground to support his flawed analysis. He saw an Indian victory as a Soviet victory over the US.

The Soviets were actually restrained in their support for India and discouraged India from going to war. They provided no help when the March 1971 massacre began, and it was only when the US had announced its rapprochement with China that they deepened their alliance with India and agreed to provide it with military equipment. At a White House meeting with Kissinger, the Russian ambassador Anatoly Dobrynin indicated that India was puzzled by his assurances, on 17 August 1971, that the US would not support Chinese aggression towards India. After his trip to Peking became public, the Indians realized that Kissinger's words were meant to reassure them.[65] It was only recently when the tapes were released that the extent of Kissinger's subterfuge was discovered.

Kissinger had decided to put pressure on India by attempting to enlist China. He hoped China would threaten India by opening up a third front on the India–China border. This was duplicitous, given that that he had previously assured the Indians that they could count on US support against Chinese aggression. Aware of the psychological dimensions that a Chinese threat would inflict on India, he was actually willing to risk escalating the war to a global level to punish the Indians. Kissinger's clandestine attempts to expand the war to include China and risk a world war was alarming and a stain on his reputation as a seasoned diplomat.

Asking the Chinese to rattle their sabres was akin to stabbing the Indians in the back and twisting the knife. Fortunately, the Chinese were cautious, and although they shared Nixon's dislike for India, they were in no hurry to enter the world stage in a state of war.

On 10 December 1971, in a remarkable meeting with Ambassador Huang Hua in New York, Kissinger tried to ingratiate himself with the Chinese by divulging classified information to which even the US Congress was not privy. He revealed the back channels through which he had arranged for Pakistan to illegally receive arms to circumvent the arms embargo and named the countries he had enlisted to participate in this enterprise.

Kissinger then offered to give Ambassador Huang Hua 'whatever information we have about the disposition of Soviet forces'. He said he could arrange it in a secure way. He went so far as to tell him, 'You don't need a master spy. We give you everything. (Hands over his file.) We read you brought a master spy with you. You don't need him. He couldn't get this by himself.' He reassured them that 'we tell you about our conversations with the Soviets; we do not tell the Soviets about our conversations with you. In fact, we don't tell our own colleagues that I see you.'[66]

The aggressive declaration of friendship by Kissinger was music to China's ears. The Chinese had for some time been anxious about becoming isolated. Russia and China competed for influence in Asia. China had aggressively courted Pakistan and discouraged it from getting close to Russia or having a rapprochement with India, going so far as to inform Pakistan that it would undermine their relations. China had also viewed US influence in Pakistan as a threat.[67] Kissinger was now offering to tip the balance in Asia unequivocally to their advantage with the offer of a US alliance.

The Chinese delegation was circumspect in its response to Kissinger's overture. Ambassador Huang did not react to Kissinger's conspiratorial tones with any great show of friendship or enthusiasm. All policy was centralized in China with political winds constantly in flux. He probably did not have the authority to share secrets or depart from his official instructions.

It is unclear why Kissinger felt he could trust the Chinese so early in their relationship. The US was involved in Southeast Asia and in highly sensitive negotiations with the Soviets. The Chinese had often disagreed with US policy in Asia and were wary of the US–Soviet talks. Kissinger was so indiscreet with the Chinese that he made the US vulnerable to a country that was unusually opaque and until recently, an enemy.

Aware of Chinese antipathy for India, Kissinger laid out his anti-Indian agenda and suggestively commented, 'If the PRC were to consider the situation on the Indian subcontinent a threat to its security, and if it took measures to protect its security, the US would oppose efforts of others to interfere with the People's Republic.' He went on, saying, 'Our judgement is if West Pakistan is to be preserved from destruction, two things are needed—maximum intimidation of the Indians and, to some extent, the Soviets, secondly, maximum pressure for the ceasefire.'[68]

It was a clear invitation to the Chinese to enter the conflict, which could potentially escalate to involve Russia and the US. Although the Chinese ambassador responded with his own critical view of India, he deflected the call to arms. Aside from supporting Pakistan at the UN, China eventually provided what amounted to a negligible skirmish on its border with India.

Kissinger's final, and possibly most dangerous, manoeuvre to tip the balance towards Pakistan was deploying the USS *Enterprise* to the Bay of Bengal. As Indians heard that an American warship with a nuclear arsenal was steaming towards them, alarm bells went off in Delhi. Defence Minister Jagjivan Ram declared that India would sink the ship. A sceptical deputy head of mission in Washington, M.K. Rasgotra, asked how this would be accomplished and Jagjivan Ram responded that several naval officers had volunteered themselves as suicide bombers—they would swim under the US ship and detonate. Chief of naval staff, Admiral S.M. Nanda, offered a more reasonable approach and said he would invite the commander of the USS *Enterprise* on board for a drink![69]

Indian leaders were confident that the war would be over by the time the USS *Enterprise* reached India. However, they felt the US had entered the war by threatening India with this aggressive action. To this day, even as the relations between the countries have improved, the US is still viewed sceptically, with this incident pointed out as an example of American high-handedness. World opinion, which had lurched from sympathy for India's refugee problem to anger when India was viewed as the aggressor when the war began, shifted back to India in sympathy as news of the US aircraft carrier's deployment spread.

## The Fallout

With all the secret channels and wars on different fronts, Kissinger, who viewed himself as the grand conductor orchestrating events on the world stage, began to unravel. A not uncommon confrontation with the State Department pushed him over the edge, and on 7 December 1971, Haldeman described him as being in a monumental flap, threatening to resign. President Nixon, Haldeman and Haig were worried about his state of mind and thought him physically exhausted. Haldeman wrote, 'I talked later this afternoon with the P [President Nixon] about the whole thing again. He feels as I do now, that there's more to this than just India, Pakistan ... In any event, I talked again with Henry [Kissinger] and played it a little brutally with him this time by saying if he was going to announce his resignation in December, he should resign in December. He couldn't just announce it then hang on, and he said, oh no, he couldn't do that because he couldn't leave the P alone to go to China, and I said you shouldn't go to China having announced your resignation … So, I've given him something to think about.'[70]

Kissinger's fragile nerves may have contributed to the perilous scenarios he sketched out for the president. They ranged from the Chinese moving against India to Indians bringing the Soviets in and Kissinger trying to persuade Nixon that the US would have to get into the mix. He even suggested lobbing nuclear weapons as a possibility. Nixon, who seemed to hesitate at this picture of Armageddon, was persuaded that if the US did not join the Chinese against Russia and India, its diplomatic initiative with China would be jeopardized.

Fortunately for the world, cooler heads prevailed. The Chinese did not threaten India, and on 12 December 1971, the Soviets conveyed a message to Nixon from Mrs Gandhi that she was not planning to take any territory in West Pakistan. The UN Security Council asked for a ceasefire, but the Russians vetoed it, protecting India's agenda on East Pakistan. India was willing to accept a ceasefire provided Bangladesh became an independent country. Unilateral recognition of Bangladesh by India alone was not sufficient. The world community needed to provide legitimacy by endorsing it. With the Russians unwilling to publicly back India by recognizing Bangladesh, India needed time for Pakistan to capitulate.

It took a few more days for Pakistan to admit defeat, but on 15 December 1971, General A.A.K. Niazi requested a ceasefire just before the USS *Enterprise* entered the Bay of Bengal.

Sending the USS *Enterprise* was an act of aggression that was the final nail in the coffin for the Gandhi–Nixon relationship. As far as the Indians were concerned, it was tantamount to a declaration of war. Many Americans were equally upset at the prospect of a conflagration involving the superpowers. The US embassy in India wondered if it should evacuate its personnel. Galen Stone, a US embassy official who delivered the Pakistani ceasefire request to Haksar, was stunned by Nixon's escalation of the crisis. He expressed his own and his colleague's dismay with his president's policies. The two officials agreed that relations between the two countries had been destroyed.[71]

On 16 December 1971, General Niazi surrendered to the Indian general in Dacca. The war was over. Sydney Schanberg wanted to write an article about the surrender of a Pakistani Muslim general to the Indian Jewish general. Ever the gentleman, General Jacob refused and had General Niazi surrender to General Aurora, a Sikh.[73]

Immediately after the surrender in the East, Mrs Gandhi declared that India had no territorial ambitions. With Bangladesh free, on 17 December 1971, she ordered a unilateral ceasefire on the western front. The Indians agreed to abide by the Geneva Convention and protect all Pakistani personnel. In a contemptuous press release, with references to the American Declaration of Independence claiming the moral high ground, she said: 'All unprejudiced persons objectively surveying the grim events in Bangladesh since 25 March have recognized the revolt of 75 million people who were forced to the conclusion that neither their life, nor their liberty, to say nothing of the possibility of the pursuit of happiness, was available to them.'[73]

Yahya Khan resigned after the defeat by India. Bhutto, who took over the government, promptly put him under house arrest. In an ironic twist, General Zia-ul Haq, another military leader, overthrew Bhutto and later hanged him. Zia released Yahya in 1977.

Close to a million people perished and almost 10 million were displaced in East Pakistan during 1970–71. It was a high cost to pay for the collective misreading and mishandling of events by the people in charge. The US possessed the ability to alter the outcome but, in pursuing its own agenda, grossly misjudged the consequences of deliberate 'inaction'.

Many members of Kissinger's own staff disagreed with the tilt to Pakistan. Some tried to persuade their boss to revaluate the policy. One can only conclude, from reading transcripts of discussions, that pandering to the president was more important to Kissinger than heeding the advice of his staff, the State Department and US ambassadors. He accepted that Nixon's attitude to India was frozen, but why he never sought to temper the response to the crisis in South Asia is hard to fathom. What is harder to overlook is that rather than advise wisely, he risked a world war by raising the stakes.

On 4 April 1972, the US formerly recognized Bangladesh. The president remained bitter towards India until the end. He harboured fantasies of punishing India, but other events, such as the 1973 Arab–Israeli war, the oil embargo and Watergate, precluded him from pursuing them. Never before had the US–India relationship sunk to such depths and been so subject to the personal prejudices of the people who made policy as they had during the Nixon years. For him, all India-related policies were personal and it clouded his judgement preventing him from making rational assessments.

The Indians, appalled by the invective and Nixon's aggressive attitude towards India, recoiled. They viewed the US policy in South Asia as anti-Indian and full of contradictions. They felt that the US has enabled the perpetrators of genocide, contravening the US's professed pro-human rights position. In refusing to support the aspirations of Bengali nationalism, the US betrayed the principles of its stated ideals, and finally, having assured India it would come to its aid if China were to attack, the US instead tried to encourage Chinese aggression. Shunned by Nixon in favour of a military dictatorship, India no longer regarded the US as a friend or even a neutral party.

Mrs Gandhi's popularity soared after the victory of the 1971 war. *The Economist* labelled her the 'Empress of India' and the Indian press unanimously sang her praises. She was deified in paintings and prayed to in villages across the country. Having faced down Pakistan, who was backed by the US, she dealt the lightning strike that Yahya had aspired to effect. She proved she had nerves of steel and claimed the moral high ground by withdrawing expeditiously when Bangladesh was declared independent.

On 14 December 1971, Kissinger, unable to reconcile himself to his failed policy in South Asia and what he considered Soviet–India collusion, told reporters that the White House was considering cancelling the Moscow Summit. The president, who considered an agreement with Moscow part of his legacy, was furious. It did not help that a member of Kissinger's staff, disgruntled by his anti-Indian policy, leaked minutes of the WSAG meetings to the press. Jack Anderson published the secret documents on the same day. Nixon cut Kissinger off and stopped taking his calls. Kissinger was beside himself, and it was not until preparations for Nixon's China visit had begun a few months later that the relationship thawed.

Nixon's visit to China in 1972 was the zenith of his popularity and presidency. The SALT agreement was signed the same year. The

Bangladesh War had receded in people's memory and Nixon was re-elected in a landslide. On 27 January 1973, the treaty to end the Vietnam War was signed in Paris.

Jubilation in the White House quickly gave way to despair as the press revealed details of the Watergate break-in. Under mounting pressure from the investigations, Nixon's administration began to fall apart. In April 1973, his closest advisors, Haldeman and Ehrlichman, resigned and Howard Dean was fired. In October 1973, Vice President Agnew was forced out over corruption charges. Kissinger's nemesis, Will Rogers, left, and Kissinger took over as the secretary of state. Finally, on 8 August 1974, Richard Milhous Nixon resigned in disgrace.

Nixon had appointed former senator Daniel Patrick Moynihan the ambassador to India as a conciliatory gesture in 1972. Moynihan had come out against the tilt to Pakistan. His wife Elizabeth (Liz), with her dedication to Indian history, won over many of the disenchanted Indian elite, but India's relationship with the US government was so severely damaged that it would take many years to repair.

# Chapter 11

# Ford: India Goes Nuclear

THE BANGLADESH WAR HAD ESTABLISHED INDIA AS THE DOMINANT power in South Asia. Although Nixon never got past his personal animosity towards India, he understood that some gesture was required to placate New Delhi. In 1973, he appointed the controversial Harvard professor Daniel Patrick Moynihan as ambassador to India and Kenneth Keating, who had disappointed Nixon, was transferred as ambassador to Israel. Nixon believed that Keating had become an advocate for India during the Bangladesh War, and was confident that Moynihan would repair relations and mollify the Indians while staying loyal to the president. Moynihan had publicly criticized the administration's tilt to Pakistan and, as a consequence, the White House assumed he would be well-received in New Delhi.

Moynihan, Kissinger and Haldeman had been the only persons in the White House with direct access to the president. Kissinger and Moynihan, both Harvard professors, had a competitive relationship. Moynihan had been the president's domestic policy tsar* and had left the administration in 1970 to resume teaching at Harvard, but he had remained in close touch with Nixon. Kissinger was not unhappy to have his old rival sent to India as ambassador in 1973. It placed one of Nixon's favourite confidants in a distant land, considered unimportant by the White House.

---

\* Professor Moynihan was a Democrat and had been an advisor to presidents Kennedy and Johnson before joining the Nixon White House.

Moynihan hardly seemed an obvious candidate for such a delicate assignment. For one thing, he had no prior affinity for India. He accepted the job knowing that relations between the two countries had plummeted. Moynihan's initial assessment of India was pessimistic. He was critical of India in a conversation with the president before departing for his ambassadorship. He concluded that India was broke and heading for starvation.

Moynihan told the president that the Indians 'have made the ridiculous assertion that they want to get rid of all foreign aid by the year 1979 ... in the end they'll have to come to us and say, "Look, as a matter of fact, we can't."'[†] He went on to explain that the PL480 had become a billion-dollar problem for India. Moynihan calculated that, by 2010, India would owe the US about $5 billion.

> Moynihan: By the year 2040 we own India.
> Nixon: Wow!
> Moynihan: (laughs) Who wants to own India?
> Nixon: God no! Please!
> Moynihan: But in a funny way, it's something in between us and them. We own a third of their currency, in effect. And we have our people, our people are always scurrying out there, picking up land to build a dam here, or save a tiger, or do some birth control.[2]

Despite Moynihan's sarcasm about the Indians and belittling the social projects of American NGOs, he actually came up with an innovative solution that was radical and pro-India. He argued that, for a limited time, the US utilize the rupees that India was using to service its debts to the US for expenses incurred in India, such as the running of the US embassy. He suggested the US consider cancelling the debt eventually and move the remainder of the money into a foundation to support activities in India run by Indians. His solutions regarding the debt restructuring

---

† India was confronting severe food shortages in 1972–73 and was trying to buy wheat. The US was the only country with surplus wheat. The Russians were also short of wheat and buying it from the US.

were insightful and generous and rectified what had become a financially destabilizing aid programme for India.

The Indians were wary of aid with strings attached. In the past, India felt that the US had used aid as leverage. Like any debtor in hock to his creditor, an inevitable distrust had singed the relationship. The Indian goal to get free from the yoke of aid was genuine. The US misinterpreted India's attitude as a bargaining position and it smacked to them of ingratitude.

When Moynihan arrived in Delhi in February 1973, India was sinking under its growing economic burden. The 1972 monsoons had failed, and part of India's limited foreign exchange reserves had to be used to meet the shortfall in food. The Arab oil embargo following the war in the Middle East had global consequences, putting an enormous strain on Indian resources. The price of oil had skyrocketed and depleted India's hard currency. The two looming problems between the US and India were the financial structure of the PL480 funds, which threatened to destabilize the fragile Indian economy, and India's need for wheat imports to feed its people.

Moynihan campaigned hard with the White House and State Department to restructure and write off most of the PL480 debt. He argued it would have little consequence to the US as the rupee account had no impact on the US economy, but forgiving the debt payments would inject life support into the ailing Indian economy. India's debts to the US totalling $3.3 billion represented the money used to buy surplus food from the US during the previous three administrations. The debt being paid back was, in essence, incurred by the grandparents of the current generation.[3]

Moynihan made a Herculean effort and succeeded where other ambassadors had failed. He initially negotiated a waiver of future interest payments of approximately $4 billion, a write-off of a third of the holdings, with the remaining two thirds for the use of the US within India. Kissinger and Moynihan, the two old White House rivals, came to appreciate each other over this period. They worked together to find creative solutions to issues like the PL480 funds, which complicated relations between the two countries. It was with Kissinger's help that Moynihan eventually got two thirds of India's debt written off, with just a billion to be held in rupees, for use by the US in India.[4]

Once he had settled into his new job, Moynihan began to understand the cultural differences between the US and India in their respective attitudes to aid. In a letter to Nixon, he explained, 'Indians are clearly influenced by the Buddhist view which holds that "gratitude, if it exists, should be felt by he who gives and not he who receives, since the latter has been the cause of good action, which to the full advantage of the former, will inevitably by the iron law of karma bring its own reward"'.[5]

Although gratitude may be too generous a description of the Indian response to the PL480 solution, they most certainly appreciated what Moynihan had done to ease India's economic pains. With Kissinger's help, Moynihan had overcome obstacles raised by members of Congress. Senator Ted Kennedy joined other liberal Democrats to override Senator Byrd's amendment attempting to prevent the agreement.

India faced severe food shortages again in mid-1973. The US did not have surplus wheat that year. The Russians, who also needed to import wheat, had bought up most of the available supply. By July, India's ambassador to the US, T.N. Kaul, began pushing Kissinger to help India with grain purchases. A month later, India's finance minister, Y.B. Chavan, along with Ambassador Kaul, called on Kissinger and pursued the issue.

On 19 July 1973, an ever-cynical Moynihan wrote in his journal: 'The starving time appears to be at hand. The words begin to appear in the press. "Famine deaths" in Orissa ... All schools have closed. And so it is America time again.'[6] Kissinger, in the meantime, made an effort to aid India's quest for food. He followed up on the requests made by Kaul, Chavan and cables from Delhi by pressuring Agricultural Secretary Earl Butz to make the grains available. Moynihan commented in his journal: 'In the afternoon an hour with [Foreign Secretary] Keval Singh, who was forthcoming, even grateful. Odd or perhaps not odd. I make clear that we are not giving them anything, merely offering to help them buy with hard cash at inflated prices.'[7]

India, short on cash, was feeling around for better terms. In the end, it waited too long as prices went against it. Kaul, never one to let a good deed go unpunished, accusingly brought this up in a meeting with Kissinger. Kissinger had extended himself to work the levers of power to find India the needed wheat allocation. He was irritated by Kaul's remarks.

Fortunately, Swaran Singh, India's more diplomatic foreign minister, who was also at the meeting, smoothed over Kaul's caustic tone.

By the end of 1973, Nixon was preoccupied and trying to salvage his legacy in Vietnam and Russia in the wake of Watergate. He had increasingly less time for foreign affairs and, by the fall of 1973, Kissinger was running foreign policy. He was busy putting out fires in the Middle East and gave Moynihan a free hand in India.

As a highly regarded Harvard professor, Moynihan was looking forward to getting to know the academic community in India. But the easy access and warmth that Galbraith had enjoyed were denied to Moynihan when he first arrived. India was still seething at the US and any representative of the Nixon administration was viewed with suspicion. In an interview with Bernard Weinraub of the *New York Times*, in March 1974, he said, 'I somehow wish I could have more of an exchange with Indian academics. But they're so lost in a kind of ritual anti-Americanism, you've got to be a masochist to try.'[8]

Although it took time, Indians grew to appreciate the acerbic professor. His dazzling intellect and wit eventually won over the intellectual elite. His occasionally abrasive personality was softened by his wife Elizabeth, who deserves a great deal of credit for opening doors for him. She immersed herself in Indian history and developed an appreciation for its culture, which broke down many barriers. She is credited with discovering a Mughal garden and established her India bona fides among the literary set in Delhi.

As he got to know India, Moynihan developed a grudging respect for its people. He summed up his feelings in a letter to President Nixon, 'The Indians have such good brains: if only they didn't have such bad ideas. They are committed to a socialism that cannot work.'[9]

One of Moynihan's great regrets was his failure to establish a rapport with Mrs Gandhi. He was not alone among the diplomatic community in this regard. His impatience with diplomatic niceties got in the way of his objectives and set him apart from his predecessors, who came across as much more pro-India. His tendency towards sarcasm did little to endear him to Indian officials. He angered the Indian government while being questioned by Indian journalists about the United States' military activities in Diego Garcia, an island 1,000 miles south of India in the Indian Ocean. He retorted, 'Why call it the Indian Ocean? One may call it the Madagascar Sea.' Moynihan admitted he had been impolitic.[10]

In private, Moynihan was incensed when he learnt about the US presence in Diego Garcia and considered resigning over it. He felt the US military had misled him. He speculated that either Kissinger was involved in some complex diplomatic manoeuvring or that it was military incompetence.[11] President Kennedy had initially raised the issue with Defense Secretary McNamara and requested he look into the potential for a US military presence in the Indian Ocean. Busy with Vietnam and an abbreviated administration, Kennedy was prevented from pursuing it further. President Johnson had shown little inclination for an aggressive policy, but that changed under Nixon.

## Relationship Under Pressure

Soon after Moynihan arrived in New Delhi, the White House announced the lifting of the arms embargo on Pakistan. It was an inauspicious beginning, making Moynihan's task of improving relations between the two countries rather difficult.

Mrs Gandhi, given her recent success in the 1971 war despite US opposition, felt no need to accommodate the new ambassador. At their very first meeting on 17 March 1973, Moynihan was on the defensive. He was in the awkward position of having to justify his country's recent decision to reinstate prior agreements of arms supply to Pakistan while trying to present the US desire for friendship with India. Referring to the arms deal, Mrs Gandhi bluntly told him that, though she wished him success, he had not made a good beginning.[12]

Approximately $1.7 million worth of military supplies for Pakistan had been held up due to an arms embargo imposed on India and Pakistan when they went to war in 1965. Most of the items that the US initially wanted to release were spare parts and military aircraft engines that were being repaired in the US. The objectionable item, from the Indian perspective, was an additional $13 million for 300 armoured personnel carriers. This was part of a package approved under a one-time exception prior to the war breaking out. Pakistan had made a down payment against the purchase and US suppliers were pushing to fill the order.

Moynihan, the State Department and members of Congress opposed the resumption of arms supplies except for the arms that Pakistan owned and was having repaired in the US. India viewed the resumption as strategic policy to rehabilitate Pakistan. It maintained that the US could have, at the very least, put pressure on Pakistan to recognize Bangladesh in exchange for releasing its equipment.

India viewed the US as creating discord in South Asia, just as bilateral peace negotiations were moving forward. It believed that Pakistan would feel emboldened by the US arms announcement and become more intransigent. Additionally, economic aid to Pakistan had resumed after the war while it had still not been announced for India. The Indian public viewed this as yet another example of the America's partiality towards their adversary.

The Simla Agreement of 1972 took place after the Bangladesh War. India and Pakistan had agreed to meet and have direct negotiations. It was a path forward for the two countries that had never been attempted before. The parties agreed to resolve issues bilaterally, including those relating to Kashmir and Bangladesh. India agreed to return Pakistan's 93,000 prisoners of war, subject to Bangladesh's approval, as well as 5,000 square miles of Pakistani territory it had captured in West Pakistan. Despite heavy criticism from various groups in India, Mrs Gandhi was determined not to humiliate Pakistan. Her principal advisor P.N. Haksar repeatedly referred to the baneful consequences of the harsh terms the Treaty of Versailles had imposed on the vanquished.[13] The two countries agreed to convert the ceasefire line in Kashmir to a 'line of control', a 450-mile-long frontier dividing the disputed region into two, with the intention of making it a permanent border. Pakistan's recognition of Bangladesh was to lead to other agreements, such as the fate of the POWs.[‡]

Following the Bangladesh War, India was playing middleman between Pakistan and Bangladesh on the POW issue. India was committed to

---

‡ The Simla Agreement was contentious and came close to failing. Mrs Gandhi was accused by many of selling India short. However, there has been no following agreement that achieved a peaceful solution to the disputes.

handling the matter in a way that adhered to the Geneva Convention. The US and India held several discussions on the issue, hoping for a peaceful solution. India urged the US to persuade Pakistan to recognize Bangladesh and agreed that it was best to avoid Pakistani officers being publicly tried in Bangladesh and for them to be repatriated to Pakistan.

Bhutto had dragged his feet on recognition due to domestic pushback. The US acknowledged Bangladesh in 1972 and pledged to provide it with aid. India requested the US to persuade Pakistan to do so as well but they only agreed to do so in 1974, after pressure was applied from several Muslim countries.

India, for its part, agreed to repatriate the POWs being held to Pakistan and dissuaded Bangladesh from putting West Pakistani officers on trial.

Bhutto, who had grown up in Sindh, was anti-Indian in the extreme. Unlike some of the other members of the military and government who had been born in India and moved to Pakistan after Partition in 1947, he lacked pleasant memories of growing up in a mixed community. He often ranted about 'Hindu imperialists' and felt India had dismembered Pakistan and would do it again. Bhutto put considerable pressure on the US to augment Pakistan's military capability with the latest US arms, and quietly began to implement plans for a covert nuclear programme in Pakistan.

By the middle of 1973, both President Nixon and Prime Minister Gandhi's domestic status had begun to erode. Watergate subsumed the president. Defections and resignations plagued the Nixon administration while Mrs Gandhi was faced a severe economic crisis.

Kissinger was one of the few loyalists left unscathed by the Watergate scandal. Nixon appointed him secretary of state in September. He also retained his role as the national security advisor. All foreign policy was now under his person. He was the plenipotentiary supreme. With Rogers gone and no rivals to challenge his policies, he became more secure. With the State Department wholly under his jurisdiction, he no longer tried to exclude its personnel. He developed a growing respect for the professionals who worked there and took their advice into consideration. His attitude to India softened and, having accomplished the opening to China, he became more even-handed with India and Pakistan.

In the fall of 1973, Kissinger was awarded the Nobel Peace Prize for negotiating an end to the Vietnam War. He had transformed himself from an ambitious, if insecure, foreign policy advisor given to rages to the diplomat of the century.

By late 1973, Mrs Gandhi's heroic leadership during the war, which had won her the admiration of her staunchest critics in India, quickly receded in the face of two failed monsoons in 1972 and 1973. With the prospect of another famine looming, inflation surged to double digits. The oil price surge of 1973 had hurt India as it had the rest of the world, and industrial growth continued to remain static. Improved health standards and lower infant mortality had increased population growth rates, straining resources. Nixon had suspended aid to India during the war and payments to the US now exceeded inflows.

Mrs Gandhi's 1971 friendship treaty with the Soviets and India's heavy reliance on them for its arms supply had become a cause for concern. Ever cautious about Russia's grip, she wanted to improve relations with the US to diversify her sources. But her only contribution towards better relations was to tone down her anti-US rhetoric and refrain from criticizing its foreign policies. The constant castigation of the US from the Indian government and press had been something of a bugbear for several US administrations.[§] Aside from fulminating about US policy in Vietnam, they accused the CIA of continual nefarious activities in India.

Uncomfortable with India's increasing dependence on Moscow, Mrs Gandhi thought it expedient to improve relations with the US. Unfortunately, she sent her trusted advisor T.N. Kaul, a pro-Soviet, intemperate man, as ambassador to the US with the directive to improve relations.

## The Explosion: India Becomes a Pariah State

By the end of 1973 and the first half of 1974, Mrs Gandhi's world was closing in on her. Having been glorified in the press as a goddess after

---

§   Much of these criticisms were for domestic consumption and to satisfy the communist elements.

winning the Bangladesh War in 1971, her star had faded. She was dealing with an opposition that was looking for any opportunity to knock her off her pedestal. Her economic policies were a failure. Food shortages were mounting, and the economy was collapsing. Separatist movements and communists were gaining traction around the country and the Indian press had become intensely critical of her government.

On 18 May 1974, India became the world's sixth nuclear power. Three months before Nixon resigned, India shocked the world by exploding an underground nuclear device in the Thar desert in Rajasthan. Indians were euphoric.

Reaction to the test earned India worldwide condemnation. Liberal, pro-India constituencies around the world were scathing. Mrs Gandhi was stung and viewed the response as a denial of India's right to progress. She insisted that the technology would only be used for peaceful purposes. The rest of the world remained sceptical.

Moynihan paid a visit to Mrs Gandhi to communicate official US reaction. He told her, 'India has made a huge mistake. Here you were the number one hegemonic power in South Asia. Nobody was number two and call Pakistan number three. Now in a decade's time, some Pakistani general will call you up and say I have four nuclear weapons and I want Kashmir. If not, we will drop them on you, and we will all meet in heaven. And then what will you do?'[14]

Mrs Gandhi resented the lecture and refused to respond. She was angry at the reaction from the West. Her critics, both inside India and in the US, felt she had exploded the bomb to distract the public from her domestic failures and failed campaign promises to decrease poverty. The US embassy reported: 'India has exploded a nuclear device at a time when India is in deep economic difficulty.'[15]

Many years later, Raja Ramanan, who had been in charge of India's nuclear programme, admitted that the test had not been just for peaceful purposes. One of the consequences of the US intent to threaten India by sending the USS *Enterprise* to the Bay of Bengal during the Bangladesh War was the exposure of India's military vulnerabilities. Mrs Gandhi had been obliged to the Soviets for sending their naval ship to the Indian Ocean to counter the US threat. Many high-ranking government officials in her circle had urged her to back down and declare a ceasefire. Although she refused and fought on to victory, she was determined to prevent India's exposure to nuclear intimidation.

Pakistan's reaction was predictably negative: 'The Indian nuclear test shocked Pakistan at many levels. It put India in a league different from Pakistan.'[16] Bhutto, still seething from the loss of East Pakistan, was furious. He resolved to retaliate by developing Pakistan's own nuclear programme. The nuclear arms race in South Asia had been put into motion.

Canada was highly critical of India's decision as the plutonium used in the test was produced in the Canadian-built CIRUS research reactor. Canada had spent $96.5 million since 1956 in nuclear assistance to India and felt that, by conducting the explosion, India had violated the understanding between the two countries. It suspended all nuclear cooperation with India.

Surprisingly, Kissinger had sent out strict instructions for the US administration to keep its responses low key. He made it clear he would not tolerate anyone making critical statements publicly. Despite Moynihan's negative comments to Mrs Gandhi, Kissinger reasoned that India already had the bomb, the US was powerless to reverse facts, and the main thrust of its efforts should be containment and non-proliferation.

Many anti-proliferation groups lobbied the US administration to follow Canada's example and disconnect India from the nuclear supply chain. The argument was that the US had supplied the heavy water for the Canadian-built reactor that had been used for the explosion. Its misuse violated the agreements between them, and the controversy enraged several US congressmen who raised objections to continued cooperation. The administrations of the two countries argued that the US was contractually obliged to fulfil its obligations to India. After some delays and written assurances from the Indian government that US supplies would only be used for peaceful purposes, the enriched uranium for Tarapur nuclear plant was shipped.

The Nuclear Suppliers Group (NSG) was formed as a response to India's 1974 test. It was an independent body whose mandate was to prevent nuclear proliferation by putting stringent safeguards in place. Controversy surrounding India's nuclear programme had only just begun and several US administrations would be forced to manage India's nuclear ambitions.

Despite Kissinger's new moderation, and Foreign Minister Swaran Singh and Foreign Secretary Keval Singh's softer approach to the US, Kaul and Moynihan could be equally abrasive. Moynihan never developed a rapport with Mrs Gandhi. He recounted a meeting with her on 18 October 1973 which was a monologue by him with her responding with nods and smiles, without saying a word until the meeting was over.[17] Throughout Moynihan's tenure, Mrs Gandhi remained impervious to his efforts to engage her. The only time she showed any interest in what he had to say was when the subject of aid was broached. She distanced herself from the US, leaving it to her ambassador, foreign minister and foreign secretary to maintain relations, just as Nixon and Kissinger left the relationship in Moynihan's hands.

Mrs Gandhi and Nixon's remoteness from foreign policy during this period was for very different reasons. Nixon became irrelevant to relations after 1973, once the prospects of his impeachment became inevitable. Mrs Gandhi was wholly preoccupied with her domestic troubles.

Although Nixon's dislike for Mrs Gandhi, and India, was rooted in his past and seemed more personal, her anger towards him was grounded in his administration's tilt to Pakistan. The two leaders had more similarities than they would have liked to admit. They both had dominating fathers and 'saintly' mothers whom they adored and had lost family members to TB. By all accounts, both had difficult childhoods, albeit for very different reasons. They were both loners and found it difficult to open up to people. They were both aloof, thin-skinned and shared the handicap of never forgetting a slight. In Nixon's case, he brought it forward into his presidency, and in Mrs Gandhi's case, it lasted through her time in government. One can only wonder if relations could have been more neutral if a resourceful staffer had pointed out commonalities they could have connected with on a personal level.

Nixon resigned in disgrace on 8 August 1974, and Gerald Ford, who had taken over from Spiro Agnew as vice president the previous December, became the 38th President of the United States.

# Gerald Ford

Ford's mother, Dorothy Gardner, made the terrible choice of falling in love with her brother's roommate, Leslie King. Tall, blonde, handsome and the son of a wealthy banker in Omaha, he swept her off her feet and they were married in 1912. On her honeymoon, she realized something was terribly wrong. His outward charm camouflaged a deeply disturbed man who was violent and prone to lying and drinking. The couple moved in with his parents in Omaha, but things did not improve. Dorothy's marriage became unbearable. Just as she decided to leave her husband, she discovered she was pregnant.

Leslie King, Jr, was born on 14 July 1913. His father tried to attack him and his mother with a butcher's knife, and the police had to be called to restrain him. Although divorce was a rarity in those days, the court granted her one, along with custody of the boy in December 1913.

The story ended happily. Dorothy moved back to her parents' home in Michigan and met a kind, decent man at a church social the following year. They were married in February 1917, and her new husband, Gerald Rudolf Ford, gave her son his name. Gerald Ford, Jr loved his parents and did not know he was adopted until he was twelve or thirteen.[18] He excelled at football and played on both his high school and college football teams. He was good enough to receive offers from professional teams but decided to go to Yale Law School. His highest grades were in the ethics class.[19]

Ford had a brief flirtation with a modelling career when he dated an aspiring model by the name of Phyllis Brown, but he was inspired to enter politics after hearing Wendell Willkie at a rally. He joined the US Naval Reserve in 1942 and saw action in the Pacific in 1944. After the war, he decided to run for office, determined to break the stronghold of the power brokers in Michigan. He was elected to Congress in 1948, holding his seat through thirteen terms and always winning with a comfortable margin.

Gerald Ford was known for his integrity. He had been in Congress for twenty-five years and was respected and liked by his peers when Nixon consulted House Speaker Carl Albert and Senate Majority Leader Mike Mansfield regarding Vice President Spiro Agnew's replacement. Nixon had always appreciated Ford's loyalty and friendship and Ford admired

Nixon's encyclopaedic knowledge of world affairs. Nixon, along with Albert and Mansfield, agreed that Ford would be the best choice for the vice president's position and easy to confirm. Speaker Albert would claim that 'Congress made Jerry Ford president'.[20] In his inaugural address, Ford acknowledged that he had not been chosen by the people and appealed to the public to 'confirm me as your president in your prayers'.

President Ford's priority was to try to 'heal' the country.[§] In addition to the pall that had befallen the country in the aftermath of Watergate, the US economy, like India, was in a downward spiral. Inflation, chronic energy shortages and distrust in government were just the beginning.

As an unelected president, Ford inherited an administration and cabinet that he had not picked. Initially, for the sake of national continuity, he kept most of his predecessor's staff. Surrounded by Nixon acolytes, in particular, Alexander Haig, the new president was boxed in by his predecessor's policies and network. Ford's pardon of Nixon on 8 September 1974 ended his honeymoon with the public and Congress.[**] Donald Rumsfeld became his chief of staff, pushing out Alexander Haig. Kissinger's portfolio was reduced. He remained secretary of state, but Brent Scowcroft became the national security advisor. Dick Cheney became Rumsfeld's top deputy and they slowly consolidated power in the White House.

The general direction of foreign policy did not change much. Its focus remained the Middle East and Southeast Asia. The ceasefire in Vietnam broke down, and Kissinger wondered if he should return his Nobel Prize. (He did not.) The country was fed up with the war; Congress refused to increase aid to Vietnam; Saigon fell to the North Vietnamese in April 1975; and the US was left with the haunting images of people clinging to the last US helicopter, as it lifted off from the helipad at the US embassy.

## Suspicions Linger

Mrs Gandhi saw the change in the US administration as an opportunity to try and revive flagging relations. She wrote letters of congratulations

---

§ Ford became president on 9 August 1974.

** Ford's decision to pardon Nixon was very controversial.

and communicated in tones much warmer than with the previous administration. India extended an invitation to President Ford to visit, to which he responded positively.

Kissinger visited India in October 1974. Before leaving his post, Moynihan had persuaded Kissinger of the importance of a visit to repair relations. In Washington, Kaul also pushed for the visit. Despite Mrs Gandhi's concern about India's increasing reliance on the Russians and her need to improve her US relationship, she was unable to alter her mindset. She had given a prickly interview to the press the day before Kissinger's arrival in Delhi. She said that India would not beg or be manipulated with aid and that the US did not treat India with the respect it deserved.[21]

Privately, Kissinger's attitudes towards India and Mrs Gandhi had not changed either. Kissinger was apoplectic when he learned of Mrs Gandhi's accusation from a cable while on route to India. Moynihan, who was travelling with Kissinger, wrote: 'The door from the forward cabin opens. The Secretary of State. Cable in hand. "The bitch." What is an ambassador to say? What I say is, "She will piss on your grave, Henry. There is nothing to be done about her. We come and we go: she remains." The door closes. Disaster.'[22]

There had been widespread allegations in the Indian press of CIA meddling in India's internal affairs prior to Kissinger's arrival. He was being denounced as Allende's murderer with stories of the Chilean leader's assassination making the rounds in the press, linking his death to the CIA and some even suggesting that Kissinger had a hand in it. Kissinger gave a press conference in Delhi denying the CIA was trying to undermine India.

During his three days in New Delhi, Kissinger made several speeches. He was careful to strike a conciliatory tone. He recognized India as the pre-eminent power in South Asia. This went a long way in placating India's bruised ego. Kissinger also acknowledged that the relationship was strained and promised a change. His diplomatic attitude received optimistic reactions from the press and the government. Some hoped it would usher in a more positive era in their relations. What he had really wanted to tell the Indians was that beggars can't be choosers, but he wisely kept his dislike in check.

A joint Indo-US commission was set up and Kissinger met with many senior members of the government, including a lunch meeting with Mrs Gandhi. She was not won over, and 'as a measure of her scorn for the US secretary of state, she pointedly departed New Delhi in the middle of his visit, leaving him to deal with lesser officials'.[23]

Kissinger had to constantly balance any overtures to India with explanations and reassurances to Pakistan, which felt insecure with the improved US ties with India. Bhutto asked his foreign minister, Aziz Ahmed, to remind Kissinger that in 1971 he had promised to teach the Indians a lesson they would never forget.[24] Kissinger deflected Pakistani accusations by attributing positive reports about Indo-US relations in the press to 'leaks' and 'imaginings'. He was trying to find ways to keep the channel with India open so that it could be distanced from the Soviet orbit. However, his determination to aid Pakistan militarily would counter any attempts to curry favour in New Delhi.

In early 1974, the Pentagon announced plans to construct a naval base in Diego Garcia, an island fifteen hundred miles south of India. The prospect of a permanent US presence in the Indian Ocean was viewed as a destabilizing presence in the region. The US wanted to counter the growing Soviet influence after the 1971 friendship treaty between India and the USSR. India's objections to the US naval base in Diego Garcia became more vocal over time. Once the US resumed arms shipments to Pakistan in 1975, relations suffered a severe setback.

Bhutto had put considerable pressure on the US to once again sell arms to Pakistan. The defeat against India in 1971 and India's nuclear explosion in May 1974 gave Pakistan substantial grounds to argue its case. Kissinger agreed that the US should help its ally. He did not perceive why India should feel threatened, as it was stronger militarily and continued to receive arms from the Soviets.

During his meetings in India in October 1974, Kissinger was unequivocally told by Swaran Singh that 'any attempt to introduce arms in Pakistan will certainly wipe out our efforts (of improving relations with Pakistan) ... any introduction of arms from American sources would create an uproar here'.[25]

On 24 February 1975, President Ford announced the lifting of the US sales embargo on lethal military equipment to India and Pakistan. The ban had been in place since the two went to war in 1965. The previous return of military equipment to Pakistan had met with a muted response by India, as it did not wish to scuttle the small steps that it had taken to improve relations with the US.

William Saxbe, Nixon's last attorney general and a former Republican senator from Ohio, replaced Moynihan as the ambassador to India. Prior to his arrival, on Kissinger's recommendation, President Ford had lifted the arms embargo on Pakistan. This meant that Pakistan would once again be able to purchase new arms and weapons from the US. Lifting the ten-year arms embargo predictably outraged India and Saxbe delayed his arrival until after the announcement. In a public statement, Saxbe stated that he had opposed the decision but was unable to persuade Kissinger.

## The Wrong Diplomat

Although Foreign Minister Y.B. Chavan cancelled his upcoming US visit in protest, it was Ambassador Kaul who wrecked the painstakingly patched-up bridges. T.N. Kaul was an odd choice to send to Washington because he was widely regarded as being pro-Soviet. When Mrs Gandhi had announced his appointment, Moynihan had cabled Washington: 'I have not yet met him, but all here agree he's inclined towards slyness, especially in his dealings with westerners. This latter quality is not only Kashmiri Brahmanical arrogance, it also reflects Kaul's propensity for misconstruing cleverness for sophistication in diplomatic dealings.' He also stated that Kaul was 'marked by pro-Soviet bias and concomitant anti-American words and deeds'.[26]

Initially, officials in Washington made an effort to welcome him, and despite the cynics, he developed a rapport with Kissinger, who joked that he dined more often at the Indian embassy than any other in Washington. Remarkable, given that Kissinger disliked Indian food![27]

Although Kaul was deputed to improve relations between the two countries, he was far from being an ideal diplomat. He would often start meetings and exchanges with the US administration in an aggressive manner. In a departure from his attitude towards India prior to becoming the secretary of state, Kissinger treated Kaul with humour and made sure the relationship remained civil. Kissinger had often called in his predecessor, L.K. Jha, for a dressing down. Jha, a far more polite and erudite man than Kaul, had worked hard during his tenure to maintain a cordial relationship. He had tried to explore commonalities and grievances with all sincerity but Kissinger at the time followed Nixon's lead in his anti-Indian, pro-Pakistan tilt, and there was no room for a relationship between the two diplomats in that hostile atmosphere.

Kaul either took Kissinger's goodwill for granted or carried away by his own hubris called a press conference where he railed against him and US policies. It was a total breach of diplomatic conduct. Kaul, given to sarcasm, could be undiplomatic. His constant haranguing was hardly conducive to better relations, but this time he went too far. The only explanation was that he probably thought he would endear himself to Mrs Gandhi.

Kissinger was furious and said that 'the comments of the Indian foreign minister are restrained and statesmanlike (might be acceptable), but those of the Indian ambassador are unacceptable'.[28] With that, the Indian dinners and attempts at friendship between the two came to an end. Kaul lost his access to the most important person in the US foreign policy establishment, who essentially gave up on improving relations with India. Mrs Gandhi, surveying the damage, recalled Kaul and sent the genteel Keval Singh as ambassador. Jagat Mehta, the most pro-US advocate in the foreign service, who had close relationships with Bunker, Galbraith and Moynihan, was appointed foreign secretary.

Mrs Gandhi may have recognized the need to repair relations with the world's most powerful democracy, but she invested little time or energy to do so. As neither Keval Singh nor Jagat Mehta were given the authority to make meaningful changes, their attempts at good relations amounted to little more than window dressing. Aside from making these pro-US foreign policy appointments, Mrs Gandhi was not incorrect in her assessment of India's importance, or lack thereof, to the US.

By 1976, President Ford was focused on the elections and India was largely forgotten. Essentially, the US viewed India and Mrs Gandhi as pro-Soviet with little strategic value. They saw no benefit in going out of their way for India. The US also found the unrelenting anti-US rhetoric offensive. Repeated requests by Kissinger and Saxbe to turn down the dial and use diplomatic channels to communicate grievances were ignored. Although Saxbe relayed to his government that much of the invective was for domestic consumption, Washington found it intolerable.

The two countries were consumed by domestic problems after 1974. The public in both countries had lost confidence in the integrity of their leaders and their ability to get them out of their economic difficulties. Ford, despite his reputation as a man of character, was weighed down by the economic downturn. He had tried to restore the country's faith in the presidency, but his pardon of President Nixon stained his otherwise clean reputation. He would always remain a transitional president.

South Vietnam was overrun by the North nine months into his administration, making a mockery of the prolonged US intervention in the region. The graphic images of defeat—of helicopters evacuating the US embassy in Vietnam—would endure as a testament to the futility of long-distance engagements in foreign cultures, where the loyalties of the civilian populations are indifferent to US interests.

Rising inflation, high oil prices and a car industry in trouble deepened the economic malaise in the US. Republicans haemorrhaged seats in Congress, as jobs disappeared and the economy shrank. President Ford tried to get the economy under control and hired as his financial advisors William Simon and Alan Greenspan, but any proposals to raise taxes alienated the conservatives. New York City, the financial and cultural capital of the US, almost went bankrupt. It was ultimately bailed out, but the enduring headline that remained was President Ford telling New York City to 'drop dead'![††]

By 1976, it became clear that President Ford would face an uphill battle against Jimmy Carter in the elections. In the end, the baggage of the Nixon presidency weighed Ford down. His lacklustre campaign did not help matters, and he lost the election to Carter in November 1976.

---

[††] President Ford did not actually utter those words. New York City was facing bankruptcy and he decided against bailing them out, and those were the words used by the newspaper headlines. It cost him politically and some say it cost him his presidency.

Faced with rising communist agencies within India challenging her government, Mrs Gandhi distanced herself from a 'capitalist USA' and lost few chances over the year to criticize it. Various members of her party echoed her lead. Communication between the two countries dried up and goodwill was reduced to a trickle. Furthermore, once Mrs Gandhi subverted democracy by imposing the infamous Emergency, she alienated American liberals who were India's strongest advocates in the US, leaving it isolated abroad.

# Chapter 12

# The Indian Emergency

SANJAY GANDHI WAS NOT QUITE THIRTY, IN 1975, BUT HAD STRONG views about how his mother should manage the affairs of India. He had recently married Maneka Anand, who had caught his attention when she won a beauty contest at the liberal arts college she attended. Maneka was the daughter of an army officer and ten years his junior. Headstrong and ambitious, the two of them were a sharp contrast to Mrs Gandhi's older son Rajiv and his wife Sonia.

Rajiv was quiet, self-deprecating and exceptionally polite. His Italian-born wife was beautiful, shy and devoted to her husband and two children. They all lived together with Mrs Gandhi in the same house. Although both brothers were interested in mechanics, neither had excelled academically and did not obtain any college degrees. Rajiv had attended Trinity College, Cambridge, and then moved to Imperial College in London to study engineering. He was passionate about flying, and trained as a pilot and obtained employment as one for Indian Airlines when he returned to India. It was a modest job by Indian standards for the son of such a prominent family. By all accounts, he led an unassuming life, kept a low profile and cherished his privacy.

After a stint at Rolls-Royce in England, Sanjay came back and attempted to start a car manufacturing company in India. Critics felt he used every available contact and did not hesitate to trade on his family connections to launch his business but was hamstrung by the very regulations that his mother's government had imposed on industry.

11 October 1949: Indian Prime Minister Jawaharlal Nehru (L), his sister and ambassador Madame Vijaya Lakshmi Pandit and US President Harry S. Truman ride from the airport to Blair House, in Washington, DC, after the Indian leader arrived in the United States for the first time. Nehru was there on a goodwill mission. It was his first visit to the US. Truman had sent his plane to pick Nehru up in London as there was no direct flight from India to the US at the time. The theme of his visit prepared by the State Department was 'the discovery of America'.

14 December 1959: President Dwight D. Eisenhower (L) with Prime Minister Jawaharlal Nehru at the Rashtrapati Bhavan in New Delhi, during Eisenhower's enormously successful goodwill tour. As the first US president to visit India, Eisenhower was greeted by thousands of well-wishers everywhere he went.

7 November 1961: US President John F. Kennedy (sitting in a rocking chair) meets with Prime Minister of India Jawaharlal Nehru, in the Oval Office, at the White House. Kennedy admired Nehru and tried to cultivate him, but would be deeply disappointed when India took over Goa without forewarning the US, shortly after the prime minister's return to India after meeting the president.

10 November 1961: Indian Prime Minister Jawaharlal Nehru arm-in-arm and deep in conversation with Jacqueline Kennedy, wife of the American president John F. Kennedy, on arrival at the White House. Nehru was charmed by Jackie Kennedy and invited her to visit India.

30 March 1966: Indian Prime Minister Indira Gandhi (C) chats with US President Lyndon B. Johnson before a dinner at the White House, during a three-day official visit to the United States. Mrs Gandhi, who had recently taken over as prime minister, had come to the US on a mission. India was facing a food crisis and she needed US aid. She had stopped in Paris on her way to visit her hairdresser, and as one State Department official wryly observed, 'She set out to vamp LBJ and succeeded.'

4 November 1971: President Richard Nixon and Prime Minister Indira Gandhi on the reviewing stand during her arrival ceremony at the South Lawn. India–US relations reached its nadir under the Nixon presidency. The two leaders quite evidently disliked one another.

12 June 1985: US President Ronald Reagan and First Lady Nancy Reagan with Prime Minister Rajiv Gandhi of India and Mrs Sonia Gandhi in the Yellow Oval Room during a state dinner.

17 September 2000: (L-R) First Lady Hillary Clinton, President Bill Clinton and Prime Minister Atal Bihari Vajpayee pose for a photograph, as the Clintons welcomed the Indian premier to the White House for a state dinner in his honour. Clinton viewed India as an important country and relations between the two nations began to thaw when the US supported India during the Kargil conflict.

18 July 2005: US President George W. Bush (R) and Indian Prime Minister Manmohan Singh (L), after a ceremony on the South Lawn, of the White House. The two leaders formed a partnership that transformed Indo-American relations, culminating in the historic nuclear deal.

President Bush (R) and Prime Minister Singh (L) toast at the White House during a state dinner. This was the first state visit by an Indian prime minister to Washington in five years that led to the nuclear deal of 2008 and began a new chapter in the India–US relationship.

25 January 2015: US President Barack Obama (L) hugs Indian Prime Minister Narendra Modi after a joint press conference in New Delhi. Obama announced they had reached an agreement to break the deadlock that had been stalling a civilian nuclear power agreement.

22 September 2019: Tens of thousands of Indian Americans converged at the NRG Stadium in Houston, Texas for the 'Howdy, Modi!' event that was attended by US President Donald Trump and Indian Prime Minister Narendra Modi. The crowd was decked out in all its finery and the event was attended by several prominent US politicians from both parties, indicating the growing importance of the Indian American community. The event kicked off in a football stadium with a Sikh blessing, boisterous bhangra dancing and, in a nod to local customs, cheerleaders in cowboy hats.

Sanjay was also attracted by politics—the family business. Unlike his mother and grandfather, who had spent years paying their dues as members of the Congress party and participants in the independence movement, he was impatient. He began to insert himself into his mother's political decisions as though it was his birthright. His sense of entitlement, coupled with his arrogance, alienated members of her government and tested the loyalty of her closest advisors. The prime minister's secretariat, with whom she used to consult, became increasingly marginalized. Her old advisors, P.N. Haksar, P.N. Dhar and other members of the 'Kashmiri mafia', as they were called, quickly realized that she was unreceptive to any criticism of Sanjay.

In 1975, Mrs Gandhi had been the prime minister for almost a decade. The pressures of the refugee crisis, the Bangladesh War and an anaemic economy were taking a toll on her. By 1975, bad harvests, high oil prices and shortages led to mass strikes and demonstrations.[‡‡] The Right increased its attacks, and the communists, with whom she had traditionally allied herself, not only turned against her but led the strikes. She was besieged and worried that she was losing control over the country. Her natural inclination to distrust outsiders and withdraw into herself in times of trouble began to take over. This time, however, things were different. Her sons were grown men and Sanjay was pushing to be actively involved in politics. She finally felt she had someone reliable she could lean on, and allowed him to exert an inordinate influence on many key decisions.

Sanjay was especially intrusive in the area of political appointments. According to various sources, he would hold grudges against people who had not assisted with his Maruti car project. He had spent years attempting to build a prototype, without success. He had finally managed to raise enough capital and used his connections to obtain a letter of intent, not an easy task in India in the 1960s. Bansi Lal, the chief minister of Haryana, befriended him, realizing that this would give him a direct line to Mrs

---

[‡‡] In 1972 and '73, the monsoons had failed, causing food prices to rise by 23 per cent and 30 per cent, respectively. The fourfold OPEC oil price hike in 1973 exacerbated the problem, sending inflation shooting up. The price of imports increased by a billion dollars, putting the economy near collapse.

Gandhi and power. Lal gave Sanjay, among other benefits, land for his factory at subsidized rates and became one of Sanjay's closest friends in the process. Sanjay was later accused of receiving help from questionable sources looking to curry favour with his mother.

Any irregularities relating to Sanjay's business were overlooked in deference to his mother's position. In a disappointing lapse of judgement, Mrs Gandhi enabled nepotism by not putting a stop to the unsavoury methods her son employed to further his interests. In Coomi Kapoor's book on the Emergency, she describes Mrs Gandhi calling her finance minister to tell him the Maruti project had run into trouble and asking him if he could look into it. The minister asked Sanjay for a project report, which he dismissed as old-fashioned. The minister explained to Mrs Gandhi that her son, despite good ideas, had no concept of how to set up a company. He offered to get him professional help, but Sanjay haughtily turned him down. The minister was left with no choice but to instruct banks not to lend the project any more money.

The Maruti project had become fodder for the gossip mill in political circles. Mrs Gandhi's trusted advisor P.N. Haksar suggested that she distance herself from the project and that, if Sanjay persisted in going ahead with it, they should consider living separately. Sanjay responded by making sure Haksar was removed from the prime minister's secretariat to a post where their interactions were limited.[1]

In 1974, students in the state of Gujarat protested the increasing cost of education and its decreasing quality. Inflation had raised food prices and colleges had passed them on to the students. The election promises of 1971 had not materialized and, with the economy in crisis, the students were angry. The state's new chief minister called in the police to restore order and seventy-four people were killed in the process, inflaming tensions further. Protests spread to other universities across Gujarat, along with calls for the resignation of the chief minister. He resigned in February 1974 and president's rule was imposed in the state. Morarji Desai now entered the fray and, in the tradition of Mahatma Gandhi, went on a fast demanding that the state assembly, dominated by the Congress party, resign as well. Mrs Gandhi yielded to the pressure and the state assembly was dissolved in 1974. The opposition was galvanized and determined not to allow the Congress to retain power in the state. Under pressure, Mrs Gandhi agreed to call elections in June for the state assembly. Her party lost, and the opposition led by Morarji prevailed.

Jayaprakash Narayan, a highly respected leader who was a member of the independence movement and a friend of Mrs Gandhi's parents, had joined the protests, giving them moral authority. He extended this into a national movement against the government. He had tapped into the disillusionment that the ordinary people were feeling. The protest movement spread to his state of Bihar, gathering national momentum. The Bihar state assembly was compelled to resign as well.

Indian Railways, the lifeblood of India, came next. It encompassed 10 per cent of the public sectors employees. Political parties in most countries try to court the unions, and India was no different. The railways had several competing unions with allegiance to different political parties, which were constantly stirring up tensions. In November 1973, a firebrand socialist, George Fernandes, took over the national union of railwaymen. He made clear that he intended to bring down Mrs Gandhi's government.

Fernandes threatened the government in a speech to union members: 'Realize the strength which you possess. A seven days' strike of the Indian Railways—every thermal station in the country would close down. A ten days' strike of the Indian Railways—every steel mill in India would close down and the industries in the country would come to a halt for the next twelve months. Once the steel furnace is switched off, it takes nine months to re-fire. A fifteen days' strike in the Indian Railways—the country will starve.'[2]

A strike was called for on 8 May 1974. Other unions, inspired by the railway workers, joined in. The strike lasted several days. Mrs Gandhi had 300,000 people arrested and the army was called to restore order. It shook her that the unions would risk the country's collapse. Many in government believe that this was the final straw that led to the Emergency.

Twelfth of June, 1975, began badly for Mrs Gandhi. One of her closest advisors, D.P. Dhar, had died. He was India's ambassador to Moscow and was in Delhi for meetings when he was taken ill and rushed to the hospital. By the time P.N. Dhar (no relation) arrived at the hospital, Mrs Gandhi was already there making funeral arrangements.

The day had begun badly but it would get worse for her.

By midday, the Gujarat election results were announced. The opposition had won, dealing a big blow to Mrs Gandhi, who had worked hard in that state for her party. However, as if things were not gloomy enough, the Allahabad judgement was handed down, and it ruled against Mrs Gandhi. In the 1971 election, she had won her seat from Raebareli. Her defeated opponent, Raj Narain, filed a case against her on a technicality to unseat her. He claimed that her election agent was a government employee and she had misused his services. Although the agent had resigned from government, the resignation was a matter of form rather than substance. The presiding Justice Sinha declared Mrs Gandhi guilty of dishonest election practices, ruled her election void, and barred her from running for elective office for six years.

The news caused a sensation. Although Mrs Gandhi announced that she would appeal the decision, the opposition was reinvigorated in calling for her resignation. The judicial process accomplished what the opposition's many protests had failed to do.

Sanjay was furious and organized masses of people to gather in front of the family home in a show of support. He employed state resources to bus people in. Day after day, Delhi traffic came to a standstill near the prime minister's residence as the rent-a-crowd milled about. Sanjay insisted she not resign.[3] Although he had never been elected to anything, he became an alternative power centre in the prime minister's circle. Mrs Gandhi remained huddled with her legal advisors Siddhartha Shankar Ray, Rajni Patel and D.K. Barooah for several days, deciding on a course of action. Sanjay and his cronies 'and various Congress party workers ... urged her to stand firm ... and not resign.'[4]

On 24 June 1975, Justice V.R. Krishna Iyer of the Supreme Court turned down Mrs Gandhi's appeal and granted her a conditional stay. She could continue as prime minister but was barred from voting in Parliament and could not receive a salary. The implications were clear. To avoid political chaos she could remain in office, for the time being, until elections could be called. But by depriving her of her seat in Parliament, her authority to govern was undermined. It was a devastating decision as it delegitimized her authority.

J.P. Narayan had called for a massive rally on 25 June 1975 to demand Mrs Gandhi's resignation. Thousands of people showed up. In the meantime, at the prime minister's residence, lists were being made of enemies to be dealt with. Mrs Gandhi, along with her coterie, had decided to suspend democracy and the freedoms in civil society for which her father had fought.

At 11p.m., a tense prime minister told P.N. Dhar that she planned to call a cabinet meeting in the morning and was going to declare an emergency in accordance with Article 352(1) of the Constitution. Officially, the president of India is the only person authorized to sign it. Fakhruddin Ali Ahmed, who was the president, did not protest as he owed his position to Mrs Gandhi.

That evening the lists of people to be apprehended were given to senior officials all over India. The arrests were made under the Maintenance of Internal Security Act, which permitted indefinite detention without a trial, a special snub to the judiciary.

By the early hours of the morning, jails around the country had begun to fill. Opposition members, journalists such as Kuldip Nayar who had written unfavourable articles about Mrs Gandhi or Sanjay in the past, publishers, and even the maharanis of Jaipur and Gwalior were rounded up. By August 1975, the total number arrested stood at 91,871. In subsequent weeks, 48,606 were released, with 43,265 remaining in prison in November 1975.[5]

Morarji was one of the lucky ones to be put up in a guesthouse. Most detainees were held in overcrowded, rat-infested and poorly ventilated jails. Several political prisoners died in prison. Lord Mountbatten intervened on behalf of his friend, the maharani of Jaipur, but to no avail.

The Indian press was muzzled. On the night of 25 June, electricity was cut to all newspapers on Bahadur Shah Zafar Marg in the capital. The government issued instructions that all newspapers were to be censored[6] and the mild-mannered minister of information and broadcasting, I.K. Gujral, was replaced by one of Sanjay's approved officers, V.C. Shukla. Editors were called in and told that they could not publish items that the government considered destabilizing. In protest, the *Indian Express* left its editorial space blank. Others published poems of bravery and freedom on the front page while some published recipes. *The Statesman* published its paper with blank spaces and an explanation that it was under censorship.

'A *Washington Post* reporter covering dissent about the Emergency gets kicked out of the country, his notebooks confiscated as he goes. The notebooks are mysteriously returned to him several months later, the names of his government sources underlined in red. Many of the sources had been picked up and taken to prison.'[7]

The Emergency, following on the heels of India's nuclear explosion, cost Mrs Gandhi the support of American liberals. She had corresponded regularly with a few friends overseas with whom she had developed a close relationship. Shocked by her assumption of dictatorial powers, they stopped writing to her. This was painful for her as it was personal.

If the power grab had invited Western condemnation, it was nothing compared to what was heaped on her from within India due to her son's actions. Although she had all the powers under the Emergency to implement any policy she wanted, little progress was made. Sanjay, who saw himself as co-consul, declared a twenty-point social welfare programme, with a special emphasis on lowering India's population. In order to legitimize his authority, he joined the Youth Congress and took its membership from a lacklustre seven lakhs to sixty lakhs. These members became his 'red guards'. The young, hitherto mostly unemployed, youths went around intimidating people. They forced people to show up for rallies and rounded them up for sterilization drives, and stories of extortion and racketeering became rampant. They even challenged Mrs Gandhi's old-time party workers, but she did nothing to rein in her son.

Sanjay set sterilization targets and handed them out to hospitals, government employees and officials all over India. Massive sterilization drives were undertaken nationally. Thousands at a time were sterilized. The medical procedure was conducted in railway stations and in schoolyards, often under the most unhygienic conditions. There was no informed consent and no follow-up care to manage complications. Many of the people were poor and had no avenues to complain. Reports of people being rounded up without explanation and taken to a centre to be sterilized began to come in. Men who were under thirty or had never had children were victims of the programme. As the demand to meet the numbers grew from the centre, even old men were sterilized to meet the targets.[8]

The literacy programme took a beating. Although it was one of Sanjay's five points, teachers were not spared. Because they had been tasked along with government employees to produce a set number of candidates to be sterilized every month, they pressured their students to get their parents to volunteer for sterilization and threatened to fail them if they refused. Parents began to pull their children out of school.[9] Despite the press censorship, reports began coming in from many sources of protests and anger. Some were conveyed to Mrs Gandhi, but she initially refused to believe them.

Sterilization was not the only area where people's rights were violated. Slum clearance was another of Sanjay's targets. People's homes containing all their possessions were bulldozed overnight. In Delhi, a widely publicized incident, involving the demolition of the area around Jama Masjid and Turkman Gate, cost Mrs Gandhi the Muslim vote that had traditionally voted for her as a bloc. Reports of harassment by minor officials with excessive power began to circulate. India had become an authoritarian state and was rapidly losing touch with the sentiments of its people.

To the dismay of many in her own government, Mrs Gandhi postponed the elections that were to have taken place in 1976. Reaction in the US was predictably negative. While Kissinger was more circumspect, Moynihan in an interview he gave to *Playboy* said, 'When India ceased to be a democracy, our actual interest there just plummeted. I mean what does it export but communicable disease?' He later told Dennis Kux he regretted the sarcasm but not the point.[10]

During this period, Sanjay gave an interview to Uma Vasudev for *Surge* magazine criticizing the USSR and India's communist party (CPI), which had supported his mother and the socialist policies of the past. This alarmed Mrs Gandhi, who was worried that he was alienating her strongest allies, especially as Moscow had supported the Emergency. She asked P.N. Dhar to squash the interview. The power orbits of mother and son were coming into conflict. Stories began to circulate that she was scared of him and that he had some secret hold over her. With newspapers suppressed, gossip circles took over. By the end of the year, Mrs Gandhi could no longer ignore the reports of atrocities that were making it past the filters.

Mrs Gandhi's decision to end the Emergency and call elections in January 1977 seemed to gather speed when she discovered that Sanjay, without consulting her, had convinced the state assemblies of Uttar Pradesh, Haryana and Punjab to pass resolutions demanding a new constituent assembly with a view to moving to a presidential system. The idea had been proposed by B.K. Nehru who felt the Westminster system model had not worked for India. Mrs Gandhi gave his carefully considered proposal to her advisors, D.K. Barooah, Rajni Patel and S.S. Ray. They responded with a paper drafted by A.R. Antulay that provided no checks and balances, and all but gave her monarchical powers, providing Sanjay with a legal basis for a power grab. Even Mrs Gandhi was unconvinced by its merits.[11]

The Emergency had become a noose around her neck, and rather than give her complete control of the country, it distanced her from her electorate and disconnected her.

The Intelligence Bureau had made it clear that the negative aspects of the Emergency would lead to law-and-order problems. Except for Sanjay and his henchmen, everyone Mrs Gandhi consulted urged her to end the Emergency. On 18 January 1977, she announced that elections would be held in eight weeks. All remaining political prisoners were freed, civil liberties were restored and all restrictions on the press were removed. The nightmare for India was finally over. In March that year, the Emergency was lifted, and the people went to the polls and voted her out of office. Depriving the people of their fundamental rights seemed to awaken political consciousness among the ordinary people. Democracy had taken root in India.

# Part Four:
# 1977–1991

# Chapter 13

# Carter: Wishful Thinking

NEW DELHI WAS RELIEVED TO SEE THE REMNANTS OF THE NIXON administration depart Washington in 1977. Mrs Gandhi's government felt that it could now reframe relations with the US, as President Jimmy Carter and his staff came with no previous baggage with respect to India. The Indians were especially optimistic since Lillian Carter, the president's mother, had volunteered with the Peace Corps as a health worker in India in 1966.*

When the president of India passed away shortly after Carter took office, he sent his mother to represent him at the funeral.† The Indians took this as a special mark of respect and perhaps attributed greater significance to it than Carter intended. A few weeks after becoming president, Carter wrote a candid letter to Mrs Gandhi in which he acknowledged that relations between their countries had not always been smooth. He hoped that while they may not agree on everything, they could move past their differences. 'Both sides no doubt have legitimate ground for complaint about actions and statements of the other, but for my part at least, I would like to put these behind us ... Our interests are not always going to coincide ... When we do have disagreements, these should not affect our overall relationship.'[1] He also made reference to

---

*   At the age of sixty-eight, Lillian Carter worked at the Godrej Colony near Mumbai for twenty-one months. She wrote a series of letters about her experience.

†   Fakhruddin Ali Ahmed died in February 1977, a few weeks after Carter took office.

his mother's time in India and indicated that it had predisposed him towards India.

Carter promised Mrs Gandhi he would appoint an ambassador with stature to represent him in New Delhi. His choice of Robert Goheen was a deliberate attempt on his part to improve relations by displaying cultural sensitivity towards India. Goheen came with stellar credentials. He had served as the president of Princeton University and was already familiar with India when he arrived, as it was the country of his birth.[‡] His parents had been missionaries there and he had maintained strong links with India throughout his life. During his tenure as ambassador he played an important part in smoothing over differences between the two countries.[§]

As Carter was settling into the White House in January, Mrs Gandhi announced she would hold elections in March, convinced that she had brought the economy under control and subjugated her critics. She ended the state of emergency in March, prior to the election, confident that the people of India were on her side. With human rights high on Carter's international agenda, it removed a potential source of conflict in their relations.

Mrs Gandhi prided herself on her ability to feel the pulse of the masses and was stunned when the country overwhelmingly voted against her and turned her out of office. The Congress party had lost power for the first time since Independence. The Janata Dal led by Morarji Desai was asked to form the government. The vote was not so much a vote for Desai but an indictment of Mrs Gandhi's authoritarian rule and the suspension of the

---

‡    Robert Goheen was born in India on 15 August 1919. He went to the US at age fifteen.

§    Cables from the US embassy to Assistant Secretary of State Saunders reveal a coherent understanding of India's political pressures and the value of India as a strategic partner to the US. It tried to explain India's opposition to arms shipments to Pakistan and Indian reservations about the Cold War rivalries in Asia. It acknowledges the role of the Soviets in supporting India and the rationale behind India's strong ties with them. The embassy put forward strong reasons to maintain the good relations that PM Desai had begun with President Carter.

Constitution during the Emergency. Desai, at the age of eighty-one, finally accomplished his long-cherished goal of becoming the prime minister.

President Carter was impressed with the election results and spoke admiringly of Indian democracy. With Mrs Gandhi defeated and her pro-Soviet advisors no longer in power, Carter saw an opportunity to place relations with India on a more positive footing. The election results proved that Indians understood the power of the vote and were not afraid to use it. In a neighbourhood replete with dictatorships, from Myanmar to the Mediterranean, it was a reminder to the US that India, the world's largest democracy, shared its core political values.[3]

Indian politicians also took note. India had survived its first major challenge to constitutional rule and no politician after the Emergency ever tried to tamper with democracy again.

## The Outsiders: Desai and Carter

When Desai finally became the prime minister, he was relatively unexposed to international affairs. Although he did not have a defined foreign policy agenda, he was clear about one thing. He was certain that the pro-Soviet tilt under Mrs Gandhi was wrong and needed rebalancing, and had regularly railed against what he considered India's excessively close relations with the Soviets. He had always been suspicious of them and saw them as a threat to India's independence and its policy of non-alignment.[¶]

The Soviets had tried to court him on several occasions, but Desai had refused their advances over the years. He argued with his ambassadors and foreign ministry officials who pressed him to visit the USSR and temper his comments about the Russians.[4] He disliked communists, and his suspicions about their motives had deep roots. Desai was viewed as pro-Western and pro-business and argued that India's friendship with

---

¶ The US government officials were aware that Desai's detractors used this to paint him as overly pro-Western. They went out of their way not to overreact to Soviet foreign minister Gromyko's visit in April 1977 or other Indo-Russian overtures.

Russia had come at the cost of Indo-US relations. This, of course, was welcome news in the US State Department.[**]

Desai was everything the worldly Nehrus were not. The Nehrus were socially liberal, firmly secular and loosely socialist. They had travelled widely, were educated overseas, and their friends included members of the international elite. Desai, on the other hand, belonged to an orthodox Hindu family from a small town in Gujarat.

When Desai was fifteen, he became the head of the household when his father took his own life by jumping into a well.[5] In accordance with his conservative upbringing, he assumed responsibility for his mother and siblings once his father died. Desai decided to proceed with his arranged marriage even though it was scheduled to take place just three days after his father's death.[††]

Desai was ascetic in his tastes. He was a vegetarian, and aside for a weakness for Swiss chocolates, he could go for long periods subsisting on just milk and dried fruit. He lived simply in the Gandhian tradition, with a minimal amount of material possessions. Desai was opinionated, known to be incorruptible, outspoken and often critical of the leadership and the party. Desai held several important posts after Independence, among them chief minister of Bombay State and home minister.

What he always wanted was to become the prime minister, but it was implicitly understood by members of the Congress party that Nehru would lead the country as long as he was alive. However, when Nehru died, Desai was disappointed when the party passed him over for Shastri. When Shastri suddenly died just eighteen months after being in office, Desai was bypassed once again as the party leadership selected Indira

---

[**] Desai's administration had tried to cultivate a closer, more pragmatic relationship with China, even trying to resolve the contentious border dispute. The overture did not go very far as, by the time the Chinese responded, Desai's tenure had grown shaky and China saw no reason to negotiate with a government that looked like it would fall.

[††] It was not uncommon in rural India for arranged marriages to take place between minors. Morarji Desai was fifteen at the time of his marriage. The couple did not live together or consummate the relationship until they were older, as was the custom.

Gandhi to head the government. Desai was furious. He was bitter about the decision and made it clear he thought she was unfit to run the country. He served in both the Nehru and Gandhi government, but resigned from Mrs Gandhi's government over her policies.

Desai and Carter both came from small towns, were deeply religious and were self-made men. In every way, Desai was, from a US perspective, the ideal prime minister. He was anti-Soviet, pro-Western and pro-business, but most significantly, it was his position on nuclear policy that was important to Carter. Desai had come out publicly against India developing its nuclear capability. He sincerely believed that it was immoral and against India's interest to develop nuclear technology for military uses.

The Desai government presented the perfect opportunity for the US to pull India in its direction and put a wedge between its relations with the Soviets. With the US military already committed to Pakistan, and years of mutual suspicion permeating relations between India and the US, it needed a president with a special interest in India to move the relationship forward.

Jimmy Carter, an evangelical Christian, was born in Plains, Georgia, and the name of the town perfectly described his lifestyle. He raised his family in a simple ranch-style house, to which he returned after he left the White House. When he became the president, any romantic notions of southern grace and grandeur becoming part of the White House social calendar were quickly dispelled. In his memoirs President Carter recalls walking, rather than driving, down Constitution Avenue after taking the oath of office. The Carters enrolled their ten-year-old daughter, Amy, in public school and insisted on frugality and informality in the White House.

Unlike Jackie Kennedy and Nancy Reagan, the Carters tried to scale back on ceremony and excessive social protocol. They sold the presidential yacht, deeming it an unnecessary expense. Although the public and press did not always appreciate their efforts, the Carters were determined to convey a message of simplicity.

Carter had grown up in a segregated south. Plains was a small place, with a population of approximately 600 when Carter was growing up. He did not have many choices when it came to his playmates and several of them were the children of black sharecroppers. By his own admission, he accepted the 'separate but equal' ruling of the US Supreme Court.[6] As a child he had not questioned the unfair standards of equality that applied to his black friends. He took for granted that they had to walk to school while he took a bus. It did not upset him that they were barred from many of the places he could frequent. Racism did not trouble him until he left Georgia and was exposed to more liberal values and a more inclusive lifestyle. 'It seems almost unbelievable, but it was only after I had gone away to serve in the Navy for eleven years and returned home to live ... that I finally came to acknowledge that black schoolchildren were still walking to their separate schools.'[7]

Although the racial disparities and prejudices in the American south offended him on his return from the navy, his conscience did not move him to action. He admitted that he did not participate in the civil rights movement that was picking up steam. 'It was deeply moving to see the end of legal segregation in the South and to observe the immediate benefits that came to all of us. I was not directly involved in the early struggles to end racial discrimination.'[8]

Barring the eleven years he spent in the navy, Carter's cultural exposure had been confined to the south. He returned to run his family's peanut farm when his father died and became gradually involved in politics. Beginning as a member of the Sumter County Board of Education, he was elected Governor of Georgia in 1970. The former governor, Lester Maddox, was a segregationist. Carter had concluded that segregation was wrong and decided to address the issue of racism the day he was sworn in as governor. In his inaugural speech he declared, 'The time for racial segregation [is] over.'[9] As the president, he supported the Voting Rights Act and attributed his election to the large numbers of African Americans who voted for him.

Carter was a complete outsider to Washington politics. This played to his advantage during his presidential campaign as he could portray himself as a candidate who was unencumbered by political obligations.

Despite the US experiencing precarious economic times with instability in the oil markets and record deficits, like Nixon, President Carter moved US foreign policy to the top of his agenda. He felt that previous administrations had lied to the American people about Vietnam, Cambodia and Chile, along with other policies, and that the trust deficit was as important as the economic one. He was deeply concerned that the US had lost its moral standing internationally. He was determined to restore America's reputation and became the most prominent advocate of human rights, both during and after his presidency.

## Non-proliferation

In his inaugural address, President Carter had vowed to work towards eliminating nuclear weapons from the world. His goal was to stop the spread of nuclear weapons to states that did not possess them and to convince nuclear-armed states to put limits on testing and stockpiles. He tried to get world leaders to commit to non-proliferation. Under President Eisenhower's Atoms for Peace programme, the US had committed to help energy-poor countries develop nuclear power for peaceful purposes.[10] India had been one of the countries that had participated in it.

Nehru was responsible for funding and setting up India's pursuit of nuclear energy, but was against the development of nuclear weapons. He enjoyed a close relationship with Homi Bhabha, the father of India's nuclear programme, but some in the Indian nuclear establishment viewed Nehru's pacifist views as soft. By 1960, in a world racing towards nuclear parity, Nehru was considered naïve by the India's Department of Atomic Energy (DAE). China's nuclear explosion in 1964 was considered sinister in the context of India's humiliating defeat two years earlier in the Sino-Indian War.

Many right-wing hawks felt India should aggressively pursue its own interest in atomic energy to counter the Chinese threat. After Nehru, every prime minister—except for Desai—approved of the work that the scientists were doing at the DAE. This put them at odds with the international nuclear community that wanted to contain the number of countries that possessed nuclear weapons. India's nuclear test in 1974 had created problems for its nuclear programme. It galvanized anti-proliferation groups to lobby against cooperation with India.

When India's CIRUS reactor was being built in the 1950s with Canada's help, an international entity regulating the transfer of nuclear technology did not exist. Bilateral agreements were the norm, and the terms varied by country. A universal understanding that the technology transfers were to be used strictly for peaceful purposes underpinned all agreements. Although the US had supplied the heavy water for the CIRUS reactor, initially its response to India's test was ambivalent. Canada however felt that India's 1974 nuclear bomb test had violated the spirit of the agreement and it ceased all nuclear cooperation going forward.

The international nuclear regime was created in 1967 and enshrined in the Treaty on the Non-Proliferation of Nuclear Weapons (NPT) were all the rules that regulated nuclear technology. The NPT recognized five countries as nuclear states. The countries that were part of the 'nuclear club' were the US, Russia, France, the UK and China. These five countries were allowed to keep their nuclear weapons as long as they agreed not to proliferate and share their technology with non-nuclear states. The privileged group of five had developed and exploded nuclear devices prior to 1967. China, the last country to be included in the club, had gone nuclear in 1964.

Non-nuclear states who signed the treaty were eligible to receive civil nuclear technology for peaceful purposes and, in return, they had to agree to submit their nuclear facilities to international safeguards and inspections and abide by a list of requirements outlined by the International Atomic and Energy Agency (IAEA). The rules excluded cooperation with countries like India that were non-signatories.

India had refused to sign the NPT claiming it was unfair and discriminatory. When India went ahead and exploded its own nuclear device in 1974, it was treated as a pariah by the international nuclear community. The NSG was set up in 1974 as a response to India's explosion to prevent nuclear proliferation. It laid down rules controlling the export of materials, equipment and technology to countries outside the NPT. The restrictions were placed in order to prevent trade in commodities used to manufacture nuclear weapons.

The US was heavily involved in India's nuclear programme before the international nuclear regime was established. India's largest nuclear power station at Tarapur, Maharashtra, was built by the US under a 1963 agreement.‡‡ It became operational in 1969. The contract, which predated the NPT, obligated the US to supply the Tarapur plant with enriched uranium for the next thirty years. The agreement further stipulated that the fuel had to come from the US; so, India was locked in on the supply side. India, in return, had to accept international safeguards and inspections at the facility. The US also had 'consent rights' on any reprocessed or spent fuel.

Due to contractual obligations, a partial amount was shipped to India during the end of the Ford administration, leaving it to President Carter to negotiate the contentious issue. As India was not allowed to seek other sources of enriched uranium, it put the plant and its energy output in jeopardy. This created intense resentment among Indians as they felt that the US was changing the terms of the original agreement. President Carter weighed the issues and decided to take a long-term view. He reasoned that India may be persuaded to sign the NPT if fulfilling the agreement to supply fuel in the short term would remove tensions with it. He pressured the US Nuclear Regulatory Commission to approve a long overdue license for the export of nine tons of enriched uranium to India.

Ambassador Goheen met with Desai in May 1977 and asked him to accept three conditions before the US shipped the long-pending low-enriched fuel for India's nuclear plant. It required India to maintain the IAEA's safeguards at Tarapur, provide assurances that the fuel would not be used in a nuclear explosive device and agree to negotiate with the US on non-proliferation questions. Desai agreed to all three conditions. In November that year, Zbigniew Brzezinski, Carter's national security advisor met with Ambassador Palkhivala in Washington to tell him that Desai should seize the moral leadership in the issue of proliferation. Palkhivala forcefully explained 'the political difficulty Desai would face if he were to agree to discriminatory controls such as the NPT or full-scope safeguards under apparent US pressure'.[11]

Carter invited Desai to visit Washington. The key objective was to eventually bring India under full-scope safeguards and commit to no

---

‡‡ General Electric (GE) built the plant.

further testing. The British chimed in, telling Americans that they should apply pressure on the Indians as 'the Indian strategy is simply to procrastinate'. But the Indians made it clear that Desai would be unable to make concessions during his visit.[12]

In March 1978, US Congress passed the Nuclear Non-Proliferation Act (PL 95242), placing strict controls on the export of nuclear equipment and material and requiring full-scope IAEA safeguards on all its nuclear facilities, including those not made by the US. There was a congressional veto provision that was tested on shipments to India in July 1978.[13] Section 123 of the US Atomic Energy Act placed restrictions on the US, only allowing it to enter into nuclear sharing agreements with countries that had signed the NPT. As a consequence, the US stopped supplying fuel to Tarapur, and it became a long-running dispute between the two countries.

The civilian use of nuclear technology remained the single-biggest unresolved issue between India and the US since India's nuclear bomb test in 1974. It would continue to cast a shadow over subsequent administrations and become a thorn in the relationship as the Indian nuclear establishment was adamant that the US and Canada had penalized India unfairly, and worse, the US was unreliable as it was reneging on its contractual obligations.

Carter understood that the US risked the cooperation of the Indians on the bigger issue of non-proliferation and the full scope of safeguards if he did not fulfil the US end of the Tarapur contract. He tried to obtain an exemption for India but was unsuccessful. In May 1978, President Carter wrote to Prime Minister Desai that he had submitted an executive order to Congress authorizing the export for Tarapur.[14] This was very well received in India and reinforced the perception that Carter was a friend, but the devil remained in the many details that had to be worked out.

Carter began writing to Desai to build channels of communication with the goal of persuading India to sign the NPT.[§§][15] This proved to be

§§ President Carter wanted PM Desai to commit to a moratorium on testing and accept a full scope of safeguards on all nuclear facilities. Carter's briefing papers prior to his India visit in January 1978 make it clear that Desai could not make concessions under US pressure. It would have been politically disastrous for Desai had he done so.

more difficult than he realized. Despite the confluence in their views on non-proliferation, India's national interests kept them far apart. Desai was sincere about the need to limit nuclear weapons and future testing, but he was unable to persuade powerful groups within the Indian government who disagreed with him.[16]

The defence establishment in India and the Congress party firmly opposed giving up India's options to develop nuclear technology for military purposes. With Pakistan now developing its nuclear capability with China's help, they thought Desai would jeopardize India's future security if he tried to roll back the nuclear programme. Even the scientific community in India ridiculed his naïveté.

Desai did not believe India should be in the nuclear arms race. Philosophically, he agreed with Carter, but his domestic political weakness prevented him from taking a strong stand. Goheen asked Desai to try to get India to sign a joint agreement with Pakistan that would commit both countries to not develop or to use nuclear weapons. Desai told the ambassador that he had already pledged to do so verbally, but deferred signing any formal agreement.

Carter made other small but significant overtures to develop the initial positive turn in the relations between the two countries. He moved away from Cold War rhetoric and was the first president to accept India's foreign policy of non-alignment as legitimate. When Carter became the president, he suspended sales of A-7 fighter-bombers to Pakistan because it was trying to purchase a nuclear reprocessing plant from France. The US had information that Pakistan was procuring sensitive technology with the goal of making a nuclear weapon. India's 1974 explosion put it in a different league militarily and Pakistan was determined to catch up. Having lost all its wars against India, it had no intention of being so disadvantaged. Bhutto famously swore that Pakistanis would eat grass if they had to, but they would get their bomb.

Carter's ambassador to Pakistan, Arthur Hummel, underplayed Pakistan's pursuit of nuclear parity with India. In a conversation with his counterpart in the US embassy, the Pakistani ambassador to Paris 'virtually admitted the purpose of the plant was military—to give the Pakistani people, Indians and others a perception of a Pakistani military capability'.[17] Pakistan had also tried to drum up support and funding from the Arabs for an 'Islamic bomb'.

Secretary of State Warren Christopher wanted to bribe Pakistan away from its nuclear ambitions by providing conventional arms that were highly sophisticated. These included A-7 aircraft, C-130 transport planes and air defence radar systems, along with food aid and economic assistance. Carter wrote 'No' in his own handwriting on virtually all of the items on the secretary's list. He also scribbled, 'Don't favor Pakistan buying nuclear processing plant from France'.[18] Under pressure from the US, the French backed out of their deal with Pakistan. In return, Carter resumed food aid and economic assistance to Pakistan.

Carter made a trip to India early in his administration and delinked India and Pakistan by simply not including a stop in Pakistan on the same trip. He also recognized India as the pre-eminent power in South Asia. The 'Delhi Declaration' that was announced at the end of the trip restated their mutual interests. It iterated platitudes about good relations but contained no significant progress in policies. It was symbolically important to India as it was a step in the right direction, but it was window dressing and lacked substance. President Carter resumed the bilateral assistance programme that had been suspended under Nixon, though it remained well below the requirements of a country the size of India.

India had been fortunate with the monsoons and had three good harvests. It had adequate food supply and the economy was growing at the rate of 7 per cent (1977–78). It looked to the US for assistance in investments and aid but was disappointed. Desai had no clear economic programme and years of regulation had made India an unattractive place for foreigners to invest. The relationship lacking mutual interests was entirely dependent on the energy that Carter and the octogenarian prime minister were willing to put in.

Desai was gracious to Carter's overtures. When an open microphone caught a private conversation between Carter and his secretary of state, Vance, in which the president complained about the Indian prime minister and confided to Vance that they needed to be 'cold and blunt' with India regarding nuclear concessions, Desai played it down.[19] He made a trip to the US following Carter's visit. He appointed Nani Palkhivala, who was known for championing human rights, as ambassador to the US.

Despite the talk of friendship and cooperation, and the occasional gesture of friendship, the pace of progress in relations between the two countries remained glacial. In fact, economic cooperation took a turn for the worse. The socialist mentality and suspicion of the US was deeply entrenched in India. Despite the pro-business rhetoric of the Desai government, it sabotaged its own plans by making the socialist politician George Fernandes minister of industries. Fernandes slapped exacting controls on foreign investors, which required them to reduce their ownership of capital shares in Indian enterprises to 40 per cent. Although the measures had been enacted under Mrs Gandhi, they had not been enforced. US companies began to regard India as unfriendly to businesses and were reluctant to invest in India. India lost Coca-Cola and IBM, both of whom pulled out. Trade barriers remained an insurmountable challenge.

From the Indian perspective, the US had not eased any critical restrictions. Aid, though restored, remained at negligible levels. India's attempts to diversify away from the Soviets by buying military hardware from the US met with continued resistance.[20] India had begun to manufacture small military hardware but it was still dependent on the Soviets for replacement parts and sophisticated weapons. Of the $200 million that India spent on overseas arms purchases in 1977, only $4 million was with the US.[21] The Indians felt that they had tried to remain non-aligned but that the US provided no help to them in their efforts to reduce their dependency on Moscow.

Carter's energy was fully engaged in other pressing areas which were placing his presidency on a path to historic success in his first two years in office. He concluded and signed the Panama Canal Treaty in September 1977, restoring the sovereignty of the canal back to Panama. It was a hard-fought victory with many in Congress opposing the handover, but Carter eventually prevailed. The US had controlled the canal since 1903 and retained the right to defend it. The conservatives had resisted relinquishing what they considered an asset vital to US interest, but the

US military presence in Panama had created friction between the two countries for decades.

Carter also pursued nuclear disarmament—one of his campaign promises and an issue close to his heart. He continued the SALT negotiations with the Soviet Union, which were begun by his predecessors to limit the respective superpowers' nuclear arsenals. His most enduring effort, however, was to bring peace to the Middle East and that is where his legacy was written. He approached the peace negotiations between Egypt and Israel with missionary zeal and began the process almost as soon as he became the president. Two years of negotiations, followed by historic talks that lasted for thirteen days in September of 1978, resulted in a treaty that remains his greatest achievement. Thanks to his Herculean efforts to bring Egyptian President Sadat and Israeli Prime Minister Begin together, the peace treaty has endured for over thirty years. No president since has broken the impasse in this forever war that is entering its seventh decade.

## The Russian Headache

If 1978 was President Carter's year of glory, 1979 would be his nadir.

Valentine's Day 1979 was a cold winter morning in Kabul. Gul Mohammed pulled up in front of the US ambassador's residence to drive him to work. It was a short distance from the residence to the embassy, where Ambassador 'Spike' Dubs planned to start his day with a staff meeting. The black Cadillac had barely driven halfway when armed insurgents in police uniforms halted the car at gunpoint. The hijacked car was ordered to the Kabul Hotel, where the ambassador was to spend his last remaining hours in Room 117. Mohammed, the driver, was ordered to go to the US embassy and inform its personnel that their ambassador had been 'arrested'.[22]

Ten thousand miles away in Washington, DC, it was close to midnight. President Carter had been preparing for a difficult trip to Mexico with which commercial ties had become strained. Emboldened by rising oil prices, Mexico had stepped back from signing trade agreements which it decided were not in its interest. Carter was scheduled to leave the next day for Mexico at 8.30 a.m. State Secretary Vance was woken up just before midnight and briefed on the situation in Kabul. He rushed to the State Department and tried to manage the situation via impossibly primitive cable and phone connections.

The message from Washington was to avoid any rash action that might endanger the ambassador's life and for the embassy officials to put pressure on the Afghan government to negotiate with the terrorists for his release. Ambassador Dubs's deputies, Bruce Amstutz, James Taylor and Bernard Woertz, frantically tried to contact everyone they could reach, from President Amin to the police chief, to intervene, but were shut out. As the morning wore on and precious moments ticked away, Afghan officials either refused to be available or were ineffectual. The insurgents were demanding the release of several political prisoners in exchange for the ambassador's life. They had set a deadline for noon. Not much was known about the abductors, who were identified as being part of an Islamic rebel group.

Four US embassy officials on site at the Kabul Hotel stood outside Room 117, trying to communicate with the insurgents and pleading with the Afghan police to not take any drastic actions that might endanger their ambassador.

By noon, Afghan commandos began to pour into the hotel. The US embassy officials observed that prominent among them were Soviet agents who seemed on familiar terms with the Afghans.

Despite the pleas for restraint from the American embassy staff, at 12.45 p.m. the police informed them that a rescue would be attempted. A Soviet advisor seemed to be overseeing the operation.[23] Americans watched in horror as the Afghan police opened fire. In forty seconds, it was over. There were no survivors. When the door to Room 117 was finally opened, there were bloodied bodies everywhere. Ambassador Dubs was dead.

President Carter's immediate response was to cut off aid, shrink the US embassy and step up its covert presence in the region. This inevitably meant using Pakistan to aid the anti-Soviet rebels. No one could have foreseen the long and complicated involvement with Afghanistan and Pakistan that would now be set into motion.

General Zia had taken over from Bhutto in July 1977 in a military coup. He was deeply religious and strategically clever. Unlike Bhutto, who was secular but would rant about India and American imperialism, Zia was quiet and self-deprecating. He slowly began the Islamization of Pakistan. He introduced public lashings and other medieval punishments as prescribed by the sharia law, much to the dismay of educated Pakistanis. Bhutto was imprisoned, and Zia began the process of promoting religious acolytes within the army and the ISI.

When Soviet tanks crossed the Amu Darya River and began a long occupation of Afghanistan, Zia knew Pakistan's fortunes were about to change. He saw the Soviet presence in Afghanistan as an opportunity to hold US interests hostage. He quickly calculated that the US would need Pakistan's help and launched an intensive marketing campaign. He talked about the communist threat in theatrical terms to frighten the West. He hinted that Pakistan could come under the Soviet sphere of influence, opening a back door to the Gulf, and tried to sell Pakistan as a force to push back Russian expansion if the US would support the effort.

The Carter administration quickly sought congressional approval to suspend the Symington and Glenn amendments that sanctioned countries thought to be proliferating or reprocessing fuel. Having censured Pakistan in the past, the Carter administration now found itself in the awkward position of going back on its policies and needing Pakistan's cooperation. Zia held out for the best deal he could extract. He pushed for the most advanced US military equipment, billions in aid and non-interference in Pakistan's nuclear programme. The Carter administration balked at his demands and offered him a more modest aid package. Zia turned it down. It was unprecedented for the Pakistanis to turn down US aid in any form. But after consulting his allies in the US and the Gulf, Zia took a calculated risk that there would soon be a new administration in the US and held out for a better deal.

The resurrected US relationship with Pakistan became a source of irritation for India, but that would soon be the least of its concerns. By the end of 1978, the US had begun to discern signs of weakness in the Desai government. Although negotiations would limp along, India had begun to slide off the US radar. By 1979, Carter was facing challenges of his own that would put India on the back-burner. By mid-1979, both Carter and Desai were beset by problems that would doom their respective administrations.

## Trouble on the Horizon

Morarji Desai's domestic problems were mounting. His government was based on a coalition and infighting between the groups undermined effective governance. Despite his pro-Western tilt, the promise of Western investments never materialized. The economy remained sluggish despite strong reserves and good harvests, with no economic vision about how to solve the distribution of resources or alleviate the grinding poverty that continued to plague the country. The prime minister's more liberal beliefs in a market economy failed to overcome barriers towards liberalization. The biggest disappointment for the commercial sector was that all the regulations and red tape that dampened business investment remained in place. Desai never won over India's civil services, which ran the country and remained suspicious of the US. Desai was viewed as old and eccentric whose personal habits also damaged him. The fact that he followed ancient cures like drinking his own urine and was not shy about extolling their virtues publicly[24] made him vulnerable to ridicule both inside and outside the country.

Desai was no match for Mrs Gandhi's extensive political apparatus, which she ceaselessly worked to weaken him. There were many allegations that the Russians also tried to undermine him behind the scenes. Desai, who could be blunt to the point of rudeness, offended USSR on more than one occasion. In a direct confrontation with Premier Kosygin, he accused the Soviet Union of interfering in India's domestic politics. He rather undiplomatically refused to accept Kosygin's denials.[25] Having failed to develop good relations with him, the Russians sought to ensure their reliable ally Mrs Gandhi's return to power.

The warming of relations between India and the US depended heavily on the efforts of the two leaders. President Carter was, by nature, reserved and somewhat cold. Although he liked India and tried to develop a rapport with Desai in order to promote his agenda on nuclear disarmament, he did not put his weight behind it once he realized that while the Indians were not guilty of proliferating, they would not sign the NPT. Constrained by the new regulations and laws governing nuclear technology, he was unable to accommodate India's requirements. As the Desai government lost altitude, he transferred his energy in other directions.

Desai, despite being aligned with President Carter on the issue of non-proliferation, was unable to persuade his own officials to abide by the new international standards demanding inspections and safeguards to ensure non-proliferation. Although his values were closer to the US than Moscow, he was not willing to sacrifice India's priorities. Desai's government had focused its attention on its immediate neighbours and distanced itself from the Soviets. India reached a historic agreement with Bangladesh, in November 1977 to share the waters of the Ganges at Farakka in West Bengal.

India and the US shared a relatively limited agenda where they could cooperate, and while it was an improvement from when the US was viewed as hostile to India, the leaders never connected on any personal level. Their shared views on disarmament, free trade and democracy were insufficient to overcome the baggage carried by their respective governments when they dealt with each other.

Events in Carter's presidency began to unfold in rapid succession. Domestically, the economy was in deep trouble. The oil price hike in 1979 had resulted in runaway inflation. The Federal Reserve Bank under Chairman Paul Volcker had applied tough measures, sending interest rates shooting up. Although the economy would calm down eventually, time was needed for policy prescriptions to take effect. Carter was running against the clock and was unable to benefit from the end results of his policies.

Internationally, events were brewing that would prove fatal to the Carter presidency. Iran, a staunch ally of the US, was going through a major political upheaval that would cast a long shadow over the world for decades. Iranians, chafing under the repressive regime of the Shah, overthrew him in a revolution in 1979. A Muslim cleric, Ayatollah Khomeini, took over and Iran became a theocracy.

Carter, who was intensely engaged in the most important negotiations of his career with Sadat and Begin, failed to recognize the enormity of the situation in Iran. The Shah departed Iran on 16 January 1979. The US administration was preoccupied with preparing for the first visit by a Chinese premier the following week.⁵⁵ Although the press covered Khomeini's triumphant return to Iran in February after years in exile, the US was focused on the highly anticipated signing of the Middle East Peace Treaty between Egypt and Israel in March 1979. No president had come this far in negotiating peace between the Arabs and Israelis. Both Yasser Arafat and Anwar Sadat were planning to attend. It was a historic achievement that should have catapulted President Carter to a second term in office.

Shortly after the peace treaty was signed on 26 March, the Salt II Treaty was signed with the Soviet premier, Leonid Brezhnev, in Vienna on 18 June. The summer of 1979 was the last time that Carter held the initiative in his presidency.

In October 1979, President Carter, under intense pressure from the Shah's powerful friends in the US, agreed to allow him to enter the country to receive medical treatment. That fateful decision cost him his presidency. Infuriated students in Iran took over the US embassy in Tehran, on 4 November 1979, and held fifty-two American diplomats hostage for 444 days. They were finally released as he left the White House. The infamous 'hostage crisis' was the pivot point in Carter's administration. It was to consume him right up to his last day in office and relegated him to a one-term presidency.

## Prelude to the Longest War

The year just kept getting worse for President Carter. In December 1979, just as the US election season was underway, the Russians invaded Afghanistan. Although events in Iran were more significant for Carter and his presidency, the invasion of Afghanistan would be the beginning of a US engagement in a country that would last longer than any war in its history. It would take different forms, from covert efforts to push back the Soviets to direct involvement in the region, and become a quagmire that sucked the US in for decades.

---

⁵⁵ Vice Premier Deng Xiaoping and his wife Madame Zhuo Lin visited Washington on 29 January 1979.

Developments in Afghanistan not only revived the Cold War matrix but, much to India's ire, revived Pakistan's status as a strategic partner for the US. India was pushed aside as an unimportant player. India looked politically unstable as Desai had been ousted in a power struggle months earlier, and his successor, Charan Singh, barely lasted 171 days. The Indian government had been in free fall for six months. The tiny window of improved US–India relations that had presented itself when the pro-Western Desai became the prime minister closed before either side was able to pry it open to give it air. Regardless of whether the US acknowledged it or not, India had strategic interests in Afghanistan.

Under the Indo-Soviet treaty of 1971, the Russians were bound to inform India about their Afghan intentions. The Soviet Union was aware that its actions would be criticized by the world and was desperately trying to reach the new interim prime minister. The Russians were not just trying to fulfil their treaty obligation. They knew that they would need a strong ally in the face of world condemnation.

Prime Minister Charan Singh was unreachable. He was ill. When Brezhnev's message was finally delivered, to Russia's surprise, the response was lukewarm. Much to their annoyance, Singh lectured them about Afghan history and their resilience to foreign invaders. Although the Indian government fell into line and publicly supported the Soviet action in the international arena, many privately condemned what they were sure was a foolhardy enterprise doomed to failure. As there was no effective government in India, there was no strategy to privately convey to the US and other world powers that they had deep reservations about Soviet aggression in Afghanistan.

Although India was unhappy at the Soviet action and tried to influence Russia to unilaterally withdraw from Afghanistan, its refusal to censure Russia in the United Nations placed it in the enemy camp. Several Indian officials, who felt that a more balanced policy would serve India better, thought the vote to abstain from censuring the Soviets was a mistake, but the damage was done and the two countries reverted to a cold peace.[26]

Once again, as in 1968 when the Soviets crushed the uprising in Czechoslovakia, India had stood on the wrong side of history. Indians capitulated to Russia, which they should not have on the principle of non-alignment. It was the last time they would allow the Russians to exert such a degree of influence over their foreign policy. Many considered it payback for Soviet support during the Bangladesh War and their consistent support on Kashmir in the UN.

Charan Singh's interim government fell. The Indian electorate was fed up with the Janata government's incompetence and infighting. They felt Mrs Gandhi had been chastised enough and she roared back to power in January 1980. The Soviet's strongest ally was back.

By 1980, the Carter presidency was in trouble. A highly respected journalist, Ted Koppel, aired a daily update on the hostage situation in Tehran on a TV show called *Nightline*, reminding the public every day about the unresolved crisis in Iran. In March 1980, a botched attempt to rescue the US embassy hostages made Carter's administration look incompetent. In May, Mount St. Helens erupted; it was the biggest volcanic eruption in the US. Over 1,000 feet of the mountain vanished with the explosion and volcanic ash fell across fifteen states. It was an ominous sign. In November 1980, Carter lost the election to the Republican Ronald Reagan, governor of California and a former Hollywood actor.

President Carter never gave up trying to bring the hostages home. It was his persistent efforts that finally got them released, but he did not receive the credit he deserved. The hostages were released on 20 January 1981 just as Reagan was being sworn in. The newly elected president got a shining start to his presidency, while Carter was deprived of a much-needed positive end to his. The India–US relationship was simply forgotten in the avalanche of world events confronting the outgoing Carter administration.

# Chapter 14

# Afghanistan: The Great Game Continues

AFGHANISTAN FLOATED SOMEWHERE ON THE PERIPHERY OF American consciousness. It was a remote, exotic country that few Americans had visited. Afghanistan in the 1960s and '70s was barely on the radar of the US government. The US was preoccupied with Soviet interests in Europe and the Middle East rather than South Asia. Iran had been cultivated as the listening post to spy on Russia during the Cold War. The US backed this resource up with a strong ally in Pakistan; the US had little need for Afghanistan, a country they viewed as backward and culturally inaccessible. They accepted Soviet hegemony there without undue concern. Their investments in the Indian subcontinent were minimal.

Although Russian influence in India had been a damper on Indo-US relations, South Asia and, in particular, Afghanistan, it was not critical enough for the US to get excited over. With Pakistan firmly in the US camp, it had hedged its bets in the region.

Russian hegemony in the region was nothing new. In the nineteenth century, during the colonial period, the British were the world's pre-eminent power and they had watched warily as the Russians expanded both territory and influence in the region.

For the British Empire, however, India, which encompassed Pakistan and Bangladesh prior to 1947, was central to their wealth and prestige, and they were willing to go to great lengths to protect India from any Russian interference. The Great Game* was played out between these two reigning world powers in the harsh landscapes of the lands east of the Hindu Kush. Afghanistan provided an important buffer for India from the steadily encroaching Russians. 'For four centuries the Russian Empire had been steadily expanding at the rate of some … 20,000 square miles a year. At the beginning of the nineteenth century, more than 2,000 miles separated the British and Russian Empires in Asia. By the end of it, this had shrunk to a few hundred, and in parts … to less than twenty.'[1] The British were determined to expand their strategic depth by keeping Afghanistan firmly under their sphere of influence. They invaded Afghanistan three times. The first invasion in 1839 ended in a disastrous defeat for the British. Everyone in the British army was slaughtered except for one man, who was left to relay the message of their defeat to the British garrison. The story has become the stuff of legend and a powerful symbol of the inability of foreign powers to subjugate Afghanistan.

The success of the second invasion in 1878 was dubious, with heavy losses for the British who, despite their victory at Kandahar, aptly demonstrated the cliché of winning the battle but losing the war. In the First Anglo-Afghan War, retreating soldiers and families who were not killed died from the cold. In 1878, cholera and searing heat decimated the British army. A tentative peace followed with the British maintaining authority over Afghanistan's foreign policy, although they withdrew all their forces from the country.

In 1919, Afghanistan attempted to rid itself of British oversight for good. The Third Anglo-Afghan War ended with Afghanistan's independence. The Durand Line was drawn to demarcate Afghanistan from British India and would become a controversial border in the future, as it cut through tribes and families.

It is hard to imagine that Afghanistan was a Buddhist country for almost a thousand years. The beautiful Buddhist statues at Bamiyan that dated from the sixth century were the evidence of another Afghanistan long

---

\* The Great Game was the competition between Russia and the British Empire for influence and territory during the nineteenth century.

past, but highly respected, until Islamic fanatics took over the country. In 2001, the statues were destroyed by the Taliban.

When Alexander's armies invaded in 330 BCE, Buddhism was widely practised in the region. Over the centuries, various invaders brought different cultural and religious influences in the area. Zoroastrianism and Hinduism were practised too at some point. Islam arrived around the eighth century but, by all accounts, the different religions coexisted peacefully. Al-Biruni and Al-Idrisi, both travellers and scholars, refer to the Afghans as Buddhists and Hindus as late as the twelfth century. However, by the fourteenth century, Afghanistan had become a Muslim-majority country.

In 1929, a Pashtun family took control, ushering in the longest period of peace in modern Afghanistan that would last until 1978. Zahir Shah ascended the throne in 1933, at the age of nineteen, after his father was assassinated. It is instructive to see how he managed the various factions and the international powers vying for influence over four decades of peace. When he became king, he waited patiently while his tribe and family members ran the government. He bided his time and slowly established control over them. He used existing rural power structures to maintain law and order, and cautiously began to introduce concepts of Western democracy, pushing for modernization while maintaining stability. He created consensus through long-standing local political systems, using the Loya Jirga, an indigenous system of representative government, which became the symbol of Afghan unity.

Not all of Zahir Shah's ministers were content with the status quo and slow pace of modernization. The king's brother-in-law, Daoud Khan, was impatient with his policies and wanted to modernize Afghanistan quickly. He took over in a coup in 1973, when Zahir Shah was overseas for medical treatment. Although concerned about US reaction, it was his neighbour, the Soviets, that he leaned on for support and approval.

The Soviets had begun to play an active role in Afghanistan in order to consolidate their influence. They had built up their bona fides with tangible assistance over the years. A popular project that was a point of pride for the Afghans was the Salang Tunnel, built by the Soviets in 1964 at a height of 11,154 feet. The 1.66-mile-long tunnel was considered a feat of engineering in Asia at the time. The Soviets, in order to strengthen alliances with their neighbours throughout the Cold War period, also provided other forms of aid to the Afghans as was their policy with India.

Under Soviet leadership, an Afghan communist party was established. Babrak Kamal and Nur Taraki become its leaders. The communists began to assert themselves and jostled for power. The Khalq faction wanted their country to modernize immediately along the Soviet model. The Parcham party was more moderate and preferred to modernize slowly after building up civic institutions. When Daoud forcibly took over the reins of government by upending the monarchy, he opened the floodgates of war, rivalries and assassinations that would scar the country and stunt development for the next thirty years. It is a testament to Zahir Shah's symbolic value embodying Afghan unity that, twenty-nine years after he was ousted, at the age of eighty-two, he was persuaded by the US to return from exile and help establish the Karzai government.

A dizzying round of assassinations and coups took place after the king's ouster in 1973. Daoud, who had signed a friendship treaty with the Soviet Union, was killed by Taraki in 1978.

On 27 April 1978, the Indian foreign secretary, Jagat Mehta received a phone call informing him that Daoud had been gunned down along with his family and entire cabinet and Taraki had taken over. Yuri Voronstsov, the Soviet ambassador to India, was sitting in his office with him. Mehta looked at the ambassador and tried to assess his reaction to the information.[2] Mehta wrote that he was convinced after watching his reactions that the Soviets had no hand in Taraki's actions.

India's immediate concern was to reassure Pakistan that it would not act in any way that would jeopardize their recent attempts at opening a dialogue. Mehta also met with Ambassador Goheen to press upon him India's view that the US treat developments in Afghanistan as a regional matter and not react by providing more arms to Pakistan.

Events in Kabul, however, moved so rapidly that diplomatic efforts by the Indians to constrain the US would soon dissipate.

It was not long before Hafizullah Amin, another prominent communist leader, challenged Taraki.

Taraki had pleaded for Soviet military assistance but Kosygin told him that Soviet troops on the ground would inflame things further.[3] With remarkable foresight, he said the Afghan population would rise up against them and it would provoke the US and Pakistan to support the rebels. Barely seven months after Ambassador Dubs's murder, Amin's supporters killed Taraki in September 1979. Each usurper undertook a 'cleansing' operation after seizing power and eliminated his enemies. The political upheavals in Kabul had turned the rivalries into a bloodbath.

The Soviet leaders had been watching the mounting body count and deteriorating political situation with increasing alarm. Complicating the Soviet calculus was concern that the US was attempting to take advantage of the chaos in Afghanistan and penetrate its leadership.

On 8 December 1979, in a private meeting of senior politburo members including Brezhnev, Andropov, Ustinov and Suslov, it was decided to have the KGB remove Amin and instal their man, Babrak Karmal, as the prime minister. In addition, they decided to send troops into the country to ensure stability.[4]

Not everyone in Moscow agreed with the decision. Nikolai Ogarkov, aware of Afghanistan's history and culture, was highly critical of the 12 December directive to invade Afghanistan. In a highly unusual move, and at great personal risk, he, along with two other generals Akhromeyev and Varennikov, filed a dissenting report to Ustinov. Their warnings fell on deaf ears. Somehow the politburo had convinced itself that the US plan was to dominate Afghanistan and threaten the Soviet Union using the Afghans as a base. On Christmas Eve, the Soviet army crossed the Amu Darya River.

The generals understood that the Afghans were a fiercely independent people with a low tolerance for interference from foreign governments in their country's affairs. Despite internal divisions, Afghans unite when threatened with outside aggression. The British learnt that to their detriment during the colonial period. It was the Afghan resistance to their efforts at subjugation that exposed the limits of British power.

The Afghans' ultimate success at wresting independence from the British became a powerful inspiration for the Indians during the struggle for India's independence. The Indians realized that the British were not invincible. If the all-powerful British, with their superior artillery, disciplined armies and complicated rules of engagement and manoeuvres, could be defeated by a ragtag group of South Asian tribesmen, the far more sophisticated Indians should be able to throw them out of India. It was the beginning of the end of the British Empire. Any great power that tried to dominate Afghanistan was undermined by it. The next great power to try would be the Soviet Union, and their involvement in the region would also be a prelude to their demise as a superpower.

Russians had remained the dominant world power in the eastern hemisphere since the Second World War and had watched carefully as British attempts at dominance had crumbled in the face of Afghan resistance. Sixty years after Afghan independence in 1919 and British withdrawal, and despite the lessons learnt, the Soviets embarked on a similar enterprise and got mired in the quicksand of Afghan politics.

Like the British, the Soviet weakness would be exposed. It quickly became their Vietnam. Their involvement in Afghanistan kept escalating in inverse proportion to their success, draining their treasury, manpower and morale. It contributed to the dismantling of the Soviet Empire. After a gruelling decade, like the British before them, the Soviets withdrew in defeat.

Soviet interference resulted in the US escalating their involvement and the unhappy consequences would bleed through several US administrations. Much to India's dismay, Pakistan became America's indispensable ally in the war to undermine the Soviets.

The US would now start its long, complicated and sometimes illegal involvement in Afghanistan. It would, in one way or another, tie the fates of the three countries[†] in a deadly embrace for the next thirty-five years. Afghanistan has become America's longest running war, a quagmire without a happy ending. No one wants to admit defeat, but like Russia and the British before them, Afghanistan may simply remain a country that is the 'Graveyard of Empires', as Seth Jones so aptly called his book on Afghanistan.[5]

---

† Pakistan would become the conduit for arms shipments to the Afghan rebels. Pakistan would use their position to get aid and arms, and the US relationship with India would wither.

## Chapter 15

# Mrs Gandhi and Reagan: A Tentative Thaw

AT 7 A.M. ON 23 JUNE 1980, AS THE NATIONAL CAPITAL WAS waking to its daily rhythms, Sanjay Gandhi, an amateur pilot, went to the Delhi Flying Club to take a spin in a two-seater Pitts S-2A plane. It was a typical clear, hot, sunny day in New Delhi. The plane was parked at Safdarjung Airport, a largely abandoned airfield in the centre of the city, less than a mile from the prime minister's residence. Barely forty-five minutes into the flight, while flying dangerously low and trying out various manoeuvres, Sanjay lost control and crashed just 500 yards from his home.[1] He and his co-pilot were killed instantly. Sanjay was thirty-four years old. He left behind his twenty-four-year-old widow, their three-month-old son and a bereft Mrs Gandhi.

Sanjay enjoyed taking people for rides in the plane and subjecting them to daredevil stunts. The Sunday before the accident, he had taken his wife Maneka and Mrs Gandhi's personal aide, R.K. Dhawan, for a ride and they had both emerged jittery. 'Civil aviation authorities had complained last May that Sanjay was ignoring safety requirements during his frequent flights.' Members of the flying club knew him 'as a skilled but wilful flier … prone to show off his dare-devilry. He had no ears for cautionary advice.'[2] Mrs Gandhi, who had heard the reports, was worried and had planned to speak to him but never got the chance.

The loss of Sanjay was both personal and political for Mrs Gandhi. Losing her child was painful but losing her political heir was a catastrophic setback for the prime minister. For an increasingly paranoid politician who relied on family, her loss was irreparable. She had shown no qualms about setting up a line of succession that ran antithetical to the institutions of democracy, and would now try to persuade Rajiv, her elder son, who had kept his distance from politics, to take Sanjay's place. There was no separation between the prime minister and her extended family. They were part of her everyday life. Sanjay, Rajiv and their families had always lived with their mother in her official residence.*

Mrs Gandhi's government had been busy consolidating its victory in the election six months ago. They had returned to power in January 1980, after a three-year period in the political wilderness following the Emergency. After losing the elections in 1978, the opposition had launched full-scale investigations† into Mrs Gandhi's abuse of power. Former colleagues and friends had avoided her. The Soviets, not wishing to antagonize the newly formed Janata government, had maintained their distance. Mrs Gandhi's circle of trusted advisors had narrowed, and she had increasingly leaned on Sanjay, choosing to ignore the glaring political impropriety of elevating her son over long-serving members of her party. Sanjay had run for office in 1980 and now held his own seat in Parliament. He had built up an alternative and independent power structure[3] from his mother that created severe misgivings within the Congress party and government circles. This, combined with the prime minister's blatant nepotism, rankled many, but with the opposition in disarray, she pushed the boundaries of her office without anyone challenging her. Although she was more contrite in public since her

---

* As is usual in many traditional Indian households, the grown sons along with their families lived under the same roof as their parents. This was not disturbing to the electorate as it was a traditional structure, but it clearly gave the new MP unusual access and power.

† The Shah Commission was appointed by the government of India in 1977 to enquire into all the excesses committed during the Emergency (1975–77). It was headed by Justice J.C. Shah, a former chief justice of India. The commission published its report on the illegal events during the Emergency and the persons responsible in three volumes, totalling 525 pages.

ouster in the 1978 election, Mrs Gandhi's innate authoritarian tendencies had not diminished.

After Sanjay's death, many, both in and out of government, felt relieved that he was no longer around to bully and push people to do his bidding. Most were hoping that with him and his cabal gone, decision-making would revert to the traditional hierarchies within government.

Rajiv, Sanjay's older, more soft-spoken brother, was a professional pilot for Indian Airlines. He had married an Italian woman with whom he had fallen in love while studying at Cambridge University. Although his wife Sonia was very close to her mother-in-law and had become her most trusted companion after Sanjay's death, neither Sonia nor Rajiv had displayed any interest in a political career. They had never taken advantage of their access to power and would now reluctantly enter public life.

Although Mrs Gandhi maintained a stoic demeanour during the funeral and went about her work, those close to her were aware of the intense loss she felt following Sanjay's death. She confided to her physician Dr K.P. Mathur that she felt she had lost her right arm.[4] She increasingly turned to religion for comfort.[5] Having shown no interest in religion prior to her defeat in 1977, she worshipped at a dozen shrines since being re-elected. After Sanjay's death, Mrs Gandhi's increasing interest in astrologers and rituals alarmed family and friends.[6]

There was little movement in foreign affairs during this period as the rest of her year was spent trying to control the domestic turmoil in the country. The economy was faltering. India had also suffered from the oil price hike that had hurt the US. Inflation had soared and growth had sagged. The border states were agitated. Assam was up in arms because a massive influx of Bangladeshi Muslims threatened to turn the Hindu Assamese into a minority in their own state. This particular demographic tension would fester for decades. Tensions between the Hindus and the Sikhs in Punjab drove the Sikhs to demand their own state. Some even proposed secession. In Kashmir, there were riots in response to Mrs Gandhi's heavy-handedness in firing elected officials who had not supported her in the past. Trying to extinguish all the fires within India left Mrs Gandhi little time for international relations.

## Reagan and the Rise of the Conservatives

In the US, President Carter's last year was mired in the Iran hostage crisis and another oil price hike that had sent the US economy into a tailspin. Interest rates had jumped to 18 per cent and every economic indicator pointed to a crisis. With the election looming, President Carter seemed to have all the cards stacked against him. The evangelicals, who had considered President Carter as one of their own, began to abandon him. He lost his solid base of support in the south. They moved over to the Republicans, ensuring Ronald Reagan's victory at the polls in November 1980.[‡]

Reagan had started out life as a liberal, not unlike many of his Hollywood friends. When reflecting on his past, he called himself a 'haemophiliac liberal'.[7] When his acting career generated an income that put him in a high tax bracket, the 84 per cent tax rate on his income appalled him.[8] As the president of the Screen Actors Guild (SAG), he had confrontations with communist organizers and this experience gradually drove him to the Right. Although he admired FDR and the New Deal, he began to view government and regulations as an impediment to progress. He endorsed Nixon in 1960 and formally became a Republican in 1962.

The political landscape in the US had begun to shift in small but significant ways that would transform its politics for the next century. Southern Democrats had been moving steadily to the Right since the 1960s and the repeal of the Jim Crow laws that enforced racial segregation in some southern states which had been enacted by white legislators to counter political and economic gains made by African Americans after the civil war. Conservative southerners resented northern liberals passing judgement on their social structures and way of life. Culture clashes around busing, affirmative action and civil rights created deep divisions and resentments within the US.

---

‡   Gerald Rafshoon, Carter's White House communications director, recounted a story to me about Jerry Falwell organizing his followers against the president. One Sunday, as the first lady, Rosalyn Carter, emerged from church, she was confronted with a long line of hostile women waving anti-Carter signs. She was shaken by the vitriol on the signs.

Despite President Carter being a southern Democrat, the conservative movement picked up steam during his presidency. Although the far right was still operating on the fringes of Washington and the Republican Party, the shifting political winds were bending in their direction. Jerry Falwell, a southern conservative pastor and founder of the political group the Moral Majority, had begun an aggressive campaign to promote a conservative agenda. They were pro-life and anti-gay, and quickly became a political powerhouse. Their nascent conservative strain was the beginning of the conservative movement that began to dominate the corridors of power in Washington.

Although the conservative American Enterprise Institute had been established in 1943, it was far from being the proactive think tank we recognize it as today. It maintained a much more low-key profile than its more liberal counterpart, the Brookings Institution. It was only from Carter's tenure that conservatives began to institutionalize their agenda and promote their policies within Congress.[§]

Big money began to pour into conservative causes and, by the end of the 1970s, Washington was overflowing with conservative entities that began to exert their influence on the Hill.[¶] Most were socially as well as politically conservative and tried to put a brake on civil rights, affirmative action and abortion. In foreign affairs they were fervently anti-communist and tended towards isolationism.

The conservatives mastered the maze of Washington's legislative process and became increasingly effective at fast tracking their agenda through government. Several religious organizations began to endorse the conservative movement and promoted socially conservative messages among their congregations. The Right was on the lookout for conservative

---

§ Two ambitious Hill staffers set out to create the Heritage Foundation and attracted big money from the Coors and Richard Mellon Scaife. Paul Weyrich, one of the founders of the Heritage Foundation, was an admirer of McCarthyism.

¶ The Manhattan Institute, Olin Foundation, Cato Institute and the National Institute for Public Policy were just a few of the many new conservative organizations mushrooming in the US, promoting less government and lower taxes.

leaders open to promoting their agenda. Reagan's telegenic personality caught the attention of conservatives early on in his career. His simple messages on lower taxes, less government and fewer regulations resonated with them. Conservative millionaires began to back him. In 1966 he ran for governor of California and won. He did not disappoint his base and, when he ran for president, they continued to support him.

Although Reagan had the backing of conservatives and had won with a clear majority, the 1980 election in the US had one of the lowest voter turnouts since 1948.[9] People were still recovering from Jimmy Carter's 'malaise' speech, nationally televised on 15 July 1979, which seemed to convey that he had lost confidence. Reagan, the ultimate optimist, provided the perfect antidote. He believed in the American dream and in American exceptionalism. The US was the land of milk and honey and endless opportunities. He believed that anything was achievable in America if one was willing to work for it. The glass was always half-full from his vantage point. His self-deprecating good humour endeared him to the public and he was never condescending. Despite the low voter turnout when he was first elected, he had the ability to project a positive outlook and make people feel optimistic about their future. He became a highly popular president and was re-elected in a landslide when he ran for a second term.

The genial manner that made Reagan so approachable camouflaged a man who seldom allowed anyone into his inner emotional life. His first marriage to actress Jane Wyman ended in divorce when she asked him to move out in 1949. By all accounts, he seemed surprised and hurt by her decision and the experience may have exacerbated his instinct to maintain an emotional distance from people. He married Nancy Reagan in 1952, but even she acknowledged his detachment. Nancy Reagan who, after his mother, was the only person he trusted completely, said, 'You can get just so far to Ronnie, and then something happens.'[10] Perhaps his remoteness was an instinctive attempt at self-preservation, initially from a difficult childhood, then as a public figure in Hollywood and later in politics.[**]

---

** Reagan's children's accounts of his remoteness towards them contradicts the perception the public had of him as a warm person. His adopted son Michael recounts how his father failed to recognize him at his graduation.

Ronald Reagan was born in Tampico, Illinois. Like Nixon, he had an unsuccessful father who was an alcoholic and a sweet, pious mother who was the anchor of the family. They moved several times, adding stress to an already tense domestic situation. Reagan would escape by immersing himself in books. He was particularly drawn to inspirational books about moral heroes who lifted themselves up.[11]

Reagan began his career in radio and enjoyed public speaking. He was once able to dramatize and recreate an entire baseball game from a spotty ticker tape for an enthralled audience. Realizing that he possessed dramatic talent, he moved to Hollywood to expand his career through acting. He was exposed to politics when he joined the Hollywood Democratic Committee and then served as the president of SAG from 1947–52. He made speeches in support of President Harry Truman and Vice President Hubert Humphrey and began to enjoy his role as a political impresario. Reagan's acting career had plateaued, and he increasingly abandoned it as he became more involved in politics. In 1964 he became a supporter of Barry Goldwater's run for the presidency. He campaigned against Lyndon Johnson and became a speaker for the Goldwater campaign. Reagan launched his ideas in the speech 'A Time for Choosing'. Goldwater lost but Reagan the politician was born.

President Reagan was sworn in on 20 January 1981, just as the US hostages in Iran were being flown out of Teheran. Although it was Carter who had worked for months negotiating their release, it was Reagan who made the announcement minutes after he was sworn in and basked in the glory of the successful conclusion to one of the most humiliating episodes in US diplomatic history. His presidency was off to a promising start.

After years of presidents with limited charisma—Nixon and Carter—the tall, attractive and disarmingly jovial former Hollywood actor was a welcome change for the American people.

Nancy Reagan and their Hollywood friends restored a glamour to the White House not seen since the Kennedys. The Reagans redecorated the White House, and dinners there included a revolving door of celebrities and many of their Hollywood friends. After disappointments in Vietnam and Iran and high oil prices, the electorate was ready for some festivity.

On 30 March 1981, barely eight weeks into his presidency, Reagan was the target of an assassination attempt. John Hinckley, Jr fired shots at the president's chest when he was leaving a conference at the Washington Hilton. The attempt was not politically motivated; it was the act of a mentally unstable man seeking to impress actress Jodie Foster. Fortunately, Reagan recovered in a few weeks, though some of his aides suffered critical injuries. The self-deprecating good humour with which he handled his injury further endeared him to the American people.

Reagan racked up several successes in his first year. He passed a major tax cut, ended an air controllers' strike and nominated the first woman to the Supreme Court, Sandra Day O'Connor.

## Conflicting Interests

Unfortunately for India, defeating communism was the foundation of Reagan's foreign policy goals. The Soviet Union was viewed as the 'Evil Empire'.[††] Reagan went beyond the Truman Doctrine of containment. He urged active engagement when necessary to roll back Soviet expansionism. After the 1956 and 1968 invasions of Hungary and Czechoslovakia, the Soviets were viewed by the West as dangerously expansionist. In both cases, India refused to censure the USSR. When they invaded Afghanistan in 1979, South Asia was propelled on to the centre stage. This time the conflict was taking place in India's backyard. Congress was united in its opposition to the Soviet invasion and failed to understand India's refusal to see the danger both to the world and itself. The refusal to publicly repudiate Soviet aggression in Afghanistan impeded any progress in Indo-American relations.

At the core of India's inability to publicly criticize the USSR was its extreme dependence on the Soviets for arms supplies. Since the US cut off arms sales to India during the India–Pakistan War of 1965, India had been obtaining close to 70 per cent of her arms from the USSR at very

---

†† Reagan's speech, on 8 March 1983, to the National Association of Evangelicals in Florida.

favourable terms. In 1980, they agreed to a $1.8 billion arms deal that had a market value of between $7 and $8 billion.[12]

Mrs Gandhi and most Indians bristled at being labelled a Soviet satellite and pointed out to anyone who would listen that they objected to any foreign power in Afghanistan, but the US was unimpressed. During the 1980 debate on Afghanistan in the United Nations, India's permanent representative noted:

- The USSR had acted at the request of the Afghan government;
- Although India was against foreign troops and bases in any country, it trusted Soviet promises to withdraw when invited to do so and;
- India was concerned by the reaction of the US, China, Pakistan and others to the Soviet action.[13]

Though India abstained on the vote to condemn the USSR, it did little to mitigate its pro-Soviet image, sounding instead like apologists for them.

The soul-searching within the Indian government did not cut any ice with the hawks in the Reagan administration, who had written the Indians off as being in the Soviet camp. Many Indian officials, such as Foreign Secretary Jagat Mehta,‡‡ lamented their position and privately communicated as much to their US friends, but there was no back channel established to finesse their alliances.[14] Within the government, the Indians perceived the invasion as an act of aggression, but they were too dependent on the Soviets militarily and their support of India's position on Kashmir at the UN to publicly censure them.

India faced a further insurmountable barrier: the impregnable bond that developed between Bill Casey of the CIA and General Zia of Pakistan. According to Bruce Riedel, 'Zia essentially became his partner and whatever Zia wanted Casey would pretty much get the US government to do, because Casey was closer to Reagan than any other member of the cabinet. Casey had unlimited access to the Oval Office because he had been Reagan's campaign manager.'[15] The Pakistanis were always badmouthing the Indians, which further prejudiced the US against India.[16] Though

---

‡‡ Jagat Mehta was foreign secretary from 1976–79.

Reagan may have been courteous to Mrs Gandhi, it did not filter down to his administration. For the Reagan administration, South Asia policy was all about one thing—defeating the Soviets in Afghanistan. Pakistan was their indispensable partner and the Indians were on the wrong side.

As Pakistanis became critical to the containment of communism in the subcontinent, the Reagan administration moved swiftly to pass a very generous aid package for them. In the spring of 1981, the US approved a $2.5 billion multi-year aid package to Pakistan. This included F-16 aircrafts previously only supplied to NATO allies, Egypt and Israel.[17] By doing this, the US had effectively raised Pakistan's status to that of a strategic partner. The US had chosen its ally in the battle against the Soviets in Afghanistan. Pakistan had proven once again, at India's expense, to be a reliable partner for the US. The US would also begin supplying Afghan resistance fighters. Most of the resources for this covert enterprise were routed through its Pakistani allies.[§§] Pakistan's intelligence agency, the ISI, became the primary contact with the Afghan resistance and the US relied on it to run its covert war against the Soviets. By 1984, the CIA was providing $250 million annually to the ISI. At its peak in 1987 and 1988, the expenditure reached at least $400 million.[18] The CIA and Casey were essentially running South Asia policy and India was just in the way.

Mrs Gandhi dispatched her closest advisors, Gopalaswami Parthasarathy and Secretary Eric Gonsalves of the Ministry of External Affairs, to lobby the US government and Congress against the arms package to Pakistan. Alexander Haig was secretary of state and a Nixon holdover. Haig had served under Kissinger during Nixon's presidency and had acquired Nixon's anti-Indian bias and was dismissive of India's concerns.[19] The Indians did not cultivate CIA Director Bill Casey, the most critical player. Even if they had tried, Casey's closeness to Zia would have likely been a barrier, according to Riedel: 'The Reagan–Casey team focused on the Cold War exclusively. Pakistan was the essential ally against Russia. India was an afterthought, if not a Soviet ally. Casey, who ran the war

---

§§   The covert war in Afghanistan is detailed in Steve Coll's book *Ghost Wars* that won the Pulitzer Prize.

in Afghanistan, was uninterested in India. Reagan's primary wish was to avoid Indian interference in Pakistan.'[20]

With the Russians in Afghanistan, the US feared Soviet expansionism might not stop there. After 1979, Tehran was lost to the US as a strategic listening post and Pakistan had offered itself as a substitute. The US had no intention of risking Pakistan to Soviet influence. With India tightly aligned with the Soviets, the US bolstered Pakistan with aid and guns. Pakistan became America's frontline against communist expansion.

In a press conference on 10 July 1981, and again in an interview with a Spanish journalist the following January, Mrs Gandhi publicly criticized the US for destabilizing the region. She was still furious about the US military assistance programme with Pakistan and was convinced that Pakistan would not use the US-supplied F-16s against the Soviets. The weapons were offensive, not defensive, and more likely to be used against India.[21] In a departure from the past, the US had not put constraints on Pakistan with a provision that the weapons not be used against India. This caused intense bitterness among the Indians, who felt that the US had become excessively pro-Pakistan at India's expense.

Indian intelligence had discovered that Pakistan was actively pursuing nuclear technology. The Indian government knew that were Pakistan to develop a nuclear bomb, it would be a game changer in the subcontinent. India needed to persuade the US to pressure Pakistan to abandon its ambitions, but it was a challenging proposition. They needed a better relationship with the US for their lobbying efforts to carry any weight, but their interests seldom aligned.

With the Soviets entrenched in Afghanistan and giving her no indication of their intention to withdraw, Mrs Gandhi was growing increasingly uncomfortable in their suffocating embrace. She, along with her advisors, had for some years considered diversifying India's sources of arms supply. This would not just be sensible from India's security perspective, but also expand India's foreign policy options and partners and create space in which to operate. Although the Soviets had been reliable allies, the political ramifications of a sole supplier were precarious for a country's security independence. India decided to turn to Europe as a neutral alternative. The Indian government entered negotiations with the French to buy Mirage 2000 fighters. They also sought Jaguar aircraft from the UK and submarines from West Germany. India was interested in technology transfers and began looking for partners to build and assemble parts domestically.

Mrs Gandhi was revaluating her foreign policy options. The US rapprochement with China was worrying for India as its relations with China had not recovered since the countries had gone to war in 1962. Border disputes that remained unresolved were a constant source of tension, and as China had emerged as the superior force, India had allied with the Soviets for regional balance while China had supported Pakistan. The stability was delicate, but the entry of the US tipped the scales in Pakistan's direction. Not only had the US supported Pakistan consistently but its budding friendship with China also threatened to encircle India.

## Mrs Gandhi Reaches Out

The stakes for India had risen and Mrs Gandhi looked for ways to rebalance the political landscape. She reached out to China to settle outstanding border disputes as a way of removing tensions between the countries. Although she was under no illusion that they would be friends, she hoped to restore a level of neutrality.[22] Poor relations between India and China increased India's dependence on the Soviets.

Most of all, Mrs Gandhi wanted to adjust her relations with the US. She turned off her standard anti-US rhetoric and refrained from the usual accusations of foreign interference in India's internal affairs. Anxious to impress upon the new president that she wished the countries to have better relations, she had dispatched her cousin and senior advisor, B.K. Nehru, to convey her message to Reagan when he took office. The president at this point was not seeing many foreign representatives and certainly not ones from countries that he considered to be low on the totem pole.

Reagan was determined to initially focus on domestic affairs and put foreign affairs on the back-burner. Nixon, whose advice he valued, had confirmed his instincts and told him not to get distracted by foreign affairs and to concentrate on the economy first.[23]

Unable to get an official meeting, the Indians went to great lengths calling in every available contact to make a connection. B.K. Nehru was a former ambassador to Washington and had many friends on the Hill. A 'chance' meeting at Senator Laxalt's office was orchestrated.[¶¶] Paul Laxalt was considered the president's closest friend in Congress and their friendship predated the presidency. It was a diplomatic coup to have engineered the rendezvous, although it is unclear if the meeting opened any channels to deepening relations. It was not until Mrs Gandhi met Reagan in person in Cancun, Mexico that relations took on a decidedly warmer tone.

Mrs Gandhi, a leading member of the non-aligned nations, had gone out of her way to persuade its delegates not to insist on Castro's attendance at the Cancun Conference. She felt this was not the time to alienate Americans and risk a US boycott of the conference.[24] It was a significant change in her attitude towards the US; in the past, she was unhesitatingly critical of their policies and would have been unlikely to accommodate them so publicly. It indicated how desperate she was to improve relations. Reagan and Mrs Gandhi exchanged letters in advance of their meeting. Reagan, while recognizing India's ascendant position in South Asia following the 1971 war with Pakistan, like Carter, did not shy away from reminding her that they had substantive differences. 'I recognize that India and the United States do not always agree on issues of common concern, but the strength of the relationship between our two democracies is that we can discuss our differences candidly.'[25] Mrs Gandhi continued to remain solicitous, sending a letter expressing concern after the attempted assassination of the president and praising his decision to participate in the Cancun Conference.

The conference was held in October 1981, as a summit on global poverty. President Reagan had been somewhat reluctant to participate in the north–south dialogue, but globalization was becoming unavoidable, with the increasing disparity between the conclaves of the rich and the

---

[¶¶] Senator Laxalt was very close to the president and one of the few people who could call him 'Ron'. President Reagan consulted him on political issues and would not have refused a request from him.

poor nations becoming a problem for both. The Cancun Conference was limited in its achievements. Reagan firmly believed in free markets and, as many international conferences often end, no concrete solutions emerged from the talks. However, the meetings served as a useful platform to start the process of negotiations. For some countries like India, the conference also provided an opportunity to meet with leaders and push industrialized countries for more favourable terms in trade and aid. For Reagan, it was a listening and learning trip as it came early in his term and, more importantly for his staff, it served as a dress rehearsal for their European trip.

It was well known among his staff that Reagan was unlikely to read the briefing books that had been painstakingly prepared for him. He did not enjoy policy papers, though he was an avid reader in his youth and as an adult had devoured the works of Whittaker Chambers, F.A. Hayek and William Hazlitt.*** As he got older, Reagan preferred biographies and *Reader's Digest*, which he mined for the many anecdotes in his speeches. He liked to get his information on three-by-five note cards. He was a visual learner, and his aides often presented information to him via graphs and films. To prepare him for his meetings with world leaders, including Mrs Gandhi, his staff had asked the CIA to make videos profiling the leaders, which he dutifully watched. His staff found that the enactment of a play was the best way to engage the president and transmit information he needed to know prior to a meeting. Staff members played the roles of the people Reagan would be meeting, with the president playing himself.[26]

In Cancun, the White House staff converted the president's hotel suite into an extension of the Oval Office. The process was made as painless for Reagan as possible. In addition to watching the films, he was briefed by his staff before he met each leader. The Indians were pleased when he referenced the Green Revolution but confused when he called it a triumph of capitalism rather than attributable to the efforts of the government.[27]

---

*** In a now famous incident, Baker, Reagan's chief of staff, noticed the president had not opened the briefing books left for him prior to an economic summit, only to be told that Reagan had watched *The Sound of Music* on TV instead.

Reagan's critics have suggested that, unlike his predecessors Nixon and Carter, who were micromanagers and pored over policy details obsessively trying to control every decision, Reagan's hands-off style made him vulnerable to manipulation. Although he did leave the details of policy to his aides, Reagan had a fairly consistent vision of what his goals were and was generally clear about his course of action.

If success can be measured in small symbolic gestures, Mrs Gandhi's efforts paid off. An invitation to visit the White House followed in 1982. The US softened its stance on India's needs at multilateral institutions like the World Bank.††† India had requested a $5.8 billion loan from the International Monetary Fund and was anxious that the US support the request.

India was not without friends in the US government. Prior to Mrs Gandhi's visit, the senator from Utah, Orrin Hatch, wrote a letter dated 21 April 1982 to Mr Clark, head of the National Security Agency (NSA), to include India in a strategic plan to reduce Soviet influence in key countries. He wrote: 'My suggestion is that you review the history of the Indian requests for military sales from us in the last few years ... we are denying the Indians arms and arming the Indians arch enemy.' He was critical of Secretary of Defense Casper Weinberger, saying: 'Cap has not visited Pakistan yet and has no plans to visit India, which I believe is a mistake.' He said Reagan had a historic opportunity to reduce Soviet influence in 'what may be Moscow's single-most important non-communist client in the world'.[28] He urged Clark to focus on India as a country to cultivate away from Soviet influence. It is revealing that Senator Hatch wrote to Clark at the NSA rather than George Shultz, the new secretary of state. At the time, Clark was trying to dominate foreign policy and Shultz, in his memoir, describes in some detail the competitive struggle between the two to decide matters of foreign policy.

The Soviets had been trying to invite Mrs Gandhi to Moscow ever since her re-election in 1980. They were anxious to cement relations with their

---

††† From the founding of the International Development Association in 1960 through July 1980, India received $8.25 billion in interest-free loans, 40.3 per cent of the total $20.57 billion lent by the IDA. Jokingly called 'India Development Assistance', it was under threat as Bangladesh and several African countries put pressure to increase their share of soft loans.

most important ally, but she was in no hurry to see them. She had not forgotten their cold behaviour towards her when she was out of power. She responded that it was President Brezhnev's turn to visit. At the age of seventy-four, and visibly tired, Brezhnev went to India in December to maintain relations, but any concessions to withdraw from Afghanistan that Mrs Gandhi may have hoped for did not materialize. This visit was a far more subdued affair than the one in 1973, when the enthusiasm with which he was greeted by the crowds had been overwhelming. He made few appearances on this trip, and their joint affirmations of friendship were pro forma. Trade commitments to India were announced but Mrs Gandhi only accepted an invitation to visit Russia after her visit to the US was confirmed.

In November 1981, M.K. Rasgotra became the foreign secretary. He was convinced that it was dangerous for India to have a single strong ally. He urged Mrs Gandhi to restore a more positive relationship with the US. Rasgotra had served in the US twice, first at the UN and later as the deputy head of mission at the Indian embassy in Washington. He had established close relations with his counterparts in the US government and was more balanced politically than the pro-Soviet advisors that surrounded Mrs Gandhi.

Mrs Gandhi confided in Rasgotra that Foreign Minister P.V. Narasimha Rao, Policy Planner G. Parthasarthy and Principal Secretary to the Prime Minister P.C. Alexander were all opposed to her going to the US. They were worried she would offend the Soviets. Rasgotra pushed through the arrangements over their objections. Once she had made up her mind to visit the White House, they all fell in line.[29]

Mrs Gandhi's visit to Washington, DC, in July 1982, was very different from her previous visit with President Nixon ten years earlier.[‡‡‡] The Tarapur supply issue that had plagued relations for almost a decade

---

‡‡‡ Reagan consulted often on a variety of issues with former president Nixon, but, for political reasons, this was done outside public scrutiny. Nixon made suggestions regarding policy and appointments. President Reagan was always polite and respectful but did not always follow his advice. This proved fortunate for his dealings with Gorbachev and luckily Nixon's anti-India prejudice did not pass to Reagan.

had been amicably resolved. France was to take over from the US as the supplier of nuclear fuel for Tarapur. Mrs Gandhi had directed Rasgotra to find a solution before her meeting with President Reagan.[30] After years of intransigence on both sides, it seemed as though the visit itself became a catalyst for a resolution, as neither government wanted to have a state visit with Tarapur's shadow darkening relations.[31] No doubt, after the positive meeting in Cancun, both leaders instructed their respective negotiators to arrive at a solution.[§§§] By 1981, the US had become India's largest trading partner, another reason for Mrs Gandhi to repair relations.

As President Reagan and Mrs Gandhi stood on the South Lawn at the White House, on a sunny July morning in 1982, participating in the welcoming ceremonies, the rapport between the two leaders was a marked contrast to her last visit. The November 1970 meeting with President Nixon had been a disaster. No doubt, President Reagan's easy manner and warmth put Mrs Gandhi at ease. In an effort to win them over, she had also become more circumspect in her rhetoric and relations with the US. The state dinner was informal and warm. A friend of Reagan, known as 'Judge', persuaded the Indian delegation to place an order for almonds from the president's home state of California. The prime minister was amenable, and almonds became a staple of US exports to India.[32]

George Shultz had just replaced Alexander Haig as secretary of state. Fortunately, he did not share his predecessor's animus towards Mrs Gandhi. Although the State Department was distracted by the war in the Middle East that had just erupted when Israel invaded Lebanon, agreements on trade and scientific exchanges were made. On the surface, relations between India and the United States seem to have been restored to a more normal, if inconsequential, level.

Mrs Gandhi visited Russia in October 1982. She had warned the Russians that their occupation was provoking stiff resistance in Afghanistan and once again urged them to withdraw. Brezhnev confided to her: 'Taraki kept asking me for 10,000 troops and I kept refusing. After much hesitation, I sent 10,000 Russian soldiers to Afghanistan in 1979. Now there

---

§§§ The US softened its requirement of perpetual safeguards and India stopped blocking all safeguards. France agreed to supply the fuel.

are 110,000 Russian soldiers in Afghanistan! I do not know what they are doing there. I want to get out of Afghanistan. Madam, you know the region well! Show me a way to get out of Afghanistan.'[33]

According to Rasgotra, Mrs Gandhi made no attempt to respond or help him find a solution to his dilemma. She had not forgiven the Russians and was willing for them to stew in the problem they found themselves in and was now contemplating a different set of alliances. As Alexander and Rasgotra whispered that she ought to say something, she icily suggested to Brezhnev that the way out was the same as the way in. The Russians were flummoxed by her elliptical response and asked her ministers to explain what she meant, but no one from her entourage dared to divine her meaning.

India began diversifying its arms purchases and the Soviet defence minister, along with the commanders of his navy and air force and thirty other generals, arrived in New Delhi in May 1982, with what a British diplomat described as 'a message of concern'. At the time, approximately 70 per cent of India's military equipment came from Moscow. It dwarfed anything that was on order from the West.[34]

The Russians were not happy about the rapprochement between Reagan and Mrs Gandhi and made several attempts at planting stories to create misunderstandings between India and the US. In March of 1983, *The Patriot*, a left-wing publication in India, claimed that there was a secret plan authored by Jeanne Kirkpatrick, the US ambassador to the UN, to Balkanize India and destroy its influence in the third world.[35] The article was timed to coincide with the Non-Aligned Conference in Delhi, which Mrs Gandhi was hosting. Kirkpatrick had irritated the Indians on a previous visit in 1981, when she refused to acknowledge that arming Pakistan was a threat to India. A letter from President Reagan was quickly sent to Mrs Gandhi, assuring her there was no basis for the allegations made in *The Patriot*. To maintain the new direction in her relationship with the US, Mrs Gandhi decided to ignore the accusation, and buried the issue.

Mrs Gandhi's reserve had begun to thaw under Reagan's charm and, when Vice President George H.W. Bush visited in 1984, she invited him to an intimate family dinner, in addition to the state functions. Though his visit would build a foundation for the future, unresolved policy differences between India and the US continued to hinder progress. One of the reasons that the bilateral relationship did not improve in any appreciable manner, despite Mrs Gandhi's attempts, lay in the differences in governance. In India, the prime minister's authority had become monarchical. Her bureaucrats interpreted her every gesture, positive or otherwise, and translated it into policy. In the US, the president was always subject to congressional oversight and cooperation. Mrs Gandhi may have placed too much emphasis on establishing a rapport with President Reagan and may have been better served by trying to win over members of Congress and the Pentagon as well.

In June, the issue of spare parts for Tarapur came up. Although the two leaders and their staff had made progress in moving the relationship forward and expanding cooperation, many members of Congress and some at the State Department still viewed India as anti-US and pro-Soviet. Another more problematic divide was the closeness that had developed between the CIA and the ISI as well as the Pentagon officials and the Pakistani army, who were now all working together against the Soviet occupation. The Pakistanis cultivated them and they proved to be a very effective lobby against India and protecting its nuclear programme and military interests. But even without Pakistan's hand, the US had several reasons for its reluctance to help India.

In 1983, India opposed the US at the UN on all ten issues that the US considered important. Pakistan voted for five of them, Bangladesh voted with the US on four, and Sri Lanka voted affirmatively to three. In general, India had voted with the Soviets 80 per cent of the time and with the US only 20 per cent.[36] When President Reagan requested Congress approve the sale of spare parts to Tarapur, Congressman Markey responded with a letter opposing the sale signed by fifty-five members, including liberals like Chuck Schumer, Barney Frank, Gary Hart and Bill Richardson.[37]

By September, the White House was preoccupied with other events. On 1 September 1983, a Soviet fighter downed Korean Air Lines Flight 007, killing all 269 passengers on board including sixty-one Americans. Marxists had overrun Grenada and, in a show of force in October 1983, President Reagan had sent troops to the tiny Caribbean island to oust them.

A more serious attack in Beirut, Lebanon from a suicide truck bomber at the US Marine barracks killed 241 marines. It would be a harbinger of a new threat, one which would, over the next decade, redirect US energies to a new enemy that would dwarf communism.⁑⁑⁑

India continued to press for US cooperation in science and technology but there was resistance from the US Departments of Defense and Energy to provide sensitive technology to India. Tireless efforts by Ambassador Harry Barnes to convince his country that India was not a Soviet satellite, combined with support from senators like Orrin Hatch, who wanted to bring India into the US orbit, created a small opening for further cooperation. Suspicions persisted on both sides that would take a long time to overcome. The Indian defence establishment had felt burned when the US suspended arms supplies to India after 1965. They mistrusted the terms the US insisted on, such as the unilateral cut-off clause⁂⁂⁂⁂ and refusal to refund money already paid for undelivered arms. The failure of the Indian government to court the US Congress and military hurt India. The Pakistanis grasped what both Nehru and Mrs Gandhi did not—that Congress wielded power over aid appropriation, military sales and nuclear technology transfers.

Secretary Shultz visited India in 1983. He recalled that the visit started awkwardly, with Mrs Gandhi sitting with him in a deafening silence, until somehow the ice was broken and a normal conversation followed. Despite her multiple overseas trips and ease on the world stage, she was often stilted with the US. Underneath her attempts to forge a closer relationship with them lay the impediment of her deep-seated distrust of Americans. Her suspicions about the US were not always misplaced.

In 1984, General Zia and Mrs Gandhi attempted to deescalate tensions between their countries. They both agreed to sign a 'no war pact' and a friendship treaty. Over a period of several months, Niaz Naik on the Pakistan side and M.K. Rasgotra on the Indian side hammered out an

---

⁑⁑⁑ Fundamentalist Islamic groups like Al Qaeda, the Taliban and the ISIS.

⁂⁂⁂⁂ If the US found that a country was in violation of an agreement, they could unilaterally cut off aid and suspend trade, including refusing to refund money already paid as a deposit against goods to be delivered in the future.

agreement acceptable to both leaders. Along with the agreement not to attack each other, they built on the Simla Treaty to resolve disputes bilaterally. They also came to an understanding on not allowing their countries to be used as foreign bases.

Naik telegraphed the agreement to his foreign minister, who happened to be visiting Washington. He shared the telegraph with his friends on the Senate Foreign Relations Committee and House Foreign Affairs Committee. The US felt the agreement went against their interests in using Pakistan for their own purposes in the region. The US advised the Pakistani minister Sahabzada Yaqub Khan to not sign the agreement. India thought that the Pakistanis had been duplicitous until Rasgotra was informed by a friend on the Hill about the US role. The US scuttled what could have been a historic treaty for peace between India and Pakistan.[38] General Zia's attitude hardened and relations between the two countries reverted to form. Mrs Gandhi renewed her accusations against Pakistan's interference in Kashmir and Punjab. By the summer of 1984, she was in the vortex of a domestic insurgency that would end her career and her life.

Mrs Gandhi had won a resounding victory at the polls in 1980 but her natural inclination to wield power from the Centre would prove to be her downfall. She incessantly interfered in state elections to ensure that her party retained the maximum number of seats needed to promote her policies.

Much of the resentment towards her in important border states such as Kashmir, Nagaland and Punjab was due to her meddling in local politics. On 24 August 1984, Sikh separatists hijacked an Indian Airlines flight with 100 passengers on board. The plane stopped in Lahore and Karachi and when it landed in Dubai, the United Arab Emirates, with US help, negotiated the safe return of the plane and passengers to New Delhi. The hijackers handed in a pistol that was traced back to Pakistan.

Pakistan was not the only country enabling the Sikh separatists. The UK, Canada and the US were home to a large number of wealthy Sikhs. The separatist Khalistan movement had many sympathizers in these communities. India had complained to the three countries about their tolerance of the activities of some of the more radical elements in these communities, but the countries had failed to clamp down on them.

## Problems in Punjab

Punjab was one of the wealthiest states in India and considered the nation's granary. Concerned by the accumulation of power in the hands of the ruling Akali party and their occasional calls for autonomy, Mrs Gandhi sought to sow dissent among them. She quietly had people identify and promote younger leaders to challenge the existing leadership. Originally, after 1947, the Akali Dal's main objective had been to maintain Punjab as a cultural and linguistic region with jurisdiction over Sikh religious sites. As the political interests of Hindu Punjabis and Sikh Punjabis diverged, the state became ungovernable in its current composition. The state was then divided into a Sikh-majority Punjab and a Hindu-majority Haryana.

The Sikhs remained dissatisfied; they addressed their grievances in a meeting in 1973 and passed the Anandpur Sahib Resolution. It affirmed their right to maintain their cultural and religious integrity.

In the 1980s, the resolution was invoked by groups frustrated by the Centre's relentless meddling in Punjab politics; between August 1980 and September 1981, the Akali Dal held seven largely peaceful demonstrations. The Congress party identified Jarnail Singh Bhindranwale, a young, orthodox leader from Faridkot who had studied at a Sikh seminary, to challenge the Akali leadership and weaken their party. Delhi underestimated both Bhindranwale's popularity and loyalty to Punjab. He had got his start by going from village to village preaching the word of the ten gurus[††††] and had steered men away from alcohol, drugs and pornography, earning not just their gratitude but that of their families.[39] He was charismatic and combined spiritual appeal with vigour and bravery. Bhindranwale became a magnet for young Sikhs ready to fight for Punjab. Sensing his growing popularity, the Akalis joined forces with him. They called for autonomy and, throughout 1983 and into early 1984, tensions mounted with the Centre. Their followers began attacking Hindus on buses, carried out bank bombings and killed politicians. The law-and-order problem became so

---

[††††] The Sikh religion is based on the spiritual teachings of the founder Guru Nanak and nine successive gurus (teachers).

severe that, in October 1983, Mrs Gandhi dissolved Punjab's legislative assembly and imposed president's rule.

There was some concern among US officials in New Delhi that the US would be blamed for meddling in destabilizing activities in Punjab. The Soviet propaganda news service, *Izvestia*, implied that the US was trying to divide India, but the Indians ignored it. In the past, Mrs Gandhi had often blamed unrest within India as being instigated by foreign elements, a euphemism for the CIA.

In Punjab, Bhindranwale and the secessionists were receiving considerable financial support from overseas. The Sikh diaspora in the UK, Canada and the US had been sending them funds for some time.

Bhindranwale was suspected of being behind most of the terror and was arrested but, as there was no concrete evidence to prosecute him, the government let him go. Keeping him without sufficient evidence was a political liability. Bhindranwale and his followers then took the dramatic step of moving into and fortifying the Golden Temple, the most sacred shrine of the Sikhs.

The final straw came in June 1984 when the Akalis stopped all food grains from leaving the state. As Punjab was the breadbasket of India, this was tantamount to holding the country hostage just as supplies were at their lowest. They also stopped paying land and water taxes to the Centre.

The government responded by sealing Punjab's borders and cordoning off the Golden Temple, in preparation of an offensive if the occupiers refused to surrender. All attempts to negotiate with the Sikhs in the temple were met with refusals.

On 4 June 1984, the government launched 'Operation Blue Star'. Two thousand army troops assaulted the temple with tanks and artillery. Bhindranwale and many of his followers were killed. The Golden Temple was badly damaged in the process. The Sikh community throughout the world was inflamed and many Sikhs in the government and military resigned in protest. The siege, however, was over and the bid by the Sikhs for autonomy quashed.

Four months later, on a cool October morning, Mrs Gandhi's Sikh bodyguards assassinated her as she walked from her residence to her office through the garden. She was wearing a saffron sari, and had taken care to dress well, as she was on her way to meet Peter Ustinov.[‡‡‡‡] Barely forty-eight hours earlier, at a public meeting, she had said, 'I am here today, I may be gone tomorrow ... Nobody knows how many attempts have been made to shoot me ... I do not care whether I live or die ... I will continue to serve until my last breath and when I die every single drop of my blood will invigorate the nation and strengthen united India.'[40]

Operation Blue Star had radicalized many Sikhs by what they considered the desecration of their holiest shrine. The reprisals and arrests of Sikhs in the months after Mrs Gandhi's assassination further alienated them. Many young Sikhs had taken oaths to exact revenge and restore their honour.

Moscow did not allow any opportunity to discredit the US to go by. Propaganda was published by Soviet news sources that the US was somehow involved in Mrs Gandhi's murder, but it was too far-fetched even for the Indian authorities to give it credence. As the US delegation touched down at Palam Airport in India, Ambassador Barnes briefed them on the Soviet allegations. The US delegation was headed by George Shultz and included Senate Majority Leader Howard Baker and all living former ambassadors to India.[§§§§]

Among the guests who came to pay their respects was Palestinian leader Yasser Arafat, who wept at the funeral and bemoaned the loss of his 'sister' Indira Gandhi.

State funerals are often another forum for world leaders to meet each other. After the funeral, Shultz went to the Soviet embassy and met with Premier Nikolai Tikhonov. He discussed Soviet–US relations and asked that the Soviets desist from all propaganda suggesting any US involvement in Mrs Gandhi's death.[41] Shultz also met with President Zia-ul-Haq of Pakistan.

Shultz described the Pakistani delegation to the funeral as all attired in black tunics over white leggings. 'Their appearance was elegant, their manner grand and gracious. I felt as if I had stumbled into the throne room of the emperor of all pandas.'[42]

---

‡‡‡‡    Peter Ustinov was a well-known British playwright and actor.

§§§§    Senator Moynihan, Professor Galbraith, Robert Goheen and Sherman Cooper.

After several other meetings, including a formal one with Rajiv to pay their condolences, they met with Prime Minister Margaret Thatcher on their final round. She lectured them on using this opportunity to get closer to India and balance it with their closeness to Pakistan. Judging from the way Secretary Shultz related the meeting with the British delegation in his memoir, the lens through which the US viewed India remained discoloured. With world events taking place that would shake up global politics, India was unimportant to the US.

## End of an Era

For India, Mrs Gandhi's assassination, on 31 October 1984, was the end of an era dominated by members of the independence movement. Independent India came into existence in 1947 just as the Iron Curtain[¶¶¶¶] descended on the world. Freed from colonial overlords, India wanted to remain unaligned, but the Cold War created difficult foreign policy choices for India, usually putting it on the wrong side of the US.[*****]

Pakistan's willingness to court the US and align its country with Washington contrasted sharply with India's insistence on non-alignment. Pakistan used its strategic location to every advantage. It consistently voted with the US and proved to be a reliable ally, always prepared to support US interests. In return, it was able to secure generous aid packages and increasingly sophisticated arms, a matter of grave concern to India. Pakistan always welcomed US leaders with pomp and show, whereas both Nehru and Mrs Gandhi had been often cool and aloof to them.[†††††]

---

[¶¶¶¶] In a famous speech on March 1946, at Westminster College in Fulton, Missouri, Winston Churchill argued for a special relationship between the US and Britain and accused Stalin and the Soviet Union of dividing Europe into a communist and non-communist bloc, with a metaphorical 'iron curtain' between them. He said the Iron Curtain had descended on Europe and behind it lay all the ancient capitals.

[*****] Although India was technically non-aligned and neutral, it usually voted against US interests at the UN and was viewed as a Soviet ally.

[†††††] Kennedy with Nehru, Nixon when out of office with Mrs. Gandhi.

Pakistan's decisions were not ideological but driven by the need for survival. It would be a mistake to hang the problems in Indo-US relations around Pakistan's neck, as critics in India have sometimes done. Pakistan wanted a protector from India. It invested in the US relationship early on, as it would later with China.

The US Congress had also become a headache for India. A case study on congressional perspectives on India, undertaken by Peter Tomsen at the State Department,[43] concluded that consensus on India had vanished over the past twenty years. This coincided with Mrs Gandhi's time in office. Not only did the Hill not pay much attention to India but, according to the report, India's image among many congressmen and staffers was largely negative. There were several problems in the Indo-US relationship that nested within each other.

One of the most consequential was America's changing relationship with China. India had been seen as a bulwark of democracy and worth propping up against the threat of Chinese communism. When China invaded India in 1962, President Kennedy fully backed support for India. According to Senator Moynihan, it was the 'high watermark of Indo-US relations'. Once the US rapprochement with China began in 1970, the perceived value of India's geo-strategic importance waned.[44]

The changes in the legislative processes on the Hill after the Johnson administration also made it easier to block support for India.‡‡‡‡‡ Although the House Foreign Affairs Committee generally supported assistance to India, the Appropriations Committee was less inclined.

There was also substantial resistance from the US Department of Defense to provide India with either sophisticated weapons or technology transfers. By contrast, the Soviets always came through for India on arms and technology. During her visit to Moscow in 1982, the prime minister asked Brezhnev for MiG-29s. This was a new advanced jet fighter that the

---

‡‡‡‡‡ From 1947 until 1968, there was bipartisan support on the Hill to support emerging democracies like India. After Watergate, influence of the over 300 sub-committees grew and issues had to clear this initial process, leaving many proposals for aid, etc., on the floor. Powerful members were no longer able to push things through as LBJ used to when he was in the Senate.

Russians had been developing under great secrecy. Ustinov and the Soviet military reluctantly admitted they had the jet and Brezhnev instructed them to make it available to India, saying, 'We should give our friends what they need.'[45] The contrast with the US attitude towards India could not have been greater.

Mrs Gandhi's constant accusations about US interference in India's internal affairs had not endeared her to members of Congress. They were also irritated by her constant criticism of US foreign policy. India's 1974 nuclear test severely tried relationships with her strongest supporters in Congress. Liberal congressmen who pushed for aid to India were unanimously opposed to it developing a bomb. When it came to its nuclear policy, India was isolated. Mrs Gandhi's gradual tilt to Moscow, culminating in the Indo-Soviet friendship treaty of 1971,[§§§§§] effectively shut the door on any remaining Indo-US cooperation.

Indira Gandhi's demise ended India's socialist mentality and reflexive hostility to the West. Pathways to development in domestic programmes and Indo-US relations opened up. Mrs Gandhi's prickly personality had disabled her from overcoming disagreements with the US on policy. Her departure from India's political stage removed the single greatest impediment to India–US relations.

---

§§§§§    Her disastrous interactions with President Nixon and the looming war in Bangladesh led her to sign the treaty.

# Chapter 16

# Shifting Winds

While India struggled to regain its balance, Americans were headed to the polls. Four days after Mrs Gandhi died, President Reagan was re-elected in a landslide carrying forty-nine of the fifty states and 59 per cent of the popular vote. It would be the first time since President Eisenhower that a US president would complete two terms in office.

With Sanjay dead, Mrs Gandhi assassinated and Rajiv reluctant to 'accept the crown', India's future looked uncertain. The Congress party was in a hurry to stabilize the country. It wanted to make sure that India's adversaries, China and Pakistan, did not take advantage of the sudden vacuum in India's leadership. It quickly appointed Rajiv to replace his mother, an assignment he was neither prepared for nor wanted. Although he had been privy to his mother's thoughts and conversations around the dining table at home, he was not experienced in the making of policy or politics. He had deliberately avoided both, which left him untainted but disadvantaged.

The reaction to Mrs Gandhi's assassination was swift. Her body was still lying in state when riots broke out in Delhi. Mobs sought revenge for her assassination and targeted the Sikh population. The capital was one of the worst-affected areas. Sikhs were attacked in their homes, places of work and in public. Until then, Sikhs had been well assimilated into India's armed forces, police and government. Many of them were members of Delhi's social elite, but even they were targeted. Women were raped, shops burnt and people set on fire as horrified witnesses looked on. Many Hindus were friends and neighbours of the Sikhs. They did what they could to protect them, but despite their efforts, Human Rights Watch estimated that over 2,700 people died in Delhi alone. It took the young prime minister a few months to calm the country and end reprisals against them. It scarred the Sikh community and converted formerly non-political members to consider radical elements that promoted Sikh nationalism* with greater sympathy. India seemed to have all but forgotten Gandhi's teachings of non-violence and tolerance.

Elections were called for December 1984. Just before Indians went to the polls on the night of 2 December, a massive gas leak at the Union Carbide plant in Bhopal killed almost 2,500 people and thousands more fell sick.† It was the world's largest industrial accident and threatened to complicate India–US relations. Tensions were running high and recriminations between India and the US multinational grew increasingly bitter. The CEO, Warren Anderson, flew to Bhopal to assess the damage and was promptly arrested. Rajiv was on the campaign trail, but sent instructions to free Mr Anderson right away. He did not want to jeopardize relations with the US so early in his term. This avoided what could have turned into a diplomatic embarrassment, but the many lawsuits against Union Carbide would drag out over the next decade.

Rajiv won the election in a landslide. Undoubtedly, he benefitted from a wave of sympathy, but that alone does not explain the sweeping victory of winning 404 out of 515 seats—comparable to the popularity his grandfather enjoyed in the 1950s. Rajiv was just forty years old when he became the prime minister, but he had a quiet dignity and humility that appealed to ordinary people as well as the power brokers in Delhi. People appreciated that he had not grabbed power, but accepted his role as a responsibility, and considered it a duty to serve his country. Tall, handsome and soft-spoken, he was welcomed as the right person to take India across the bridge into a more politically neutral world where growth rather than ideology drove decisions. For a country where most of the

---

\*   The Khalistan movement was a Sikh separatist movement that called for a Sikh homeland.

†   Some estimate the death toll as high as 8000.

population was under thirty-five, the young prime minister represented their future hopes and dreams.

## A New Approach

Rajiv maintained some of his mother's advisors but many of the hardcore socialists retired or faded away. He removed the old, corrupt, sycophantic politicians he inherited from his mother's regime and replaced them with younger, more dynamic officials. Twenty-five powerful secretaries in the civil service were transferred in one swoop soon after he was elected. A new group of junior ministers were installed, and he made it clear that members of government would be judged on their performance, not loyalty. He summoned V.N. Gadgil, the minister of state for communications, to his house for a midnight meeting to let him know that the failure of the telecommunication system during the Sikh riots was unacceptable. He was replaced by a younger man who was ordered to modernize the system.[1] Rajiv changed his ministers and cabinet several times, including going through six external affairs ministers, leading to some insecurity among the bureaucrats.[2]

Rajiv brought a more modern, technocratic perspective to government and was fascinated by anything to do with technology. He loved gadgets and tinkered with them in his spare time. While living in London during his college days he had dismantled a car engine and, much to amusement of his friends, the various parts lay strewn all over his living room floor.[3] Rajiv tried to introduce computers into all aspects of government. He used one himself to write out his talking points before any speech. Indians affectionately referred to him as 'Computerji'.[‡,4]

Like President Reagan, Rajiv disliked long-winded written or oral exposés on policy. Despite the new dynamism that he tried to inject into the process of governing, he had to contend with continual pushback from the long-established civil service who viewed their jobs as sinecures and operated with a sluggish deliberation. Their ability to clog decisions to enhance their power was built into the system. Bureaucratic resistance

---

‡    Loosely translated as 'Mr Computer'.

ensured that the changes the new prime minister wished to introduce proceeded at a glacial pace.

Government officials had been raised on a system of five-year plans borrowed from the Soviet model and had internalized a socialist outlook on development. Although Nehru had borrowed the planned economy from the Soviets, his daughter Mrs Gandhi had strangled it with regulations. The economy, dominated by the public sector, required multiple licenses for any business to operate, leading to immense corruption and inhibition of business investment. Bureaucratic red tape maintained the power and privileges of the civil service who were loath to give up the system of patronage that it encouraged.[5] India was nicknamed the 'Licence Raj'.

Rajiv wanted to make a mark internationally. He made forty-eight foreign trips in four years and, like his grandfather, wanted India to be a presence on the global stage. His immediate concern was to establish good relations within the neighbourhood. He made an effort to reach out to all the countries in South Asia and his approach was conciliatory and humble. He came across as sincere and India's neighbours welcomed the outreach.

Rajiv entered negotiations with Bangladesh to resolve outstanding water-sharing disputes, although the disagreements would ultimately be resolved by his successor. He was the first Indian prime minister to visit China since the 1962 war. His meeting with Deng was accompanied by extensive publicity and ushered in the phrase 'peace and tranquility' as the way to manage the border dispute.

Rajiv also tried to play a helpful role in the Sri Lankan Civil War. The British had brought the Tamil population to Sri Lanka from India as labourers during colonial rule. The Tamils had eventually settled on the island but felt discriminated against and demanded autonomy. Rajiv tried to help negotiate a settlement and sent a peacekeeping force to Sri Lanka but ended up incurring the wrath of the Tamil rebels and taking a heavy toll of lives. He would pay dearly for his attempts to mediate between the Sri Lankan government and the Tamils.

His relations with Pakistan were more problematic. Initially, Zia and Rajiv began on a positive note following Mrs Gandhi's funeral, but the relationship was encumbered by long-standing grievances which precluded any co-operation between the two leaders. Ongoing border disputes and the arms build-up by Pakistan made India nervous. It was convinced that the arms would be used against it rather than Afghanistan. Evidence that Pakistan was developing nuclear capabilities also clouded communications.

## A Difficult Courtship

The US viewed Rajiv's leadership as an opportunity to wean India away from Soviet influence, and Rajiv was responsive to their overtures. He was invited to visit Washington in 1985 and inaugurate the Indian Cultural Festival that his mother was to have attended. He was keen to dispel the notion that India was a Soviet puppet. He accepted on condition that adequate security be provided during the trip to protect him from known live assassination operations. 'Extraordinary measures were taken. On 13 May, Attorney General Edwin Meese forced through the order to arrest five Sikhs in New Orleans, then in the final stages of preparing to murder Mr Gandhi during his trip here. The day before the prime minister's arrival, two other Sikhs with the same mission were arrested in Puerto Rico.'[6] The US had no intention of risking any embarrassing security breach on their watch.

Rajiv was also invited to address the US Congress, an honour not extended to Mrs Gandhi. The Americans welcomed his quiet, calm, friendly manner, which was a contrast to his occasionally moody and sarcastic mother. Vice President Bush, who had developed close relations with the family when he visited India, had been assigned to look after him and accompanied the new prime minister to Texas for his visit to the National Aeronautics and Space Administration (NASA).

Rajiv had inherited a relatively stable economy with growth at 6 per cent. Food production was adequate, and India had been able to export some of its surplus for the first time. Still heavily dependent on oil imports, it was facing a worsening balance of payments deficit as its exports were growing slowly. India's available overseas development assistance at preferential rates had declined as had workers' remittances, putting pressure on resources. Its ever-increasing population mitigated any gains in growth. Rajiv was convinced that the path out of poverty was through technological modernization of the economy,[7] but for this he needed the World Bank, and IDA[§] loans, in particular. Since the IDA's founding in 1960, India had received approximately 40 per cent or $8.25 billion over twenty years in interest-free loans which carried fifty-year maturities.[8] China was understandably competing for a share of the funds, and Rajiv needed Reagan's help to preserve India's prerogatives there.

The young prime minister arrived in the US with three objectives. He wanted to make sure that the US: (1) continued to support India's share of IDA financing; (2) would agree to transfer technology including supercomputers; and (3) would reduce the flow of money and arms to Pakistan.

Rajiv's visit to the US accomplished some forward movement on the issue of India's share of IDA loans at the World Bank. Congress, which provided 20 per cent of the World Bank funding, had begun to cut its contribution to IDA, which would mean that other countries would follow suit, resulting in a reduction of soft loan money. During the Carter administration, the US lowered its contribution from $1.1 billion to $750 million. Now, conservatives were pushing to reduce it further to $520 million. In the end, they voted for the $750 million allocation.

President Reagan was genial and warm and liked Rajiv. His administration was happy to help out with the World Bank, but when it came to foreign policy, India was not a priority as Reagan was singularly focused on the Soviet threat. India had so far been unable to influence the Soviets or play any role that was helpful in this theatre that mattered so much to him.

Although the goodwill the two leaders established diffused tensions on several contentious occasions, over the years, distrust of the Indian bureaucracy among US officials prevented progress in cooperation on technology between the two countries.

---

§   IDA (International Development Agency) loans from the World Bank were 'soft loans' at very favourable terms. With China's entry, India's percentage had shrunk. The US and the World Bank also felt that many African countries had a greater need than India of IDA's support and India should graduate to IBRD loans that had stiffer terms.

India wanted the US to provide the Cray XMP-24 computer to the Indian Institute of Science. It was among the world's most advanced computers at the time. India wished to use it to predict weather conditions, in particular, the erratic monsoon that its agricultural sector was so dependent on. The computer's provision to India remained a controversial issue as the dual-use product could be used for the development of nuclear missiles and had several other sensitive military applications.

Acquiring the computer was of personal interest to Rajiv given his obsession with technology. He wanted to upgrade India's systems but the various US departments involved were unwilling to sign off on the transaction. They simply did not trust the Indians and felt the technology risked being shared with the Russians. In the end, the US persuaded India to accept the lower level Cray XMP-14 that could not be used for defence purposes. Scientists and government officials in India were bitter about the decision and the inability of the US to trust them but hoped they could build on the relationship and acquire the Cray XMP-24 at a later date.

In 1985, India expressed an interest in acquiring the GE 404 engine used in the F-18 fighter planes for manufacture in India. Once again, Washington dragged its heels and took so long over the approval process that Ambassador John Gunther Dean was worried it would breed mistrust. As one Indian junior minister for external affairs quipped, 'India-US relations were like the titles of two Dickens novels: *Great Expectations* and *Hard Times*.'[9]

Although technology transfer and IDA loans were the two immediate concerns for India, the larger foreign policy issues regarding Pakistan's arms build-up and its pursuit of a nuclear weapons programme had become a major concern for India.

Despite President Reagan's warm reception of Rajiv, with the CIA and the Pentagon using the Pakistani military establishment as a proxy to fight its covert war against the Russians, the US gave Pakistan the increasingly sophisticated arms it wanted and turned a blind eye to its pursuit of nuclear technology. Rajiv did his best to thaw relations with the US and point out the consequences of a nuclear arms race in the region, but the cards were stacked against him. The US military and the CIA were deeply embedded with the Pakistani army and intelligence services, which poisoned their attitudes towards India.

In his effort to improve relations with the US, Rajiv was helped enormously by the US ambassador to India, Harry Barnes. Rajiv trusted Barnes' low-key style and over time, the ambassador, who worked quietly, won over the Indians. Barnes was a career diplomat but, after the likes of Galbraith, Moynihan, and Goheen, Indians initially wondered if they had been downgraded when he was first appointed. Barnes lacked the high profile and strong links to the White House that several of his predecessors had enjoyed and the unassuming ambassador had arrived in India after dodging a scandal.

During his previous posting as ambassador to Romania, Barnes's wife had an affair with their chauffeur, who doubled as an intelligence agent. He had used Mrs Barnes to gain access to the US embassy, where he had planted listening devices. When the affair was exposed, Barnes reported it to his superiors at the State Department. They decided to conceal the information from Congress during his confirmation hearings as ambassador to India.[10]

The Indian ambassador to the US together with Barnes proved a helpful partnership in the Indo-American relations exercise. Shankar Bajpai had lived in Washington when his father was India's first representative to the US before Independence. He was a skilled diplomat and built relationships with the US Departments of Defense, Energy and Commerce. The two ambassadors negotiated a memorandum of understanding for technology transfer that India desperately wanted. Although the details were initially ironed out with Foreign Secretary Rasgotra, and then with Romesh Bhandari, it was the two ambassadors' behind-the-scenes efforts that overcame hesitations within the US. The agreement was finally signed in May 1985 before Barnes was sent to Chile as the ambassador to the Pinochet government.

John Gunther Dean succeeded Ambassador Barnes. Like him, Dean was also a career foreign service officer and had been hand-picked by the White House for the posting in Delhi. The White House did not want the State Department making the decision. Ambassador Dean realized that, despite Rajiv being more disposed towards the US than his mother,

Washington had done precious little to improve relations between the countries from its end. He tried to advocate on India's behalf: 'When all is said and done, India counts for more and will continue to count for more than any other nation in this part of the world whether we help them in this or not. In the India–US relationship there is a lot of history that has to be put behind us.'[11]

In the end, it all boiled down to a matter of trust. Prejudices had become so ingrained within both bureaucracies that it would take an investment from the leadership of both countries to change existing perceptions. This was the case not just between the two bureaucracies, but also with the US Congress where all the appropriations are made. India was slow to invest in its relationships on the Hill.

Ambassador Dean acknowledged in his memorandum to Richard Murphy at the bureau of Near Eastern Affairs that the US showed no willingness to transfer anything but old technology to India and India could get newer and better technology from the Europeans.[12]

Dr Fred Ikle, under secretary at the Pentagon, came to India in May 1985 to discuss the development in India of light combat aircraft. Vernon Orr, secretary of the air force, followed him. All of these were encouraging signs and held out the hope of possible defence cooperation down the line.

It would be an uphill battle as prejudices take time to expunge. One staffer told Peter Tomsen at the State Department that India was 'at best an apologist, at worst a stooge of the Soviet Union.'[13] The Hill found it outrageous that India proposed the US take the first step in resolving the Afghanistan problem by stopping its support to the mujahedin, who were armed to their teeth and, with the Soviets gone, were using the weapons against each other. According to the Tomsen report, congressmen sometimes wanted to punish India and when it came to the long-standing issue of Tarapur, the often-heard complaint was 'what have they done for us?'[14]

With Rajiv at the helm and with his more pro-Western stance, the respective ambassadors worked behind the scenes to change the negative attitudes that had developed during Mrs Gandhi's time in office.

The Indian defence ministry had fifteen export licences pending before the US, eleven of which had been previously turned down. In an effort to improve relations, the National Security Council eventually recommended they be reviewed again and fast-tracked.

India had also been placed on the 'priority watch list' under the Omnibus Trade Act of 1988. A special trade clause called the 'super 301' put countries that had trade barriers on a special list for retaliatory action. US action could have grave negative consequences for India because it was India's biggest trading partner. India thought the US was being unfairly aggressive, as Dinesh Singh, India's commerce minister, pointed out in a statement to the press on 26 May 1989. The trade relationship was asymmetrical, with India barely registering on the US balance sheet.

India's primary concern remained the arms build-up in Pakistan. The State Department and NSA were aware of India's concerns. Although positive in their assessments of the new leadership in India, they were reluctant to shift gears. Old prejudices and preferences remained. A paper written for internal use in December 1984 states: 'We must try not to get a new friend (India) at the expense of our old friend (Pakistan).'[15] The preferred method was to encourage improvements in India's relations with China and Pakistan. In the lexicon of the US administration, India and Pakistan were linked, and as long as there was an 'Afghan problem', Pakistan was needed by the US and India was the dispensable nation.

The US acceded to President Zia's demands for sophisticated weapons and continued to increase aid to Pakistan. Zia was helped by William Casey, who was one of the most influential members of the administration. A particular grievance of India was the US refusal to give assurances that the arms provided to Pakistan would not be used against it. General Zia, who had executed Bhutto in April 1979, cancelled elections and made himself head of government, was a religious fundamentalist. He had recruited and encouraged religious members into the ISI and army. They became the conduits of US aid to the mujahidin in Afghanistan. The US had outsourced the war to Zia and would have to grapple with the consequences of those decisions at a later date.

Pakistan's covert pursuit of nuclear technology to build a bomb was viewed by New Delhi as destabilizing to the region. President Zia was as shrewd as he was religious. Appalled by Pakistan's defeat in the 1971 war, he was determined to restore Pakistan's military parity with India.

He was convinced that they could not win a conventional war against India and they had to go nuclear. By 1979, US intelligence had obtained information that Pakistan had secretly built a uranium-enrichment facility in response to India.[16] Although President Carter had cut off aid to Pakistan, once the Soviets occupied Afghanistan, aid was restored and was increased under Reagan.

There was mounting evidence that Pakistan was pursuing a nuclear weapons programme during the Reagan administration, but the US was unwilling to invoke the Pressler Amendment, which forbade them from providing aid to countries that developed nuclear weapons. Robert Einhorn, one of the leading non-proliferation negotiators for the US, confirmed that the US was aware of the existence of the Pakistani programme. 'As the eighties wore on, it became clear that Pakistan was pursuing nuclear weapons; this was when the United States was cooperating with Pakistan, in particular the ISI, to funnel aid to the mujahidin in Afghanistan. The key objective was to bleed the Soviets and get them out of Afghanistan. Pakistan was the indispensable component of that important national objective.'[17]

The US was not prepared to alter its policy or police Pakistan so long as the Soviets remained in Afghanistan. When visiting Zia during Mrs Gandhi's funeral, Secretary Shultz asked the Pakistani president about rumours that Pakistan was pursuing a nuclear bomb. In his memoir, Shultz seemed remarkably unconcerned by the president's evasive response: 'We are nowhere near it. We have no intentions of making such a weapon. We renounce our right to make such a weapon. But please do not discriminate against Pakistan. Look at what is happening in the region.'[18] With Pakistan remaining the only viable conduit to arm the Afghan resistance, the US was lenient towards their ally until the Soviets withdrew.

The US used the CIA to manage the covert war through their proxies in Pakistan. As with any clandestine war involving vast amounts of cash, arms and dark characters, there was corruption that found its way to the top.[¶] Ambassador Dean felt the heat from the covert war that was being run between Washington, Afghanistan and Pakistan, all the way in New Delhi:

---

¶    The story of the covert war is covered in Steve Coll's book *Ghost Wars*.

'I found that in India the ambassador was at times not the coordinator of US activities in the field, but behind the ambassador's back Washington took initiatives on major issues without keeping the ambassador directly informed.'[19]

## Drugs, Guns and Aid[**]

In December 1983, a young Pakistani man was arrested at Oslo airport with three and a half kilos of heroin. Links led directly back to the president of Pakistan. Zia's 'adopted son' Hamid Hasnain was a kingpin in the drug trade. The police found chequebooks and bank statements belonging to Zia and his family on Hasnain.[20] According to Ambassador Dean, drug dealing was intertwined with the flow of arms to the Afghan resistance. The US Drug Enforcement Agency (DEA) had identified at least forty drug syndicates operating out of Pakistan, but their investigations were subordinated to the CIA's agenda overseas. The DEA could not recruit informants or initiate inquires without CIA approval. This enabled the CIA to steer it away from sensitive clandestine operations.[21]

In 1986, the BBC aired a documentary on *Panorama* involving an interview with a Japanese courier, Hisayoshi Maruyama. He had been caught carrying seventeen kilos of heroin when he was arrested. He described the drug syndicate in Pakistan and identified its top man who, despite being well known to authorities, was freely operating his business. A senior Pakistani narcotics officer said the 'boss', Iqbal Baig, was protected. He noted that there was an apparent US policy not to press for arrests that led to embarrassing connections with government officials allied with the US.[22]

In July 1986, Major Zahooruddin Afridi was arrested while driving to Karachi from Peshawar carrying 200 kilos of high-grade heroin. Two months later, Flight Lieutenant Khairur Rahman was also intercepted carrying 220 kilos of heroin. He confessed it was his fifth mission. The street value of the drugs amounted to approximately $4 billion. It was the

---

** Much of the information in this section is derived from Ambassador John Gunther Dean's oral history.

equivalent of the entire covert budget for the Afghan war over eight years. Both men 'escaped' mysteriously before trial.[23]

Lawrence Lifschultz reported that the *Herald*, a Pakistani paper, repeatedly noted that the main channel by which weapons were sent to the Afghan resistance was the same route used to transport heroin. It is hard to conceive that any of this could have been done without the knowledge or direction of the Pakistani intelligence services. The implication was that the CIA knew what was going on but looked the other way.

## Caught Between the Superpowers

The US wanted to isolate the Soviets and show firmness in the face of Soviet aggression in the developing world. Its goals were to weaken the Soviets, deny them a base in Afghanistan and convince them the that their long-term strategy there was doomed.

The Reagan administration put considerable pressure on India to push for a Soviet withdrawal but, despite India's close ties with the Russians, they were unable to make headway. With no deliverables, India's security concerns were ignored in Washington.

For now, the world was dominated by two superpowers and the Cold War dictated their alliances and priorities. Reagan had started out in politics with an uncompromising view of communism. He had viewed Nixon and Kissinger's opening to China with a degree of scepticism. His views were aligned with the far right's opinion that Roosevelt's 1945 meeting with Stalin at Yalta was a sell-out.

His view was fairly simplistic. He believed the Soviet system was a façade and, therefore, unsustainable. He was a military hawk whose views that US superiority needed to be maintained at all costs, were supported by Secretary of State Alexander Haig,[††] Secretary of Defense Casper Weinberger and William Casey of the CIA. He called for the Strategic Defense Initiative (SDI), which would defend against a first strike and make it difficult for any nuclear missile to penetrate the US. Its massive cost would outspend anything Russia could contemplate as a response.

---

†† Alexander Haig was the secretary of state from January 1981 to July 1982.

Reagan was certain that the Soviet economy was under pressure and trying to compete with the US could possibly bankrupt it and end the Cold War. He was not far off the mark.

Reagan increased military spending from $171 billion to $229 billion in his first term. 'They cannot vastly increase their military productivity because they've already got their people on a starvation diet,' Reagan observed of the Russians in October 1981. 'But now they're going to be faced with the fact that we could go forward with an arms race and they can't keep up.'[24] The hope was that they would curtail their activities in Afghanistan, Africa and elsewhere.[‡‡] He viewed his spending and SDI as a means to an end, but by his second term, his convictions softened.

President Reagan began to get increasingly concerned about the perils of nuclear weapons in his second term. He went from wanting to defang the Soviets to nuclear disarmament. Confronted with the fallout of nuclear war, as demonstrated to him by Pentagon simulations, he was shocked.

Graphic films reinforced the president's views. The ABC television film, *The Day After,* showed in gruesome detail the obliteration of Lawrence, Kansas in the event of a nuclear attack. According to Reagan's biographer Lou Cannon, his thinking was also influenced by the 1983 film *War Games*, which concludes there are no winners in a nuclear war.[§§]

When the two sides met in Reykjavik, Iceland in October 1986, Gorbachev had already proposed eliminating all intermediate-range nuclear missiles in Europe and a phased plan for the bilateral elimination of all nuclear weapons by the year 2000. The Chernobyl disaster in April

---

‡‡ Many reliable sources have also referenced another more mystical influence in the president's thinking that affected his worldview. He believed in Armageddon. He made references to it in his conversations with his national security advisor, 'Bud' McFarland, regarding SDI. He brought it up in an interview with Jim Bakker's PTL television network as something they could see in their lifetime. It was the sort of conversation that spooked rational policy makers and opened Reagan up to ridicule. Reagan's conviction that in a conflagration with the Soviets, the US representing the force of good would win allowed him to pursue his high-stakes policy.

§§ Another film that had a great impact on President Reagan was *The Day the Earth Stood Still*. His aides rolled their eyes when he brought it up.

1986, when radioactive material fanned out towards Europe after the No. 4 reactor at the Chernobyl nuclear power plant failed, convinced the world that the risks of nuclear contamination could not be confined and helped bring hardliners on board.

Gorbachev, who was more forward thinking than his older, stauncher communist party members, had to find a way to persuade them of the more radical plan to eliminate nuclear weapons. A freak incident in Russia provided Gorbachev with the opportunity he was looking for to shake up his military leadership and rid him of the old guard. On 27 May 1987, a young man from West Germany flew a small plane into the Kremlin with a message for Gorbachev. Shocked that he had breached security without detection, Gorbachev used this as an excuse to reorganize the military leadership and get rid of those who disagreed with him.

Although Reykjavik did not produce any agreements, it was the first time the US realized that the Russians, and particularly Gorbachev, were sincere about arms control.[55] They finally signed the Intermediate-Range Nuclear Forces (INF) Treaty in December 1987. In the intervening months, the two leaders learnt to trust each other and became friends. Gorbachev, unlike his predecessors, was charming and less formal. Combined with Reagan's easy manner that smoothed out tense moments, the two formed an alliance in the challenges they shared. This included having to convince members of their own teams that the elimination of nuclear weapons was in the best interests of their respective countries and the world. Many Republicans repudiated Reagan's policy. Nixon and Kissinger actively lobbied against it. Reagan ended up looking for and finding support among the Democrats on the Hill.

Rajiv was impressed by Gorbachev and saw no reason to diminish the Indo-Russian alliance. Unlike the past, when Russia looked at India's efforts at a US alliance with suspicion, Gorbachev was sanguine. He himself was working to develop relations with Reagan and recognized that the tracks of diplomacy needed to be rearranged. Although it was not visible to India or the US, Gorbachev was worried that the existing political

---

[55] SDI became a roadblock. Gorbachev insisted they confine it to a lab. Reagan refused.

and economic structures within Russia were in trouble and needed to change. He was more concerned about keeping the country competitive and strong internally than maintaining the complicated network of client states within their Cold War status.

## Relations Wither

While Reagan and Gorbachev were making history in Reykjavik on 11–12 October 1986, Casper Weinberger visited India to discuss the transfer of military technology to India. His non-committal trip, which was hailed as a success by the US, was considered uneventful in India as he did not deliver on the technology that India had hoped for. The first trip ever made by a US secretary of defence was a disappointment. Rajiv left the country for an overseas trip before the secretary's trip was over. It was interpreted as a putdown by Indians. Weinberger's stop in Pakistan, and his subsequent announcement there, nearly pulled out the threads of the fragile repair undertaken in Indo-US relations.

While in Pakistan, the defence secretary reaffirmed US commitments to Pakistan's aid and arms supply. He then added that Pakistan's request for AWACs (airborne warning and control system) and Abrams tanks was under consideration. The Indians were caught off guard and were incensed that they had not been forewarned about the impending announcement.

On 11 November 1986, a special discussion on the AWACs sale in the Lok Sabha induced a bipartisan attack on the US. The four-hour debate railed about US actions destabilizing South Asia. A comment by the US administration, in support of Pakistan, stating that '[t]he US government would not come down on the Zia regime with a heavy hand even if a bomb were found in Zia's basement',[25] further inflamed the situation and confirmed to the nuclear hawks that Rajiv's efforts at friendship with the US had not yielded any results and the US had not softened its pro-Pakistan tilt. Senior State Department official Bruce Riedel agreed with Rajiv that despite Vice President Bush's friendly gestures and Reagan's genial manner, the US had acted against India's interests. 'The US support for Pakistan in the 1980s emboldened the hawks, including Zia, to heat up the pressure in Kashmir, but, more broadly, against India across the board.'[26]

In December 1987, relations slid to rock bottom when the Senate Appropriation Committee, tacitly admitting it was aware of Pakistan's nuclear programme, said that Pakistan was justified in pursuing a nuclear bomb as India had one.

Ken Adelman, Reagan's arms control director, tried to point out to his colleagues, including Colin Powell, that this gutted the US policy on non-proliferation. It was tantamount to the US blessing an arms race in South Asia. Rajiv and the Indian defence establishment were stunned. Rajiv had met with Reagan, in 1985 on a state visit and again informally when he went for the UN meetings, and believed he had built up goodwill with the Reagan administration, which inoculated India against any negative actions.

The US had subordinated non-proliferation, a key foreign policy objective, to the war in Afghanistan. They had effectively become complicit in Pakistan's quest to acquire nuclear weapons. US intelligence agencies had all the evidence they needed to confront Pakistan and shut down its drive to become a nuclear weapon state, but they chose to look the other way. The White House and the US military went further. They wilfully broke US laws regarding proliferation to protect Pakistan by lying to Congress about Pakistan's nuclear programme.

Ambassador Dean was called in to meet with Rajiv and his senior advisor, Ronen Sen, on 4 December 1987. India had always gone out of its way to state that its nuclear resources would be used for peaceful purposes and warned against a nuclear arms race in South Asia. It had also made it clear that it viewed itself as the pre-eminent power in South Asia and resented being 'twinned' with Pakistan by the US. Rajiv wanted the US to use its influence to rein in Pakistan's nuclear ambitions. In his memorandum to the State Department, Dean described the prime minister as sad and deeply disappointed by the US. Rajiv had gone out of his way to foster Indo-US relations and thought he had developed a good relationship with both President Reagan and Vice President Bush. He felt politically betrayed.[27]

In a dramatic meeting with the American ambassador on 7 December, Ronen Sen, secretary to the prime minister, accused the US of undermining Rajiv. He complained that US actions had emboldened the nuclear hawks in India, and they were demanding that India advance its nuclear weapons capability. To emphasize his point, he offered to provide the ambassador with a list of their names.[28]

Indian cooperation on various programmes stalled or was put on hold. The prime minister was faced with having to walk back on the glowing state of Indo-US relations that he had painted for Parliament on his return from the US earlier in the year. Rajiv was being criticized in the Indian press for being naïve and misreading US intentions.

The Indian ambassador in Washington did not escape censure. Members of Parliament insisted he be recalled for failing to protect India's interests. The Reagan administration, including Vice President Bush and the State Department, worked furiously to try to salvage the situation and tone down the infamous Inouye-Kasten Amendment, which equated India and Pakistan and used India's nuclear programme to justify appropriating money for Pakistan. The White House eventually persuaded the Senate Appropriation Committee to pass a diluted version that was less offensive to India. India and Pakistan were de-linked; an important clause for India. Further, in order for Pakistan to continue receiving arms, waivers would have to be obtained to satisfy the Symington Amendment, which required the suspension of aid to countries acquiring nuclear weapons.[29]

Rajiv was genuinely interested in eliminating nuclear weapons. However, he did not offer to end India's nuclear programme. Morarji Desai had also believed in disarmament but had been opposed by the military and scientific establishment in India. Rajiv did not make Desai's mistake in trying to overrule the Indian nuclear community, but this did not prevent him from pushing his views internationally. He advocated for a nuclear-free world and submitted extensive proposals to the UN on behalf of the non-aligned group. At the UN General Assembly in June 1988, he presented a comprehensive 'Action Plan for Ushering in a Nuclear Weapon Free and Non-Violent World'. Reagan and Gorbachev shared his views, but they viewed the issue as a bilateral problem for Russia and the US to resolve; they saw no role for India in their discussions.

As 1987 ended, Reagan and Gorbachev signed the INF Treaty that began the end of the Cold War. They began the laborious process of a drawdown of nuclear weapons.*** The following spring, in April 1988, the Soviets finally started their withdrawal from Afghanistan. The Soviet withdrawal decreased the flow of money and arms to Pakistan, removing a major impediment to closer relations between India and the US. Although the AWACs sale was not confirmed, it cast a shadow over relations. It would take time to recover from the Inouye-Kasten saga of the previous year. Afghanistan had been hovering below the radar, but now thrust itself on to everyone's plate. The US took the lead in trying to determine what a post-Soviet political solution would look like.

Afghanistan was a significant contributory factor to end the Cold War. The US played the starring role with Pakistan as the supporting actor. US support of the mujahidin had strained the Russian occupation for years. It bled the Soviets in terms of resources and manpower and exposed their vulnerability as a superpower—it became their Vietnam. It was a highly unpopular war in Russia, and the US had made sure the occupation became an unbearable burden for them.

India's primary concern was preventing Afghanistan from becoming an Islamic fundamentalist state. It was worried that Zia, who was an Islamist and had encouraged conservative Islam in Pakistan, would encourage fundamentalism in Afghanistan. These concerns were shared by Gorbachev and would prove to be correct. The US was overly dependent on its Pakistani partners and failed to assess the potential for Afghanistan to be taken over by religious fundamentalists.[30] Reagan had taken office as the US hostages in Iran were released, and a fundamentalist government had taken over the state, but Americans overlooked the regional implications. Reagan and the US administration were unable to see the consequences of Zia's Islamification of Pakistan's military and secret service or the groups they supported to evict the Soviets from Afghanistan. Their minds were

***The INF treaty saved Reagan's presidency from the Iran-Contra scandal (a secret arms deal that sold missiles to Iran to free American hostages held in Lebanon, and used funds from the deal to support rebels in Nicaragua) that had made his approval ratings plummet. It was particularly controversial as it broke US laws as Iran was under sanctions.

occupied by the communist threat and the Islamic fundamentalist one was a distant idea.

On 17 August 1988, General Zia, several of Pakistan's top military commanders, Arnold Raphael, the US ambassador to Pakistan, and a US general died when the flight they were on exploded upon take-off. Many conspiracy theories circulated as to the cause of the explosion. Zia had accumulated many enemies while in office. John Gunther Dean was convinced that there was a cover up of what really happened. He speculated that the Israeli secret service Mossad had been responsible, as they did not want Pakistan to develop an 'Islamic bomb'. His speculation resulted in his removal from the foreign service in 1989.[31]

India was determined to play a role in the Afghan resolution. Pakistan, which had done all the heavy lifting, wanted India kept away and to keep Afghanistan under its sphere of influence. The US would walk a fine line between keeping India informed on a need-to-know basis, while also maintaining distance between India and Pakistan on the issue.

As the US began to replace the Russians as the primary interlocutors in the constantly mutating Afghan war, the Soviet Empire began to disintegrate. The Soviets became increasingly preoccupied with their internal problems and the break-up of their partnerships in Eastern Europe.

Reagan's success in ending the Cold War was due to the partner he had in Gorbachev, as well as his insight into the economic pressure Russia was under and his negotiating skills. Andropov's death in 1984, followed by a short tenure by an ailing Chernenko allowed Gorbachev to take the helm of Soviet affairs. Gorbachev would prove the ideal partner and one with the vision and philosophical flexibility to move his country towards a new world order. Like Reagan, he understood that there would be no winners in a nuclear confrontation and actively worked to negotiate arms reduction.

All US presidents had, in one way or another, formed policies around the containment of communism since the Cold War began. It was not until Nixon penetrated China with his historic diplomatic initiative that the West was able to contemplate the normalizations of relations with a communist country.

The end of the Reagan presidency would change the balance of power in the world. President Reagan had stood in front of the Berlin Wall and, against the advice of his lieutenants, challenged Gorbachev to 'tear down this wall'. Although the Berlin Wall did not physically come down until George Bush took over as president in 1989, Reagan's actions caused it to symbolically crack. He had followed his instincts, decided this was the moment for peace, and pushed to end a forty-year stand-off that had polarized the world.

Reagan had started out as a domestic policy president, but he left an enduring legacy in foreign affairs that made the world a safer place.

By ending the Cold War, and removing the contentious Afghan problem, Reagan inadvertently created an opportunity for a new relationship between India and the US. The Reagan presidency also witnessed the end of an era in India with the passing of Mrs Gandhi. She had compromised India's non-alignment policy and tilted the country towards the Soviets. In her pursuit of power, she had strayed from the democratic principles of the founders of independent India, including her father, who had always had reservations about the Soviets. She had surrounded herself with pro-Soviet advisors that fed her own natural inclination towards anti-Americanism. Her political weaknesses had left her vulnerable to the communist factions in India, pushing her left of where she wanted to be. Her poor relations with Nixon snuffed out whatever embers may have been burning among the ashes of Indo-US relations.

India's increasingly influential diaspora were firmly invested in the West and had become global entrepreneurs. They now began to exert pressure on India to abandon its socialist mentality and align itself with the West both politically and economically. With communism crumbling and technology levelling the global space, the stage was set for a new world order. The US had emerged as the dominant superpower. Nixon's opening to communist China would, in time, change the balance further as China became a more active participant in the world economy. India, under its young leader and his West-leaning advisors, would finally begin a long overdue correction in its foreign relations and join the march towards liberalization and improved relations with the US.

# Chapter 17

# Bush 41: The End of an Era

GEORGE HERBERT WALKER BUSH AND RAJIV GANDHI HAD BEEN surrounded by politics their entire life. Both leaders had been born into established political dynasties. Bush, the son of a former US senator, served two terms as a congressman before becoming the forty-first president, and his son would continue the tradition and become the forty-third president of the US, placing the Bushes among America's leading political families, alongside the Roosevelts and the Kennedys. Rajiv's mother and grandfather had both served as prime ministers of India. Between them, they had governed India for more than thirty years.

Both men were, by nature, kind, self-deprecating and outwardly humble. But whereas Rajiv had entered political life reluctantly, Bush was motivated by his personal ambition to become president. Rajiv had been pressured to accept the leadership of the Congress Party by those wanting to retain power after his mother's assassination in 1984. The Congress party had persuaded him that he was the only unifying force that could keep the enterprise together.

Unlike previous Republican presidents Eisenhower, Nixon and Reagan, who grew up in humble circumstances, Bush's lineage derived from the elite of the East Coast establishment. Growing up, he divided his time between Greenwich, Connecticut, Kennebunkport, Maine and his maternal grandfather's plantation in South Carolina. The family had emphasized the value of public service and he had grown up with the mantra: 'To whom much is given, much is expected.' Bush had both academic and athletic ability, was considered handsome and, uncharacteristically for his generation, was somewhat emotional.

Bush felt a profound sense of duty to his country and enlisted when the war broke out. He would be the last president to have voluntarily enlisted and seen combat: 'It was a red, white and blue thing. Your country's attacked, you'd better get in there and try to help.'[1] He served as a pilot from 1942 to 1945. Before the war ended with the Japanese surrender, George Bush had flown fifty-eight combat missions, made 128 carrier landings and been shot down once.

The war injected a harsh dose of reality into his otherwise sheltered world, and according to his autobiography, had a profound effect on him. He was still young when the war ended, and after graduating from Yale, he moved to Texas to make his fortune with a view to entering politics.

Bush's political career spanned several presidents from Johnson to Reagan, but his rise in politics did not follow a straight line. It was always one step forward, two steps back. Despite all his political and financial connections, the prize of the presidency eluded him until 1989. His move to Texas coincided with a shift in the political climate of the south. Texas and the south were steadily moving to the right, and Bush joined this seismic shift. The socially conservative old southern Democrats were unhappy with the liberal direction of the country. They had started their steady conversion to the Republican Party in the 1960s, but the pace accelerated once Reagan, who appealed to their values, ran for president.

Bush was a moderate Republican and believed in bipartisan cooperation. He was a conservative in fiscal policy, but had also voted against many aspects of the Civil Rights Act, in subservience to the growing right-wing voices in his party that had become more vocal in the 1960s. It was a political decision, as he was personally against segregation. He wrote, 'I opposed discrimination of any kind and abhorred racism.'[2] In a letter to a friend, he confessed, 'My heart is heavy … I want to win but not at the expense of justice, nor at the expense of the dignity of any man—not at the expense of hurting a friend nor teaching my children a prejudice I do not feel.'[3] Later, he tried to compensate by voting for the Fair Housing Act and had to face considerable anger from his constituents. His personal moderation did not sit well with the extreme right wing of his party and the struggle between his personal, more moderate social beliefs and those of his more conservative constituents would remain a continual challenge for him.

Congressman Bush did not always give in to the conservatives in his party. In 1954, he was among the twenty-two Republicans who voted against McCarthy. He said, 'I realize that anybody who takes a stand against McCarthy is apt to be subjected through the lunatic fringe to all sorts of abuse.'[4] He had encountered the extremists early on when he ran for the Senate in 1964 and found them distasteful. The John Birch Society, an anti-communist, far-right political group, had campaigned against him and Bush lost, but in 1966 Bush felt vindicated when he won a Congressional House seat despite them.

Still, Bush hankered after the Senate and in 1969 sought advice from his fellow Texan, President Lyndon Johnson. He was weighing the risk of losing his safe congressional seat. The former president's response was classic Johnson: 'The difference between being a member of the Senate and a member of the House is the difference between chicken salad and chicken shit.'[5] With that advice, Bush went to President Nixon, who also encouraged him to run for the Senate. Once again, things did not work out and Bush lost the race to Lloyd Bentsen. As compensation, Nixon made him ambassador to the UN.

Bush discovered that he enjoyed foreign policy immensely. He went about establishing relationships with the representatives of foreign countries, immersing himself in international issues. He soon encountered the first of Henry Kissinger's tantrums. Kissinger had zero tolerance for sharing the spotlight on the foreign policy stage. When he and Bush clashed over the status of Taiwan at the UN, Kissinger gave Ambassador Bush a dressing down: 'I want to treat you as I do four other ambassadors, dealing directly with you, but if you are uncooperative, I will treat you like any other ambassador.' Bush described it as a very heated exchange.[6] When President Nixon was re-elected, he removed Bush from the UN and made him chairman of the Republican National Committee (RNC). Bush had hoped to remain in foreign policy, and he wanted to be the number two at the State Department, but it is unlikely that Kissinger would have allowed it.

When Nixon resigned in disgrace and Ford became president, Bush paid him a visit. Bush had been short-listed to be Ford's vice president and was disappointed at being passed over.* He took the opportunity, in his capacity as chairman of the RNC, to advise Ford to relieve Kissinger of his dual role as secretary of state and national security advisor.

Bush was sent as the ambassador to China, a post that had been his second choice as he would have preferred a cabinet position. Although President Ford had consulted Kissinger, who had a hand in the decision, he may not have been the only one to push Bush away from the centre of politics. Donald Rumsfeld's star was rising. The former congressman had been sidelined under Nixon and sent to Brussels as the US representative. Rumsfeld was brought to the centre of power by President Ford and appointed as chief of staff, a job Bush would have liked better than the ambassadorship.

Kissinger's influence began to wane as Rumsfeld, with his deputy Dick Cheney, took over the White House. In November 1975, President Ford made several changes in his administration in preparation for the 1976 election. Rumsfeld became secretary of defence, Cheney replaced him as chief of staff, and Bush was recalled from China to head up the CIA, where presidential ambitions were said to die. Bush was devastated and thought his rival Rumsfeld was behind his appointment.

Bush had really wanted to be vice president on the Ford ticket as it would have been the perfect springboard for a future presidential run, whereas the CIA was not considered a good assignment for that purpose. The organization was going through a crisis in confidence, with failed assassination plots against foreign leaders and illegal black operations that had been revealed under post-Watergate scrutiny. Bush, ever the team player, agreed to take the job against his best instincts. In the end, it would barely last a year.

Jimmy Carter defeated President Ford in 1976 and Bush returned to Texas to plot his path to the presidency. He ran against Reagan in 1980

---

\* A damaging report was released by *Newsweek* that implicated Bush's 1970 senate campaign in the receipt of funds from a Nixon slush fund called the 'Townhouse Operation'. Bush was cleared but the damage was done.

and lost. After some reluctance, Reagan offered Bush the job of vice president, which would provide Bush with the launch pad to the 1989 presidency.

## Getting Along

Rajiv Gandhi and George Bush had first met when Rajiv accompanied his mother and prime minister Mrs Gandhi to the US on a state visit in 1982. Two years later, Bush came to India. There was commentary in the Indian press that the vice president was visiting India to compensate for President Reagan's official visit to China in April 1984. During the visit, the US agreed to sell nuclear reactors to China. The US also agreed to let China reprocess the spent fuel. This irked the Indians as they had consistently been denied the same privilege.

From the Indian perspective, the US practice of following a hard line in its nuclear policy towards India smacked of double standards. India was a democracy and China was a communist state. India suspected that China was proliferating by helping Pakistan's nuclear ambitions and was offended that the US showed a preference for communist China over democratic India.

The Indians wondered if the US stand on proliferation was just used to pressure specific countries. To aggravate misgivings, a visiting Canadian parliamentary delegation made it clear that India was unlikely to receive nuclear aid unless they signed the Non-Proliferation Treaty (NPT).

There was considerable pressure from the pro-Soviet factions within the Indian government to retaliate, but Mrs Gandhi had made up her mind. She felt things had gone in the wrong direction with the US far enough and was determined to patch up relations. She went out of her way to welcome Vice President Bush during his visit and invited him to her home for an intimate dinner instead of an official one. It was meant to confer a special status to his visit. The dinner was limited to the Bushes, Mrs Gandhi and Rajiv.

The points of discussion were mutually agreed upon in advance. However, the private dinner invitation, aside from being a highly unusual gesture, enabled frank discussions away from the press and hangers on.

Prior to departing, Bush told the press, 'I came away from my meetings with the prime minister with renewed appreciation of the Indian perspective on the problems that confront our world.'[7] The visit was deemed a success, and a more empathetic relationship seemed to have been established between the two countries.

Bush had held some pre-trip interviews where he had gone out of his way to reassure the Indians. He stated that the US was not trying to encircle India in any way, emphasized India's strategic importance and laid the groundwork for warmer relations.[8] His trip was a social success, even if there were no concrete agreements reached. The Indian government also helped to get a US couple released who had been held by kidnappers in Sri Lanka. The effort was appreciated by the US and resulted in a warm exchange of letters.

In 1985, when Rajiv visited the US as prime minister after his mother's assassination, Vice President Bush spent considerable time with him. He became President Reagan's point person for managing the relationship with India. He accompanied Rajiv to Texas and introduced him to many of his business and personal contacts. The visits during Bush's time as vice president laid the foundations for a more balanced approach towards India once he became president.

Rajiv's visit to the US in 1985 substantially reduced the animosity that the US government had built up towards India. Like Bush in India, Rajiv charmed the US officials he met with his self-deprecating demeanour and willingness to listen.

'President Reagan's closest advisors, hidebound curmudgeons like CIA Director William Casey and United Sates Information Agency Chief Charles Wick, stated in separate interviews to *India Today* that despite continuing differences between the two countries, Rajiv's visit had proved a "turning point" in Indo-US ties. "He's quite a guy," remarked the usually tight-lipped Casey.'[9]

When Rajiv returned to attend the UN General Assembly meetings, Bush invited him to stay at his family home in Maine. He added, in his own handwriting, 'Oh yes, one more thing—no formal clothes, no protocol up there at all!!'[10]

## Differences

Despite an increased rapport in personal relations between Rajiv and Bush, it was hard to overcome the long years of antipathy towards India that had developed within the different branches of the US government. Not only were the Congress and Pentagon often unsympathetic to India, but during a confidential conversation with Vice President Bush and members of the bureaucracy, Ambassador Barnes said that the prevailing attitude in the US Treasury was 'If it's India, we don't want to help,' or 'It can go away.'[11] This made assisting India on the World Bank's IDA and Asian Development Bank loans even more challenging. Although the Indian economy had been steadily improving, it was at a very low rate. The World Bank's soft loans were regarded by India as critical to its economic development, particularly for its industrial development.

The continuing military aid to Pakistan was a constant thorn in India's dealings with the US. The increased flow of aid and military equipment to Pakistan continued to destabilize Indo-Pakistan relations. India wanted a US commitment that it would not allow Pakistan to use its bases or arms against India, but despite Bush's public assurances, privately the US administration, especially the military, were pro-Pakistan, and thought India was stepping on Pakistan's sovereignty.[12]

The US attitude inevitably prevented Rajiv from warming to them. According to Mani Shankar Aiyar, who served in the Prime Minister's Office and helped write his speeches, Rajiv was unfailingly polite, but he was cynical about America's motivations and intentions; when it really mattered, the US seldom came through for India. But Rajiv tried to work with the US in areas of mutual concern, such as Afghanistan, despite his hesitations.

Gorbachev announced a plan to withdraw troops from Afghanistan on 15 May 1988, and to be completed over a period of ten months. Rajiv, who had received early reports about the Soviet plan, had informed the US. There was some disagreement between the two superpowers over support to the rebels in the interim. The Soviets insisted that the US terminate all support to the rebels prior to withdrawal, but the US refused to define when that would occur. UN-sponsored talks were held in Geneva to oversee the process, with the US acting as guarantor. The Geneva accords were to include Pakistan and Afghanistan, but the Soviets were chagrined that the US continued to funnel aid and arms to the rebels and felt that they were not acting impartially. As Pakistan was the conduit for the arms supply to the rebels, it continued to receive both military and economic assistance from the US until the Soviets left.

Another area of conflict with the US was the militarization of the Indian Ocean. The US had established a base at Diego Garcia and refused to accede to India's requests to vacate the island.

## New Challenges

On his first day in office as president, Bush had tears in his eyes as he walked Reagan to the presidential plane that would carry him and his family to Los Angeles for the final time. At the age of sixty-five, and with almost twenty-two years devoted to public service, George Herbert Walker Bush became the forty-first president of the United States.

Almost every new president begins his tenure by trying to address domestic problems but, inevitably, events on the world stage intrude and demand immediate attention. On 8 February 1989, as the newly elected president was rolling out his plan to solve the savings and loan crisis in the US, terrorists bombed the British library in Karachi, followed by another bombing in Peshawar on 15 March. The consensus was that fundamentalist Muslims were behind the attack. They were retaliating against the publication of Salman Rushdie's *The Satanic Verses* in the UK.

In March 1989, President Bush was mopping up the fallout from the Exxon Valdez oil spill. The extensive damage to wildlife and the environment would take years to litigate, but soon momentous political events in the East overwhelmed these concerns and swamped the White House.

The attention of the US administration and the world at large would be riveted by events in the communist world, which would end the dual superpower structure of the Cold War that had been in place since the Second World War.

In May 1989, the communist regime in China reversed course and stepped away from liberalization. It clamped down on student protesters. It was personally discouraging for the president, who had been an ambassador to China. The Tiananmen Square Massacre, when the Chinese government brutally put down a pro-democracy movement led by students calling for free speech and freedom of the press, became a migraine for the Bush administration. The US had welcomed China into the free world with exchanges in technology, including nuclear reactors and arms, but China was falling backwards. The Bush administration had to now strongly condemn China.

While communism was reasserting itself in China, the Soviet Empire was in disarray. There was considerable pressure on the president to follow up on the Reagan–Gorbachev talks and make sure that the Soviet dissolution did not destabilize Europe. In November 1989, the Berlin Wall fell and thousands of East Germans streamed across to the West. The most robust symbol of Soviet power was gone. The East European satellite states began to peel away from the Soviet Union, leaving the US as the sole superpower in the world.

Barely a week after Bush became president, the 'shake and bake' case made headlines. India had contracted with a US company, MB Dynamics of Ohio, to supply a combined acceleration, vibration and climatic test system (CAVCTS), also known as 'shake and bake'. The US government had held up its export and kept requesting additional assurances from India.[†] According to a memorandum written by Tyrus Cobb, special assistant to the president, the Commerce Department had issued the licence for export and the State Department had signed off on it but the Department of Defense objected, so Secretary Carlucci had referred the matter to the president.[13]

While India was mired in its usual stalemate with the US, Rajiv's domestic problems were mounting. By the time Bush became president in January 1989, Rajiv Gandhi's government was in trouble. Rajiv's economic reform programme had slowed due to pushback from the agrarian sector,

---

† The US was concerned that India could pass on the dual-use technology to Russia.

which was unconvinced that liberalization was going to benefit it. Foreign investment in India was barely $200 million, of which the US share was a mere $38 million in 1989. By 1990, the US investment had dropped to $19 million.[14]

India was still regarded as operating a protectionist and closed economy. Indian businesses, wanting foreign investment without foreign competition, lobbied hard to keep international companies out of India to avoid exposing their inefficiencies and inferior products.

There was little demand for Indian products in the West due to their inferior quality and production inefficiencies but the Soviets, in an effort to court India, were willing to buy them and became an important outlet for Indian goods.

There was little incentive to invest in Indian industry as the government had laced the industrial sector with red tape that protected Indian businesses, but not in a way that made them prosper and grow. Foreigners were not allowed controlling interests in companies they invested in, international intellectual property rights were not enforced, and the licences required to operate within India inhibited entry. Pepsi had tried to break into the Indian market in the 1980s but a massive lobbying effort led by Ramesh Chauhan, a businessman and owner of one of the largest soft drink companies, including Bisleri and Thums Up, put obstacles in the way. Chauhan had benefitted when Coco-Cola was thrown out of India and sales of Thums Up, a substitute produced by him, soared. Chauhan galvanized the media and politicians to support him and Pepsi's headquarters in New York found the entry terms to doing business in India 'suicidal'.[15] In an ironic twist, several years later, an immigrant from India, Indra Nooyi, would head Pepsi in the US.

The newly wealthy non-resident Indian (NRI) community from the US was trying to invest in India and led the push against Indian protectionism. The behemoth that was the Indian government was not yet ready to change, and the NRIs were unable to break through its barriers.

With economic reforms at a crawl, their benefits had yet to materialize. This created discontent among the electorate. A rash of electoral defeats at the state level galvanized the socialists within the Congress party to oppose Rajiv's economic platform. The die-hard socialists in the party saw their defeat as an ominous sign for the future of the party.

India had been living beyond its means and was headed towards a balance of payments crisis. Rajiv's popularity among the people was further eroded by the Bofors scandal, alleging that the government had taken kickbacks from a Swedish arms manufacturer to supplement the coffers of the Congress party.

Rajiv's honeymoon was over. Rajiv was in his fifth year as prime minister and would overlap with President Bush for just ten months before losing to the opposition.

## The 1990 Crisis: Gates Mission

In 1990, India and Pakistan exchanged skirmishes along their border that quickly began to escalate. Three years earlier, both sides had conducted massive military exercises called 'Brasstacks' along the border in Rajasthan. In December 1989, Pakistan conducted the largest military exercise in its history in Punjab. It included '2,00,000 soldiers, four army corps, seven infantry divisions, one armoured division, three independent infantry and armour brigades, a squadron of the army's cobra helicopters, air defence units and several air squadrons'.[16] However, the military and civilian leaders communicated and de-escalated the crisis.

In 1990, unrest in Kashmir created a much more volatile situation. Large numbers of militants had crossed the border quietly, the Indian Army had overreacted, and the dismissal of the Kashmir state assembly had angered Kashmiris. The Indian government had a history of repressing free and fair elections in the Kashmir valley. The local population had been living under tension and the political situation had spun out of control.

Pakistan had encouraged the separatists, with Bhutto proclaiming that they would fight for a thousand years for Kashmir. India did nothing to win over the hearts and minds of the Kashmiris, and Pakistan did everything it could to inflame the situation. Pakistan was determined to display that it had recovered from the defeat of 1971. Dr A.Q. Khan, considered the father of the Pakistani atomic bomb, gave an interview in which he confirmed that Pakistan had developed its nuclear weapons programme.[17]

Pakistanis wanted to make sure that India understood that it would never defeat Pakistan again.

A flurry of diplomatic activity between the two countries only served to extend the tensions. The US worried about the nuclear arsenals of the two adversaries and a possible drift to war, with potentially catastrophic consequences. On 19 May 1990, Defense Secretary Bob Gates was dispatched by President Bush to try to diffuse the crisis.[18] The US administration was genuinely concerned that tensions could erupt into a nuclear confrontation. Bob Gates, Richard Haass and John Kelly met with both the Indians (whom they found very reasonable) and the Pakistanis. They told the Pakistanis that 'Washington had war-gamed a potential India–Pakistan conflict, and Pakistan was a loser in every scenario. They also firmly told the Pakistanis, "In the event of war, Pakistan would not receive American assistance."'[19]

This was the first time that a US administration took the Indian side in an Indo-Pakistan conflict. It was a fork in the road that other US administrations would take and was a significant departure from past policy. With the Cold War over and the Soviets out of Afghanistan, US interest in South Asia and its unequivocal support for Pakistan did not just wind down, it evaporated.

Richard Haass perhaps summed up US policy in South Asia best in a speech before the Asia Society, on 11 January 1990; he said: 'Our interest in these two countries was at best uneven. The tendency was to ignore South Asia except when local tensions boiled up and forced themselves on to our agenda. We would then engage in some crisis diplomacy, only to pull back once the crisis had passed.'[20] He affirmed that the US had a 'special relationship' with Pakistan and they followed a policy that often made them choose one country over the other, explaining that 'more than once we did enough on Pakistan's behalf to alienate India but not so much that we managed to please Pakistan'.[21]

The former Indian military commander General Sundarji, in the first public discussion of the role of nuclear weapons in India's security, suggested that both countries' nuclear status would act as a deterrent from any precipitous action.[22]

## Nuclear Concerns

Once Afghanistan was no longer an issue, proliferation became the only window through which the US looked at South Asia. The prospect of two states with contentious issues armed with nuclear weapons alarmed the US. South Asia policy was now driven by the non-proliferation group headed by Robert Einhorn. Following the 1990 incident, Secretary James Baker met with his counterparts in the Indian, Chinese and Soviet governments to discuss non-proliferation and regional nuclear stability. India remained cool to regional proposals and US pressure. It saw itself as a stable power and 'refused to accept a regional Indo-Pak solution, citing its strategic concerns with China and its philosophical position that resolution of the South Asia nuclear issue should be linked to global disarmament'.[23] The regional proposal went nowhere.

US policy towards Pakistan also hardened as it became impossible to deny the evidence that Pakistan was in the advanced stages of developing a nuclear weapon. Even Einhorn admitted that: 'By 1989, once the Soviets had been evicted from Afghanistan, the evidence had mounted to the point that it was just laughable not to invoke Pressler and that is what the Bush administration did.'[24] Larry Pressler, Stephen Solarz and other members of Congress pushed to censure Pakistan.[‡] In an op-ed, Solarz wrote: 'We have had a decade to persuade the Pakistanis that we are serious about non-proliferation. But every time they took steps that ran counter to US law, we looked the other way. Their assistance in Afghanistan was too valuable, we were told. Or we didn't want to undermine Pakistan's transition to democracy by cutting off aid to the military establishment whose support would be essential if political pluralism were to take root.'[25]

---

‡   The Solarz Amendment, passed in 1985, requires a cut-off in all aid and military sales to non-nuclear countries trying to illegally source nuclear-related material from the US. The Pressler Amendment compelled the president to certify each year that Pakistan did not have nuclear weapons before providing aid.

On 19 September 1990, Congressman Solarz wrote to the president requesting that the Pressler Amendment,§ which barred countries who pursue nuclear weapons from receiving aid, be applied to Pakistan.[26] This came as a relief for India, which felt that Pakistan had been given a pass under Reagan, who had been willing to certify that Pakistan was in compliance with US law and had not pursued a nuclear programme in order to receive military aid and other forms of assistance. In an interview with an Indian journalist in 2004, Benazir Bhutto openly admitted that Pakistan had developed the bomb back in 1989. During her state visit to Washington in June 1989, the CIA director, William H. Webster, gave Ms Bhutto a detailed briefing on Pakistan's nuclear capability. He even offered to provide her with a mock-up, making it clear that the US was fully aware of Pakistan's activities.[27] Initially, the army in Pakistan had excluded Ms Bhutto from their nuclear activities, but once she was made aware of their progress, she threatened to fire the scientists unless she was briefed on a regular basis. She made it clear that the US was aware of their capabilities, as it was monitoring the enrichment plant via satellite. She asserted in the interview that, in return for maintaining enrichment levels below weapons grade, the Pressler Amendment was waived and Pakistan received $4.6 billion and a promise for 60 F-16s, the highly desirable fighter jets. She stated it was a 'quid pro quo'.[28]

When Benazir Bhutto was elected as prime minister, in December 1988, the US felt that Pakistan's return to democracy should be supported. In January 1989, National Security Advisor Brent Snowcroft wrote to Stephen Solarz saying that Pakistan's return to democracy was good for broader US interests but that it was understood that the army would continue to play an important role.[29] He felt that for her government to survive, the US needed to continue its support. He acknowledged 'our ability to continue US assistance will be affected by any developments in Pakistan's nuclear programme'.[30] In February 1989, Bush and Bhutto had met in Tokyo at Emperor Hirohito's funeral. President Bush was impressed by the Americanized Bhutto

§   The Pressler Amendment adopted in 1985 was a new section 620E in the Financial Administration and Audit Act.

and invited her to Washington for a state visit. The optimism about Pakistan's democratic potential was premature, as Bhutto's tenure was short-lived. Ms Bhutto was toppled by a military coup in August 1990 after barely twenty months in office.

With the Russians evicted from Afghanistan, the US government was willing to rein in Pakistan. In October 1990, President Bush refused to certify Pakistan, and the Pressler Amendment⁵ finally went into effect. India was elated and Pakistan was incensed. Not only was Pakistan denied delivery of the coveted F-16s that it had already paid for, they were charged $50 million for storage as the planes sat on the ground while the US looked for another buyer.[31]

Pakistan believed that it had discharged its debt to the US by ousting the Russians from Afghanistan and that it had been discarded now that it was no longer needed. Pakistan was not alone in this belief. There was considerable loyalty for Pakistan within the US government. At an NSC meeting held at the White House Cabinet Room, on 9 October 1990, President Bush said, 'I understand that we've run into considerable congressional resistance to our proposed suspension of the Pressler sanction on aid.'[32] The Pakistani military, many of whom had trained in the US, had developed strong ties with the US military. The Department of Defense was steadfastly pro-Pakistani. According to journalist Seymour Hersh, Pakistan had acquired more nuclear-related goods clandestinely inside the US than Iraq. A former CIA officer, Richard M. Barlow, told Hersh that the CIA and State Department had misled Congress intentionally regarding Pakistan's activities. Pakistan's relationships with the US were deep. India had never developed such relationships.

---

§ The Pressler Amendment requires all US military and economic assistance, including sales and transfers of military equipment, spare parts and military technology end immediately if the president is unable to certify in writing that the recipient country does not possess a nuclear weapons programme. The storage of the F-16 was considered aid and was charged to Pakistan.

Section 518 of PL101-167 directs that assistance be immediately terminated to any nation in which the democratically elected head of government is removed by military coup or decree. Since Pakistan agreed to hold elections in October, aid was not suspended for this reason.

## Gulf War

On 2 August 1990, Saddam Hussein invaded Kuwait. The invasion by Iraq would shift the US foreign policy needle firmly to the Middle East. The Cold War would be replaced by a war against militant Islam.

Barely nine months after Rajiv's defeat, the government of the new prime minister, V.P. Singh, was already on the brink of collapse and would fall in October, with Singh having been in office less than a year. V.P. Singh had been Rajiv's finance minister. He had discovered compromising details of the Bofors scandal, revealing kickbacks from an arms dealer that bolstered the coffers of the Congress party. As the revelations became public, he was moved to the Ministry of Defence, where he learned even more about the details of the pay-offs. He resigned from the Congress party in disgust and joined the opposition, becoming prime minister in 1989. No one in the US government paid much attention to him. South Asia was swept aside as the US focus shifted to Kuwait and Iraq. Benazir's dismissal a few days after the Iraqi invasion briefly took up some energy in the White House, but with the Soviets no longer a threat, all eyes were on Iraq.[**]

India had its own concerns with the Iraq war. Close to 2,00,000 Indians were working in Kuwait as guest workers. Prime Minister V.P. Singh took the decision to evacuate them. An Indian delegation, headed by Foreign Minister I.K. Gujral, visited various countries, including Washington and Moscow, to try to diffuse the situation in the Gulf. Gujral, who was left wing and anti-American, had sent a communiqué to the Indian missions 'indicating that the crisis was the creation of Western imperialism to control the supply of crude oil to the world'.[33] Neither Moscow, Jordan nor Egypt had any interest in opposing US actions to liberate Kuwait and defeat Saddam Hussein. Saddam was defiant and told Gujral, 'Let them come. They [Americans] will be buried in the sands of the area.'[34]

This did not sit well with President Bush, who viewed the Gulf War as a defining moment in his presidency in the post-Cold War period and

---

[**] According to Hussain Haqqani in his book, *Magnificent Delusions* (p. 281), Benazir Bhutto's dismissal was timed just after the Gulf War began so that the US would be distracted and not pay too much attention to her dismissal by a military coup.

hoped that the world would choose to be on his side. Iraq had invaded another country and was in the wrong. You were either with the US or not. India had a weak interim government at the wrong moment and vacillated. With Rajiv no longer there, there was no personal relationship to smooth things over, and once again the friendly relationship between the two countries fell victim to circumstance.

India was refused permits to use its military aircraft in Iraq to rescue its citizens; however, after some negotiations with the UN and Iraqis, India was assured safe passage for its nationals to Jordan. Air India airlifted 1,70,000 Indian citizens, operating 488 flights over a period of fifty-nine days. It was a heroic evacuation. India came in for sharp criticism by the US for not condemning Saddam when he invaded Kuwait. They did so under international pressure, once their citizens were safely home.

## Shock and Awe

The Gulf War, codenamed 'Operation Desert Storm', was conducted in two phases. The first, called 'Operation Desert Shield' (to shield Saudi Arabia), built capacity in Saudi Arabia by sending troops and military equipment to the kingdom. Saddam had threatened the Saudis and their king requested US help. The US believed that the world would be thrown into turmoil if Iraq tried to take over the oil fields in Saudi Arabia. The UN sanctioned Iraq and ordered it to withdraw from Kuwait by 15 January 1991. It did not.

The second phase of the war, Operation Desert Storm, began on 24 February 1991. By 27 February it was all over. The US, together with its coalition partners, launched a lightning offensive and defeated the Iraqis in 100 hours.

This was the first war that people all over the world watched from their living rooms. CNN made its debut in the international domain with its round-the-clock coverage, liberal use of satellites and the latest technology to facilitate broadcasts to a global audience. It was a war won as much by media as by military might. The generals controlled the narrative. They released the footage and decided which reporters to allow in and where. The sleek display of American superiority on the battlefield was an advertisement for military hardware, as the Abrams tanks, M1 tanks, Apache helicopters and Bradley fighting vehicles destroyed the Iraqi army. At the battle of 73 Easting, twenty-three Iraqi tanks were destroyed in twenty-three minutes.

As American fighter jets strafed the skies and lit up the night over Baghdad, people the world over watched in awe. The fantastic display of disciplined American military power, equipped with planes and technology that was almost futuristic, left no one in any doubt about who the superpower was. American power was at its zenith. George H.W. Bush had restored US military prowess from the debacle of the Vietnam War. The US military had become heroic overnight and its generals had all become household names.

Critics of the war have alleged that Saddam did not want war with the US. He had been an ally and been on friendly terms with the US when Khomeini took over in Iran. He believed that the US ambassador to Iraq, April Glaspie, had indicated the US would not get involved in his fight with the Kuwaitis. Sources say Saddam had offered to negotiate but the US either ignored him or they misread each other's signals. Iraq was no match for the US and General McMaster. In an interview he gave to Peter Bergen, he described it as a somewhat unfair fight: 'It's like we called Saddam's army out into the schoolyard and beat up that army.'[35]

## Disaster Looms in Delhi

Despite the successful extraction of its citizens from the Gulf, V.P. Singh's government was in trouble. His coalition, like the others before it, was strung together with weak alliances, with different factions vying for power. The primary connection keeping them together was the anti-Rajiv consensus among them. The economy was under strain, and the various groups were unable to make decisions. VP's coalition government fell in less than a year.

Chandra Shekhar became the next prime minister. He had been a member of the old Congress party. Chandra Shekhar had split with Mrs Gandhi when she was the prime minister and had been jailed along with Morarji Desai during the Emergency. He had led the coalition against V.P.

Singh, causing the government to fall, and took over as prime minister in November 1990 while the US was preparing for war.

Chandra Shekhar opted for an alliance with Rajiv and the Congress party, rather than the right-wing, Hindu-oriented BJP. This was a political risk, as Rajiv had 197 seats to his 57. It would leave him vulnerable to Rajiv's political manoeuvrings. Chandra Shekhar had inherited an unstable economy and political situation.

Affirmative action called 'reservations' in India was dividing castes. Opening the controversial Babri Masjid to Hindu claims was dividing religious groups, and corruption in defence procurements was dividing politicians. No one was paying attention to rising deficits. While politicians in New Delhi were expending their energy arguing, India was eating its way through its reserves at an alarming pace.

In October 1990, New Delhi was shocked when Moody's, the credit rating agency for global capital markets, downgraded India and put it on its watch list. Overseas Indians grew nervous and began to withdraw their money from Indian banks, while the spike in oil prices drained foreign reserves. India was perilously close to defaulting.

In December 1990, a team was dispatched to the International Monetary Fund (IMF) to obtain a loan, but the IMF imposed politically difficult conditions that were hard to overcome in a coalition government. Besides, Rajiv had lent his support to Chandra Shekhar as an interim measure while he canvassed the country for the upcoming elections. He saw no advantage in his rival's success. Finance Minister Yashwant Sinha tried to implement the structural adjustments and fiscal stabilization measures that the IMF sought, but time was running out.

The US was getting ready to go to war and requested permission from the Indian government to refuel in India. The president and prime minister acquiesced. They knew that they needed US support if they were to obtain the IMF loan. 'Over the next month, two US military aircraft landed every day at the Bombay, Madras and Agra airports ... Agra was a military airport ... the fact that India allowed US military aircraft to land at a military airfield was in itself seen as an important gesture. The US also sought and secured transit facilities for its navy.'[36]

Once the media broke the story, anti-US groups criticized the decision. Surprisingly, Rajiv joined this group—even though he would likely have made the same concessions had he been the prime minister. The issue became a lightning rod during elections. Chandra Shekhar, under great political pressure, withdrew the permit granted to the US, and refuelling stopped on 12 February 1990.

The US had decided to back India's IMF request as a reward for the fuelling facilities extended to them. The US understood that elections had made the politics of refuelling toxic but decided to support India's application for a loan from the IMF. In January 1991, $1.8 billion was made available to India from the IMF as a standby arrangement. It was a special facility that had been created by the IMF to help countries that had developed temporary balance of payments problems due to unpredictable events outside their control.

One of the conditions of the IMF loan was that the government had to pass a budget. The Indian government tried to do that in February 1991, but Rajiv asked for a postponement, knowing this would put the loan and his country's economy in jeopardy. Manmohan Singh, the prime minister's economic advisor, was worried. Rajiv now raised the ante, knowing he had all the power as the largest coalition partner. He claimed the government was spying on him.

The Indian president had warned Rajiv not to destabilize the government, as the all-important IMF loan was essential for India, but Rajiv was on the warpath, with the goal of coming back to power. Chandra Shekhar, finding his situation untenable, resigned in anger on 6 March 1991. He had been prime minister for just five months. India had gone from two unstable coalition governments to a caretaker one. Elections were to be held in May and June 1991, and he was asked to remain as caretaker prime minister until a new one was elected. He obliged.

## Selling India's Gold

Standard and Poor, considered one of the three big credit rating agencies along with Moody's, downgraded India's sovereign rating to a BBB minus, further damaging its international economic credibility. The caretaker government had to abandon its efforts to secure the IMF loan.

The government's inability to repay loans eliminated external sources of revenue, as no one was willing to lend to India. The urgency to pay for imports of oil and food left the government few solutions. Backed into a corner, the only solution left was to sell India's gold with a repurchase option. 'I don't want to be known as the prime minister who sold the country's silver,' lamented Chandra Shekhar. Naresh Chandra, a future ambassador to the US, responded, 'You would hardly like to be known as the prime minster who declared bankruptcy.'[37] As a compromise, the Reserve Bank of India (RBI) used 20 tons of gold held by the government that had been confiscated from persons such as smugglers, rather than the gold held in their vaults.

The Union Bank of Switzerland insisted that the gold bullion be physically sent to them. Gold bars of acceptable quality were required. The gold had to be inspected, then removed from the vaults and transported by vans through the congested streets of Bombay to the airport. A special plane had to be chartered as no commercial flight was willing to take the cargo. The movement of the gold was undertaken in utmost secrecy. It was a complex and nerve-racking undertaking.

## The Final Assassination

Rajiv had agreed to let Chandra Shekhar become prime minister so that he could consolidate his base in time for the next election. He used the same strategy utilized by his mother in toppling Morarji Desai—pulling his support for Chandra Shekhar at the last minute and undermining his reforms, causing the government to fall. History was repeating itself. After Mrs Gandhi's government was ousted in 1977, the opposition splintered after a short time in office, and the Congress party headed by Mrs Gandhi won when the electorate got fed up with the bickering opposition.[††] Rajiv

---

†† Elections in India take place over several weeks due to the remoteness of some areas, requiring complicated logistical arrangements of staff and security.

was hoping for a similar outcome in the elections to be held in May and June 1991.

May is often the most brutal month in India. The heat before the monsoons arrive is intense. Rajiv was busy campaigning near Chennai in the south. It was scorching hot and he had been campaigning all day. He was running late and driving from Madras to the small town of Sriperumbudur. It was late, everyone was tired and likely not as alert as they would have been had it been morning. As usual, there was a large crowd waiting to see Rajiv. It was past 10 p.m. A woman in her mid-thirties wearing a peculiar red wig approached him and bowed. There was an explosion as she detonated her suicide vest. Seventeen people, including Rajiv, were killed in the explosion.

Rajiv was assassinated at the age of forty-seven. Politically motivated assassins had killed both Rajiv and his mother. The dynasty was finished. His children were too young and his wife too consumed by grief to understand the compulsions of the Congress party, and the claims it had on the family.

The Congress won the election on a 'sympathy wave' but, for the first time, there was no Gandhi to lead it. P.V. Narasimha Rao became the prime minister.

With the Gulf War successfully concluded, George H. W. Bush turned his attention to Russia. Gorbachev and Bush were preparing for an arms summit and it had become increasingly clear to the US that Gorbachev was in trouble internally. Power within the Kremlin has shifted to Boris Yeltsin. Between the dissolution of the Soviet Empire and a faltering US economy, India slipped out of American consciousness.[‡‡] Without Rajiv, the personal link to President Bush was broken. Even though the relationship was transactional in 1991, it was not as negative as it had been in the seventies. Rajiv and the US president would leave behind a legacy of greater empathy between the countries that their respective successors would build on.

---

[‡‡] During the Gulf War, the Indian government had reluctantly allowed the US to refuel in India.

George H.W. Bush was the last of the US presidents who came of age during the Cold War. He was also the last president to have fought for his country on the battlefield. He may not be remembered for his domestic policies, but he was one of the more successful US presidents when it came to the conduct of international affairs. He was president at a pivotal time, overseeing the end of the Cold War, reuniting Germany, evicting the Iraqis from Kuwait and successfully transitioning the US to a new world order, with the US as the reigning superpower.

George H.W. Bush was a thorough gentleman and self-deprecating in the extreme. He always put his country before himself. His aversion to personal confrontation and understated demeanour invited the label of 'wimp' and he was accused of having no vision. He ran an administration that included men like James Baker and Colin Powell, who would be admired and held up as the gold standard for future presidential advisors. He remains one of the most underrated US presidents of the twentieth century.

# Part Five:
## 1991–2020

# Chapter 18

# Rao and Clinton: Economic Reforms

ONCE THE RUSSIANS WITHDREW FROM AFGHANISTAN IN 1989, the Soviet Union imploded, and by December 1991 it had ceased to exist. The Cold War was over, and the US had emerged as the world's uncontested superpower. If there was any doubt in anyone's mind, the Gulf War had confirmed US military superiority to the world. Traditional alliances were rearranging themselves and Islamic terrorism had not yet replaced the Cold War as a priority for the US.

India's policy of non-alignment was no longer an irritant for the US. Other pressure points such as India's dependence on food aid were now in the distant past. The US had long accepted that Kashmir would be resolved bilaterally, removing a major source of contention. As the traditional irritants of aid and non-alignment disappeared, non-proliferation and the issues around security came to dominate the relationship.

Pakistan was adept at exploiting the Cold War to its advantage and had differentiated itself from India by aligning itself with US interests. Whenever the US intervened in the region, it inevitably tipped the regional balance in Pakistan's favour, pushing India closer to the communists.* Deputy secretary of state Strobe Talbott once observed that the reason why India and the US had such poor relations was that 'each was on such good terms with the other's principal enemy'.[1] The US was convinced that India was pro-Soviet,

---

\*  Until 1960, Nehru tried to develop a rapport with Communist China. Under Mrs. Gandhi, India moved close to the Soviets signing a friendship treaty in 1971.

[ 381 ]

while the Indians blamed America's consistent preference for Pakistan and the arms build-up for pushing it closer to the Soviets.

When Afghanistan became the battlefield of the post-colonial Great Game in 1980, Pakistan's fortunes and relations with the US became intimately linked to its fate. The US decided to defeat Russia in Afghanistan and Pakistan became indispensable in achieving that objective. Pakistan was fully aware of its strategic importance to the US and extracted money, arms and indulgence while it could.

Once the Soviets retreated in 1988, Pakistan lost its leverage with the US, which was now no longer willing to expend political capital on its behalf. A decade later, all the players would be back, except this time it was the US, not Russia, with boots on the ground in Afghanistan. After 9/11, the US became engaged in the longest war in its history. The same Afghan resistance that had been aided by Pakistan and the US and successfully bled the Russians into retreat, would now find themselves fighting the Americans.

In 1991, the US was heading into elections and India became consumed with an economic crisis. On 21 May 1991, the powerful Indian National Congress, which had dominated Indian politics since Independence, found itself for the first time without a member of the Gandhi family to lead it. The party had been weakened over the course of Mrs Gandhi's tenure. She had needed help from the Left on more than one occasion to form her government, and in return for its support, the communist party had extracted a heavy toll, pushing Indian economic policy to the Left. Since 1989, coalition governments had become the norm, leading to political paralysis and bringing the economy close to collapse. Rajiv's withdrawal of support from the previous government had prevented India from getting a much-needed IMF loan. Public debt of the state and central government rose to 71 per cent of GDP, inflation had reached double digits, reserves had dipped to just three weeks of imports and India was on the brink of default.

Finding a leader to negotiate India out of this disaster was now urgent, but when Rajiv was assassinated, the Congress party had lost its deity. It had won the largest number of seats but failed to get a majority. Headless, its members splintered into different power groups within the party.

Rao's nomination as prime minister was a remarkable turn of events for him. In April 1991, Rajiv had summoned Rao for a meeting and suggested he retire from the party. He was not given a seat despite having won eight consecutive elections from his state. As a consolation, the deposed man was given the task of preparing the party manifesto. He did this obediently, even though he had been denied a future in the party he had served for most of his adult life.

Without a seat, Rao had packed his bags and was on his way home in Andhra (now Telangana) when he was summoned back to Delhi. At the age of seventy, this shy, self-effacing man was asked to form the government. He would confound his critics by going on to serve a full term.

Rao had spent most of his life in public service. He had served as the chief minister of Andhra Pradesh, as well as the home minister and minister of external affairs at the national level. Although he was well respected in this home state and within the Congress party, he was by no means a public figure. Had he walked into the street without the trappings of office, few people would have recognized him. Rao canvassed his supporters in the Congress to become party president but was not their first choice. He was only offered the position after Shankar Dayal Sharma turned it down. The Congress party seemed destined for another short-term coalition government in 1991. If the past was any indication of how minority governments performed, Rao was set up for failure.

Rao was an unlikely replacement for Rajiv. They had nothing in common. Rajiv was young, urbane and westernized. Rao was just four years younger than Indira Gandhi. Unlike the Gandhis, he had been born in a village in Andhra and was married at the age of ten to a bride chosen for him. His first trip overseas was in 1974, when he was fifty-three. He was a man of simple tastes, preferred vegetarian food and enjoyed relaxing in traditional lungis at home. His outward appearance may have been unsophisticated but his vast intellect was anything but simple.

Rao had shown an aptitude for learning early in his childhood. He was sent away to school so he could obtain a better education than what was available in the district in which his family lived. He was a gifted linguist and taught himself several languages during his lifetime, including

Persian, Arabic and several Indian languages. He also learnt Spanish and French while in Delhi. On overseas trips he often had a dictionary of the country he was visiting. He wrote poetry and translated literature in his spare time. Rao's mental curiosity was inexhaustible, and he was fascinated by technology. He brought computers back when he went overseas and taught himself computer programmes[†] by studying manuals.

According to his biographer, Narasimha Rao was able to devote time to his various hobbies because he spent long periods away from his family. His loneliness led him to develop close friendships with two women. The first, Lakshmi Kantamma, became a Member of Parliament. According to one of Narasimha's political rivals, J. Vengala Rao, 'He was so obsessed with Lakshmi Kantamma that he sits when she asks him and stands when she asks him to.'[2] Later, he became close to the journalist Kalyani Shankar. Rao was also close to several swamis and, in particular, used the well-connected Chandraswami to help him politically. Although Rao was a practising Hindu, he was secular in his outlook. He was well versed in the scriptures and, while contemplating retirement, he seriously considered an invitation to head up a religious order.

Rao was determined to continue India's move towards liberalization and wanted to convey to the world that India was open for business. When he visited the US in 1994, he requested the Indian embassy in Washington to arrange for him to meet with the business community. According to his biographer Vinay Sitapati, he even pressed his astrologer Chandraswami to open his personal rolodex to set up introductions during his visit to the US.

### An Economic Crisis

Rao had an understated manner, but faced with an economic crisis, he knew he had to take bold decisions. The socialist model of development was broken, revenue collection was in an abysmal state, deficits were soaring, and foreign capital and investments were negligible. He immediately put his team into place. Dr Manmohan Singh was made finance minister and the formidable Amar Nath Varma became principal secretary. Dr

---

[†] Rao taught himself BASIC and COBOL.

Rakesh Mohan provided the blueprint for industrial reform. Together they would overhaul policy, loosen India's regulatory chokehold and put the country on the path to economic growth.

The first order of business was to manage the looming balance of payments crisis and shore up the dwindling foreign exchange reserves. The new prime minister wasted no time. On 22 June 1991, the day after he was sworn in, he addressed the problems to the people head on, in an unusually forthright television appearance. He said: 'The economy is in crisis. The balance of payments situation is exceedingly difficult. Inflationary pressures on the price level are considerable. There is no time to lose. The government and the people cannot keep living beyond their means and there are no options left. We must tighten our belts and be prepared to make the necessary sacrifice to preserve our economic independence.' He then described his plan, saying that 'the government is committed to removing the cobwebs that come in the way of rapid industrialization'. He vowed to make India internationally competitive by making it part of the global economy.[3] In one fell swoop, he cut loose the red tape that had stunted industrial development.

Mrs Gandhi imposed the complex maze of regulations and licences that Rao inherited. She was handicapped by a poor understanding of economics and her choices were often dictated by political considerations. They did not lead to growth or good industrial policy. In the 1980s, she had begun to accept that India was stagnating but did little to alleviate the malaise that had settled across the economy.

Her successor Morarji Desai, the pro-Western, free-market prime minister, had recruited Dr Manmohan Singh to come to India to address the problem, but his government was short-lived and unable to change the policies in time. Coalition governments like Desai's found that the room for manoeuvre to change policy was limited. Any move towards the free-market or pro-US policy, even when it was in India's interest, was always politically difficult as it was perceived as caving to American pressure.[‡]

Rajiv Gandhi did not subscribe to his mother's economic model and wanted to shift India in a new direction in 1984, which was market-

---

‡   This was true during Mrs Gandhi's time in the sixties as well.

based and pro-West. His ideas were more modern and he wanted to bring technological innovation to India, and for that he needed Western cooperation.[4] He was keen to free India from its regulations but lacked the political will to bring the government along. It took a monumental crisis six years later to pull the country out of the quicksand.

Dr Singh, a Cambridge-educated economist and highly respected among his peers, convinced several talented Indian colleagues from Ivy League universities and institutions (like the World Bank) to return to India and use their expertise to assist their country.

Montek Singh Ahluwalia and Dr Rakesh Mohan were among the people he recruited, who would play a prominent role in reforming India's economy. It took time and political will for this elite economic dream team and their ideas to gain acceptability. The continual collapse of governments following assassinations impeded the implementation of meaningful reforms. The politicians were too distracted by power struggles to focus on the economy that was in free fall.

With the country skating on the edge of an economic precipice, and a possible default staring them in the face, Rao and his ministers knew that they would need the support of the people across the board if they wanted to turn the country around. Being a minority government made the rescue especially challenging. On 24 June 1991, senior leaders of the Congress, along with the leading members of the various opposition parties, were called in for briefings with Manmohan Singh. They were given the unvarnished truth about the country's potential economic collapse. Manmohan Singh remembers that the opposition was stunned; they had not realized the gravity of the situation.[5] They quickly agreed to support the government's radical measures. The strategy to include the opposition was wise, as they not only went along with the government in the short term but in the long term better understood and continued the reform process when they took power.

Prime Minister Rao's government was barely two weeks old when he announced the dire situation to the public, on 22 June, and convinced the bureaucrats to support him. He then turned his attention to the impending default. With time ticking by and barely enough reserves to cover three weeks of imports, drastic measures had to be taken. Once again, the country's gold came to the rescue. This time it was not the confiscated gold from smugglers, but actual reserves held by the RBI in its vaults that were used.

This second tranche was twice the amount of the first. About 46.9 tons of gold was to be sold and, once again, the buyers insisted on delivery. This time the logistics were twice as difficult as the government was moving twice the amount of gold. India's economic survival depended on the gold getting to its destination. It was moved from the RBI vaults to the airport under heavy security. In the middle of the journey through Bombay's crowded streets, the truck transporting the bullion broke down. Everyone was in a panic till the convoy resumed its journey.[6]

India was not the only country where a potentially disastrous situation involving the transport of gold was averted. In 1914, as the Germans advanced towards France, the Banque De France decided to ship all its gold reserves, including 38,800 gold ingots and innumerable bags of gold coins, out to safety. The massive logistical operation ran into a hitch when one of the trains carrying the coins derailed and the coins spilled out. It took 500 men to get things back on track and secure the gold before the evacuation resumed.[7]

Still, the economic crisis was far from over, and far more invasive interventions were required to staunch the bleeding. India was on life support and every remedy was being tried. Nothing was sacred. Next, the Rao government decided to devalue the currency. Devaluation was not a decision the prime minister took lightly. Mrs Gandhi's decision to devalue the rupee by 57 per cent in 1966, under advisement from the World Bank, had been unpopular. The political fallout was seared into people's memory.

The devaluation project was code-named 'hop skip jump'. It was done in two stages, with the intention of jump-starting the economy. The first devaluation took place on 1 July, followed by a second devaluation on 3 July. The two together accounted for an 18 per cent decline in the value of the rupee.[8]

As news about the sale of the gold leaked out, there was an uproar. That, coupled with devaluation, incited rebellion in the coalition, and on 15 July, Narasimha Rao faced a no-confidence motion in Parliament. The vote was

241-111 for Rao. It was a comfortable margin and gave him the green light to continue.

## Emerging India

The long-term or structural reforms that were announced on 22 June 1991 were now implemented. Once again, the government wisely reached out to stakeholders. They met with industrialists and reassured the hardliners by prefacing their new policies with a nod to Nehru. They softened the socialists by comparing India to the rising countries in Asia as a model to emulate rather than the West. Manmohan Singh's team made the case that India was being left behind by countries half its size, like South Korea, Indonesia and even Thailand.[§][9] In his budget speech on 24 July 1991, Manmohan Singh quoted Victor Hugo: 'No power on earth can stop an idea whose time has come.'[10]

In order to stimulate long-term growth, the implementation of structural reforms in the industrial sector was critical. India's industrial policy had derived from the Defence of India Act that predated Independence. 'The system originated in the war powers act of 1939. Given these origins, the system was much more for control and less for development. This was also consistent with the colonial bureaucratic mindset ... as if these old set of controls was not enough, new forms of control were added over the years ... by 1990 as many as 836 items of production were reserved for production in small-scale enterprises.'[11] It is no wonder that India fell far behind its Asian counterparts, as many of the industries that stimulated its growth were among the 836 industries under controls in India. Indian manufacturing was simply uncompetitive.

India had acquired the reputation of being one of the world's most prohibitive countries to do business in. 'In the short space of two years, investment controls on the private sector were more or less abolished, and the rigid import-licensing system was also dismantled, and all items of capital goods, components, intermediaries and raw materials were made

---

§ By the mid-1990s, India had fewer than 10 million organized manufacturing-sector workers; China had more than a hundred million.

freely importable.'¹² Dismantling the Licence Raj was a critical step towards growth but it required time to succeed. External investors would need convincing that India had changed course before they could be induced to invest in the country. Domestically, industry would need to restructure to take advantage of the newly liberated business environment. It had been able to get away with being inefficient and providing second-rate goods to the domestic market for too long. It would have to restructure to remain competitive.

Until 1991, 'most decisions for an Indian corporation were made by bureaucrats sitting in Delhi and, in some cases, state capitals. But after 1991 those decisions were discussed and debated and decided by the board of directors in the boardrooms of corporations.'¹³ Narayana Murthy, the co-founder of Infosys, said this single act was instrumental in unleashing India's entrepreneurial spirit.

In April 1992, capital markets and the Security and Exchange Board of India was made a statutory regulator. Insider trading, cronyism and corruption ended as operators were forced to register and follow rules. Foreign investors were invited to invest in India and Enron made a splash by committing to invest $3 billion in the energy sector.

In the eighties, the government had launched a marketing campaign to attract dollar deposits from Indians living overseas. Money had flowed in as NRIs, keen to invest in India, were seduced by high interest rates and attractive terms. As foreign currency came in, it buoyed reserves. When the economy began to teeter, the NRI money fled the Indian banks, destabilizing the reserves further. The NRIs would need to be convinced that India's economy was stable.

As 1992 approached, the economy had begun to show signs of stabilizing. The doctors who had worked day and night to keep the patient alive began to breathe a little easier. India was undergoing a massive transformation. Although industrial policy had been unchained, many constraints remained. Infrastructure was inadequate and small-scale industries still needed to be reformed, and they would take much longer to solve. The pace and scale of reforms were unprecedented, and it was more than the Left could bear. They brought a no-confidence vote against Rao on 17 July 1992, but he prevailed once again, and his coalition held.

The Rao government also took an unusual step of formally recognizing Israel and establishing formal diplomatic relations in 1992. According to Bruce Riedel, the impact of this one foreign policy decision should not be underestimated. It likely won India several friends in Congress and in the US administration. Krishnan Srinivasan, Rao's foreign secretary, said: 'I think he felt he could never get a good relationship with the US going while he did not have a diplomatic relationship with Israel.'[14]

In December 1991, India supported the US at the UN to rescind the resolution equating Zionism with racism. It was a significant overture on India's part and the US noticed. Rao then invited Yasser Arafat to India for an official visit in January 1992, before announcing full diplomatic relations with Israel.[§] Rao had covered all his bases.

Just as the economic crisis receded in India, Rao's political problems threatened the peace. The BJP had begun to grow in strength. This right-wing, pro-Hindu, pro-business party had tapped into a resurgent Hindu fundamentalist vein that ran through the heartland of India. A sixteenth-century mosque called Babri Masjid was the victim of corrosive religious prejudices, because it had supposedly been built on the site claimed to be the birthplace of Ram. On 6 December 1992, Hindu fundamentalists destroyed the mosque. Predictably, riots followed and, although estimates vary, reports of almost 2,000 Muslims being killed began to pour in.[15]

Again, Rao faced a no-confidence vote in Parliament. This was the second crisis that lent itself to the prime minister's advantage. Secularists were alarmed at the actions of the BJP's followers and were determined to keep them from obtaining power. The communist party joined other opposition groups to support Rao. The Congress was the flagbearer of secularism and Rao got 334 votes to 106. It was a massive mandate for Rao. He had now survived three no-confidence votes in Parliament. It was quite an accomplishment for a party that did not have a majority.

Rao may have been understated but it would be a mistake to underestimate him. He was an astute politician. Some have called him

---

§    Pictures of Arafat and Rao hugging each other appeared in the press, which were meant to appease the Muslims. Arafat was meant to be seen as having given his blessing to the opening of diplomatic relations with Israel.

wily. He once told Shyam Saran that 'to be a successful leader in India you must be ruthless but also ascetic'.[16] He understood that the crisis also presented an opportunity. He used the economic crisis to push through much-needed reforms. Both Rakesh Mohan and Montek Ahluwalia have praised his deft use of the crisis to transform India's economy. He did not let the Babri debacle go without deriving political capital from it.[**] He reminded his coalition partners about the dangers of anti-secular parties and consolidated his position.

On 12 March 1993, thirteen explosions ricocheted through the commercial heart of Mumbai, killing 257 people in response to the Babri incident. The Bombay Stock Exchange, the railway station and buildings owned by the Birlas and Tatas were among the targets. It would not be an isolated event. It is a credit to the government that it neither stopped reforms nor emboldened the opposition.

In April 1992, the Rao government embarked on a 'Look East' policy. China's rapid rise as an Asian economic powerhouse and its increasing assertiveness had raised tensions in the region. The prime minister visited China, South Korea and Thailand to promote India as a logical counterbalancing force for regional stability. He was the first prime minister to visit South Korea and was impressed by the economic progress he saw there. India saw Asia as a source for capital but also as a model for export-driven growth.

The next leap forward took place in January 1993. As the new president was being sworn in in the United States, Rao pushed reforms one step further by allowing private banks to obtain licences to operate. This opened up India's credit markets. All of a sudden, credit lines were available to small- and medium-sized businesses. A new middle class began to emerge, with software companies leading the way. Infosys was listed on the stock exchange. The technology companies had strong links with overseas companies in the US, connecting India to the global technology marketplace and propelling it to its next stage of development.

---

** Rao was criticized for not doing enough to stop the riots and control the tensions at the Babri Masjid.

The reformists allowed private airlines to enter the market and Jet Air gave customers a decent alternative to the substandard Indian Airlines. Perhaps the most revolutionary change was the opening up of telecom and TV to the private sector. In 1995, the Supreme Court ruled that the airways belonged to all people. This ended the government monopoly. In 1991, five million people in India had telephones and not all of them worked. By 2016, one billion people had phones, most of them mobile.[17] Villagers in far-flung rural areas could instantly check market prices for their products. Access to doctors, stock markets, government services and general information began to transform society.

The US had just elected a president who wanted to pursue a more robust relationship with India. India was pursuing economic policies that were more in line with the rest of the world. Although it had a long way to go before catching up with its Asian counterparts, it was emerging on the world stage as a democratic country with economic potential. Global alliances were starting to shift, and it was impacting both East–West and regional politics. William Jefferson Clinton decided that developing a close relationship with India was a priority for his administration.

## Clinton

The Clinton presidency began as the new world order was taking shape. Clinton recognized that China, East Asia and India were emerging from the shadows and would become increasingly important economically and politically. He had read *A Passage to India* while at Oxford and had developed a fascination for India early on.[18] Hillary Clinton also shared her husband's interest in India and had wanted to visit India as a student.

Clinton was everything his predecessor was not. He was young, extroverted in the extreme, brilliant but undisciplined and exuded energy. He grew up poor and his family life was tinged with domestic abuse and difficult stepfathers. His ambitions lay beyond his childhood circumstances. The combination of his academic ability, natural charisma and support from people who believed in him put him on the path to politics early on. He went to Georgetown and then to Yale Law School, where he met Hillary Rodham. After attending Oxford as a Rhodes scholar, where he met Strobe Talbott, he moved to Arkansas and entered politics.

Unlike the elder Bush, Clinton had avoided the draft and had not served his country by joining the military. He felt no compulsion to participate in a war he did not believe in. Although he had been the governor of Arkansas and was becoming more well known in the Democratic Party, he was still considered a long shot when he first announced his candidacy for president.

Clinton's time in the White House was marred by a sex scandal that would haunt him through the rest of his presidency. As a southern Democrat with working-class roots, he understood that jobs and the economy were going to decide the election. He had campaigned as a centrist and vowed to be a 'domestic' president. The key to winning, as he once famously said, was: 'The economy, stupid!'[††]

Clinton marked a turning point in American politics. For the first time, the first lady was given a role in government. The Clintons reflected their generation, where women were often as well qualified as the men and had careers of their own. Clinton told the country that they were getting 'two for the price of one', but it had not gone over well. The US electorate was sensitive when it came to its leaders and did not appreciate an unelected official being promoted on to the centre stage, even if she was the first lady and highly qualified. As president, Clinton put Hillary in charge of health care reform, but it met with stiff resistance among lawmakers. It would take the Clintons some time to accommodate to the ways of Washington.

Clinton was determined to focus on domestic and economic issues, but, as every president discovers, the world outside provides little time to settle in before demanding attention. The Clinton presidency marked the shift of the primary international threat from communism to Islamic fundamentalism. A month after taking his oath of office, Clinton was faced with the first Islamic terrorist act on US soil. On 26 February 1993, there was an explosion at the World Trade Center. Although the building

---

[††] James Carville, a campaign strategist working for Clinton's 1992 campaign, originally coined the phrase to remind the campaign workers to focus their messaging on the economy. It then became a de facto slogan of the Clinton election campaign.

remained standing, six people were killed. One month later, on 12 March 1993, thirteen explosions killed 257 people and injured 700 others in Mumbai. Although they were unrelated, both countries would suffer from Islamic extremism incubated in Pakistan.

Clinton told his staff that he would like to visit India. The president's interest in India puzzled his staff. Although the non-proliferation gurus still dominated policy towards India, Clinton did not want it to hinder bilateral relations. His pursuit of India would have to be postponed as, between 1993 and 1996, he had many other pressing issues that would occupy him. First, his team needed to focus on the potential for nuclear proliferation that the post-Soviet era presented.

The new countries in Eastern Europe had many of the old Soviet 'nukes' distributed among them. The Clinton administration tried to secure them before they fell into the wrong hands. Strobe Talbott, a friend of President Clinton, joined the government as ambassador-at-large and was tasked with the assignment. Talbott was fluent in Russian and had translated Khrushchev's memoirs at the age of twenty-three while he was a student at Oxford. A former editor of *TIME* magazine, he was an author of several books on disarmament. In 1994, he became the deputy secretary of state and would take a keen interest in India.

Talbott had tried to 'dissuade the Russians from supplying rocket engines and related technology to India for use in its missile programme'.[19] In April 1994, two weeks after becoming deputy secretary of state, Clinton asked him to go to South Asia to discuss bringing the nuclear arms race under control. Talbott also carried with him a formal invitation for the prime minister to visit Washington in May. Although the US administration wanted to support Rao's reforms, and found him to be erudite and reasonable, they were insistent that India refrain from testing its nuclear capability.

Rao visited Washington in May 1994. It was a short visit. 'Krishnan Srinivasan remembers that Rao was unsure of himself, (and) perhaps felt inadequate to handle President Clinton.'[20] Rao was eager to establish warm relations with the US and find support for his reforms. He was looking for US investors but needed to be careful to resist pressure on the nuclear front.

Clinton was not ready to fully engage with India yet. Somalia was Clinton's first foreign policy challenge and it did not end well. The galling image of US soldiers being dragged through Somalian streets by a pickup truck driven by rebels was depicted in the film *Black Hawk Down*. US troops, which had arrived in October 1994 to keep the peace in Somalia, were brought home the following year in ignominy. It was Clinton's first foreign policy failure. After the success of the Gulf War, America had looked invincible. Somalia undercut the perception and indicated to the Islamic rebels that this powerful country was vulnerable in an asymmetric war. Osama Bin Laden was paying attention.

Unable to find the time to focus on India in his first term, Clinton sent his wife there in March 1995. He wanted to send a signal to the Indians that extending the relationship between the two countries was a priority for him. Hillary Clinton's trip convinced them that stronger ties with India should be a key foreign policy objective for the Clinton administration.

India's economic reforms opened a window through which better relations could be promoted. General Electric (GE) was one of the few companies that already had a presence in India and was cooperative. It had built the Tarapur plant. Unfortunately, GE had not found enough customers in India who could afford its highly sophisticated products. But GE discovered that India had plenty of highly educated software engineers, and started to use India to support its information technology needs. Outsourcing to India caught on, and in the 1990s many international firms like American Express, Chase Manhattan Bank and others had begun to use India for their back-office support. Indian technology firms like Wipro and Infosys teamed up with them and propelled the growth of other Indian technology companies, which would create a new class of entrepreneurial wealth. As the new century was ushered in, 60 per cent of the Fortune 500 companies had established similar business operations in India.[21] India's emergence as a global economic power had begun.

The economic reform process in India was new and much of it was uneven. Interest groups often tried to block reforms. As Montek Ahluwalia insightfully pointed out, 'Democracy is not a consensual form of government: It is inherently an adversarial form, in which it is the business of the opposition to oppose.'[22] Rao had consciously chosen a slower pace in certain sectors that required legislative changes. All the components had not been worked out and power was perhaps the most glaring deficit.

An Indian delegation had come to the US in 1992 to attract US corporate investments in India. They met with senior executives at Enron, who decided to invest in a large power plant in Maharashtra. It was a complicated deal involving price guarantees and commitments from the Indian government. The World Bank refused to get involved, judging the project unviable. Despite the World Bank's reservations, the Indian government decided to move ahead with it. From the outset, it ran into problems. Many of these early projects had been rushed through and were ill-conceived.

The Indian government decided to fast-track certain projects that they deemed to be in the national interest. Many of them were in the power sector where India suffered from acute shortages. Enron, Cogentrix, CMS Electric and the AES Corporation were all fast-tracked as an incentive to attract federal deposit insurance. Due to several complicated structural problems, the cost overruns and agreements ran into trouble with finger-pointing on both sides. Enron finally pulled out in August 1995. The companies sold out their interests and most left India by 2003. The failure fed the critics of the economic reforms and cast a long shadow over foreign investments. India's attempts to project itself as a business-friendly country after its 1991 reforms had backfired. It would take time to persuade foreign investors to return to India.[23]

Clinton asked his commerce secretary, Ron Brown, to prepare a delegation with US business leaders to visit India and look for economic opportunities and relationships. India was to be part of the Big Emerging Markets Initiative that Jeffrey Garten, under secretary for international trade, and Secretary Brown had incorporated into their international policy. Getting busy CEOs to accompany Brown to India turned out to be a lot harder than anticipated. Raymond Vickery, an assistant secretary at commerce, wrote: 'Active persuasion was necessary in many instances. The value of taking CEOs' time to go to India with a secretary of commerce was not obvious to many of the busy executives. The argument that participation would serve both the national and companies' interests was not always appreciated.'[24] Vickery also had to persuade his colleagues, who were cynical: 'I was the only one interested in India. Other officials at the department admonished that I would be wasting my time trying to promote US–India engagement.'[25]

The two ambassadors, Frank Wisner and S.S. Ray, put their muscle behind the initiative. Efforts to create alliances between business leaders from both countries and their respective trade associations were also tried, but several sticking points hindered cooperation.

The protection of US patents and copyrights was an ongoing dispute that put India on a special '301' list of priority countries, which fail to adequately protect US patents, copyrights and intellectual property. The Office of the United States Trade Registration had taken a firm stand on the issue, but after Secretary Brown's visit in 1995, Clinton quietly decided to put it aside in order to promote relations. 'Secretary of Commerce Ron Brown accompanied by 26 CEOs visited India from 14–19 January. They concluded commitments on projects worth $7 billion.'[26] The following year Secretary Brown led a similar mission to the Balkans, where tragically his plane crashed, killing all thirty-five people on board.

The secretary of defence, Bill Perry, also initiated dialogues between his counterparts in India and Pakistan. He was convinced that better relations and back channels needed to be established in order to avoid a nuclear catastrophe in South Asia. Rather than attempting to get the two countries to roll back their arsenal, which he recognized was unrealistic, he preferred to accept reality and put safeguards in place.

## Nuclear Stalemate

Despite Rajiv's public push for global disarmament, he had fully supported an Indian covert military nuclear programme. Rao inherited a nuclear programme that was secret and no longer purely for peaceful purposes. In February 1993, the Prithvi I missile was test launched successfully. India now had a delivery system. It had become a nuclear weapons state. In February 1994, it test fired the Agni missile which had a longer range.

India's position on the global nuclear disarmament regimes was at odds with that of the US. The Indian view was that the nuclear club was arbitrary and discriminatory. India viewed itself as a responsible state and wanted to be accepted as a nuclear power. It continued to refuse to sign the NPT or the Comprehensive Test Ban Treaty (CTBT).

By 1994 the Indian diaspora in the US had become increasingly influential politically. Indian Americans made substantial contributions to political campaigns and pushed for pro-Indian policies. The Indian government enlisted their help to promote its point of view. Their influence began to counter the pro-Pakistan constituency in Congress and change relations, so they were less discriminatory towards India. During 1994 and 1995 they put considerable pressure on senators Jesse Helms and Sam Brownback, who were persuaded that the CTBT was not in the best interests of the US.

In May 1995, under the leadership of the US, the NPT was extended indefinitely over India's objections. The Indians were furious. They saw the US slamming the door shut in their face, denying them any possibility of joining the nuclear club, despite all their efforts to persuade the world that they would be a responsible nuclear power. The hawks in India were straining at the bit to go ahead and test, as a universal acceptance of the CTBT would have prevented India from any further testing.

On 18 September, Clinton sent Rao a letter asking him to reconsider India's refusal to support the NPT. It was a non-starter. Clinton, in the meantime, was also promoting the CTBT and managed to get 146 countries to sign it. If the CTBT went through, all testing would have to stop. Countries like the US that had tested for years would be unaffected, but India, whose nuclear programme was in its infancy, would be adversely impacted. The US had conducted 1,054 nuclear tests, Russia 715, France 210 and China and the United Kingdom had tested 45 times each.[27] By November 1995, Rao was under intense pressure from the Department of Atomic Energy and the Defence Research and Development Organization to test at Pokhran before the CTBT deal was signed.

In early December 1995, US satellites passing over the Pokhran test site in Rajasthan picked up suspicious images indicating an underground blast was about to take place. Cables were shown running through L-shaped tunnels, presumably to transmit data from an underground blast. US Ambassador Frank Wisner, who happened to be in Washington, received a full briefing from the CIA. He flew to New Delhi, where he confronted Principal Secretary A.N. Varma with the images. The unflappable Varma looked at the image and at the furious ambassador and politely asked him to sit down, offered him a cup of tea and calmly denied that they were about to test.

On 21 December 1995, Clinton called Rao and warned him not to proceed with the test; he reminded him that the Glenn Amendment would be invoked if India went ahead and sanctions would be enforced. He pressed exactly the right button with Rao by asking him to consider the impact that sanctions would have on the reforms India had so recently undertaken. On Christmas Day, he followed up by again urging Rao to delay testing.

Rao was under pressure from all sides and elections were underway in India. The US was threatening sanctions that would jeopardize his reform programme and the hawks in the Indian security establishment were pushing him to test. On 14 January 1996, A.P.J. Abdul Kalam, who was then scientific advisor to the defence minister, pushed him to boycott the CTBT and test. On 19 January, Rao met with his defence minister, principal secretary and atomic minister to discuss the CTBT, but Clinton's threat of sanctions hung over him like the sword of Damocles. Finally, he asked the finance ministry to prepare a document that would analyse the potential economic fallout from testing.

While Rao was vacillating, on March 1996 Clinton called him again hoping to both cajole and threaten. He ended with a firm message: desist from testing. The Indian prime minister decided to keep all his options open and kept the test site on standby. As the election results came in, his resolve faltered, and he felt he had to call it off. Having lost the election, he did not feel he had the authority to proceed with testing. Instead, he kicked the can down the road. As he left office, he passed along the message to Vajpayee that all systems were ready and loaded.

## Ready to Go But No One to Visit

President Clinton was re-elected in 1996. He was finally ready to visit India, but with Rao gone, there was no stable head of state to visit. It was an exceedingly frustrating time for the White House to plan a visit, and Clinton's staff was wondering if they had lost their opportunity. Prime

Minister Rao had provided stability, served a full term and pursued policies that were pro-Western. His successor Atal Bihari Vajpayee had lasted just thirteen days. The coalitions trying to form the next government were divided and there was no dominant leader among them. The next agreed-upon prime minister, H.G. Deve Gowda, was a regional politician with no national profile. He had no exposure to foreign affairs and barely lasted eleven months.

The musical chairs for prime minister had another round to play before stability returned. This last chord saw I.K. Gujral take the prime minister's seat. Gujral, a former follower of the communist party and ambassador to Moscow, had been Gowda's foreign minister. Unlike his boss, he had no regional base but was well known in Delhi. His family knew the Nehrus, and he had served as translator for his deaf brother Satish Gujral, a famous artist who had painted portraits of Mrs Gandhi. He had seen the Soviet edifice collapse and had adjusted his politics by moving closer to the centre over the years.

By the time Gujral became prime minister, he was no longer the firebrand communist of his youth. In a talk to the Council of Foreign Relations in New York, he promoted democratic values, pluralism, the rule of law and the dignity of the individual.[28] His party, the United Front, should have held elections, but knowing it was unlikely to win, opted for a weak coalition government that it knew was likely to be short-lived. Gujral assumed office knowing that unpacking his suitcase would be a waste of time. He was in office just under a year.

Gujral met President Clinton during the UN General Assembly meetings in New York in September 1997, but the new prime minister was not secure in his position and unable to provide any political breakthroughs. He also spoke so softly that no one could hear what he said at the meeting.[29] During his brief tenure, Gujral focused on strengthening India's ties in Asia. He developed a good personal relationship with Pakistan president Nawaz Sharif. They not only got on well but spoke the same language, as they were both Punjabis. Gujral had grown up in Lahore before Partition. But both men were politically weak. Nawaz was unable to advance relations with India with the hawks looking over his shoulder, and the Gujral government was unable to survive the domestic challenges to his party.

Eventually, elections were held in India and the BJP won. Atal Bihari Vajpayee was back as prime minister in March 1998 and Clinton's wait was finally over. Clinton called to congratulate Vajpayee and instructed his office to begin making plans for him to visit India.

## Atal Bihari Vajpayee

Vajpayee's family migrated from Uttar Pradesh to Gwalior, Madhya Pradesh where he grew up. His parents were humble schoolteachers and India was in the throes of the independence movement when Vajpayee was born in 1925. Like many of his contemporaries, he got involved in politics and was swept up in the nationalist fervour.

Unlike the secular politics of Nehru and Gandhi, Vajpayee was drawn to Hindu nationalism. In 1942, when he was just sixteen years old, he joined the Rashtriya Swayamsevak Sangh (RSS), a right-wing militant branch of the nationalist Hindu movement. Its adherents wanted India to be based on Hindu principles and viewed non-Hindus as second-class citizens. Its members exercised daily, were highly disciplined and many forswore marriage. Many Indians viewed the RSS as a cult. Vajpayee was one of its more moderate members and, after Independence, some of the RSS members like Vajpayee became politicians and joined parties like the Jana Sangh, predecessor to the BJP. The party was more moderate on the surface than the RSS, in order to attract voters and counter the Congress.

Although Vajpayee belonged to a right-wing orthodox Hindu party, he was far from conservative. He had developed a crush on a Kashmiri girl in his youth and the story is that he wrote her a love poem and sent it to her in a book. She responded but he somehow did not get her response. She married and moved on but many years later they met in Delhi. It seems that their feelings for each other were still strong. They moved in together, along with her husband, and he officially adopted one of her daughters. It was a rather unusual arrangement. When she died, Sonia Gandhi and several cabinet ministers came to pay their respects, which was an indication of her importance in Vajpayee's life.[30]

Vajpayee had been Morarji Desai's foreign minister. He had attracted political attention in Parliament as a talented orator. By the time he became prime minister he was seventy-two years old. He had spent most of his life in the opposition and, though he did not subscribe to the anti-Muslim views of his party, he seemed unable to bring its worst elements under control.

The BJP and the Congress held very different values on domestic policies, but they were united when it came to India's security interests. Both parties had turned away from the pacifism of the Nehru years and fully supported India's nuclear programme.

## Engaging India

The Clinton administration was apprehensive when the BJP came to power. According to Strobe Talbott, 'Americans had grown used to dealing with the Congress party, and not just for reasons of familiarity. Congress represented continuity with Gandhi's and Nehru's commitment to secularism and pluralism as the basis for Indian statehood. On the nuclear question, the combination of restraint and ambiguity that had marked Indian policy since Indira Gandhi's time, while hardly ideal, was better than the alternative that was now staring us in the face.'[31]

They did not have to wait long for their fears to be justified. Vajpayee had held on to the information, passed on to him by Prime Minister Rao when he left office, about India being ready for another nuclear test. Rao had been unable to test once he lost the election and Vajpayee had only been in office for less than two weeks during his first round as a prime minister in 1996. This time, confident in the election results, India conducted three underground nuclear tests at Pokhran, on Monday, 11 May 1998, at 15.45 hours. They were quickly followed two days later by a second set of tests. The Indian press was universally positive. Clinton was apoplectic. The Security Council unanimously condemned India's tests on 6 June 1998, under resolution 1172.[‡‡]

---

‡‡ The resolution required India to halt development of nuclear-capable ballistic missiles and production of any fissile materials that could be used for weapons. It also banned India from all further tests.

'We're going to come down on those guys like a ton of bricks,' said President Clinton as he opened a meeting in the Oval Office.[32] According to Strobe Talbott, it was not unusual for the president to throw a volcanic fit when things went wrong in the world, and it took a few days to calm him down.

Sanctions were placed on India in accordance with US law and the US also used its muscle to deter the World Bank and IMF from providing assistance to India.[§§] Vajpayee, in turn, wrote to 177 heads of state explaining India's position.

Senators Sam Brownback and Jesse Helms, former supporters, now turned against India and declared it was a nuclear threat, while Kissinger and Moynihan were both more realistic and conceded that India's nuclear programme was a reality to which the US would have to adjust.

One of the reasons Clinton was so angry was that he knew this would set off a nuclear arms race between India and Pakistan. He was not wrong. He gave Talbott the unenviable task of persuading the Pakistanis not to follow suit. The Talbott team jokingly referred to their task as 'mission impossible' as they flew to Pakistan.[33] They tried in vain to offer Pakistan aid incentives, but on 28 May 1998, and again on 30 May, Pakistan followed India and tested its own nuclear device.

The Clinton administration's reaction to the nuclear test and its insistence that India observe standards of human rights in Kashmir did not help to build bridges between the two countries. 'Just when the two sides needed to build trust and confidence in each other, US diplomacy on Kashmir and nuclear non-proliferation stirred deep anxieties in India about American intentions and motivations.'[34] India was also peeved that the US reaction to Pakistan, which followed India's tests with its own nuclear explosions, was far more muted.

---

§§ The Glenn Amendment went into effect, but unlike 1996 when India was recovering from its economic crisis, in 1998 it was stronger economically and able to withstand the sanctions. Among the sanctions imposed was a halt to all military sales and assistance, as well as all US loan guarantees and credit assistance. Prohibitions were imposed on loans and credits from US banks and a hold on Export-Import Bank loans was also affected.

The result of the explosions in South Asia was a serious engagement with India, led by the deputy secretary of state Strobe Talbott. Over the next two years Talbott met with Jaswant Singh, the minister of external affairs. They met fourteen times, in seven countries and three continents, to try to work out a nuclear deal. Although a deal was never concluded, it was an extraordinary dialogue chronicled by Talbott in his book, *Engaging India*. The relations that were built laid the groundwork for a friendship between the two countries, which definitively carried the relationship past the sludge that had bogged it down for decades.

The year 1998 was a miserable one for President Clinton. In his autobiography, *My Life*, he wrote: 'When 1998 began, I had no idea it would be the strangest year of my presidency, full of personal humiliation and disgrace.'[35] It was the year of the Monika Lewinsky scandal and the Ken Starr investigation that ended in impeachment proceedings.

In August 1998, the militant Islamic organization Al Qaeda attacked the US embassies in Kenya and Tanzania, killing 257 people including twelve Americans. Osama Bin Laden, the leader of Al Qaeda, was living in Afghanistan under the protection of the Taliban. The Taliban was being supported by Pakistan's ISI. Although Pakistan was a US ally, its unwavering support for the Taliban would place it at odds with American interests. The US began to conduct missions against Al Qaeda without the knowledge of its Pakistani counterparts. Diverging interests between Pakistan and the US over its support of terrorists seeded mutual suspicion, which germinated over the next decade as Indian perspectives increasingly found a more sympathetic ear among US officials.

## Kargil

The skirmish that took place between India and Pakistan at 17,000 feet, in 1999, where the air is thin and conditions harsh, permanently altered their relations with the US in ways that surprised the two warring neighbours in South Asia.

India had been on a quest to build better relations with its neighbours including Pakistan since the Simla Agreement, but progress had stalled. Vajpayee had decided to jump-start it by promising to visit Pakistan and open up trade between the countries, and Nawaz Sharif had accepted the proposal in principle. Vajpayee had kept his promise and, in a dramatic gesture, in February 1999, crossed the border by bus to inaugurate a bus service between the two countries as a precursor to establishing trade relations.

The Lahore Declaration followed, to reduce the possibility of nuclear war between the countries. It was an agreement about which the US was cautiously optimistic. The nuclear pundits in the administration felt both leaders had stuck their neck out, but they were more worried about Sharif as he was on shakier political ground. His new head of the army, Pervez Musharraf, was a hawk and saw India through a singular lens—as an enemy to be defeated.

Musharraf had emigrated from India during Partition and had limited patience with civilian politicians and long-winded diplomacy. He felt humiliated by the defeat of the 1971 war and was firmly committed to wresting Kashmir away from India. In the spring of 1999, he was chief of the Pakistani army and decided to cross the LOC to occupy the small outpost of Kargil, high on the Himalayan Mountains between Srinagar and Leh in Ladakh. It was five miles inside Indian territory, in an area usually abandoned by troops during the winter months. It was a provocative act conducted at 17,000 feet. The Indians retaliated and the skirmish quickly escalated, with casualties mounting and additional planes and troops being called in on both sides.

In Washington, the administration was following the situation with alarm, worried that there could be a nuclear confrontation in the Himalayas. On 16 June 1999, India's national security advisor, Brajesh Mishra, met his US counterpart, Sandy Berger, and told him that the Indians were acting with restraint but could not be held back for much longer.[36]

The US got the message. General Zinni went to Pakistan to ask for an immediate withdrawal of Pakistani troops from Kargil. 'For the first time ever in a Pakistani-Indian conflict, the United States was unequivocally and publicly siding with India. They called Pakistan the aggressor and demanded it withdraw its troops. Islamabad was devastated, and New Delhi could hardly believe it.'[37] Bruce Riedel, who was involved in the negotiations, said that the Indian ambassador called him to confirm the

US position and he responded that the US was fully behind India. It was a sea change in the relationship.

Pakistan panicked. The US threatened Pakistan with putting holds on its IMF loans if it did not withdraw its troops. Nawaz Sharif ran to China for support but came back empty-handed. Nawaz Sharif asked the US for a face-saving gesture for resolving the Kashmir dispute, with Clinton's personal involvement in exchange for withdrawal. President Clinton refused. He insisted that Pakistan withdraw its troops before any discussions take place.[38]

Sharif showed up uninvited to Washington during the Fourth of July weekend. The US was receiving worrying intelligence that Pakistan was readying its nuclear arsenal while Sharif was in Washington, which only further irritated the White House. India was looking increasingly like the adult in South Asia, and US goodwill had swung in its direction. Clinton wanted to make sure the Indians understood that he would protect their interests, and their past experiences of being passed over in deference to Pakistan would not be repeated. President Clinton kept Prime Minister Vajpayee informed of the discussions.

Each time the two sides took a break, Clinton called Vajpayee to brief him but barely got a response. "'What do you want me to say?" he responded after listening silently to Clinton's detailed report. "Nothing," Clinton replied: he just wanted Vajpayee to know he was holding firm.'[39] Years of American indifference towards India's security concerns had made India cynical of any hope for a balanced approach from the US in South Asia. 'That guy's from Missouri big-time,' said Clinton afterward, 'he wants to see those boys get off that mountain before he's going to believe any of this.'[40]

Kargil had fed the Pakistan sceptics in India. Sharif had squandered his goodwill and Vajpayee's Lahore expedition was now in tatters. Sharif had lost that political ground to the fundamentalists in his party after Kargil. Although the Indians eyed the discussions warily, they were relieved at the outcome. In a phone call to Talbott, Jaswant Singh observed the change in the relations. 'Something terrible has happened these past several months between us and our neighbours,' said Singh, 'but something quite good and new has happened between our own countries, yours and mine—

something related to the matter of trust. My prime minister and I thank you for that.'[41]

According to C. Raja Mohan, some analysts felt that the Indian Army would have succeeded in evicting the Pakistanis regardless of the American diplomatic intervention, but he states that they underestimated the diplomatic space that American support provided in isolating Pakistan internationally and limiting the cost of military operations in vacating the aggression. 'American neutrality in the conflict would have significantly expanded India's political burden.'[42]

The US also recognized the LOC as the international boundary between India and Pakistan, the violation of which would not be tolerated without censure. The US had used its diplomatic weight to get Saudi Arabia and China to sign on to the status quo. This was a major win for India in a world where Russia's star had faded, and it could no longer be counted on to back India.

Sharif was in a precarious position. He was under considerable pressure from his military not to give in to the US demands for withdrawal but, in the end, Clinton convinced him he had no choice but to withdraw his troops in order to diffuse the situation. The compromise weakened Sharif within Pakistan. He then compounded his situation by trying to arrest Musharraf, who rebelled and deposed him in a coup. Sharif was sentenced to death like his predecessor Bhutto, but this time the US intervened successfully. President Clinton arranged for Nawaz Sharif to live in exile in Saudi Arabia, where he survived to return to Pakistan a decade later to star in a rerun of his previous role. As Pakistan took on its familiar military mantle, India, by contrast, held elections and the BJP won a solid majority, thus giving Vajpayee a full term in office.

President Clinton was now nearing the end of his presidency. His desire to visit India was finally looking like a reality. In advance of the trip he waived a significant number of sanctions incurred in the aftermath of the 1998 explosion. Twenty-five years had passed since the last American president had visited India. Clinton's trip to India in March 2000 marked a high point in Indo-US relations. The president was invited to address Parliament, where he was received with great enthusiasm. He spent five days visiting different parts of India from small villages to hi-tech centres in Hyderabad. He loved every minute of his trip—the cheering crowds, the budding entrepreneurs, the grassroots NGOs and young leaders. Describing his visit in his autobiography, Clinton said he wished he had another week to absorb India's beauty and mystery.

On 25 March 2000, a smaller group accompanied Clinton to Pakistan, where they touched down just for a few hours. The Pakistanis had cleared an area a mile wide around the runway for security reasons, and the president described the landing as a 'bracing experience'. The motorcade travelled down an empty highway to a location where the president had some meetings. The contrast with India could not have been greater.[43]

With the growing warmth in US-Indo relations, India took another stab at trying to convince the Clinton White House about the duplicity of the Pakistani government. The Indians tried to convince the US that Pakistan's continued support of Islamic extremists was now being turned against the US. India had complained for years about Pakistan's interference in Kashmir, but the US had generally turned a blind eye to the extremist groups that it had supported. Now the US began to take an interest in their activities and viewed India's complaints with increased empathy.

As the Clinton administration came to a close, both sides softened their positions on the nuclear issues that had divided them. The US had grudgingly accepted that India as a nuclear power was here to stay and could not be persuaded to roll back its programme. It also conceded that India had acted responsibly, in contrast to Pakistan. The US had received intelligence that A.Q. Khan was sharing Pakistan's nuclear technology with rogue countries like North Korea and Iran.

Although President Clinton had signed the CTBT, he had failed to get it ratified by the US Senate. This provided cover to the Indians, who were reluctant to sign a treaty that limited their options to test without being welcomed into the nuclear club. The nuclear negotiators on the Clinton team, led by Strobe Talbott and Robert Einhorn, tried until the end to persuade India to sign the CTBT even though the US Senate had not ratified it, but they privately conceded it was unlikely to happen.[44] The clock had run out on the negotiations as the Clinton administration was ending. India and the Vajpayee government saw no point in concessions as presidential candidate George Bush seemed unlikely to promote the

CTBT. The acceptance of India as a responsible nuclear power and a country worth cultivating carried through to the next administration, extending the goodwill established by the Clinton team.

As the political situation in Afghanistan deteriorated and Pakistan's role in the evolving battleground became more complicit, the US once again revived its relations with Pakistan. This time, however, rather than doing so at India's expense, the US went to great lengths to maintain a balanced relationship. It was the beginning of a shift in the alliances between the US and its Asian allies.

# Chapter 19

# 9/11: A Changed World

URING THE ADMINISTRATION OF GEORGE W. BUSH TWO significant events had a lasting impact on US–India relations. The first, the terrorist attack on 11 September 2001, occurring just nine months after Bush was sworn in, defined his presidency and determined much of his foreign policy agenda. Afghanistan and Pakistan's role as safe havens for terrorists swiftly began to preoccupy his administration and shifted US attention to South Asia.

The second was the Bush administration's deliberate decision to court India, enabling the countries to finally forge a partnership. The two countries concluded a historic nuclear agreement in 2008, which took several years of difficult negotiation and almost brought down the Indian government.

Bush had won by a handful of votes in a hotly contested election. The results were inconclusive and had been challenged by both parties. The dispute ended up in the Supreme Court, which declared Bush the winner, a verdict that was not embraced by the Democrats.

Just four months into his presidency, Bush took some provocative international actions that indicated he intended to pursue an aggressive foreign policy. In February 2001, he ordered an attack on Iraqi radar sites to enforce a 'no-fly' zone, calling it a routine action. He rejected the Kyoto Protocol, an international agreement to reduce greenhouse emissions that had been ratified by 192 countries. In April, a US spy plane flying too close to Chinese territory was forced down, creating a diplomatic incident. He then angered the Chinese further by pledging military support for Taiwan in the event it was attacked by China. It was a significant departure from recent US policy. This was all done just four months into his presidency.

While the new administration was busy flexing its political muscle, it ignored the outgoing Clinton administration's warning of a real threat. The CIA and intelligence community had picked up signals that something 'big' was going to happen soon after the US election. The Clinton White House had left briefing papers marked 'urgent' for the incoming administration. They warned the Bush administration that they had picked up chatter on the airwaves of an impending terrorist attack in the US which would dwarf previous attacks in scale and fallout. The Bush administration failed to heed the warning seriously.

Bush, a former governor of Texas, was only the second son of a president to occupy the White House, after John Quincy Adams in 1825. Like many, he wanted to establish his own identity. He brought few of his father's advisors into his administration, even though many of them had legendary reputations—starting with Baker. Instead, he appointed Dick Cheney as his vice president. Cheney wielded enormous power in the West Wing* easily establishing himself as the most powerful vice president in US history and redefined the role of a vice president. He was conservative and believed in executive privilege and pre-emptive war. His default position in foreign affairs was the exertion of hard power in preference to diplomacy. There was considerable speculation as to whether Vice President Cheney's office was behind the early aggressive foreign policy moves.

Bush appointed his father's nemesis, Donald Rumsfeld, as secretary of defence. It almost appeared that, rather than just trying to differentiate himself from his father, Bush was trying to poke the elder statesman in the eye. According to senior officials, Senator Dan Coates had been initially tapped for the job of secretary of defence, but Cheney made sure his friend Rumsfeld was appointed instead.†

Donald Rumsfeld was arrogant, chauvinistic and exceptionally close to the vice president. Together, they were a formidable force and determined

---

\* The US president's offices are located in the West Wing of the White House.

† Rumsfeld had brought Cheney into the Ford administration.

to 'control Washington'. They often belittled Condoleezza Rice, the national security advisor; Secretary of State Colin Powell often found himself at odds with the two powerful men. The atmosphere in the Bush administration was far from harmonious.

In June 2001, the CIA included a warning in the president's daily brief that Osama Bin Laden was planning to attack the US. Cofer Black and George Tenet of the CIA went to see Rice at the White House to convey the seriousness with which they were taking the intelligence, though they were unable to pinpoint the time or method. Their warnings went unheeded.

On 9 September 2001, the Afghan Northern Alliance leader Ahmad Shah Masoud was assassinated. He was the main opposition to the Taliban within Afghanistan and had warned that any harm to him should be taken as an ominous sign.

The morning of 11 September was clear and sunny on the East Coast when hijacked planes turned the skies over the US into a horror show. Two planes struck the two tallest buildings in New York City. The dramatic collapse of the World Trade Center towers, the burning bodies and people jumping to their deaths are all images that are still fresh wounds in the American psyche. A third plane crashed into the Pentagon, and the fourth was brought down by passengers in Pennsylvania, killing everyone on board.

A powerful silence filled the skies over the country as all flights were grounded and security protocols were introduced, which changed the way Americans lived forever. The US outlook on the world shifted dramatically after 9/11, as the country withdrew into a self-protective mode and the administration reoriented its foreign policy. Although Europe and Russia remained areas of interest, the post-9/11 world saw a permanent shift eastward as the Middle East, South Asia and China became the focus of US foreign policy.

Deputy Secretary of State Richard Armitage, who met with Bush almost every day, said that Bush was almost uncomfortable in his position as president when he first arrived in Washington, as his election had been contested and decided by a Supreme Court decision. But when 9/11 happened, 'A light bulb lit up and he said this is why I am president, I am being tested. I can do this. After that I saw a change in his demeanour, and he became more confident.'[1]

When the Bush administration first took office, the right-wing hawks had brought out plans to finish what they felt had not been done in Iraq, namely regime change. Now, confronted with a monumental attack on America, they had no choice but to shelve the Iraq plans and respond to what was clearly an attack organized by Al Qaeda and its leader Osama Bin Laden. The immediate goal was to go after the militant group and prevent any future terror attacks against the homeland.

Initially, a group of highly skilled horsemen, belonging to the Special Forces, landed in Afghanistan and within a hundred days had Al Qaeda on the run and Osama within their sights. The terrorists had agreed to surrender, but the US military wanted a grand display of military power and brought in troops and the air force, which nullified the agreed-upon surrender. Osama escaped and evaded capture for almost a decade until President Obama finally tracked him down and had him killed.

The US obliterated whatever strongholds in Afghanistan they could in an intensive bombing campaign. 'Operation Enduring Freedom' was launched on 7 October 2001. Within a month Mazar[‡] fell, and by December, Mullah Omar and much of the Taliban leadership abandoned their base in Kandahar and moved across the border to Pakistan. By then, Al Qaeda was on the run and Osama was hiding in Pakistan.

The US flooded Afghanistan with troops and non-military personnel and attempted to remake Afghanistan, a tribal, conservative Islamic, ethnically diverse and backward state, into a democracy. India and Pakistan both watched with concern as the outcome in Afghanistan had direct consequences for their regional politics. Pakistan lost its foothold in Afghanistan via its proxy, the Taliban. It gave the Taliban shelter in Pakistan and allowed it to set up its headquarters in Quetta.

Pakistan was given an ultimatum and Musharraf was asked if he was 'with the US'. He quickly confirmed his support. Pakistan had been somewhat discredited after the Kargil conflict with India during the

---

[‡]    The Taliban had captured the city of Mazar-i-Sharif in Afghanistan and had it under their control since 1998.

Clinton administration, but it now saw an opportunity to revive its alliance and became an important partner for the US in its 'war on terror'. There was close cooperation between the two countries and Pakistan took its share of losses in the fight against Islamic terrorists. The first two to three years after 9/11 were the golden years of cooperation between Pakistan and the US. India watched helplessly from the sidelines as, once again, events in Afghanistan gave Pakistan a logistical advantage in its relationship with the US.

India was pleased to see the Taliban on the run and the dismantling of Afghanistan as a terrorist training camp. But the chaos and lack of stability that followed worried India. It decided to provide aid to Afghanistan and establish a bilateral partnership to counter the influence that Pakistan had with the Taliban, hoping that under US supervision a more balanced approach would be encouraged. Initially, India discovered that the US was resistant to its involvement in Afghanistan, as it was anxious not to antagonize its partnership with Pakistan. The US attitude towards India would change over time, as it became clear that terrorist activities against US soldiers and international personnel were often aided by the Taliban, who were supported by the ISI.

To conduct the war in Afghanistan, the US was heavily dependent on Pakistan for routes, transport, logistical help and intelligence; though, as time went on, Pakistan became increasingly suspect as a partner. Pakistan did not want a long-term US presence in Afghanistan. It entered a duplicitous alliance with the US, helping the military logistically with its war in Afghanistan, while its Directorate S, the ultra-secret wing of the ISI, protected the Taliban and Al Qaeda, the very enemies the US was trying to eliminate. They were 'assets' that Pakistan needed in order to maintain its strategic depth in the region. Pakistan turned into a 'frenemy' and the US–Pakistan relationship deteriorated into one of mutual suspicion.

In a major break from the past, rather than marginalize India in lieu of America's need for Pakistani assistance, Bush broke precedent and decided to elevate India as an ally. India had never been able to expunge the Pakistani factor from its relationship with the US during previous administrations. Now, for the first time, the US was willing to delink them.

Many books have been written about the mistakes made in Bush's pursuit of the wars in Afghanistan and Iraq, and it is not a subject that can be covered in these pages. George W. Bush's strategy of war will be counted among his biggest failures. Suffice it to say, Afghanistan is the longest-running war for the US and one that it seems unable to 'win', as the goalposts and the definition of success keep shifting. Just as the British and the Soviets discovered, Afghanistan did not take kindly to foreign interference in its affairs.

## Pakistan: A Shared Headache

After 9/11, the administration's strategic priorities were subordinated to the 'war on terror', and entering into a nuclear deal with India was not yet on the horizon in 2001.

On 13 December 2001, five terrorists, armed with guns, explosives and suicide vests, entered and attacked the Indian parliament using fake IDs. Fortunately, the suicide vests failed to detonate, and the terrorists were shot by security guards as they entered the building—but not before they had killed several people on their way in.

The terrorists had two car accidents on their way to Parliament. During the first accident, they had to get out of their vehicle and placate the driver of the car they had collided with, by offering the customary payment on the spot for the damage they had caused. This entailed some bargaining, using up valuable time. They then had a second accident, this time running into the vice president's car as it entered the grounds of Parliament. This panicked the already nervous gang: they decided to abandon their car and make a run for it, shooting their way into Parliament on foot. The delays likely saved lives as the parliamentary session went into recess and, though there were almost a hundred people, including some ministers still in the building when the terrorists finally entered, the potential to cause fatalities was less than it would have been had they arrived forty minutes earlier and been able to use their explosives when the house was in full session. The failure of the suicide vests also reduced what could have turned into a bloodbath.

Jaswant Singh, India's foreign minister, confronted the Pakistani high commissioner in New Delhi with incontrovertible proof that the terrorists were members of two well-known terrorist organizations, Lashkar-e-Taiba and Jaish-e-Mohammed, based in Pakistan and demanded the handover of its leaders. Pakistan refused. The investigation also turned up evidence that the terrorists were supported and directed by the ISI, Pakistan's intelligence service.

The US, worried about the potential for nuclear war on the subcontinent, intervened at several diplomatic levels to avoid an escalation of the crisis. Their decision to delink India and Pakistan from their decision-making process was put to the test. Ambassador Bob Blackwill visited the Indian parliament on 14 December and stated that 'the assault was no different in its objective from the terror attacks in the US on 11 September'.[2] The US was struggling with its dependence on Pakistan, without whom they could not conduct military operations in Afghanistan, and the administration's new policy in South Asia in which India was the cornerstone.

Rice said that the US and Britain put pressure on Musharraf to condemn the attacks, which he reluctantly did, but he accompanied it with a warning to India not to react, which undercut any goodwill he might have generated.[3]

Vajpayee was under intense public pressure to retaliate. India mobilized its forces along the border, and Pakistan did the same. By 27 December, the US received confirmation that a million troops were massed along the border. Powell tried to convince Jaswant Singh to meet with the Pakistanis to deescalate the situation, but the Indians did not trust Musharraf and refused. The US, wishing to steer the situation away from any potential for a nuclear conflict, tried to deescalate the crisis by continuing to talk to both sides.

Bush massaged Pakistan and Musharraf, providing various incentives to encourage responsible behaviour. Bush called Pakistan a major non-NATO ally and approved a $1.2 billion aid package,[4] with half of it designated for military use, which, much to India's anger, the Pakistanis used to go on a military shopping spree.

Six months later, Pakistani terrorists launched another attack in Jammu on 14 May 2002, killing thirty-four and injuring fifty. This time the victims were the wives and children of Indian soldiers. Armitage was dispatched to meet with Musharraf to make it clear that the US would not tolerate any aggression by Pakistan and sought assurances that he could take to India to broker a stand-down.

Brajesh Mishra, the urbane, erudite, calm Indian national security advisor in the Vajpayee government, warned the US that the calls for going to war were getting harder to ignore, and something had to be done to rein in Pakistan. He emphasized that India had shown considerable restraint until then, in contrast to Pakistan's condonation of terrorist attacks on Indians. He suggested the US follow a balanced role in the region.

After 9/11, the US was more sympathetic to India's accusations about Pakistani support of terrorist activities in India. In her memoir, *No Higher Honor*, Condoleezza Rice described the State Department's efforts to calm the situation and the US's recognition of India's right to self-defence, which was a direct consequence of its own experience with recent terrorist attacks and a departure from previous government attitudes.

By then Musharraf had irritated the US administration, which began to view him as a 'flawed partner' at best and a headache most of the time. He further alienated Bush by conducting a series of tests of short- and medium-range missiles capable of carrying nuclear warheads. The president called Musharraf to warn him to stop the sabre-rattling against India and rein in the militants on both sides of the border.

During Bush's first term, the US administration obtained proof that Pakistan was also proliferating. Although Pakistan's pursuit of nuclear weapons had by now been well established, proliferation was a different category of offence, especially since Pakistan was selling the technology to America's enemies—Iran and North Korea. Bush decided to confront Musharraf. To placate the US, Musharraf placed A.Q. Khan, the father of Pakistan's nuclear programme, under house arrest.

As secretary of state, Colin Powell had been busy responding to 9/11, the Iraq war and purported weapons of mass destruction. The bombing of the Indian parliament and other terrorist activity that had created tensions along the Indo-Pakistani border had usurped whatever time he had available for India. He had little time to develop a long-term strategy for an Indo-US partnership during President Bush's first term. His time in office was complicated by a difficult relationship with Vice President Cheney and Defense Secretary Rumsfeld.

Bush, who had made up his mind that the relationship with India needed to be advanced, relied on Condoleezza Rice, national security advisor, to carry out his wishes. Ashley Tellis, one of the members of the US team that negotiated the nuclear agreement, believed the 'Bush administration had decided to do something big with India during its first term, but, I think, it was politically impossible to pursue something like the nuclear deal at the time because it was so revolutionary. There would have been a tremendous political risk going into a re-election with a controversial agreement that broke a lot of China.'[5]

In 2002, Rice began the process of transforming the relationship incrementally. The US began to share intelligence on counterterrorism with India and, for the first time, began a political-military dialogue. As a result, a joint military engagement was initiated. In 2002, the Indian navy escorted US ships through the Strait of Malacca for six months. Following the tsunami over Christmas 2004, the Indian navy worked on humanitarian missions in Sri Lanka and Indonesia along with US naval ships. Both encounters helped develop a professional appreciation between the two sides and the potential for a partnership was considered.

Rice was fully aware that, while these were important gestures, nuclear cooperation would be the game changer.

## Bush and India

Bush's interest in India predated his presidency. He had met many Indians over the years as governor of Texas and admired their entrepreneurial spirit. India's commitment to democracy appealed to him, and he believed that they shared common values. When he was on the campaign trail before he was elected, Bush made public comments about India being the largest democracy in the world and developing a partnership with it was a goal he intended to pursue. According to Tellis, 'Bush liked India, but central to his interest in the country was India's commitment to democracy. During his first term, when Vajpayee was prime minister, he saw in him a new kind of leader and wanted to build a relationship for the long term.[6]

At the height of the Cold War in the fifties and sixties, India was viewed as a barrier against communist China, but that perception fell away after Nixon's opening with China in the seventies. China had gone from being a political threat to an economic worry. Steve Hadley, who became national security advisor and was instrumental in negotiating the nuclear deal, explained President Bush's thinking and said the relationship with India had nothing to do with countering China. He told me: 'The president had decided that India was going to be emerging on the world scene as a global power, and that it was important that we have a good relationship with India so that when it did emerge on the global scene it would be a potential partner and not an adversary of the US. India was coming of age as a power and it being a democracy made it especially attractive, given his [Bush's] freedom agenda, as he believed our relationship is strongest with countries whom we share values with.'[7]

Other members of the administration believe China's rise was definitely a contributing factor in Bush's pivot to India. Tellis argued that it was hard to imagine the US making such a huge leap of faith and changing forty years of standing US policy—which is essentially what it took to get the nuclear deal with India done—if China played no role in their calculation. 'We saw this very much in terms of the China question. Everything we wrote from 2001–03 arguing for this deal was all pegged to strengthening US–India ties to manage China's rise. Our strongest allies in the State Department and Department of Defense all bought it on the grounds of the China argument but, for various understandable reasons, no one wanted to package this initiative as a China balancing act.'[8] Tellis acknowledged that Hadley did not share his perspective on this, but Blackwill and Rice did.

From the very beginning of his administration, Bush embarked on a series of steps designed to improve ties with New Delhi. As a gesture of his intentions, he lifted the sanctions that had been imposed on India after its explosion of a nuclear device in 1998. The US began to explore its potential commercial relationships with India for the first time and discussed the possibility of using Indian spaceships to launch US satellites.[9] The US administration began a conversation on space cooperation with India. In return, when the Bush administration announced the US was pursuing missile defence, India did not react negatively as it normally would have, and the US, in turn, agreed to give India periodic briefings on missile defence technology.[§]

Bush decided to accelerate relations early on by inviting Prime Minister Vajpayee to visit Washington. The visit took place in November 2001 in the wake of 9/11. Bush wished to demonstrate that he intended to embark on a relationship that would be beneficial to both countries. He directed his staff to find out what it would take to wipe out some of the irritants that had prevented the two democracies from becoming strategic partners in the past.

## Prelude to the Deal

India had long made it clear that its number one priority from the West was cooperation on civilian nuclear technology to help build power plants for its booming economy and recognition that it was a responsible nuclear state.

The Bush administration had a steep domestic hurdle to overcome before it could proceed with a nuclear agreement with India, due to US laws governing the sharing of nuclear technology. Section 123 of the US Atomic Energy Act placed restrictions on the US, only allowing it to enter into nuclear sharing agreements with countries that had signed the NPT, which India had refused to sign.

To understand why the process was so complicated, it is essential to understand the history of the nuclear regime that governed all international nuclear agreements. (A brief description is provided in Chapter 13, page 288.)

Under the agreement, the US stopped supplying nuclear material for Tarapur following India's 1974 nuclear explosion. The Indian Department of Atomic Energy (DAE) had always viewed the US with suspicion after it reneged on its Tarapur commitment. Indian nuclear scientists took pride

---

§    This did not involve any technology transfer at this stage.

in their work and chafed at being constrained in their progress by the rules that other countries had devised. They preferred to remain outside the international nuclear regime rather than give up their 'sovereign rights'.

Rice, exceptionally close to the president, was entrusted with channelling Bush's strategic priorities into action. She worked with Steve Hadley and together they began to lay out a framework for a deal that would enable India to obtain the civilian technology it wanted, while retaining its nuclear weapons so long as it submitted its civilian nuclear facilities to international controls and inspections.

In 2003, Steve Hadley and Kenneth Juster⁵ went to India with a proposal called the 'Next Steps in Strategic Partnership' (NSSP). It was the precursor to the nuclear deal and contained all the changes in the rules and regulations that needed to be in place before India could be offered a nuclear deal by the US. It required India to upgrade its export control regulations to make them consistent with international norms. The US negotiators could then proceed with confidence, knowing that India was serious. It also provided the White House with the ammunition it needed to make the case to Congress that India deserved a waiver of Section 123, allowing an 'India exception'. This would permit the US to cooperate on civil nuclear technology with India.

The US began negotiations with a firm, if somewhat tough, position. It wanted India to put catch-all legislation in place based on UN Security Council resolution 1540, which spelled out the requirements for the prevention of non-proliferation. Furthermore, the US insisted India sign an end-use agreement that guaranteed sensitive technology would not be transferred to any third country. After the conditions were met, the US agreed to start removing sanctions and begin cooperation with India,

Both teams painstakingly laid the foundations, one layer at a time, until the roadmap for a future agreement was presented.

Hadley recalled that there was enormous resistance to India within the US government from the non-proliferation priesthood, who wanted to protect the nuclear regime that was already in place. When it came to

---

⁵    Kenneth Juster currently serves as the US ambassador to India. At the time, he worked at the state department.

nuclear issues, they considered India a renegade nation and had censured it in the past. Both sides quickly realized that it would take more than hard work and meeting requirements to get over the prejudices that had built up over the years against India. When Hadley met with Brajesh Mishra, he was told emphatically, '*You* [personally] have to do it! The only way it will get done through your bureaucracy is if you drive it through the White House and the NSC.' Hadley recalls that that is exactly what they did.[10]

India would need to satisfy the US regarding the use of dual-use technology items and agree to comply with its regulations. The US would then start the process of slowly lifting restrictions on technology transfers and shipments to India. 'We identified four key areas of what we needed to do and then told the Indians what they needed to do and so on. It was like building blocks.'[11]

The first disruption in the negotiations were a result of domestic politics in India. By the end of 2003, Vajpayee was in trouble. Progress on the NSSP had slowed to a crawl due to the differences between what the US required and what the Indians were willing to concede. The Vajpayee government was no longer in a position to make historic changes in foreign policy.

By early 2004, India was headed to the polls and major policy decisions were put on hold. In May 2004, India elected a new government. The Congress party came back to power with a comfortable majority. Rajiv Gandhi's widow had thrown herself into the family profession and won her way to victory at the polls, even though she had exhibited a dislike for politics when she was Mrs Gandhi's daughter-in-law and a somewhat reluctant participant when her husband Rajiv became the prime minister. As the party leader, she had the right to be the prime minister, but she astutely appointed the technocrat and highly respected Manmohan Singh. Manmohan Singh came from an academic background and was not a political man. An economist by training, he had been recruited to change India's sagging economic structures of the past and give the country a new direction. He had served on both sides of the aisle and was a quiet, thoughtful man.

As the father of India's economic reforms, Manmohan Singh's appointment sent a clear message to the public and India watchers abroad that India was going to continue its progressive course. Although he was unelected, Singh's appointment as prime minister was applauded. By stepping away from the highest job the country had to offer, Sonia's popularity soared. The economy was growing at 6 per cent, and Indians were full of hope.

The new government was anxious to continue the work on nuclear cooperation. Singh assembled a dream team to manage the process. Ronen Sen was sent as ambassador to Washington. Earlier, he had been secretary to the Atomic Energy Commission when Prime Minister Singh had been a member of the finance ministry. Sen had handled atomic energy and defence under previous prime ministers and came to Washington with an extensive resume and great diplomatic skill.

S. Jaishankar, joint secretary for the Americas, whose power extended beyond his station, was also assigned to the nuclear deal. An unusually competent foreign service officer, he would later serve as foreign secretary, ambassador to Washington, survive opposition governments in India and have bipartisan support in running India's foreign policy. He recalls Singh describing to Senator Kerry that their differences over the nuclear issue had 'become like a thorn stuck in the throat of the US–India relationship'.[12]

Jaishankar and National Security Advisor J.N. Dixit were determined to advance relations with the US. They were joined in their efforts by Shyam Saran, the brilliant, hawkish negotiator, fully committed to the nuclear deal but equally to maintaining India's independence. Later, they would be joined by Shivshankar Menon, the cool, elegant, cerebral diplomat, who worked in tandem with Shyam Saran to find solutions acceptable to both countries and push past impediments to get the deal done. Jaishankar praised his colleagues and said that on the Indian end, without Saran, the deal would not have been negotiated and without Menon it would not have been concluded.

In the US, Bush's second term ushered in some changes as well. Condoleezza Rice succeeded Colin Powell as secretary of state and Steve Hadley took over as national security advisor. They both were committed to securing a nuclear deal and, in her new position, Rice carried the weight to get it done. She visited Delhi in March 2005, and she and Prime Minister Singh agreed to start the process of negotiations towards a comprehensive nuclear deal. They also entered into a major ten-year defence cooperation agreement, which was launched in June 2005 just ahead of the nuclear deal.

With India's growth rate projected to rise to 8 per cent over the next two years, its growing need for energy demanded an expansion of its energy sector. Nuclear energy was cleaner and better for the environment, and Saran explained to Rice that civil nuclear cooperation would need to be part of the equation if the US wanted India as a strategic partner. Rice was thoughtful. She told Saran that Bush was also interested in reviving nuclear energy domestically in the US, where no new reactors had been built for twenty years. Saran, aware of the burden of the historical relationship between the two countries, was unequivocal: 'We need to get away from the negative legacies of the past if we want to do the big things together. We are dealing with a new world and an increasingly dominant China. We would like to cooperate with the US.'[13]

Secretary Rice appointed Nick Burns as her chief negotiator on the nuclear deal, which would be the signature achievement in the Indo-US relationship. Foreign Secretary Shyam Saran was his counterpart in India. The goal was to have an agreement by mid-July, in time for Singh's state visit to the US. Americans planned to announce a strategic partnership with India during the visit, giving it top billing. 'Your PM is coming. We want this to be a big visit. What is it that you want to see from the Indian side?'[14] Saran replied that India had maintained an impeccable record on proliferation, unlike Pakistan and China, and deserved to be recognized as a responsible nuclear power.

Initially, the US team wanted the Indians to sign the CTBT, which they refused to do. India stuck to its earlier position that the CTBT was discriminatory. Saran did, however, agree to reaffirm India's earlier declaration on a moratorium on testing. The US also wanted India to commit to not enrich or reprocess fuel. Again, India refused as it had a fast breeder reactor programme. The Indian team agreed to a freeze on fissile material but insisted it be allowed to keep existing stocks.

Saran asked the US, as a show of goodwill, to supply India with nuclear fuel as its supplies were dangerously low due to sanctions, and some plants were at risk. Phil Zelikow, from the US side, responded that his legal team could review it, but he reflected that since even a one-time exception would require an act of Congress to alter the Atomic Energy Act, why not go the whole way and ask for a permanent nuclear deal? It was a revelatory moment. They all agreed to go ahead and try.

Rice made it clear that the NSSP had to be concluded before discussions on the nuclear deal could begin, which some considered a waste of time once they had decided to go all the way for a comprehensive deal. Jaishankar pointed out that the NSSP had been inherited by the Singh government and was a compromise agreement that was a result of 'some people who wanted to change the US–India relationship and their policies and others who wanted to change the relationship without changing policy'.[15] The two teams were far apart. Saran, who was leading the Indian team, explained: 'We had many red lines when we began our talks. Finally, we selected three areas that were essential to India where we needed to reach an agreement.'[16] It would take several rounds over many months before a breakthrough.

# Chapter 20

# Bush 43: The Big Transformation

T HE NUCLEAR DEAL TRANSFORMED US–INDIA RELATIONS. THE two countries developed a strategic partnership based on long-term cooperation rather than one that was plagued with conflicts, misunderstandings and the vagaries of prejudices and personalities. The negotiations spanned most of Bush's second term and were often contentious. There were times when the talks almost collapsed and then one side or other would revive the project. On one infamous occasion, the US delegation snapped and walked out of a dinner after failing to find a compromise and headed back to Washington. The lead negotiators texted and spoke until dawn before agreeing to continue.* The US president or the Indian prime minister had to personally intervene on more than one occasion to save the talks from getting derailed. The current foreign minister, S. Jaishankar, was one of the key players and remembers it vividly. 'When I look back on it today, I was deeply, passionately involved—in what can only be called a high-voltage negotiation that spanned several continents and took place in different capitals. It was wholly unique and probably the most difficult negotiation in the history of US–India relations. It had a Rashomon quality to it, with many players and agendas; but in the end, we all came together and achieved something historic.'

The two sides had barely four months before the state visit to find solutions to very complicated problems that were also politically sensitive.

---

\* The two negotiators who texted were Ashley Tellis (US) and Foreign Minister S. Jaishankar (India), who at the time was joint secretary for the Americas.

Following Secretary Rice's visit to New Delhi earlier that year, Burns and Saran spent several intense closed-door meetings, between April and July 2005, to address the outline of an agreement and tackle outstanding issues, like Tarapur and the technical problems of processing its spent fuel, which had cast a shadow over so many previous negotiations.

In July 2005, the Indian team arrived in Washington three days before the prime minister to finalize the joint agreement. The deal almost fell through over two issues. The first was semantic and over the recognition of India's status as a nuclear state. The second was India's requirement that its military nuclear programme remain off-limits to US supervision.

The US wanted guarantees that the civil nuclear cooperation was not going to be misused to enhance India's military capability. Bringing India, a nuclear pariah, in and formally recognizing it as a nuclear state without giving it the same status as the original five proved to be a challenge. India was sensitive about being recognized as a responsible nuclear power. In the end, the issue was resolved by some inventive language that satisfied both parties. It was agreed that India would reciprocally agree that it would be ready to assume the same responsibilities and practices and acquire the same benefits and advantages as other leading countries with advanced nuclear technology, such as the United States.

The US had to make sure that India would agree to inspections to satisfy the non-proliferation critics, who claimed the whole deal undermined the rationale for aiding countries which gave up nuclear arms, as first put forward under Eisenhower's Atoms for Peace programme. But India resisted even minimal steps to allow inspections. The Indian position was 'that we could not risk the cooperation of the US on the civilian side, which allowed inspections, and have them flow into our military side. We had started with a civilian and then morphed into a weapons programme, so it was hard to separate the facilities.'[2]

The US had accommodated many of India's requirements while trying to abide by US law, although the issue of inspections and safeguards remained a major hurdle. But when the prime minister's plane landed, the joint statement that the US and Indian teams had worked on together started to fall apart. Saran and his team briefed the prime minister and his delegation about the status of the negotiations, and an extensive debate broke out among the Indians.

Anil Kakodkar, head of the Department of Atomic Energy (DAE), effectively killed the deal by raising many red flags. After being subjected to thirty years of sanctions, DAE was wary of US intentions and reluctant to contractually obligate India to open its facilities to international inspectors, for a civil nuclear agreement Kakodkar did not know he could trust. Tellis remembers the interactions well: 'They [the Indians] were suspicious that our motives were not as altruistic as we imagined, and it hung over the negotiations like a dark cloud.'[3]

Kakodkar was not the only person who questioned the agreement on the Indian side. In the absence of a consensus, Saran was directed to inform his counterpart in the US that the prime minister was not in agreement with the nuclear cooperation section of the joint declaration. Saran was asked to find a more neutral formulation and frame it as positively as possible, and inform the other side that they were continuing deliberations.

Saran conveyed the message to Burns on 17 July, the night before the heads of the two governments were to meet. Burns informed Rice that the big announcement, and strategic partnership, was not happening, despite the months of negotiations and mutual concessions. There was palpable disappointment among the US team.

Rice recalled it had been a long day, and they were all tired. 'Well, if they don't want to get out of the nuclear ghetto, I can't do anything about it,' she told her team. They had worked so hard and come so far; they felt let down by the India team. She went to sleep and woke up at 4.30 a.m. 'I am not letting this go down ... I am not prepared to let this fail.'[4] She decided to give the negotiations one last try. She woke Nick Burns half an hour later and asked to see Manmohan Singh at 8 a.m. at Blair House, before his 10 a.m. meeting with Bush, but the prime minister turned her down as he did not want to say no to her. Rice refused to take no for an answer and insisted on meeting with him. It was Natwar Singh who finally persuaded the prime minister, saying he could not deny the secretary who had put so much of her own muscle into the partnership.

Rice tried to convince the soft-spoken prime minister by framing this as a historic opportunity: 'Mr Prime Minister, this is the deal of a lifetime. You and President Bush are about to put US–Indian relations on a fundamentally new footing … let's get it done before you see the president.'[5] She also explained that, without the guarantees and inspections, Congress would not approve the deal. Manmohan Singh admitted to Rice that they had not reached a consensus within their own delegation, and given the issues raised, he was concerned that he could not sell the current agreement to Parliament. Rice asked what the obstacles were from their side that were preventing an agreement and offered to see if she could find a solution.

The prime minister nodded and asked Natwar Singh, his foreign minister who was with him in the room, to call in Anil Kakodkar. Kakodkar was asked to write down on a piece of paper the requirements that would satisfy the scientific community in India. He listed a set of demands such as India-specific safeguards and full civil nuclear cooperation from A to Z, and that the US not be able to cherry-pick which aspects of civil nuclear technology they would share. Rice looked at the list and agreed to the conditions. It was done. Manmohan Singh left to meet Bush.

The principals, Bush and Singh, began their meeting, while Saran and Burns huddled in the Roosevelt Room and found language that was acceptable to both sides. Minutes before the press briefing, as the leaders emerged from the meeting, they were handed the document and the strategic partnership was announced on the White House lawns on 18 July 2005. It took many officials in both countries by surprise. Ambassador Sen and Saran credit Rice's persistence and hard work with getting it done.[†]

## Negotiations

As part of the agreement, India agreed to separate its military and civilian facilities. India's nuclear programme had grown organically. Excluded from the international nuclear organizations since 1974, Indian-built facilities were not subject to international requirements and inspections.

---

[†]   The announcement of the strategic partnership was a framework for civil nuclear cooperation. Although some important criteria had been negotiated, there were many details that still needed to be agreed on, like the separation agreement.

Some civilian facilities had military components and separating the facilities was a monumental task for the DAE to undertake. The DAE's claim on resources and its special status in the Indian government derived from the strategic programme. The department was naturally reluctant to see it split and its jurisdictions interfered with. Although this was an internal political issue for India, it was a major consideration for the DAE and contributed to the pushback encountered during the negotiations.

Sovereignty continued to be a sensitive issue. A relevant question that had arisen was, Who decides which facilities remain civilian and come under international inspections and which remain dark? India insisted that it be the sole decision maker. This created a great deal of unease between the parties. The US said it needed to satisfy its non-proliferation people and were willing to designate only two reactors as strategic and, therefore, off-limits to inspectors. The Indians were furious and made it clear this was not a decision they would allow the US to appropriate. At the time, India's fast breeder reactors were listed as civilian on the DAE website, so the US argued, 'Since you yourself say its civilian, why can't they be inspected?' India said no way.[6]

President Bush was slated to arrive in India in March 2006. The goal was to complete the bilateral agreement based on the framework that had been announced the previous year, during Manmohan Singh's visit to the US. Once the bilateral agreement was in place, it could be presented to the respective governments for approval. But the negotiations proved even more contentious than the last one leading to the July 2005 agreement. Once again, the DAE wanted assurances regarding fuel security[‡] and resisted any constraints on its freedom to test or open its breeder reactors to international scrutiny.

Indian political turf wars between the DAE, the Ministry of External Affairs and the Prime Minister's Office brought negotiations close to collapse. The US team, frustrated at what they saw as Indian obduracy and angry because they felt they had worked hard and with sincerity to

---

[‡]  Tarapur was never far from their minds. The US withdrew as a supplier of fuel after India's explosion. India wanted the US to guarantee lifetime supplies of nuclear fuel.

get a deal done, often felt the DAE was being churlish and uncooperative. The ghosts of Tarapur were never fully exorcised and hovered over the discussions. Recalling Tarapur, India wanted to link fuel security to safeguards. If fuel supply was ever stopped for any reason again, as it had been with Tarapur, India wanted to be released from all obligations to observe safeguards and be free to pursue its nuclear programme as it saw fit.

When Air Force One landed in Delhi, Bush was told there was no agreement and no announcement for him to make. Just as the trip looked like it was a wasted opportunity, Hadley and Burns disappeared into a room with M.K. Narayanan (MK) and Saran. They worked past midnight reworking the language to satisfy the objections. Mulford, the US ambassador, kept saying that they were wasting their time, that they should go to bed and that it was getting late. Hadley recalls he decided to continue negotiating to see if they could come to an agreement, but by dawn, they conceded defeat. In the morning, Hadley came back to MK and said the president really wanted to get it done and would personally give his assurance on fuel security and a couple of other sticking points, after which DAE gave it its blessing; finally, they had an agreement.

Most crucially, the agreement had the support of the senior DAE official, Secretary Kakodkar; though, according to some attendees, he still wore a glum expression the day after the agreement. The DAE had clung to the position that no deal was better than one that compromised India's freedom.

The 'separation plan' was announced by India in March 2006 during President Bush's visit. The agreement was announced at a state dinner at Rashtrapati Bhavan, to which Rice wore a shimmering gown by Ralph Lauren and President Bush wore a tuxedo, with the *New York Times* carrying the picture on the front page.[7] US cooperation was strictly limited to India's civilian facilities, which it agreed to place under international safeguards in accordance with the IAEA regulations. It was agreed that fourteen out of India's twenty-two facilities would be subject to international safeguards. India also agreed to voluntarily continue its moratorium on nuclear testing.

The negotiations between the two democracies seldom went smoothly. There were many hiccups along the way. The agreement would often get stuck and MK would call Hadley and tell him he needed to come and break the logjam. Hadley would help them find a way out of the impasse. 'MK was getting a lot of resistance from the Indian negotiators. When there was a problem, the question was to give some political impetus to the negotiations and find a workaround. I would take the various pieces, put them in a memo and get it blessed by the president. Narayanan would do the same with the PM. We knew the only way we would get this done is if this was viewed as the personal project of the PM and the president. Every time the negotiation would get stuck, I would bring it back to the political level and reaffirm the commitment of the president and prime minister. Then MK would take it back to his bureaucracy, and things would get unstuck.'[8]

The level of cooperation between the teams and opposing parties was both unique and unprecedented. While there were many moments of tension, and hard negotiations, once the two sides had agreed among themselves, they went out of their way to help each other bring their dissenting members along.

It had taken two years and multiple meetings to find an agreement that the leaders of both countries found acceptable, but this was just the beginning. Now they had to sell it to their respective governments. Manmohan Singh returned to India and made a formal announcement to Parliament, providing members with the broad outlines of the agreement, and Bush presented it to Congress.

## Congressional Approval

Congress was furious. The president had decided to make a major change in US nuclear policy without taking members of the Senate Foreign Relations Committee or the Armed Services Committee into confidence. Historically, the US Congress had consistently denied nuclear cooperation with India, based on its pursuit of nuclear power and refusal to sign the NPT. The regimes were built to keep India out. For thirty-five years Congress had considered itself the guardian of non-proliferation.

The Bush administration was now asking Congress to do a 180-degree turn and change its attitude and voting behaviour on the nuclear issue, with the purpose of creating an ally and improving relations with India. The approval process through Congress and the Indian parliament would prove to be long and acrimonious. Ambassador Sen remembers Senator Lugar, chairman of the Foreign Relations Committee, was livid that he had been bypassed on a major initiative and described Congress as being 'shell-shocked'.

Condoleezza Rice and her deputy, Nick Burns, poured their energy into canvassing congressmen to support the administration's position on nuclear cooperation with India. Knowing the passage of the bill would not be easy, they encouraged the US–India business council and Indian diaspora lobby groups to promote the agreement. They also asked Indian officials, who were somewhat new to the Washington lobbying machine, to put their weight behind the process. The two negotiating teams worked together to promote the deal, helping each other with their respective governments. Again, this was both extraordinary and unprecedented in the history of US–India relations.

Indian government officials met with as many US lawmakers as possible and they began to understand—perhaps for the first time—the importance of lobbying in Washington. Saran said he had never before visited so many members of Congress. Sen met forty-nine senators, including all ranking members of important committees such as those on finance and armed services. He said he met over 250 congressmen, many in their own constituencies.

The first hearings were held in front of the Senate Foreign Relations Committee on 2 November 2005. Rice testified before the House and the Senate, which was highly unusual for a secretary of state. Nick (Burns) spent many hours explaining to sceptical senators and representatives why amending US law to permit civilian nuclear trade with India made sense. One argument that gained traction particularly with Democrats was its environmental friendliness. 'Questions remained on how aligned India would be with us, how significant the costs of the India exception would be to nuclear diplomacy and the broader nuclear non-proliferation regime, and whether the economic benefit for the American nuclear industry would ever live up to the hype.'[9]

Critics of the deal were nicknamed the 'nuclear ayatollahs', as their zeal to protect existing structures blinded them to the new realities of a changing world and the potential for expanded alliances and developing new assets.[10] Congressman Henry Hyde, chairman of the House International Relations Committee, had to be persuaded and his meeting with Saran was hardly encouraging. Senators Tom Lantos, Joe Biden and Barack Obama were all highly critical of the Bill. According to Shivshankar Menon, 'It was a big swallow for Lantos, but Lugar was also critical and needed a lot of persuading. Obama would lecture us on non-proliferation whenever we saw him.'[11]

The winds had begun to shift towards India on the Hill. The US was mired in two wars and the success of the war in Afghanistan had increasingly put the US at the mercy of Pakistani cooperation. It had increasingly begun to think of Pakistan as a 'frenemy', never quite sure if it was helping the US or the Taliban. Having India as a reliable ally was looking increasingly attractive, and it didn't hurt that India was considered an 'emerging market' and of interest to US businesses.

The Indian diaspora, which had recently emerged as a wealthy and dynamic force in American society, played a critical role in pulling the nuclear deal over the finish line in Congress. Within one generation the Indian community in the US had become the highest per capita income group by ethnicity. Persons of Indian descent had risen to head several Fortune 500 companies and were doctors, educators and Silicon Valley entrepreneurs. They had also become politically active. They were deeply committed to the US improving relations with India and lobbied hard knowing Congress was always receptive to its constituents and donors.

Ronen Sen invited several of them to dinner at the embassy in Washington and explained the importance of what was at stake in the passage of the nuclear deal. He asked for their help, urging them to make sure that whatever they did was transparent: 'If it's not good for the US, don't do it. I'm not going to ask you to do something that's just good for India. It has to serve the interests of both countries.'[12]

The Indian Americans listened, then fanned out. Swadesh Bose was elected to coordinate their efforts. He had been politically active for several years and understood how Congress worked. Ambassador Sen proudly recalls that it was the largest-ever mobilization of the Indian American community to date. The response from the diaspora was overwhelming. Some held fundraisers for reluctant lawmakers; others wrote substantial cheques, took out advertisements in major newspapers and contacted affiliated organizations to support them. They reached out to Jewish and African American organizations. They even found ways to get help from the Israeli prime minister.[13] Ambassador Richard Verma, who worked in the Senate majority leader's office at the time, remembers them as a great force: 'The nuclear deal would not have happened without their help.'

The embassy reached out to corporations. 'While I was ambassador, India was growing at 8.7 per cent. Corporations were very interested in India and looking for long-term partnerships. It was a democracy and had the rule of law—both important to investors. CEOs like Jeff Immelt of GE were very helpful and made calls. Bilateral trade was growing and US exports to India had almost trebled in my time, so people were helpful.'[14]

By December 2006, the combined efforts of the White House, Rice, Hadley and the Indians paid off and Congress passed the Hyde Act on December 6, permitting civil nuclear cooperation with India and giving it a waiver on Sector 123. President Bush signed it on 18 December 2006.

## Finding a Consensus: The 123 Agreement

In mid-2006, Saran termed out and was replaced as foreign secretary by Shivshankar Menon, another seasoned diplomat. Saran, who had guided the nuclear deal through some of its most difficult stages, was asked to stay on as special envoy to see it through. The two diplomats got on well and had known each other a long time. Menon brought a soothing personality that took the edge off many contentious negotiations, and he was liked and respected by Condoleezza Rice, her deputy Bill Burns and his US counterparts. Menon had spent four years in Vienna as part of the Indian delegation to the IAEA. His experience and contacts would come in useful as India negotiated the next phase of the deal—international approvals. He had also worked in Bombay with the Indian atomic energy people. 'I knew everyone involved and it helped enormously.'

It would take almost eight months after the passage of the Hyde Act that the various clauses in the 123 Agreement would be acceptable to all parties. This would lay down much of the eventual bilateral agreement to be submitted to Congress after the international approvals were obtained. Menon admiringly talks about the 123 Agreement as 'a unique document. You could not solve one side's problems without addressing the other side's objections. That is why it is such a creative document. The Hyde Act included some objectionable items such as forbidding India to support Iran, and although we knew they were not actionable, it created a stir in Parliament.'

The Indian team would have long arduous debates, and the discussions were never easy. Jaishankar explained that they were all worried for different reasons. 'The MEA was a diplomatic institution and naturally looked for opportunities to negotiate, whereas the atomic energy agency was the custodian of India's security capabilities and had military assets to protect.'[15] Menon worried that the excessive transparency was draining the patience of their US counterparts, who sometimes found the Indian way of conducting talks confusing.

Jaishankar recalls that the US also disagreed among themselves, with arguments between the non-proliferation hawks in the bureaucracy and the White House which wanted to move ahead. Everyone approached the deal from their own institutional perspective.[16]

The challenge faced by the Indian team was to accommodate the Hyde Act and reconcile it with India's requirements. 'We had defined the end but weren't sure how to get there, so building trust between the negotiators and forming good relationships was critical to its success.'[17]

Although they had a text by February 2007, that is, two months after the Hyde Act was passed and signed by President Bush, it was only finalized and initialled on 27 July 2007. The first stage of the nuclear deal was finally agreed on. It had taken sixteen months and eight meetings in several countries to complete.

With the bilateral deal finally in place and the 123 Agreement approved, the hard work of the negotiators was paying off and there was a sense of real accomplishment. The US and Indian teams were now ready to proceed to the next stage: obtaining international approvals before bringing it back to Congress for final legislation. It was a high point in Indo-US relations.

## Controversy in India

In the US the restraints in the nuclear deal had been viewed as too weak, but in India they were viewed as too strong. The US team had contacted key members of the Indian parliament and tried to 'sell' the benefits of the deal. Both sides held joint press conferences and made sure they projected a unified message.

When the initial framework had been announced by Prime Minister Singh in Parliament in 2005, few people thought much would come of it. The response was tepid. After the separation agreement was announced in March 2006, people in India began to pay closer attention—it looked like nuclear cooperation with the US could actually happen.

In his presentation to Parliament in August 2006, Singh listed twelve criteria by which the deal should be judged, which addressed all of India's concerns. The nuclear deal was proving popular in India. According to Jaishankar, the prime minister made his decision to go ahead with the deal in 2005 because of the enormous support he had from the people. Menon, who was following it closely, confirmed that approval ratings for the deal were consistently polling at 90 per cent. Public opinion not only agreed with the government's decision, it was in favour of improving relations with the US. The problem lay with the politicians.

Once the Hyde Act was passed, the Indian opposition raised objections to various conditions in it, framing it as a departure from India's policy of non-alignment and independence. The prime minister patiently addressed the objections and tried to convince critics to watch 'what we do rather than worrying about the act'.

The operational part of the act had three very important and permanent entitlements that were given to India. This made the deal invaluable and urgent for India. Those entitlements were:

1. Under US law any country that had carried out a nuclear test was banned from nuclear cooperation. India was granted a permanent waiver.
2. In order to receive civil nuclear cooperation, a country could not have an active programme to manufacture nuclear explosive devices. India was given a permanent waiver.

3. A country receiving nuclear cooperation had to put all its facilities under full-scope safeguards. India's military facilities were excluded in a special waiver.[18]

'India got permanent waivers with no ifs or buts, so it was worth every bit of the deal. In three key respects we got what we wanted. There may have been small things we did not like, but we got all the big things.'[19]

Although the 123 Agreement was ironed out after the Hyde Act, and a text was finalized in July 2007, Singh was not in a position to present it to Parliament for approval just yet. As details of the text were revealed, the domestic political situation deteriorated. The BJP opposition was determined to sabotage the deal. Having started the process, they were angry and upset that the Congress party and Prime Minister Singh were going to get all the credit for this historic achievement. This was despite the fact that the deal was universally popular. The Congress was in power with the help of a coalition. The communist party was vehemently against cooperation with the US and threatened to pull its support and bring down the government.

Members of the government claim that Manmohan Singh reached out to the opposition and gave them credit for initiating the process with the US, saying that he had merely built on what they had begun. According to a WikiLeaks cable, the BJP told Ambassador Mulford that they liked the deal and should have no cause for concern, but that they had to play politics. Ashley Tellis did not think the government had acknowledged the BJP's contribution adequately. 'There was no acknowledgement of the role Vajpayee played and that's when the BJP became obstructionist. Congress did not appreciate how much goodwill the BJP government had built up with the Bush administration. They somehow thought this deal was conjured up between Bush and Singh, which is simply not true.'[20]

In October 2007, Manmohan Singh called Bush to inform him the agreement had to be held in abeyance for now. Washington was watching the political setback in New Delhi with growing alarm. The beleaguered negotiators on both sides were distraught that three years of hard work was being destroyed by domestic political jockeying. The US was silent and refrained from public statements, hoping the crisis in Delhi would blow over. At the *Hindustan Times* conclave in October, Sonia Gandhi announced in public that there was no rush to do the deal, which was as good as putting it on ice.

Menon felt that if the government of India was not planning to proceed with the deal after all the investment, they owed it to the Americans to tell them. He argued that both President Bush and Prime Minister Singh's prestige was on the line, and leaving things hanging could lead to misunderstandings. Cognisant that Tarapur had poisoned relations, he believed India should make every effort to avoid adding to that legacy. Singh, as always, listened carefully, and then told everyone not to give up. He said it was their obligation to try to manage the politics and to give him time to get it done.

As 2008 rolled in, both sides were increasingly anxious. The US was in full election mode, and the Indians were aware that the two frontrunners, McCain and Obama, were unlikely to support the deal. 'India had a truly remarkable friend in Bush. He was doing this deal because he said it was the right thing to do. He said it had nothing to do with pay-off or contracts and made that evident to us. It was the biggest move in Indo-US relations. He, with Condi's help, transformed it.'[21] Time was running out; 2008 was Bush's last year in office. After 2006, the Republicans had lost the Senate, and Bush would have to put all his political heft behind the deal to conclude it in the new Congress. The White House kept sending messages to New Delhi to be conscious of the US political deadlines, as multilateral approvals still had to be obtained before it was brought back to the Hill and signed into law.

The Bush administration was greatly diminished by 2008. The wars in Iraq and Afghanistan had dragged on and achieved little. His European allies were disenchanted with his wars. The premise of going to war in Iraq had been undermined by a lack of verifiable evidence of the existence of weapons of mass destruction. Bush's popularity had plummeted, and the economy was in trouble. The entire banking system was on the verge of collapse and Republicans running for re-election were distancing themselves from Bush. India, where he had staked so much, was gridlocked.

On 7 July 2008, the Indian embassy in Kabul was bombed. The US not only condemned the attack but shared intelligence with India and supported its accusation that Pakistan's ISI was behind the bombing. The US was proving to be an ally of India in the 'terror war', its sympathy and cooperation draining the opposition's anti-US stand on the nuclear deal.

It had been almost a year since the US Congress had passed the India exemption and the opposition in India had tried to use the agreement to bring down the government. A delegation, including John Kerry and Joe Biden, arrived in India and warned Singh that time was running out: 'If you think a post-Bush administration headed by either McCain or Obama will conclude this deal, you are mistaken, because everyone in the US hates this deal.'[22] They warned that if it did not get cleared during the Bush term is was a dead deal. It was a wake-up call for Singh, who went to Sonia Gandhi in June 2008 and offered to resign. He is reported to have told her that if he could not proceed with the nuclear deal, he should not be prime minister.

In the end, with just one legislative session left in the US Congress, Prime Minister Singh decided to stake his government and put his job on the line to get the deal done. The communist party had pulled their support from the coalition, so he had scrambled to work out the politics and get the support of the Samajwadi Party. Once he had that in place, he requested a no-confidence vote in Parliament. His view was that if his word as prime minister did not count for anything, he could not function effectively. The vote took place on 22 July 2008. Singh won and that night the team, led by Menon, rushed to Vienna to get the international approvals for the nuclear deal and get it through to the finish line in the US Congress.

## Multilateral Negotiations

India had already negotiated various safeguards with the IAEA and was on good terms with its chairman, Mohamed ElBaradei. The IAEA approval came within two weeks, on 1 August 2008 (by May 2009, it was enforceable). By the time the IAEA had signed the agreement, there was just a month left before Bush finished his last legislative session and a new president was announced. The last component of the nuclear deal was for the NSG to sign off on it and give India a waiver of its normal requirements of full-scope safeguards. Once this was complete, it would all come back to the US Congress to be passed into law.

Saran and Menon travelled to several capitals and tried to persuade governments and foreign ministers to support their application. They had a monumental task before them. Forty-eight countries had to agree to an India-specific waiver. Saran recalls it being a daunting task. He visited twenty NSG member countries to try to win their consent.[23] Although the US was not part of the negotiating team any more, it acted as a proxy for India and went out of its way, working behind the scenes, to ensure its safe passage. Having worked for so many years on the bilateral agreements, Bush, Rice, Hadley and Burns had a lot riding on its success.

Despite all the permutations, negotiations and agreements, when the two sides arrived at the NSG for final approval, there were differences and somewhat different recollections of events. According to the US side, when the Indian team arrived in Vienna, they came armed with a document that the US quickly saw was unacceptable and would not go over well with the NSG. At first, the US team set about trying to rework the documents, but Steve Hadley decided to do what the Indians wanted and make them happy because 'that's the reason we are doing this deal'.

The Indians remember it differently. 'India had agreed with the US that the clearance would be clean, with no conditions, and it would be an India-specific exception. But the ayatollahs of non-proliferation started to raise objections; we told them they could not start changing the terms now and putting conditions on. When we got a whiff of this, we told them there was a problem. People in India will feel you don't keep your word.'[24] By 6 September 2008, they reconciled their differences.

The NSG remained the most difficult to get approval from and the Bush administration pulled out all the stops to obtain it now that they were on the same page.

In New Delhi, the US ambassador invited the unpersuaded countries' representatives to lunch to try to convince them to vote yes, while Secretary Rice was on the phone with their ministers at home.

Bill Burns, who had taken over from Nick Burns and was now in the thick of the NSG negotiations, was concerned that the Indians needed to be more flexible to see the last part of the process through but that they were constrained by domestic politics from making the necessary accommodations. Burns was asked to lead the US delegation to the NSG board meeting in Vienna, to signal how seriously the US was taking this. In the end, Burns said persuasion and elegant diplomacy was set aside when he asked member countries to vote for India. 'This was about power, and we were exercising it ... I had to wake up senior Swiss and Irish officials in their capitals at four in the morning for a final yes. I argued our case but didn't belabour it. The point was simply that we needed this vote and were calling in a chit.'[25]

Menon, after briefing board members, flew to China, where he was told that though they did not approve of the deal, they would not be the only holdout. The others were Australia, Ireland and New Zealand.

On 5 September 2008, India's foreign minister, Pranab Mukherjee agreed to put a voluntary unilateral testing moratorium on record, removing a major hurdle for the NSG. Menon admiringly recalls, 'Everyone was squeezed for time, but what the Americans accomplished was an amazing feat. I watched the US display her diplomatic power.'[26]

John Rood, the US representative to the NSG, called Hadley from Vienna to say they had all the votes except China. The board members had been sequestered in a room; Rood locked the door and would not let anyone go home until all the votes were in and they had agreed. The White House put pressure on China to sign off. China, sensing it was isolated in its disapproval, gave in. They were there till 11.30 p.m. on Friday, 5 September 2008, until the votes were committed. Then, the next morning, the NSG signed the approval papers.

The White House rushed it through Congress, with just weeks before its final legislative session ended and a new president was elected in November. On 27 September 2008, the legislation was passed by the US Congress and President Bush signed it into law.

A month before Barack Obama was elected president, at a jubilant State Department ceremony on 8 October 2008, the administration breathed a sigh of relief as they celebrated one of George W. Bush's most remarkable achievements: a historic nuclear deal with India inaugurating an alliance that permanently shifted the relationship.

Prime Minister Singh hosted a dinner for 700 Indian Americans in New York in September, when he came for the UN General Assembly meetings. He thanked them for their help in the passage of the nuclear deal through Congress. It was a moving occasion for the people present, many of whom had been born in India, to be recognized and appreciated by the gracious prime minister.

On 26 November 2008, just two weeks after Barack Obama won the nomination to be the next president, a series of terrorist attacks carried out by Lashkar-e-Taiba terrorized the residents of Mumbai over four days. In the end, 166 people died including nine terrorists, who hit high-profile targets like the five-star Taj Hotel, a Jewish centre and a well-known crowded café frequented by tourists and journalists. The FBI and other US intelligence agencies asked to come to India and assist in the investigation. According to Indian officials, in the past such a request would have been turned down, but the goodwill and trust generated between the countries was such that they were now welcomed. Intelligence and counterterrorism experts set up channels of communication and alliances replaced suspicions.

President Bush was leaving the White House with his legacy in ashes. The ill-conceived and poorly executed wars in Afghanistan and Iraq had damaged US prestige. The banking system was in free fall and the economy had tumbled. But for one brief shining moment, he could savour a significant foreign policy success that no previous president had managed to achieve. The strategic partnership with India was as transformational for India as Nixon's opening to China. In the US, it got lost in the avalanche of criticism that surrounded the departing Bush administration, but it permanently shifted the US–India relationship. In India, George W. Bush was considered a man of integrity and a true friend of India—a president you could count on.

# Chapter 21

# Obama and India: Deepening Ties

B ARACK HUSSEIN OBAMA, THE FRESHMAN SENATOR FROM ILLINOIS with the thousand-watt smile, swept past Hillary Clinton to become the Democratic nominee for president in the 2008 US presidential election.

Hillary Clinton, a former first lady, was well known, highly vetted and expected to win easily. But people wanted something new and the electorate found Obama's message of hope and change inspiring. After fifteen years in Washington, the Clintons represented the establishment.

Eight years of Bush, two endless wars with no end in sight and a failing economy had worn people out. Obama promised to end America's involvement in the Middle East. Unlike Bush, he did not come from wealth and privilege, and unlike the Clintons, he carried no political baggage. He was a gifted orator, and his youth and energy were contagious. Thousands turned out to hear him speak wherever he went.

Obama came across as intelligent and sincere. He had worked his way up, which appealed to the working class. His autobiography, *Dreams from My Father,* revealed a vulnerability that people could relate to. The story of being raised by a single mother, abandoned by his father and learning how to cope as a biracial child growing up in the different cultures his mother exposed him to only added to his allure. He was the kid that could have gone off the tracks but chose the right path. He was the example every parent wanted for their child, white or black. He embodied the American dream.

Obama won against McCain in a landslide. He carried 365 electoral votes to McCain's 173. He won states that had not voted for Democrats before.

Obama inherited a Democrat majority in Congress when he became president. Aware that, historically, presidents usually lost their majority in the mid-term elections, he came fully prepared to push through his most important goals immediately.

His first and most pressing problem was the banking crisis. He had to hit the ground running, putting several fires out at once. Simultaneously, he chose to fix the US healthcare system. Obamacare was big, bold and something that would define his legacy. His campaign promises to end the wars in Iraq and Afghanistan and close Guantanamo* proved more difficult to achieve.

The reaction in Delhi to Obama's election was one of cautious observation. The Democrats had traditionally been supportive of India during the sixties and seventies when it needed foreign aid, and Clinton had shown an interest in India as an emerging economic power. He had also supported India during the Kargil conflict with Pakistan.

But all this had paled in comparison to what Bush, a Republican, had done for India. Bush had used his presidential powers to recognize India as a nuclear power, brought it out of its pariah status, and made it a strategic military partner. The Democrats, on the other hand, had historically penalized India for developing a nuclear programme.

Not only was there anxiety about Obama's commitment to the newly established Indo-US strategic partnership, there was some concern that his priorities on climate change and Afghanistan were not aligned with India's. New Delhi was somewhat relieved at his choice of Hillary Clinton as secretary of state for the continuity it promised.

## New Directions in Foreign Policy

The election had been contentious and the race against Hillary Clinton had been close. As the president, Obama wanted to bring the Democratic Party together and the choice of Clinton to be his secretary of state was

---

\* The detention camp in Guantanamo Bay, Cuba, is held by the US military. There have been multiple reports of indefinite detention without trial and torture of captives, leading to gross human rights violations.

seen as a peace offering. She was highly respected as a senator and well known by world leaders. She was the third woman to occupy the office. The first, Madeleine Albright, had been appointed by Bill Clinton; she was followed by Condoleezza Rice, a George W. Bush appointee.

President Obama's first State of the Union address, and subsequent talks by Hillary, contained some of his campaign pledges to end the quagmire in Iraq and Afghanistan and focus on climate change and the Indo-Pacific region. Europe was absent from the conversation, and it became increasingly apparent that NATO and the Europeans, once the most important partnership for the US, were now of secondary importance. The Europeans were troubled by the developments, but there was little they could do. The shift had begun under the Bush administration, but it seemed more incontrovertible under Obama.

Obama and Singh first met in London at the G-20 meeting, in early April 2009. It was the second meeting of the group and the countries collectively made a series of decisions to prevent the global economy from collapsing. Protesters had lined the streets outside the building where the meetings were being held; inside, Italy's Silvio Berlusconi caused a stir when he tried to get Obama's attention by shouting too loudly and had to be reprimanded by the Queen.

Obama and Singh liked each other at once. Menon said: 'Their chemistry was really good whenever I saw them talking to each other. They were both intellectuals and they really respected each other. Manmohan Singh found in him someone he could talk to at his own level. That's not common among alpha males in the political class.'[1] After the meeting, Obama mentioned an interest in visiting India and it filtered back to the administration, which made it easier for communication between the officials of both countries. According to Menon, 'The strength of the US are her institutions; even though it looks like everyone is changing when a new administration changes, there is an institutional memory and an establishment that is ultimately stable. Thanks to people like Bill Burns, there was continuity. Our bilateral cooperation was bipartisan, but it helps enormously when the president indicates an interest.'[2]

But as time went on, Indian officials noted the difference between Bush, whose commitment to India won their trust and admiration, and Obama, who seemed less focused on India. When Obama made a speech in Japan about the rising powers in Asia, in mid-November 2009, he insulted the Indians by not mentioning India.

According to a senior State Department official during Obama's first term, India was a low priority for the administration. 'There were senior, substantial people, good people, on most countries they considered important. Dennis Ross was doing the Middle East, General Lute and Holbrook were representing Pakistan and Afghanistan, Jeff Bader was overseeing Asia and Mike McFaul was the Russia hand. There was no one of equivalent stature on India. No senior official had been assigned to India. I believe the omission was deliberate. They did not want a serious India voice in policy discussions. There was no one who had the stature of an Ashley Tellis. General Petraeus had no mandate on India. He did not go to Delhi for consultations, and because of the way the bureaucracy at the Pentagon was divided, India came under the Pacific command.'[3]

When Nixon and Kissinger opened the gateway to China and brought them into the mainstream, they did not anticipate it would become a global economic power within two decades, threatening US manufacturing and becoming a major creditor of the US. By the time George W. Bush became president, China, in addition to establishing itself as a global economic power, had begun to invest heavily in its military.

Obama recognized that China was an important stakeholder in the international system, and investing in the Indo-Pacific relationship became a priority for him. He decided to visit China during his first year as president in late November 2009. The US delegation prepared a joint statement in advance, recognizing a convergence in their shared areas of interest. It laid the foundation of a G-2 with China as an ascending power, cooperating with the US on the global stage. It was a powerful and positive document that treated China as an equal.

India found sections of the document objectionable. According to Shyam Saran, 'There was a paragraph in the joint statement saying that the US and China pledge to work together to ensure there is stability and security in South Asia. We got very, very angry and upset about that—if we're your strategic partners, then why are you working with the Chinese on South Asian interests? To us, it sounded like collusion. This whole new concept of a G-2 was a completely new world order being presented to us, dominated by the two countries.'⁴ According to US officials, India misunderstood the reason for its inclusion.

In 2009, Obama was still preoccupied with getting the war in Afghanistan under control and managing Pakistan. Knowing that China could exert a great deal of pressure on Pakistan, the US hoped to enlist its help in restraining Pakistani support of terrorist activities and tolerance of terrorist groups from operating from within its borders.

Obama was focused on China and may not have seen the final draft of the China statement until it was too late. The contrast with Bush, under whose administration the directive to make India a priority came directly from the Oval Office, could not have been starker. Bill Burns thinks that some of these incidents 'initially unnerved the Indian leadership. Fresh from their partnership with Bush, Singh and his chief advisors were worried that Obama was less enthusiastic.'⁵

Some of these early oversights could be attributed to the inexperience of the incoming administration, which had to get used to coordinating its positions with various departments before rolling out a speech or position paper. The China statement was likely drawn up by the China experts who neglected to run it past the South Asia hands at the State Department or at the White House.

Obama had overestimated his diplomatic skills in handling China. His trip was far from a success. Helen Cooper wrote in the *New York Times* that 'China effectively stage-managed President Obama's public appearances, got him to make statements endorsing Chinese positions of political importance to them, and effectively squelched discussions of contentious issues such as human rights and China's currency policy'.⁶ The Chinese found they could stand up to the Americans and not bend to their will.

The US was also disappointed that China took a hands-off approach towards Pakistan. Although the US officials maintained the trip was a success, Obama realized he had been played. India believed that after his disappointment with China, Obama reverted to the pro-India policies of Bush, hoping that India would be a useful counterbalance to the growing power of China in Asia.

His earlier reservations† about the nuclear deal were put aside, and the White House decided they needed to maintain strong ties with India. To signal India was a priority. The state dinner for the Indian prime minister that took place in November 2009 was elevated into a grand affair, with a big banquet and a star-studded guest list. Many of the one-on-one meetings between Obama and Singh centred around the rise of China. Obama also committed to visit India the following year.

The decision by the White House to host the Indian prime minister was to assuage the bad feelings that had resulted from the president's trip to China. The Indians interpreted it as a sort of consolation prize for the president's 'excessive' overture to China. Not only had Obama dented relations with India, his visit to China had not gone well.

Manmohan Singh's visit to the White House was a success, except for a bizarre breach in security when a couple gatecrashed the state dinner.

Nisha Biswal, who became assistant secretary of state for South and Central Asia in 2013, recalls that there was already a strong team on East Asia, including China, Japan and Korea, but not one in place on India during Obama's first term. She explained:

> Frankly, there wasn't early on a real sense of what the India opportunity was, until they had the series of engagements. And even then, when I came in, I was brought in because we had not achieved what we thought was possible on the India–US relationship. There was a recognition by the end of the first term we were not where we needed to be on US–India ties. That while the relationship with India was stable, it wasn't really ascending. You had the two visits, but when I came in 2013 it had not translated into any ambitious agenda. Contentious issues such as the WTO negotiations and if India would support the second round dominated the relations.[7]

With the Obama administration, it sometimes felt as though they were catching up from behind when it came to the relationship.

---

† When he was a senator.

## Climate Change and Engaging India

The Democrats had been appalled by the rapid pace of climate change and had been waiting to do something significant to stop further deterioration in this area.

A major summit on climate change was scheduled to take place in Copenhagen, in mid-December 2009, where the leaders of all the major countries and their ministers and delegations would meet to debate the future of the planet. It appeared to be an ideal forum for Obama to follow up on his campaign promise to help reverse global warming and display his leadership skills. With just enough votes to pass legislation, he saw an opportunity to accomplish a key goal.

The West, which had been the leading polluter for years and had contributed vastly to climate change, now wanted to pull the ladder up behind it. The developing countries were trying to catch up and argued that they needed more time to build their economies. The contention lay in the amounts of pollution controls and the timeline that they were willing to accept.

India, with its rapidly developing economy, had resisted pressure from the West to accede to controls. Saran explained: 'Prior to the Copenhagen Summit, we were seen as the bad boys. We were viewed as climate deniers and standing in the way of any agreements. The Chinese may have been bigger polluters, but they were seen to be doing something about it and taking a leadership role. Despite the Chinese being critical of the West and their climate policies, they were treated with deference and as a positive partner.'[8]

The Indians observed that after Obama's disastrous trip to China, the US attitude towards them changed. 'China, which was the toast of the multilateral negotiations leading up to Copenhagen, was now the villain,' according to Saran. 'When it came to financing, there was nothing earmarked for China; when it came to technology, again, there was nothing for China.'[9] As antipathy towards India receded into the background, it saw an opportunity to promote itself at China's expense at the conference. And Jairam Ramesh, India's representative, did just that.

The Chinese discovered they were being isolated at the conference and reached out to India. They suggested they work together to come up with a joint position. China, having miscalculated its earlier steps with the US president, now needed allies, and tried to woo India for the first time. The Chinese requested a meeting with Singh. Initially, Manmohan Singh refused as he was at the conference for a limited time; but the Chinese insisted, so he agreed to an early morning meeting.

The two countries had only recently sparred over minor border incidents involving the Dalai Lama and the prime minister's visit to the border area. Although Nehru had been a champion of China after Independence, relations between India and China had never been good since the 1962 war. India had been dismayed at the way Nixon and the US had cultivated China since the seventies. They had watched as China had grown into an economic force in the world and become an increasingly powerful military presence in Asia.

Here was China now, for the first time since the fifties, needing India's help internationally.

The Chinese went out of their way to flatter the Indians, telling them that India was the most important country in South Asia. They even tried to convince them that the irksome paragraph in the joint statement, which had so angered the Indians during Obama's China visit, was an American insertion and not their doing.[10] Saran said: '[Premier] Wen Jiabao said to our PM, "I know our Indian friends are not very happy about this formulation in the joint statement. Let me tell you that it was put in by the Americans. We recognize India is the lead country in South Asia." After the meeting, everything changed.'[11]

India and China, along with Brazil and South Africa, formed a group called BASIC. They held similar views on emissions and pollution controls. They were not alone—other emerging economies were also trying to catch up to the West and resented having rules imposed on them. The leaders of the BASIC countries convened at China's request at 6 p.m. China and India had agreed they would coordinate their positions prior to the summit, which was to take place the following day. Some of the issues at stake were a 30 per cent cut in emissions by 2030 and financing mechanisms.

There were extensive debates on the extent that any agreement should be legally binding.

The Chinese premier had told everyone that President Obama was coming at 7 p.m. to meet with him. Instead, before the BASIC countries had finished their meeting or arrived at a joint position, Obama surprised them with an earlier than expected arrival.

According to press reports, the Americans were unaware that the BASIC heads of state were meeting 'behind their back'. Earlier that day, the president had met with the Chinese, and the meeting had not gone well. The Chinese premier had not attended a subsequent gathering of world leaders.

The US had been keeping track of all the disparate factions, world leaders and interest groups at the conference, to try to forge a consensus on climate control. Considerable political horse-trading had taken place on the margins of the formal meetings, which had turned the conference into a highly political event. When Obama heard that the Chinese premier was holding a separate meeting with like-minded countries prior to his 7 o'clock appointment, he decided to surprise him by arriving early. 'But just before he entered the room, he was told that the other three leaders were there too. "Good," he told his aides and strode in with the words "Are you ready for me?" The Americans were particularly taken aback by the presence of Manmohan, the Indian premier, as they were told he had already headed to the airport.'[12]

Saran, who was present at the meeting, said the BASIC countries had not arrived at any consensus among themselves. There just had not been enough time before Obama walked in and proceeded to take control of the meeting. He tried to formulate an agreement, which he then tried to sell to the Europeans.

The general perception was that Obama wanted an agreement even if it was weak and ineffective. He had taken a leadership role at Copenhagen and did not want to leave empty-handed. The Europeans were furious and felt he had sold them down the river. They were the only bloc that had a good track record, as they had taken a lot of steps to reduce climate change. Obama threw out many of their requirements when he made the deal in the room with the Chinese.

The US head of Greenpeace said Obama would be known as 'the man who killed Copenhagen'. Climate change advocates felt he had compromised his plans to control global warming and squandered a golden opportunity to make significant changes to improve conditions for the world. He had scored political points as a leader who could forge agreements, but the price he paid was the health of the planet. He had disappointed his progressive base and the agreement was viewed as devoid of value by the liberals who had supported him.

## Counterterrorism

The September 11 attacks were such a watershed moment in US history that they would reorient the country's foreign policy for decades. Every president since has been obsessed with keeping America safe from terrorists. President Obama had promised to end the war in Iraq, focus efforts to locate Osama Bin Laden and find a solution to the terror networks in Afghanistan. He was aware that his presidency could not sustain an attack like Bush did with 9/11. In May 2010, a Pakistani American man unsuccessfully tried to detonate a truck bomb in Times Square. Obama knew that his presidency would have been over had it succeeded.

By the time Obama became president, the Musharraf myth had been cracked open. He played the liberal Muslim card but there was no doubt that Pakistan had played a double game with the US. Musharraf had promoted the theory that there were rogue elements within Pakistan and the ISI had attacked the Indian embassy in Kabul and US assets, but the administration had become cynical about his explanations. There was a great deal of frustration with Pakistan.

The US military had become disillusioned in the partnership as many of its troops were continually attacked in Afghanistan, and the Americans suspected Pakistan's hand in this. There were a lot of bureaucratic arguments within the US about Pakistan and its duplicity, but Obama was clear he was not going to war with Pakistan over Afghanistan. Obama knew Pakistan better than any US president. He had travelled there as a student, was well informed about Islam and the Middle East and was under no illusion that he had a difficult task. 'We were trying to work out what Pakistan's strategic calculus was. How do we get them to change? Can we make them strategic partners like India?'[13]

As the US began to rely less on Pakistan for counterterrorism and their partnership became ineffective, it enabled the government to pivot back to India. Towards the end of 2014, President Obama told Peter Lavoy, assistant secretary of defence, 'I seem to spend all my time and attention on Pakistan, but I see so much more upside and potential with our relationship with India. There is so much India can do internationally, and I'd like to be spending time on that relationship.'[14]

Lavoy took it as a deliberate directive from the president. He said that even though the administration had serious grievances with Pakistan, and did not want to throw it under the bus, the US decided to shift its focus away from Pakistan and became more India-centric. As Lavoy explained, their thinking was that 'India has the potential for doing global good and Pakistan, we hoped, could play a similar role. But it never lifted its head off to do that. It never showed any inclination or capacity for it, whereas India did, and it was very positive dealing with India.'[15]

Discovering Osama Bin Laden, in April 2011, living within minutes of Pakistan's military academy and a short distance from its army bases made the US lose all confidence in Pakistan as an ally. The US military now looked at India as a far more reliable and stable partner in the region. The long, complicated entanglement of the US–Pakistan–India triangulation, which had cast a shadow over the India–US relationship for half a century, was finally dislodged.

Pakistan did not want the US in Afghanistan creating a strong government there. They did not want to risk the CIA and US military wandering around in the region trying to locate Pakistan's nukes. Obama intensified the drone programme and handed it to the CIA. Vali Nasr, an Iranian American academic and member of the State Department, believed that 'deep down Obama was fairly cynical about Pakistan and the Arabs—he didn't think the Arab Spring would go anywhere. It came from knowledge and experience. He understood their shortcomings and was not naïve, as some in the administration, to think that Egypt would emerge as Poland had—as a democratic state.'[16]

## A Steady Partnership: Obama Visits India

With a degraded relationship with Pakistan and China flexing its muscles at the expense of the US, Clinton and Obama were open to extending the relationship with India at the level that Bush had placed it.

In November 2010, Obama visited India to highlight his commitment to the Indo-US partnership. While addressing the Indian parliament, Obama indicated for the first time that the US would support India as a permanent member of the Security Council.

The announcement was a major public relations coup in New Delhi and was applauded by the Indian press. Obama was hailed as progressive and a friend of India, but privately, he warned the prime minister that there were many obstacles to this becoming a reality. There was considerable opposition to expanding the permanent membership, and many other aspirants, such as Germany, resented Obama's endorsement of India. Susan Rice, the US ambassador to the UN, had also objected to the endorsement. She had pointed out that India had voted against the US on most issues at the UN and had strong reservations about supporting India. Obama never pursued the cause, nor did he put any presidential weight behind trying to persuade any UN members to vote for India, and the effort just died on the vine.

When he was a presidential candidate, Obama ignoring his own advice about learning the lessons that history teaches us. He publicly underlined that Kashmir was 'obviously a tar pit diplomatically' and spoke about the need to 'figure out a plausible approach',[17] setting off alarm bells in New Delhi. Outside interventions on Kashmir had been abandoned after the Kennedy era and left to be decided bilaterally. Indians were caught off guard by the resurrection of what they saw as US interference in a regional issue. It was considered particularly insensitive as it came on the heels of the Mumbai attacks. During the visit, Obama was able to soften his ill-conceived comments and retreat from his position on Kashmir that had irritated the Indians.

## Defence Cooperation Takes Off

Two areas that saw a genuine development in cooperation between India and the US were security and defence. A bilateral counterterrorism initiative was signed in July 2010. The two countries began a dialogue on security issues, and for the first time, regular communication channels were set up between India's Ministry of Home Affairs and the US Department of Homeland Security.

One of the signature events that took place was the designation of India as a major US defence partner in 2016. It gave India a unique status with the US that no one else in the world has. The European countries fall under the NATO umbrella, and the Pacific architecture is an alliance-based framework. The US has not entered into a mutual defence alliance for at least fifty years. It put India somewhere above a strategic partner but below a treaty ally. In order to ensure that the arrangement was durable and would survive multiple administrations, Obama passed it through Congress to institutionalize it and make it binding. It is now formally part of US legislation and allows US cooperation with India at the highest level. It removed the barriers to sensitive technology transfer between the two countries, such as fifth-generation fighter jets that India had wanted to acquire.

One of the most inspired appointments made during this time was assigning Deputy Secretary of Defense Ashton Carter to oversee the India–US defence relationship in 2012. He put energy and intellectual effort into the relationship to find solutions to issues that pushed the countries apart. He worked closely with Shivshankar Menon and members of India's defence establishment to set up India-specific protocols to streamline the process of procurement and sales.

Carter introduced proposals for the two countries to co-produce advanced defence systems. This won a lot of Indians over. Discussions to co-produce a maritime helicopter, a naval gun, a surface-to-air missile system and a scatterable anti-tank system were initiated. When Carter was appointed as secretary of defense a year later, it was welcome news in India.

Defence cooperation took off during this period; although it was a little slow during Obama's first term, as the process was being ironed out and suspicion on both sides being erased, by the second term it rose exponentially. 'By the end of Obama's first term, India was conducting more military exercises with the Unites States than any other country, and its acquisition of defence equipment had risen from a little over $200 million to $2 billion.'[18] Sales between 2008–20016 reached $14 billion.

The two countries still needed to close the gap between their systems, as their protocols and pipelines were different and they were not used to working with each other. When India would express interest in a particular technology, often by the time the various US departments were consulted the technology was no longer available, as procurement and licensing were time-sensitive. Carter established the Defense Trade and Technology Initiative (DTTI) to streamline the process for India. Nisha Biswal said, 'We identified some key areas to work on, but it did not progress as smoothly as hoped, as the protocols in both countries were complicated with tenders and aligning contracts. On the US side, technology transfers had a cumbersome process of clearances.'[19]

India remained hesitant to go as far as the US wanted in the relationship. The US was often more interested in conducting joint exercises, whereas India wanted to proceed carefully. There was strong support within the Indian military to engage with the US, but the political class had not shed its non-aligned posture. They worried they could come under attack for lining up too closely with the US. A.K. Anthony, India's minister of defence in 2014, refused to allow joint exercises in the Indian Ocean and insisted they be done in the Pacific. Petty domestic squabbles muddied the waters that were already difficult to negotiate.

Budgetary constraints were another factor. The formulas for importing equipment versus manufacturing it in India took time to work out. There was a strong movement to develop the defence ecosystem in India, and the US was amenable to helping it become a defence manufacturing hub and eventually an exporter of defence equipment, but India's internal financial limitations slowed the process down. This is where DTTI was helpful. 'The DTTI was really an effort to get beyond our history of mutual distrust. It provided a platform to bring people together. Army commanders, air force chiefs, naval commanders from both countries would sit together for the first time and facilitate communication and develop linkages. It was a concept, not a thing. It was meant to study, discuss and enable the process to get to the next level.'[20]

India wanted to ensure they got the latest technology and were on par with Pakistan, and the US needed assurances that firewalls would exist so that technology could not be transferred to third parties. 'We were changing a strategic doctrine that was decades in the making and the internal processes in both countries and dealing with significant concerns,' explained Nisha Biswal.[21] It took patience and diplomatic skill to bring the two countries into alignment.

India has now signed three out of the four foundational agreements and been accepted by the various international organizations that make it eligible for higher levels of technology. These include admission into all the nuclear groups.

## A Lull

The enthusiasm that President Obama felt towards India and Prime Minister Singh began to wane after Obama visited New Delhi in 2010. Although Singh was admired for his personal honesty and high ethical standards, he was accused of tolerating corruption within his administration and looking the other way. Concessions for coal mines had been given out at a pittance to private individuals and the press had taken the government to task. Any enthusiasm that Obama had felt for him was dampened by the reality that the Singh government, by 2011, was too weak to get any of the big things done. The only area that made any progress was defence, and that was largely running independently of the prime minister.

Nisha Biswal explained, 'The US has long approached the relationship with India from the perspective that we have a long way we want to go with India, and they accepted they would need to invest on the front end in building this relationship and putting more on the table. The Obama administration looked at India as "the long game". But when I came in, there was also a lot of frustration with the relationship. The question was being asked: Is this a strategic relationship? Is there a long game? Everyone saw there was potential, but we could not realize the potential. Burns said we needed a more creative approach to realize this potential.'

Obama's attention for the rest of 2011 and 2012 were given to domestic concerns as he headed into another election. He was re-elected in November 2012, but the Singh government was running into trouble. Inflation, sluggish economic growth and a string of corruption scandals had weakened the government. The Indian National Congress was feudal in structure, and its culture of nepotism and entitlement grated with a demographic where more than half of the population was under twenty-five and aspirational. They wanted change. With elections around the corner, Indians were also focused on domestic affairs in 2011 and 2012.

## Khobragade Crisis: A New Low

At 9.30 a.m. on a cold December day in Manhattan, a young thirty-nine-year-old Indian diplomat was arrested by US federal marshals as she was leaving her children's school after dropping them off.

Devyani Khobragade was handcuffed and taken to the US district court building downtown, where she was strip-searched and, according to her, subjected to the indignity of a cavity search. She was accused of one count of visa fraud and one count of lying on her visa application about the wages she paid her domestic worker.

Khobragade had brought a domestic worker from India a year ago and within seven months the worker ran away. Khobragade reported her as missing to the US authorities, with whom her lawyers had a contentious meeting a month later. Their issues remained unresolved prior to Khobragade's arrest. Khobragade and the Indian government claimed that she had diplomatic immunity and the case should be dismissed, but by then the press in both countries had turned it into a big story. The image of a mother being handcuffed in front of her children's school won her sympathy in India. Her treatment by the arresting officers, when she looked harmless, incensed women who felt the strip search was unduly aggressive. The Indian government demanded an apology from Washington.

There was no one on the India desk in Washington when the incident happened. Nisha Biswal was going through her confirmation process and there was no one at the NSC. Burns says, with some regret, that it fell through the cracks. Law enforcement had taken it into its own hands to pursue an offence, and there was no internal process to manage the interagency process to navigate a law enforcement investigation with a diplomatic crisis.

Biswal explained, 'Everything is siloed to protect the integrity of criminal investigations, so State Department was unable to interfere in a law enforcement operation. No one wanted it to unfold the way it did.'[22] At the Indian embassy, Ambassador Nirupama Rao had recently departed and the new ambassador, S. Jaishankar, had not arrived in Washington yet, so there was no senior person to manage the public relations fallout.

New Delhi decided to recall Khobragade to India, and she was flown out with the help of the State Department after her original indictment was dismissed. A new indictment was issued against her soon after, but she was by then safely in India.

Although the situation was salvaged, it was a costly lesson. There is no question that it set the relationship back. It also forced both countries to take a long hard look at what they wanted from the partnership. Looking back at the incident, Biswal was philosophical, 'When you are in danger of losing the relationship, you really look at it carefully. I credit Jaishankar, who said, "I did not come here to see the demise of the US–India relationship; we are going to clean this up." And I had the full backing of the US administration to resolve the problem. We were all looking for a way out.'[23]

India was in the throes of elections and anti-US sentiments were whipped up by the incident by those who were against the new closeness that had developed between the countries. The Congress party used this incident to prove they were being tough with the US and as a political issue all the way to the polls.

The Congress fell victim to its own inequitable system of political entitlement and favours dispensed by the Gandhi family. The Indian electorate was fed up with the corruption and arrogance of officials, who seemed indifferent to the growing income inequality in the country. They turned away from the Congress party, which was seen as elitist.

## The Modi Phenomenon

By late 2013, the BJP announced that Narendra Modi would be their candidate for prime minister. It was a highly unusual move and allowed Modi to run a presidential-style campaign, based on a person rather than a party. His rise within the BJP was by no means a given as he was an outlier within his party. His base of support came from extreme right-wing fringe elements like the Rashtriya Swayamsevak Sangh (RSS), the Hindu nationalist paramilitary organization devoted to making India a Hindu nation.[24]

Modi made his reputation as an effective chief minister of Gujarat. He was business-friendly at a time when India was moving towards economic reforms, and he decided to make his state a model for attracting businesses. His reputation took a beating in 2002, when communal riots broke out in his state and thousands of Muslims were killed and displaced. His government was blamed for allowing the targeting of Muslims and news reports alleged that the police and state officials colluded in the crimes that were committed. After that he became a pariah both nationally and internationally. A visa ban prevented him from travelling to the US and the elders in his party shunned him. After the BJP defeat at the polls in 2009, and Modi's rising popularity among the masses, the party revaluated its options.

Unlike the aristocratic Gandhis and the highly educated Manmohan Singh, Modi was a man of the people. He was the son of a local tea stall owner and had just a few years of school. He had grown up in the company of the RSS *pracharak* (key worker) community. For the first time, people saw in him a prime minister that came from their rank and file. He was charismatic and, like Obama, a great orator. He represented a change and a departure from nepotism and feudal favours. He came without the baggage of family and party obligations. He had left his wife years ago and had no children. He owed the BJP hierarchy nothing.

Eight months before the election, the elders of the BJP swallowed their reservations and invited him to be their candidate for prime minister. He campaigned on a platform of clean government. It appealed to the people, who were tired of the corruption associated with the ageing Congress party. Modi won a resounding victory, decimating the Congress for the foreseeable future. It was a new dawn in Indian politics.

## Obama and Modi

Washington had mixed reactions to the Indian election. The liberal elite was worried about the right-wing turn in Indian politics. Obama was practical. He called Modi to congratulate him and invited him to visit the White House. He recognized that the massive election victory gave Modi a mandate, which was an opportunity that should not be wasted. The president's eye was on the long game, and he recognized there was an opportunity to work on issues and advance US–India ties.

Modi was very interested in a good relationship with the US. When he was a young member of the RSS, he had visited the US and spent some time doing community outreach with the Indian diaspora. It was a formative experience, and he had been impressed by the US and saw it as a natural ally. As chief minister he had never criticized the US, unlike other politicians who thought that standing up to the US was a way of showing strength.

In late 2013, once the BJP had recruited Modi, the Europeans and Canadians reached out to him. Nancy Powell, the US ambassador to Delhi, also met with him. The State Department wanted to make sure that the US was bipartisan during the elections. Nisha Biswal was asked several times by reporters if the US would grant Modi a visa and her unequivocal response was, 'We have welcomed every Indian prime minister to the White House, and we will welcome the next one.' The message the US wished to convey was that they would respect the wishes of the Indian electorate.

Modi invited Xi Jinping as his first head of state to visit India in August 2014. It was an honour he hoped would be acknowledged. India laid out the red carpet for him. The theme of the visit was 'let's do business together'. Modi, who placed a high premium on his personal charm and relationships with world leaders, hoped the visit would put some of their differences aside. They had a photo opportunity on a swing together, which invited a great deal of commentary on the budding friendship. Instead, the Chinese embarrassed Modi with an incursion on the border, which took place at the same time as the visit and completely undermined Modi's first attempt at diplomacy as prime minister.

The following month, Modi visited Washington after the UN meeting in New York. Obama lavished attention on a grateful Modi. He took him in his car for a private tour of the Martin Luther King Jr Memorial. Vice President Biden hosted a lunch for him at the State Department, and in return, Modi invited President Obama to be India's honoured guest for the Republic Day celebrations.

President Obama was not oblivious to Modi's past and the growing concern that minorities were under threat in India. When he arrived in New Delhi for a state visit in January 2015, he gave a speech at Siri Fort Auditorium, where he recognized the Constitution and the principle of non-violence as values to cherish. He paid tribute to Martin Luther King, Jr and Gandhi and spoke at length about respecting women. At the end, he spoke with passion about embracing and protecting the rights of minorities, citing the example of his own family's background, and specifically appealed for tolerance towards religious minorities.

The visit was an emotional one. No US president had ever been invited to stand with an Indian prime minister in public on Republic Day. Prime ministers like Nehru and Mrs Gandhi were not inclined towards the US, and after them no one would have dared, as they would have been accused by the opposition of being too close to the US.

Modi could not have been more different from Manmohan Singh, but Obama warmed to him over time. He made an effort to meet with him on multiple occasions to try to advance the relationship and build trust. He had one unfinished task he wanted to complete before leaving office, and India was a critical player in accomplishing it.

## The Paris Climate Accord

The Copenhagen Accord had not satisfied anyone, but it laid some benchmarks for the Paris talks that were set to take place during the last week of November 2015. President Obama had wanted to make a significant contribution during his second term, which he would be remembered for, and put his energy into doing something about climate change.

China and India were critical for a strong Paris agreement, as they were the fastest-growing pollution emitters. The strategy was to get China and India to accept the same kinds of obligations on emissions as developed countries and not insist on being treated as developing countries. Obama's first job was to get China on board. Once it had agreed, India effectively became the swing vote. Obama wanted to prevent what had happened at Copenhagen with the Chinese and the Indians colluding to make their own deal without the knowledge of the US.

The quest for a climate agreement led Obama to intensify relations with Modi. He had multiple meetings with Modi during either state visits and on the margins of the G-20 and UN sessions. It became a priority for Obama, largely in order to get the Paris agreement done. Ambassador Richard Verma, who was present for some of the interactions between the two leaders, was categorical, 'If you ask Obama, he would say there would be no Paris Agreement without India's leadership. Once India came on, South Africa, Brazil, Saudi Arabia and a bunch of other countries signed on. They had been waiting to see which way the wind was blowing. It was a perfect representation of what's possible when India has a seat at the high table.'[25] Everyone had come a long way from Copenhagen. Rich Verma, the first Indian American to be sent as the US ambassador to India, spoke admiringly of how much give and take he observed in the relationship that evolved during the talks between the two leaders. 'They invested a lot of time on this. Obama would come out of the meetings saying India had a point and things needed to be more balanced, and Modi would emerge and concede on things, saying Obama had a point and India should not be an outlier and blow things up like they did in Copenhagen.'[26]

India agreed to reduce the emission intensity of its GDP by 33 to 35 per cent by 2030. India also pledged to try to derive 40 per cent of its electric power from renewable energy rather than fossil fuels by 2030. It stated that it would need financial help to achieve these targets. There were 197 countries that signed the agreement, which was then ratified by 187 countries. The US had agreed to cut its greenhouse gas emissions by 26 to 28 per cent by 2025, taking it to below 2005 levels. It also committed up to $3 billion in aid for poor countries by 2020, to help them while they met their targets. On 30 November 2015, the Paris talks concluded with an agreement signed by both China and India.

## Liberalism Fades

Modi met enthusiastic members of the Indian diaspora in Silicon Valley when he visited the US in 2015, and again, the next year, when he addressed Congress. He gave a speech in which he talked about 'going beyond the hesitations of history' and overcoming past differences. He emphasized his desire to forge an enduring partnership with the US. Pepsi, Google and Microsoft were all run by members of the Indian diaspora, who had been born in India. Modi was not shy about showing US officials the strength and following he had among prominent Indian Americans. It did not hurt that it also played well to his base at home. On an earlier visit to the US in 2014, an event at Madison Square Garden with the Indian American community sold out. Congressmen and senators took notice.

Although by the time Modi became prime minister climate change was a priority for Obama, they covered multiple subjects during the course of Obama's conversations with Modi on their various visits. Over time they developed a certain chemistry and appreciation of one another. There was a vitality and energy in the relationship. Both leaders saw in each other a partner in what they wanted to achieve.

Ambassador Verma said that Modi has been good for the India–US relationship. He notes, 'I give Modi a lot of credit. He worked hard on a lot of important international issues like climate change. He was ready and willing to advance the relationship. It takes two to tango.' There were irritations that remained, such as trade disagreements that would take time and perseverance, but it seemed that the relationship was on a path on which even Modi and Obama, two people with such divergent values, could find common ground.

As the pace of elections picked up in the US, Obama turned his attention to the Iran nuclear deal that John Kerry had spent much of the last two years trying to negotiate. It was signed in January 2016, much to India's relief. India had an interest in Iran being removed from the sanction list as it was one of its oil suppliers. In March 2016, Obama tried to normalize relations with Cuba.

In November, the US, and much of the world, was caught by surprise when Donald J. Trump won the presidency. Both the US and India now had two populist leaders and were in unchartered territory for the first time.

Manmohan Singh had observed these trends when he was prime minister. When President Obama visited India during his tenure in 2010, the country was still recovering from the 2008 Mumbai attacks. Singh had shown restraint in dealing with Pakistan but it had cost him politically. He had confided to Obama: 'In uncertain times, Mr President, the call of religious and ethnic solidarity can be intoxicating. And it is not hard for politicians to exploit that, in India or anywhere else.'[27]

# Chapter 22

# Trump: An Unpredictable President

## A New Kind of President

The election in November 2016 that voted in Donald J. Trump as the next president of the United States sent shockwaves around the world. His opponent, Hillary Clinton, won the popular vote but failed to secure the required votes in the Electoral College. She was so confident of victory that she later admitted she had not prepared a concession speech.

Trump, the host of a reality TV show in which he seemed to take great pleasure in firing people, was a real estate magnate who had fallen in and out of bankruptcy. As a presidential candidate, he was unrestrained, lacked discipline and liked to brag about his prowess with women. Shunned by the Republican Party leadership, who did not view him as a serious candidate, he surprised them by winning the party's nomination and eventually the presidency.

Deep down, Trump knew that many viewed his election as illegitimate, as he was elected under a cloud of allegations of Russian interference. Trump used social media to attack his opponents and continued to rail against his critics after he took office, targeting Democrats with particular venom. Officials who testified against him under oath were later summarily removed from office.

As Maggie Haberman of the *New York Times* put it: 'Over four decades in public life, President Trump has sought to bend business, real estate and political rivals to his will. Facts that cut against his position have been declared false. Witnesses who have questioned his motives have been declared dishonest. Critics of his behaviour are part of a corrupt, shadowy effort aiming to damage him. And as he like to put it, his own actions are always, to one degree or another, "perfect".[1]

Trump's popularity among Republicans remains high even though he polls below 50 per cent nationally. He relies on a core group of loyal extreme right-wing supporters and derives great energy from holding large rallies to stir up his base. He has successfully managed to intimidate the Republican Party into submission, remaking it into his own image.

As the president, Trump had control over the most powerful platform on the planet. He decided to exert his authority by undermining long-established policies and ignoring the advice of his cabinet. In a now infamous meeting at the Pentagon on 20 July 2017, Trump revealed himself to be a president like no other. General Mattis, Secretary of State Rex Tillerson and all senior members of the military and cabinet had assembled in a room called 'The Tank' to brief the president. Mattis began by stating that the 'post-war, international, rules-based order was the greatest gift of the greatest generation'.[2] Senior members of the team took turns to show the president where 'US personnel were positioned, at military bases, CIA stations and embassies, and how US deployments fended off the threats of terror cells, nuclear blasts and destabilizing enemies in places like Afghanistan, Iran, Iraq, the Korea Peninsula and Syria'.[3]

Trump interrupted the presentation, saying it was crazy and stupid to pay for bases and arguing that South Korea should be charged rent for the protection provided by American troops. He became agitated and raised his voice declaring that 'we should make money off of everything'.[4] He went on to say that NATO was worthless, and the Europeans were in arrears, using transactional real estate terms.

When Mattis attempted to convince the president that NATO kept the US safe as well as Europe, Trump insisted that the Europeans were 'ripping us off'. He insulted the military, saying it had lost the ability to win wars. He called Afghanistan a 'loser war'. When it came to the Persian Gulf, he said, 'We spent $7 trillion: they're ripping us off ... where is the fucking oil?'⁵ When he left the meeting, everyone was shell-shocked.*

Tillerson was the only person who supposedly stood up to him. It was leaked to the press that, after the meeting, he called the president 'a fucking moron'. He was fired soon after. 'The mood in the Tank was funereal. The president had just launched a cruise missile through seven decades of American national security policy and trade agreements.'⁶

After the Second World War, the US built an architecture of alliances that sought to achieve global stability, starting with NATO in Europe and extending to the Pacific. The US tried to achieve its foreign policy goals, from handling climate change to regime change in Iraq, by relying on its allies for support at the UN and other multilateral institutions. Trump not only disregarded standing US policy, he jettisoned the traditional pillars of Republican foreign policy—free trade, a strong alliance with Europe and opposition to Russia.

From the start of his presidency, Trump alienated his NATO allies, accusing them of not contributing enough to the alliance. He went out of his way to please Russia and entered into a confrontation on trade with Mexico and Canada, much of it embellished with hard-to-forgive and impossible-to-forget insults. He described Mexicans as rapists and throughout his campaign and presidency threatened to build a border wall and make Mexico pay for it.

Trump had decided from the outset to change the way US foreign policy was conducted. His doctrine of 'America First' viewed the world in terms of bilateral relations rather than through the prism of global alliances. He has often been called a 'transactional president' who judges each country by asking first if they are 'ripping off the US' or if they support 'terrorists'. He seems obsessed with overturning everything his predecessor, President Obama, accomplished: he pulled the US out of the Trans-Pacific Partnership, the Paris Climate Accord and the Iran nuclear deal. Domestically, he tried to repeal Obamacare.

---

* One senior official was incensed that Trump was treating the US military as mercenaries.

## Trump and Modi

New Delhi watched the developments in Washington with increasing trepidation. It had taken over fifty years to form a partnership with the US, and Modi was determined to make sure it stayed on course.

Trump was unpredictable and could hardly be relied on to think of long-term mutual interests. He was motivated by projects that stroked his ego. With an eye on the Nobel Peace Prize, Trump naïvely convinced himself that his personal charm could bring Kim Jong-un, the belligerent North Korean leader, to the negotiating table. Trump's efforts were unsuccessful, but Modi noted that Trump had personalized US foreign policy to an extreme. Remaining on good terms with the US would require his personal engagement with Trump.

On 13 November 2017, Modi met with Trump in Manila, Philippines at the margins of the summit they were both attending. According to the book, *A Very Stable Genius,* Trump had failed to retain any of the briefing material and kept veering off on tangents during the discussion. When Modi tried to refocus the dialogue on the threats India faced from Afghanistan, China and Pakistan, Trump shocked Modi by saying: 'It's not like you've got China on your border.' Modi's eyes bulged out in surprise.[7] Modi, used to working with Obama whose intellect and command of the issues were prodigious, was taken aback.

Trump's lack of knowledge about the region is all the more surprising given that the Trump organization's largest investments outside the US are in India. Typically, the Trump organization franchises its name, investing little money in the country or project. With India's real estate market going through a slump, Trump's visit to India in February 2020 was seen as giving the Trump-branded properties a boost. 'Trump has faced constant questions about whether he is using his presidential perch to line his own pockets … for three years, Trump's company has worked to promote its four developments in India that have earned Trump millions of dollars in royalties.'[8]

During the election campaign, Trump declared, somewhat awkwardly, that he was a 'big fan of Hindu and India', confusing the religion with the people of India. It had also been reported that he often mimicked Modi's accent and treated India's concerns dismissively. However, unlike NATO and countries like Mexico that have been the subject of Trump's vitriol, Trump has been neutral in his policy demands towards India except on long-standing trade conflicts, which he uses as leverage.[†] Some of his policies have even benefitted India.

Trump's stand on China—his negotiations on technology and attempts to create divisions between Russia and China—were viewed as helpful by India. Despite his bellicosity towards Iran, his reluctance to be provoked into a war in the Middle East was met with considerable relief in New Delhi. With over six million workers in the Middle East, India has a vested interest in maintaining peace in the region.[‡]

Trump's popularity in India soared in September 2018, when his administration cancelled $300 million in military aid to Pakistan.[§] The Pentagon accused Islamabad of not doing enough to root out terrorists, signalling a new low in relations between the two countries. It played well in India, but the Modi government worried that Trump shot from the hip with very little prior knowledge about the region.

When Imran Khan, the president of Pakistan, visited the White House in July 2019 to repair relations, Trump claimed that 'Indian Prime Minister Narendra Modi had asked him to play the role of mediator between the two countries and offered to get involved in a bid to resolve the long-standing dispute over the Kashmir issue. These remarks caused an immediate political furore in India, as they upended India's long-standing position: that there is no room for a third party in the Kashmir conversation between India and Pakistan.'[9] Foreign policy experts in New Delhi speculate that it may have prompted Modi to pre-emptively go ahead with his plans to

---

[†] During the 2020 pandemic, he wanted India to release the drug hydroxychloroquine, which he was convinced was therapeutic for treating the novel coronavirus. When Modi hesitated, he threatened to retaliate on trade issues.

[‡] John Bolton, Trump's third national security advisor, was pushing to attack Iran.

[§] According to a Pew survey, Trump's popularity in India went from 14 per cent in 2016 to 56 per cent in 2019. It is still below President Obama, who was at 58 per cent when he left office.

abrogate Article 370 of the Indian Constitution, which gave special status to Jammu and Kashmir.¶ His plan to negotiate a peace settlement with the Taliban without including the Afghan government also worried India.

In the past, US presidents highlighted human rights as a litmus test, often using aid as leverage with countries. The US saw itself all too often as the policeman of the world, trying to resolve long-standing disputes, such as the Arab–Israeli and India–Pakistan conflicts. Although he paid lip service to being helpful, Trump abandoned intervening in issues that he did not believe were central to US interests. He quickly backed away from the 'Kashmir problem'. Trump's lack of concern in the internal affairs of countries and his tendency towards isolationism suited Modi.

Modi had established a close relationship with Obama, but Trump posed a challenge. Not only was he egotistical and insecure, he could be dangerously volatile. Two years after his inauguration, Trump was still arguing about the size of the crowd that attended the occasion as compared to President Obama's inauguration. Crowd size had become such an obsession for him that it gave Modi a pathway to both 'manage' Trump and placate his ego.

When Modi visited the US in November 2019, he invited Trump to be the guest of honour at the 'Howdy Modi' event in Houston, Texas, attended by 50,000 Indian Americans. Trump was impressed and referred to the turnout at Houston several times after the visit. The rally took place a month after the Modi government rescinded Article 370, which had once protected Kashmiris and guaranteed them autonomy. The government arrested civilians, imposed a curfew, shut off mobile phone services and prevented foreign observers from visiting the state. The government also threatened Muslim migrants in Assam with deportation.[10]

During Obama's second term, Modi projected himself as a pro-Western, pro-business leader who was above corruption. Following the BJP's massive landslide in the 2019 election, Modi has come out of the fundamentalist closet. He chose to interpret the BJP's victory at the polls

---

¶ Revoking Article 370 had been part of the BJP's political platform but the party had never acted on it until 2019. The Congress government under Nehru had also at one point considered rescinding Article 370 but had never acted on it.

as a mandate to fulfil the party's extreme right-wing agenda to remake India into a 'Hindu nation'.[11]

After Trump's efforts to impose a 'Muslim ban' on travel to the US and his controversial policy of separating undocumented families on the southern border, Modi was confident that the US administration was not in a position, nor had any inclination, to challenge India's record on human rights or interfere in its domestic policies. Ambassador Verma sees the US–India relationship as unique. 'The US–India relationship is a series of concepts and values going back decades based on social justice, inclusion, fairness, freedom and democracy. It's about people and principals, not just selling stuff to each other.'[12]

But while Modi successfully handled Trump, a new and complicated element in the conduct of US relations with India is the growing influence of the Indian diaspora. Not everyone in the diaspora supports Modi and his right-wing agenda of radical socio-religious change. During the Howdy Modi rally, several thousand people protested outside the stadium against what they saw as Trump and Modi's divisive and discriminatory policies.

Modi's policies received unfavourable press coverage in the US and high-profile members of the diaspora spoke out against his policies. On 6 December 2019, the Indian American congresswoman Pramila Jayapal introduced a resolution in the House of Representatives urging India to lift all restrictions on communications in Kashmir, protect the religious freedom of its residents and end mass detentions without charge. She posted a message on her Twitter account: 'I have fought to strengthen the special US–India relationship, which is why I am deeply concerned.' She declared that preventing neutral observers from visiting Kashmir was harmful to 'our close, critical bilateral relationship'.

In January 2020, Satya Nadella, the CEO of Microsoft who was born and raised in India, criticized the Modi government for trying to pass the Citizenship Amendment Act (CAA). The CAA provided a path for citizenship to immigrants from other South Asian countries, but excluded Muslims. Protests broke out all over India and various states resisted enforcing the law, declaring it unconstitutional. 'I think what's happening is sad ... it's just bad,' said Nadella in a press interview.[13] Although members of the BJP vilified Nadella and Jayapal, they remain powerful voices within the Indian diaspora in the US. The Modi government is still learning to manage dissenting voices within this group that it had previously tried so hard to cultivate. When External Affairs Minister Jaishankar visited Washington in December 2019, he abruptly cancelled a meeting with a group of bipartisan US lawmakers because the delegation included Congresswoman Jayapal. Several Democrats criticized his actions in the press.

Modi's problems were about to get worse. On the domestic front, the Indian economy, which had been his selling point, stagnated at 4 per cent in 2019 and steadily declined. The protests in India over the controversial CAA continued to spread when Modi's investment in Trump suddenly paid off, providing him with a badly needed distraction.

Trump accepted Modi's invitation to visit India in February 2020. For a president who has made very few overseas trips, it was a pointed message. Trump's earlier gaffes seem to have given way to a growing recognition that India could be useful. He also needed to divert attention away from his domestic accusations. He had spent three years of his presidency being investigated by the Justice Department** for obstruction of justice and colluding with Russians during the elections. Following an attempt to have a foreign government investigate a political opponent, the House of Representatives impeached him. After being acquitted by the Senate, he accepted the invitation to visit India to project himself as a world leader.

Knowing how much Trump liked to boast about big crowds turning out to see him, Modi arranged for 1,00,000 people to welcome him at a cricket stadium in Gujarat's capital, Ahmedabad, where he served as chief minister. The thirty-six-hour trip, in February 2020, was a welcome change for Trump after the gruelling impeachment process. Modi consistently held out his hand in friendship, even at times when Trump could no longer count on a warm reception in many countries. The visit went smoothly, and Trump was flattered by the crowds, but no

---

** A special independent counsel under Robert Mueller was set up to investigate him. He was not charged.

trade issues were resolved. While the military relationship continued to grow with substantial agreements to share technology, intelligence and resources, little of substance was accomplished beyond establishing a personal connection between two men who were about to head into a storm during the visit.

## The Pandemic

Just days after Trump returned from India, a global pandemic that began in Wuhan, China swept across the world, infecting over 50 million people and killing more than a million worldwide. While Trump watched in dismay, as all the economic gains during his administration evaporated and unemployment reached levels not seen since the Great Depression, he struggled to manage the political fallout.

The world economy came to a virtual standstill for several months as entire countries went into quarantine to contain the virus and raced to find a vaccine and cures. The US was no longer the superpower providing the leadership through which aid and relief could be distributed globally. That space was ceded to China, while the US faced shortages and turned inwards as the crisis threatened to overwhelm its healthcare system and weaken its economy. Award-winning journalist George Packer described America's slide into dysfunction: 'From the president came wilful blindness, scapegoating, boasts, and lies. From his mouthpieces, conspiracy theories and miracle cures ... When a government doctor tried to warn the public of the danger, the White House took the mic and politicized the message ... Every morning in the endless month of March, Americans woke up to find themselves citizens of a failed state.'[14]

Trump took to television every night for the first two months to control the message, but it became a bizarre political reality show. On one occasion, he announced thinly veiled threats to India with trade retaliation if Modi did not supply the US with the anti-malaria drug hydroxychloroquine, a banned export which India needs for its own population.[††] Modi

---

†† Hydroxychloroquine was found ineffective against Covid-19 in trials and its use was not recommended.

complied.[15] Trump made himself the butt of jokes when he suggested on television that scientists explore injecting disinfectants as a possible cure. At the peak of the pandemic he cut off funding to the WHO, infuriating the rest of the world.

Trump showed an increasing reluctance to impose the draconian lockdown undertaken by China and Korea and invest in the massive testing and contact tracing done by the Europeans. While China acted quickly to get the virus under control and mitigate its spread, the US ended up with the highest number of infected cases and deaths, with African Americans getting infected and dying at higher rates than the rest of the population.

Modi, heavily invested in the US relationship at a time when the US star was in decline, was facing domestic challenges of his own. He responded to the pandemic by locking down the country swiftly and early, but it was poorly planned.

As he lifted the lockdown, infection rates soared. Migrant labourers endured untold hardships as thousands were stranded without food and shelter for weeks. The economy, already precariously weak, now faced a banking crisis, production losses and a looming recession. By June the virus had spread throughout the country. By October the number of infected cases had doubled.

In June 2020, Chinese and Indian troops clashed in the border area in Ladakh. It was the most serious altercation since the 1962 war. India lost twenty soldiers in Galwan while trying to defend border positions along the LAC (Line of Actual Control).[16] It was an unprovoked action that took India by surprise. Trump offered to mediate but Modi wisely did not take it seriously. Trump had hardly proved himself a masterful statesman and the Chinese did not show him the deference they showed Kissinger. After all, he had been unaware that China and India shared a border.

In the US, the brutal arrest and murder of an unarmed black man by police officers in the summer sparked a 'Black Lives Matter' protest across the country. Protesters demolished statues of offensive civil war slaveholders and Confederate generals, inflaming Trump's conservative base in the south. Trump threatened to deploy the US military to suppress the protests, alarming both governors and retired generals.

Alarmed, General Mattis, who had resigned as defence secretary in December 2018, publicly denounced Trump as a threat to the US Constitution. He said, 'Donald Trump is the first president in my lifetime who does not try to unite the American people—does not even pretend to try. Instead he tries to divide us.'[17] He was joined in his condemnation by General John Allen, who took over as head of the Brookings Institution after Strobe Talbott retired. General John Kelly defended Mattis and said, 'Americans should look harder at who we elect.'[18] The censure of a sitting US president from the top brass of ex-military was unprecedented.

Trump had no foreign policy achievements to brag about. Korea had snubbed him, Mexico had not paid for the wall, and he had taken on China without any clear path to success. He had tried to negotiate with the Taliban, and US intelligence sources confirmed on 29 June that the Taliban had been instead paid by the Russian military to kill US military personnel.

On the domestic front, unemployment had reached 15 per cent and the coronavirus had claimed nearly 4,00,000 lives by the time of the election of 2020. The consequences of the pandemic were everywhere and the republicans lost the house, senate and presidency.

Although Trump lost the election to Biden, 75 million Americans voted for four more years of Trump, revealing the deep divide in the country. Trump refused to accept his loss gracefully and contested the results for weeks, sowing doubt about the election. The country was thrown into chaos by his futile attempts to hold on to power. On 6 January a crowd of his supporters, after listening to a speech by him in front of the White House where he repeatedly claimed the election was fraudulent, breached the Capitol where the election results were in the process of being certified. The insurrection with protesters in Trump hats carrying Confederate flags through the US Capitol was unprecedented in US history.

Biden's presidency has been welcomed with a collective sigh of relief from America's European and Far Eastern allies but he will face several challenges when he assumes the presidency. In a repeat of what happened when Obama took office, Biden will inherit an economy in crisis that will need his immediate attention and a raging pandemic to manage.

Although he will come with an experienced team, without a majority in the Senate, he will be obstructed in his domestic agenda by the Republicans. While Trump may have left the White House, Trumpism may not be easy to eradicate, and the fissures in American society that Trump so effectively exploited to his advantage will exhaust much of Biden energy in his first term. Few Republican senators were willing to confront Trump when he refused to accept the results of the election. They were all mindful of the numbers that had voted for him.

Biden will rejoin the WHO and the Paris Climate Accord, restore his alliances with NATO that Trump so badly fractured and work on bringing the country together. Perhaps his greatest contribution will be to restore a sense of civility to the presidency. President-elect Biden called Prime Minister Modi after he won, but while India will remain a significant country for the US, barring an escalation in the Himalayas, it will not command the attention of the US in the immediate future that China will.

# Epilogue

THE PANDEMIC OF 2020 IS ONE OF THOSE SEISMIC EVENTS THAT has the potential of rearranging the world order. It has exposed the many weaknesses within the US, both socially and economically. Under a divisive leader like Trump, incompetent in the face of a global crisis, America's vulnerabilities have deepened, putting her leadership of the free world into question. When the Second World War ended, colonialism was finished; Great Britain, along with other European powers, lost its position as the world's pre-eminent global power. Although Europe recovered economically, it never dominated global politics again.

The two titans that emerged in the post-war period were the Soviets and the Americans. They were locked in a cold war, competing for military and nuclear superiority in a race that lasted almost forty years. It ended in 1989, when the US was left standing as the world's uncontested superpower.

We have left behind the rigid divisions of the world into communist and non-communist blocs. As we entered the twenty-first century, the world became a global platform for trade and ideas. Today, the world is so interconnected via trade and travel that it would be counterproductive for the great powers to contemplate war.

We have moved from the nuclear age to the digital age where technology and data drive competition. The US and China are the new protagonists in the race to dominate the global space. For now, the US is still ahead but China is catching up, quickly.

The competition with China is no longer just over trade, but over the future of the world. The clash of systems between the techno-authoritarian model versus the democratic model has become the prism through which the national security system views the future. President Xi has made it China's goal to achieve supremacy in the field of artificial intelligence (AI) by 2030. Three of the world's top ten AI universities are in China, and they are in the process of building fifty new AI research centres.

Xi has already used AI applications to exert social control within China. 'China already has hundreds of millions of surveillance cameras in place. In the near future every person who enters a public space could be identified, instantly, by AI matching them to an ocean of personal data, including every text communication, and their body's one-of-a-kind protein-construction schema … China's government could soon achieve an unprecedented political stranglehold on more than a billion people … In a sophisticated digital system of social control, codes could be used to score a person's perceived political pliancy as well.'[1]

This is of great concern to democratic governments like the US. Tensions over these issues were expressed during an interview with Jake Sullivan, who has been appointed as President-elect Biden's national security advisor: 'For a long time, US foreign policy thinking was dominated by the idea of convergence—that societies would eventually move to a more open and liberal model. But now we see that technology is not driving democracy but enabling autocracy.'[2]

This is all the more worrying if China exports the surveillance systems to dictators or countries which do not have democratic governments. 'The country is now the world's leading seller of AI-powered surveillance equipment.'[3] Equally worrying is who controls the data. According to experts who have studied the issue, when China sets up a surveillance system for a country, it generally controls the networks and the data. This puts it in a powerful position. 'The emergence of an AI-powered authoritarian bloc led by China could warp the geopolitics of this century. It could prevent billions of people, across large swaths of the globe, from ever securing any measure of political freedom.'[4]

Sullivan considers India as central to the larger strategic competition with China; and the US has begun to court India with a view to containing

China, just as it did during Eisenhower and Kennedy. The policy of containing China and using India has a frontline state has come full circle, but Xi's China is different to Mao's China. China has grasped its position in the new interconnected world, and years of commercial success has made it more assertive about pursuing its global interests.

After years of accepting the line of actual control along its border with India, it has in recent years taken aggressive actions that it knew could escalate. During Xi's state visit to India in September 2014, a thousand People's Liberation Army troops entered Chumar on the Indian side of the LAC and only vacated it three weeks after Xi's departure from India. This was followed by an incursion in the Doklam plateau in 2017, which ended when both sides withdrew after seventy-two days. This was despite Prime Minister Modi going out of his way to invest in his relationship with Xi, whom he has met with eighteen times, more than any other head of state. He either failed to establish a rapport or Xi was sending India a message. Perhaps Xi wanted to remind India that despite its growing friendship with the US, China has the potential to hurt it regionally.

'China has stepped up her assertiveness in disputes across the board: submarine patrols and military flights in the East China Sea around the Senkakus; military aircraft in Taiwanese airspace; sinking Vietnamese vessels in the South China Sea and declaring new administrative structures in those contested waters; and starting a tariff war with Australia. Assertiveness on the LAC with India would then be part of a broader pattern of China's "wolf warrior" behaviour and diplomacy.'5

Both the US and India have an ascendant China in their rear-view mirror, but China has made it clear to India that it has the ability to cause it considerable pain. A repeat of Galwan after Doklam could undermine Modi's government and make him look weak. Why else would they choose to act during the pandemic when the government was under pressure for its handling of the migrant crisis and facing an economic slowdown?

If a report in the *New York Times* is correct, and the shut down of the Indian stock market and trains in Mumbai that occurred on 13 October four months after Galwan were not an accident, there is a reason for concern. According to the report, China has penetrated India's power grid as a broad cyber campaign to remind India who calls the shots in the region. 'Stuart Solomon, Recorded Future's chief operating officer, said that the Chinese state-sponsored group, which the firm named Red Echo, "has been seen to systematically utilize advanced cyber intrusion techniques to quietly gain a foothold in nearly a dozen critical nodes across the Indian power generation and transmission infrastructure".[6]

A closer alliance with the US will need to be carefully calibrated by India. India needs friends like Russia in the region to balance China. While India has steadily become closer to the QUAD countries, 'The time has also come for India to reconsider its stand on joining the Regional Comprehensive Economic Partnership.' As former Foreign Secretary Nirupama Rao rightly points out, if India wants to build its capacities and capabilities in manufacturing and supply chain networks closer to home, it needs to take a long-term view.[7]

* * *

For now, the US still remains the world's richest economy, but the pandemic has knocked it off its sole superpower pedestal, largely due to a lack of leadership. Without the world noticing, China is now referred to by CNN and other news outlets as a 'superpower'. The pandemic seems to have rotated the kaleidoscope once again and pointed us towards a new multipolar world order.

Nehru's policy of non-alignment may still be the gold standard that plots a safe course for India through the unchartered waters that lie ahead.

# Endnotes

## Chapter 1: Introduction

1. 1949 Congressional Records 14431. House of Representatives. Proceeding and Debates of the Unites States Congress. October 13, 1949 law.
2. Stephen Phillip Cohen, *India: Emerging Power*. (Washington, DC: Brookings Institution Press., 2001), p. 4.
3. Douglas Brinkley and Luke A. Nichter, *The Nixon Tapes: 1971-1972* (Boston: Mariner Books, 2016), p. 312.
4. Source: World Bank Data, data.worldbank.org.
5. C. Raja Mohan, *Crossing the Rubicon*. (New York, NY: Palgrave Macmillian, 2003), pp. 57–58.
6. US census data
7. 'Indian immigrants are tech's new titans,' Paresh Dave, *Los Angeles Times*, 11 August 2015.
8. Sunil Khilnani, *The Idea of India* (New York: Farrar, Straus and Giroux, 1997), p. 188.

## Chapter 2: Independence

1. Stephen Broadberry and Bishnupriya Gupta, 'Indian GDP, 1600–1871: Some preliminary estimates and a comparison with Britain', Department of Economics, University of Warwick, UK, 28 April 2010.
2. Marie Seton, *Panditji: A Portrait of Jawaharlal Nehru* (New York: Taplinger Publishing Co. Inc., 1967), p. 30.
3. ibid.
4. David M. Malone, *Does the Elephant Dance* (Oxford University Press, 2011), p. 76.

5.  Jawaharlal Nehru, *An Autobiography* (India: Penguin Viking, 1936), p. 17.
6.  Frank Moraes, *Jawaharlal Nehru: A Biography* (Mumbai: Jaico Publishing House, 1959), p. 18.
7.  'Nehru, The Nation Remembers,' in tributes, Indian Science Congress.
8.  'Nehru—A Queer Mixture of East and West,' *New York Times*, 28 May 1964.
9.  Pupul Jayakar, *Indira Gandhi: An Intimate Biography* (New Delhi: Penguin, 1992), pp. 10-11.
10. Nehru, *An Autobiography*, 142.
11. Jayakar, *Indira Gandhi*, 104.
12. ibid., 386.
13. Jawaharlal Nehru Speeches (1949–53), 29 November 1952. Message to International Buddhist Cultural Conference, Government of India.
14. *The Duff Cooper Diaries: 1915–1951*, edited by John Julius Norwich (Phoenix, 2007). Date of entry: 4 November 1920.
15. Michael Brecher, *Nehru: A Political Biography* (London: Oxford University Press, 1959), p. 282.
16. H.W. Brands, *India and the United States* (Boston: Twayne Publishers, 1990), p. 13.
17. ibid.
18. M. Srinivas Chary, *The Eagle and the Peacock* (Westport, Connecticut: Greenwood Press, 1995), p. 11.
19. Arthur Herman, *Gandhi and Churchill* (New York, Bantam Books, 2008), p. 474.
20. ibid., 16.
21. Truman Presidential Library. Presidents Security Files. Box 221. 4 October 1949.
22. Brecher, *Nehru*, 372.
23. Interview with Jagat Mehta.
24. Giles Boquerat, *No Strings Attached* (New Delhi: Manohar, 2003), p. 80.
25. 1941 and 1951 Census of India.
26. Speech at the inauguration of Indian Council for Cultural Relations, 9 April 1950.
27. Sarvepalli Gopal, *Jawaharlal Nehru: A Biography*, Vol. 1 (Cambridge, MA: Harvard University Press), p. 13.
28. ibid.

## Chapter 3: Kashmir

1.  1941 Census of India.
2.  Prem Shankar Jha, *Kashmir, 1947: Rival Versions of History* (Bombay: Oxford University Press, 1996), p. 17.
3.  See fortnightly reports by British officers in Kashmir W.F. Web India Office Records Library. Files L/P&S/13/1266. Also Gen. Scott. 13/1845//b

4.  Mehr Chand Mahajan, *Looking Back: The Autobiography of Mehr Chand Mahajan* (New Delhi, India: Har-Anand Publications, 1994), p. 113, p. 124.
5.  Jha, *Kashmir, 1947*, 128.
6.  C. Dasgupta, *War and Diplomacy in Kashmir 1947–48* (New Delhi: Sage Publications, 2002), p. 48.
7.  Ramachandra Guha, *India After Gandhi* (New York: HarperCollins, 2007), p. 83.
8.  Dasgupta, *War and Diplomacy*, 51.
9.  Dasgupta, *War and Diplomacy*, 52.
10. Dasgupta, *War and Diplomacy*, 44.
11. ibid.
12. Sarvepalli Gopal, *Jawaharlal Nehru: 1947–1956*, Vol. 2 (Boston, MA: Harvard University Press, 1979), p. 22.
13. Dasgupta, *War and Diplomacy*, 111.
14. ibid., 110.
15. Gopal, *Nehru* Vol. 2, 26.
16. Francine R. Frankel, *When Nehru Looked East: Origins of India-US Suspicion and India-China Rivalry* (New York, Oxford University Press, 2020), p. 73.
17. ibid., 77.
18. Gopal, *Nehru* Vol. 2, 28.
19. Howard Schaffer, *Limits of Influence: America's Role in Kashmir* (Washington, DC: Brookings Institute Press, 2009), p. 16.
20. Truman Presidential Library. Presidential Security Files. Note on Kashmir. January 1950. Box 215.
21. Joseph Korbel, *Danger in Kashmir* (Princeton, NJ: Princeton University Press, 2015), p. 122.
22. Frankel, *Nehru looks East*, 74.
23. Korbel, *Danger in Kashmir*, 130.
24. Korbel, *Danger in Kashmir*, 135.
25. Korbel, *Danger in Kashmir*, 143.
26. Nehrus Speeches: 'Our Pledge to Kashmir'. Speech to Lok Sabha, 17 February 1953, New Delhi.
27. Dasgupta, *War and Diplomacy*, 75.
28. Tapan Bose, Dinesh Mohan, Gautam Navlakha, Sumanta Banerjee, 'India's Kashmir War,' *Economic and Political Weekly*, Vol. 25, Issue No. 13, 31 March 1990; Jason Burke, 'Indian forces in Kashmir accused of Human rights abuses cover up,' *The Guardian*, 11 September 2015; 'Kashmir: UN reports serious abuses,' Human Rights Watch, 10 July 2019.

## Chapter 4: Truman and Nehru

1.  Howard B. Schaffer, *Chester Bowles: New Dealer in Cold War* (Boston, MA: Harvard University Press, 1993), p. 37.

2. Sven Raphael Schneider, 'The Shoe Collection of Harry S. Truman', *The Gentleman's Gazette*, 15 May 2013. https://www.gentlemansgazette.com/harry-s-truman-shoe-collection/.

3. Oral History. Transcriptions of conversations between Justice William O. Douglas and Professor Walter Murphy. Cassette No 16: June 5, 1963. Princeton Library. Special Collections.

4. Escott Reid, *Envoy to Nehru* (Delhi: Oxford University Press, 1981), p. 93.

5. Reid, *Envoy to Nehru*, 95.

6. Harry S. Truman Presidential Library and Museum. Oral history interview with Elbert G. Matthews, Asst. Chief, Division of South Asia Affairs, Department of State, 1947-48; Director of South Asian Affairs, 1950-51. June 13, 1975. By Richard D. McKinzie.

7. Harry S. Truman Library. Henry Grady Papers. Box 1.

8. Harry S. Truman Library. Henry Grady Papers. Box 1.

9. Henry Grady, *The Memoirs of Ambassador Henry Grady: From the Great War to the Cold War* (Columbia, MO: University of Missouri Press, 2009), p. 124.

10. Vijaya Lakshmi Pandit, *The Scope of Happiness: A Personal Memoir* (Delhi: Vikas Publishing House Pvt. Ltd, 1979), p. 308.

11. Grady, *Memoirs*, 3

12. Grady, *Memoirs*, 3.

13. S. Gopal, *Nehru*, Vol. 1, 64.

14. Oral History. Transcripts of conversations between Justice William O. Douglas and Professor Walter F. Murphy. Princeton Special Papers Collection. Cassette No 16. June 5, 1963.

15. ibid.

16. Harry S. Truman Library. Oral history, interview June 14, 1973. Loy Henderson oral history, interview with Mr. McKenzie.

17. ibid.

18. Robert Beisner, *Dean Acheson: A Life in the Cold War* (New York, NY: Oxford University Press, 2006), p. 216.

19. G. Balachandran, *The Reserve Bank of India, 1951–1967* (Delhi, New York: Oxford University Press, 1997), p. 593.

20. S. Gopal, *Jawaharlal Nehru*, Vol. 2, 24; Michael Edwardes, *Nehru* (England: Penguin, 1971), pp. 232-233.

21. S. Gopal, *Nehru*, Vol. 1, 59.

22. Harry S. Truman Presidential Library. Oral History Interview with Elbert G. Matthews. Wash., D.C. June 13, 1975.

23. S. Gopal, *Nehru*, Vol. 1, 60.

24. Harry S. Truman Presidential library. Oral History Interview with Elbert G. Matthews. Wash., D.C. June 13, 1975.

25.  Dean Acheson, *Present at the Creation: My Years in the State Department* (New York, NY: W.W. Norton & Co., 1969), p. 336.
26.  S. Gopal, *Nehru*, Vol. 1, 60.
27.  Beisner, *Dean Acheson*, 217.
28.  Beisner, *Dean Acheson*, 218.
29.  Aparna Basu, *G.L. Mehta: A Many Splendoured Man* (New Delhi: Concept Publishing, 2001), p. 143.
30.  ibid.
31.  Vijaya Lakshmi Pandit, *The Scope of Happiness*, 296.
32.  Inder Malhotra, 'Swallowing the Humiliation', *Nation*, 12 July 2010.
33.  Jay Hauben, *The UN Role in Korea in the Division of the Korean Nation*, Columbia University, 2012.
34.  Biswamohan Mishra, 'The Indian U.N. Policy during the Korean Crisis', *The Indian Journal of Political Science* 25, no. 3/4 (1964), pp. 145–51. Accessed 16 April 2020.
35.  Michael Beschloss, *Presidents of War* (New York, NY: Crown, 2018), p. 457.
36.  Robert Barnes, 'Between the Blocs: India, the United Nations, and Ending the Korean War', *The Journal of Korean Studies* 18, no. 2 (2013), pp. 263–86.
37.  Beisner, *Dean Acheson*, 506.
38.  ibid.
39.  Chester Bowles, *Ambassador's Report* (New York, NY: Harper, 1954), p. 242.
40.  Robert Barnes, 'Between the Blocs', 263–86.
41.  Andrew J. Rotter, *Comrades at Odds* (Ithaca, NY: Cornell University Press, 2000), pp. 103–105.
42.  ibid.
43.  ibid.
44.  'Bowles Makes Hit in New Delhi Post', *New York Times*, 6 November 1951.
45.  Chester Bowles, *Promises to Keep: My Years in Public Life, 1941–1969* (New York, NY: Harper and Row, 1971), p. 246.
46.  Beisner, *Dean Acheson*, 506.

## Chapter 5: Eisenhower

1.   Interview with Aparna Basu, daughter of Ambassador G.L. Mehta.
2.   Aparna Basu, *G.L. Mehta: A Many Splendoured Man* (New Delhi: Concept Publishing, 2001), p. 147.
3.   B.K. Nehru, *Nice Guys Finish Second: Memoirs* (New Delhi: Penguin Books, 1997), p. 423.
4.   ibid.
5.   Sunil Khilnani, *Incarnations: A History of India in Fifty Lives* (New York, NY: Farrar, Straus and Giroux, 2016), p. 345.
6.   Gopal, *Nehru*, Vol. 1, 141.

7. Khilnani, *Incarnations*, 344.
8. ibid.
9. Townsend Hoopes, *The Devil and John Foster Dulles* (Boston: Little Brown Co., 1973), p. 132.
10. Hoopes, *The Devil and Dulles,* 53.
11. James B. Reston, 'John Foster Dulles and his Foreign Policy', *LIFE* magazine, 4 October 1948; Hoopes, *The Devil and Dulles*, 71.
12. Hoopes, *The Devil and Dulles*, 64–66.
13. Richard Immerman, *John Foster Dulles and the Diplomacy of the Cold War* (Wilmington, DE: SRB Books, 1999), p. 61.
14. Hoopes, *The Devil and Dulles*, 149.
15. Robert L. Beisner, *Dean Acheson: A Life in the Cold War* (Oxford University Press, 2006), p. 476.
16. Hoopes, *The Devil and Dulles*, 297.
17. Evan Thomas, *Ike's Bluff: President Eisenhower's Secret Battle to Save the World* (New York, NY: Back Bay, 2013), p. 11.
18. Evan Thomas, *Ike's Bluff: President Eisenhower's Secret Battle to Save the World* (Little Brown Co., 2012), p. 76.
19. Dennis Kux, *India and the United States: Estranged Democracies, 1941–1991* (Washington, DC: National Defense University, 1992), p. 101.
20. Rudra Chaudhuri, *Forged in Crisis* (New York, NY: Oxford University Press, 2014), p. 75.
21. Kux, *Estranged Democracies*, 105.
22. Eisenhower Presidential Library. Papers as President. 1953-61. Ann Whitman Files. International series Box 29.
23. Sarvepalli Gopal, *Nehru*, Vol. 3, 441; Letter 15 November 1953.
24. Jawaharlal Nehru, *Letters to his Chief Ministers,* Government of India publication, New Delhi.
25. S. Gopal, *Nehru*, Vol. 3, 247.
26. Brendon, Piers. *The Decline and Fall of the British Empire*. (London: Jonathan Cape, 2007), p. 104.
27. Derek Leebaert, *Grand Improvisation: America Confronts the British Superpower, 1945–1957* (New York: Farrar, Straus and Giroux, 2018), 385.
28. John Foster Dulles. Press Statement. Department of State. 13 September 1956.
29. Eisenhower Presidential Library. Papers as President. 1953–61. Ann Whitman File. International series. Box 29. Dept. of State. MR82-31. 6 November 1956. 2.45 p.m.
30. Eisenhower Presidential Library. Papers as President. 1953–61. Ann Whitman File. International series, box 31.
31. Eisenhower Presidential Library. Papers as President. 1953–61. Ann Whitman File. International series, box 31. Memo of conversation with PM Nehru of India, 17–18 December 1956.

32. Hoopes, *The Devil and Dulles*, 384–387.
33. Reid, *Envoy*, 144.
34. Robert Schulman, *John Sherman Cooper the Global Kentuckian* (Lexington, KY: Kentucky University Press, 1976), p. 67.
35. Srinath Raghavan, *Fierce Enigmas.* (New York: Basic Books, 2018), pp. 213–219.
36. National Security Council. Operations Coordinating Board. 18 March 1959. US policy towards South Asia. NSC5701
37. John F. Kennedy Library. Papers of John F. Kennedy. Pre-presidential papers. Senate Files. Series 12. Speeches and the press. Box 900, Folder 'The choices in Asia-Democratic Development in India.' Senate Floor, 25 March 1958.
38. Kux, *Estranged Democracies*, 150.
39. Eisenhower Presidential Library. Papers as President. 1953–61. Ann Whitman File. International series. Box 28. Department of State. No. 318, 14 August1953.
40. 'US Backs India Against Red China's Use of Force,' *The Brattleboro Daily Reformer*, 13 November 1959.

## Chapter 6: Nehru and the Kennedys

1. Arthur M. Schlesinger, Jr., *A Thousand Days* (Boston, MA: Houghton Mifflin Co., 1965), p. 522.
2. Schlesinger, *Thousand Days*, 298.
3. Dorothy Norman, *Indira Gandhi: Letters to an American Friend, 1950–1984* (New York, NY: Harcourt Brace Jovanovich, 1985), p. 84.
4. John Kenneth Galbraith, *Ambassador's Journal: A Personal Account of the Kennedy Years* (Boston, MA: Houghton Mifflin Co., 1969), p. 105.
5. ibid.
6. FRUS. S. Asia files.1061-63. Kennedy, JF. Doc 201-351. Telegram 3607 from Embassy to US Dept of State. March 18.
7. Schlesinger, *Thousand Days*, 524.
8. Schlesinger, *Thousand Days*, 525.
9. Gopal, *Nehru* Vol. 1, 190.
10. Jacqueline Kennedy and Arthur M. Schlesinger, *Jacqueline Kennedy: Historic Conversations on Life with John F. Kennedy, Interviews with Arthur M. Schlesinger, Jr., 1964* (New York, NY: Hyperion, 2011).
11. Schlesinger, *Thousand Days*, 524.
12. See Chapter 9 on Mrs Gandhi.
13. B.K. Nehru, *Nice Guys Finish Last*, 412.
14. B.K. Nehru, *Nice Guys Finish Last*, 413.
15. Norman, *Indira Gandhi: Letters*, 88.
16. Schlesinger, *Thousand Days*, 525.

17. Ted Sorensen, *Kennedy: The Classic Biography* (New York: Harper and Row, 1965), p. 578.
18. Papers of John F. Kennedy. JFK Library. Box 106A. Country India. CIA. Telegram, 3 December 1961.
19. Gopal, *Nehru* Vol. 1, 191.
20. NS Files Box 155A. NLK-78-138. Telegram from Galbraith. To Rusk. Dec. 22, 1961.
21. JFK Library, NS files, Box 155A, Department of State. Telegram No. 1867, 22 December 1961, New Delhi, Galbraith.
22. JFK Library, NS files, Box 155A Dept of State, Telegram No. 867, 22 December 1961, New Delhi, Galbraith.
23. JFK library. Box 111 NS Files. Country India. NLK 87-50. Letter from JFK to Nehru Jan. 18, 1962.
24. Jay Mulvaney, *Jackie: The Clothes of Camelot* (New York, NY: St. Martin's Press, 2014).

## Chapter 7: The War with China

1. Bruce Riedel, *JFK's Forgotten Crisis* (Washington, DC: Brookings Institution Press, 2017), p. 110.
2. According to Jagat Mehta, he saw a 'flowering of friendship between China and India'. *Rescuing the Future* (New Delhi: Manohar, 2008), p. 317.
3. Jagat Mehta, *Rescuing the Future*, 317
4. The treaties of Aigun, 1858 and Peking, 1860.
5. Neville Maxwell, *India's China War* (New York, NY: Pantheon Books, 1970), p. 31.
6. Eds. David M. Malone, C. Raja Mohan and Srinath Raghavan, *The Oxford Handbook of Indian Foreign Policy* (UK: Oxford University Press, 2015), p. 58.
7. Maxwell, *India's China War*, 70.
8. ibid.
9. Interview with Jagat Mehta.
10. John W. Garver, *Protracted Contest: Sino-Indian Rivalry in the Twentieth Century* (Seattle, London: University of Washington Press, 2001), pp. 100-101.
11. Maxwell, *India's China War*, 332.
12. J.P. Dalvi, *Himalayan Blunder* (London, England: Natraj Publishers, 1969), p. 271.
13. Ted Sorensen, *Kennedy*, 672.
14. John F. Kennedy, Address During the Cuban Missile Crisis, October 22, 1962, JFK Library, JFKWHA-142-001.
15. Galbraith, *Ambassador's Journal*, 431.
16. John F. Kennedy Papers. JFK Presidential Library. NSC Files. Country. India. Box 111. NLK98-77.

17.  Maxwell, *India's China War*, 278.
18.  'Chinese open new front; use tanks against Indians,' *The New York Times*, 23 October 1962.
19.  Papers of President Kennedy. JFK Presidential Library. NS Files 718. India 1961-63 Folder 2 of 4. Chronology of the Sino-Indian border Dispute and related developments.
20.  Charles Stuart Kennedy and Lindsey Grant, *Interview with Lindsey Grant*, 1990, Manuscript/Mixed Material, https://www.loc.gov/item/mfdipbib000440/.
21.  Galbraith, *Ambassador's Journal*, 445.
22.  Galbraith, *Ambassador's Journal*, 466.
23.  John F. Kennedy Presidential Papers. Dept of State. Action 3777. Telegram. 3922. N.S.F. Box 107.
24.  Interview with Jagat Mehta.
25.  'The case of Nehru's Dog', *TIME*, 30 August 1963, p. 27.
26.  JFK presidential Library. NSF Country Files. Komer Files. NIN-D-7 *US-Indian relation. Aid to India*. Sept 1963
27.  JFK Library. NS Files. Box 111. Country. India. NLK98-77: Oct 26,1962 Letter from Nehru to JFK; 2 Letters Nov 19, Nehru to JFK.NLK91-54; Letter Nov 12, 1962 Nehru to JFK.
28.  B.K. Nehru, *Nice Guys*, 453.
29.  ibid., 454.
30.  Riedel, *JFK's Forgotten Crisis*, 135.
31.  Galbraith, *Ambassador's Journal*, 487.
32.  JFK presidential Library. NS Files Box 111A NLK 77-484. Aug 11, 1963. Letter to JFK from Nehru.
33.  John F. Kennedy Presidential papers. JFK Presidential Library. Box 111A
34.  JFK Library Country Files. India. NS Files 418. India 1961-63. Folder 2 of 4: Sino-Indian talking paper for Nassau. Dec 17, 1962; Dept of State Telegram 2692. Dec 24, 1962; Letter from President Kennedy to Nehru Dec 6, 1962. Box 112 NSF JFK Library.
35.  JFK Library. Presidential Papers. India: General Economic Data. Dept of State. Telegram 4034. May 16, 1963. NLK-OLR 112-2-7-8.
36.  JFK Library. Presidential papers. Box 419. Dept of State. Telegram 4680. May 30, 1963.
37.  Memo. April 26, 1963. President's views on India as expressed at 25 April meeting. JFK lib. NSF files. Box 107.
38.  NARA NLK oir-419-4-7-6 May 28, 1963. Western Military Assistance. President Radhakrishnan's visit.
39.  Memo. April 26, 1963. President's views on India as expressed at 25 April meeting. JFK lib. NSF files. Box 107.

40. JFK Presidential Library. NS Files. Robert W Komer Box 430 Papers of President Kennedy.
41. Dept of State. Talbot. Telegram: 1047 May 9, 1963. JFK Library.
42. Draft from President to Prime Minister, dated 16 May 1963. NLK oir-419 6.4.7.
43. B.K. Nehru, *Nice Guys*, 456.
44. M. Srinivas Chary, *The Eagle and the Peacock* (Wesport, CT: Greenwood Press, 1995), p. 123.
45. Kennedy Presidential Papers. JFK Library. Memo of Conversation JFK/ TTKOon May 20, 1963. Komer files. NLKOIR 4196.4.7
46. Ibid.
47. B.K. Nehru, *Nice Guys*, 457.
48. S. Gopal, *Nehru* Vol. 1, 289.
49. JFK presidential papers. JFK Library. Box 110. Galbraith to Rusk. April 17, 1963. Bhilai was a much smaller steel plant set up by the Soviets.
50. JFK Presidential Library. Komer Files Box 110.
51. JFK presidential papers. JFK Library. Box 110. Galbraith to Rusk. April 17, 1963.

## Chapter 8: Johnson and Shastri

1. Interview with Arthur Schlesinger.
2. https://en.wikipedia.org/wiki/List_of_dignitaries_at_the_state_funeral_ of_John_F._Kennedy
3. Merle Miller, *Lyndon: An Oral Biography* (New York, NY: GP Putnam's Sons, 1980), pp. 284–285.
4. Miller, Lyndon, 334.
5. Miller, *Lyndon*, 345.
6. ibid.
7. Miller, *Lyndon*, xvii.
8. Miller, *Lyndon*, xv.
9. Miller, *Lyndon*, xviii.
10. Schaffer, *Chester Bowles*, 220.
11. Schaffer, *Chester Bowles*, 228.
12. Chester Bowles, *Promises to Keep*, 482-483.
13. ibid.
14. ibid., 483–484.
15. Eds. Praveen K. Chaudry and Marta Vanduzer-Snow, *The United States and India: A History through Archives* (Sage India, 2011), p. 167.
16. ibid., 166.
17. ibid., 161–162.
18. Marie Seton, *Panditji: A Portrait of Nehru* (New York, NY: Dobson Books, 1967), 468.

19. Tully, Mark. Masani, Zareer, *India: Forty Years of Independence* (New York: George Braziller, 1988), p. 105.
20. Harish Kapur, *Foreign Policies of India's Prime Ministers* (New Delhi: Lancer, 2009), p. 77.
21. FRUS. 1964–68. Volume XXV, South Asia. Telegram from the Embassy in the Philippines to the Department of State, 7 March 1965.
22. Kux, *Estranged Democracies*, 233.
23. Mike Dash, 'Khrushchev in Water Wings: On Mao, Humiliation and the Sino-Soviet Split', Smithsonian Magazine (online), May 4, 2012.
24. Kux, *Estranged Democracies*, 240.
25. ibid., 243.
26. Treaty of Rome. FRUS State Dept. Volume XXV 1964-68 South Asia India. Embassy of Italy. Telegram 263. Nov 26, 1965.
27. Kux, *Estranged Democracies*, 244.
28. Doris Kearns Goodwin, *Lyndon Johnson and the American Dream* (Norwalk, CT: Easton Press, 1976), 112.
29. Robert Komer, Oral History. Lyndon B. Johnson Library. NAID 24617781. LBJ Presidential Library.
30. Chaudhry, *The United States and India*, 214.
31. H.W. Brands, *India and the United States*, 109.
32. Hussain Haqqani, *Magnificent Delusions: Pakistan, the United States, and an Epic History of Misunderstanding* (New York, NY: Public Affairs, 2013), p. 111.
33. Shuja Nawaz, *Crossed Swords: Pakistan, Its Army, and the Wars Within* (New York, NY: Oxford University Press, 2008), p. 205.
34. FRUS. 1964–68. Volume XXV, South Asia. Memorandum from Executive Secretary of the Department of State to the President's special assistant for NSA (Bundy), 27 January 1964.
35. FRUS. 1964–68. Volume XXV, South Asia. Memorandum from Robert Komer of the NSC staff to the President's special assistant for NSA (Bundy), 26 March 1964.
36. Major Agha Humayun Amin, 'Grand Slam: A Battle of Lost Opportunities,' Washington, DC: *Defense Journal*; Shuja Nawaz, Crossed Swords, 206.
37. Haqqani, *Magnificent Delusions*, 111.
38. Nawaz, *Crossed Swords*, 208.
39. ibid., 236.
40. Robert Komer, Oral History. Lyndon B. Johnson. NAID 24617781 LBJ Presidential Library.
41. Kux, *Estranged Democracies*, 238.
42. FRUS.1964–68. Volume XXV, South Asia, 23 November 1965.
43. FRUS. 1964–68 Volume XXV, South Asia, Memorandum from Secretary of Agriculture Freeman to President Johnson, 7 January 1966.
44. Chaudhry, *The United States and India*, 247.

## Chapter 9: Mrs Gandhi

1.  Uma Vasudev, *Indira Gandhi: Revolution in Restraint*, Vol. 1, 1917–1971 (New Delhi, India: Shubhi Publication, 2011), p. 258.
2.  Krishna Hutheesing, *Dear to Behold: An Intimate Portrait of Indira Gandhi* (London: The Macmillan Co., 1969), p. 19.
3.  Pupul Jayakar, *Indira Gandhi: An Intimate Biography* (New Delhi: Penguin, 1992), p. 22.
4.  ibid., 44.
5.  Katherine Frank, *Indira: The Life of Indira Nehru Gandhi* (London: Harper Collins, 2001), p. 91.
6.  Jayakar, *Intimate Biography*, 204.
7.  Frank, *Indira*, 40.
8.  Frank, *Indira*, 88.
9.  Frank, *Indira*, 89.
10. Jairam Ramesh, *Intertwined Lives* (New Delhi: Simon and Schuster, 2018).
11. Jayakar, *Indira Gandhi*, 117.
12. Frank, *Indira*, 202.
13. Jayakar, *Indira Gandhi*, 154.
14. Dorothy Norman, *Indira Gandhi: Letters to an American Friend, 1950–1984* (New York, NY: Harcourt Brace Jovanovich, 1985), p. 57.
15. Norman, *Letters*, 69.
16. Norman, *Letters*, 89.
17. ibid., 96.
18. ibid., 97.
19. Uma Vasudev, *Two Faces of Mrs Gandhi* (New Delhi: Vikas Publishing House, 1977).
20. ibid., 4.
21. Vasudev, *Indira Gandhi: Vol. 1*, 283.
22. ibid., 263.
23. ibid., 120.
24. FRUS. 1964-68. Volume xxv, South Asia. Telegram 285.
25. Inder Malhotra, *Indira Gandhi: A Personal and Political Biography* (London: Hodder and Stoughton, 1989), 95.
26. Kux, *Estranged Democracies*, 250.
27. Frank, *Indira*, 297.
28. Jayakar, *Intimate Biography*, 190.
29. Praveen K. Chaudhry and Marta Vanduzer-Snow, *The United States and India through Archives*, Vol. 1 (New Delhi: Sage, 2011), p. 252.
30. Kux, *Estranged Democracies*, 257.
31. Jayakar, *Intimate Biography*, 203.

32. Amol Agrawal, 'Why Indira Gandhi Nationalized India's Banks,' Bloomberg-Quint, 12 July 2019.

## Chapter 10: Nixon

1. Adam Taylor, 'Say Goodbye to the Weirdest Border Dispute in the World,' *The Washington Post*, August 2015.
2. Sydney Schanberg, 'After Pakistani Storm: Grief, Indifference,' *The New York Times*, 30 December 1970.
3. M.A. Jinnah, public meeting in Dacca (now Dhaka), 21 March 1948.
4. Third Five-Year Plan of Pakistan, p. 11; Report of the Panel of Economists on the Fourth Year Plan (1970–75), p. 132.
5. Asadullah Mohammad Niaz, 'Educational Disparity in East and West Pakistan, 1947–71,' University of Oxford, Discussion Papers in Economic and Social History, No. 63 (July 2006).
6. Roger Volger, 'The Birth of Bangladesh: Nefarious Plots and Cold War Sideshows,' *Pakistaniaat: A Journal of Pakistan Studies* 2, No. 3 (2010).
7. Owen Bennett-Jones, *Pakistan: Eye of the Storm* (New Haven, CT: Yale University Press, 2002), p. 227.
8. Jones, *Pakistan: Eye of the Storm*, 147.
9. Robert Payne, *Massacre: The Tragedy at Bangla Desh and the Phenomenon of Mass Slaughter Throughout History* (New York, NY: Macmillan Company, 1973).
10. Mark Dummett, 'Bangladesh War: The Article that changed History,' BBC News, 16 December 2011.
11. ibid.
12. Anthony Mascarenhas, 'Genocide,' London: *The Sunday Times*, 13 June 1971.
13. ibid.
14. ibid.
15. The Australian doctor working with women in Bangladesh was Dr Geoffrey Davis. Interview with Bina D' Costa.
16. Dept of State. Cables 959 and 958. 1971
17. Henry Kissinger, *The White House Years* (Boston, MA: Little, Brown, 1979).
18. Samuel Hopkinson, Memo to the NSA, March 28,
19. Richard Reeves, *President Nixon: Alone in the White House* (New York, NY: Warner, 1982), pp. 105-106.
20. Rick Perlstein, *Nixonland: The Rise of a President and the Fracturing of America* (New York, NY: Scribner, 2008), pp. 569-570.
21. Sultan Muhammad Khan, *Memories & Reflections of a Pakistani Diplomat* (Karachi: Paramount Publ. Enterprise, 1997), pp. 185-186.
22. Reeves, *President Nixon*, 43.
23. ibid., 31.

24. Reeves, *President Nixon*, 42.
25. Perlstein, *Nixonland*, 23.
26. Robert Dallek, *Nixon and Kissinger: Partners in Power* (New York, NY: Harper Collins, 2007), p. 9.
27. Evan Thomas, *Being Nixon: A Man Divided* (New York: Random House, 2015) p. 198.
28. Henry Kissinger, *On China* (New York, NY: Penguin, 2011), 221.
29. Kissinger, *White House Years*, 699.
30. Kissinger, *White House Years*, 700.
31. Dallek, *Partners*, 336.
32. Gary Bass, *The Blood Telegram: Nixon, Kissinger, and a Forgotten Genocide* (New York, NY: Alfred A. Knopf, 2013), pp. 34–35.
33. Archer Blood, Dissent Cable. Dept of State. Dacca 1138. 4/06/ 71
34. Walter Isaacson, *Kissinger: A Biography* (New York, NY: Simon and Schuster, 2013), p. 376.
35. Memcon 29740, HK office, 3 June 1971.
36. Gary Bass, 'The Terrible Cost of Presidential Racism,' *The New York Times*, 3 September 2020.
37. Sydney Schanberg, 'West Pakistan Pursues Subjugation of Bengalis,' *The New York Times*, 14 July 1971.
38. 1941 Census of India, 2011 Census of Bangladesh.
39. Gary Bass, *The Blood Telegram: Nixon, Kissinger, and a Forgotten Genocide* (New York, NY: Alfred A. Knopf, 2013), p. 141.
40. *The Washington Star*, 19 May 1971. Quoted in Kissinger's *White House Years*, p. 856.
41. Dallek, *Partners*, 337.
42. Roger Volger, 'The Birth of Bangladesh: Nefarious Plots and Cold War Sideshows,' *Pakistaniaat: A Journal of Pakistan Studies* Vol. 2, No. 3 (2010), pp. 24–46.
43. Dallek, *Partners*, 336.
44. Gary Bass, 'The Terrible Cost of Presidential Racism,' *The New York Times*, 3 September 2020.
45. Kissinger, *White House Years*, 857.
46. WH action memo 27876. April 28, 1971.
47. Reeves, *President Nixon*, 105.
48. Dallek, *Partners*, 338.
49. Richard Nixon, *Leaders: Profiles and Reminiscences of Men who Have Shaped the Modern World* (New York, NY: Simon and Schuster, 2013), p. 270.
50. Nixon, *Leaders*, 271.
51. Nixon, *Leaders*, 272.
52. Kux, *Estranged Democracies*, 280. Interview with Kux.

53. Gary Bass, 'The Terrible Cost of Presidential Racism,' *The New York Times*, 3 September 2020.
54. Kissinger, *White House Years*, 848.
55. Telephonic conversation between Sisco and Kissinger, 1.45 p.m., 17 February 1970.
56. Walter Isaacson, *Kissinger,* 356.
57. Kissinger, *White House Years*, 916.
58. Brinkley, Nichter, *The Nixon Tapes*, transcripts of phone conversation.
59. WH memcon. 00323.HK/ Ambassador Jha, 9 August 1971.
60. Bass, *Blood Telegram*, 252.
61. Haldeman, Haldeman Diaries, 377.
62. Bass, *Blood Telegram*, 262.
63. Bass, *Blood Telegram*, 264.
64. Dallek, *Partners*, 341.
65. William Burr (Ed.), *The Kissinger Transcripts: The Top Secret Talks with Beijing and Moscow* (New Press, 1998), WH. Secret Memo, 17 August, p. 46.
66. Burr, *Kissinger Transcripts*, 51.
67. Khan, *Memories & Reflections*.
68. Burr, *Kissinger Transcripts*, 52.
69. Maharaja Krishna Rasgotra, *A Life in Diplomacy* (Gurgaon: Penguin, Viking, 2016), p. 265.
70. Haldeman, Haldeman Diaries, 380–381.
71. Bass, *Blood Telegram*, 318.
72. Bass, *Blood Telegram*, 320.
73. Reeves, *President Nixon*, 407.

# Chapter 11: Ford

1. FRUS. Volume E8. Documents on South Asia, 1973-1976. Document 106. Conversation between Nixon and Ambassador Moynihan, Washington, 8 February 1973. 2.34–3.07 p.m.
2. FRUS. Volume E8. Documents on South Asia, 1973-1976. Document 106. Conversation between Nixon and Ambassador Moynihan, Washington, 8 February 1973. 2.34–3.07 p.m.
3. Steve Wiesman, *Daniel Patrick Moynihan: A Portrait in Letters of an American Visionary* (New York: Public Affairs, 2010), p. 291.
4. Kux, *Estranged Democracies*, 313.
5. Weisman, *Moynihan*, 276.
6. Wiesman, *Moynihan*, 300.
7. Wiesman, *Moynihan*, 300.
8. Bernard Weinraub, 'Daniel Moynihan's passage to India,' *The New York Times*, 31 March 1974.

9. Wiseman, *Moynihan*, 276.
10. Bernard Weinraub, 'Daniel Moynihan's passage to India,' *The New York Times*, 31 March 1974.
11. Wiseman, *Moynihan*, 328.
12. FRUS Vol E-8. Document 118. Documents on South Asia. Telegram 49943. Mar 17/73.
13. P.N. Dhar, *Indira Gandhi, the 'Emergency', and the Indian Democracy* (New York: Oxford University Press, 2000), p. 205.
14. Kux, *Estranged Democracies*, 315.
15. Haqqani, *Magnificent Delusions*, 209.
16. Haqqani, *Magnificent Delusions*, 210.
17. Wiesman, *Moynihan*, 310.
18. Douglas Brinkley, *Gerald R. Ford* (New York: Times Books, 2007), p. 3.
19. ibid.
20. James Cannon, 'Gerald R. Ford' in *Character Above All: Ten Presidents from FDR to George Bush* (Simon & Schuster, 1996).
21. Mrs Gandhi's interview with *The National Herald* newspaper, founded by the Nehru family.
22. Wiesman, *Moynihan*, 355.
23. H.W. Brands, *India and the United States* (Boston: Twayne Publishers, 1990), p. 150.
24. FRUS Vol E8. Document 176. Sept 30/74.
25. FRUS, E-8 document 180. New Delhi. Oct. 24, 1974. Conversation with Kissinger, Swaran Singh and others.
26. 'Moynihan said T.N. Kaul was sly, arrogant by birth,' *Times of India*, 9 April 2013.
27. FRUS Vol E-8. Document 187. Jan 27/75. Conversation between HK and ambassador designate Saxbe
28. Kux, *Estranged Democracies*, 332.

## Chapter 12: The Indian Emergency

1. Coomi Kapoor, *The Emergency: A Personal History* (New York, NY: Penguin Books, 2016), Chapter 10.
2. V. Krishna Ananth, *India Since Independence* (New Delhi: Pearson, 2010), p. 132.
3. T.V. Rajeswar, *India: The Crucial Years* (New Delhi: Harper Collins, 2015).
4. P.N. Dhar, *Indira Gandhi, the 'Emergency' and Indian Democracy*, (New York: Oxford University Press, 2000), p. 260.
5. Rajeswar, *India*, 77.
6. Vasudev, *The Two Faces of Mrs Gandhi*, 93.
7. Khilnani, *Incarnations*, 364.
8. Inder Malhotra, *Indira Gandhi*, 180-181.

9. My direct observations while working in Delhi as a social worker.
10. Kux, *Estranged Democracies*, 343; *Playboy*, March 1977, p. 78.
11. Dhar, *Indira Gandhi*, 336-337.

## Chapter 13: Carter

1. The Carter Center. Letter from President Carter to Prime Minister Gandhi, 24 February 1977.
2. NLC16-48-3-17-1. 4/13/79
3. NLC 16-48-3-17-1. Memo from US Embassy Delhi to Asst. Sec. Saunders. 4/13/79. Sit report.
4. Kapur, *Foreign Policies*, 158.
5. Kapur, *Foreign Policies of India's Prime Ministers*, 151.
6. Jimmy Carter, *Keeping Faith: Memoirs of a President* (New York, NY: Bantam Books, 1982), p. 141.
7. ibid.
8. Carter, *Keeping Faith*, 141–142.
9. Carter Center. Jimmy Carter, Governor's inaugural address. Atlanta, 12 January 1971.
10. NLC -4-5-5-2-5. Background paper, 22 December 1977.
11. Carter Center. National Security Council. Memo, 9 November 1977. NLC-10-6-5-5-4.
12. Carter Center. NLC 4-5-5-2-5
13. Carter Center. NLC 43-64-1-4-9 *Congressional Quarterly*. John Felton, 'Non-Proliferation Law Violation', 17 May 1980, p. 1367.
14. Carter Center NLC 128-3-2-6-8. White House letter from President Carter to Prime Minister Desai, 8 May 1978.
15. Carter Center NLC 1-2-1-14-2. WH memo to President from Z. Brzezinski, 23 April 1977.
16. NLC 129-15-1-10-0, p. 3.
17. Haqqani, *Magnificent Delusions*, 236.
18. Haqqani, *Magnificent Delusions*, 221.
19. Kux, *Estranged Democracies*, 354–355.
20. NLC 10-6-7-17-9. Memo from Thornton to Brzezinski. Nov 25,1977; NLC 10-8-4-6-2 Alert item from Thornton; NLC 132-152-1-6-9. Memo for Brzezinski from Dept. of State, 11 August 1977.
21. NLC 132-152-1-6-9. Memo for Brzezinski from Dept of State, 11 August 1977.
22. Katherine Brown, 'The Day Embassy Kabul Forever Changed: Remembering the 1979 Assassination of Adolph "Spike" Dubs and The Dismantling of the American Civilian Mission in Afghanistan,' *Small Wars Journal*, 14 February 2011.

23. Brown, *Embassy Kabul*; USDS 'Kidnapping of Ambassador Dubs': Situation Report No. 8/9, 14 February 1979.zulu declass. The Assassination of Ambassador Dubs, Association for Diplomatic Studies and Training, USAID. Interview with Bruce Flatin, political counsellor in Kabul, 1993.
24. Dan Rather's interview with Morarji Desai, on the CBS news show *60 Minutes*.
25. Kapur, *Foreign Policies*, 164–165.
26. Jagat Mehta, *March of Folly in Afghanistan, 1978–2001*, (New Delhi: Manohar Publishers, 2002), p. 23.

## Chapter 14: Afghanistan

1. Peter Hopkirk, *The Great Game* (New York: Kodansha International, 1990), p. 5.
2. Mehta, *March of Folly*.
3. Seth Jones, *In the Graveyard of Empires: America's War in Afghanistan* (New York, NY: W.W. Norton & Co., 2009), p. 15.
4. Jones, *Graveyard*, 17.
5. ibid.

## Chapter 15: Mrs Gandhi and Reagan

1. Sunil Sethi, 'Sanjay Gandhi: Flight of Destiny,' *India Today*, 15 July 1980.
2. ibid.
3. Vasudev, *Two Faces of Mrs Gandhi*, 102, 120.
4. 'The Death that devastated Indira Gandhi,' rediff.com, 20 July 2017.
5. Kapur, *Foreign Policies*, 186.
6. Jayakar, *Intimate Biography*, 418.
7. Sean Wilentz, *The Age of Reagan* (New York, NY: Harper Collins, 2008), p. 31.
8. Jacob Weisberg, *Ronald Reagan: The American Presidents Series: The 40th President, 1981–1989* (New York, NY: Times Books, 2016), p. 30.
9. Wilentz, *Age of Reagan*, 124.
10. Lou Cannon, *President Reagan: The Role of a Lifetime* (New York, NY: Public Affairs Books, 2008), p. 19.
11. Wilentz, *Age of Reagan*, 130.
12. June Kronholz, *Wall Street Journal* (Asia), 14 June 1982, p. 21.
13. Reagan Presidential Library. Kemp, /Geoffrey: files Box 2 Anderson, Walter. Dept. of State. Rebalancing the Indo Soviet Relationship.
14. Interview with Jagat Mehta.
15. Interview with Bruce Riedel.
16. ibid.

17. Bernard Gwertzman. 'Pakistan Agrees to A U.S. Aid Plan and F16 Delivery,' *The New York Times*, 16 September 1981.

18. Riedel, *Avoiding Armageddon*, 96.

19. Kux, *Estranged Democracies*, 379.

20. Riedel, *Avoiding Armageddon*, 100.

21. Rashmi Jain, *The United States and India 1947–2006* (New Delhi: Radiant Publishers, 2007), p. 72.

22. Reagan presidential Library. Kemp, /Geoffrey: files Box 2 Anderson, Walter. Dept. of State, 18 May 1983. Floor Statement. US relations with India. Orrin Hatch to G. Kemp.

23. Cannon, *Role*, 56.

24. Kapur, *Foreign Policies*, 193.

25. President Reagan letter, The White House, 12 March 1981. FOIA 1998-0387-F. George HW Bush Vice Presidential Records. Gregg, Donald. P, files. 19767-013 George HW Bush Library.

26. Cannon, *President Reagan*. 127.

27. Cannon, *Role*, 412.

28. Reagan Presidential Library. Hatch, Orrin. US Senate, 21 April 1982. NLS F96-110#54.

29. Maharaja Krishna Rasgotra, *A Life in Diplomacy* (Gurgaon: Penguin, Viking, 2016), p. 324.

30. Rasgotra, *Life in Diplomacy*, 327.

31. Bernard Weinraub, 'Reagan and Mrs Gandhi resolve dispute on nuclear fuel for India,' *The New York Times*, 30 July 1982.

32. Rasgotra, *Life in Diplomacy*, 329.

33. Rasgotra, *Life in Diplomacy*, 336.

34. June Kronholz, 'Is India Romance with Russia Losing its Thrill?,' *The Wall Street Journal*, 14 June 1982.

35. Reagan Library. NSC. Psn 071225. Csn:hce250

36. Kux, *Estranged Democracies*, 396–397.

37. Reagan Presidential Library. National Security Affairs. Asst to the President for Chron. Files. 8590547 Box 90582.

38. India 1983. Congress of the US, House of Representatives, 30 June 1983.

39. Rasgotra, *Life in Diplomacy*, 334.

40. Meredith Weiss, 'The Khalistan Movement in Punjab,' Yale Center for International & Area Studies, June 2002.

41. Frank, *Indira*, 490.

42. George P. Shultz, *Turmoil and Triumph: My Years as Secretary of State* (New York, NY: Charles Scribner, 1993), p. 493.

43. ibid.

44. Peter Tomson, *U.S. Congressional Perspectives of India: A Case Study, Twenty-Sixth Session, 1983–84* (Washington, DC: Department of State, n.d.).

45. Peter Tomson, *U.S. Congressional Perspectives of India: A Case Study, Twenty-Sixth Session, 1983–84* (Washington, DC: Department of State, n.d.).

46. Rasgotra, *Life in Diplomacy*, 338.

## Chapter 16: Shifting Winds

1. Sumit Mitra, 'Rajiv Gandhi Reshuffles his Party and Administration According to a Flight Plan,' *India Today*, 15 December 1984.

2. D.P. Satish, '5 Foreign Ministers in 25 Years: Is MEA jinxed?,' *News18*, 26 June 2015.

3. From the recollections of Mahmud Ahamed, Rajiv Gandhi's roommate in London.

4. Kux, *Estranged Democracies*, 401.

5. Reagan Presidential Library. NLS. Memo, 6 August 1985. NLSF96-128/2#51 Shirin Tahir-Kheli Files. Box 91882

6. Linda de Hoyes, 'Rajiv Gandhi and President Reagan set Basis for US-India relations,' EIR Vol 12 No 25, 25 June 1985.

7. Reagan Presidential Library. NLS Memo, 6 August 1985. NLSF96-128/2#51 Shirin Tahir-Kheli Files box 91882

8. Stuart Auerbach, 'World Bank Cuts India's Share of No Interest loans,' *The Washington Post*, 23 January 1982.

9. Srinath Raghavan, *Fierce Enigmas* (New York, Basic Books, 2018), p. 340.

10. Christopher Drew, 'Envoy Wife's Affair Used in Marine's Spy Case,' *Chicago Tribune*, 12 May 1987.

11. Dept. of State. May 86. F96-128/2 #26. State.132657.

12. Reagan Presidential Library. Dept. Of State. Telegram. May 86.NLS. F96-128/2#26

13. Ambassador Peter Tomsen, *US Congressional Perspectives of India*. A case Study. Twenty-sixth session.1983-84. Washington DC Department of State.

14. Tomsen, *Congressional Perspectives*.

15. Reagan library. South Asia files. F96-112/1#36. 12/84.

16. Lawrence Wright, 'The Double Game,' *The New Yorker*, 16 May 2011.

17. Interview with Robert Einhorn, 26 June 2018.

18. Shultz, *Turmoil and Triumph*, 494.

19. Carter Center, John G. Dean, oral history.

20. ibid.

21. ibid.

22. Lifschultz, Lawrence, 'The Heroin Trail: Pakistan authorities are deeply involved,' *Times of India*, 24 October 1988. Quoted in John G. Dean's oral history, Carter Center.

23. ibid.

24. Sean Wilentz, *The Age of Reagan* (New York, NY: Harper Perennial, 2009), p. 154.

25. Reagan Presidential Library. NSC. Nov 86.NLC F96-128/2#46.

26. Interview with Bruce Riedel.
27. Telegram. Ambassador Dean to State Dept, 4 December 1987. E.O. 12356. NLC. 131-5-8-11-0
28. Telegram, 7 December 1987. New Delhi. Ambassador Dean to State Department. EO 12356. NLC 131-5-8-15-6.
29. Reagan Library. South Asia. File 6. JG Dean's chronological files of messages to and from Am. Embassy New Delhi. July-Dec.1987.
30. NSC. May 23,1988. Meeting with Ambassador Oakley and P.K. Singh. Add. Sec. NLS F96-128/2#17.
31. Dean, John Gunther. Oral History. The Jimmy Carter Presidential Library.

## Chapter 17: Bush 41

1. Jon Meacham, *Destiny and Power: The American Odyssey of George Herbert Walker Bush* (New York, NY: Random House, 2013), p. 38.
2. ibid.
3. George W. Bush, George *All the Best* (New York, NY: Scribner, 1999), p. 88.
4. Meacham, Jon *Destiny and Power*, 108.
5. ibid., 144.
6. Meacham, *Destiny and Power*, 160.
7. W. H. Situation room. May 1984. George H.W. Bush Vice Presidential records. NSA office. Donald Gregg files. FOIA 1998-0387F. OA/ID 19870-020.
8. Bush Library. Vice Presidential Records. NSA. Donald Gregg Files. FOIA: 1998-0387-F. WH situation Room. May 84.
9. Inderjit Bhardhwaj and Madhu Trehan, 'Rajiv Gandhi's visit proves "a turning point" in Indo-US ties,' *India Today*, 15 July 1985.
10. Bush, H.W. Personal letter. George H.W. Bush Presidential Library. Donald Gregg files. NSA. FoIA 1889-0387F.OA/ID 19808-006.
11. Memcon. George H.W. Bush vice presidential records. NSA. Donald Gregg Files. April 2/1985.0OA/ID 19870 -020. FOIA 1998-0387-F
12. George H.W. Bush Vice presidential records. NSA. Donald Gregg Files. FOIA 1998-0387-F. OA//ID 19780-007
13. Cobb Tyrus W. Memo. India Test System Export Case. NSC. 9, 1989. 980387-F
14. UNCTAD-World Investment Report
15. Surajeet Das Gupta, 'How Pepsi became India's right choice,' *Business Standard*, 28 March 2014.
16. P.R. Chari, Pervaiz Iqbal Cheema and Stephen Philip Cohen, *Four Crisis and a Peace Process* (Washington, DC: Brookings, 2007), p. 86.
17. Ramindar Singh and Dilip Bobb, 'Dr A. Q. Khan's Pak N-Bomb Revelation ...,' *India Today*, 31 March 1987.

18. John F. Burns, 'US Urges Pakistan to End Feud with India Over Kashmir,' *The New York Times*, 21 May 1990.

19. Chari, Cheema and Cohen, *Four Crisis and a Peace Process*, 97.

20. Richard Haass, Speech South Asia Society, 11 January 1990.

21. ibid.

22. Chari, Cheema and Cohen, *Four Crisis and a Peace Process*, 94.

23. George Bush Presidential records. NSA. Richard Haass Files. FoIA 1998-0387-F. OA/ID CF01625-029.

24. Interview with Robert Einhorn, 26 June 2018.

25. Stephen Solarz, 'No Blinking at Pakistan's Bomb,' *The Christian Science Monitor*, 21 November 1990.

26. Stephen Solarz, George H. W. Bush Presidential records. NSA. Richard Haass files. FOIA 1998-0387-F. OA/ID CF1304-006.

27. Seymour M. Hersh, 'On the Nuclear Edge,' *The New Yorker*, 29 March 1993.

28. Shyam Bhatia, The Rediff interview with Benazir Bhutto, *India Abroad*, 9 March 2004.

29. Brent Snowcroft, The White House. January 1989.George H. W. Bush presidential records. NSA.FOIA 1998-0387-F. OA/ID CF01361-005.

30. Brent Snowcroft, The White House. January 1989.George H. W. Bush presidential records. NSA.FOIA 1998-0387-F. OA/ID CF01361-005.

31. Interview with Bruce Riedel, 6 June 2018.

32. 28 George Bush Presidential records. NSA. Richard Haass Files. FOIA 1998-0387-F. OA/ID CF01625-029.

33. Harish, *Foreign Policies*, 267.

34. Harish, *Foreign Policies*, 268.

35. Peter Bergen in *American War Generals*, National Geographic Channel, September 2014.

36. Sanjaya Baru, *1991: How P.V. Narasimha Rao made History* (New Delhi: Aleph Book Company, 2016), p. 25.

37. Naresh Chandra, 'Selling the Country's Jewels,' *The Hindu*, 1 August 2016.

## Chapter 18: Rao and Clinton

1. Strobe Talbott, *Engaging India: Diplomacy, Democracy and the Bomb* (Washington, DC: Brookings Institution Press, 2004), p. 7.

2. Vinay Sitapati, *Half Lion: How P.V. Narasimha Rao Transformed India* (New Delhi: Penguin Books India, 2016), p. 43.

3. Sanjaya Baru, *1991*, 87–88.

4. Interview with Mani Shankar Aiyar.

5. Sitapati, *Half Lion*, 118.

6. C. Rangarajan, '1991's golden transaction,' *The Indian Express*, 28 March 2016.

7. Liaquat Ahamed, *Lords of Finance: The Bankers Who Broke the World* (New York, NY: Penguin Press, 2009).

8. Omkar Goswami, 'Remembering 1991 ... and Before' in *India Transformed*, ed. Rakesh Mohan (Washington, DC: Brookings Institution Press, 2018), p. 73.

9. ibid., 7.

10. Rakesh Mohan, *India Transformed* (Washington, DC: Brookings Institution Press, 2018), p. 5.

11. Rakesh Mohan, *India Transformed*, 13.

12. Montek Singh Ahluwalia, 'India's 1991 Reforms' in *India Transformed*, p. 50.

13. N.R. Narayana Murthy, 'From Bureaucrats to Boardrooms,' *Business Standard*, 30 October 2014

14. Sitapati, *Half Lion*, 261.

15. 'Babri Masjid demolition: A day that lives in infamy,' *India Today*, 6 December 2018.

16. Shyam Saran, *How India Sees the World* (New Delhi: Juggernaut Books, 2017), p. 44.

17. Rakesh Mohan, *India Transformed*, 13.

18. Talbott, *Engaging India*, 23.

19. Talbott, *Engaging India*, 29.

20. Sitapati, *Half Lion*, 273.

21. Raymond E. Vickery, *The Eagle and the Elephant* (Washington, DC: Woodrow Wilson Center Press, 2004), pp. 118–119.

22. Rakesh Mohan, *India Transformed*, 54.

23. Sunil Jain and Hardev Santora, 'Shiv Sena-BJP alliance scraps Enron power project,' *India Today*, 31 August 1995.

24. Vickery, *Eagle and the Elephant*, 38.

25. ibid.

26. Robin Rafael, Statement by Asst. Sec. for South Asia. Before House CFA Sub-Committee on Asia and Pacific. February 1995. Extract.

27. Bruce Riedel, *Avoiding Armageddon: America, India and Pakistan to the Brink and Back* (Washington, DC: Brookings Institution Press, 2013), p. 125.

28. Kapur, *Foreign Policies*, 349.

29. Bruce Riedel, *Avoiding Armageddon*, 119.

30. Kingshuk Nag, 'Vajpayee: Love, Life and Poetry,' *Outlook India*, 15 February 2016.

31. Talbott, *Engaging India*, 44.

32. Talbott, *Engaging India*, 52.

33. Interview with Robert Einhorn.

34. Raja C. Mohan, *Crossing the Rubicon* (New York, NY: Palgrave Macmillan, 2003), p. 88.

35. William J. Clinton, *My Life*. (New York: Alfred A. Knopf, 2004), p. 771.

36. Riedel, *Avoiding Armageddon*, 132.

37. ibid.
38. Interview with Bruce Riedel.
39. Talbott, *Engaging India*, 168.
40. Talbott, *Engaging India*, 169.
41. ibid.
42. Raja Mohan, *Crossing*, 190.
43. Clinton, *My Life*, 902.
44. Interview with Robert Einhorn.

## Chapter 19: 9/11

1. Interview with Richard Armitage.
2. Interview with Shyam Saran.
3. Condoleezza Rice, *No Higher Honor* (New York, NY: Broadway Paperbacks, 2011), p. 122.
4. Rice, *No Higher Honor*, 128.
5. Interview with Ashley Tellis.
6. ibid.
7. Interview with Steve Hadley.
8. Interview with Ashley Tellis.
9. Interview with Shyam Saran.
10. Interview with Steve Hadley.
11. ibid.
12. Interview with Foreign Minister S. Jaishankar.
13. Interview with Shyan Saran.
14. ibid.
15. Interview with S. Jaishankar.
16. Interview with Shyam Saran.

## Chapter 20: Bush 43

1. Interview with S. Jaishankar.
2. Interview with Shyam Saran.
3. Interview with Ashley Tellis.
4. Rice, *No Higher Honor*, 438–39.
5. ibid., 419.
6. Interview with Shyam Saran.
7. Elizabeth Bumiller, *Condoleezza Rice: An American Life* (New York, NY: Random House, 2007).
8. Interview with Steve Hadley.
9. Rice, *No Higher Honor*.

10. William Burns, *The Back Channel* (New York, NY: Random House, 2019), p. 258.
11. Interview with Shivshankar Menon.
12. Interview with Ronen Sen.
13. ibid.
14. ibid.
15. Interview with S. Jaishankar.
16. ibid.
17. Interview with Shivshankar Menon.
18. Interview with Shyam Saran. He also discusses these entitlements in his book, *How India Sees the World*.
19. Interview with Shyam Saran.
20. Interview with Ashley Tellis.
21. Interview with Ronen Sen.
22. Interview with Ashley Tellis.
23. Shyam Saran, *How India Sees the World* (New Delhi: Juggernaut Books, 2017), pp. 228-229.
24. Interview with Shivshankar Menon.
25. Burns, *Back Channel*, 260.
26. Interview with Shivshankar Menon.

## Chapter 21: Obama and India

1. Interview with Shivshankar Menon.
2. ibid.
3. Interview with Vali Nasr.
4. Interview with Shyam Saran.
5. Burns, *The Back Channel*, 261.
6. Helen Cooper, 'China Holds Firm on Major Issues in Obama's Visit,' *The New York Times*, 17 November 2009.
7. Interview with Nisha Biswal.
8. Interview with Shyam Saran.
9. ibid.
10. ibid.
11. ibid.
12. Philip Sherwell, 'Barak Obama Denies Accusations that he "crashed" secret Chinese climate change talks,' *The Telegraph*, 19 December 2009.
13. Interview with Vali Nasr.
14. Interview with Peter Lavoy.
15. ibid.
16. Interview with Vali Nasr.
17. Rudra Chaudhuri, *Forged in Crisis* (Oxford University Press, 2014), p. 260.

18. Burns, *The Back Channel*, 262.
19. Interview with Nisha Biswal.
20. ibid.
21. ibid.
22. ibid.
23. ibid.
24. 'Gandhi's Killer Evokes Admiration as Never Before,' Sameer Yasir, *The New York Times*, 4 February 2020.
25. Interview with Ambassador Richard Verma.
26. ibid.
27. Barack Obama, *A Promised Land* (New York, Crown), p. 601, Kindle edition.

## Chapter 22: Trump

1. Maggie Haberman, *New York Times*, 22 November 2019.
2. Phillip Rucker and Carol Leonnig, *A Very Stable Genius: Donald J. Trump's Testing of America* (New York, NY: Penguin Press, 2020) 132.
3. ibid.
4. ibid.
5. Rucker and Leonnig, *Stable Genius*, 132.
6. Peter Bergen, *Trump and his Generals: The Cost of Chaos* (New York: Penguin, 2019), p. 14.
7. Rucker and Leonnig, *A Very Stable Genius*, 163.
8. Anita Kumar, 'Trump visits a big foreign market-for the U.S. and for Trump org,' *Politico*, 22 February 2020.
9. Barkha Dutt, 'Trump's ignorance was on full display in his meeting with Imran Khan,' *The Washington Post*, 22 July 2019.
10. Mili Mitra, 'This is the Modi government's darkest moment,' *The Washington Post*, 6 August 2019.
11. Amy Kazmin, 'Modi's emphatic victory cements India's nationalist shift,' *Financial Times*, 24 May 2019.
12. Interview with Rich Verma.
13. Pranav Dixit, 'Microsoft CEO Satya Nadella Harshly Criticized The Indian Law That Discriminates Against Muslim Immigrants: "I Think It's Just Bad",' Buzz Feed News, 13 January 2020.
14. George Packer. 'We Are Living in a Failed State,' *The Atlantic*, June 2020.
15. Hannah Ellis-Peterson, 'India releases hydroxychloroquine stocks amid pressure from Trump,' *The Guardian*, 7 April 2020.
16. Shivshankar Menon, 'India-China: Time for a Reset,' *India Today*, 27 July 2020.
17. Jeffrey Goldberg, 'James Mattis Denounces President,' *The Atlantic*, 3 June 2020.

18. Martin Pengally, 'John Kelly Says…,' *The Guardian*, 5 June 2020.

## Epilogue

1. Ross Anderson, 'The Panopticon Is Already Here,' *The Atlantic*, September 2020.
2. Interview with Jake Sullivan, head of policy planning, Department of State, in Obama administration.
3. Ross Anderson, 'The Panopticon Is Already Here,' *The Atlantic*, September 2020.
4. ibid.
5. Shivshankar Menon, 'India–China: Time for a Reset,' *India Today*, 27 July 2020.
6. David E. Sanger, Emily Schmall, 'Power Outage in India May Stem from China,' *The New York Times*, 1 March 2021.
7. Nirupama Rao, 'Galwan: Postscript to a tragedy,' *The Hindu*, 19 June 2020.

# Acknowledgements

I wrote this book with two audiences in mind: an Indian one and an American one. The book was not written for academia, but for ordinary people to enjoy history and get to know the people that participated in its making. I owe my inspiration to many talented writers who made history a joy to read: Ramachandra Guha, William Dalrymple, Antonia Frasier and William Manchester, among others.

As I read the many books, papers and memoirs that laid the foundations of my research, I realized how many dazzlingly talented personalities shaped the trajectory of the relationship between the two largest democracies. The book is an attempt to put the main characters, along with their actions and motivations, back on the centre stage.

This book would not have been written if Prannoy and Radhika Roy hadn't brought me to NDTV all those years ago and inducted me into the world of journalism. Thank you to Mala and Tejbir Singh and M.J. Akbar, for giving me the opportunity to move to print journalism, and to Strobe Talbott and the late Brooke Shearer for mentoring me through this transition. Thanks also to my great friend Peter Bergen for opening the doors at *Foreign Policy*, which led to other venues in the US. It takes a village.

We all stand on the shoulders of those who went before us and to the recorders of history, I owe a debt of gratitude. There are many wonderful biographies too numerous to mention here that I probably spent more time on than I should have. Galbraith's journal while he was ambassador is worth reading just for its wit and prose. On the US side, Dennis Kux painstakingly recorded much of the interactions from Independence until the 1980s and was an invaluable source, as were the many books by Howard and Teresita Schaffer and Bruce Riedel. Strobe Talbott's book, *Engaging India*, was an invaluable guide on the pre-nuclear deal negotiations. They all were kind enough to guide me, answer my endless questions and give generously of their time. The works of Ramachandra Guha, Srinath Raghavan and Sarvepalli Gopal were invaluable research references in India, as were the memoirs of various diplomats, as unlike the US, where the presidential libraries are a goldmine for historical researchers, India is still a relatively closed shop. I am grateful to the many archivists at the presidential libraries in the US, who were all very helpful, as well as those at the Nehru Memorial Museum & Library in New Delhi.

Not only were the eminent historian Evan Thomas's biographies on Nixon and Eisenhower illuminating, but he shared his thoughts and graciously connected me to the archivists at the relevant presidential libraries, which made my work there very efficient. The historian and biographer Scott Berg was a great support on the West Coast, and opened his library to me when I was in dire need of certain books there.

Many mentors and friends gave generously of their time and shared their thoughts. I had the good fortune of speaking with many people over the years it took to write this book, but I want to thank in particular: Michael Beschloss, Jim Fallows, who was Carter's speechwriter, Vali Nasr and Jake Sullivan. Steve Wiseman, Bill Hamilton, Robert Einhorn, Nisha Biswal, Martha Kessler, Armeane Choksi, Ed Luce, Neal Katyal, Josh Geltzer, Swadesh Bose, Ambassador Frank Wisner, Ray Vickery, Anish Goel, Steve Hadley, Gary Bass, Bill Burns, David Bradley, Ashley Tellis, Karan Mahajan, Alyssa Ayres and Ambassador Rich Verma, on the US side. In India, National Security Advisor Shivshankar Menon, Ambassador Shyam Saran, Ambassador Nirupama Rao, Sunil Khilnani, Foreign Minister S. Jaishankar, Dhruva Jaishankar, Vikram Mehta, Navin Chawla, the late Jagat Mehta, the late Aparna Basu and Mani Shankar Aiyar were all kind enough to speak with me.

Dr Rakesh Mohan was a mentor for many of the economic points in the book, especially the reform period. He was exceptionally generous with his time, and his suggestions and corrections vastly improved the book.

Both Ambassadors Menon and Saran were remarkably patient with my endless questions, going over timelines, details and clarifying facts. I am in awe of their prodigious knowledge, memory and grace.

Bim Bissell, who worked at the American embassy in Delhi during the critical early years and had a ring-side seat to some of the most interesting events, such as Jackie Kennedy's visit to India, was a treasure of memories and one of my first interviews. She has encouraged and helped the project in countless ways and remains one of the people I most admire. Dr Akeel Bilgrami of Columbia University never questioned my credentials when I told him about my intention to embark on this rather ambitious project, and at once brought me a pile of books on Nehru to get me started. The historian Derek Leebaert read my work, urged me to continue when I flagged, corrected misconceptions and was always available with advice.

My dear friends Joy de Menil and Scott Moyers chimed in with valuable guidance and advice, taking time from their own overloaded editing schedules at Harvard University Press and Penguin, respectively, to encourage and keep me pointed in the right direction, as did Cullen Murphy of *The Atlantic*.

Most people were unaware that I was working on the book for the first six years. It is only in the last two years when it started taking shape that I told people about my project. I could not have done it without the support of my amazing friends: Margaret Warner, Jane Mayer, Sheri Fink (who offered her help right at the start), Carole Geithner, Margaret and David Hensler, Mary Haft, Maryam Irvani, Ketaki Seth, Tresha Bergen, Priya Basu, Jyoti Singh, Rupika Chawla, my Sun Valley pals, my nieces Rukmini and Mrinalini, and sister Dr Gauri Gandhi, who looked after me in Delhi.

Lekha and Ranjan Poddar gave me a quiet place to work in Delhi for months at a time, away from the distraction of family and friends. I spent many months over the years holed up there, with just visits to the Nehru library. I cannot repay them. The wonderful connection with HarperCollins was thanks to Navin Chawla, who has been a generous friend and shared his political insights.

On a short stop in Mumbai, Aurobind Patel decided my manuscript needed a makeover in its design layout and with a few magical strokes made it all look so much more elegant. Some people are just gifted. My daughter Shabu bailed me out often with tech support. After long days at her Harlem clinic looking after patients, she would help her tech-challenged mother format documents and fix typos and fonts. Although her efforts to teach me computer skills were an experience in frustration, I was grateful for the attempt.

Emily Schneider not only helped with preliminary copy edits but kept my manuscript in order. Diya Patel dug up articles from Indian news archives. The team at HarperCollins has been a joy to work with and my editors, Krishan Chopra and Suchismita Ukil, have been supportive in the way an author can only pray for. I am grateful to my agent Lynn Nesbitt for falling in love with my book and telling me it was a worthy project. She is remarkable.

I have always been inspired by my husband Liaquat's writing. He taught me that words have poetry and sentences need to be elegant. Watching him work and play with the construction of sentences when he writes has made me more conscious of my own writing.

Some years are more trying than others and I could not have completed this book without the kindness and moral support of Katherine Bradley, and my sister Tara Sinha, two of the wisest people I know. My daughters Shabu and Tara were always there for me and remain my biggest champions. Tara held my hand when I needed it most. My book is for them. My many thanks to my son-in-law Jonathan Tucker for bailing me out on multiple occasions, especially this past year while I was preoccupied.

Everyone deserves to have a 'brilliant friend' and I was fortunate to have one. We go back to boarding school in India. Rima Singh is an accomplished lawyer and lives in California. She was my first reader and copy editor, and lectured me about commas and pointed out assertions that needed to be verified. She also told me she learnt a lot from the book, and coming from her, it meant something.

Lastly, I'd like to thank the elders in my family, who went through Partition, left the homes they grew up in and started their lives across the border in India, but brought us up without any trace of bitterness or prejudice. My late father, Balwant Ram Narula, always spoke of Lahore in poetic terms. H.K. Lall took me for walks among ancient monuments and made me fall in love with history by bringing them to life and recreating all the stories that took place in them. Prabha and Shiv taught me about my culture and to believe in myself, and were a second set of parents to my great fortune.

My mother, Nirmala Bogra Narula, raised me on stories of her grandfather Lala Dunni Chand's role in the Independence movement in Punjab. One of the most gratifying moments of my research was seeing references to him in people's memoirs.

I grew up in India and left reluctantly for college, but I have come to admire the founding principles of the US and the warmth of the American people. The book is a tribute to the country of my birth and where I now live.

# Bibliography

Acheson, Dean. *Present at the Creation*. New York, NY: W. W. Norton & Co., 1969.

Ahamed, Liaquat. *Lords of Finance: The Bankers Who Broke the World*. New York, NY: Penguin Press, 2009.

Ambrose, Stephen. *Nixon, Vol. 2*. New York, NY: Simon and Schuster, 1989.

Anderson, Jack and George Clifford. *The Anderson Papers*. New York, NY: Random House, 1973.

Akbar, M.J. *Nehru: The Making of India*. United Kingdom: Penguin, 1971.

Baru, Sanjaya. *1991: How P.V. Narasimha Rao Made History*. New Delhi: Aleph Book Company, 2016.

Bass, Gary. *The Blood Telegram: Nixon, Kissinger and a Forgotten Genocide*. New Delhi: Random House India, 2013.

Basu, Aparna. *G.L. Mehta*. Concept Publishing Co. New Delhi, 2001.

Beisner, Robert. *Dean Acheson*. New York, NY: Oxford University Press, 2006.

Bennett-Jones, Owen. *Pakistan: Eye of the Storm*. New Haven, CT: Yale University Press, 2002.

Beschloss, Michael. *Presidents of War*. New York, NY: Crown, 2018.

Bose, Sugata and Jalal, Ayesha. *Modern South Asia: History, Culture, and Political Economy*. New York, NY: Routledge, 1999.

Bowles, Chester. *Promises to Keep: My Years in Public Life, 1941-1969*. New York, NY: Harper, 1971.

Bowles, Chester. *Ambassador's Report*. New York, NY: Harper and Brothers, 1954.

Boquerat, Gilles. *No Strings Attached? India's Policies and Foreign Aid 1947-1966*. New Delhi, India: Manohar, 2003.

Branch, Taylor. *The Clinton Tapes*. New York, NY: Simon and Schuster, 2009.

Brands, H.W. *India and the United States*. Boston, MA: Twayne Publishers, 1990.

Brecher, Michael. *Nehru: A Political Biography*. London, England: Oxford University Press, 1959.

Brendon, Piers. *The Decline and Fall of the British Empire*. London: Jonathan Cape, 2007.

Broadberry, Stephen N. and Gupta, Bishnupriya. 'Indian GDP Before 1870: Some Preliminary Estimates and a Comparison with Britain.' *CEPR Discussion Paper* No. DP8007, September 2010. Available at SSRN: https://ssrn.com/abstract=1707897.

Brown, Katherine. 'The Day Embassy Kabul Forever Changed: Remembering the 1979 Assassination of Adolph "Spike" Dubs and The Dismantling of the American Civilian Mission in Afghanistan.' *Small Wars Journal*, 14 February 2011.

Bumiller, Elizabeth. *Condoleezza Rice: An American Life*. New York, NY: Random House, 2007.

Burns, John F. 'US Urges Pakistan to End Feud with India Over Kashmir.' *The New York Times*, 21 May 1990.

Burns, William. *The Back Channel*. New York, NY: Random House, 2019.

Bush, George. *All the Best*. New York, NY: Scribner, 1999.

Califano, Joseph A., Jr. *The Triumph & Tragedy of Lyndon Johnson*

Cannon, Lou. *President Reagan: The Role of a Lifetime*. New York, NY: Public Affairs Books, 2008.

Carter, Jimmy. *Keeping Faith: Memoirs of a President*. New York, NY: Bantam Books, 1982.

Chandra, Naresh. 'Selling the Country's Jewels.' *The Hindu*, 1 August 2016.

Chari, P. R.; Cheema, Pervaiz Iqbal and Cohen, Stephen P. *Four Crises and a Peace Process*. Washington, DC: Brookings Institution Press, 2007.

Chaudhry, Praveen K., and Vanduzer-Snow, Marta. *The United States and India: A History Through Archives*. Vol 1. Sage Publications. New Delhi. 2011.

Chaudhuri, Rudra. *Forged in Crisis*. New York, NY: Oxford University Press, 2014.

'Civilian Mission in Afghanistan.' *Small Wars Journal*, 14 February 2011.

Cohen, David. *Churchill & Attlee: The Unlikely Allies Who Won the War*. London, England: Biteback, 2019.

Cohen, Stephen Phillip. *India: Emerging Power*. Washington, DC: Brookings Institute, 2001.

Cooper, Helen. 'China Holds Firm on Major Issues in Obama's Visit.' *The New York Times*, 17 November 2009.

Crocker, Walter. *Nehru*. India: Random House, 2009.

Dallek, Robert. *Nixon and Kissinger: Partners in Power*. New York, NY: HarperCollins, 2007.

Dalvi, J.P. *Himalayan Blunder*. London, England: Natraj Publishers, 1969.

Dasgupta, C. *War and Diplomacy in Kashmir 1947-48*. New Delhi, India: Sage Publications, 2002.

Dash, Mike. 'Khrushchev in Water Wings: On Mao, Humiliation and the Sino-Soviet Split.' *Smithsonian* (magazine), 4 May 2012.

Das Gupta, Surajeet. 'How Pepsi became India's right choice.' *Business Standard*, 28 March 2014.

Dauer, Richard P. *A North-South Mind in an East-West World*. Westport, CT: Praeger, 2005.

Dhar, P.N. *Indira Gandhi: The 'Emergency' and Indian Democracy*. India: Oxford University Press, 2000.

Drew, Christopher. 'Envoy Wife's Affair Used in Marine's Spy Case.' *Chicago Tribune*, 12 May 1987.

Ferguson, Niall. *Kissinger: 1923-1968: The Idealist*. New York, NY: Penguin, 2015.

Frank, Katherine. *Indira: The Life of Indira Nehru Gandhi*. London, England: HarperCollins, 2001.

Frankel, Francine R. *When Nehru Looked East*. Oxford University Press, 2020.

Galbraith, John K. *Ambassadors Journal: A Personal Account of the Kennedy Years*. Boston, MA: Houghton Mifflin Co., 1969.

Garver, John W. *Protracted Contest*. Seattle, WA: University of Washington Seattle, 2001.

Goodwin, Doris Kearns. *Lyndon Johnson and the American Dream*. Norwalk, CT: Easton Press, 1976.

Gopal, Sarvepalli. *Jawaharlal Nehru: A Biography, 1889-1947,* Vol. 1. Boston, MA: Harvard University Press, 1976.

Gopal, Sarvepalli. *Jawaharlal Nehru: A Biography, 1947-1956,* Vol. 2. Boston, MA: Harvard University Press, 1979.

Gopal, Sarvepalli. *Jawaharlal Nehru, 1956-1964,* Vol. 3. New York, NY: Vintage/Ebury, 1984.

Grady, Henry. *The Memoirs of Ambassador Henry Grady: From the Great War to the Cold War.* Columbia, MO: University of Missouri Press, 2009.

Guha, Ramachandra. *Makers of Modern Asia.* Cambridge, MA: Belknap Press, 2014.

Guha Ramachandra. *India After Gandhi.* New York, NY: HarperCollins, 2007.

Guthrie, Anne. *Madam Ambassador.* New York, NY: Harcourt Bruce and World, 1962.

Haldeman, H.R. *The Haldeman Diaries.* New York, NY: Putnam 1994.

Haqqani, Hussain. *Magnificent Delusions: Pakistan, the United States, and an Epic History of Misunderstanding.* New York, NY: Public Affairs, 2013.

Herman, Arthur. *Gandhi & Churchill: The Epic Rivalry That Destroyed an Empire and Forged Our Age.* New York, NY: Bantam Books, 2008.

Hoopes, Townsend. *The Devil and John Foster Dulles.* Boston, MA: Little Brown & Co., 1973.

Hutheesing, Krishna. *Dear to Behold: An Intimate Portrait of Indira Gandhi.* London: The Macmillan Co., 1969.

Immerman, Richard. *John Foster Dulles and the Diplomacy of the Cold War.* Wilmington, DE: SRB Books, 1999.

Isaacson, Walter. *Kissinger: A Biography.* New York, NY: Simon and Schuster, 2013.

Jain, Rashmi. *The United States and India, 1947-2006.* New Delhi, India: Radiant Publisher, 2007.

Jayakar, Pupul. *Indira Gandhi: An Intimate Biography.* New Delhi: Penguin Books India, 1992.

Jha, Prem Shankar. *Kashmir, 1947: Rival Versions of History.* Bombay: Oxford University Press, 1996.

Jones, Seth. *In the Graveyard of Empires: America's War in Afghanistan.* New York, NY: W.W. Norton & Co., 2009

Kapoor, Coomi. *The Emergency: A Personal History*. New York, NY: Penguin Books, 2016.

Kapur, Harish. *Foreign Policies of India's Prime Ministers*. New Delhi: Lancer, 2009.

Kaul, T.N. *A Diplomat's Diary: 1947-99*. New Delhi: Macmillan, 2000.

Kemp, Geoffrey. *The East Moves West*. Washington, DC: Brookings Institution Press, 2010.

Kennedy, Charles Stuart, and Grant, Lindsey. *Interview with Lindsey Grant*. 1990. Manuscript/Mixed Material. https://www.loc.gov/item/mfdipbib000440/.

Kennedy, Jacqueline and Schlesinger, Arthur M. *Jacqueline Kennedy: Historic Conversations* on Life *with John F. Kennedy, Interviews with Arthur M. Schlesinger, Jr., 1964*. New York, NY: Hyperion, 2011.

Khan, Sultan Muhammad. *Memories & Reflections of a Pakistani Diplomat*. Karachi: Paramount Publ. Enterprise, 2006.

Khasru, B. Z. *Myths and Facts Bangladesh Liberation War*. New Delhi: Rupa Publications, 2010.

Khilnani, Sunil. *The Idea of India*. New York: Farrar, Straus and Giroux, 1997.

Khilnani, Sunil. *Incarnations: A History of India in Fifty Lives*. New York, NY: Farrar, Straus and Giroux, 2016.

Kissinger, Henry. *The White House Years*. Boston, MA: Little, Brown, 1979.

Kissinger, Henry. *On China*. New York, NY: Penguin, 2011.

Korbel, Joseph. *Danger in Kashmir*. Princeton, NJ: Princeton University Press, 2015.

Kux, Dennis. *India and the United States Estranged Democracies, 1941-1991*. Washington, DC: National Defense University, 1992.

Leebaert, Derek. *Grand Improvisation: America Confronts the British Superpower, 1945-1957*. New York, NY: Farrar, Straus and Giroux, 2018.

Mahajan, Mehr Chand. *Looking Back: The Autobiography of Mehr Chand Mahajan, former Chief Justice of India*. New Delhi: Har-Anand Publishing, 1994.

Malhotra, Inder. *Indira Gandhi: A Personal and Political Biography*. Carlsbad, California: Hay House, Inc.,1975.

Malhotra, Inder. *Indira Gandhi: A Personal and Political Biography*. London: Hodder and Stoughton, 1989.

Malone, David M. *Does the Elephant Dance*. Oxford: Oxford University Press, 2011.

Malone, David M., Raja Mohan, C. and Raghavan, Srinath (eds.). *The Oxford Handbook of Indian Foreign Policy*. UK: Oxford University Press, 2015.

Mann, James. *The Rebellion of Ronald Reagan: A History of the End of the Cold War*. New York, NY: Viking/ Penguin Group, 2009.

Maxwell, Neville. *India's China War*. New York, NY: Pantheon, 1970.

McCullough, David. *Truman*. New York, NY: Simon and Schuster, 1992.

Meacham, Jon. *Destiny and Power: The American Odyssey of George Herbert Walker Bush*. New York, NY: Random House, 2013.

Mehta, Jagat. *March of Folly in Afghanistan, 1978-2001*. New Delhi: Manohar Publishers, 2002.

Menon, V.P. *Choices: Inside the Making of India's Foreign Policy*. Washington, DC: Brookings Institution Press.

Menon, V.P. *The Transfer of Power in India*. New Delhi: Orient Longman, 1957.

Miller, Merle. *Lyndon: An Oral Biography*. New York, NY: GP Putnam's Sons, 1980.

Mohan, Raja C. *Crossing the Rubicon*. New York, NY: Palgrave Macmillan, 2003.

Mohan, Rakesh. *India Transformed*. Washington, DC: Brookings Institution Press, 2018.

Moraes, Frank. *Nehru*. Mumbai: Jaico Publishing House, 1959.

Morgan, Ted. *FDR: A Biography*. New York, NY: Simon and Schuster,1985.

Mosley, Leonard. *Dulles: A Biography of Eleanor, Allen, and John Foster Dulles and Their Family Network*. New York, NY: Dial Press, 1978.

Mukherjee, Aditya and Bipan Chandra. *India after Independence 1947-2000*. New Delhi: Penguin Books India, 1999.

Mulvaney, Jay. *Jackie: Clothes of Camelot*. New York, NY: St. Martin's Press, 2014.

Nehru, Jawaharlal. *An Autobiography*. New Delhi: Penguin Viking, 1936.

Nehru, Jawaharlal. *Discovery of India*. New York, NY: Anchor Books Doubleday and Company, 1959.

Nehru, Jawaharlal. *Letters for a Nation: From Jawaharlal Nehru to His Chief Ministers 1947-1963*. New York, NY: Penguin, 2014.

'Nehru: A Queer Mixture of East and West.' *New York Times*, 28 May 1964.

Niaz, Asadullah Mohammad. 'Educational Disparity in East and West Pakistan, 1947–71.' University of Oxford Discussion Papers in Economic and Social History, No. 63, July 2006.

Nixon, Richard. *Leaders: Profiles and Reminiscences of Men Who Have Shaped the Modern World.* New York, NY: Warner, 1982.

Nixon, Richard. *RN: The Memoirs of Richard Nixon.* New York, NY: Simon and Schuster, 1978.

Norman, Dorothy. *Indira Gandhi: Letters to an American Friend, 1950-1984.* New York, NY: Harcourt Brace Jovanovich, 1985.

Norman, Dorothy. *Nehru: The First Sixty Years,* Vol. 1. New York, NY: John Day Publishing House, 1950.

Obama, Barack. *A Promised Land.* New York: Crown, 2020

Pandit, Vijaya Lakshmi. *The Scope of Happiness: A Personal Memoir.* Delhi: Vikas Publ. House Pvt Ltd., 1979.

Parker, Richard. *John Kenneth Galbraith.* Chicago, IL: University of Chicago, 2005.

Paul, T.V., ed. *The India-Pakistan Conflict.* Cambridge: Cambridge University Press, 2006.

Payne, Robert. *Massacre: The Tragedy at Bangla Desh and the Phenomenon of Mass Slaughter Throughout History.* New York, NY: Macmillan Company, 1973.

Perlstein, Rick. *Nixonland.* New York, NY: Scribner, 2008.

Raghavan, Srinath. *1971: A Global History of the Creation of Bangladesh.* Harvard, MA: Harvard University Press, 2013.

Raghavan, Srinath. *Fierce Enigmas: A History of the United States in South Asia.* New York: Basic Books, 2018.

Rajeswar, T.V. *India: The Crucial Years.* New Delhi: HarperCollins, 2015.

Rao, P.V. Narasimha. *The Insider.* New Delhi: Penguin, 1998.

Rasgotra, Maharajakrishna. *A Life in Diplomacy.* Gurgaon: Penguin, Viking, 2016.

Reeves, Richard. *President Kennedy.* New York, NY: Papermac, 1993.

Reeves, Richard. *President Nixon: Alone in the White House.* New York, NY: Simon and Schuster, 2001.

Reid, Escott. *Envoy to Nehru.* New Delhi: Oxford University Press, 1981.

Reston, James B. 'John Foster Dulles and his Foreign Policy.' *LIFE* (magazine). October 4, 1948.

Rice, Condoleezza. *No Higher Honor*. New York, NY: Broadway Paperbacks, 2011.

Riedel, Bruce. *Avoiding Armageddon: America, India, and Pakistan to the Brink and Back*. Washington, DC: Brookings Institution Press, 2013.

Riedel, Bruce. *JFK's Forgotten Crisis*. Washington, DC: Brookings Institution Press, 2017.

Rotter, Andrew J. *Comrades at Odds: The United States and India, 1947-1964* (Ithaca, NY: Cornell University Press, 2001).

Rucker, Phillip and Carol Leonnig. *A Very Stable Genius: Donald J. Trump's Testing of America*. New York, NY: Penguin Press, 2020.

Rudra, Chaudhuri. *Forged in Crisis*. Oxford: Oxford University Press, 1994.

Rusk, Dean. *As I Saw it*. New York, NY: W.W. Norton & Co., 1990.

Schaffer, Howard B. *Chester Bowles: New Dealer in Cold War*. Boston, MA: Harvard University Press, 1993.

Schaffer, Howard B. *Ellsworth Bunker*. Chapel Hill, NC: University of North Carolina Press, 2003.

Schaffer, Howard B. *Limits of Influence: America's Role in Kashmir*. Washington, DC: Brookings Institution Press, 2009.

Schaffer and Schaffer, *India at the Global High Table*. Washington, DC: Brookings Institute.

Schlesinger, Arthur Jr. *A Thousand Days*. Boston, MA: Houghton Mifflin Co, 1965.

Schlesinger, Arthur Jr. *Gerald R. Ford: The American Presidents Series: The 38th President, 1974-1977*. New York, NY: Times Books, 2007.

Schneider, Sven Raphael. 'The Shoe Collection of Harry S. Truman.' *The Gentleman's Gazette*, May 15, 2013. https://www.gentlemansgazette.com/harry-s-truman-shoe-collection/.

Schulman, Robert. *John Sherman Cooper the Global Kentuckian*. Lexington, KY: Kentucky University Press, 1976.

Seton, Marie. *Panditji: A Portrait of Nehru*. New York, NY: Dobson Books, 1967.

Sethi, Sunil. 'Sanjay Gandhi: Flight of Destiny.' *India Today*, 15 July 1980.

Shankar, Kalyani. *India and the United States*. India: Macmillan, 2007.

Sherwell, Phillip. 'Barak Obama Denies Accusations that he "crashed" secret Chinese climate change talks.' *The Telegraph*, 19 December 2009.

Shultz, George P. *Turmoil and Triumph: My Years as Secretary of State*. New York, NY: Charles Scribner, 1993.

Sitapati, Vinay. *Half Lion: How P.V Narasimha Rao Transformed India*. New Delhi: Penguin Books India, 2016.

Snedden, Christopher. *Understanding Kashmir* and *Kashmiris*. Oxford University Press, 2015.

Solarz, Stephen. 'No Blinking at Pakistan's Bomb.' *The Christian Science Monitor*, 21 November 1990.

Solomon, Richard Hugh and Quinney, Nigel. *American Negotiating Behavior*. Washington, DC: United States Institute of Peace, 2010.

Sorenson, Ted. *Counselor*. New York, NY: Harper Perennial, 2009.

Sultan, Nancy. 'Jackie Kennedy and the Classical Ideal.' Center for Hellenic Studies, Harvard University, 2011. https://chs.harvard.edu/CHS/article/display/4767.

Talbott, Strobe. *Engaging India: Diplomacy, Democracy, and the Bomb*. Washington, DC: Brookings Institution Press, 2004.

Theroux, Paul and Nichter, Luke. *The Nixon Tapes*. Boston, MA: Houghton Mifflin Harcourt, 2015.

Thomas, Evan. *Ike's Bluff: President Eisenhower's Secret Battle to Save the World*. New York: Back Bay, 2013.

Tomsen, Peter. *US Congressional Perspectives of India: A Case Study, Twenty-Sixth Session, 1983-84*. Washington, DC: Department of State, n.d.

Vasudev, Uma. *Indira Gandhi: Revolution in Restraint*, Vol. 1. New Delhi: Shubhi Publications, 2011.

Vasudev, Uma. *Two Faces of Mrs Gandhi*. New Delhi: Vikas Publishing House, 1977.

Vickery, Raymond E. *The Eagle and the Elephant*. Washington, DC: Woodrow Wilson Center Press, 2004.

Volger, Roger. 'The Birth of Bangladesh: Nefarious Plots and Cold War Sideshows,' in *Pakistaniaat: A Journal of Pakistan Studies 2*, No. 3 (2010), pp. 24–46.

Weisberg, Jacob. *Ronald Reagan: The American Presidents Series: The 40th President, 1981-1989*. New York, NY: Times Books, 2016.

Weiss, Meredith. 'The Khalistan Movement in Punjab.' Yale Center for International & Area Studies, June 2002.

Weisman, Steve. *Daniel Patrick Moynihan: A Portrait in Letters.* New York, NY: Public Affairs, 2012.

Weinraub, Bernard. 'Reagan and Mrs Gandhi Resolve Dispute on Nuclear Fuel for India.' *New York Times*, 30 July 1982.

Wilentz, Sean. *The Age of Reagan.* New York, NY: HarperCollins, 2008.

Wright, Lawrence. 'The Double Game.' *The New Yorker*, 16 May 2011.

Zeiler, Thomas. W. *Dean Rusk: Defending the American Mission Abroad.* Wilmington, DE: Scholarly Resources Books, 2000.

# Interviews

Acheson, David C. Son of Dean Acheson, Secretary of State. (2016)

Armitage, Richard. Deputy Secretary of State. (7 January 2020)

Ayres, Alyssa. US Deputy Assistant Secretary of State for South Asia. (5 November 2019)

Basu, Aparna. Daughter of Ambassador G.L. Mehta. (July 2014, March 2016)

Basu, Prahlad. Secretary to Krishna Menon, Secretary of Steel and Mines. (July 2014)

Bergen, Peter. CNN terrorism analyst. (2019)

Bissell, Bim. Social Secretary to Ambassador Kenneth Galbraith, US Embassy, New Delhi. (2012–18)

Biswal, Nisha. Assistant Secretary of State. (3 January 2020)

Burns, William J. Deputy Secretary of State. (19 November 2019)

Chawla, Navin. Indian Civil Servant IAS officer. (2012)

Choksi, Armeane. (17 November 2019)

Einhorn, Robert. Assistant Secretary of State. (26 June 2018)

Goel, Anish. State Department. (5 November 2019)

Haass, Richard. Director of Policy Planning, State Department. President, Council of Foreign Relations. (31 May 2018)

Hadley, Steve. National Security Advisor. (8 November 2019)

Helms, Cynthia. Wife of Richard Helms, CIA Director. (2015)

Jaishankar, S. Minister of External Affairs. Foreign Secretary. Indian Ambassador to the US. (21 March 2020)

Khilnani, Sunil. Historian. (21 February 2020)

Kux, Dennis. Ambassador, State Department. Served in Pakistan and India. Author. (2012–16)

Lavoy, Peter. Assistant Secretary of Defense. (17 January 2020)

Mehta, Jagat. Foreign Secretary. (2011)

Menon, Shivshankar. National Security Advisor. Foreign Secretary. (17 January 2020)

Mohan, Rakesh. Deputy Governor, Reserve Bank of India.

Nasr, Vali. State Department, Senior Advisor to Richard Holbrooke. Dean of Johns Hopkins SAIS. (8 January 2020)

Nehru, Mrs B.K. Chandigarh, India. (2014)

Newhouse, John. Journalist (2014).

Rao, Nirupama. Foreign Secretary. Indian Ambassador to the US.

Riedel, Bruce. CIA, expert on South Asia. Brookings Institution. (6 June 2018)

Saran, Shyam. Foreign Secretary. (10–12 December 2019)

Schaffer, Howard. US Ambassador to Bangladesh.

Schaffer, Teresita. Ambassador.

Sen, Ronen. Indian Ambassador to the US. (9 December 2019)

Singh, Jyoti Karan. Grandaughter of Hari Singh, Maharaja of Kashmir.

Sorenson, Ted. Counsellor and Speechwriter to President Kennedy. (2009)

Sullivan, Jake. National Security Advisor to President-elect Biden. Head of Policy Planning, Department of State. Hillary Clinton's Chief of Staff. (17 January 2020)

Talbott, Strobe. Deputy Secretary of State. President of Brookings Institution. (2002–17)

Tellis, Ashley. Senior Advisor to State Department on Indo-US civil nuclear deal.

Thomas, Evan. Historian. Biographer of Nixon and Eisenhower. (16 February 2019)

Verma, Rich. US Ambassador to India. (21 January 2020)

Vickery, Raymond. US Assistant Secretary of Commerce. (22 June 2018)

Wisner, Frank. US Ambassador to India. (9 October 2018)

# Index

# About the Author

**Meenakshi Narula Ahamed** was born in 1954 in Calcutta, India. After finishing school in India, she obtained an MA from Johns Hopkins University's School of Advanced International Studies in 1978. She has had a varied career as a journalist and prior to that as a development consultant.

She has worked at the World Bank in Washington, DC as well as for the Ashoka Society. In 1989, she moved to London and became the foreign correspondent for New Delhi Television (NDTV). Among the leaders she interviewed were Nelson Mandela, John Major and Bill Clinton during his presidential campaign. She covered the race riots in London and reported on the rise of Indian entrepreneurs in the US in the mid-nineties. After returning to the US in 1996, she worked as a freelance journalist. Her op-eds and articles have been published in *Asian Age*, *Seminar*, *Foreign Policy*, *The Wall Street Journal* and *The Washington Post*.

She has served on the board of Doctors Without Borders, The Turquoise Mountain Foundation and Drugs for Neglected Diseases. She divides her time between the US and India.